INTERNATIONAL BIBLIOGRAPHY
OF THE SOCIAL SCIENCES
BIBLIOGRAPHIE INTERNATIONALE
DES SCIENCES SOCIALES

Publications of the ICSSD / Publications du CIDSS

INTERNATIONAL BIBLIOGRAPHY OF THE SOCIAL SCIENCES / BIBLIOGRAPHIE
INTERNATIONALE DES SCIENCES SOCIALES

[published annually in four parts / paraissant chaque année en quatre
parties, until 1961 / jusqu'en 1961: UNESCO, Paris].

International bibliography of sociology / Bibliographie internationale de sociologie [red cover/couverture rouge].
Vol. 1: 1951 (Publ. 1952).

International bibliography of political science / Bibliographie internationale de science politique [grey cover/couverture
grise]. Vol. 1: 1952 (Publ. 1954).

International bibliography of economics / Bibliographie internationale de science économique [yellow cover/couverture
jaune]. Vol. 1: 1952 (Publ. 1955).

*International bibliography of social and cultural anthropology / Bibliographie internationale d'anthropologie sociale
et culturelle* [green cover/couverture verte]. Vol. 1: 1955 (Publ. 1958).

Prepared by / Etablie par
THE INTERNATIONAL COMMITTEE FOR SOCIAL SCIENCE INFORMATION AND DOCUMENTATION
LE COMITÉ INTERNATIONAL POUR L'INFORMATION ET LA DOCUMENTATION EN SCIENCES SOCIALES

27, rue Saint-Guillaume, 75007 Paris

Members / Membres, 1984

John B. Black, *University of Guelph*
Abdelwahab Bouhdiba, *Université de Tunis*
Isac Chiva, *École des hautes études en sciences sociales, Paris*
Derek Clarke, *British Library of Political and Economic Science, London*
Robert L. Cliquet, *Centrum voor Bevolkings- en Gezinsstudien, Bruxelles*
Géry d'Ydevalle, *Universiteit te Leuven*
Tamás Földi, *Bureau d'information économique, Académie des Sciences de Hongrie, Budapest*
Herbert Giersch, *Institut für Weltwirtschaft, Universität Kiel*
Jean Laponce, *University of British Columbia, Vancouver*
Kéba M'Baye, *Cour Internationale de Justice, La Haye*
Robert Mdivani, *Institut d'information scientifique des sciences sociales, Moscou*
Luis Ramallo, *Escuela Superior de Administración y Dirección de Empresas, Barcelona*
Gerhard J. A. Riesthuis, *Vakgroep Boek- en Bibliotheekwetenschap, Amsterdam*
Janusz Šach, *Centre d'information scientifique de l'Académie polonaise des Sciences, Varsovie*

General Secretary / Secrétaire Général

JEAN MEYRIAT

École des hautes études en sciences sociales, Paris

Assistant General Secretary and Managing Editor
Secrétaire Général Adjoint et Secrétaire de Rédaction

JEAN VIET

Maison des sciences de l'homme, Paris

Associate Editor / Co-rédacteur

JOHN B. BLACK

University of Guelph, Ontario

INTERNATIONAL BIBLIOGRAPHY OF THE SOCIAL SCIENCES

BIBLIOGRAPHIE INTERNATIONALE DES SCIENCES SOCIALES

1983

International Bibliography of SOCIOLOGY

Bibliographie internationale de SOCIOLOGIE

VOL. XXXIII

Prepared by the
International Committee for Social Science Information and
Documentation

Établie par le
Comité international pour l'information et la documentation
en sciences sociales

TAVISTOCK PUBLICATIONS
LONDON AND NEW YORK

Manuscript prepared under the auspices of the International Sociological Association by the ICSSD with the financial support of Unesco (Subvention — 1984-1985, DG/7.6.2/SUB. 15 (SHS))

Manuscrit préparé sous les auspices de l'Association Internationale de Sociologie par le CIDSS avec le concours financier de l'Unesco (Subvention — 1984-1985, DG/7.6.2/SUB. 15 (SHS))

Published in 1986 by
Tavistock Publications Ltd.
11 New Fetter Lane,
London EC4P 4EE

Published in the USA by
Tavistock Publications
in association with Methuen, Inc.
29 West 35th Street, New York, NY 10001

British Library Cataloguing in Publication Data

International bibliography of sociology. —
(International bibliography of the social
sciences) Vol. 33

1. Sociology — Bibliography
I. International Committee for Social Science
Information and Documentation II. Series
016.301   Z7164.S68

ISBN 0-422 81070 3
ISSN 0085-2066

*Printed in Great Britain
by Richard Clay & Co. Ltd
Bungay, Suffolk*

TABLE OF CONTENTS
TABLE DES MATIÈRES

PRÉFACE

This issue takes its place in the annual four volume series of the *International Bibliography of the Social Sciences,* regularly published since 1952. These volumes are respectively dedicated to Sociology, Economics, Political Science and Social and Cultural Anthropology.

Each of these volumes is intended to index the main primary publications of a given year pertaining to one social science discipline; in addition, some publications not covered by the previous volumes are also mentioned. So a cumulative but at the same time selective memory is enriched with a new stratum. It is intended to make possible retrospective search rather than current awareness. Our criteria for selection are explained on next page.

Each volume is expected to satisfy in most cases the requirements of people working in a given discipline. For this purpose some citations of publications related to several disciplines are duplicated in two or even three of our volumes.

However, it will be often useful, in order to collect more information, to search not only this volume but also one of the three others in the same series, or a bibliography published by another organization pertaining to a neighbouring field : a list of the main bibliographical journals is given as an annex.

For some years the edition of our Bibliography has been computerized. In this way we are developing a database which is already available on-line and will be soon made publicly accessible. The published volumes are therefore a product of this base.

PREFACE

Ce nouveau tome prend place dans la série annuelle en quatre volumes, désormais bien connue, de la *Bibliographie Internationale des Sciences Sociales*, régulièrement publiée depuis 1952. Ces volumes sont respectivement consacrés à la Sociologie, à la Science Economique, à la Science Politique et à l'Anthropologie Sociale et Culturelle.

Chacun de ces volumes a pour objet de recenser les principales publications originales parues pendant un an dans la discipline qu'il couvre. Il signale en outre les titres qui n'avaient pas pu l'être l'année précédente. Il enrichit d'une nouvelle strate une mémoire cumulative mais sélective destinée à permettre la recherche rétrospective plus encore que l'information courante. Nos critères de sélection sont expliqués ci-après.

Chaque volume doit pouvoir suffire dans la plupart des cas aux spécialistes de la discipline couverte; c'est pourquoi certaines des références à des publications intéressant plusieurs disciplines sont repétées dans deux ou même trois de ces volumes.

Néanmoins, on aura souvent intérêt, pour obtenir davantage d'informations, à compléter l'utilisation du présent volume par celle de l'un des trois autres de notre série, ou encore d'une bibliographie publiée par une autre organisation et couvrant un domaine voisin : quelques-unes des plus importantes parmi ces dernières sont indiquées en annexe.

Depuis plusieurs années la préparation de notre Bibliographie est informatisée. Nous constituons ainsi une banque de données qui est d'ores et déjà consultable, et dont l'accès va bientôt être rendu public. Les volumes imprimés représentent ainsi un produit de cette banque.

CRITERIA FOR THE SELECTION OF ITEMS

	Included	**Left out**
Subject	Documents relevant to one of the main social sciences : political science, economics, sociology, social and cultural anthropology; or to an interdisciplinary field, e.g. political philosophy, history of ideas, economic history, constitutional law, public international law, social psychology, demography, urban planning...	general philosophy, general or political history, law and jurisprudence, experimental or clinical psychology, humanities, human biology, physical anthropology, archaeology...
Nature of Items	Writings of a scientific nature, i.e. intending to communicate new knowledge on a subject, with a theoretical component	
	Up-to-date writings, bringing new ideas or making use of new materials	Purely informative or popular papers, presentation of primary data, legislative or judicial texts, description of a current situation without general implications
		Monographs on a topic of a parochial relevance only (Exception : in *Anthropology*, even local monographs may have a general significance and deserve inclusion)
Type of Documents *Books*	Scholarly books Advanced level textbooks (but with discretion) Collections of original articles	Popular books elementary textbooks
	First edition, or new and completely revised edition	2nd, 3rd ... editions

	Included	**Left out**
	Translation into a more known language of a book originally published in a language known by few people	Translation into languages with a limited area of utilization
Articles	Scholarly articles published in specialised journals (monthly or less frequent)	Articles in newspapers or journals published several times each month
	Authored articles	Unsigned articles
	Articles of relevance to one of the social sciences published in a journal of some other speciality	
	Review articles, significant book reviews	
		Redundant articles (by the same author on the same topic in several journals)
		Partisan or polemical articles
		Very short articles, brief communications (unless of major significance)
Serials	First issue only of a new specialised journal or yearbook	
Research reports, thesis, dissertations	If published, or if publicly available from a known repository	
Unpublished governmental documents	If containing analysis with general significance, and if easily available for loan or photocopy	If purely administrative per nature, or containing only data
Microforms	If micro-edition of works not available under other form	If reproduction of documents previously published
Bibliographic materials	Specialised (social science) bibliographies, progress reports, specialised glossaries or dictionaries	

CRITÈRES POUR LA SÉLECTION DES RÉFÉRENCES

	Sont retenus	Sont exclus
Sujet	Les documents concernant l'une des principales sciences sociales : science politique, science économique, sociologie, anthropologie sociale et culturelle; ou un domaine interdisciplinaire, ex. : philosophie politique, histoire des idées, histoire économique, droit constitutionnel, droit international public, psychologie sociale, démographie, planification urbaine...	philosophie générale, histoire générale ou politique, législation et droit, psychologie expérimentale ou clinique, humanités, biologie humaine, anthropologie physique, archéologie...
Nature des Références	Ecrits de nature scientifique, c'est à dire destinés à communiquer des connaissances nouvelles sur un sujet avec une composante théorique	
	Ecrits à jour, apportant des idées nouvelles ou utilisant des données nouvelles	Ecrits uniquement informatifs ou destinés au grand public, recueils de données primaires, textes législatifs ou juridiques, description d'une situation ne présentant pas d'implication de portée générale
		Etudes monographiques d'un sujet d'intérêt purement local (Exception : en *Anthropologie*, même des monographies locales peuvent être pertinentes et mériter d'être retenues)
Type de Documents *Livres*	Ouvrages de recherche Manuels de niveau post-universitaire (avec modération) Recueils d'articles originaux	Livres pour grand public, manuels élémentaires
	1ère édition, ou alors édition entièrement revue et complétée	2ème, 3ème ... éditions

	Sont retenus	**Sont exclus**
	Traduction en une langue largement diffusée d'un livre originellement publié dans une langue de faible diffusion	Traduction dans des langues de faible diffusion
Articles	Articles "savants" publiés dans des revues spécialisées (mensuelles ou paraissant moins fréquemment)	Articles de journaux ou de périodiques paraissant plusieurs fois par mois
	Articles signés	Articles anonymes
	Articles relevant d'une des sciences sociales publiés dans une revue de spécialisation différente	
	Articles critiques, comptes rendus critiques substantiels	Articles répétitifs (publiés par le même auteur sur le même sujet dans des revues différentes)
		Articles de nature partisane ou polémique
		Articles très courts, communications brèves (sauf si elles sont d'une portée exceptionnelle)
Publications en séries	La première livraison seulement d'un nouveau périodique spécialisé ou annuaire	
Rapports de recherche, thèses	S'ils ont été publiés, ou s'ils sont à la disposition du public dans un dépot bien identifié	
Documents officiels inédits	S'ils contiennent des analyses de valeur générale, et si l'on peut facilement les emprunter ou les photocopier	S'ils sont de nature purement administrative ou contiennent seulement des données
Microformes	Les éditions sur microforme de livres qui ne seraient pas disponibles autrement	Les reproductions de documents antérieurement publiés
Matériaux bibliographiques	Les bibliographies spécialisées en sciences sociales, les rapports sur l'avancement de recherches, les glossaires ou dictionnaires spécialisés	

ANNEX / ANNEXE
OTHER BIBLIOGRAPHICAL JOURNALS
AUTRES REVUES BIBLIOGRAPHIQUES

I. ABSTRACTING JOURNALS (covering the same fields as the *International Bibliography of the Social Sciences*)
RECUEILS DE RÉSUMÉS ANALYTIQUES (couvrant les mêmes disciplines que la *Bibliographie internationale des sciences sociales.*)

Economics / Science économique:
Economic Titles / Abstracts. The Hague, Nijhoff, 1974 — . 24 x (per year/par an)
Journal of Economic Literature. Pittsburgh, American Economic Association, 1962 — . 4 x (per year/par an)

Political Science / Science politique:
International Political Science Abstracts / Documentation politique internationale. Paris, International Political Science Association, 1951 — . 6 x (per year/par an)

Social and Cultural Anthropology / Anthropologie sociale et culturelle:
Abstracts in Anthropology. New York, Baywood Publishing Co., 1970 — . 4 x (per year/par an)

Sociology / Sociologie:
Bulletin signaletique — Centre national de la recherche scientifique. Section 521. Sociologie, ethnologie. Paris, CNRS, 1969 — . 4 x (per year/par an)
Sociological Abstracts. San Diego, CA, Sociological Abstracts Inc., 1952 — . 8 x (per year/par an)

II. CURRENT BIBLIOGRAPHIES (in related fields)
BIBLIOGRAPHIES COURANTES (dans des disciplines voisines)

Social Sciences in general / Sciences sociales en général:
London Bibliography of the Social Sciences. London, Mansell, 1975 — . 1 x (per year/par an)
Novaja Inostrannaja Literatura po Obscestvennym Naukam. Moskva, INION, 1947 — . (7 series) 12 x (per year/par an)
Social Sciences Citation Index. Philadelphia, Institute for Scientific Information, 1973 — . 2 x (per year/par an)
Social Sciences Index. New York, Wilson Co., 1974 — . 4 x (per year/par an)

Biological Sciences / Sciences biologiques:
Biological Abstracts. Philadelphia, BioSciences Information Service of Biological Abstracts, 1927 — 24 x (per year/par an)

Business Economics / Économie d'entreprise:
Business Periodicals Index. New York, Wilson Co., 1958 — . 12 x (per year/par an)

Demography / Démographie:
Population Index. Princeton, Office of Population Research, 1935 — . 4 x (per year/par an)

Economics / Science économique:
Bibliographie der Wirtschaftswissenschaften. Göttingen, Vandenhoeck und Ruprecht, 1968 — .2 x (per year/par an)

Geography / Géographie:
Bibliographie géographique internationale. Paris, Centre National de la Recherche Scientifique, 1891 — 1976 : 1 x; 1977 — . 4 x (per year/per an)
Geo-abstracts. Norwich, University of East Anglia, 1960 — . (7 series) 6 x (per year/par an)

History / Histoire:
Bibliographie internationale des sciences historiques. Paris, Colin, 1926 — . 1 x (per year/par an)
Historical Abstracts. Santa Barbara, CA, American Bibliographical Center-Clio Press, 1955 — . 4 x (per year/par an)

Law / Droit:
Index to Foreign Legal Periodicals. London, Institute of Advanced Legal Studies, 1960 — . 4 x (per year/par an)

Linguistics / Linguistique:
Bibliographie linguistique. Utrecht, Spectrum, 1949 — .1 x (per year/par an)

Philosophy / Philosophie:
Bibliographie de la philosophie. Paris, Vrin, 1937 — . 4 x (per year/par an)

Psychology / Psychologie:
Psychological Abstracts. Washington, DC, American Psychological Association, 1927 — . 12 x (per year/par an)

ACKNOWLEDGEMENTS

The data contained in this Bibliography were compiled by combining the work of our editorial office, which uses all possible sources, and the communications of our foreign contributors who give us first-hand knowledge of their country's publications.

We acknowledge with many thanks the contributions made : for *Argentina* by Fundación José María Aragón, Buenos Aires; for *France* by Fondation nationale des sciences politiques and Maison des sciences de l'homme, Paris; for *Hungary* by Fövárosi Szabó Ervin Könyvtár, Budapest, and Mr. János BÁTHORY and Mrs Mária VÁGH; for *India* by Social Science Documentation Centre, Indian Council of Social Science Research, New Delhi, and Mr. S.P. AGRAWAL; for *Japan* by Japan Sociological Society, Tokyo; for *Poland* by Ośrodek Informacji Naukowej, Polska Akademia Nauk, Warszawa, and by Dr Kazimierz MARDOŃ; for *Spain* by Instituto Balmes de Sociología, Madrid, and Mrs Valentina FERNÁNDEZ VARGAS; for the *USSR* by Institut Naučnoj Informacii po Obščestvennym Naukam, Moskva, and Prof. V. VINOGRADOV and Dr Robert MDIVANI.

We also thank Germaine GEORGE and Agnès MAJOROS, who helped the editors for collecting and classifying the bibliographical data; and the data creation and production staff located in Guelph, Canada : Audrey KITCHING, Dorothy KARL, Elizabeth SMITH, Ruth JOHNSTON, Linda DAEHN.

REMERCIEMENTS

Les données bibliographiques contenues dans ce volume ont été réunies en combinant le travail de notre bureau de rédaction, qui exploite toutes les sources possibles, et les contributions de divers correspondants étrangers qui nous font connaître de première main les publications de leur pays respectif.

Nous sommes heureux de remercier particulièrement les institutions et les personnalités qui nous ont aidés cette année, et dont les noms sont donnés ci-dessus.

Nous remercions aussi Germaine GEORGE et Agnès MAJOROS, qui ont assisté les responsables de la publication pour rassembler et classer les données; et les membres de l'équipe de création et de production des données informatisées à Guelph, Canada : Audrey KITCHING, Dorothy KARL, Elizabeth SMITH, Ruth JOHNSTON, Linda DAEHN.

LIST OF PERIODICALS CONSULTED
LISTE DES PÉRIODIQUES CONSULTÉS

Accounting Review	Columbus, OH
Acta Baltica	Taunus
Acta Geographica	Paris
Acta Marxistica Leninistica. Filozofiai Tanulmányok	Hungary
Acta Sociologica	København
Actes de la Recherche en Sciences sociales	Paris
Actualité économique	Montréal, PQ
Administration (Dublin)	Dublin
Administrative Science Quarterly	Ithaca, NY
Advances in Librarianship	New York, NY
Affari sociali internazionali	Milano
Africa (London)	London
Africa Quarterly	New Delhi
Africa Report	Washington, DC
Africa Today	Denver, CO
African Studies Review	Boston, MA
Afrika Spectrum	Hamburg
Afrique contemporaine	Paris
Ageing and Society	Cambridge, MA
Aggiornamenti sociali	Milano
Aichi kyoiku daigaku Aikyodai kenpo, kyoiku-kagaku-hen	[Nihon]
Aizu tanki daigaku gakuho	Aizuwakamatsu
Allemagnes d'aujourd'hui	Paris
Allgemeines Statistisches Archiv	Göttingen
Alternatives	Amsterdam
América indígena	México
American Behavioral Scientist	Beverly Hills, CA
American Economic Review	Nashville, TN
American Economist	New York, NY
American Journal of Agricultural Economics	Lexington, KY
American Journal of Economics and Sociology	New York, NY
American Journal of Political Science	Austin, TX
American Journal of Sociology	Chicago, IL
American Political Science Review	Washington, DC
American Politics Quarterly	Beverly Hills, CA
American Psychologist	Lancaster, PA
American Review of Canadian Studies	Washington, DC
American Sociological Review	Washington, DC
American Statistical Association. Proceedings of the Social Statistics Section	Washington, DC
Amérique latine	Paris
Ampo	Tokyo
Análise social	Lisbon
Analyses de la SEDEIS	Paris
Annales de l'Université des Sciences sociales de Toulouse	Toulouse
Annales de Vaucresson	Vaucresson
Annales internationales de Criminologie	Paris
Annales Universitatis Scientiarum budapestiensis de Rolando Eötvös nominatae. Sectio philosophica et sociologica	Budapest
Annales-Économies, Sociétés, Civilisations	Paris
Annals of the American Academy of Political and Social Science	Philadelphia, PA
Année sociologique	Paris
Annuaire de l'URSS et des Pays socialistes européens	Strasbourg
Annuaire du Tiers-Monde	Paris
Annual Review of Information Science and Technology	New York, NY
Annual Review of Sociology	Palo Alto, CA
Anthropology UCLA	Los Angeles, CA

Applied Economics	London
Archipel	Paris
Archipelago	France
Archiv des Völkerrechts	Tübingen
Archiv für Kommunalwissenschaften	Berlin
Archiv für Rechts- und Sozialphilosophie	Budenheim-bei-Mainz
Archiv für Sozialgeschichte	Bonn
Archives de politique Criminelle	France
Archives de Sciences sociales des Religions	Paris
Archives européennes de Sociologie	Paris
Argument	Berlin
Armed Forces and Society	Chicago, IL
Artha Vijnana	Poona
Asahikawa daigaku kiyo	Asahikawa
Asian Affairs	New York, NY
Asian Affairs (London)	London
Asian Profile	Hong Kong
Asian Survey	Berkeley, CA
Asien	Hamburg
Atarashii kazoku	[Nihon]
Atarashii shakaigaku no tameni	[Nihon]
Atlantic	London-Boston, MA
Aussenpolitik	Stuttgart
Australian and New Zealand Journal of Sociology	Melbourne
Australian Foreign Affairs Record	Canberra
Australian Journal of Politics and History	St. Lucia [Queensland]
Australian Quarterly	Sydney
Autogestions	Paris
AWR Bulletin	Wien
Azija i Afrika Segodnja	Moskva
Bangladesh Development Studies	Dacca
Behavior Science Research	New Haven, CT
Behavioral Science	Ann Arbor, MI
Benelux	Brussels
Berichte über Landwirtschaft	Hamburg
Berkeley Journal of Sociology	Berkeley, CA
Bevolking en Gezin	Voorburg
Biuletyn Instytutu Gospodarstwa Społecznego	Warsaw
Boletín CEIL	Buenos Aires
Boletín de Estudios latinoamericanos y del Caribe	Amsterdam
Bolletino di psicologia applicata	Firenze
British Journal of Industrial Relations	London
British Journal of Political Science	London
British Journal of Sociology	London
Bulletin d'Information du CENADDOM	Talence
Bulletin de l'Institut d'Histoire du Temps présent	Paris
Bulletin de Liaison de la Recherche en Informatique et Automatique	Rocquencourt
Bulletin de Psychologie	Paris
Bulletin du Centre de Documentation d'Études juridiques, économiques et sociales	Cairo
Bulletin of Concerned Asian Scholars	San Francisco, CA
Bulletin of Indonesian Economic Studies	Canberra
Bulletin of Latin American Research	Oxford
Bulletin of Peace Proposals	Oslo
Bungaku	Tokyo-San Francisco, CA
Cadmos	Genève
Cahiers d'Études Africaines	La Haye-Paris
Cahiers de l'Analyse des Données	Paris
Cahiers de la Communication	Paris

Cahiers de Sociologie et de Démographie médicales	Paris
Cahiers du Centre d'études de l'emploi	Paris
Cahiers européens	Hamburg
Cahiers internationaux de Sociologie	Paris
Cahiers ORSTOM. Série Sciences humaines	Paris
Cahiers québécois de Démographie	Québec, PQ
California Management Review	Los Angeles, CA
Cambridge Journal of Economics	London
Canadian Journal of African Studies	Ottawa
Canadian Journal of Economics / Revue canadienne d'Économique	Montreal, PQ
Canadian Journal of Political and Social Theory	Winnipeg, MB
Canadian Journal of Political Science	Waterloo, ON
Canadian Journal of Sociology	Edmonton, AB
Canadian Journal of Sociology / Cahiers canadiens de Sociologie	Edmonton, AB
Canadian Public Administration	Toronto, ON
Canadian Review of Sociology and Anthropology	Calgary, AB
Canadian Slavonic Papers	Ottawa
Capital and Class	London
Caribbean Geography	Kingston
Catalyst	Peterborough, ON
Chiba daigaku kyoyobu kenkyu hokoku	Chiba
Chiba kenritsu eisei tanki daigaku kiyo	Chiba
Chicago Anthropological Exchange	Chicago, IL
China Quarterly	London
China Report	New Delhi
Chinese Law and Government	New York, NY
Chingin jutsumu	[Nihon]
Chuo daigaku bungakubu kiyo	[Nihon]
Chuo daigaku daigakuin kenkyu nenpo	[Nihon]
Chuo daigaku shakai-kagaku kenkyujo-ho	Tokyo
Ciência e Trópico	Recife
Civilisations	Bruxelles
Columbia Journal of Transnational Law	New York, NY
Commentaire	Paris
Common Market Law Review	Leyden
Communautés	Paris
Comunicación	Buenos Aires
Communication	Newark, NJ
Communications	Paris
Communications (Sankt Augustin)	Sankt Augustin
Community Development Journal	London
Comparative Education Review	Chicago, IL
Comparative Political Studies	Beverly Hills, CA
Comparative Politics	New Brunswick, NJ
Comparative Social Research	Greenwich, CT
Comparative Studies in Society and History	Cambridge
Comunicación y cultura	Buenos Aires
Conflict	New York, NY
Conflict Studies	London
Conjoncture (Tunis)	Tunis
Connexions	Paris
Conscience et Liberté	Berne
Consommation	Paris
Contemporary Crises	Amsterdam
Contemporary French Civilization	Bozeman, MT
Contradictions	Paris
Contrepoint	Paris
Contributions to Indian Sociology	Bombay
Convergence	Fribourg-Toronto, ON
Cristianismo y sociedad	Argentina
Critica marxista	Roma
Critica sociologica	Roma
Critique	Paris

Critiques de l'Économie politique	Paris
Crossroads	Israel-New York, NY
Cuadernos americanos	Mexico
Cuadernos de economía	Santiago
Cuadernos hispanoamericanos	Madrid
Cuadernos médico-sociales	Rosario
Culture technique	Neuilly-sur-Seine
Cultures	Paris
Cultures et Développement	Louvain-La-Neuve
Current Population Reports. Special Studies	Washington, DC
Current Sociology / Sociologie contemporaine	London
Dados	Rio de Janeiro
Daedalus	Cambridge, MA
Daigaku-shi kenkyu	[Nihon]
Debreceni Szemle	Debrecen
Défense nationale	Paris
Demográfia	Budapest
Demografía y Economía	México
Demografie	Praha
Demography	Ann Arbor, MI
Demosta	Praha
Desarrollo económico	Buenos Aires
Desarrollo indoamericano	Bogotá
Deutsche Studien	Bleckede
Deutsche Zeitschrift für Philosophie	Berlin
Deutschland Archiv	Köln
Development and Change	The Hague
Development and Peace	Budapest
Development Dialogue	Uppsala
Déviance et Société	Genève
Dialectics and Humanism	Florence
Diogène	Paris
Documentación Social	Madrid
Documentation européenne	Bruxelles
Documentation sur l'Europe centrale	Louvain
Documents	Paris
Documents CEPESS	Bruxelles
Dōto daigaku kiyō	[Nihon]
Dritte Welt	Meisenheim am Glan
Droit social	Paris
East European Quarterly	Boulder, CO
Eastern Anthropologist	Lucknow
Econometrica	Chicago, IL
Economia e Lavoro	Padova
Economic and Industrial Democracy	London
Economic and Social Review	Dublin
Economic Development and Cultural Change	Chicago, IL
Economic Inquiry	Los Angeles, CA
Economic Journal	London
Economic Record	Melbourne
Economica	London
Économie et Humanisme	Lyon
Économie et Statistique	Paris
Économies et Sociétés	Paris-Geneva
Economisch en Sociaal Tijdschrift	Antwerpen
Economy and Society	London
Education et Formations	Vanves
Educational Analysis	Sussex
Edukacja polityczna	Warszawa
Égypte contemporaine	Le Caire
Eichi daigaku Sapienchia	[Nihon]

Einheit	Berlin
Ekistics	Athens
Ėkonomičeskie Nauki	Moskva
Ekonomický Časopis	Bratislava
Enfance	Paris
Equal Opportunities International	Hull [UK]
Espace géographique	Paris
Espaces et Sociétés	Paris
Esprit	Paris
Estudios sociales centroamericanos	San José
Ethics	Chicago, IL
Ethnic and Racial Studies	Henley-on-Thames
Ethnology	Pittsburgh, PA
Études	Paris
Études canadiennes — Canadian Studies	Talence
Études internationales	Québec, PQ
Études rurales	Paris
EURE	Santiago
Europäische Rundschau	Vienna
Europe	Paris
European Journal of Political Research	Amsterdam
European Journal of Social Psychology	The Hague
European Judaism	London
Evaluation Studies	Beverly Hills, CA
Family Planning Perspectives	New York, NY
Filosofija i Naučnyj Kommunizm	Minsk
Filosofskie Nauki	Alma-Ata
Filosofskie Problemy Sovremennogo Ėstestvoznanija	Kiev
Fletcher Forum	Medford, MA
Formation emploi	Paris
Foro internacional	México
Forschungsinstitut der Friedrich-Ebert-Stiftung	Hannover
Fragen der Freiheit	Boll-Eckwaelden [BRD]
Frankfurter Hefte	Frankfurt-am-Main
Futures	Guildford
Futuribles	Paris
Gazdaág és Jogtudomány	Budapest
Gekkan Asia-Africa kenkyū	[Nihon]
Gendai shakaigaku	Tokyo
Genève-Afrique	Genève
Genus	Roma
Geographical Review	New York, NY
Geographische Rundschau	Braunschweig
Gérontologie et Société	Paris
Geschichte und Gesellschaft	Bielefeld
Gewerkschaftliche Monatshefte	Köln
Gledišta	Beograd
Government and Opposition	London
H Histoire	Paris
H: revue de l'habitat social	Paris
Hamburger Jahrbuch für Wirtschafts- und Gesellschaftspolitik	Hamburg
Hanzai shakaigaku kenkyū	Tokyo
Hanzai to hiko	Tokyo
Harvard Educational Review	Cambridge, MA
Harvard Law Review	Cambridge, MA
Hérodote	Paris
Higher Education	Amsterdam
Hirosaki daigaku jinbungakubu bunkei ronso	[Nihon]
Hiroshima daigaku ronshu	Hiroshima

Hiroshima shudai ronshu	Hiroshima
Hiroshima taiikugaku kenkyu	Hiroshima
Historical Social Research / Historische Sozialforschung	Köln
History and Theory	Middletown, CT
History of European Ideas	Elmsford, NY-Oxford
Hitotsubashi kenkyu	Tokyo
Hokkaido daigaku Environmental Science	[Nihon]
Hokkaido kyoiku daigaku jinbun ronkyu	[Nihon]
Hokkaido toshi	[Nihon]
Homme	Paris
Homme et Société	Paris
Hommes et Migrations	Paris
Hosei daigaku kyoyobu kiyo shakai-kaguku-hen	[Nihon]
Human Organization	New York, NY
Human Relations	London
Human Systems Management	Amsterdam
Humanisme	Paris
Humanisme et Entreprise	Paris
IBLA	Tunis
IDOC internazionale	Roma
India Quarterly	New Delhi
Indian Journal of Economics	Allahabad
Indian Journal of Politics	Aligarh
Indian Journal of Social Research	Uttar Pradesh
Indian Journal of Social Work	Maharashtra
Indian Labour Journal	Simla
Indian Political Science Review	Delhi
Indonesian Quarterly	Djakarta
Industrial and Labor Relations Review	Ithaca, NY
Industrial Relations	Berkeley, CA
Industry of Free China	Taiwan
Information Society	New York, NY
Informationen zur Raumentwicklung	Bad Godesberg
Informations sociales	Paris
Inquiry	Oslo
Insurgent Sociologist	Eugene, OR
Inter-American Economic Affairs	Washington, DC
Interchange	Toronto, ON
Internasjonal Politikk	Bergen
International and Comparative Law Quarterly	London
International Journal	Toronto, ON
International Journal of Comparative Sociology	Leiden
International Journal of Group Tensions	London
International Journal of Lifelong Education	Lewes [UK]
International Journal of Middle East Studies	London
International Journal of Political Education	Amsterdam
International Journal of Politics	White Plains, NY
International Journal of Public Administration	New York, NY
International Journal of Social Economics	Bradford
International Journal of Sociology	Armonk, NY
International Journal of Sociology and Social Policy	Humberside
International Journal of the Sociology of Language	The Hague
International Journal of the Sociology of Law	London
International Journal of Urban and Regional Research	London
International Library Review	London
International Migration	The Hague
International Migration Review	New York, NY
International Political Science Review	London
International Review of History and Political Science	Meerut
International Social Science Journal / Revue Internationale des Sciences Social	Paris
International Social Science Review	Winfield, KS

International Studies Quarterly	Detroit, MI
Internationales Afrika Forum	München
Internationales Asien Forum	München
Investigación económica	México
IPW Berichte	Berlin
IPW Forschungshefte	Berlin
Israel Yearbook on Human Rights	Tel Aviv
Issue	Los Angelos, CA
Istorija SSSR	Moskva
Izvestija Akademii Nauk Gruzinskoj SSR. Serija Filosofii i Psihologii	Tbilisi
Izvestija Akademii Nauk Kirgizskoj SSSR	Frunze
Izvestija Akademii Nauk SSSR. Serija Ėkonomičeskaja	Moskva
Izvestija Severo-Kavkazskogo Naučnogo Centra Vysšej Školy. Obščestvennye Nauki	Rostov
Izvestija Sibirskogo Otdelenija Akademii Nauk SSSR. Serija Obščestvennyh Nauk	Novosibirsk
Jahrbuch der Wirtschaft Osteuropas	München-Wien
Jahrbuch für christliche Sozialwissenschaften	Münster-Göttingen
Jahrbuch für Geschichte von Staat, Wirtschaft und Gesellschaft Lateinamerika	Köln
Jahrbuch für Neue Politische Ökonomie	Berlin
Jahrbuch für Ostrecht	Munich
Jahrbuch für Regionalwissenschaft	Göttingen
Jahrbuch für Theorie und Praxis des Demokratischen Sozialismus	
Japanese Journal of Religious Studies	Tokyo
Jerusalem Quarterly	Jerusalem
Jewish Journal of Sociology	London
Jewish Social Studies	New York, NY
Jinko mondai kenkyu	Tokyo
Jogtudományi Közlöny	Budapest
Journal de la Société de Statistique de Paris	Paris
Journal for the Theory of Social Behaviour	Oxford
Journal für Sozialforschung	Vienna
Journal of African Law	London
Journal of African Studies	Berkeley, CA
Journal of Applied Behavioral Science	New York, NY
Journal of Asian and African Studies	Leiden-Tokyo
Journal of Asian Studies	Ann Arbor, MI
Journal of Biosocial Science	Cambridge
Journal of Black Studies	Los Angeles, CA
Journal of Broadcasting	Philadelphia, PA
Journal of Communication	Austin, TX
Journal of Conflict Resolution	Ann Arbor, MI
Journal of Consumer Affairs	Columbia, MO
Journal of Contemporary Asia	Stockholm
Journal of Contemporary History	London
Journal of Development Studies	London
Journal of Economic Issues	Lincoln, NE
Journal of Economic Literature	Nashville, TN
Journal of Family History	Minneapolis, MN
Journal of Health, Politics Policy and Law	Durham, NC
Journal of Human Resources	Madison, WI
Journal of Information Science	London
Journal of Inter-American Studies and World Affairs	Beverly Hills, CA
Journal of Interdisciplinary History	Cambridge, MA
Journal of International Affairs	New York, NY
Journal of Jewish Communal Service	New York, NY
Journal of Law and Society	Oxford
Journal of Marriage and the Family	Minneapolis, MN
Journal of Mathematical Sociology	London
Journal of Modern African Studies	Cambridge [UK]
Journal of Peasant Studies	London

Journal of Personality and Social Psychology	Washington, DC
Journal of Philippine Statistics	Manila
Journal of Political and Military Sociology	Dekalb, IL
Journal of Political Economy	Chicago, IL
Journal of Politics	Gainesville, FL
Journal of Public Policy	Cambridge
Journal of Religion in Africa	Leiden
Journal of Social Issues	New York, NY
Journal of Social Policy	Cambridge
Journal of Social Psychology	Provincetown, MA
Journal of Social, Political and Economic Studies	Washington, DC
Journal of the American Planning Association	Washington, DC
Journal of the History of Sociology	Boston, MA
Journal of the Market Research Society	London
Journal of the Royal Statistical Society	London
Journal of Vocational Behaviour	Ann Arbor, MI
Journalism Quarterly	Minneapolis, MN
Jugoslovenski Pregled	Beograd
Juventud	Washington, DC-Buenos Aires
Kagoshima joshi-daigaku kenkyū kiyō	Hayato-Cho
Kagoshima keizai daigaku shakaigakubu ronshu	[Nihon]
Kansai daigaku shakaigakubu kiyo	Osaka
Kateika kyoiku	[Nihon]
Kazoku kenkyu nenpo	[Nihon]
Keio gijuku daigaku daigakuin shakaigaku kenkyuka kiyo	[Nihon]
Keio gijuku daigaku shinbun kenkyujo nenpo	[Nihon]
Keio gijuku daigaku tetsugaku	[Nihon]
Khamsin	London
Kikan jinruigaku	Kyoto
Kikan shakai hosho kenkyu	Tokyo
Kinjō gakuin daigaku ronshū	[Nihon]
Kinjō gakuin daigaku ronshū shakai-kagaku-hen	[Nihon]
Kinki daigaku Kindai fudo	[Nihon]
Kobe daigaku bunkagaku nenpo	[Nihon]
Kokumin seikatsu kenkyu	Tokyo
Kokuritsu minzokugaku hakubutsukan kenkyu hokoku	[Nihon]
Kokusai kirisutokyo daigaku shakai-kagaku journal	Tokyo
Kölner Zeitschrift für Soziologie und Sozialpsychologie	Köln-Opladen
Komazawa shakaigaku kenkyu	[Nihon]
Kommunist (Moskva)	Moskva
Korea Journal	Seoul
Koriyama joshi daigaku kiyo	[Nihon]
Közgazdasági Szemle	Budapest
Kultúra és Közösség	Budapest
Kultura i Społeczeństwo	Warszawa
Kursbuch	Berlin
Kyklos	Berne
Kyoiku shakaigaku kenkyu	[Nihon]
Kyōto University Economic Review	Kyōto
Land Economics	Madison, WI
Language Problems and Language Planning	Austin, TX
LARU Studies	Toronto, ON
Latin American Perspectives	Riverside, CA
Latin American Research Review	Austin, TX
Latinskaja Amerika	Moskva
Law and Policy Quarterly	Beverly Hills, CA
Law and Society Review	New York, NY
Leviathan	Wiesbaden
Liberal (Bonn)	Bonn
Library Trends	Champaign, IL

Littérature	Paris
Loisir et société	Québec, PQ
Luso-Brazilian Review	Madison, WI
Majalah Demografi Indonesia	Djakarta
Man	London
Manchester School of Economic and Social Studies	Manchester
Masses ouvrières	Paris
Matsuyama shoka daigaku Matsuyama shodai ronshu	[Nihon]
Media, Culture and Society	London
Međunarodni Problemi	Belgrade
Medvetánc	Budapest
Meiji gakuin ronso	Tokyo
Mens en Maatschappij	Amsterdam
Miasto	Warszawa
Micropolitics	New York, NY
Milbank Memorial Fund Quarterly	Cambridge, MA
Minerva	London
Mita tetsugakukai tetsugaku	[Nihon]
Mitarbeit (Die)	Heidelberg
Mitteilungen aus der Arbeitsmarkt- und Berufsforschung	Stuttgart
Miyagigakuin joshi daigaku kenkyu ronbunshu	[Nihon]
Modern China	Beverly Hills, CA
Mois en Afrique	Paris
Momoyama gakuin daigaku shakaigaku ronshu	Sakai, Osaka
Mondes en Développement	Brussels
Monthly Review	New York, NY
Mouvement social	Paris
Mozgó Világ	Magyarország
Műhely	Budapest
Musashi daigaku junbungakukkai zasshi	[Nihon]
Nagano daigaku kiyo	[Nihon]
Nakamura gakuen kenkyu kiyo	[Nihon]
Narody Azii i Afriki	Moskva
National Institute Economic Review	London
Nationalities Papers	Omaha, NB
Naučnoe Upravlenie Obščestvom	Moskva
Naučnye Doklady vysšej Školy. Naučnyj Kommunizma	Moskva
Naučnye Trudy (Kurskij Pedagogičeskij Institut)	Kursk
Naučnye Trudy (Tjumenskij Universitet)	Tjumen
Nauka i Religija	Moscow
Nekotorye Problemy Sozdanija Material'no-Tehničeskoj Bazy Kommunizma v Uslovijah Naučno-Tehničeskoj Revoljucii	
Netherlands Journal of Sociology	Assen
Neue Politische Literatur	Wiesbaden
Neue Praxis	Neuwied
New Hungarian Quarterly	Budapest
New Left Review	London
New Universities Quarterly	Oxford
Nihon daigaku bunrigakubu Mishima kenkyu nenpo	[Nihon]
Nihon daigaku Mishima gakuen seikatsukagaku kenkyujo hokoku	[Nihon]
Nihon daigaku seisan kogakubu hokoku B.	[Nihon]
Nihon daigaku shakaigaku ronso	[Nihon]
Nihon daigaku Soshiorojikusu	[Nihon]
Nihon joseigaku kenkyu	[Nihon]
Nihon joseigaku kenkyukai Joseigaku nenpo	[Nihon]
Nihon minzokugaku	Tokyo
Nihon toshi-gakkai nenpo	[Nihon]
Niigata daigaku jinbun kagaku kenkyu	[Nihon]
Notas de Población	Santiago
Notes, critiques et débats de l'Institut des Sciences économiques	Paris
Nouvelles campagnes	Toulouse

Novos Estudos CEBRAP	São Paulo
Nowe Drogi	Warszawa
Nueva Sociedad	Caracas
Obščestvennye Nauki	Moskva
Obščie Problemy Kul'tury i kul'turnogo Stroitel'stva-naučno-referativnyj Sbornik	
Observations et diagnostics économiques	Paris
Ochanomizu joshi daigaku jinbun-kagaku kiyo	[Nihon]
Oeconomica polona	Warszawa
Ohtani daigaku tetsugaku ronshu	[Nihon]
Ohtani gakuho	Kyoto
Oita daigaku kyoikugaku-bu kiyo	Oita
Okayama daigaku kyōikugakubu kenkyū shūroku	[Nihon]
Okinawa Kirisutokyo tanki daigaku kiyo	Okinawa
Optima	Johannesburg
Optimum	Ottawa
Orbis	Louvain
Organization Studies	New York, NY-Berlin
Orient	Opladen
Orientation scolaire et professionnelle	Paris
Osaka daigaku Nenpo ningen kagaku	Osaka
Osaka furitsu daigaku shakai mondai kenkyu	Osaka
Osaka furitsu-daigaku ningen kagaku ronshu	Osaka
Osaka gaikokugo daigaku gakuho	Osaka
Osaka kyoiku daigaku kiyo	Osaka
Osaka kyoiku daigaku kyoikugaku ronshu	Osaka
Osaka shiritsu daigaku shakai fukushi ronshu	Osaka
Österreichische Zeitschrift für Politikwissenschaft	Wien
Osteuropa	Stuttgart
Otemae Joshi Tanki-Daigaku Otemae Bunka Gakuin Kenkyu Shuroku	[Nihon]
Pacific Affairs	New York, NY
Pacific Viewpoint	Wellington
Pakistan Development Review	Karachi-Islamabad
Pakistan Year Book	Karachi
Papers. Revista de Sociologia	Barcelona
Patterns of Prejudice	London
Penant	Paris
Pensée	Paris
Pensiero politico	Firenze
Personnel	New York, NY
Personnel Journal	Santa Monica, CA
Personnel Psychology	Baltimore, MD
Perspectives (UNESCO)	Paris
Peuples Méditerranéens / Mediterranean Peoples	Paris
Peuples Noirs — Peuples Africains	Paris
Philippine Journal of Public Administration	Manila
Philippine Studies	Quezon City
Philosophical Forum	Boston, MA
Philosophy and Public Affairs	Princeton, NJ
Philosophy of the Social Sciences	Aberdeen
Phylon	Atlanta, GA
Planning and Administration	The Hague
Planning Bulletin	Santiago de Chile
Plánované Hospodářství	Praha
Planovoe Hozjajstvo	Moskva
Plural Societies	The Hague
Pluriel	Paris
Policy Review	Washington, DC
Policy Studies	London
Policy Studies Journal	Urbana, IL
Policy Studies Review	Urbana, IL

Polish Sociological Bulletin	Warsaw
Politica ed Economia	Roma
Political Affairs	New York, NY
Political Behavior	New York, NY
Political Economy of the World-System Annuals	Beverly Hills, CA
Political Methodology	Los Altos, CA
Political Power and Social Theory	Greenwich, CT
Political Psychology	Los Angeles, CA
Political Science	Wellington
Political Science Quarterly	New York, NY
Political Science Review	Jaipur
Political Science Reviewer	Pennsylvania, PA
Political Studies	Oxford
Political Theory	London
Političeskaja Organizacija Obščestva i Upravlenie pri Socializme	
Politička Misao	Beograd
Politico	Pavia
Politics	Canberra
Politics and Society	Washington, DC
Politiikka	Helsinki
Politique africaine	Paris
Politische Studien	München
Polity	New York, NY
Polityka społeczna	Warszawa
Population	Paris
Population and Development Review	New York, NY
Population Bulletin of the United Nations	New York, NY
Population et Famille	Bruxelles
Population Research and Policy Review	Wilmington, DE
Population Studies	London
Populi	New York, NY
Pouvoirs	Paris
Poznań Studies	Poznań
Praca i Zabezpieczenie społeczne	Warszawa
Prakseologia	Warszawa
Praxis International	Oxford
Présence africaine	Paris
Priroda	Moskva
Problemi del Socialismo	Milan
Problems of Communism	Washington, DC
Problemy Dal'nego Vostoka	Moskva
Problemy Dialektiki	Leningrad
Problemy Filosofii	Kiev
Problemy Marksizmu-Leninizmu	Warszawa
Problemy naučnogo Kommunizma	Moskva
Problemy vysšej Školy	Moskva
Projet	Paris
Przegląd Humanistyczny	Warszawa
Przegląd zachodni	Poznań
Psichologičeskij Žurnal	Moscow
Psychologie française	Paris
Public Administration	London
Public Administration and Development	London
Public Administration Review	Chicago, IL
Public Choice	Blacksburg, VA
Public Finance Quarterly	Gainesville, FL
Public Interest	New York, NY
Public Opinion	Washington, DC
Public Opinion Quarterly	New York, NY
Publizistik	Münster-in-Westfalen
Quality and Quantity	Padova
Quarterly Journal of Economics	Cambridge, MA

Quarterly Review — National Westminister Bank	London
Quarterly Review of Economics and Business	Champaign, IL
Queen's Quarterly	Kingston
Questions actuelles du Socialisme	Belgrade
Rabočij Klass i sovremennyj Mir	Moskva
Race and Class	London
Radical Humanist	New Delhi
Raison présente	Paris
Rassegna economica	Napoli
Rassegna italiana di Sociologia	Bologna
Rassegna sindicale. Quaderni	Roma
Razón y Fe	Madrid
Recherche	Paris
Recherche sociale	Paris
Recherches économiques et sociales	Paris
Recherches internationales	Paris
Recherches sociographiques	Québec, PQ
Recherches sociologiques	Louvain
Recht der Arbeit	München
Recht der Internationalen Wirtschaft	Heidelberg
Recht in Ost und West	Berlin
Reflets et Perspectives de la Vie économique	Bruxelles
Regional Science and Urban Economics	Philadelphia, PA
Regional Studies	Oxford
Rekishi koron	[Nihon]
Relations industrielles	Québec, PQ
Res publica	Bruxelles
Research in Corporate Social Performance and Policy	Greenwich, CT
Research in Economic Anthropology	Evanston, IL
Research in Labor Economics	Greenwich, CT
Research in Organizational Behaviour	Greenwich, CT
Research in Political Economy	Greenwich, CT
Research in Race and Ethnic Relations	Greenwich, CT
Research in Social Movements, Conflicts and Change	Greenwich, CT
Review (F. Braudel Center)	Binghamton, NY
Review of African Political Economy	London
Review of Economic Conditions in Italy	Roma
Review of Economic Studies	Edinburgh
Review of Politics	Notre Dame, IN
Review of Radical Political Economics	Ann Arbor, MI
Revija za Sociologiju	Zagreb
Revista Argentina de Administración Pública	Buenos Aires
Revista brasileira de Economia	Rio de Janeiro
Revista brasileira de Estatística	Rio de Janeiro
Revista brasileira de Estudos políticos	Belo Horizonte
Revista de Administração municipal	Rio de Janeiro
Revista de Ciencias sociales	Fortaleza [PR]
Revista de ciencias sociales (San José)	San José
Revista de Ciencias Sociales de la Universidad de Costa Rica	San José
Revista de Direito administrativo	Rio de Janeiro
Revista de Economía política	Madrid
Revista de Educación	Madrid
Revista de Estudios agro-sociales	Madrid
Revista de Estudios de la Vida local	Madrid
Revista de Estudios internacionales	Madrid
Revista de Estudios políticos	Madrid
Revista de Filozofie	Bucureşti
Revista de Fomento social	Madrid
Revista de la Cooperación	Buenos Aires
Revista de la Facultad de Ciencias Económicas de la Universidad de Cuyo	Mendoza
Revista de la Facultad de Derecho de México	México
Revista de Planeación y Desarrollo	Bogotá

Revista de Política Social	Madrid
Revista de Statistică	Bucureşti
Revista española de Investigaciones Sociológicas	Madrid
Revista interamericana de Planificación	Bogotá
Revista internacional de Sociología	Madrid
Revista javeriana	Bogotá
Revista mexicana de ciencias politicas y sociales	México
Revista mexicana de Sociología	México
Revue algérienne des Sciences juridiques, économiques et politiques	Algiers
Revue belge de Sécurité sociale	Bruxelles
Revue d'Économie politique	Paris
Revue d'Économie régionale et urbaine	Paris
Revue d'Études comparatives Est-Ouest	Paris
Revue d'Intégration européenne	Montréal, PQ
Revue de Corée	Seoul
Revue de droit rural	Paris
Revue de Géographie alpine	Paris
Revue de Géographie de Lyon	Lyon
Revue de l'Institut de Sociologie	Bruxelles
Revue de la Coopération internationale	Londres
Revue de Science criminelle et de Droit pénal comparé	Paris
Revue des Études coopératives	Paris
Revue des Pays de l'Est	Bruxelles
Revue des Sciences morales et politiques	Paris
Revue économique et sociale	Lausanne
Revue européenne des Sciences sociales	Geneva
Revue fiduciaire	Paris
Revue française d'Administration publique	Paris
Revue française d'Études américaines	Paris
Revue française d'Histoire d'Outre-mer	Paris
Revue française de Finances publiques	Paris
Revue française de Gestion	Paris
Revue française de Science politique	Paris
Revue française de Sociologie	Paris
Revue française des Affaires sociales	Paris
Revue française du Marketing	Paris
Revue géographique des Pyrénées et du Sud-Ouest	Toulouse
Revue internationale d'action communautaire	Montreal, PQ
Revue internationale de Droit pénale	Paris
Revue internationale de Sécurité sociale	Genève
Revue internationale de Sociologie / International Review of Sociology	Rome
Revue internationale des Sciences administratives	Bruxelles
Revue internationale du Travail	Genève
Revue juridique et politique. Indépendance et Coopération	Paris
Revue nouvelle	Tournai
Revue politique et parlementaire	Paris
Revue roumaine des Sciences sociales. Série de Sociologie	Bucharest
Revue roumaine des Sciences sociales. Série des Sciences juridiques	Bucharest
Revue tunisienne de Communication	Tunis
Revue tunisienne de Géographie	Tunis
Revue tunisienne des Sciences sociales	Tunis
Ricerca sociale	Milan
Rikkyo daigaku oyo shakaigaku kenkyu	[Nihon]
Rissho daigaku bungakubu ronso	Tokyo
Rissho daigaku jinbun-kagaku kenkyujo nenpo	[Nihon]
Ritsumeikan daigaku Sangyo shakai ronshu	[Nihon]
Rivista internazionale di Scienze economiche e commerciali	Milano
Rivista internazionale di Scienze sociali	Milano
Rivista italiana di scienza politica	Bologna
Rivista trimestrale di Diritto pubblico	Milano
Ronen shakai-kagaku	Tokyo
Rozprawy z filozofii i socjologii	Toruń
RS. Cuadernos de realidades sociales	Madrid

Ruch prawniczy, ekonomiczny i socjologiczny	Poznań
Rural Sociology	Lexington, KY
Ryukoku daigaku ronshu	Kyoto
Ryūkokū kiyo	[Nihon]
Sage Annual Reviews of Communication Research	Beverly Hills, CA
Sage Yearbook in Women's Policy Studies	Beverly Hills, CA
Sage Yearbooks in Politics and Public Policy	Beverly Hills, CA
Sapporo daigaku keizai to keiei	Sapporo
Sbornik naučnyh Trudov (Leningradskij Institut Kultury)	Leningrad
Sborník Prací filozofické Fakulty Brnenské University	Brno
Scandinavian Economic History Review	Copenhagen
Scandinavian Journal of Materials Administration	Oslo
Scandinavian Political Studies	Helsinki
Schema	Seattle, WA
Schmalenbachs Zeitschrift für Betriebswirtschaftliche Forschung	Berlin
Schweizer Monatshefte	Zürich
Schweizerische Zeitschrift für Soziologie	Genève
Science and Public Policy	London
Science and Society	New York, NY
Sciences sociales — Académie des Sciences de l'URSS	Moscou
Sciences Sociales du Japon Contemporain	[Japan]
Scientific American	New York, NY
Scientometrics	Budapest
Search	Miami, FL
Seijo daigaku communication kiyo	[Nihon]
Seiroka kango daigaku kiyo	[Nihon]
Seminar	New Delhi
Senden kaigi	[Nihon]
Senshu daigaku shakai-kagaku nenpo	[Nihon]
Shakai kyoiku	[Nihon]
Shakai rōnengaku	[Nihon]
Shakaigaku hyoron	Tokyo
Shakaigaku kenkyu	Tokyo
Shakaigaku nenpo	Tokyo
Shakaigaku nenshi	Tokyo
Shakaigaku ronso	Tokyo
Shakaigaku-shi kenkyu	[Nihon]
Shihoku gakuin daigaku ronshū	[Nihon]
Shinbungaku hyōron	[Nihon]
Shisō	[Nihon]
Shizuoka joshi tanki-daigaku kenkyu kiyo	Haniamatsu
Shumu jiho	[Nihon]
Signs	New York, NY
Sistema	Madrid
Sloan Management Review	Cambridge
Social Action	New Delhi
Social and Economic Studies	Mona
Social Compass	The Hague
Social Dynamics	Capetown
Social Forces	Chapel Hill, NC
Social Indicators Research	Dordrecht
Social Networks	Bethlehem, PA
Social Policy	New York, NY
Social Problems	New York, NY-Rochester, MI
Social Psychology Quarterly	Albany, NY
Social Research	New York, NY
Social Science Information / Information sur les Sciences Sociales	London
Social Science Information Studies	Borough Green
Social Science Journal (Fort Collins)	Fort Collins, CO
Social Science Journal (Seoul)	Seoul
Social Science Quarterly	Austin, TX

Social Science Research	Ann Arbor, MI
Social Sciences in China	Beijing
Social Service Delivery Systems: an International Annual	Beverly Hills, CA
Social Service Review	Chicago, IL
Social Theory and Practice	Tallahassee, FL
Social'no-Ékonomičeskie Problemy Truda	[Kujbysev]
Socialismo y participación	Lima
Socialist Review	San Francisco, CA
Society	New Brunswick, NJ
Socijalizam	Beograd
Socio-Economic Planning Sciences	Oxford
Sociología	Caracas
Sociologia	Roma
Sociologia internationalis	Berlin
Sociologia ruralis	Assen
Sociological Analysis	San Antonio, TX
Sociological Focus	Akron, OH
Sociological Inquiry	Toronto, ON
Sociological Methodology	San Francisco, CA
Sociological Methods and Research	Beverly Hills, CA
Sociological Perspectives	Beverly Hills, CA
Sociological Quarterly	Carbondale, IL
Sociological Review	Keele
Sociological Review Monograph	Keele
Sociologičeskie Issledovanija	Moskva
Sociologie du Travail	Paris
Sociologie et Sociétés	Montréal, PQ
Sociologija	Beograd
Sociologija Sela	Zagreb
Sociologische Gids	Meppel
Sociologos	[Nihon]
Sociologus	Berlin
Sociology	London
Sociology and Social Research	Los Angeles, CA
Sociology of the Sciences	Dordrecht
Soka daigaku daigakuin kiyo	Hachioji, Tokyo
Soka daigaku Soshiorojika	[Nihon]
Soshioroji	Kyoto
South Africa International	Johannesburg
Southern Economic Journal	Chapel Hill, NC
Sovetskaja Pedagogika	Moskva
Sovetskoe Gosudarstvo i Pravo	Moskva
Soviet Geography	New York, NY
Soviet Jewish Affairs	London
Soviet Studies	Glasgow
Soziale Welt	Göttingen
Sozialer Fortschritt	Bonn
Spółdzielczy Kwartalnik naukowy	Warszawa
Sprawy międzynarodowe	Warszawa
SŠA	Moskva
Staat (Dcr)	Berlin
Staat und Recht	Potsdam
Statistika	Praha
Statistiques du travail. Supplément au bulletin mensuel	Paris
Stato e Mercato	Bologna
Statsvetenskaplig Tidskrift	Lund
Studi di Sociologia	Milano
Studi Emigrazione	Roma
Studia Demograficzne	Warszawa
Studia Filozoficzne	Warszawa
Studia Nauk Politycznych	Warszawa
Studia Socjologiczne	Wrocław
Studies in Family Planning	New York, NY

Südosteuropa — Zeitschrift für Gegenwartsforschung	München
Svensk Juristtidning	Stockholm
Szociológia	Budapest
Taamuli	Dar es Salaam
Taisho daigaku counseling kenkyujo kiyo	[Nihon]
Tamagawa daigaku bungaku-bu kiyo	[Nihon]
Társadalmi Szemle	Budapest
Társadalomkutatás	Budapest
Társadalomtudományi Közlemények	Budapest
Teachers College Record	New York, NY
Teaching Political Science	Beverly Hills, CA
Teaching Politics	Delhi
Teaching Sociology	Beverly Hills, CA
Technological Forecasting and Social Change	New York, NY
Telos	St. Louis, MO
Temps modernes	Paris
Területi Statisztika	Budapest
Testnevelés és Sporttudomány	Budapest
Theory and Society	Amsterdam
Third World Planning Review	Liverpool
Three Banks Review	Edinburgh
Tiers-Monde	Paris
Tocqueville Review	Rochester, MI
Tohoku fukushi daigaku kiyō	Sendai
Tohoku toshi gakkai kaiho	[Nihon]
Tokei	Tokyo
Tokushima daigaku gakugei kiyō (shakai-kagaku)	[Nihon]
Tokyo daigaku kyoikugakubu kiyo	Tokyo
Tokyo gakugei daigaku kiyo	Tokyo
Tokyo keizai daigaku jinbun shizen kagaku ronshu	Tokyo
Tokyo keizai daigaku kaishi	Tokyo
Tokyo toritsu daigaku jinbungaku-ho	Tokyo
Tokyo toritsu daigaku shakaigaku ronko	Tokyo
Tokyo toritsu daigaku sogo toshi kenkyu	Tokyo
Tokyo toritsu shoka tanki daigaku kenkyu ronso	Tokyo
Tokyo toritsu shoka tanki-daigaku	Tokyo
Tonan Asia kenkyu	[Nihon]
Toshi keikaku bessatsu	[Nihon]
Toshi mondai	Tokyo
Toshi mondai kenkyu	Osaka
Toyama daigaku kyoikugakubu kiyo	[Nihon]
Toyo daigaku shakaigakubu kiyo	[Nihon]
Travail et Emploi	Paris
Travail et Méthodes	Paris
Travail et Société	Genève
Travail humain	Paris
Travaux de l'Association Henri Capitant	Paris
Trimestre económico	México
Tsukuba daigaku Latin American Studies	[Nihon]
Tsuruoka kogyo koto senmon gakko kenkyu kiyo	[Nihon]
Universitas	Stuttgart
Urban Affairs Annual Reviews	Beverly Hills, CA
Urban Affairs Quarterly	Beverly Hills, CA
Urban and Social Change Review	Boston, MA
Urban Geography	Silver Spring, MD
Urban Studies	Edinburgh
Utafiti	Dar es Salaam
Verfassung und Recht in Übersee	Hamburg
Verwaltung	Heidelberg
Vestnik Harkovskogo Universiteta	Harkov

Vestnik Leningradskogo Universiteta. Serija Ėkonomika, Filosofija Pravo	Leningrad
Vestnik Moskovskogo Gosudarstvennogo Universiteta. Serija Geografija	Moskva
Vestnik Moskovskogo Universiteta. Serija Filosofija	Moskva
Vestnik Moskovskogo Universiteta. Serija Pravo	Moskva
Vestnik Moskovskogo Universiteta. Serija Teorija naučnogo Kommunizma	Moskva
Vestnik Statistiki	Moskva
Vierteljahreshefte für Zeitgeschichte	Stuttgart
Vierteljahreshefte zur Wirtschaftsforschung	Berlin
Viitorul social	Bucarest
Vita e Pensiero	Milano
Volunteer katsudo kenkyu	[Nihon]
Voprosy Ateizma	Kiev
Voprosy Ėkonomiki	Moskva
Voprosy Filosofii	Moskva
Voprosy Filosofii (Ėrevan)	Ėrevan
Voprosy Istorii	Moskva
Voprosy Istorii KPSS	Moskva
Voprosy političeskoj Ėkonomii	Kiev
Vorgänge	Hamburg
Vozes	Petropolis [Brazil]
Wallonie	Namur
Waseda daigaku kotogakuin kenkyu nenshi	Tokyo
Waseda daigaku shakai-kagaku tokyu	Tokyo
Waseda daigaku shakaigaku nenshi	Tokyo
Waseda daigaku shaken kenkyu series — soren touou shakai no shin-kenkyu	Tokyo
West European Politics	London
Western Political Quarterly	Salt Lake City, UT
Wieś i Rolnictwo	Warszawa
Wieś Współczesna	Warszawa
Wirtschaftswissenschaft	Berlin
Women and Politics	New York, NY
Women's Studies International Forum	Oxford
Work and Occupations	Beverly Hills, CA
Work and People	Melbourne
World Affairs	Washington, DC
World Politics	Princeton, NJ
World Today	London
WSI Mitteilungen	Köln
Yahata daigaku ronshu	Yahata
Yale Law Journal	New Haven, CT
Yamaguchi joshi daigaku kenkyu hokoku	[Nihon]
Yearbook of Population Research in Finland	Helsinki
Yearbook of Social Policy in Britain	London
Yugoslav Survey	Belgrade
Yuibutsuron kenkyu	[Nihon]
Zagadnienia Ėkonomiki rolnej	Warszawa
Zaïre-Afrique	Kinshasa
Zeitschrift der Gesellschaft für Kanada-Studien	Neumünster
Zeitschrift für Bevölkerungswissenschaft	Wiesbaden
Zeitschrift für das Gesamte Genossenschaftswesen	Göttingen
Zeitschrift für Nationalökonomie	Wien-New York, NY
Zeitschrift für Parlamentsfragen	Opladen
Zeitschrift für Politik	Berlin
Zeitschrift für Soziologie	Stuttgart
Zeitschrift für Wirtschaftspolitik	Köln
Życie Szkoły Wyższej	Warszawa

CLASSIFICATION SCHEME
PLAN DE CLASSIFICATION

10100   SOCIAL SCIENCES. SOCIOLOGY
SCIENCES SOCIALES. SOCIOLOGIE

1   ABRAMS, Philip. *Historical sociology.* Near Shepton Mallet, Somerset, Open Books, 82, xviii-353 p.

2   ACCARDO, Alain. *Initiation à la sociologie de l'illusionnisme social: invitation à la lecture des oeuvres de Pierre Bourdieu.* Bordeaux, Éditions le Mascaret, 83, 211 p.

3   ADAMS, Robert McCormick; SMELSER, Neil J.; TREIMAN, Donald; [eds.]. *Behavioral and social science research: a national resource.* Washington, DC, National Academy Press, 82, xiii-121 p.

4   ATAL, Yogesh. "Using the social sciences for policy formulation", *International Social Science Journal* 35(2), 83 : 367-377.

5   ATOJI, Yoshio. "Ferdinand Tönnies and Georg Simmel", *Soka daigaku Soshiorojika* 7(2), 83 : 1-41.

6   ATOJI, Yoshio. "Georg Simmel and Emile Durkheim", *Soka daigaku Soshiorojika* 8(1), 83 : 15-71.

7   BAKLIEN, Bergljot. "The use of social science in a Norwegian Ministry: as a tool of policy or mode of thinking?", *Acta Sociologica* 26(1), 83 : 33-47. [Ministry of Transport and Communication]

8   BERLAGE, Gai; EGELMAN, William. *Experience with sociology: social issues in American society.* Reading, MA, Addison-Wesley Publishing Co., 83, x-108 p.

9   BERNERT, Chris. "From cameralism to sociology with Albion Small", *Journal of the History of Sociology* 4(2), 82 : 32-63. [USA]

10   BESNARD, Philippe. "Histoire de la sociologie", *Année sociologique* 33, 83 : 355-380. [Compte rendu bibliographique]

11   BIE, P. de. "Les débuts de la sociologie en Belgique. I. La fondation du premier Institut de sociologie Solvay", *Recherches sociologiques* 14(2), 83 : 109-140.

12   BIFFOT, Laurent. *Grandes tendances de la sociologie et de la psychologie sociale.* Libreville, chez l'auteur, 83.

13   BÍNA, V. "Tsjechische sociologie en marxisme-leninisme" (Czech sociology and Marxism-Leninism), *Mens en Maatschappij* 58(1), feb 83 : 53-77.

14   BLAGOJEVIĆ, Stevan. "Social sciences and humanities", *Yugoslav Survey* 24(1), feb 83 : 91-104.

15   BLALOCK, Hubert M. Jr.; [et al.]. "How to improve the quality of introductory sociology courses", *Teaching Sociology* 10(2), jan 83 : 149-230. [USA]

16   BOURDIEU, Pierre. *Leçon sur la leçon.* Paris, Éditions de Minuit, 82, 55 p.

17   BOURDIEU, Pierre. "Les sciences sociales et la philosophie", *Actes de la Recherche en Sciences sociales* 47-48, jun 83 : 45-52.

18   BOVENKERK, Frank; BRUNT, Lodewijk. "Where sociology falls short: how Dutch sociologists observe social reality", *Netherlands Journal of Sociology* 19(1), apr 83 : 65-78.

19   BULMER, Martin; [ed.]. "Social science and policy-making. The use of research by governmental commissions", *American Behavioral Scientist* 26(5), mai-jun 83 : 555-680.

20   CARDOSO, Fernando H.; [et al.]. *Medina Echavarría y la sociología latinoamericana* (Medina Echavarría and Latin American sociology). Madrid, Ediciones Cultura Hispánica del Instituto de Cooperación Iberoamericana, 82, 159 p.

21   CHENG, L.; SO, A. "The reestablishment of sociology in the PRC: toward the signification of Marxian sociology", *Annual Review of Sociology* (9), 83 : 471-498.

22   CLIQUET, R. L. "De betekenis van de sociobiologie voor de emancipatie van de vrouw" (The meaning of social biology for women's liberation), *Bevolking en Gezin* (2), 83 : 255-272.

23   COLOMBO, Miriam. "La sociologia di fronte alla cooperazione negli anni ottanta" (Sociology and cooperation in the '80s), *Studi di Sociologia* 20(3-4), jul-dec 82 : 361-368.

24   COSTEA, Ştefan; LARIONESCU, Maria; UNGUREANU, Ion. *Sociologie românească contemporană* (Romanian sociology today). Bucureşti, Editura Ştiinţifică şi Enciclopedică, 83, 423-1 p.

25   CZARNOWSKI, S. *Wybór pism socjologicznych* (Choice of sociological writings). Warszawa, Książka i Wiedza, 82, xxix-481 p. [Poland]

26   DANIELS, Douglas F. "Can North American sociology be applied to China?", *Monthly Review* 34(7), dec 82 : 19-30.

27   DAS, Man Singh; [ed.]. *Contemporary sociology in the United States.* New Delhi, Vikas, 83, x-329 p.

28   DE GENNARO, Antonio. *Modelli e storiografia nelle scienze sociali: temi e problemi* (Models
      and historiography in social sciences: themes and problems). Milano, F. Angeli, 83, 224 p.
29   DEEGAN, Mary Jo. "Sociology at Wellesley College: 1900-1919", *Journal of the History
      of Sociology* 5(1), 83 : 91-115. [USA]
30   DIESING, Paul. *Science and ideology in the policy sciences.* New York, NY, Aldine, 82, 460 p.
31   DONATI, Pierpaolo. "Quale sociologia? L'approccio del realismo critico e le tesi della
      sociologia relazionale" (What kind of sociology? The critical realism approach and the
      theses of the relational sociology), *Studi di Sociologia* 21(2), apr-jun 83 : 126-146.
32   DRIESSEN, Patrick A. "The wedding of social science and the courts: is the marriage
      working?", *Social Science Quarterly* 64(3), sep 83 : 476-493.
33   EISENSTADT, Shmuel N. "Die soziologische Tradition: Ursprünge, Grenzen, Innovations-
      muster und Krisenformen" (The sociological tradition: origins, limits, innovation models
      and crisis forms), *Kölner Zeitschrift für Soziologie und Sozialpsychologie* 35(2), jun 83 : 205-229.
34   FAVRE, Pierre. "Gabriel Tarde et la mauvaise fortune d'un 'baptême sociologique' de
      la science politique", *Revue française de Sociologie* 24(1), jan-mar 83 : 3-30.
35   FEDOSEEV, P. N. "K voprosy o predmete marksistskoleninskoj sociologii" (Question on
      the Marxist-Leninist sociology object), *Sociologičeskie Issledovanija* (3), 82 : 27-29.
36   FRICK, Jean-Paul. "Les détours de la problématique sociologique de Saint-Simon", *Revue
      française de Sociologie* 24(2), apr-jun 83 : 183-202.
37   GAREAU, Frederick H. "The multinational version of social science", *International Social
      Science Journal* 35(2), 83 : 379-389.
38   GHEORGHIU, Mihnea. "New trends in the social and political sciences", *Revue roumaine
      des sciences sociales. Série de sociologie* 26(2), dec 82 : 107-116.
39   GRAYSON, John Paul; [ed.]. *Introduction to sociology: an alternate approach.* Toronto, ON,
      Gage, 83, x-598 p.
40   HAGEDORN, Robert; [ed.]. *Sociology.* Dubuque, IA, W. C. Brown Co. Publishers,
      83, xxi-601-12 p.
41   HALLEN, G. C. "The state of contemporary sociology", *Indian Journal of Social Research*
      23(3), dec 82 : 203-211.
42   HARRIS, Reuben T.; CAHN, Meyer Michael. "Use of behavioral science and technology:
      an international perspective", *Journal of Applied Behavioral Science* 19(3), 83 : iv-239-407.
43   HARRISON, Deborah. "The limits of liberalism in Canadian sociology: some notes on
      S. D. Clark", *Canadian Review of Sociology and Anthropology* 20(2), mai 83 : 150-166.
44   HARVEY, Charles E. "John D. Rockfeller, Jr., and the social sciences: an introduction",
      Journal of the History of Sociology 4(2), 82 : 1-31.
45   HAZARD, Barbara P. "Chinese Marxist sociology: recent development and future trends",
      Internationales Asien Forum 14(1), mar 83 : 5-34.
46   HERSENI, Traian. *Sociologie: teoria generală a vieţii sociale* (Sociology: general theory of social
      life). Bucureşti, Editura Ştiinţifică, 82, 658-2 p.
47   HILLER, Harry H. *Society and change: S. D. Clark and the development of Canadian sociology.*
      Toronto, ON-Buffalo, NY, University of Toronto Press, 82, xvi-207 p.
48   HIMMELSTRAND, Ulf. "The relationship between sociology and social practice", *Praxis
      International* 2(4), jan 83 : 408-420.
49   HIRSCHHORN, Monique. "Max Weber et les durkheimiens. Brève histoire d'un rendez-
      vous manqué", *Revue de l'Institut de Sociologie* (3-4), 83 : 293-310.
50   HOLZER, Horst. *Soziologie in der BRD* (Sociology in the GFR). Frankfukrt-am-Main,
      Marxistische Blätter, 82, 128 p.
51   IAKHIEL, Niko. *Sotšiologiiă i sotsialna praktika* (Sociology and social practice). Sofiia,
      Partizdat, 82, 345 p. [Bulgaria]
52   INKELES, Alex. "The sociological contribution to advances in the social sciences", *Social
      Science Journal (Fort Collins)* 20(3), jul 83 : 27-44.
53   IZZO, Alberto. "La sociologia critica in Italia" (Critical sociology in Italy), *Critica sociologica*
      66, 83 : 19-42.
54   JANISZEWSKI, Ludwik; SOSNOWSKI, Adam. "Socjologia morska: jej przedmiot i
      funkcje" (Maritime sociology: its subject and functions), *Studia Socjologiczne* 90 (3), 83 : 35-59.
55   JAVEAU, Claude. "La sociologia e la crisi del positivismo: per un'antropologia ontologica"
      (Sociology and crisis of positivism: for an ontological anthropology), *Critica sociologica*
      68, 83-84 : 6-15.
56   JONES, Frank; [et al.]. "Dialogue: crisis in sociology", *Australian and New Zealand Journal of
      Sociology* 19(2), jul 83 : 195-215.
57   JONES, Robert Alun. "The new history of sociology", *Annual Review of Sociology* (9), 83 : 447-469.

58   KELLER, Berndt. "Individualistische Sozialwissenschaft. Zur Relevanz einer Theorie-
        diskussion" (Individualistic social science. On the relevance of a theory discussion),
        Kölner Zeitschrift für Soziologie und Sozialpsychologie 35(1), mar 83 : 59-82.

59   KOVAČ, Tereza. "Savremena madarska sociologija" (Hungarian modern sociology),
        Sociologija 25(2-3), 83 : 325-339.

60   KULCSÁR, Kálmán. *Historical outlook and politics: notes to the evolution of the historical outlook
        of Hungarian sociology.* Budapest, Magyar Tudományos Akadémia Szociologiai Intézete,
        83, 45 p.

61   KWAŚNIEWICZ, Władysław. "Socjologia w sto lat po Marksie" (Sociology one hundred
        years after Marx), *Problemy Marksizmu-Leninizmu* 3-4, 83 : 81-95.

62   LEE, Alfred McClung. "Riumanizzare le scienze sociali" (To rehumanize social sciences),
        Critica sociologica 66, 83 : 10-18.

63   LEPENIES, Wolf. "Contribution à une histoire des rapports entre la sociologie et la
        philosophie", *Actes de la Recherche en Sciences sociales* 47-48, jun 83 : 37-44.

64   LEPSIUS, M. Rainer. "The development of sociology in Germany after World War II
        (1945-1968)", *International Journal of Sociology* 23(3), 83 : 3-88.

65   LINDENBERG, Siegwart. "Zur Kritik an Durkheims Programm für die Soziologie" (On
        the critique of the Durkheim's program for sociology), *Zeitschrift für Soziologie* 12(2), apr
        83 : 139-151.

66   LOPREATO, Joseph; RUSHER, Sandra. "Vilfredo Pareto's influence on USA sociology",
        Revue européenne des Sciences sociales 21(65), 83 : 69-122.

67   LOPREATO, Joseph; [et al.]. "Sociologies d'hier et d'aujourd'hui", *Revue européenne des
        Sciences sociales* 21(65), 83 : 69-198.

68   LÜSCHEN, Günther. "Zwei Soziologien? Deutsche und amerikanische Soziologie in
        repräsentativen Kompendien" (Two sociologies? German and American sociologies
        through two representative works), *Kölner Zeitschrift für Soziologie und Sozialpsychologie* 35(1),
        mar 83 : 133-141. [Joachim Matthes and James Short]

69   LYON, David. "Sociology and humanness: the action-structure tension in secular and
        Christian thought", *Sociologia internationalis* 21(1-2), 83 : 51-68.

70   MAFFESOLI, Michel. "L'imaginaire et le quotidien dans la sociologie de Durkheim",
        Revue européenne des Sciences sociales 21(65), 83 : 123-133.

71   MATLOCK, Donald T.; SHORT, Alvin P. "The impact of high school sociology. Some
        preliminary test results from the college introductory course", *Teaching Sociology* 10(4),
        jul 83 : 505-516. [USA]

72   MCGUIRE, Patrick; DAWES, Kenneth. "Sociology as social contribution: University of
        North Dakota as a case study of the contradictions of academic sociology", *Sociological
        Quarterly* 24(4), 83 : 589-603.

73   MEYER, Peter. *Soziobiologie und Soziologie: eine Einführung in die biologischen Voraussetzungen
        sozialen Handelns* (Sociobiology and sociology: an introduction to the biological premises
        of social action). Darmstadt, Luchterhand, 82, 152 p. [Edited by Johannes BERGER]

74   MIKHAĬLOV, Stoian. *Sotsiologicheski studii* (Sociological studies). Sofiia, Izd-vo Nauka i
        Izkustvo, 82, 304 p.

75   MONGARDINI, Carlo. "Per una sociologia umanistica" (For a humanistic sociology),
        Studi di Sociologia 21(2), apr-jun 83 : 147-159.

76   MORGAN, J. Graham. "Courses and texts in sociology", *Journal of the History of Sociology*
        5(1), 83 : 42-65. [USA]

77   MORI, Shigeo. "Durkheim to Durkheim-izen" (Durkheim and his precedents), *Tokyo
        daigaku kyoikugakubu kiyo* 22, 83 : 193-202.

78   MURPHY, Raymond. "The struggle for scholarly recognition. The development of the
        closure problematic in sociology", *Theory and Society* 12(5), sep 83 : 631-658.

79   NAGAMI, Isamu. *Ryokai to kachi no shakaigaku* (Understanding and the value aspects of
        sociology). Tokyo, Idemitsu Shoten, 83, 215 p.

80   NAITO, Kanji. "Durkheim gakuha no jitsuzo" (What is Durkheimian school?), *Rissho
        daigaku jinbun-kagaku kenkyujo nenpo* 20, 83 : 50-60.

81   NOCK, David A. "S. D. Clark in the context of Canadian sociology", *Canadian Journal
        of Sociology / Cahiers canadiens de Sociologie* 8(1), 83 : 79-97.

82   NOVÁK, Vladimír J. A. *The principle of sociogenesis.* Praha, Czechoslovak Academy of
        Sciences, Academia Publishing House, 82, 214 p.

83   ŌGANE, Takeshi. "Shakaigakuteki keishiki no mondaisei: Georg Simmel to Emile
        Durkheim" (The problematic nature of sociological forms: George Simmel and Emile
        Durkheim), *Dōto daigaku kiyō*, 83 : 83-96.

84   PEŠIĆ, Vesna. "Etnometodologija i sociologija" (Ethnomethodology and sociology),
        Sociologija 25(2-3), 83 : 261-286.

85   POLLAK, Michael. "Institutionalisierung, Wachstum und Wandel der heutigen französischen
        Soziologie" (Institutionalization, growth and change in current French sociology),
        Historical Social Research (25), jan 83 : 4-23. [résumé en anglais]
86   PREWITT, Kenneth. "Social science and the Third World: constraints on the United
        States", *International Social Science Journal* 35(4), 83 : 757-765.
87   QUIJANO, Anibal. "Sociedad y sociologiía en América latina" (Society and sociology
        in Latin America), *Revista de Ciencias sociales* 23(1-2), jun 81 : 225-249.
88   REX, John. "British sociology 1960-80: an essay", *Social Forces* 61(4), jun 83 : 999-1009.
89   REYES, R. "Ciencias Sociales: hacia un modelo alternativo de programa" (Social sciences:
        towards an alternative programme model), *Sistema* (57), nov 83 : 141-145.
90   RIPEPE, Eugenio. "Après Karl Marx est-ce le temps de Gaetano Mosca?", *Revue européenne
        des Sciences sociales* 21(65), 83 : 135-141.
91   RJABUŠKIN, T. V.; OSIPOV, G. V.; [eds.]. *Sovetskaja sociologija. I. Sociologičeskaja teorija
        i social'naja praktika. II. Dinamika social'nyh processov v SSSR* (Soviet sociology. I. Sociological
        theory and social practice. II. Dynamics of social processes in the USSR). Moskva,
        Nauka, 82, 287 p.
92   SABERWAL, Satish. "For a sociology of India. On multiple codes", *Contributions to Indian
        Sociology* 16(2), jul-dec 82 : 289-294.
93   SARGENT, Magaret J. *Sociology for Australians.* Melbourne, Longman Cheshire, 83, xvi-254 p.
94   SCHRAG, Francis. "Social science and social practice", *Inquiry* 26(1), mar 83 : 107-124.
95   SEBALD, Hans. "Freud: instinctivist or bahaviorist? The mirages of American sociology",
        Journal of the History of Sociology 4(2), 82 : 64-89.
96   SEIDMAN, Steven. "Beyond presentism and historicism: understanding the history of
        social science", *Sociological Inquiry* 53(1), 83 : 79-94.
97   SICA, Alan. "Sociology at the University of Kansas, 1889-1983: an historical sketch",
        Sociological Quarterly 24(4), 83 : 605-623.
98   SIMICH, J. L.; TILMAN, Rick. "On the use and abuse of Thorstein Veblen in modern
        American sociology. I. David Riesman's reductionist interpretation and Tallcott Parsons'
        pluralist critique", *American Journal of Economics and Sociology* 42(4), oct 83 : 417-429.
99   SINGH, Ujagar. "New horizon in teaching and research in sociology in India", *Indian
        Journal of Social Research* 23(1), apr 82 : 71-79.
100   SOCIÉTÉ FRANÇAISE DE SOCIOLOGIE. *Enquête sur l'enseignement de la sociologie.
        I. Analyse des réponses au questionnaire d'enquête.* Paris, SFS, 83, 73 p. [France]
101   SOWA, Kazimierz Z.; [ed.]. *Szkice z historii socjologii polskiej* (Essays on the history of Polish
        sociology). Warszawa, Instytut Wydawniczy PAX, 83, 427 p.
102   STEIN, Nancy Wendlandt; [ed.]. "The use of mass media in sociology curricula", *Teaching
        Sociology* 10(3), apr 83 : 283-405. [USA]
103   SZACKI, Jerzy. *Historia myśli socjologicznej* (History of the sociological thought). Warszawa,
        Państwowe Wydawnictwo Naukowe, 83, 918 p.
104   SZMATKA, Jacek. "Correspondence principle as a tool explaining the growth of social
        science", *Philosophy of the Social Sciences* 13(1), 83 : 47-53.
105   TANABE, Yoshiaki. "Reimeiki no Chugoku shakaigaku: Chugoku shakaigaku-shi josetsu"
        (The early stage of China's sociology), *Shakaigaku-shi kenkyu* 5, 83 : 63-73.
106   TARAS, Ray. "Polish sociology and the base-superstructure debate", *Philosophy of the Social
        Sciences* 13(3), sep 83 : 307-324.
107   THURSTON, Anne F.; PASTERNAK, Burton; [eds.]. *The social sciences and fieldwork in
        China: views from the field.* Boulder, CO, Westview Press, 83, xv-161 p.
108   UTAGAWA, Takuo. "Parsons shakaigaku to kindaiteki profession" (Parsons' sociology
        and modern professions), *Hokkaido kyoiku daigaku jinbun ronkyu* 43, 83 : 13-26.
109   VAN BERG, Victor. "The rebirth of utilitarian sociology", *Social Science Journal (Fort Collins)*
        20(3), jul 83 : 71-78.
110   WALLACE, Walter L. *Principles of scientific sociology.* New York, NY, Aldine, 83, xiv-545 p.
111   YI, Man-gap. *Sociology and social change in Korea.* Seoul, Seoul National University Press,
        82, v-336 p.
112   YOKOTOBI, Nobuaki; [ed.]. *Gendai shakaigaku no shiten* (Contemporary sociology: a survey).
        Kyoto, Horitsu Bunkasha, 83, 230 p.
113   ZANOTTI, Angela. "Sui rapporti tra sociologia e potere in Italia: gli anni '50 e '60" (On the
        relations between sociology and power in Italy: the fifties and sixties), *Critica sociologica*
        66, 83 : 54-74.

10200   RESEARCH WORKERS. SOCIOLOGISTS
CHERCHEURS. SOCIOLOGUES

114   "Psychologues (Les): fonctions et formation", *Psychologie française* 28(1), mar 83 : 5-83. [France]

115   "Sociologo (Il) nel servizio sanitario nazionale" (The sociologist in national health service), *Ricerca sociale* 10(30), 82 : 11-251. [Italy]

116   BOËNE, Bernard. "Les décisions américaines en matière de défense. Comment les sociologues y contribuent", *Revue française de Sociologie* 24(2), apr-jun 83 : 203-226. [résumés en anglais, allemand et espagnol]

117   CARO, Jean-Yves. *Les économistes distingués: logique sociale d'un champ scientifique*. Paris, Presses de la Fondation Nationale des Sciences Politiques, 83, 287 p.

118   ELIAS, Norbert. "Über den Rückzug der Soziologen auf die Gegenwart" (On sociologists' retreat on the present), *Kölner Zeitschrift für Soziologie und Sozialpsychologie* 35(1), mar 83 : 29-40.

119   FABIANI, Jean-Louis. "Les programmes, les hommes et les oeuvres. Professeurs de philosophie en classe et en ville au tournant du siècle", *Actes de la Recherche en Sciences sociales* 47-48, jun 83 : 3-20. [France]

120   GIERYN, Thomas F. "Boundary-work and the demarcation of science from non-science: strains and interests in professional ideologies of scientists", *American Sociological Review* 48(6), dec 83 : 781-795.

121   JOGAN, Maca. "Sociologija i sociolozi u praksi" (Sociology and sociologists in practice), *Sociologija* 25(1), 83 : 77-92. [Yugoslavia]

122   LYSON, Thomas A.; SQUIRES, Gregory D. "Oversupply or underutilization? The sociology job market in the 1980's", *Sociological Focus* 16(4), oct 83 : 275-283. [USA]

123   MATSUMOTO, Miwao. "Sangyō shakai ni okeru kagaku no senmon shokugyōka no kōzō: Jūkyū-seiki Eikoku kagaku seidoshi o jirei toshite" (The structure of the professionalization of science in industrial society: a case of the history of scientific institution in the 19th century Britain), *Shisō* 713, 83 : 80-97.

124   MULKAY, Michael; GILBERT, G. Nigel. "Scientists' theory talk", *Canadian Journal of Sociology / Cahiers canadiens de Sociologie* 8(2), 83 : 179-197.

125   PEŁKA-PELIŃSKA, Elżbieta. *Nauka: zawód i specjalność badacza* (Science: the profession and specialization of a researcher). Wrocław, Ossolineum, 83, 176 p.

126   PINTO, Louis. "L'école des philosophes. La dissertation de philosophie au baccalauréat", *Actes de la Recherche en Sciences sociales* 47-48, jun 83 : 21-36.

127   RAŠKOVSKIJ, É. "Tradicii i sovremennost' v trudah indijskih sociologov (70-80-e gg.)" (Traditions and contemporary era in the Indian sociologists' works: seventies-eighties), *Azija i Afrika Segodnja* (11), 82 : 38-41. [continued in ibid. (12), 1982 : 35-38]

10300   ORGANIZATION OF RESEARCH. RESEARCH POLICY
ORGANISATION DE LA RECHERCHE. POLITIQUE DE RECHERCHE

10310   Current research
Recherche en cours

128   "Nekotorye sravnitel'nye ėmpiričeskie sociologičeskie issledovanija, provedennye v SSSR v 1960-1982 gg." (Some comparative empirical sociological research, realized in the USSR during the 1960th-1982th years), *in: Metodologičeskie i metodičeskie problemy sravnitel'nogo analiza v sociologičeskih issledovanijah. II.* Moskva, 1982 : 217-224.

129   ABGARJAN, É. A.; ABGARJAN, R. É. *Problemy matematizacii sociologičeskih issledovanij* (Problems of the use of mathematics in sociological research). Moskva, Izdatel'stvo Moskovskogo Universiteta, 83, 112 p.

130   DIEJOMAOH, Vremudia P. "Nigerian social science research priorities for development", *Afrika Spectrum* 17(2), 82 : 151-161. [résumé in French]

131   GRAY, David J. "Value-relevant sociology: the analysis of subjects of social consequence, including implications for human well-being", *American Journal of Economics and Sociology* 42(4), oct 83 : 405-416.

132   GREHNEV, V. S. "K voprosu o specifike social'nofilosofskogo issledovanija" (Question on the specificity of socio-philosophical research), *Vestnik Moskovskogo Universiteta. Serija Filosofija* 36(5), 82 : 3-14.

133   HUDSON, Herschel C.; [et al.]. *Classifying social data: new applications of analytic methods for social science research*. San Francisco, CA, Jossey-Bass, 82, xxii-270 p.

134   HUTMACHER, Walo. "Peter Heinz et l'institutionnalisation de la recherche sociologique en Suisse", *Schweizerische Zeitschrift für Soziologie / Revue suisse de Sociologie* 9(1), 83 : 13-16.

135 KOZLOV, D. F. "Mesto i rol' sociologičeskih issledovanij o sisteme obščestvennyh nauk" (Place and role of sociological research in the social sciences system), *Vestnik Moskovskogo Universiteta. Teorija naučnogo Kommunizma* (5), 82 : 47-55.

136 LAU, Thomas; WOLFF, Stephan. "Der Einstieg in das Untersuchungsfeld als soziologischer Lernprozess" (Enhance in research field as a sociological learning process), *Kölner Zeitschrift für Soziologie und Sozialpsychologie* 35(3), sep 83 : 417-437.

137 LAUTMAN, Jacques. "Les sciences sociales et le CNRS, entre la culture et la demande bureaucratique", *Commentaire* 6(21), spr 83 : 186-197. [France]

138 MATSUMOTO, Kazuyoshi. "Shakaigaku to rinsetsu kagaku: Shakaigaku no kozoteki kinoteki riron to keikeiteki chosa ni tsuite" (Sociology and the adjacent disciplines: on a structural-functional theory and empirical research in sociology), *Niigata daigaku jinbun kagaku kenkyu* 63, 83 : 33-62. [continued in ibid. 64, 1983: 15-45]

139 NELLIS, John. "Social science research and technical assistance: two African experiences", *Cultures et développement* 14(2-3), 82 : 297-329.

140 PEREDA, C.; PRADA, M. A. "La investigación sociológica en España" (Sociological research in Spain), *Documentación Social* (50), jan-mar 83 : 247-267.

141 POPPING, Roel. "Overeenstemming en associatie in sociologisch onderzoek" (Agreement and association in sociological research), *Mens en Maatschappij* 58(2), mai 83 : 132-150.

142 REMETE, László. "A szociológiai kutatás könyvtári és információellátásáról" (The informational and documentational supply of sociological research in libraries), *Szociológia* 11(4), 82 : 597-609.

143 ROSE, Gerry. *Deciphering sociological research.* London, Macmillan, 82, x-325 p.

144 STATERA, Gianni. *Metodologia e tecniche della ricerca sociale: una introduzione sistematica* (Methodology and techniques of social research: a systematic introduction). Palermo, Palumbo, 82, 324 p.

145 TITMA, M. H.; [ed.]. *Sociologičeskie issledovanija v Sovetskoj Pribaltike: tematičeskij sbornik posvjaščennyj 60-letiju obrazovanija SSSR* (Sociological research in Soviet Baltic republics: a subject collection consecrated to the 60th anniversary of the USSR formation). Vil'njus, Institut Filosofii, Sociologii i Prava Akademia Nauk Lit. SSR, 82, 364 p.

146 VAN DER ZEE, Hendrik. *Tussen vraag en antwoord: beginselen van sociall-wetenschappelijk onderzoek* (Between question and answer: principles of social science research). Meppel, Boom, 83, 255 p.

10320 Applied research. Interdisciplinary research
Recherche appliquée. Recherche interdisciplinaire

147 ADAM, Franko. "Prilog teoretskom i metodološkom utemeljenju akcionog istraživanja" (Contribution to theoretical and methodological foundation of action research), *Sociologija* 24(4), 82 : 435-448.

148 BAUM, Richard. "Science and culture in contemporary China: the roots of retarded modernization", *Asian Survey* 22(12), dec 82 : 1166-1186.

10330 Research centres
Centres de research

10340 Organization of research. Research policy
Organisation de la recherche. Politique de la recherche

149 "Economía y sociología agraria en Iberoamérica y España: posibilidades de cooperación científica y técnica" (Agrarian economy and sociology in Spanish America and Spain: opportunities for scientific and technical co-operation), *Revista de Estudios agro-sociales* 32(122), mar 83 : 9-202. [with contributions by Pedro MORAL LOPEZ, Manuel VIDAL HOSPITAL, Fernando BARRIENTOS FERNANDEZ]

150 ARIMOTO, Akira. "Nihon no gakkai no kokusai hyoka to tokushitsu" (The international evaluation and characteristics of the scientific community of Japan), *Osaka kyoiku daigaku kiyo* IV-32(1), 83 : 1-16.

151 BENCHIKH, Madjid; [et al.]. *Politiques scientifiques et technologiques au Maghreb et au Proche-Orient.* Paris, Éditions du CNRS, 82, 359 p.

152 BISOGNO, Paolo. *Prometeo: la politica della scienza* (Prometheus: science policy). Milano, A. Mondadori, 82, 417 p.

153 BROOKMAN, Henry. "The development of science policy in the Netherlands, 1945-1975", *Science and Public Policy* 10(3), jun 831 : 134-141.

154   DARVAS, György. *International scientific co-operation and its effects on society; proceedings of a symposium held in Siíofok, 10-14 May, 1982*. Budapest, Akadémiai Kiadó, 83, 315 p.

155   FISHER, Donald. "The role of philanthropic foundations in the reproduction and production of hegemony: Rockefeller Foundation and the social sciences", *Sociology (London)* 17(2), mai 83 : 206-233.

156   KHADER, Bichara. "La politique scientifique et technologique dans les pays arabes. Situation présente et propositions pour un plan d'action", *Cultures et Développement* 14(2-3), 82 : 425-462.

157   PIGOROV, S. V. *Upravlenie naukoj: social'no-èkonomičeskij aspekt* (Science management: the socio-economic aspect). Moskva, Mysl', 83, 180 p.

158   SCHUBERT, András; ZSINDELY, Sándor; BRAUN, Tibor. "Scientometric analysis of attendance at international scientific meetings", *Scientometrics* 5(3), 83 : 177-187.

159   VAN HOUTEN, J.; VAN VUREN, H. G.; LEPAIR, C.; DIJKHUIS, G. "Migration of physicists to other academic disciplines: situation in the Netherlands", *Scientometrics* 5(4), 83 : 257-267.

160   WHITLEY, Richard D. "From the sociology of scientific communities to the study of scientists' negotiations and beyond", *Social Science Information* 22(4-5), 83 : 681-720.

10350   Research equipment
Équipement de la recherche

161   ARDIGÓ, Achille. "Un nuovo processo mimetico: le ricerche di 'intelligenze artificiali'. Interrogativi ed ipotesi di rilevanza" (A new process of mimesis: research on 'artificial intelligence'. Questions and relevant assumptions), *Studi di Sociologia* 21(3), jul-sep 83 : 233-244.

162   BERLEUR, J.; [et al.]. *Une société informatisée: pour qui? pour quoi? comment? Actes des Journées de réflexion sur l'informatique, Namur, 21-23 mai 1983*. Namur, Presses Universitaires de Namur, 82, 540 p.

163   BERTASIO, Danila. "Il potenziale evolutivo dell'informatica e la crisi del sistema scolastico" (Evolution potential of informatics and crisis of the school system), *Sociologia (Roma)* 17(1), jan-apr 83 : 271-282.

164   ELGIE, Kae; [ed.]. *Proceedings of the Forum on the Social Impacts of Computerisation*. Waterloo, ON, Waterloo Public Interest Research Group, University of Waterloo, 82, iv-229 p.

165   LOHISSE, Jean. "L'artefact informatique ou la communication asservie", *Diogène* 123, jul-sep 83 : 101-120.

166   NAIMAN, Adeline. *Microcomputers in education: an introduction*. Chelmsford, MA, Northeast Regional Exchange; Cambridge, MA, Technical Education Research Centers, 82, 76 p.

167   PASK, Gordon; CURRAN, Susan. *Micro man: living and growing with computers*. London, Century Publishing Co., 82, 222 p.

10360   Sociological associations
Associations de sociologie

168   "XIIth Congress of the European Society for rural sociology. Budapest, July 25-29, 1983", *Sociologia ruralis* 23(3-4), 83 : 199-275.

169   GAY, David E.; WATERS, Alan R.; [eds.]. "Western Social Science Association silver anniversary: transformations in the social sciences", *Social Science Journal (Fort Collins)* 20(3), jul 83 : 1-96.

170   KILBORNE, Benjamin. "Anthropolitical thought in the wake of the French Revolution: the 'Société des observateurs de l'homme'", *Archives européennes de Sociologie* 23(1), 82 : 73-91.

10400   CONGRESSES. MEETINGS
CONGRÈS. RÉUNIONS

10500   DOCUMENTS. INFORMATION PROCESSING
DOCUMENTS. TRAITEMENT DE L'INFORMATION

10510   Documentation
Documentation

171   "Militarismo y manipulación informativa" (Militarism and information manipulation), *Communicación* (39), sep 82 : 3-107. [Latin America] [with contributions by José MARTINEZ TERRERO, Héctor MUJICA, Fred LANDIS, Juan Carlos ZAPATA]

172   BRAVO, J. "La información: viejos y nuevos problemas" (Information: old and new problems), *Papers. Revista de Sociología* (20), 83 : 175-198.
173   CLEVELAND, Harlan. "L'information en tant que ressource", *Revue économique et sociale* 41(1), feb 83 : 7-16.
174   DUKIĆ, Zvjezdana. "Izvori snanstvenih informacija u sociologiji" (Sources of scientific information in sociology), *Revija za Sociologiju* 11(3-4), 81 : 191-204. [Yugoslavia]
175   GLASSNER, Barry; CORZINE, Jay. "Library research as fieldwork: a strategy for qualitative content analysis", *Sociology and Social Research* 66(3), apr 82 : 305-319.
176   GREWLICH, Klaus W. "Les flux transfrontières de données — plaidoyer pour un effort de connaissance et de coopération", *Revue économique et sociale* 41(1), feb 83 : 17-29.
177   LICHNEROWICZ, André; PERROUX, François; GADOFFRÉ, Gilbert; [eds.]. *Information et communication; séminaires interdisciplinaires du Collège de France.* Paris, Maloine, 83, 294 p.
178   MARINO, Jean-Bernard. *Utilisation de la théorie mathématique de la communication en sciences de l'information.* Reims, Bibliothéque Universitaire, Section des Sciences et Techniques, 82, 48 p.
179   MARKUS, M. Lynne; ROBEY, Daniel. "The organizational validity of management information systems", *Human Relations* 36(3), mar 83 : 203-225.
180   ROSENBERG, Victor. "National information policies", *Annual Review of Information Science and Technology* 17, 82 : 3-32.
181   SEEGER, T. "Changes in the occupation and profession of information work: the impact of the new communication technologies", *Social Science Information Studies* 3(4), oct 83 : 199-208. [Germany FR]
182   SHARMA, C. L.; PATHRIA, R. K.; KARMESHU. "Diffusion of information in a social group", *Journal of Mathematical Sociology* 9(3), 83 : 211-226.
183   SMITH, Barry N. P. "Is there a place for the professional sceptic?: a comment on information transfer and the relationship between social policy and social research", *Australian and New Zealand Journal of Sociology* 17(3), nov 81 : 20-26.
184   SZYPERSKI, Norbert; [et al.]. *Assessing the impacts of information technology: hope to escape the negative effects of an information society by research.* Braunschweig, Vieweg, 83, ix-210 p.
185   VORST, Harrie C. M. *Gids voor literatuuronderzoek in de sociale wetenschappen* (Guide for literature survey in social sciences). Meppel, Boom, 82, 242 p.

10520   Documentary analysis. Reference works
Analyse documentaire. Ouvrages de référence

186   LAPOINTE, François H. *Georg Lukács and his critic: an international bibliography with annotations (1910-1982).* Westport, CT, Greenwood Press, 83, 403 p.
187   PERITZ, Bluma C. "A classification of citation roles for the social sciences and related fields", *Scientometrics* 5(5), 83 : 303-312.
188   VARET, Gilbert; [ed.]. *Bibliographie et informatique. Les disciplines humanistes et leurs bibliographies à l'âge de l'informatique.* Paris, Éditions de la Maison des Sciences de l'Homme, 83, 176 p.

10530   Information services
Services d'information

189   "Current trends in reference services", *Library Trends* 31(3), wint 83 : 361-510. [with contributions by Bill HATZ, Samuel ROTHSTEIN, Mary-Jo LYNCH, Robert KLASSEN, Jack R. LUSKAY, Geraldine B. KING]
190   "Sciences (Les) humaines et l'informatique. Les banques de données: comment les utiliser au bénéfice de la recherche scientifique", *Bulletin de Liaison de la Recherche en Informatique et Automatique* (78), mai 82 : 1-25. [supplément]
191   CHANDLER, G. "The Japanese library and information system: a broad comparative survey of its evolution and structure 1947-82", *International Library Review* 15(4), oct 83 : 389-407.
192   DYAB, M. M. "University libraries in Arab countries", *International Library Review* 15(1), jan 83 : 15-29.
193   LINE, M. B. "Libraries in Saudi Arabia", *International Library Review* 15(4), oct 83 : 365-373.
194   LUO, Xingyun. "Libraries and information services in China", *Journal of Information Science* 6(1), mar 83 : 21-31.
195   MAACK, Mary N. "The colonial legacy in West African libraries: a comparative analysis", *Advances in Librarianship* 12, 82 : 174-245.
196   SITARSKA, A.; MOCZULSKA, A. "Central social science research libraries in Poland: origins and selected problems for investigation", *Social Science Information Studies* 3(1), jan 83 : 21-31.

197   UNESCO. SOCIAL SCIENCE DOCUMENTATION CENTRE; INTERNATIONAL
         COMMITTEE FOR SOCIAL SCIENCE INFORMATION AND DOCUMENTATION.
         Selective inventory of information services (Inventaire sélectif des services d'information). Paris,
         UNESCO, 81, xxi-140 p.

         10540   Documentalists
                   Documentalistes

198   HEIM, Kathleen M. "The demographic and economic status of librarians in the 1970s,
         with special reference to women", *Advances in Librarianship* 12, 82 : 2-45. [USA]

         10550   Terminology
                   Terminologie

199   CALLON, Michel; [et al.]. "From translations to problematic networks: an introduction
         to co-word analysis", *Social Science Information* 22(2), 83 : 191-235.
200   ENDRUWEIT, Günter. *Dreisprachiges Wörterbuch der Soziologie* (Trilingual dictionary of
         sociology). Königstein/Ts., Athenäum, 82, 2nd enl., 133 p.
201   LADMIRAL, Jean-René. "Problèmes psychosociologiques de la traduction", *Connexions* 39,
         83 : 115-125.
202   SOEKANTO, Soerjono. *Kamus sosiologi* (Dictionary of sociology). Jakarta, Rajawali, 83, vii-403 p.

         10560   Biographies
                   Biographies

203   BALANDIER, Georges. "Raymon Aron (1905-1983)", *Cahiers internationaux de Sociologie*
         75, 83 : 354 p.
204   BOUDON, Raymond. "In memoriam Raymond Aron (1905-1983)", *Année sociologique*
         33, 83 : 3-5.
205   FERRAROTTI, Franco. "Biography and the social sciences", *Social Research* 50(1), 83 : 57-80.
206   FERRAROTTI, Franco. "Raymond Aron, o della neutralità appassionata" (Raymond
         Aron, or the passionate neutrality), *Critica sociologica* 68, 83-84 : 3-5.
207   GROHS, Gerhard. "Zum Wandel der sozialen Funktionen afrikanischer Autobiographien"
         (Change of the social functions of African autobiographies), *Kölner Zeitschrift für Soziologie
         und Sozialpsychologie* 35(2), jun 83 : 334-340.
208   HAUBTMANN, Pierre. *Pierre-Joseph Proudhon, sa vie et sa pensée, 1809-1849.* Paris,
         Beauchesne, 82, 1-140 p.
209   KELLERHALS, Jean; LAZEGA, Emmanuel; TROUTOT, Pierre-Yves. "Quelques notes
         sur l'utilisation interactive du récit de vie", *Schweizerische Zeitschrift für Soziologie / Revue
         suisse de Sociologie* 9(1), 83 : 127-136.
210   LENGYEL, Peter. "Peter Heintz, 1920-1983", *International Social Science Journal* 35(3), 83 : 559-560.
211   SCHWARTZMAN, Simon. "Peter Heinz, 1920-1983", *Dados* 26(1), 83 : 5-7.
212   YAMAGISHI, Haruo. "Kojin no seikatsushi kenkyu no imi" (The meaning of the research
         on the individual life history), *Ōita daigaku kyoikugaku-bu kiyo* 6(5), 83 : 109-118.

         10570   Articles. Periodicals
                   Articles. Périodiques

213   NAITO, Kanji. " 'Shakaigaku nenpo' koto hajime" (Origins of 'L'Année Sociologique'),
         Rissho daigaku bungakubu ronso 75, 83 : 35-54.
214   SASAKI, Kōken. "Shakaigaku nenpo to Weber-ke no hitobito" (History of sociology and
         Weber's families), *Soka daigaku Soshiorojika* 8(1), 83 : 68-88.
215   WEPSIEC, Jan. *Sociology: an international bibliography of serial publications, 1880-1980.* London,
         Mansell Publishers, 83, xii-183 p.

         10580   Proceedings. Reports
                   Actes. Rapports

         10590   Textbooks. Theses
                   Manuels. Thèses

216   "Manuel (Le) scolaire dans les pays en développement", *Perspectives (UNESCO)* 13(3),
         83 : 339-399. [with contributions by Philippe G. ALTBACH, Douglas PEARCE, S.
         GOPINATHAN, K. YADUNANDAN]

217   HENKE, Ursula; BOEHNER, Ulrich; ODENWALD, Eva-Maria. "Soziologische Lehr-
       bücher. Ergebnisse einer Expertenbefragung" (Sociological textbooks. Results of a ques-
       tionnaire for experts), *Sociologia internationalis* 21(1-2), 83 : 159-174.
218   KRETSCHMER, Hildrun. "Representation of a complex structure measure for social
       groups and its application to the structure of citations in a journal", *Scientometrics* 5(1),
       83 : 5-30.
219   LAW, John. "Enrôlement et contre-enrôlement: les luttes pour la publication d'un article
       scientifique", *Social Science Information* 22(2), 83 : 237-251.
220   PERITZ, Bluma C. "Are methodological papers more cited than theoretical or empirical
       ones? The case of sociology", *Scientometrics* 5(4), 83 : 211-218.
221   URQUIDI, Arturo. *Sociología* (Sociology). La Paz, Librería Editorial Juventud, 83, 285 p.

METHODOLOGY. THEORY
MÉTHODOLOGIE. THÉORIE

11100 **EPISTEMOLOGY. RESEARCH METHODS. THEORY**
EPISTÉMOLOGIE. MÉTHODES DE RECHERCHE. THÉORIE

11110 **Philosophy. Theory**
Philosophie. Théorie

222 "Class, politics and the State", *New Left Review* (138), apr 83 : 11-68. [with contributions by Eric Olin WRIGHT, Göran THERBORN, Ralph MILIBAND]

223 "Karl Marx in contemporary perspective", *Social Science Quarterly* 64(4), dec 83 : 777-861.

224 "Kritika antimarksistskih teorij" (Criticism of anti-Marxist theories), *Ékonomičeskie Nauki* 24(10), 82 : 78-89.

225 "Marx plus cent", *Temps modernes* 39(440), mar 83 : 1656-1791. [with contributions by Louis GRUEL, Robert CHENAVIER, Lahouari ADDI, Grégoire MADJARIAN, Michel HERLAND, Henri NADEL]

226 "Marx y el marxismo" (Marx and Marxism), *Sistema* (54-55), jun 83 : 1-190. [with contributions by Agnes HELLER, Immanuel WALLERSTEIN, Alessandro BARATTA, Juan TRIAS VEJARANO, José COLINO, Ramón VARGAS-MACHUCA ORTEGA, Gabriel BELLO REGUERA]

227 "Marxisme (Le) et l'analyse sociologique du monde contemporain", *Revue roumaine des sciences sociales. Série de sociologie* 27(2), 83 : 85-114.

228 "Le marxisme et la libération humaine", *La pensée*, 1983 Numéro spécial : 5-212.

229 "Pensare Marx" (Marx's thought), *Critica marxista* 21(2-3), jun 83 : 5-218. [with contributions by Agnès HELLER, Su SHAOZHI, Giulio GIARDI, Oskar NEGT]

230 "Special issue in memory of Alvin W. Gouldner", *Theory and Society* 11(6), nov 82 : 731-940. [with contributions by Charles LEMERT, Paul PICCONE, Ivan SZELENYI, Theda SKOCPOL, Dennis H. WRONG]

231 "Zum Karl-Marx Jahr 1983" (1983: Karl Marx's year), *Deutsche Zeitschrift für Philosophie* 31(2), 83 : 133-212. [with contributions by E. FROMM, R. RAFFEL, H. STEINER]

232 AGGER, Ben. "Marxism 'or' the Frankfurt School?", *Philosophy of the Social Sciences* 13(3), 83 : 347-365.

233 AKIBA, Setsuo. " 'Doitsu ideorogi' no kaikyuron; shokojin no jissen keisei no kanten kara" (The class theory of 'Die Deutsche Ideologie'), *Shakaigaku kenkyu* 44, 83 : 109-128.

234 ANTONIO, Robert J. "The origin, development and contemporary status of critical theory", *Sociological Quarterly* 24(3), sum 83 : 325 351.

235 AREF'EVA, G. S. "Istoričeskij materializm kak nauka" (Historical materialism as a science), *Filosofskie Nauki* 24(4), 82 : 143-153. [continued in ibid. 24 (6), 1982: 131-141]

236 BAGATURIJA, G. A. "O nekotoryh osobennostjah razvitija marksizma kak teoretičeskoj sistemy" (On some characteristics of development of Marxism as a theoretical principle), *Voprosy Filosofii* 36(1), 83 : 49-59.

237 BARZAGHI, Mario. *Dialettica e materialismo in Adorno* (Dialectics and materialism in Adorno). Roma, Bulzoni, 82, 243 p.

238 BEVERS, A. M. *Geometrie van de samenleving: filosofie en sociologie in het werk van Georg Simmel* (Geometry of social life: philosophy and sociology in Georg Simmel's works). Deventer, Van Loghum Slaterus, 82, 262 p.

239 BOKSZAŃSKI, Zbigniew. "On the concept of residues in the theory of Vilfredo Pareto", *Polish Sociological Bulletin* 51(2), 81 : 39-50.

240 BOUDON, Raymond. "Progrès récents de la théorie sociologique", *Revue des Sciences morales et politiques* 138(2), 83 : 295-315.

241 BROWN, Richard Harvey. "Theories of rhetoric and the rhetorics of theory: toward a political phenomenology of sociological truth", *Social Research* 50(1), 83 : 126-157.

242 BROWNSTEIN, Larry. *Talcott Parsons' general action scheme: an investigation of fundamental principles.* Cambridge, MA, Schenkman Publishing Co., 82, xiii-309 p.

243 CLAIRMONT, Don; APOSTLE, Richard; KRECKERL, Reinhard. "The segmentation perspective as a middle-range conceptualization in sociology", *Canadian Journal of Sociology / Cahiers canadiens de Sociologie* 8(3), 83 : 245-271.

244 CLARKE, Simon. *Marx, marginalism and modern sociology: from Adam Smith to Max Weber.* London, Macmillan, 82, vi-250 p.

245   COASSIN-SPIEGEL, Hermes. *Gramsci und Althusser: eine Kritik der althusserschen Rezeption von Gramscis Philosophie* (Gramsci and Althusser: a critique of the Althusserian understanding of Gramsci's philosophy). Berlin, Argument-Verlag, 83, 258 p.

246   COLLINS, Randall; [ed.]. *Sociological theory, 1983.* San Francisco, CA, Jossey-Bass Publishers, 83, xxiii-355 p.

247   DANDEKER, Christopher. "Theory and practice in sociology: the critical imperatives of realism", *Journal for the Theory of Social Behaviour* 13(2), jul 83 : 195-210.

248   DELMOTTE, Gino. "Schatting van de toegang voor natuurlijke selectie in de Nederlandstalige gemmenschap in Belgie" (Evaluation of natural selection opportunities within the Dutch-speaking Belgian community), *Bevolking en Gezin* (2), 82 : 171-184. [Belgium]

249   DREYFUS, Hubert L.; RABINOW, Paul. *Michel Foucault, beyond structuralism and hermeneutics.* Chicago, IL, University of Chicago Press, 82, xxiii-231 p.

250   ELIAESON, Sven. *Bilden av Max Weber: en studie i samhällsvetenskapens sekularisering* (Considerations on Max Weber: a study on social sciences secularization). Stockholm, Norstedt, 82, 340 p.

251   ELSTER, Jon; [et al.]. "Marxism, functionalism, game theory: a debate", *Theory and Society* 11(4), jul 82 : 453-459.

252   FARR, James. "Popper's hermeneutics", *Philosophy of the Social Sciences* 13(2), 83 : 157-176. [with comments by John KING-FARLOW, Wesley E. COOPER: 177-182, Karl-Otto APEL: 183-193, and Tom SETTLE: 195-202]

253   FLITNER, Elisabeth H. "Revolte gegen den Rationalismus. Beziehungen zwischen Max Webers und Hegels Analysen zur Dialektik der Verwissenschaftlichung" (Revolt against nationalism. Relations between Max Weber's and Hegel's analysis of the scientific approach dialectics), *Kölner Zeitschrift für Soziologie und Sozialpsychologie* 35(2), jun 83 : 255-273.

254   FOTEV, Georgi. *Printsipite na pozitivistkata sotsiologiia* (Principles of positivist sociology). Sofiia, Bŭlgarskata Akademiia na Naukite, Institut po Sotsiologiia, 82, 259 p.

255   FRASER, John. "Dopo lo storicismo, l'organicismo e il meccanicismo: ci serve una nuova sistematica?" (After historicism, organicism and mechanicism: a new systematics for what use?), *Critica sociologica* 67, 83 : 56-63.

256   GABITOVA, R. "Filosofija i kul'tura" (Philosophy and culture), *Obščestvennye Nauki* (1), 83 : 193-197.

257   GALLINICOS, Alex. *Marxism and philosophy.* Oxford, Clarendon Press, 83, 177 p.

258   GEORGOUDI, Marianthi. "Modern dialectics in social psychology: a reappraisal", *European Journal of Social Psychology* 13(1), jan-mar 83 : 77-93.

259   GRAFSTEIN, Robert. "Structure and structuralism", *Social Science Quarterly* 63(4), dec 82 : 617-633.

260   GRESKOVITS, Béla. "Ellentmondásos értékek és értékes ellentmondásuk Polányi Károly elméleti rendszerében" (Contradictional values and valuable contradictions in the theory of Karl Polányi), *Szociológia* 11(2), 82 : 201-213.

261   GUILBERT, Philippe; DORNA, Alejandro. *Significations du comportementalisme.* Toulouse, Privat, 82, 231 p.

262   HALFPENNY, Peter. "A refutation of historical materialism?", *Social Science Information* 22(1), 83 : 61-87.

263   HALJAVIN, G. M. "Problema sociologičeskogo nasledija K. Marksa" (Problem of K. Marx's sociological heritage), *Vestnik Moskovskogo Universiteta. Teorija naučnogo Kommunizma* (5), 82 : 73-79.

264   HAMAYA, Masao. *Kojin, to shudan no koiron* (The action theory of individual and group). Tokyo, Kobundo Shuppansha, 83, 258 p.

265   HEIMANN, Horst. "Die Krise des Marxismus und das Verhältnis zwischen sozialistischen Intellektuellen und organisierter Arbeiterbewegung" (The crisis of Marxism and the relations between the socialist intellectuals and organized labour movements), *Jahrbuch für Theorie und Praxis des Demokratischen Sozialismus*, 81 : 96-145.

266   HENNIS, Wilhelm. "Max Weber's 'central question'", *Economy and Society* 12(2), 83 : 135-180.

267   HOLMWOOD, John. "Talcott Parsons and the development of his system", *British Journal of Sociology* 34(4), dec 83 : 573-590.

268   HOLMWOOD, John M. "Action, system and norm in the action frame of reference: Talcott Parsons and his critics", *Sociological Review* 31(2), mai 83 : 310-336.

269   HUERTAS VÁZQUEZ, Eduardo. *Teoría sociológia de las creaciones culturales: el estructuralismo genético de Lucien Goldmann* (Sociological theory of cultural creations: Lucien Goldmann's genetic structuralism). Madrid, Centro de Investigaciones Sociológicas, 82, 404 p.

270   ILLUMINATI, Augusto. "Il marxismo oggi — un bel problema" (Marxism today — a fine problem), *Critica sociologica* 66, 83 : 75-78.

271   JACOB, André. *Cheminements: de la dialectique à l'éthique.* Paris, Anthropos, 82, 226 p.

272   JONES, Robert Alun. "On Merton's 'theory' and 'systematics' of sociological theory", *Sociology of the Sciences* 7, 83 : 121-142.

273   KAWAMURA, Nozomu. "Shakaigaku-sha toshiteno Marx" (K. Marx as a sociologist), *Yuibutsuron kenkyu* 8, 83 : 47-57.

274   KEARN, Michael. "Understanding George Simmel", *Sociological Focus* 16(3), aug 83 : 169-279.

275   KILLAK, T. I. "O predmete mirovozzrenija" (On the object of the world conception), *Problemy vysšej Školy* (5), 82 : 12-30.

276   KILMAN, Ralph H. "A dialectical approach to formulating and testing social science theories: assumptional analysis", *Human Relations* 36(1), jan 83 : 1-21.

277   KITANO, Yuhji. "Weber minshu-shugi shiso no sai-kento: Mommsen no mondai to hoho o tegakarini" (Max Weber's thought of democracy and politics: an application of Wolfgang J. Mommsen's study of Weber), *Osaka daigaku Nenpo ningen kagaku* 4, 83 : 159-175.

278   KUMADA, Toshio. "Kankei gainen toshiteno 'Kino': Kinoshugi riron sai-kosei no tameni" ('Function' as a concept of relation: for the reconstruction of functionalism), *Keiogijuku daigaku daigakuin shakaigaku kenkyuka kiyo* 23, 83 : 87-95.

279   KURCZEWSKA, Joanna. "Peculiarities of the Polish Marxism at the turn of the last century", *Polish Sociological Bulletin* 54(2), 81 : 51-62.

280   KUVAKIN, V. A.; TITOVA, L. G. "Filosofskaja nauka v SSSR: nekotorye osobennosti i zakonomernosti razvitija" (Philosophical science in the USSR: some characteristics of development laws), *Vestnik Moskovskogo Universiteta. Serija Filosofija* 36(6), 82 : 3-10.

281   LAVERS, Annette. *Roland Barthes, structuralism and after.* Cambridge, MA, Harvard University Press, 82, 300 p.

282   LEDUC, Victor. "Fondements du marxisme et mouvement ouvrier cent ans après la mort de Marx", *Raison présente* (66), trim. 2, 83 : 59-66.

283   LIEBERSOHN, Harry. "Leopold von Wiese and the ambivalence of functionalist sociology", *Archives européennes de Sociologie* 23(1), 82 : 123-149.

284   LUBAN, David. "Explaining dark times: Hannah Arendt's theory of theory", *Social Research* 50(1), 83 : 215-248.

'285   LUHMANN, Niklas. "Insistence on systems theory: perspectives from Germany: an essay", *Social Forces* 61(4), jun 83 : 987-998.

286   MALRIEU, Philippe. "Vers une recherche marxiste en psychologie", *La pensée* (235), oct 83 : 19-38.

287   MARKIEWICZ, Władysław. "Karol Marks czy Max Weber: dylemat rzeczywisty czy urojony?" (Karl Marx or Max Weber: a real or fictitious dilemma?), *Studia Socjologiczne* 89(2), 83 : 7-26.

288   MAYHEW, Bruce H. "Structuralism and ontology", *Social Science Quarterly* 63(4), dec 82 : 634-639.

289   MCINTOSH, Donald. "Max Weber as a critical theorist", *Theory and Society* 12(1), jan 83 : 69-109.

290   MIXON, Don. "A theory of actors", *Journal for the Theory of Social Behaviour* 13(1), mar 83 : 97-110.

291   MORI, Mototaka. "System riron to hihan riron: J. Habermas to gendai shakaigaku riron" (System and critical theory: J. Habermas and modern sociological theory), *Shakaigaku nenshi* 24, 83 : 1-18.

292   MUCCHIELLI, Alex. *L'analyse phénoménologique et structurale en sciences humaines.* Paris, Presses Universitaires de France, 83, 324 p.

293   NAGAO, Mari. "G. H. Mead to pragmatism: Jikanron o kijiku toshite" (G. H. Mead and pragmatism: with special reference to the theory of time), *Mita tetsugakukai Tetsugaku* 76, 83 : 123-147.

294   NOWAK, Leszek. "Marxian methodology leads to the generalization of historical materialism", *Poznań Studies* 7, 82 : 9-30.

295   OLIVER, Ivan. "The 'old' and the 'new' hermeneutic in sociological theory", *British Journal of Sociology* 34(4), dec 83 : 519-553.

296   OVČINNIKOVA, Z. L. "Istoričeskij materializm — metodologičeskaja osnova obščestvennyh nauk" (Historical materialism, the methodological basis of social sciences), *in: Otraženie obščestvennyh processov v kategorijah istoričeskogo materializma.* Moskva, 1982 : 36-42.

297   RAM, Jagdish. "The existentialist predicament", *Indian Journal of Social Research* 23(3), dec 82 : 245-252.

298   RATH, Norbert. *Adornos kritische Theorie: Vermittlungen und Vermittlungsschwierigkeiten* (Adorno's critical theory: bargaining and bargaining difficulties). Paderborn, F. Schöningh, 82, 266 p.

299   RAY, Larry. "Review essay: systematic functionalism revisited", *Journal for the Theory of Social Behaviour* 13(2), jul 83 : 231-241.

300   RIPEPE, Eugenio. "Due apparenti paradossi nell'opera di Gaetano Mosca: meritrocrazia
           come democrazia e idealismo come realismo sociologico" (Two apparent paradoxes in
           Gaetano Mosca's work: meritocracy as democracy and idealism as sociological realism),
           Pensiero politico 15(3), 82 : 514-524.

301   ROMANOVA, A. P. "Kritika filosofskih osnov fenomenologičeskoj sociologii" (Critics of
           philosophical bases of the phenomenological sociology), *in: Kritika religioznoj ideologii i
           problemy ateističeskogo vospitanija.* Moskva, 1982 : 83-89.

302   RUTIGLIANO, Enzo. "L'influenza della teoria critica sulla sociologia italiana" (The
           influence of critical theory on Italian sociology), *Critica sociologica* 66, 83 : 43-53.

303   SAKUTA, Keiichi; [ed.]. *Durkheim.* Tokyo, Kodansha, 83, 344 p.

304   SARVER, Vernon Thomas Jr. "Ajzen and Fishbein's 'Theory of reasoned action': a critical
           assessment", *Journal for the Theory of Social Behaviour* 13(2), jul 83 : 155-163. [about Icek
           Ajzen and Martin Fishbein: 'Understanding attitudes and predicting social behaviour',
           Englewood Cliffs, NJ, Prentice-Hall, 1980]

305   SCAGLIA, Antonio; GARZIA, Mino; APICELLA, Enrico. *Illusione capitalistica e utopia
           marxista: elementi di teoria sociologica e problematiche istituzionali* (Capitalist illusion and Marxist
           utopia: elements of sociological theory and institutional problems). Milano, F. Angeli,
           82, 305 p.

306   SHIOBARA, Tsutomu. *Shakigaku no riron* (Sociological theory). Tokyo, Obunsha, 83, 166 p.

307   SKVORETZ, John. "Salience, heterogeneity and consolidation of parameters: civilizing
           Blau's primitive theory", *American Sociological Review* 48(3), jun 83 : 360-375.

308   STAUDER, Paulo. "Sistema d'azione e psicologia dell'io. Talcott Parsons e Heinz
           Hartmann" (Action system and ego psychology. Talcott Parsons and Heinz Hartmann),
           Studi di Sociologia 20(3-4), jul-dec 82 : 333-350.

309   STOĬCHEV, Todor Stoĭchev. *Kategorii na istoricheskiia materializum* (Categories in historical
           materialism). Sofiia, Izd-vo Nauka i Izkustvo, 83, 242 p.

310   STREL'COV, N. N. "Obščaja teorija dejstvija T. Parsonsa: nekotorye itogi razvitija"
           (The T. Parsons' general theory of action and some results of its development), *Voprosy
           Filosofii* 36(1), 83 : 139-145.

311   STRESIUS, Lothar. *Theodor W. Adornos negative Dialektik: eine kritische Rekonstruktion* (Theodor
           W. Adorno's negative dialectics: a critical reconstruction). Frankfurt-am-Main, P. Lang,
           82, 280 p.

312   STUART-FOX, Martin. "Marxism and Theravada Buddhism: the legitimation of political
           authority in Laos", *Pacific Affairs* 56(3), aut 83 : 428-454.

313   ŠUČENKO, V. A. "Nacional'naja filosofija kak forma obščestvennogo soznanija i èlement
           duhovnoj kul'tury" (National philosophy as a form of social consciousness and the element
           of the spiritual culture), *Sbornik Naučnyh Trudov (Leningradskij Institut Kultury)* 57, 81 : 32-41.
           [USSR]

314   SUDAKOV, V. I. "Obščaja sociologičeskaja teorija kak teoretiko-metodologičeskaja osnova
           kompleksnogo social'nogo poznanija" (The general sociological theory as a theoretical
           and methodological basis of complex social consciousness), *in: Voprosy teorii i metodov
           sociologiceskih issledovanij.* Moskva, 1981 : 9-14.

315   TITTENBRUN, Jacek. "Teoria struktur w świetle materializmu historycznego" (Structure
           Theory in the light of historical materialism), *Studia Filozoficzne* 208(3), 83 : 131-144.

316   TSUNEMATSU, Naoyuki; HASHIZUME, Daisaburo; SHIDA, Kiyoshi. "Kino riron wa
           fukano de aru" (Functional theory cannot survive), *Sociologos* 7, 83 : 155-163.

317   TUCHAŃSKA, Barbara. "Marksowska koncepcja człowieka" (Marxist concept of man),
           Studia Socjologiczne 89(2), 83 : 41-63.

318   TURNER, Denys. *Marxism and Christianity.* Oxford, Basil Blackwell, 83, xii-256 p.

319   VAN DETH, Jan W. "The persistence of materialist and post-materialist value orientations",
           European Journal of Political Research 11(1), mar 83 : 63-79.

320   ZIMIN, A. I. "Strukturnaja antropologija kak raznovidnost' strukturalizma" (Structural
           anthropology as a variety of structuralism), *Filosofskie Nauki* 24(6), 82 : 109-119.

**11120   Epistemology. Explanation. Understanding
           Epistémologie. Explication. Compréhension**

321   "Qu'est-ce que classer?", *Actes de la Recherche en Sciences sociales* 50, nov 83 : 3-99. [with
           contributions by Dominique MERLLIÉ, Gérard MAUGER, Claude FOSSÉ-POLIAK,
           Gabrielle BALAZS, Jean-Pierre FAGUER]

322   AMUNDSON, Ron. "The epistemological status of a naturalized epistemology", *Inquiry*
           26(3), sep 83 : 333-344.

323 ANDREENKOV, V. G.; TOLSTOVA, Ju. N.; [eds.]. *Tipologija i klassifikacija v sociologiceskih issledovanijah* (Typology and classification in sociological research). Moskva, Nauka, 82, 296 p.

324 BAUMRIND, Diana. "Specious causal attributions in the social sciences: the reformulated stepping-stone theory of heroin use as exemplar", *Journal of Personality and Social Psychology* 45(6), dec 83 : 1289-1298.

325 COHEN, G. A. "Functional explanation, consequence explanation and Marxism", *Inquiry* 25(1), mar 82 : 27-56.

326 EIDLIN, Fred H. "Popper's fact-standard dualism contra 'value-free' social science", *Social Science Quarterly* 64(1), mar 83 : 1-18.

327 FARR, James. "Humean explanations in the moral sciences", *Inquiry* 25(1), mar 82 : 57-80.

328 GULLVÅG, Ingemund. "Depth of intention", *Inquiry* 26(1), mar 83 : 31-83.

329 HAMILTON, V. Lee; SANDERS, Joseph. "Universals in judging wrongdoing: Japanese and Americans compared", *American Sociological Review* 48(2), apr 83 : 199-211.

330 JARVIE, I. C. "Rationality and relativism", *British Journal of Sociology* 24(1), mar 83 : 44-60.

331 KASAVIN, I. T. "Nauka i ideologija v ėpistemologičeskom anarhizme P. Fejerabenda" (Science and ideology in P. Feyerabend's epistemological anarchism), *Vestnik Moskovskogo Universiteta. Serija Filosofija* 37(1), 83 : 49-59.

332 KRAUSZ, Ernest; TULEA, Gitta. "Indeterminism versus determinism in contemporary sociological thought", *International Journal of Comparative Sociology (Leiden)* 24(3-4), sep-dec 83 : 218-228.

333 LEVŠINA, I. S. "K traktovke otdel'nyh ponjatij, upotrebljaemyh v dannom sbornike statej ('Social'noe', 'social'no-psihologičeskoe', 'sociologičeskoe', 'tipologija', 'massovoe', 'funkcionirovanie', 'vosprijatie', 'upravlenie')" (Interpretation of separate concepts used in a collection of papers ('social', 'socio-psychological', 'sociological', 'typology', 'mass', 'functioning', 'perception', 'management')), *in: K voprosu social'nogo funkcionirovanija iskusstva: teoretičeskie i ėmpiriceskie aspekty*. Moskva, 1982 : 205-216.

334 LONGINO, H. E. "Scientific objectivity and the logics of science", *Inquiry* 26(1), mar 83 : 85-106.

335 MORGAN, Timothy M.; ANESHENSEL, Carol S.; CLARK, Virginia A. "Parameter estimation for mover-stayer models. Analyzing depression over time", *Sociological Methods and Research* 11(3), feb 83 : 345-366.

336 PARDI, Franceso. "Sogge-tività e sistema sociale: problemi de metodo" (Subjectivity and social system: methodological problems), *Rassegna italiana di Sociologia* 24(4), oct-dec 83 : 553-574.

337 RADEV, Dinko. *Nauchnoto obiasnenie v obshtestvoznanieto* (Scientific explanation in the social sciences). Sofiia, Izd-vo na Bŭlgarskata Akademiia na Naukite, 82, 127 p.

338 ROBLIN, D W "Meaningful actions: problems and procedures of interpretation in the social sciences", *Chicago Anthropological Exchange* 15(1), 82 : 32-44.

339 ROLLE, Pierre. "Une logique de la recherche sociale. L'épistémologie de Pierre Naville", *Homme et Société* 67-68, jan-jun 83 : 115-130.

340 SIDOTI, Francesco. *I limiti della razionalità pubblica: evoluzionisti razionalisti nella teoria sociologica* (The limitations of public rationality: evolutionist rationalists in the sociological theory). Milano, Edizioni di Comunità, 83, 225 p.

341 SOBEL, Michael E. "Some large-sample standard errors for components of a mean difference under a linear model", *Sociological Methodology*, 83-84 : 169-193.

342 STINCHCOMBE, Arthur L. "Linearity in log-linear analysis", *Sociological Methodology*, 83-84 : 104-125.

343 WINSHIP, Christopher; MANDEL, Michael. "Roles and positions: a critique and extension of the blockmodelling approach", *Sociological Methodology*, 83-84 : 314-344.

11130 Research techniques. Sociological analysis
Techniques de recherche. Analyse sociologique

344 "Temps (Le)", *Loisir et société* 5(2), aut 82 : 251-472. [with contributions by Jacques HAMEL, Octavio de Lima CAMARGO, Gÿorgy FUKAZS, Joffre DUMAZEDIER]

345 ACEDO, Clemy Machado de. *Introducción al análisis sociológico* (Introduction to sociological analysis). Caracas, Universidad Central de Venezuela, Ediciones de la Biblioteca, 82, 149 p.

346 ALLEN, Michael Patrick. "The identification of interlock groups in large corporate networks: convergent validation using divergent techniques", *Social Networks* 4(4), dec 82 : 349-366.

347 ALVIRA, Francisco. "Perspectiva cualitativa-perspectiva cuantitativa en la metodología sociológica" (Qualitative-quantitative approaches in sociological methodology), *Revista española de Investigaciones sociológicas* 22, apr-jun 83 : 53-75.

348   ARDOINO, Jacques. "À propos de la notion de 'structure' dans l'univers des 'organisateurs' et des 'organisations'", *Connexions* 39, 83 : 7-19.

349   ARMER, J. Michael; MARSH, Robert M.; [eds.]. *Comparative sociological research in the 1960s and 1970s.* Leiden, Brill, 82, 287 p.

350   ARMINGER, Gerhard. "Multivariate Analyse von qualitativen abhängigen Variablen mit verallgemeinerten linearen Modellen" (Multivariate analysis of qualitative dependent variables with generalized linear models), *Zeitschrift für Soziologie* 12(1), jan 83 : 49-64.

351   BERGMANN, Werner. "Das Problem der Zeit in der Soziologie. Ein Literaturüberblick zum Stand der 'zeitsoziologischen' Theorie und Forschung" (The problem of time in sociology. A literature survey on the state of time sociological theory and research), *Kölner Zeitschrift für Soziologie und Sozialpsychologie* 35(3), sep 83 : 462-504.

352   BERMUDEZ, Marlen. "El análisis de contenido: procedimientos y aplicaciones" (Content analysis: procedures and applications), *Revista de Ciencias Sociales de la Universidad de Costa Rica* 24, 83 : 71-80.

353   BERNERT, Christopher. "The career of causal analysis in American sociology", *British Journal of Sociology* 24(2), jun 83 : 230-254.

354   BONACICH, Phillip. "Representations for homomorphisms", *Social Networks* 5(2), jun 83 : 173-192.

355   BORDET, Jean-Pierre; KOKOSOWSKI, Alain; LEMAIRE, J. *Analyse multidimensionnelle et typologie.* Issy-les-Moulineaux, Éditions EAP; Mont-Saint-Aignan, Publications de l'Université de Rouen, 82, 447 p.

356   BOUDON, Raymond; [ed.]. "Méthodologie et épistémologie. II.", *Année sociologique* 32, 82 : 3-525. [Première partie publiée en 1981]

357   BOYD, John Paul. "Structural similarity, semi-groups and idempotents", *Social Networks* 5(2), jun 83 : 157-172.

358   BRUCE, Steve; WALLIS, Roy. "Rescuing motives", *British Journal of Sociology* 24(1), mar 83 : 61-71.

359   BULMER-THOMAS, V. *Input-output analysis in developing countries: sources, methods and applications.* New York, NY-Chichester-Toronto, ON-Brisbane, Wiley, 82, xvi-297 p.

360   CAVALLARO, Renato. "Analisi sociologica e teoria dei gruppi sociali. Alcune proposte della sociologia contemporanea" (Sociological analysis and theory of social groups. Some prospects of contemporary sociology), *Sociologia (Roma)* 17(1), jan-apr 83 : 89-113.

361   CIBOIS, Philippe. "Tri-deux: une méthode post-factorielle de dépouillement d'enquête", *Année sociologique* 32, 82 : 61-80.

362   CRAIN, Robert L.; MAHARD, Rita E. "The effect of research methodology on desegregation-achievement studies: a meta-analysis", *American Journal of Sociology* 88(5), mar 83 : 839-854.

363   CUIN, Charles-Henry. "Analyse systémique et sociologie de la mobilité sociale", *Année sociologique* 33, 83 : 249-269.

364   DATTA, Lois-Ellin. "Strange bedfellows. The politics of qualitative methods", *American Behavioral Scientist* 26(1), sep-oct 82 : 133-144.

365   EHARA, Yumiko. "Ningen chushinshugi karano datsu-chushinka e: Gendai shakaigaku no ichi-doko" (From humanistic approach to de-centred analysis: a trend of recent sociology), *Ochanomizu joshi daigaku jinbun-kagaku kiyo* 36, 83 : 1-25.

366   GORDY, Michael. "Reading Althusser: time and the social whale", *History and Theory* 22(1), 83 : 1-21.

367   HAŁAS, Elżbieta. "Floriana Znanieckiego koncepcja definicji sytuacji a interpretacyjny paradygmat socjologii" (Florian Znaniecki's concept of the definition of situation and interpretative paradigm of sociology), *Studia Socjologiczne* 88(1), 83 : 32-42.

368   HECHTER, Michael; [ed.]. *The microfoundations of macrosociology.* Philadelphia, PA, Temple University Press, 83, 287 p.

369   HEKMAN, Susan. "Beyond humanism: Gadamer, Althusser, and the methodology of the social sciences", *Western Political Quarterly* 36(1), mar 83 : 98-115.

370   HOELTER, Jon W. "The analysis of covariance structures. Goodness-of-fit indices", *Sociological Methods and Research* 11(3), feb 83 : 325-344.

371   HOPPE, Hans-Hermann. *Kritik der kausalwissenschaftlichen Sozialforschung: Untersuchungen zur Grundlegung von Soziologie und Ökonomie* (Critique of causal social research: investigations on laying the foundations of sociology and economics). Opladen, Westdeutscher Verlag, 83, 108 p.

372   ISAMBERT, François-A. "De la définition: réflexions sur la stratégie durkheimienne de détermination de l'objet", *Année sociologique* 32, 82 : 163-192.

373   JAVEAU, Claude. "Comptes et mécomptes du temps", *Cahiers internationaux de Sociologie* 74, 83 : 71-82.

374 KOZAKIEWICZ, Helena. *Inna socjologia: studium zapoznanej metody* (Another sociology: a study of a misunderstood method). Warszawa, Państwowe Wydawnictwo Naukowe, 83, 369 p.

375 LAUMANN, Edward O.; MARSDEN, Peter V. "Microstructural analysis in interorganizational systems", *Social Networks* 4(4), dec 82 : 329-348.

376 LENSKI, Gerhard; [ed.]. "Current issues and research in macrosociology", *International Journal of Comparative Sociology (Leiden)* 24(1-2), jan-apr 83 : 1-136.

377 MANISCALCO, Maria Luisa. "La riscoperta del 'soggetto' nell'analisi sociologica: F. Alberoni e A. Ardigò" (The rediscovery of the 'subject' in sociological analysis: F. Alberoni and A. Ardigo), *Sociologia (Roma)* 17(3), sep-dec 83 : 3-32.

378 MARIOLIS, Peter. "'Region' and 'subgroup': organizing concepts in social network analysis", *Social Networks* 4(4), dec 82 : 305-328.

379 MARSDEN, Peter V. "On interaction effects involving block variables", *Sociological Methods and Research* 11(3), feb 83 : 305-323.

380 MASLOVA, O. M. "Rol' sravnitel'nogo analiza pri obosnovanii metodiki sociologičeskogo sprosa" (The role of comparative analysis to design the sociological survey methods), *in: Metodologičeskie i metodičeskie problemy sravnitel'nogo analiza v sociologičeskih issledovanijah. I.* Moskva, 1982 : 21-39.

381 MASON, William M.; WONG, George Y.; ENTWISLE, Barbara. "Contextual analysis through the multi-level linear model", *Sociological Methodology*, 83-84 : 72-103.

382 MCKAY, David; SCHOFIELD, Norman; WHITELEY, Paul; [eds.]. *Data analysis and the social sciences.* London, F. Pinter, 83, ix-291 p.

383 MILLER, Steven I. "Mapping, metaphors and meaning. A note on the case of triangulation in research", *Sociologia internationalis* 21(1-2), 83 : 69-79.

384 MOMDŽJAN, H. N. "Dialektiko-materialističeskij analiz sovremennogo hoda istorii" (The dialectical and materialist analysis of the contemporary course of history), *Problemy naučnogo Kommunizma* (6), 83 : 240-254.

385 MÜNCH, Richard. "From pure methodological individualism to poor sociological utilitarianism: a critique of an avoidable alliance", *Canadian Journal of Sociology / Cahiers canadiens de Sociologie* 8(1), 83 : 45-77.

386 NIEDERMAYER, Oskar. "Zur Theorie, Methodologie, und Praxis international vergleichender Sozialforschung" (On theory, methodology and practice of international comparative social research), *Kölner Zeitschrift für Soziologie und Sozialpsychologie* 35(2), jun 83 : 304-320.

387 NISHIYAMA, Toshihiko. "'Mono' no shosō to kachi kiban: shakaigakuteki ritsuron eno yobi kosatsu" (Things, phenomena, facts, and value-premises: a preliminary note toward sociological analyses), *Eichi daigaku Sapienchia* 17, 83 : 1-19.

388 PANIOTO, V. I.; MAKSIMENKO, V. S. *Količestvennye metody v sociologičeskih issledovanijah* (Quantitative methods in sociological research). Kiev, Naukova Dumka, 82, 272 p.

389 PELLICCIARI, Giovanni; TINTI, Giancarlo. *Tecniche di ricerca sociale* (Social research techniques). Milano, F. Angeli, 82, 401 p.

390 PESCOSOLIDO, Bernice A.; KELLEY, Jonathan. "Confronting sociological theory with data: regression analysis, Goodman's log-linear models and comparative research", *Sociology (London)* 17(3), aug 83 : 359-379.

391 POLULJAH, I. A. "O nekotoryh metodologičeskih funkcijah special'nyh sociologičeskih teorij" (On some methodological functions of special sociological theories), *in: Voprosy teorii i metodov sociologičeskih issledovanij.* Moskva, 1981 : 14-19.

392 POUPART, Jean; RAINS, Prudence; PIRES, Alvaro P. "Les méthodes qualitatives et la sociologie américaine", *Déviance et Société* 7(1), mar 83 : 63-91.

393 PUGH, Judy F. "Into the almanac: time, meaning and action in North Indian society", *Contributions to Indian Sociology* 17(1), jan-jun 83 : 27-49.

394 RAGIN, Charles; ZARET, David. "Theory and method in comparative research: two strategies", *Social Forces* 61(3), mar 83 : 731-754.

395 RAPOPORT, V. S. "Metodologičeskie problemy sistemnogo issledovanija organizacionno-ėkonomiceskogo mehanizma upravlenija" (Methodological problems of systemic research on organizational and economic mechanism management), *in: Sistemnye issledovanija: metodologičeskie problemy, 1982.* Moskva, 1982 : 159-181.

396 REJZEMA, Ja. V. *Informacionnyj analiz social'nyh processov: problemy sociologičeskoj informatiki* (Informational analysis of social processes: problems of sociological informatics). Moskva, Nauka, 82, 199 p.

397 ROIG, Charles. "Leninist dialectic seen from the point of view of Kenneth Burke's dialectic: theory, analysis and ideology in Lenin's speech", *Poznań Studies* 7, 82 : 49-64.

398 SEIDMAN, Stephen B. "Network structure and minimum degree", *Social Networks* 5(3), sep 83 : 269-287.

399   SHINN, Terry. "Construction théorique et démarche expérimentale: essai d'analyse sociale et épistémologique de la recherche", *Social Science Information* 22(3), 83 : 511-554.
400   SILVA SANTISTEBAN, Luis. *Ensayo sobre metodología de las ciencias sociales* (Essay on methodology of social sciences). Lima, Centro de Investigaciones Económicas y Sociales de la Universidad de Lima, 82, 210 p.
401   STOTO, Michael A.; EMERSON, John D. "Power transformations for data analysis", *Sociological Methodology*, 83-84 : 126-168.
402   SUPEK, Rudi. "Tri razine sociološke analize: epistemološko-logička, strukturano-historijaska i antropološko-ontološka" (Three levels of sociological analysis: epistemological-logical, structural-historical and anthropological-ontological), *Sociologija* 24(1), 82 : 1-24.
403   THOMPSON, John B. "Ideology and the analysis of discourse: a critical introduction to the work of Michel Pécheux", *Sociological Review* 31(2), mai 83 : 212-236.
404   TIHONOV, A. M. "Metodologičeskie principy sociologičeskogo izučenija social'noj struktury sovetskogo obščestva" (Methodological principles of sociological study on the Soviet society social structure), *Problemy Filosofii* 57, 82 : 81-85.
405   TITTENBRUN, Jacek. "Strukturalne antynomieu" (Structural antinomies), *Kultura i Społeczeństwo* 27(3), 83 : 157-173. [with a comment by Andrzej PIOTROWSKI: 175-177]
406   TOURAINE, Alain; [et al.]. *La méthode de l'intervention sociologique*. Paris, Atelier d'Intervention Sociologique, 83, 99 p.
407   TURNER, Stephen P. "Durkheim as a methodologist. I. Realism, teleology, and action", *Philosophy of the Social Sciences* 13(4), 83 : 425-450.
408   WADLEY, Susan S. "The rains of estrangement: understanding the Hindu yearly cycle", *Contributions to Indian Sociology* 17(1), jan-jun 83 : 51-85.
409   WEISBROD, R. L. "Systems analysis in the human sciences", *Anthropology UCLA* 12, 82 : 1-159.
410   WINDISCH, Uli. "Le temps: représentations archétypes et efficacité du discours politique", *Cahiers internationaux de Sociologie* 75, 83 : 263-282.
411   WU, Lawrence L. "Local blockmodel algebras for analyzing social networks", *Sociological Methodology*, 83-84 : 272-313.
412   YAMAGUCHI, Kazuo. "Impermeability and distance: a method for the analysis of some structural characteristics underlying social processes", *Sociological Methodology*, 83-84 : 225-247.
413   ZADRA, Dario. "Symbolic time: the Christian liturgical year", *Sociologia (Roma)* 17(1), jan-apr 83 : 41-87.

**11200   DATA COLLECTION. EXPERIMENTS
RASSEMBLEMENT DES DONNÉES. EXPÉRIENCES**

**11210   Experimentation. Observation
Expérimentation. Observation**

414   BONSS, Wolfgang. *Die Einübung des Tatsachenblicks: zur Struktur und Veränderung empirischer Sozialforschung* (The rehearsal of fact perception: on the structure and change of social research). Frankfurt-am-Main, Suhrkamp, 82, 341 p.
415   DE PINA CABRAL, João. "Notas críticas sobre a observação participante no contexto da etnografia portuguese" (Critical notes on the participant observation in the context of the Portuguese ethnography), *Análise social* 19(2), 83 : 327-339.
416   FLAP, H. D. "Het betrekkelijke succes van de sociographische beweging" (The relative success of the sociographic movement), *Sociologische Gids* 30(1), jan-feb 83 : 4-17. [Netherlands]
417   GUARNIERI, Giuseppe. "Max Weber in Italia: studi dopo il '68" (Max Weber in Italy: studies after 1968), *Studi di Sociologia* 21(1), mar 83 : 87-106.
418   GUARNIERI, Giuseppe. "Max Weber in Italia: studi italiani tra il 1945 e il 1968" (Max Weber in Italy: Italian studies between 1945 and 1968), *Studi di Sociologia* 20(3-4), jul-dec 82 : 369-384.
419   KANTOWSKY, Detlef. "Max Weber on India and Indian interpretations of Weber", *Contributions to Indian Sociology* 16(2), jul-dec 82 : 141-174.
420   MICHAELS, James W. "Systemic observation as a measurement strategy", *Sociological Focus* 16(3), aug 83 : 217-226.
421   MITCHELL, J. Clyde. "Case and situation analysis", *Sociological Review* 31(2), mai 83 : 187-211.
422   PATEL, S. C. "Empirical research", *Indian Journal of Social Research* 23(1), apr 82 : 51-70.

11220 **Sampling. Surveys**
Échantillonnage. Enquêtes

423 ANDREWS, Frank M.; HERZOG, A. Regula. *The quality of survey data as related to age of respondent.* Ann Arbor, MI, Survey Research Center, Institute for Social Research, University of Michigan, 82, 19 p.

424 BERK, Richard A. "An introduction to sample selection bias in sociological data", *American Sociological Review* 48(3), jun 83 : 386-398.

425 CAPLOW, Théodore. "La répétition des enquêtes: une méthode de recherche sociologique", *Année sociologique* 32, 82 : 9-22.

426 FREEMAN, Howard E.; SHANKS, J. Merrill; [eds.]. "The emergence of computer-assisted survey research", *Sociological Methods and Research* 12(2), nov 83 : 115-216.

427 GIBBAL, Jean-Marie; [et al.]. "Position de l'enquête anthropologique en milieu urbain africain", *Cahiers d'Études africaines* 21(1-3), 81 : 11-24.

428 MERLO, Jean. *Une expérience de conscientisation par enquête en milieu populaire.* Paris, Éditons L'Harmattan, 82, 142 p.

429 NEUBÄUMER, Renate. *Die Eigenschaften verschiedener Stichprobenverfahren bei wirtschafts- und sozialwissenschaftlichen Untersuchungen* (The characteristics of various sample survey processes in economic and social scientific researches). Frankfurt-am-Main, Lang, 82, 227 p.

430 SUDMAN, Seymour. "Survey research and technological change", *Sociological Methods and Research* 12(2), nov 83 : 217-230.

431 TANUR, Judith M. "Methods for large-scale surveys and experiments", *Sociological Methodology,* 83-84 : 1-71.

432 VAN DOORNE, J. H. "Situational analysis: its potential and limitations for anthropological research on social change in Africa", *Cahiers d'Études africaines* 21(4), 81 : 479-506.

433 WEISSBERG, Robert. "The politically relevant in measuring public opinion", *Micropolitics* 2(4), 83 : 379-400. [USA]

11230 **Interviews. Questionnaires**
Entretiens. Questionnaires

434 ANDERSEN, Bjarne Hjorth; CHRISTOFFERSEN, Nygaard. *Om spørgeskemaer: problemer ved spørgsmålsformulering i interviewundersøgelser* (Questionnaires: problems of questions wording in interview surveys). København, Teknisk Forlag, 82, 214 p.

435 CHABROL, Claude. "À qui parle-t-on dans un entretien d'enquête?", *Connexions* 38, 82 : 107-121.

436 CHRISTOFFERSEN, Mogens Nygaard; ANDERSEN, Bjarne Hjorth. *Åbent interview: en gennemgang af tidligere anvendelser af ikke-standardiserede, intensive interviewsamtaler* (Open interview: a review of previous uses of non-standardized intensive interviews). København, Socialforskningsinstituttet, Teknisk Forlag, 82, 140 p.

437 LIEBHERR, Françoise. "L'entretien, un lieu sociologique", *Schweizerische Zeitschrift für Soziologie / Revue suisse de Sociologie* 9(2), 83 : 391-406.

438 LUTYŃSKA, Krystyna; WEJLAND, Paweł; [eds.]. *Wywiad kwestionariuszowy* (The questionnaire interview). Warszawa, Ossolineum, 83, 436 p.

439 MOLINEAUX, Dorothy; LANE, Vera W. *Effective interviewing: techniques and analysis.* Boston, MA, Allyn and Bacon, 82, viii-244 p.

440 SINGLY, François de. "Questionnaire et figuration", *Revue de l'Institut de Sociologie* (3-4), 83 : 311-325.

441 SOBAL, Jeff. "Disclosing information in interview introductions: methodological consequences of informed consent", *Sociology and Social Research* 66(3), apr 82 : 348-361.

442 WEBSTER, Edward C. *The employment interview: a social judgment process.* Schomberg, ON, SIP Publications, 82, x-144 p.

11240 **Personality measurement. Tests**
Mesure de la personnalité. Tests

443 KLINE, Paul. *Personality, measurement, and theory.* London, Hutchinson, 83, 174 p.

11250 **Sociodrama**
Sociodrame

11300 **MATHEMATICAL ANALYSIS. STATISTICAL ANALYSIS**
ANALYSE MATHÉMATIQUE. ANALYSE STATISTIQUE

11310   Algebra. Calculus. Logic
Algèbre. Calcul. Logique

444   ALEXANDER, Jeffrey C. *Theoretical logic in sociology. I. Positivism, presuppositions, and current controversies.* Berkeley, CA, University of California Press, 82, s.p. p.
445   CERRONI, Umberto. *Logica e societO1a: pensare dopo Marx* (Logic and society: to think after Marx). Milano, Bompiani, 82, 161 p.
446   COLLINS, Randall; RESTIVO, Sal. "Robber barons and politicians in mathematics: a conflict model of science", *Canadian Journal of Sociology / Cahiers canadiens de Sociologie* 8(2), 83 : 199-227.
447   DIEKMANN, Andreas; MITTER, Peter. "The 'sickle-hypothesis': a time dependent Poisson model with applications to deviant behavior and occupational mobility", *Journal of Mathematical Sociology* 9(2), 83 : 85-101.
448   LOESER, Franz. "What is dialectical logic?", *Poznań Studies* 7, 82 : 95-96.
449   NAVILLE, Pierre. *Sociologie et logique: esquisse d'une théorie des relations.* Paris, Presses Universitaires de France, 82, 280 p.
450   PARRA LUNA, Francisco. "Por una matematización de lo social" (For a mathematization of the social), *Revista internacional de Sociología (Madrid)* 41(46), apr-jun 83 : 297-312.
451   STARTUP, Richard. "The evolution of number", *Sociological Focus* 16(2), apr 83 : 107-116.

11320   Statistical analysis
Analyse statistique

452   BÉLAND, François. "Interpretation of strength and relations between variables in log-linear analysis", *Canadian Review of Sociology and Anthropology* 20(2), mai 83 : 208-221.
453   BERGER, Horst; PRILLER, Eckhard; [eds.]. *Indikatoren in der soziologischen Forschung* (Indicators in sociological research). Berlin, Akademie Verlag, 82, 149 p. [German DR]
454   COHEN, Ayala. "Comparing regression coefficients across subsamples: a study of the statistical test", *Sociological Methods and Research* 12(1), aug 83 : 77-94.
455   COOPER, Ron A.; WEEKES, A. J. *Data, models, and statistical analysis.* Totowa, NJ, Barnes and Noble Books, 82, xv-400 p.
456   GARCÍA FERRANDO, Manuel. *Socioestadistica* (Sociostatistics). Madrid, Centro de Investigaciones Sociologicas, 82, 461 p.
457   GEPHART, Robert P. Jr. "Multiple R, the 'parametric strategy', and measurement imprecision", *Sociological Perspectives* 26(4), oct 83 : 473-503.
458   GLISSON, Charles A.; MOK, Henry Man-Kwong. "Incorporating nominal variables in path analysis: a cross-cultural example with human service organizations", *Journal of Applied Behavioral Science* 19(1), 83 : 95-102.
459   GUMPRECHT, Nancy. "Block grants and funding decision: the case for social indicators", *Social Service Review* 57(1), mar 83 : 137-148.
460   HUJER, Reinhard; KNEPEL, Helmut. "Spezifikation und Schätzung sozialökonomischer Indikatormodelle" (Specification and evaluation of socioeconomic indicator models), *Allgemeines Statistisches Archiv* 66(2), 82 : 174-194.
461   JOHNSON, David Richard; CREECH, James C. "Ordinal measures in multiple indicator models: a simulation study of categorization error", *American Sociological Review* 48(3), jun 83 : 398-407.
462   LAND, Kenneth C. "Social indicators", *Annual Review of Sociology* (9), 83 : 1-16.
463   LORENZI-CIOLDI, Fabio. "L'analyse factorielle des correspondances dans les sciences sociales", *Schweizerische Zeitschrift für Soziologie / Revue suisse de Sociologie* 9(2), 83 : 365-390.
464   MANGAHAS, Mahar. "Measurement of poverty and equity: some ASEAN social indicators experience", *Social Indicators Research* 13(3), oct 83 : 253-279. [ASEAN countries]
465   MOHAN, Raj P. "The problem of social indicators", *Indian Journal of Social Research* 23(3), dec 82 : 224-228.
466   NURIUS, Paula S. "Use of time-series analysis in the evaluation of change due to intervention", *Journal of Applied Behavioral Science* 19(2), 83 : 215-228.
467   SCOTT, Wolf; MATHEW, N. T. *Levels of living and poverty in Kerala.* Geneva, United Nations Research Institute for Social Development, 83, iv-107 p.
468   SEMENOV, I. S. "O poznavatel'noj roli metodov statistiki" (On the cognitive role of statistical methods), *Filosofskie Problemy Sovremennogo Estestvoznanija* 53, 82 : 96-105.
469   TANAKA, Shohei. "Fukushi no sokutei ni tsuite: Hokkaido ni okeru shakai shihyo eno shiko" (On the measurement of welfare: social indicators in Hokkaido), *Sapporo daigaku keizai to keiei* 14(1), 83 : 1-30.

470   VISVALINGAM, M. "Area-based social indicators: signed chi-square as an alternative to ratios", *Social Indicators Research* 13(3), oct 83 : 311-329.
471   WACKER, Friedrich. "Konstruktion sozialer Indikatoren, dargestellt am Bereich Bildung" (Construction of social indicators, by the example of the education field), *Berichte über Landwirtschaft* 61(3), 83 : 466-485. [résumé in English and French]
472   WINSHIP, Christopher; MARE, Robert D. "Structural equations and path analysis for discrete data", *American Journal of Sociology* 89(1), jul 83 : 54-110.

11330   Cybernetics. Information theory
Cybernétique. Théorie de l'information

473   KUNCZIK, Michael. "Elemente der modernen Systemtheorie im soziologischen Werk von Herbert Spencer" (Elements of modern systems theory in the sociological work of Herbert Spencer), *Kölner Zeitschrift für Soziologie und Sozialpsychologie* 35(3), sep 83 : 438-461.
474   KURIHARA, Takashi. "J. Habermas no communication noryokuron" (The communication theory of Jürgen Habermas), *Hitotsubashi kenkyu* 7(4), 83 : 33-48.
475   MUIR, Donal E. "An adaptive systems theory: toward reductionism", *Sociological Inquiry* 53(4), 83 : 435-448.
476   WILLKE, Helmut. *Systemtheorie: eine Einführung in die Grundprobleme* (Systems theory: an introduction to the basic problems). Stuttgart, F. Fischer, 82, 163 p.

11340   Graph theory
Théorie des graphes

477   BARNES, J. A.; HARARY, Frank. "Graph theory in network analysis", *Social Networks* 5(2), jun 83 : 235-244.
478   CHEN, Huey-Tsyh. "Flowgraph analysis for effect decomposition: use in recursive and nonrecursive models", *Sociological Methods and Research* 12(1), aug 83 : 3-29.
479   EVERETT, Martin G. "EBLOC: a graph theoretic blocking algorithm for social networks", *Social Networks* 5(4), dec 83 : 323-346.
480   EVERETT, Martin G. "An extension of EBLOC to valued graphs", *Social Networks* 5(4), dec 83 : 395-402.
481   FREEMAN, Linton C. "Spheres, cubes and boxes: graph dimensionality and network structure", *Social Networks* 5(2), jun 83 : 139-156.
482   WHITE, Douglas R.; REITZ, Karl P. "Graph and semigroup homomorphisms on networks of relations", *Social Networks* 5(2), jun 83 : 193-234.

11350   Stochastic processes. Statistical decision. Game theory
Processus stochastiques. Décision statistique. Théorie des jeux

483   FRIEDMAN, Samuel R. "Game theory and labor conflict: limits of rational choice models", *Sociological Perspectives* 26(4), oct 83 : 375-397. [USA]
484   GERCHAK, Yigal. "Durations in social states: concepts of inertia and related comparisons in stochastic models", *Sociological Methodology*, 83-84 : 194-224.
485   GERCHAK, Yigal. "On interactive chains with finite populations", *Journal of Mathematical Sociology* 9(3), 83 : 255-258. [USA]
486   LINDENBERG, Seigwart. "Utility and morality", *Kyklos* 36(3), 83 : 450-468.
487   RUSCONI, Gian Enrico. "Teoria dei giochi e spegazione sociologica" (Game theory and sociological explanation), *Stato e Mercato* (8), aug 83 : 251-270. [résumé en anglais]

11360   Attitude scales
Échelles d'attitude

488   COOK, Wade D.; SEIFORD, Lawrence M.; WARNER, Stanley L. "Preference ranking models: conditions for equivalence", *Journal of Mathematical Sociology* 9(2), 83 : 125-137.
489   GROSS, Jonathan L. "Information-theoretic scales for measuring cultural rule systems", *Sociological Methodology*, 83-84 : 248-271.
490   KOCH-WESER AMMASSARI, Elke. "Sources of error in rating scale measurements", *Revue internationale de Sociologie* 18(1-2-3), apr-aug-sep 82 : 89-108.
491   LARSEN, Knud S.; LEROUX, Jeff. "Item analysis vs. factor analysis in the development of unidimensional attitude scales", *Journal of Social Psychology* 119(1), feb 83 : 95-101.

492   TAYLOR, Marylee C. ''The black-and-white model of attitude stability: a latent class
         examination of opinion and nonopinion in the American public'', *American Journal of
         Sociology* 89(2), sep 83 : 373-401.
493   WEGENER, Bernd. ''Category-rating and magnitude estimation scaling techniques: an
         empirical comparison'', *Sociological Methods and Research* 12(1), aug 83 : 31-75.

12100   PSYCHOLOGY. SOCIAL PSYCHOLOGY. SOCIOMETRY
         PSYCHOLOGIE. PSYCHOLOGIE SOCIALE. SOCIOMÉTRIE

12110   Psychoanalysis. Social psychology
         Psychanalyse. Psychologie sociale

494   "Judaism and psychotherapy", *European Judaism* 17(2), wint 82 : 2-46. [with contributions by Jeff AITMAN, Paul BROWN, Jonathan MAGONET]

495   "Psicología social" (Social psychology), *Revista mexicana de Sociología* 45(2), apr-jun 83 : 641-726.

496   "Psychology in the public forum: psychotherapy", *American Psychologist* 38(8), aug 83 : 907-955. [USA] [with contributions by Daniel K. INOUYE, David H. BANTA, Leonard SAXE, Gerald L. KLERMAN]

497   "Social psychology in South Africa", *Journal of Social Psychology* 121(2), dec 83 : 161-311. [Special issue]

498   ABRAHAM, Georges; ANDRÉOLI, Antonio. *La psychothérapie aujourd'hui.* Villeurbanne, Simep, 82, 211 p.

499   AMERIO, Piero. *Teorie in psicologia sociale* (Theories in social psychology). Bologna, Il Mulino, 82, 439 p.

500   BADCOCK, C. R. *Madness and modernity: a study in social psychoanalysis.* Oxford, B. Blackwell, 83, 180 p.

501   BEVLI, Updesh Kaur. *Concept formation in children: eco-cultural context.* New Delhi, National, 82, viii-230 p.

502   BJÖRKLID, Pia. *Children's outdoor environment: a study of children's outdoor activities on two housing estates from the perspective of environmental and developmental psychology.* Lund, CWK Gleerup, 82, 255 p.

503   CRANO, William D.; MESSÉ, Lawrence Allen. *Social psychology: principles and themes of interpersonal behavior.* Homewood, IL, Dorsey Press, 82, xv-559 p.

504   DOISE, Willem; MOSCOVICI, Serge. *Current issues in European social psychology.* Cambridge, Cambridge University Press; Paris, Éditions de la MSH, 83, xviii-316 p.

505   DURANDEAUX, Jacques. *Poétique analytique: des langues et des discours dans la psychanalyse.* Paris, Seuil, 82, 185 p.

506   FISHER, Ronald J. *Social psychology: an applied approach.* New York, NY, St. Martin's Press, 82, viii-712-103 p.

507   JADCZAK, Ryszard. "Związki między psychologią a socjologią w ujęciu Tadeusza Szczurkiewicza" (Connections between psychology and sociology in Tadeusz Szczurkiewicz's formulation), *Rozprawy z filozofii i socjologii*, 83 : 19-34.

508   MASCHINO, Maurice T. *'Votre désir m'intéresse': enquête sur la pratique psychoanalytique.* Paris, Hachette Littérature Générale, 82, 253 p.

509   MCKINNEY, John Paul; FITZGERALD, Hiram E.; STROMMEN, Ellen A. *Developmental psychology, the adolescent and young adult.* Homewood, IL, Dorsey Press, 82, xi-260 p.

510   MUHINA, É. N. "Istoričeskaja psihologija v sisteme nauk o kul'ture" (Historical psychology in the sciences system on culture), *Sbornik Naučnyh Trudov (Leningradskij Institut Kultury)* 57, 81 : 51-61.

511   NEDERHOF, Anton J.; ZWIER, A. Gerard. "The 'crisis' in social psychology, an empirical approach", *European Journal of Social Psychology* 13(3), jul-sep 83 : 255-280.

512   QUAGLINO, Gian Piero. *Temi di ricerca in psicologia sociale: rappresentazione e intergruppo* (Research themes in social psychology: representation and intergroup). Torino, G. Giappichelli, 82, 121 p.

513   RABOW, Jerome. "Psychoanalysis and sociology", *Annual Review of Sociology* (9), 83 : 555-578.

514   ROSENBERG, Seymour; GARA, Michael A. "Contemporary perspectives and future directions of personality and social psychology", *Journal of Personality and Social Psychology* 45(1), jul 83 : 57-73.

515   TOUZARD, Hubert. "Psychologie sociale", *Année sociologique* 32, 82 : 195-224. [Compte rendu bibliographique]

516   VANNIKOVA, N. R. "Social'nye funkcii kliničeskoj psihologii v SŠA" (Social functions
        of clinical psychology in the USA), *Psichologičeskij Žurnal* (3-4), 82 : 124-130.
517   ZLOTNIKOV, V. G.; JANUŠKO, A. V. "O sootnošenii obščestvennoj psihologii
        i obščestvennogo soznanija" (On correlation of social psychology and social conscious-
        ness in: *Problemy social'nogo poznanija: voprosy formirovanija social'noj aktivnosti.* Moskva,
        1981 : 59-68.

        12120   Psychological factors
        Facteurs psychologiques

        12200   INDIVIDUALS. PERSONALITY
        INDIVIDUS. PERSONNALITÉ

        12210   Ego. Identity
        Ego. Identité

518   "Problem (The) of personhood: biomedical, social, legal and policy views", *Milbank Memorial
        Fund Quarterly* 61(1), wint 83 : 1-147. [USA] [with contributions by Willy de CRAEMER,
        Leonard GLANTZ, Dorothy NELKIN, Fenée C. FOX, David P. WILLIS]
519   "Sozialstruktur und gesellschaftliche Individualisierungstendenzen" (Social structure and
        social individualization trends), *Soziale Welt* 34(3), 83 : 270-371. [résumé en anglais,
        with contributions by Josef MOOSER, Elisabeth BECK-GERNSHEIM]
520   "XXV Congrès de l'Institut international de Sociologie: La liberté individuelle et l'organisation
        sociale", *Revue internationale de Sociologie* 18(1-2-3), apr-aug-sep 82 : 5-485. [Lisbonne,
        10-16 apr 80]
521   BOLTANSKI, Luc; THÉVENOT, Laurent. "Finding one's way in social space: a study
        based on games", *Social Science Information* 22(4-5), 83 : 631-680.
522   COTESTA, Vittorio. "Kant e E. Durkheim. Elementi per una sociologia dell'individuo
        moderno" (Kant and Durkheim. Elements for a sociology of the modern individual),
        Critica sociologica 60, 82 : 16-59.
523   WATASE, Hiroshi. *Soshiki to ningen* (Organization and individual). Tokyo, Dobunkan,
        83, 281 p.

        12220   Egocentrism. Self concept
        Égocentrisme. Conception de soi

524   "Studi sull'identità" (Identity study), *Rassegna italiana di Sociologia* 24(1), jan-mar
        83 : 3-130.
525   ARNDT, Hans-Joachim. "Identitätsstörungen bei Jugendlichen und Geschichtsbewusstsein.
        Neuere Entwicklungen bei der Pflege eines deutschen Geschichtsbildes in der Bundes-
        republik" (Identity crisis in youth and historical consciousness), *Hamburger Jahrbuch für
        Wirtschafts- und Gesellschaftspolitik* 27, 82 : 115-134.
526   BOSKI, Pawel. "Egotism and evaluation in self and other attributions for achievement
        related outcomes", *European Journal of Social Psychology* 13(3), jul-sep 83 : 287-304.
527   COOPER, Robert. "Some remarks on theoretical individualism, alienation, and work",
        Human Relations 36(8), aug 83 : 717-723.
528   DAHRENDORF, Ralf. "Die Grenzen der Gleichheit: Bemerkungen zu Fred Hirsch"
        (The limits of identity: remarks on Fred Hirsch), *Zeitschrift für Soziologie* 12(1), jan
        83 : 65-73.
529   DELHEZ-SARLET, Claudette; CATANI, Maurizio; [eds.]. "Individualisme et auto-
        biographie en Occident", *Revue de l'Institut de Sociologie* (1-2), 82 : 13-293. [Colloque
        tene Au Centre Culturel International, Cerisy-la-Salle, 10-20 juillet 1979]
530   DEMO, David H.; SAVIN-WILLIAMS, Ritch C. "Early adolescent self-esteem as a function
        of social class: Rosenberg and Pearlin revisited", *American Journal of Sociology* 88(4), jan
        83 : 763-774. [USA] [about Morris ROSENBERG, Leonard I. PEARLIN, 'Social class
        and self-esteem among children and adults', ibid. 84, 79: 53-77]
531   DUMONT, Louis. "A modified view of our origins: the Christian beginnings of modern
        individualism", *Contributions to Indian Sociology* 17(1), jan-jun 83 : 1-26.
532   ESCOBAR, Modesto. "La autoidentidad. Problemas metodológicos del Twenty Statements
        Test" (Self identity. Methodological problems of the Twenty Statements Test), *Revista
        Española de Investigaciones Sociológicas* 23, jul-sep 83 : 31-51.

533 FUNATSU, Mamoru. "Jiga to jiko hyogen" (Self and self presentation), *Shakaigaku kenkyu* 45, 83 : 173-200.

534 FUNATSU, Mamoru. "Jigaron no kadai" (Problems of self theory), *Gendai shakaigaku* 17, 83 : 104-124.

535 GECAS, Viktor; SCHWALBE, Michael L. "Beyond the looking-glass self: social structure and efficacy-based self-esteem", *Social Psychology Quarterly* 46(2), jun 83 : 77-88.

536 GRAUMANN, Carl F. "On multiple identities", *International Social Science Journal* 35(2), 83 : 309-321.

537 GREENBERG, Jerald. "Self-image versus impression management in adherence to distributive justice standards: the influence of self-awareness and self-consciousness", *Journal of Personality and Social Psychology* 44(1), jan 83 : 5-19.

538 HALL, Peter M. "Individualism and social problems: a critique and an alternative", *Journal of Applied Behavioral Science* 19(1), 83 : 85-94.

539 HARGREAVES, David J.; COLMAN, Andrew M.; SLUCKIN, Wladyslaw. "The attractiveness of names", *Human Relations* 36(4), apr 83 : 393-401.

540 HOELTER, Jon W. "Factorial invariance and self-esteem: reassessing race and sex differences", *Social Forces* 61(3), mar 83 : 834-846. [USA]

541 IRIBARNE, Philippe d'. "Crise de l'identité moderne", *Futuribles* 62, jan 83 : 61-72.

542 KRAUSE, Neal. "The racial context of black self-esteem", *Social Psychology Quarterly* 46(2), jun 83 : 98-107.

543 LASKER, G. W. "Surnames in five English villages: relationship to each other, to surrounding areas, and to England and Wales", *Journal of Biosocial Science* 15(1), jan 83 : 25-34.

544 MACKIE, Marlene. "The domestication of self: gender comparisons of self-imagery and self-esteem", *Social Psychology Quarterly* 46(4), dec 83 : 343-350.

545 MEMMENDEY, Amélie; SCHREIBER, Hans-Joachim. "Better or just different? Positive social identity by discrimination against, or by differentiation from outgroups", *European Journal of Social Psychology* 13(4), oct-dec 83 : 389-397.

546 MISIEWICZ, Halina. *Poczucie własnej wartości u młodzieży* (Self-esteem of young people). Warszawa, Instytut Wydawniczy Związków Zawodowych, 83, 140 p.

547 PROSS, Helge. "Wertdefizit und Integration. Der neue Individualismus in der Bundesrepublik" (Value deficit and integration. The new individualism in the Federal Republic), *Hamburger Jahrbuch für Wirtschafts- und Gesellschaftspolitik* 27, 82 : 145-151.

548 SCHÄFER, Alfred. "Identität und sekundäre Anpassung. Zum theoretischen Bezugsrahmen Erving Goffmans" (Identity and secondary adaptation. On Erving Goffman's theoretical relations framework), *Kölner Zeitschrift für Soziologie und Sozialpsychologie* 35(4), dec 83 : 631-654.

549 STAGER, Susan F.; CHASSIN, Laurie; YOUNG, Richard David. "Determinants of self esteem among labelled adolescents", *Social Psychology Quarterly* 46(1), mar 83 : 3-10.

550 STOLTE, John F. "The legitimation of structural inequality: reformulation and test of the self-evaluation argument", *American Sociological Review* 48(3), jun 83 : 331-342.

551 TESSER, Abraham; PAULHUS, Del. "The definition of self: private and public self-evaluation management strategies", *Journal of Personality and Social Psychology* 44(4), apr 83 : 672-682.

552 TOTH, Michael A. "Why sociology is difficult: emergence, structure, and the peculiar location of self-consciousness in nature", *Social Science Journal (Fort Collins)* 19(4), oct 82 : 1-7.

553 VAN DER PLIGT, Joop; EISER, J. Richard. "Value connotations, perspective and self-perception", *European Journal of Social Psychology* 13(2), apr-jun 83 : 129-141.

554 WALSH, Edward J.; TAYLOR, Marylee C. "Occupational correlates of multidimensional self-esteem: comparisons among garbage-collectors, bartenders, professors, and other workers", *Sociology and Social Research* 66(3), apr 82 : 252-268.

555 WELLS, L. Edward; RANKIN, Joseph H. "Self-concept as a mediating factor in delinquency", *Social Psychology Quarterly* 46(1), mar 83 : 11-22.

12230 Personality
Personnalité

556 ABUL'HANOVA-SLAVSKAJA, K. A. "O putjah postroenija tipologii ličnosti" (On the ways of the personality typology elaboration), *Psichologičeskij Žurnal* 4(1), 83 : 14-29.

557   EYSENCK, Hans Jurgen. *Personality, genetics, and behavior: selected papers.* New York, NY, Praeger, 82, x-340 p.

558   GATCHEL, Robert J.; MEARS, Frederick G. *Personality: theory, assessment, and research.* New York, NY, St. Martin's Press, 82, xiv-559 p.

559   GREBEN'KOV, N. N. "Organizacionnoe samoopredelenie ličnosti v kollektive" (Organizational self-determination of the personality in the collectivity), *Naučnye Trudy (Kurskij Pedagogičeskij Institut)* 215, 81 : 34-44.

560   LEYENS, Jacques-Philippe. *Sommes-nous tous des psychologues? Approche psychosociale des théories implicites de la personnalité.* Bruxelles, Mardago, 83, 284 p.

561   MARTINDALE, Don Albert. *Personality and milieu: the shaping of social science culture.* Houston, TX, Cap and Gown Press, 82, vii-207 p.

562   PETROVA, Ju. N.; [ed.]. *Problemy hudožestvennogo razvitija ličnosti: social'no-psichologičeskie aspekty priobščenija k iskusstvu* (Problems of the personality artistic development: sociopsychological aspects of the access to art). Moskva, VNII Iskusstvoznanija, 82, 247 p.

563   SERŽATOV, V. F.; [ed.]. *Teorija ličnosti* (The theory of personality). Leningrad, Izdatel'stvo Leningradskogo Universiteta, 82, 185 p.

564   TITARENKO, A. I.; [ed.]. *Nravstvennye problemy razvitija ličnosti* (Moral problems of the personality development). Moskva, Izdatel'stvo Moskovskogo Universiteta, 82, 144 p.

565   VOLKOV, L. B.; [et al.]. *Naučnoe upravlenie obščestvom i vsestoronnee razvitie ličnosti* (Scientific management of society and personality total development). Moskva, INION AN SSSR, 82, 208 p.

12240   Cognition. Emotion. Motivation
**   Cognition. Émotion. Motivation**

566   "Investigación (La) psicosocial sobre problemas de aprendizaje en Costa Rica" (Psychosocial research on learning problems in Costa Rica), *Revista de ciencias sociales (San José)* (23), mar 82 : 7-40. [with contributions by Sandra QUIROS CESPEDES, Ana Teresa ALVAREZ HERNANDEZ, Luis OTERO REYES]

567   "Terror and State terrorism", *Telos* (54), wint 82-83 : 1-154. [with contributions by Max HORKHEIMER, Juan E. CARRABI, Istvan LOVAS, Ken ANDERSON, Jadwiga STANISZKIS, Michal REIMAN; Frederick JOHNSTONE, Norberto BOBBIO]

568   AGNEW, Robert S. "Social class and success goals: an examination of relative and absolute aspirations", *Sociological Quarterly* 24(3), sum 83 : 435-452.

569   AMABILE, Teresa M. "The social psychology of creativity: a componential conceptualization", *Journal of Personality and Social Psychology* 45(2), aug 83 : 357-376.

570   ANGELUSZ, Róbert; CSEPELI, György. "Love your enemies, bless them that curse you. To the criticism of the theories of cognitive balance", *Annales Universitatis Scientiarum budapestiensis de Rolando Eötvös nominatae. Sectio philosophica et sociologica* 16, 82 : 223-240.

571   ARGYRIS, Chris. "Action science and intervention", *Journal of Applied Behavioral Science* 19(2), 83 : 115-135. [with comments by Michael L. LAUDERDALE: 136-138 and a reply by the author: 139-140]

572   BARDO, John W.; BARDO, Deborah J. "A re-examination of subjective components of community satisfaction in a British new town", *Journal of Social Psychology* 119(2), apr 83 : 35-43.

573   BASS, Bernard M. *Organizational decision making.* Homewood, IL, R. D. Irwin, 83, xiii-223 p.

574   BOUWEN, R. "Behavioral strategies in complex decision making process", *Scandinavian Journal of Materials Administration* 9(2), 83 : 25-41.

575   CARRIER, James G. "Masking the social in educational knowledge: the case of learning disability theory", *American Journal of Sociology* 88(5), mar 83 : 948-974.

576   CHAVARRIA, Ma. Celina. "La estimulación temprana: apuntes sobre sus fundamentos teóricos, bases empíricas, raíces socio-históricas. Elementos para una discusión" (The early estimulation: outline on its theoretical bases, empirical bases, socio-historical roots. Elements for a discussion), *Revista de Ciencias Sociales de la Universidad de Costa Rica* 23(1), 82 : 41-56.

577   CORRADI, Juan. "Une forme de destruction: la terreur en Argentine", *Amérique latine* (15), sep 83 : 3-11.

578   COURBON, Jean-Claude. "Processus de décision et aide à la décision", *Économies et Sociétés* 16(12), dec 82 : 1455-1476.

579   DINITZ, Simon; BETO, George. "In fear of each other", *Sociological Focus* 16(3), aug 83 : 155-167.

580   DINKELBACH, Werner. *Entscheidungsmodelle* (Decision models). Berlin-New York, NY, W. de Gruyter, 82, xv-285 p.

581   FOURASTIÉ, Jean. *Le rire, suite.* Paris, Denoël/Gonthier, 83, 263 p.

582   FYANS, Leslie J.; [et al.]. "A cross-cultural exploration into the meaning of achievement", *Journal of Personality and Social Psychology* 44(5), mai 83 : 1000-1013.

583   GEREBEN, Ferenc. *A falusi lakosok olvasási és könyvbeszerzési szokásai* (Reading and book purchasing habits of villagers). Budapest, Könyvkiadók és Könyvterjesztők Egyesülete, 82, 93 p. [Hungary]

584   GUBRIUM, Jaber F.; LYNOTT, Robert J. "Rethinking life satisfaction", *Human Organization* 42(1), 83 : 30-38. [USA]

585   GUIMOND, Serge; DUBE-SIMARD, Lise. "Relative deprivation theory and the Quebec Nationalist Movement: the cognition-emotion distinction and the personal-group deprivation issue", *Journal of Personality and Social Psychology* 44(3), mar 83 : 527-535. [Canada]

586   HOEDE, C.; MEEK, A. "Structural aspects of decisional power", *Journal of Mathematical Sociology* 9(3), 83 : 243-253.

587   HUNT, Morton M. *The universe within: a new science explores the human mind.* Brighton, Sussex, Harvester Press, 82, 415 p.

588   KERR, Norbert L. "Motivation losses in small groups: a social dilemma analysis", *Journal of Personality and Social Psychology* 45(4), oct 83 : 819-828.

589   LEATHER, Phil. "Desire: a structural model of motivation", *Human Relations* 36(2), feb 83 : 109-122.

590   LYSYJ, I. Ja. "Problema mesta potrebnostej v sisteme social'noj determinacii" (Problem of the needs place in the social determination system), *Problemy Filosofii* 55, 82 : 72-80.

591   MARTIN, Rod A.; LEFCOURT, Herbert M. "Sense of humor as a moderator of the relation between stressors and moods", *Journal of Personality and Social Psychology* 45(6), dec 83 : 1313-1324.

592   MATALON, Benjamin. "La psychologie et l'explication des faits sociaux. II. L'analyse des processus de décision", *Année sociologique* 32, 82 : 115-161.

593   MDIVANI, L. V. "O nekotoryh aspektah issledovanija kategorii potrebnostej" (On some aspects of research on the needs categories), *Izvestija Akademii Nauk Gruzinskoj SSR. Serija Filosofii i Psihologii* (4), 82 : 31-35.

594   NEMETH, Charlan Jeanne; WACHTLER, Joel. "Creative problem solving as a result of majority vs. minority influence", *European Journal of Social Psychology* 13(1), jan-mar 83 : 45-55.

595   OKSENBERG RORTY, Amelie. "Imagination and power", *Social Science Information* 22(6), 83 : 801-816.

596   PADIOLEAU, Jean-G.; EYMERIAT, Michel. "L'étude des styles cognitifs dans la pensée sociale ou poltique. Note de recherche", *Année sociologique* 32, 82 : 39 59.

597   PAVETT, Cynthia M. "Evaluation of the impact of feedback on performance and motivation", *Human Relations* 36(7), jul 83 : 641-654.

598   PENNINGS, Johannes M.; [ed.]. *Decision making: an organizational behavior approach.* New York, NY, M. Wiener Publications, 83, viii-391 p.

599   PESTELLO, H. Frances Geyer. "Fear and misbehavior in a high school", *Sociological Quarterly* 24(4), 83 : 561-573. [USA]

600   PORPORA, Douglas V. "On the post-Wittgensteinian critique of the concept of action in sociology", *Journal for the Theory of Social Behaviour* 13(2), jul 83 : 129-146.

601   ROSENFELD, Paul; GIACALONE, Robert A.; TEDESCHI, James T. "Humor and impression management", *Journal of Social Psychology* 121(1), oct 83 : 59-63.

602   ROY, Bernard; [ed.]. *La décision: ses disciplines, ses acteurs.* Lyon, Presses Universitaires de Lyon, 83, 194 p.

603   SANTORO, Jean-Louis. "Le discours audio-visuel: une méthode d'apprentissage de la lecture", *Humanisme et Entreprise* 137, feb 83 : 19.

604   SCHEFF, Thomas J. "Toward integration in the social psychology of emotions", *Annual Review of Sociology* (9), 83 : 333-354.

605   SCHERER, Klaus R.; SUMMERFIELD, Angela B.; WALLBOTT, Harald G. "Cross-national research on antecedents and components of emotion: a progress report", *Social Science Information* 22(3), 83 : 355-385.

606   TERADA, Atsuhiro. "Setsumei zushiki toshiteno koiteki approach I" (Action approach: a conceptual scheme), *Nihon daigaku bunrigakubu Mishima kenkyu nenpo* 31, 83 : 53-62.

607   TOURRETTE, Catherine. "L'intérêt pour la lecture chez les enfants de 6 à 12 ans. L'accès au livre et le contenu des lectures", *Bulletin de Psychologie* 36(361), aug 83 : 747-756. [France]

608   TURNER, Stephen P. "Weber on action", *American Sociological Review* 48(4), aug 83 : 506-519.
609   VAN LIERE, Kent D.; DUNLAP, Riley E. "Cognitive integration of social and environmental beliefs", *Sociological Inquiry* 53(2-3), spr 83 : 333-341.
610   VAN ZUUREN, F. J. *Fobie, situatie en identiteit: een studie over de situatie-vermijding en identiteits-problematiek van twee soorten fobici* (Phobia, situation and identity: a study on situation evasion and identity problems in two types of phobia). Lisse, Swets en Zeitlinger, 82, ix-230 p.
611   VAYER, Pierre; TOULOUSE, Pierre. *Psychosociologie de l'action: le motif et l'action.* Paris, Doin, 82, xvii-173 p.
612   VENGERENKO, N. A. "Istoričeskoe tvorčestvo, ègo formy i mehanizm razvitija" (Historical creation: its forms and mechanisms of development), *in: Tvorčestvo o obščestvennyj progress.* Moskva, 1982 : 26-67.
613   VORONCOV, B. N. "Razumnye potrebnosti kak potrebnosti kollektivistskoj ličnosti" (Judicious needs as needs of the collective personality), *Naučnye Doklady vysšej Školy. Naučnyj Kommunizma* (4), 82 : 30-38.
614   WINDISCH, Uli. *Pensée sociale, langage en usage et logiques autres: l'exemple de la causalité dans la vie quotidienne en acte.* Lausanne, L'Âge d'Homme, 82, 127 p.
615   WIŚNIEWSKI, Wiesław. "Przemiany w poczuciu zaspokojenia niektórych potrzeb w społeczeństwie polskim w latach 1977-1981" (Transformations of the sense of satisfaction of needs in Polish society between 1977-1981), *Studia Socjologiczne* 90 (3), 83 : 95-118.
616   WOOLSEY BIGGART, Nicole. "Rationality, meaning, and self-management: success manuals, 1950-1980", *Social Problems* 30(3), feb 83 : 298-311. [USA]
617   YIN, Peter. "Fear of crime as a problem for the elderly", *Social Problems* 30(2), dec 82 : 240-245. [USA]
618   ZIJDERVELD, Anton C. "Sociology of humour and laughter", *Current Sociology* 31(3), 83 : 1-103.

12300   INTERPERSONAL RELATIONS
RELATIONS INTERPERSONNELLES

12310   Human relations. Sociability
Relations humaines. Sociabilité

619   BRANDSTÄTTER, Hermann. "Emotional responses to other persons in everyday life situations", *Journal of Personality and Social Psychology* 45(4), oct 83 : 871-883.
620   CHEATWOOD, Derral. "Sociability and the sociology of humor", *Sociology and Social Research* 67(3), apr 83 : 324-338.
621   DEGENNE, Alain. "Sur les réseaux de sociabilité", *Revue française de Sociologie* 24(1), jan-mar 83 : 109-118.
622   DESSLER, Gary. *Applied human relations.* Reston, VA, Reston Publishing Co., 83, xv-427 p.
623   FERGE, Zsuzsa. "Emberi viszonyok és társadalmi értékek" (Human relations and social values), *Társadalomtudományi Közlemények* 13(1), 83 : 102-125.
624   FOURNIER, Daniel. "Consanguinité et sociabilité dans la zone de Montréal au début du siècle", *Recherches sociographiques* 24(3), sep-dec 83 : 307-323.
625   GÖBEL, Adrieke. *De mens en zijn relaties: een inleiding in de gedragswetenschappen* (Human persons and their relations: an introduction to behavioural sciences). Deventer, Van Loghum Slaterus, 82, 194 p.
626   KEUPP, Lutz. *Interpersonale Beziehungen und Devianz: eine normdissonante Gruppe (Strafgefangene) und eine normkonsonante Gruppe (Polizeibeamte) im empirischen Vergleich* (Interpersonal relations and deviance: a norm-dissonant group and a norm-consonant group in empirical comparison). Heidelberg, Kriminalistik Verlag, 82, viii-198 p.
627   KING, Gillian A.; SORRENTINO, Richard M. "Psychological dimensions of goal-oriented interpersonal situations", *Journal of Personality and Social Psychology* 44(1), jan 83 : 140-162.
628   LAWLER, Edward J. "Cooptation and threats as 'divide and rule' tactics", *Social Psychology Quarterly* 46(2), jun 83 : 89-98.
629   MEFFORD, Dwain. "A comparison of dialectical and Boolean-algebraic models of the genesis of interpersonal relations", *Poznań Studies* 7, 82 : 31-47.
630   PAMPEL, Fred C. "Changes in the propensity to live alone: evidence from consecutive cross-sectional surveys, 1960-1976", *Demography* 20(4), nov 83 : 433-488.
631   RIDDER, Guido de. *Du côté des hommes: à la recherche de nouveaux rapports avec les femmes.* Paris, L'Harmattan, 82, 218 p.
632   RODRIGUES, Aroldo; DELA COLETA, José Augusto. "The prediction of preferences for triadic interpersonal relations", *Journal of Social Psychology* 121(1), oct 83 : 73-80.

633   SCHMIDT, Nancy; SERMAT, Vello. "Measuring loneliness in different relationships", *Journal of Personality and Social Psychology* 44(5), mai 83 : 1038-1047.

634   SEMIN, G. R.; MANSTEAD, A. S. R. *The accountability of conduct: a social psychological analysis.* London-New York, NY, Academic Press, 83, xiii-204 p.

635   SWAP, Walter C.; RUBIN, Jeffrey Z. "Measurement of interpersonal orientation", *Journal of Personality and Social Psychology* 44(1), jan 83 : 208-219.

636   WHEELER, Ladd; REIS, Harry; NEZLEK, John. "Loneliness, social interaction, and sex roles", *Journal of Personality and Social Psychology* 45(4), oct 83 : 943-953.

637   WIDEGREN, Örjan. "The general principles of sociability: developing Sahlns' theory of 'primitive exchange' ", *Sociology (London)* 17(3), aug 83 : 319-338.

12320   Social perception
Perception sociale

638   AMBERT, Anne-Marie; SAUCIER, Jean-François. "Adolescents' perception of their parents and parents' marital status", *Journal of Social Psychology* 119(2), apr 83 : 101-110.

639   BOLDT, Edward D.; FINNBOGASON, Eve M.; SEGALL, Alexander. "Psychiatric labelling and the imputation of mental illness by jurors", *Sociological Focus* 16(2), apr 83 : 91-98.

640   CRITTENDEN, Kathleen S. "Sociological aspects of attribution", *Annual Review of Sociology* (9), 83 : 425-446.

641   GULOTTA, Guglielmo. *I processi di attribuzione nella psicologia interpersonale e sociale* (Attribution processes in interpersonal and social psychology). Milano, F. Angeli, 82, 103 p.

642   JASPARS, Jos; FINCHAM, Frank D.; HEWSTONE, Miles. *Attribution theory and research: conceptual, developmental, and social dimensions.* London-New York, NY, Academic Press, 83, xvi-415 p.

643   KRAJEWSKI, Krzysztof. "Podstawowe tezy teorii naznaczania społecznego" (Essential propositions of the social labelling theory), *Ruch prawniczy, ekonomiczny i socjologiczny* 45(1), 83 : 225-245.

644   KRUGLANSKI, Arie W.; AJSEN, Icek. "Bias and error in human judgment", *European Journal of Social Psychology* 13(1), jan-mar 83 : 1-44.

645   LEWICKI, Pawel. "Self-image bias in person perception", *Journal of Personality and Social Psychology* 45(2), aug 83 : 384-393.

646   SANDERS, Glenn S.; MULLEN, Brian. "Accuracy in perceptions of consensus: differential tendencies of people with majority and minority positions", *European Journal of Social Psychology* 13(1), jan-mar 83 : 57-70.

647   SCHUL, Yaacov; BURNSTEIN, Eugene; MARTINEZ, James. "The informational basis of social judgments: under what conditions are inconsistent trait descriptions processed as easily as consistent ones?", *European Journal of Social Psychology* 13(2), apr-jun 83 : 143-151.

648   VAN DER PLIGHT, Joop; EISER, J. "Actors' and observers' attributions, self-serving bias and positivity bias", *European Journal of Social Psychology* 13(1), jan-mar 83 : 95-104.

12330   Interpersonal attraction
Attraction interpersonnelle

649   AMATO, Paul R. "Helping behavior in urban and rural environments: field studies based on a taxonomic organization of helping episodes", *Journal of Personality and Social Psychology* 45(3), sep 83 : 571-586.

650   BIGELOW, Brian. "Assessing children's friendship expectations: supplementing the semistructured interview with picture sequence tasks", *Human Relations* 36(3), mar 83 : 285-308.

651   DAVIS, Mark H. "Measuring individual differences in empathy: evidence for a multi-dimensional approach", *Journal of Personality and Social Psychology* 44(1), jan 83 : 113-126.

652   DUCK, Steve. *Friends, for life: the psychology of close relationships.* Brighton, Sussex, Harvester Press, 83, 181 p.

653   FRY, P. S.; CORFIELD, V. K. "Social attraction ratings of divorced males and females", *Journal of Social Psychology* 120(2), aug 83 : 259-272.

654   GONZÁLEZ, M. Hope; [et al.]. "Interactional approach to interpersonal attraction", *Journal of Personality and Social Psychology* 44(6), jun 83 : 1192-1197.

655   HUCKFELDT, R. Robert. "Social contexts, social networks, and urban neighborhoods: environmental constraints on friendship choice", *American Journal of Sociology* 89(3), nov 83 : 651-669. [USA]

656   ISCHER, Claude S.; OLIKER, Stacey J. "A research note on friendship, gender, and the life cycle", *Social Forces* 62(1), sep 83 : 124-133.

657   JOHNSON, John A.; CHEEK, Jonathan M.; SMITHER, R. "The structure of empathy", *Journal of Personality and Social Psychology* 45(6), dec 83 : 1299-1312.

658   LEUNG, Angela Kiche. "L'amour en Chine. Relations et pratiques sociales aux XVIIIᶜ et XIVᶜ siècles", *Archives de Sciences sociales des Religions* 56(1), jul-sep 83 : 53-76.

659   LEVIN, Jack; ARLUKE, Arnold. "Attitude similarity and parent-child attractiveness", *Journal of Social Psychology* 120(2), aug 83 : 223-228.

660   MCPHERSON, Miller. "An ecology of affiliation", *American Sociological Review* 48(4), aug 83 : 519-532.

661   POPE, Whitney; JOHNSON, Barclay D. "Inside organic solidarity", *American Sociological Review* 48(5), oct 83 : 681-692.

662   VERBRUGGE, Lois M. "A research note on adult friendship contact: a dyadic perspective", *Social Forces* 62(1), sep 83 : 78-83.

12340   Interpersonal influence
Influence interpersonnelle

663   HECKATHORN, Douglas D. "Extensions of power-dependence theory: the concept of resistance", *Social Forces* 61(4), jun 83 : 1206-1231. [with a response by Richard M. EMERSON, pp. 1232-1247, and an answer by the author: pp. 1248-1259]

664   WATASE, Hiroshi. "Identification and identity: a problem of 'organization and man' ", *Kyoto University Economic Review* 53(1-2), apr-oct 83 : 16-24.

665   WICHER, Czesław. "Wzór osobowy jako kategoria etyczna i socjologiczna" (Personal model as an ethical and sociological category), *Rozprawy z filozofii i socjologii*, 83 : 171-179.

666   ZAPATA, Cesar Rafael. "Dependencia: racionalización y legitimación de la dominación" (Dependence: rationalization and legitimation of domination), *Revista de Ciencias sociales* 22(3-4), dec 80 : 331-357.

12350   Interpersonal conflicts
Conflits interpersonnels

667   FELSON, Richard B. "Aggression and violence between siblings", *Social Psychology Quarterly* 46(4), dec 83 : 271-285.

668   MUELLER, Charles W.; DONNERSTEIN, Edward. "Film-induced arousal and aggressive behavior", *Journal of Social Psychology* 119(1), feb 83 : 61-67.

669   SHOKEID, M. "The regulation of aggression in daily life: aggressive relationships among Moroccan immigrants in Israel", *Ethnology* 21(3), 82 : 271-281.

12360   Intergroup relations
Relations intergroupes

670   "Political negotiation", *European Journal of Political Research* 11(2), jun 83 : 129-195. [with contributions by Ronald P. BARSTON, Christer JONSSON, Knut MIDGAARD, Volker RITTBERGER]

671   ALTHABE. "Les luttes sociales à Tananarive en 1972", *Cahiers d'Études africaines* 20(4), 80 : 407-447.

672   BECKER, Gary S. "A theory of competition among pressure groups for political influence", *Quarterly Journal of Economics* 98(3), aug 83 : 371-400.

673   BEDNAR, David A.; CURINGTON, William P. "Interaction analysis: a tool for understanding negotiations", *Industrial and Labor Relations* 36(3), apr 83 : 389-401.

674   BIAŁYSZEWSKI, Henryk. *Teoretyczne problemy sprzeczności i konfliktów społecznych* (Theoretical problems of social contradictions and conflicts). Warszawa, Państwowe Wydawnictwo Naukowe, 83, 304 p.

675   FARRO, Antimo. "Conflitti sociali enll'area urbana di Napoli, 1970-1980" (Social conflicts in the urban area of Naples, 1970-1980), *Critica sociologica* 65, 83 : 106-118.

676   FREUND, Julien. *Sociologie du conflit*. Paris, Presses Universitaires de France, 83, 380 p.

677   HART, Sergiu; KURZ, Mordecai. "Endogenous formation of coalitions", *Econometrica* 51(4), jul 83 : 1047-1064.

678   HOLSTEIN-BECK, Maria. *Konflikty* (Conflicts). Warszawa, Instytut Wydawniczy Związków Zawodowych, 83, 232 p.

679   JOGAN, Matilda. "Teorija konflikata kod L. Kozera" (L. Coser's theory of conflict), *Sociologija* 24(1), 82 : 45-56.

680   KOMORITA, S. S.; NAGAO, Dennis. "The functions of resources in coalition bargaining", *Journal of Personality and Social Psychology* 44(1), jan 83 : 95-106.

681   LANDAZÁBAL REYES, Fernando. *Conflicto social* (Social conflict). Medellín, Beta, 82, 510 p. [Latin America]

682   MAGENAU, John M. "The impact of alternative impasse procedures on bargaining: a laboratory experiment", *Industrial and Labor Relations* 36(3), apr 83 : 361-377.

683   MARKIEWICZ, Władysław. *Konflikt społeczny w PRL* (Social conflict in People's Republic of Poland). Poznań, Krajowa Agencja Wydawnicza, 83, 92 p.

684   MARSH, Robert M. "Sources of Japanese university conflict: organizational structure and issues", *Journal of Conflict Resolution* 26(4), dec 82 : 730-756.

685   NEALE, Margaret A.; BAERMAN, Max H. "The role of perspective-taking ability in negotiating under different forms of arbitration", *Industrial and Labor Relations* 36(3), apr 83 : 378-388.

686   O'TOOLE, Laurence J. "Interorganizational cooperation and the implementation of labour market training policies: Sweden and the Federal Republic of Germany", *Organization Studies* 4(2), 83 : 129-150.

687   OBATA, Masatoshi. "Kokanzai no bunrui to sokutei" (Classification and measurement of exchange), *Waseda daigaku shakaigaku nenshi* 24, 83 : 37-52.

688   ROTH, Alvin E.; SCHOUMAKER, Françoise. "Expectations and reputations in bargaining: an experimental study", *American Economic Review* 73(3), jun 83 : 362-372.

689   TRIST, Eric. "Referent organizations and the development of inter-organizational domains", *Human Relations* 36(3), mar 83 : 269-284.

690   ÜSDIKEN, Behlül. "Interorganizational linkages among similar organizations in Turkey", *Organization Studies* 4(2), 83 : 151-164.

691   WILKE, H.; VAN KNIPPENBERG, A. "Integration, differentiation and coalition formation", *Journal for the Theory of Social Behaviour* 13(2), jul 83 : 181-194.

12400   **GROUPS**
              GROUPES

12410   **Group dynamics**
              Dynamique de groupe

692   ALCALAY, Rina. "Health and social support networks: a case for improving interpersonal communication", *Social Networks* 5(1), mar 83 : 71-88.

693   FARARO, Thomas J. "Biased networks and the strength of weak ties", *Social Networks* 5(1), mar 83 : 1-11.

694   MCALLISTER, Ian. "Social contacts and political behaviour in Northern Ireland, 1968-1978", *Social Networks* 5(3), sep 83 : 303-313.

695   MILARDO, Robert M. "Social networks and pair relationships: a review of substantive and measurement issues", *Sociology and Social Research* 68(1), oct 83 : 1-18.

696   OBERT, Steven L. "Developmental patterns of organizational task groups: a preliminary study", *Human Relations* 36(1), jan 83 : 37-52.

697   PARKS, Malcolm T.; STAN, Charlotte M.; EGGERT, Leona L. "Romantic involvement and social network involvement", *Social Psychology Quarterly* 46(2), jun 83 : 116-131.

698   SNOW, David A.; ZURCHER, Louis A. Jr.; EKLAND-OLSON, Sheldon. "Further thoughts on social networks and movement recruitment", *Sociology (London)* 17(1), feb 83 : 112-120.

699   SORRELS, J. Paul; MYERS, Bettye. "Comparison of group and family dynamics", *Human Relations* 35(5), mai 83 : 477-492.

700   YALOM, Irvin D. *Inpatient group psychotherapy.* New York, NY, Basic Books, Inc., 83, xiv-350 p.

12420   **Primary groups. Training groups**
              Groupes primaires. Groupes de formation

701   EISENHART, Margaret A.; HOLLAND, Dorothy C. "Learning gender from peers: the role of peer groups in the cultural transmission of gender", *Human Organization* 42(4), 83 : 321-332.

702   SCHOFIELD, Janet Ward; WHITLEY, Bernard E. Jr. "Peer nomination vs. rating scale measurement of children's peer preferences", *Social Psychology Quarterly* 46(3), sep 83 : 242-251.

703   SZMATKA, Jacek. "Próba strukturalistycznej koncepcji małej grupy społecznej" (Attempt at a structuralist concept of a small group), *Studia Socjologiczne* 89(2), 83 : 153-170.

704   TANFORD, Sarah; PENROD, Steven. "Computer modeling of influence in the jury: the role of the consistent juror", *Social Psychology Quarterly* 46(3), sep 83 : 200-212.

12430   Group size
Dimension du groupe

705   "Slovenes (The) of Northeastern Italy", *Nationalities Papers* 11(2), aug 83 : 148-204. [with
       contributions by Joze PIRJEVIC, Alessio LOKAR, Emidio SUSSI]
706   BAYES, Jane H. *Minority politics and ideologies in the United States.* Novato, CA, Chandler
       and Sharp, 82, 144 p.
707   CAPOBIANCO, Michael; PALKA, Zbigniew. "The distribution of popular persons in a
       group", *Social Networks* 5(4), dec 83 : 383-393.
708   DALSTRA, Koos. "The South Moluccan minority in the Netherlands", *Contemporary Crises*
       7(2), apr 83 : 195-208.
709   FREUND, Wolfgang Slim. "Minderheiten und Entwicklung" (Minority and development),
       Dritte Welt 9(3-4), 81 : 261-269.
710   FREUND, Wolfgang Slim. "Türken in Deutschland: die sozio-kulturelle Barriere", *Dritte
       Welt* 9(3-4), 81 : 270-278.
711   HASEGAWA, Kohichi. "Daiado kankei to funsō katei" (Dyad relations and social conflict),
       Shakaigaku hyoron 34(3), 83 : 354-373.
712   KAPLAN, Kalman J.; [et al.]. "Distancing in dyads: a comparison of four models", *Social
       Psychology Quarterly* 46(2), jun 83 : 108-115.
713   LEE, Yong Len. "Ethnic differences and the State: minority relationship in South-East
       Asia", *Ethnic and Racial Studies* 6(2), apr 83 : 213-220.
714   LEGER, Robert G. "Race, class and conflict in a custodial setting: toward the development
       of a theory of minority-group politicalization", *Human Relations* 36(9), sep 83 : 841-863.
       [USA]
715   NAKANO GLENN, Evelyn. "Split household, small producer and dual wage earner: an
       analysis of Chinese-American family strategies", *Journal of Marriage and the Family* 45(1),
       feb 83 : 35-46.
716   VIRK, J.; AGGARWAL, Y. P.; BHAN, R. N. "Similarity 'versus' complementarity in
       clique formation", *Journal of Social Psychology* 119(2), apr 83 : 27-34.

12440   Group integration
Intégration du groupe

717   GURR, Ted Robert; [ed.]. "Group protest and policy responses: new cross-national
       perspectives", *American Behavioral Scientist* 26(3), jan-feb 83 : 283-416.
718   MIKAMI, Takeshi. "Utopia keisei to shudan doitsusei" (Group identity and utopia),
       Shakaigaku hyoron 34(1), 83 : 18-35.
719   PIPER, William E. "Cohesion as a basic bond in groups", *Human Relations* 36(2), feb 83 : 96-108.
720   RUTKOWSKI, Gregory K.; GRUDER, Charles L.; ROMER, Daniel. "Group cohesiveness,
       social norms, and bystander intervention", *Journal of Personality and Social Psychology* 44(3),
       mar 83 : 545-552.
721   SHARRON, Avery. "Time and space bias in group solidarity: action and process in musical
       improvisation", *International Social Science Review* 58(4), 83 : 222-230.
722   SWANK, Duane H. "Between incrementalism and revolution: group protest and the growth
       of the welfare state", *American Behavioral Scientist* 26(3), jan-feb 83 : 291-310.

12450   Group membership
Appartenance au groupe

723   EDER, Donna. "Organizational constraints and individual mobility: ability group formation
       and maintenance", *Sociological Quarterly* 24(3), sum 83 : 405-420.
724   GORNSTEIN, Gershon; [et al.]. "On the measurement of social orientations in the minimal
       group paradigm", *European Journal of Social Psychology* 13(4), oct-dec 83 : 321-350. [with
       comments by John C. TURNER: 351-367 and a reply by the authors: 369-381 and
       a second reply by John C. TURNER: 383-387]
725   SELL, Jane; MARTIN, Michael W. "The effects of group benefits and type of distribution
       rule on noncompliance to legitimate authority", *Social Forces* 61(4), jun 83 : 1168-1185.
726   SMITH, Peter B. "Back-home environment and within-group relationship as determinants
       of personal change", *Human Relations* 36(1), jan 83 : 53-67.
727   TACHI, Itsuo; NANAMORI, Katsushi. "Junkyo shudanron no tenbo III: T. M. Newcomb
       to M. Sherif o megutte" (Perspectives in the theory of reference group: a study of T. M.
       Newcomb and M. Sherif), *Meiji gakuin ronso* 338-339, 83 : 1-20.

728   WATANABE, Yūko. "Junkyo shūdan riron no mondaiten" (The problems on the reference group theory), *Tokyo toritsudaigaku shakaigaku ronko* 4, 83 : 1-22.

729   WOLF, Sharon; LATANE, Bibb. "Majority and minority influence on restaurant preferences", *Journal of Personality and Social Psychology* 45(2), aug 83 : 282-292.

12460   Group performance
Performance du groupe

730   ANCOCK, Djamaludin; CHERTKOFF, Jerome M. "Effects of group membership, relative performance, and self-interest on the division of outcome", *Journal of Personality and Social Psychology* 45(6), dec 83 : 1256-1262.

731   BURGER, Jerry M.; RODMAN, John L. "Attributions of responsibility for group tasks: the egocentric bias and the actor-observer difference", *Journal of Personality and Social Psychology* 45(6), dec 83 : 1232-1242.

732   TAYLOR, Donald M.; DORIA, Janet; TYLER, J. Kenneth. "Group performance and cohesiveness: an attribution analysis", *Journal of Social Psychology* 119(2), apr 83 : 187-198.

12500   BUREAUCRACY. ORGANIZATION
BUREAUCRATIE. ORGANISATION

12510   Sociology of organization
Sociologie des organisations

733   AKTOUF, Omar. "Les théories des organisations et leurs implications dans les rapports de travail", *Revue algérienne des Sciences juridiques, économiques et politiques* 19(4), dec 82 : 571-623.

734   BACHARACH, Samuel B.; [ed.]. *Research in the sociology of organizations.* Greenwich, CT-London, JAI Press, 82, x-329; 276 p. [2 vols.]

735   BECKMANN, Martin J. *Tinbergen lectures on organizational theory.* New York, NY-Berlin-Tokyo, Springer, 83, x-176 p.

736   BOSCHKEN, Herman L. "Organization theory and federalism. Interorganizational networks and the political economy of The Federalist", *Organization Studies* 3(4), 82 : 355-373.

737   JENSEN, Michael C. "Organization theory and methodology", *Accounting Review* 58(2), apr 83 : 319-339. [with comments by Robert S. KAPLAN: 340-346 and Joel S. DEMSKI: 347-349]

738   KILMANN, Ralph H. "A typology of organization typologies: toward parsimony and integration in the organizational sciences", *Human Relations* 35(6), jun 83 : 523-548.

739   KUHN, Alfred; BEAM, Robert D. *The logic of organization.* San Francisco, CA-London, Jossey-Bass, 82, xxxix-495 p.

740   LAMMERS, Cornelis Jacobus. *Organisaties vergelijkenderwijs: ontwikkeling en relevantie van het sociologisch denken over organisaties* (Organizations in a comparative view: development and relevance of the sociological thought on organizations). Utrecht, Spectrum, 83, 552 p.

741   RAELIN, Joseph A. "A policy output model of interorganizational relations", *Organization Studies* 3(3), 82 : 243-267.

742   SCHENK, Karl-Ernst. "Institutional choice und Ordnungstheorie" (Institutional choice and organization theory), *Jahrbuch für Neue Politische Ökonomie* 2, 83 : 70-85.

743   SCHOFIELD, Norman; ALT, James. "The analysis of relations in an organisation", *Quality and Quantity* 17(4), aug 83 : 269-279.

744   SHARMA, K. L. "Values and behavioural sciences in industrial organizational analysis", *Indian Journal of Social Research* 24(2), aug 83 : 125-132. [India]

745   SHIROM, Arie. "Toward a theory of organization: development interventions in unionized work settings", *Human Relations* 36(8), aug 83 : 743-763.

746   VEEN, P. *Mensen in organisaties: een inleiding in de organisatiepsychologie* (Men in organizations: an introduction to organizational psychology). Deventer, Van Loghum Slaterus, 82, 275 p.

12520   Complex organizations
Organisations complexes

747   CABANES, Robert. "Identités du territoire limouxin", *Sociologie du Travail* 25(2), apr-jun 83 : 160-178. [associations professionnelles et socio-culturelles de la ville de Limoux, France; résumé en anglais]

748   FRANDA, Marcus F. *Voluntary associations and local development in India: the Janata phase.* New Delhi, Young Asia Publications, 83, vi-356 p.

749   KNOKE, David. "Organization sponsorship and influence reputation of social influence associations", _Social Forces_ 61(4), jun 83 : 1065-1087. [USA]
750   LAUTMAN, Jacques. "Renouveau des sociétés locales: volonté ou résultat?", _Sociologie du Travail_ 25(2), apr-jun 83 : 233-242. [France] [résumé en anglais]
751   MCPHERSON, Miller. "The size of voluntary organizations", _Social Forces_ 61(4), jun 83 : 1044-1064.
752   MORRIS, Robert. "Government and voluntary agency relationships", _Social Service Review_ 56(3), sep 82 : 333-345.
753   REYNAUD, Emmanuèle. "Groupes secondaires et solidarité organique: qui exerce le contrôle social?", _Année sociologique_ 33, 83 : 181-194.
754   SAINSAULIEU, Renaud. "La régulation culturelle des ensembles organisés", _Année sociologique_ 33, 83 : 195-217.
755   SATO, Yoshiyuki. "Jihatsuteki kessha no soshikiron" (Organizational theory of voluntary association), _Gendai shakaigaku_ 17, 83 : 3-17.
756   STARBUCK, William H. "Organizations as action generators", _American Sociological Review_ 48(1), feb 83 : 91-102.

12530   Bureaucracy
Bureaucratie

757   "Enseñenza de la planificación en América latina" (Teaching of planning in Latin America), _Revista interamericana de planificación_ 17(67), sep 83 : 7-150. [with contributions by Alejandro ROFMAN, Mario R. dos SANTOS, Abelardo SANCHEZ-LEON]
758   ALBANESE, Robert; VAN FLEET, David D. _Organizational behavior: a managerial viewpoint._ Chicago, IL, Dryden Press, 82, x-598 p.
759   BEAUVOIS, Jean-Léon. "Structures organisationnelles: hiérarchie et autogestion", _Connexions_ 39, 83 : 47-64.
760   BONAZZI, Giuseppe. "Scapegoating in complex organization: the results of a comparative study of symbolic blame-giving in Italian and French public administration", _Organization Studies_ 4(1), 83 : 1-18.
761   BRIEF, Arthur P.; DOWNEY, H. Kirk. "Cognitive and organizational structures: a conceptual analysis of implicit organizing theories", _Human Relations_ 36(12), dec 83 : 1065-1089.
762   BRUNS, John P. "Reforming China's bureaucracy, 1979-82", _Asian Survey_ 23(6), jun 83 : 692-722.
763   BRUSCAGLIONI, Massimo; SPALTRO, Enzo; [eds.]. _La psicologia organizzativa_ (Organizational psychology). Milano, F. Angeli, 82, 827 p.
764   CONATY, Joseph; [et al.]. "Social structure and bureaucracy: a comparison of organizations in the United States and prerevolutionary Iran", _Organization Studies_ 4(2), 83 : 105-128.
765   CUNNINGHAM, J. Barton. "Gathering data in a changing organization", _Human Relations_ 36(5), mai 83 : 403-420.
766   CZAJKOSKI, Eugene H.; WOLLAN, Lawrin A. "Bureaucracy and crime", _International Journal of Public Administration_ 5(2), 83 : 195-216. [USA]
767   DIMAGGIO, Paul J.; POWELL, Walter W. "The iron cage revisited: institutional isomorphism and collective rationality in organizational fields", _American Sociological Review_ 48(2), apr 83 : 147-160.
768   FREEMAN, John; HANNAN, Michael T. "Niche width and the dynamics of organizational populations", _American Journal of Sociology_ 88(6), mai 83 : 1116-1145.
769   FRIEDKIN, Noah E. "Horizons of observability and limits of informal control in organizations", _Social Forces_ 62(1), sep 83 : 54-77.
770   GEBERT, Diether. "Genossenschaftsdemokratie aus organisations-psychologischer Sicht" (Cooperative democracy from the organizational psychology point of view), _Zeitschrift für das Gesamte Genossenschaftswesen_ 33(3), 83 : 176-182.
771   GRANGER, Yves. "Le management en question", _Année sociologique_ 33, 83 : 85-100.
772   HAMAGUCHI, Haruhiko. "Romania no rodosha jishukanri eno shiko" (Trends toward self-management in Romania), _Waseda daigaku shaken kenkyu series — soren touou shakai no shin-kenkyu_ 15, 83 : 117-138.
773   HAYASHI, Yatomi. "Shoyu to tosei no bunri ni kansuru sho-mondai" (On the separation of ownership and control), _Osaka gaikokugo daigaku gakuho_ 61, 83 : 21-44.
774   HSU, Cheng-Kuang; MARSH, Robert M.; MANNARI, Hiroshi. "An examination of the determinants of organizational structure", _American Journal of Sociology_ 88(5), mar 83 : 975-996.
775   ISHIKAWA, Akihiro. "Shihonshugi-ka ni okeru rodosha jishu kanri no tenkai to genkai" (Development and restriction of workers' self-management under capitalism), _Gendai shakaigaku_ 17, 83 : 29-47.

776 ISHIMARU, Hiroshi. "Kanryoseiteki shihai no soshiki renkan: Nihon ni okeru tokatsu kancho no rekishiteki ichi kosatsu" (Interorganizational relations of bureaucratic domination: a historical study of integration agencies in Japan), *Osaka daigaku Nenpo ningen kagaku* 4, 83 : 141-158.

777 JECAUC, Anton. "L'autogestion et le progrès technique et technologique", *Questions actuelles du Socialisme* 33(2), feb 83 : 25-38. [Yugoslavia]

778 JENKINS, Bill; GRAY, Andrew. "Bureaucratic politics and power: developments in the study of bureaucracy", *Political Studies* 31(2), jun 83 : 177-193.

779 KONIG, Klaus. "Bürger und Staat: Zur Bürokratie in einer demokratischen Gesellschaft" (Citizen and State: about bureaucracy in democratic society), *Politische Studien* 34(269), jun 83 : 279-291.

780 KOOT, Willem. "Organizational dependence. An exploration of external power relationships of companies", *Organization Studies* 4(1), 83 : 19-38.

781 LI, Vladimir. "The formation and evolution of bureaucracy in developing countries of the East", *Development and Peace* 3(2), 82 : 32-46.

782 MAURICE, Marc; [et al.]. "The production of hierarchy in the firm", *International Journal of Sociology* 13(4), 83-84 : 3-76.

783 MILBURN, Thomas; [et al.]. "Organizational crisis. I. Definition and conceptualization. II. Strategies and responses", *Human Relations* 36(12), dec 83 : 1141-1160. [continued in ibid. 36 (12), dec 83 : 1161-1179]

784 MONTANARI, John R.; MORGAN, Cyril P. "The impact of technology and functional unit on centralization in organizations", *Human Relations* 36(8), aug 83 : 705-715.

785 NEHMY, Rosa. "Organisations à projet", *Année sociologique* 33, 83 : 67-84.

786 NOTTENBURG, Gail. "Scarcity in the environment. Organizational perceptions, interpretations and responses", *Organization Studies* 4(4), 83 : 317-337.

787 OLDSON, William O. "The bureaucratization of the academy: the impact on scholarship and culture of professional staff", *Sociologia internationalis* 21(1-2), 83 : 81-91.

788 OTTAWAY, Richard N. "The change agent: a taxonomy in relation to the change process", *Human Relations* 36(4), apr 83 : 361-392.

789 POUPARD, Raymond. "Pour une approche praxéologique du management des hommes", *Humanisme et Entreprise* 138, apr 83 : 49-71. [France]

790 RAIMBAULT, Michel; SAUSSOIS, Jean-Michel. *Organiser le changement: dans les entreprises et les organisations publiques.* Paris, Éditions d'Organisation, 83, 219 p.

791 RAMÍREZ, Rafael. "Action learning: a strategic approach for organizations facing turbulent conditions", *Human Relations* 36(8), aug 83 : 725-742.

792 ROGGEMA, J.; SMITH, M. H. "Organizational change in the shipping industry: issues in the transformation of basic assumptions", *Human Relations* 36(8), aug 83 : 765-790.

793 ROMEI, Piero. *La dinamica della organizzazione: le costanti di comportamento dei sistemi organizzativi aziendale in azione* (Organization dynamics. Behavioural constants of industrial organization systems in action). Milano, F. Angeli, 83, 209 p.

794 SENTER, Richard; [et al.]. "Bureaucratization and goal succession in alternative organizations", *Sociological Focus* 16(4), oct 83 : 239-253.

795 SZENTPÉTERI, István. "A modern társas-szervezet 'gyárszerűsége'" (The 'factory-similarity' of modern social organizations), *Társadalomkutatás* 1(2), 83 : 91-111.

796 TACCHI, Enrico Maria. "Considerazioni sullo sviluppo sociologico del concetto di 'controllo organizzativo'" (Considerations on the sociological development of the 'organizational control' concept), *Studi di Sociologia* 21(2), apr-jun 83 : 211-220.

797 THORNBERENS, Rainer. *Zur Innenstruktur ausgewählter Hierarchievorstellungen.* Frankfurt-am-Main, Lang, 82, 219 p.

798 VROOM, V. H. "Reflections on leadership and decision-making", *Scandinavian Journal of Materials Administration* 9(2), 83 : 5-24.

799 ZEITZ, Gerald. "Structural and individual determinants of organization morale and satisfaction", *Social Forces* 61(4), jun 83 : 1088-1108.

12600 LEADERSHIP. ROLE
COMMANDEMENT. RÔLE

12610 Authority
Autorité

800 ALTIERI, Leonardo; [et al.]. *Nuove forme del potere: stato, scienza, soggetti sociali* (New shapes of power: state, science, social topics). Milano, F. Angeli, 82, 162 p.

801   BROCCOLI, Angelo. *Il potere tra dialettica e alienazione* (Power between dialectics and alienation). Cosenza, Pellegrini, 83, 408 p.

802   CHOMBART DE LAUWE, Paul H. "Oppressione, sovversione e espressione" (Oppression, subversion and expression), *Critica sociologica* 65, 83 : 35-49.

803   COOK, Karen S.; [et al.]. "The distribution of power in exchange networks: theory and experimental results", *American Journal of Sociology* 89(2), sep 83 : 275-305.

804   FOMBURN, Charles J. "Attributions of power across a social network", *Human Relations* 35(6), jun 83 : 493-507.

805   IKEDA, Yoshisuke. "Ken'i no ritasei" (On the altruistic aspect of authority), *Ohtani daigaku tetsugaku ronshu* 29, 83 : 1-15.

806   KEJZEROV, N. M. "O sootnošenii kategorij 'vlast' i 'političeskaja kul'tura': kritika burzuaznhy koncepcij" (On the correlation of the 'power' and 'political culture' categories: criticism of bourgeois concepts), *Sovetskoe Gosudarstvo i Pravo* 56(1), jan 83 : 77-86.

807   KIMURA, Kunihiro. "Kenryoku kōshi ni okeru senryaku to kihan: enshutsuteki yūi to dorameteki yūi" (Strategic and normative aspects of power: directive dominance and dramatic dominance), *Shakaigaku nenpo* 12, 83 : 101-119.

808   LEMOYNE, Aimé. "Le pouvoir: langage de l'action politique", *Cahiers internationaux de Sociologie* 75, 83 : 283-304.

809   MANZ, Charles C.; GIOIA, Dennis A. "The interrelationship of power and control", *Human Relations* 36(5), mai 83 : 459-475.

810   MARSDEN, Peter V. "Restricted access in networks and models of power", *American Journal of Sociology* 88(4), jan 83 : 686-717.

811   MIYAHARA, Kojiro. "Charisma: from Weber to contemporary sociology", *Sociological Inquiry* 53(4), 83 : 368-388.

812   RUSH, Gary B. "State, class, and capital: demystifying the westward shift of power", *Canadian Review of Sociology and Anthropology* 20(3), aug 83 : 255-289. [Canada]

813   SAMU, Mihály. *Hatalom és állam* (Power and State). Budapest, Közgazdasági és Jogi Kiadó, 82, 595 p.

814   SIERKSMA, Rypke. *Plan, partijdigheid en politiemoraal: over Foucault, macht en maatschappelijke kennis* (Plan, partiality and police moral: on Foucault, power and social consciousness). Delft, Delftse Universitaire Pers, 82, v-170 p.

815   WATARI, Akeshi. "Kenryoku no simulation: Baudrillard no Foucault hihan o megutte" (The simulation of power: about Baudrillard's criticism of Foucault), *Hiroshima shudai ronshu* 23(2), 83 : 193-218.

816   WICKHAM, Gary. "Power and power analysis: beyond Foucault?", *Economy and Society* 12(4), 83 : 468-498.

**12620   Leadership
Commandement**

817   "Leaders and leadership", *International Journal* 37(4), aut 82 : 507-635. [with contributions by J. D. B. MILLER, Janice GROSSTEIN, Timothy SHAW, Naomi GHAZAN, David COX, P. M. EVANS]

818   "Leadership and followership: changing conditions and styles", *Journal of Applied Behavioral Science* 18(3), 82 : 257-414. [with contributions by Linda SMIRCICH, Gareth MORGAN, King E. DAVIS, Andrea J. BAKER]

819   ARIES, Elizabeth J.; GOLD, Conrad; WEIGEL, Russell H. "Dispositional and situational influences on dominance behaviour in small groups", *Journal of Personality and Social Psychology* 44(4), apr 83 : 779-786.

820   ASHOUR, Ahmed Sakr; JOHNS, Gary. "Leader influence through operant principles: a theoretical and methodological framework", *Human Relations* 36(7), jul 83 : 603-626.

821   BEN-YOAV, Orly; HOLLANDER, Edwin P.; CARNEVALE, Peter J. D. "Leader legitimacy, leader-follower interaction, and followers' ratings of the leader", *Journal of Social Psychology* 121(1), oct 83 : 111-115.

822   FLETCHER, D. M. "The good citizen as hero in Chinese fiction 1968-76", *Australian Journal of Politics and History* 28(2), 82 : 266-280.

823   HODGKINSON, Christopher. *The philosophy of leadership.* New York, NY, St. Martin's Press, 83, viii-247 p.

824   HOWARD, Ann; WILSON, James A. "Leadership in a declining work ethic", *California Management Review* 24(4), 82 : 33-46.

825   KOTANI, Satoshi; SUMITANI, Akio. "Opinion leader no kōzō to dōtai" (The structure and dynamics of opinion leader), *Shinbungaku hyoron* 32, 83 : 5-24.

826   MARTIN, Michael; SELL, Jane. "Self-awareness, information utilization, and social influence in cooperative task settings", *Sociological Focus* 16(2), apr 83 : 147-153.

827   RONIGER, Luis. "Modern patron-client relations and historical clientelism. Some clues from ancient Republican Rome", *Archives européennes de Sociologie* 24(1), 83 : 63-95. [550 à 74 A.C.]

828   SCHWARZ, Barry. "George Washington and the Whig conception of heroic leadership", *American Sociological Review* 48(1), feb 83 : 18-33.

829   SUGIOKA, Naoto; SAWADA, Hiroshi, Kasai, Shunji. *Hokkaido no chiiki leader ni kansuru chosa kenkyu hokokusho* (A research report on community leaders and their leadership). Hokkaido, Hokkaido Nogyo Kaigi, 83, 60 p. [Japan]

830   SVENCICKIJ, A. J. *Rukovoditel': slovo i delo; social'no-psihologičeskie aspekty* (The leader: the work and the practice; socio-psychological aspects). Moskva, Politizdat, 83, 159 p.

831   THEOBALD, Robin. "The decline of patron-client relations in developed societies", *Archives européennes de Sociologie* 24(1), 83 : 136-147.

832   TJOSVOLD, Dean; ANDREWS, Robert. "Cooperative and competitive relationships between leaders and subordinates", *Human Relations* 36(12), dec 83 : 1111-1124.

12630   Role
Rôle

833   BEDEIAN, Arthur G.; [et al.]. "Role perception-outcome relationships: moderating effects of situational variables", *Human Relations* 36(2), feb 83 : 167-183.

834   BEEHR, Terry A.; LOVE, Kevin G. "A meta-model of the effects of goal characteristics, feedback, and role characteristics in human organizations", *Human Relations* 36(2), feb 83 : 151-166.

835   FROST, Dean E.; FIEDLER, Fred E.; ANDERSON, Jeff W. "The role of personal risk-taking in effective leadership", *Human Relations* 36(2), feb 83 : 185-202.

836   GREENWOOD, John Derek. "Role-playing as an experimental strategy in social psychology", *European Journal of Social Psychology* 13(3), jul-sep 83 : 235-254.

837   GUPTA, Kuntesh. "The role theory of alienation", *Indian Journal of Social Research* 24(1), apr 83 : 15-21.

838   HOELTER, Jon W. "The effects of role evaluation and commitment on identity salience", *Social Psychology Quarterly* 46(2), jun 83 : 140-147.

839   KURIHARA, Takashi. "Yakuwari nōryokuron no kōsatsu: J. Habermas no jinkakuron ni yosete" (An analysis of role-competence theory: Jürgen Habermas' theory of personality development), *Shakaigaku hyoron* 34(3), 83 : 57-74.

840   LUUKKONEN-GRONOW, Terttu; STOLTE-HEISKANEN, Veronica. "Myths and realities of role incompatibility of women scientists", *Acta Sociologica* 26(3-4), 83 : 267-280. [Finland]

841   MANDEL, Michael J. "Local roles and social networks", *American Sociological Review* 48(3), jun 83 : 376-386.

842   NIEMEYER, Harald. "Die Rezeption der Rollen- und der Statustheorie für die Beurteilung von outsidern" (The adoption of role and status theory for the assessment of outsiders), *Sociologia internationalis* 21(1-2), 83 : 145-157.

843   VAN DE VLIERT, Evert; [et al.]. *Rolspanningen* (Role conflicts). Meppel, Boom, 83, 252 p.

844   VISSER, A. P.; [et al.]. *Rollen: persoonlijke en sociale invloeden op het gedrag* (Roles: personal and social factors of behaviour). Meppel, Boom, 83, 328 p.

845   WORACH-KARDAS, Halina. *Wiek a pełnienie ról społecznych* (Age and the social roles). Warszawa, Państwowe Wydawnictwo Naukowe, 83, 220 p.

12700   ATTITUDES. OPINION
ATTITUDES. OPINION

12710   Behaviour
Comportement

846   DE PALMA, André; LEFÈVRE, Claude. "Individual decision-making in dynamic collective systems", *Journal of Mathematical Sociology* 9(2), 83 : 103-124.

847   FORD, Jill. *Human behaviour: towards a practical understanding.* London-Boston, MA, Routledge and Kegan Paul, 83, viii-159-14 p.

848   HEINER, Ronald A. "The origin of predictable behavior", *American Economic Review* 73(4), sep 83 : 560-595.

849   JENSEN, Henning. "Sobre la relación entre teoría y práctica en la modificación del comportamiento" (About the relation between theory and practice in the modification of behaviour), *Revista de Ciencias Sociales de la Universidad de Costa Rica* 23(1), 82 : 57-69.

850   MANGAN, Gordon L. *The biology of human conduct: East-West models of temperament and personality.* Oxford-New York, NY, Pergamon Press, 82, xi-571 p.

851   MCPHAIL, Clark; WOHLSTEIN, Ronald T. "Individual and collective behaviors within gatherings, demonstrations, and riots", *Annual Review of Sociology* (9), 83 : 579-600.

852   MYTYCH, Michał. "Postawy jako przedmiot zainteresowań psychologii społecznej oraz nauki o polityce" (Attitudes as subject of interest of social psychology and policy science), *Zeszyty Naukowe Akademii Ekonomicznej w Krakowie* 155, 82 : 31-51.

853   RASTOGI, Krishna Murari. "Class differences in respect of attitudes and beliefs towards various social institutions and customs", *Indian Journal of Social Research* 24(3), dec 83 : 249-261. [India]

854   SAGARIN, Edward. "Behavior and responsibility: individual and collective", *Sociological Inquiry* 53(1), 83 : 100-112.

12720   Cognitive dissonance. Prejudice
Dissonance cognitive. Préjugé

855   CARTWRIGHT, D.; [et al.]. "Studies in imagery and identity", *Journal of Personality and Social Psychology* 44(2), feb 83 : 376-384.

856   COHEN, Claudia E. "Inferring the characteristics of other people: categories and attributes accessibility", *Journal of Personality and Social Psychology* 44(1), jan 83 : 34-44.

857   COOPER, Joel; MACKIE, Diane. "Cognitive dissonance in an intergroup context", *Journal of Personality and Social Psychology* 44(3), mar 83 : 536-544.

858   EUBBEN, Marie-Claire; VAN DER HAEGEN, Claude. "Les stéréotypes féminin et masculin dans la bande dessinée pour enfants et adolescents d'expression française", *Revue de l'Institut de Sociologie* (3-4), 82 : 433-457.

859   HEPBURN, Christine; LOCKSLEY, Anne. "Subjective awareness of stereotyping: do we know when our judgments are prejudiced?", *Social Psychology Quarterly* 46(4), dec 83 : 311-318.

860   KANEGAE, Haruhiko. "Chiiki shakai ni okeru 'Dōwa' kyōiku to sabetsu ishiki" ('Dowa' education and discriminative consciousness in community), *Senshu daigaku shakai-kagaku nenpo* 17, 83 : 269-307.

861   LILLI, Waldemar. *Grundlagen der Stereotypisierung* (Foundations of stereotyping). Göttingen, Hogrefe, 82, x-142 p.

862   MILLAR, Elaine; PHILLIPS, Julia. "Evaluating antidiscrimination legislation in the UK: some issues and approaches", *International Journal of the Sociology of Law* 11(4), nov 83 : 417-429.

863   NAGASAWA, Richard; LITTLE, Ronald L. "Formal theory of balance revisited", *Sociological Perspectives* 26(1), jan 83 : 51-69.

864   ROSENFELD, Paul; GIACALONE, Robert A.; TEDESCHI, James T. "Cognitive dissonance 'versus' impression management", *Journal of Social Psychology* 120(2), aug 83 : 203-211.

865   SAUVAGE, Léo. *Les Américains: enquête sur un mythe.* Paris, Mazarine, 83, 766 p.

866   WYLIE, Laurence; HENRIQUEZ, Sarella. "French images of American life", *Tocqueville Review* 4(2), wint 82 : 176-274.

12730   Dogmatism. F Scale
Dogmatisme. Échelle F

867   CAMACHO, Daniel; [et al.]. *Autoritarismo y alternativas populares en América Latina* (Authoritarianism and popular alternatives in Latin America). San José, Facultad Latinoamerica de Ceincias Sociales, 82, 220 p.

868   CASPI, Dan; SELIGSON, Mitchell A. "Toward an empirical theory of tolerance: radical groups in Israël and Costa Rica", *Comparative Political Studies* 15(4), jan 83 : 385-404.

869   KOOL, Vinod K.; RAY, John J. *Authoritarianism across cultures.* Bombay, Himalaya, 83, 198 p.

870   LÖVEY, Imre. "A tekintélyelvű gondolkodás vizsgálata és néhány mérési eredménye a vezetők köreből" (The principle of authority, as reflected and measured in managerial thinking), *Szociológia* 11(3), 82 : 351-372.

871   NEAL, Richard G.; JOHNSTON, Craig D. *Countering strikes and militancy in school and government services.* Manassas, VA, the authors, 82, vii-200 p.

872   PEIRANO, Mariza G. S. "Etnocentrismo às avessas: o cenceito de 'sociedade complexa'" (Ethnocentrism the wrong way around: the concept of a 'complex society'), *Dados* 26(1), 83 : 97-115.

873   RAY, J. J.; LOVEJOY, F. H. "The behavioral validity of some recent measures of authoritarianism", *Journal of Social Psychology* 119(2), apr 83 : 91-99.

874   RAY, John J.; JONES, Jennifer M. "Attitudes to authority and authoritarianism among school-children", *Journal of Social Psychology* 119(2), apr 83 : 199-203.

875   SEELAND, Klaus. "Ethnozentrismus und die Rationalität traditionaler Gesellschaften" (Ethnocentrism and the rationality of traditional societies), *Internationales Asien Forum* 14(2-3), 83 : 231-242.

876   SORANAKA, Seiji. *Ken'i-shugiteki ningen: Gendaijin no kokoro ni hisomu fascism* (The authoritarian: potential fascist in our time). Tokyo, Yuhikaku, 83, 366 p.

12740   Opinion
Opinion

877   DUCKWORTH, Frank C. "On the influence of debate on public opinion", *Political Studies* 31(3), sep 83 : 463-478.

878   FELOMAN, Stanley. "Economic individualism and American public opinion", *American Politics Quarterly* 11(1), jan 83 : 3-29.

879   GILOVICH, Thomas; JENNINGS, Dennis L.; JENNINGS, Susan. "Causal focus and estimates of consensus: an examination of the false-consensus effect", *Journal of Personality and Social Psychology* 45(3), sep 83 : 550-559.

880   KULIK, James A. "Confirmatory attribution and the perpetuation of social beliefs", *Journal of Personality and Social Psychology* 44(6), jun 83 : 1171-1156.

881   LANGE, Rense; FISHBEIN, Martin. "Effects of category differences on belief change and agreement with the source of a persuasive communication", *Journal of Personality and Social Psychology* 44(5), mai 83 : 933-941.

882   LÓPEZ PINTOR, Rafael. *La opinión pública española del franquismo a la democracia* (Spanish public opinion from franquism to democracy). Madrid, Centro de Investigaciones Sociológicas, 82, 214 p.

883   MENDRAS, Marie. "L'opinion publique en URSS: conceptualisation et sondages depuis vingt ans", *Annuaire de l'URSS et des Pays socialistes européens*, 82 : 281-296.

884   MICHELAT, Guy; SIMON, Michel. "Les 'sans-réponses' aux questions politiques: rôles imposés et compensation des handicaps", *Année sociologique* 32, 82 : 81-114.

885   MINJUŠEV, F. I. "Obščestvennoe mnenie pri socializme kak faktor vospitanija" (Public opinion under socialism as a factor of education), *Naučnye Doklady vysšej Školy. Naučnyj Kommunizma* (5), 82 : 74-80.

886   MONGARDINI, Carlo. "The conditions of consensus", *Revue internationale de Sociologie* 18(1-2-3), apr-aug-sep 82 : 12-29.

887   STRAY, S. J.; SILVER, M. S. "The measurement of change in the popularity of governments in United Kingdom by-elections", *Political Methodology* 8(1), 82 : 93-106.

888   TAMURA, Kenji. "Shitsuke to ippu-ippu-sei o meguru ishiki: Kokusai hikaku to kokunai jokyo" (Opinions about child discipline and marriage systems: international comparative and intranational study), *Toyo daigaku shakaigakubu kiyo* 20, 83 : 1-53.

889   WEBER, Renée; CROCKER, Jennifer. "Cognitive processes in the revision of stereotypic beliefs", *Journal of Personality and Social Psychology* 45(5), nov 83 : 961-977.

12750   Ideology
Idéologie

890   "Ideology/power", *Canadian Journal of Political and Social Theory* 7(1-2), spr 83 : 5-183. [with contributions by Jürgen HABERMAS, Claude LEFORT, Wayne HUDSON]

891   BILLIG, Michael. *Ideology and social psychology, extremism, moderation and contradiction.* Oxford, B. Blackwell, 82, 243 p.

892   BÜCHNER, Bernd. *Ideologie und Diskurs: zur Theorie von Jürgen Habermas und ihrer Rezeption in der Pädagogik* (Ideology and discourse: on Jürgen Habermas' theory and its acceptance in educational science). Frankfurt-am-Main, Haag + Herchen, 82, ii-308-9 p.

893   CREAGH, Ronald. *Laboratoires de l'utopie. Les communautés libertaires aux États-Unis.* Paris, Payot, 83, 224 p.

894   GUIBERT-SLEDZIEWSRI, Elisabeth. "Comment penser l'idéologie?", *La pensée* (231), feb 83 : 30-49.

895   KURKIN, B. A. "Gumanističeskaja utopija É. Fromma" (E. Fromm's humanist utopia), *Voprosy Filosofii* 36(2), 83 : 85-94.

896   KUZNECOV, P. É. "Suščnost', struktura i funkcii ideologičeskogo processa v socialističeskom
        obščestve" (Nature, structure and functions of the ideological process in the socialist
        society), *Naučnye Doklady vysšej Školy. Naučnyj Kommunizma* (5), 82 : 65-74.
897   MITI, Katabaro. "The role of ideology in Tanzania's political and economic developments",
        Taamuli 9(1), dec 79 : 41-49.
898   MURAV'EV, V. I. "O sistemno-strukturnom issledovanii ideologii" (On the systemic
        and structural research on ideology), *in: Voprosy socialističeskogo obščestvennogo soznanija.*
        Tomsk, 1982 : 24-31.
899   NOWICKA, Ewa. "The typology of Black ideologies in the United States", *Polish Sociological
        Bulletin* 53(1), 81 : 59-70.
900   PETITFILS, Jean Christian. *La vie quotidienne des communautés utopistes au XIX siècle.* Paris,
        Hachette Littérature Générale, 82, 319 p.

        12760   Collective behaviour
        Comportement collectif

901   AGUIRRE, Benigno E.; QUARANTELLI, E. L. "Methodological, ideological, and
        conceptual-theoretical criticism of the field of collective behavior: a critical evaluation
        and implications for future study", *Sociological Focus* 16(3), aug 83 : 195-216.
902   BLAIS, André. "Le Public Choice et la croissance de l'État", *Canadian Journal of Political
        Science* 15(4), dec 82 : 783-807.
903   CHAPMAN, Bruce. "Individual rights, good consequences, and the theory of social choice",
        Journal for the Theory of Social Behaviour 12(3), oct 82 : 317-328.
904   EKIERT, Grzegorz. "Działania zbiorowe a struktura społeczna, czyli o możliwości zmiany
        struktury społecznej popŕzez działania zbiorowe" (Collective actions and social structure,
        or on a possibility of changing the social structure through collective actions), *Studia
        Socjologiczne* 90 (3), 83 : 77-94.
905   GRANOVETTER, Mark; SOONG, Roland. "Threshold models of diffusion and collective
        behavior", *Journal of Mathematical Sociology* 9(3), 83 : 165-179.
906   SAWADA, Zentaro. "Power kōzō to shūgōteki kettei" (Power structure and collective
        decision), *Osaka furitsu-daigaku ningen kagaku ronshu* 15, 83 : 33-52.

13100   CULTURE. SOCIAL ENVIRONMENT. VALUE
         CULTURE. MILIEU SOCIAL. VALEUR

13110   Social and cultural anthropology
         Ethnologie

907   BOZON, Michel. "La mise en scène des différences. Ethnologie d'une petite ville de province", *Homme* 22(4), dec 82 : 63-76. [France] [résumé en anglais]
908   KŁOSKOWSKA, Antonina. *Socjologia kultury* (Sociology of culture). Warszawa, Państwowe Wydawnictwo Naukowe, 83, 607 p.
909   RASSEM, Mohammed H. *Aspekte der Kultursoziologie* (Aspects of culture sociology). Berlin, Reimer, 82, 441 p. [Edited by Justin STAGL]
910   WOOD, Geoffrey. "Frazer's magic wand of anthropology: interpreting 'the golden bough'", *Archives européennes de Sociologie* 23(1), 82 : 92-122. [in regards to the monograph: Frazer, J. G., 'The golden bough', London, Macmillan, 1922]
911   ZIJDERVELD, Ancon C. *De culturele factor: een cultuursociologische wegwijzer* (The cultural factor: an indicator in cultural sociology). 's-Gravenhage, VUGA, 83, 177 p.

13120   Civilization. Culture. Society
         Civilisation. Culture. Société

912   "Culture and politics in Latin America", *LARU Studies* 4(3), jun 82 : 3-97. [with contributions by José Luis NAJENSON, Nain NOMEZ, Julio Garcia ESPINOSA, José NUN]
913   "Cultures, religions, civilisation: questions d'hier et de demain", *Économie et Humanisme* 272, aug 83 : 7-47. [with contributions by Georges C. ANAWATI and René LUNEAU]
914   "National identity, miscegenation and cultural expressions: a comparison between the United States and Brazil", *Social Science Information* 22(2), 83 : 165-168.
915   "On national character: a symposium on what makes us what we are", *Seminar* (276), aug 82 : 11-44. [with contributions by Jai B. P. SINHA, Kapila VATSYAYAN, Raj THAPAR, K. K. SINCH, K. F. RUSTAMSI, O. U. VIJAYAN, Santi P. CHOWDHURY; A. K. JOSHI]
916   "Socialisme 'réel' et marxisme. Culture de masse et société de consommation", *Homme et Société* 65-66, jul-dec 82 : 3-189.
917   "Sociologie de la vie quotidienne et de récits de vie", *Schweizerische Zeitschrift für Soziologie / Revue suisse de Sociologie* 9(1), 83 : 17-185.
918   APINJAN, T. A. "Krizis buržuaznoj kul'tury i koncepcija igry J. Hejzingi" (Crisis of bourgeois culture and J. Huizinga's conception of play), *Filosofskie Nauki* 24(4), 82 : 78-85.
919   BALANDIER, Georges. "Essai d'identification du quotidien", *Cahiers internationaux de Sociologie* 74, 83 : 5-12.
920   BARDN, Panos D. "Society and culture", *Indian Journal of Social Research* 23(1), apr 82 : 29-50.
921   BARULIN, V. S. *Dialektika sfer obščestvennoj žizni* (Dialectics of the social life spheres). Moskva, Izdatel'stvo Moskovskogo Universiteta, 82, 230 p.
922   BELLASI, Pietro. "L'iconographie de la vie quotidienne: Lilliput et Brobdingnag", *Cahiers internationaux de Sociologie* 74, 83 : 47-56.
923   BERTAUX-WIAME, Isabelle. "Vie quotidienne, pratiques féminines et historicité", *Schweizerische Zeitschrift für Soziologie / Revue suisse de Sociologie* 9(1), 83 : 99-110.
924   BOUVIER, Pierre. "Pour une anthropologie de la quotidienneté du travail", *Cahiers internationaux de Sociologie* 74, 83 : 133-142.
925   BRÄMER, Rainer. "Sozialistische Bildungsrealität" (Socialist cultural reality), *Deutschland Archiv* 16(8), aug 83 : 858-868. [German DR]
926   BROMLEJ, Ju. V.; KULIČENKO, M. I. "Nacional'noe i internacional'noe v obraze žizni sovetskogo čeloveka" (The national and the international in the Soviet man's way of life), *Naučnye Doklady vysšej Školy. Naučnyj Kommunizma* (4), 82 : 3-12.
927   CAMPAGNAC, Elisabeth. "Transformation des modes de vie: des stratégies patronales aux pratiques sociales ouvrières", *Critiques de l'économie politique* (23-24), sep 83 : 43-65. [France]
928   CECCARELLI, Fabio. "Modelli di interazione fra biologia e cultura" (Models of interaction between biology and culture), *Rassegna italiana di Sociologia* 24(4), oct-dec 83 : 575-615.

929   CRESPI, Franco. "Le risque du quotidien", *Cahiers internationaux de Sociologie* 74, 83 : 39-45.
930   ČUPRYNIN, A. I.; [et al.]. *SŠA glazami amerikanskih sociologov. Social'nye aspekty amerikanskogo obraza žizni* (The USA in the American sociologists eyes. Social aspects of the American way of life). Moskva, Nauka, 82, 264 p.
931   DUPRÉ, Louis. *Marx's social critique of culture.* New Haven, CT-London, Yale University Press, 83, ix-299 p.
932   DZIOEV, O. I. "Kul'tura — nacija — ličnost' " (Culture — nation — personality), *Voprosy Filosofii* 35(10), 82 : 76-82.
933   ERNY, Pierre. "L'esprit de l'éducation au Rwanda ou le 'caractère national' décrit par un groupe d'étudiants", *Genève-Afrique* 21(1), 83 : 25-54.
934   FÀBREGAS, Xavier. *El fons ritual de la vida quotidiana* (The ritual background of the everyday life). Barcelona, Edicions 62, 82, 252 p.
935   FALCAO, Jaoquim A. "A favor de nova legislação de proteção ao bem cultural" (For a new legislation of cultural property protection), *Ciência e Trópico* 9(1), jun 81 : 21-34. [Brazil]
936   FEDOROV, V. M. "Problema vzaimodejstvija obščestva i prirody v teorii naučnogo kommunizma" (The problem of interaction between society and nature in the theory of scientific communism), *Vestnik Moskovskogo Universiteta. Serija Teorija naučnogo Kommunizma* (1), 83 : 60-68.
937   FISHMAN, Joshua A. "Cultural pluralism and the American school", *Plural Societies* 12(3-4), wint 81 : 5-12.
938   FISHWICK, Marshall William; [ed.]. *Bangladesh: inter-cultural studies.* Dhaka-Ananda, Dhaka University Book Society, 83, 122-iii-2 p.
939   FRANKENBERG, Ronald; [ed.]. *Custom and conflict in British society.* Manchester, Manchester University Press, 82, iv-361 p.
940   GLAZIER, Stephen D. "Cultural pluralism and respectability in Trinidad", *Ethnic and Racial Studies* 6(3), jul 83 : 351-355.
941   HAJRULLAEV, M. M.; ŠIRMATOVA, G. "Vzaimodejstvie kul'tur i duhovnoe obogaščenie ličnosti" (Interaction of culture and the personality cultural enrichment), *Filosofskie Nauki* 24(5), 82 : 3-12.
942   HANAFI, Hasan. "Arab national thought in the balance", *Jerusalem Quarterly* (25), aut 82 : 54-67.
943   HOPPÁL, Mihály. "Életmód-modellek és/mint kulturális paradigmák" (Models of way of life as/and cultural paradigms), *Műhely* 6(1), 83 : 56-69.
944   ISHIKAWA, Minoru. *Nichijo sekai no kyo to jitsu: irony no shakaigaku* (Images and realities of everyday social phenomena: sociology of irony). Tokyo, Yuhikaku, 83, 298 p.
945   JAHODA, Gustav; WOERDENBAGCH, Adrienne. "Awareness of supra-national groupings among Dutch and Scottish children and adolescents", *European Journal of Political Research* 10(3), sep 82 : 305-312.
946   JANNE, Henri. "Le pluralisme culturel dans la société contemporaine", *Cultures* 8(3), 82 : 29-40. [Europe]
947   JÄRVELÄ-HARTIKAINEN, Marja; AHPONEN, Pirkkoliisa; TAPONEN, Matti. *The frame of ways of life in Finland: an overview.* Helsinki, Helsingin Yliopisto, Sosiaalipolitiikan Laitos, 82, 307 p.
948   KOZLOV, A. P.; SALOV, M. A. "Socialističeskij obraz žizni i razvitie ličnosti" (The socialist way of life and personality development), *Naucnye Doklady vyssej Skoly. Naucnyj Kommunizma* (5), 82 : 58-64.
949   KRAUS, Richard. "China's cultural 'liberalization' and conflict over the social organization of the arts", *Modern China* 9(2), apr 83 : 212-227.
950   KRUGLOVA, L. K. "Sistemnyj podhod k kul'ture" (Systemic approach to culture), *Problemy Dialektiki* (10), 82 : 146-149.
951   KUNERT, Günter. "Auf der Suche nach dem verlorenen Selbst oder: was ist des DDR-Deutschen Vaterland?" (In search of lost identity or: what is the Eastern German fatherland?), *Deutsche Studien* 21(82), jun 83 : 109-121.
952   LABAHN, Thomas. "Staatliche Identitätsfindung und Sprache — Das Beispiel Somalia" (Search for national identity and language: the example of Somalia), *Verfassung und Recht in Übersee* 16(3), sem. 3, 83 : 267-278. [résumé en anglais]
953   LALIVE D'EPINAY, Christian. "La vie quotidienne. Essai de construction d'un concept sociologique et anthropologique", *Cahiers internationaux de Sociologie* 74, 83 : 13-38.
954   LAMBERT, Ronald D.; CURTIS, James E. "Opposition to multiculturalism among Québécois and English-Canadians", *Canadian Review of Sociology and Anthropology* 20(2), mai 83 : 193-207.
955   LEE, Joseph. "Society and culture", *Administration (Dublin)* 30(2-3), 82 : 1-18. [Ireland]

956   LOHOF, Bruce. *American commonplace: essays on the popular culture of the United States.* Bowling
        Green, OH, Bowling Green State University Popular Press, 82, 128 p.

957   LUCAS, Philippe. "Les travaux et les jours", *Cahiers internationaux de Sociologie* 74, 83 : 143-150.

958   MAEYAMA, Takashi. "Culture and value system in Brazil: a preliminary report", *Tsukuba
        daigaku Latin American Studies* 6, 83 : 153-168.

959   MAFFESOLI, Michel. "Épistémologie de la vie quotidienne", *Cahiers internationaux de
        Sociologie* 74, 83 : 57-70.

960   MARCZUK, Stanisław. "Swiadomość narodowa młodego pokolenia w świet le badań
        socjologicznych" (National awareness of the young generation in the light of sociological
        research), *Studia Socjologiczne* 90 (3), 83 : 119-141. [Poland]

961   MARKIEWICZ-LAGNEAU, Janine. *La formation d'une pensée sociologique: la société polonaise
        de l'entre-deux-guerres.* Paris, Éditions de la Maison des Sciences de l'Homme, 82, 349 p.

962   MARWICK, Arthur. *British society since 1945.* London, A. Lane, 82, 303 p.

963   MARX, Roland. *La vie quotidienne en Angleterre au temps de l'expérience socialiste: 1945-1951.*
        Paris, Hachette, 83, 323 p.

964   MATEJKO, Alexander J. "The fate of Canada between underdevelopment and post-
        industrialism", *Études canadiennes / Canadian Studies* (14), jun 83 : 35-47.

965   MATTHEWS, P. W. . "Multiculturalism in Australia: an interpretation", *Plural Societies*
        12(3-4), wint 81 : 65-92.

966   MEJÍA-RICART GUZMÁN, Tirso; [ed.]. *La sociedad dominicana durante la Segunda República*
        (Dominican society during the Second Republic). Santo Domingo, Editora de la Univer-
        sidad Autónoma de Santo Domingo, 82, 399 p. [1865-1924]

967   MEŽNARIĆ, Silva. "Nacionalni identitet i krizapokušaj tipologije procesa u međuetničkom
        prostoru u Sloveniji" (National identity and crisis: an attempt at a typology of processes
        in inter-ethnic space in Slovenia), *Revija za Sociologiju* 11(3-4), 81 : 167-178.

968   MEŽUEV, V. M. "Kul'tura kak filosofskaja problema" (Culture as a philosophical problem),
        Voprosy Filosofii 35(10), 82 : 42-52.

969   MIYAJIMA, Takashi. "Évolution du mode de vie et des attitudes à l'égard du travail au
        Japon", *Sciences Sociales du Japon Contemporain* 4, 83 : 7-55.

970   MOLNÁR, Miklós. "Pouvoir et société civile dans les pays de l'Europe de l'Est: concepts
        et réalités", *Cadmos* 5(19), aut 82 : 34-53.

971   MORIOKA, Kiyomi. "Nichijo seikatsu ni okeru shihika" (Privatization in everyday life),
        Shakaigaku hyoron 34(2), 83 : 12-19.

972   NASYROV, A. *Ėkonomičeskaja osnova socialističeskogo obraza žizni* (Economic bases of the socialist
        way of life). Taškent, Uzbekistan, 83, 247 p.

973   NEVIS, Edwin C. "Cultural assumptions and productivity: the United States and China",
        Sloan Management Review 24(3), spr 83 : 17-29.

974   NIŽNIK, Jízef. *Społeczne przesłanki działalności kulturalnej* (Social premises of cultural activity).
        Warszawa, Centralny Ośrodek Metodyki Upowszechniania Kultury, 83, 120 p.

975   NOVIKOVA, L. I. "Civilizacija i kul'tura v istoričeskom processe" (Civilization and
        culture in the historical process), *Voprosy Filosofii* 35(10), 82 : 53-63.

976   NUSUPOV, Č. T. "Rol' marksistko-leninskoj ideologii v soveršenstvovanii socialističeskogo
        obraza žizni" (Role of the marxist-leninist ideology in the improvement of
        the socialist way of life), *Izvestija Akademii Nauk Kirgizskoj SSSR* (3), 82 : 62-66.

977   OLANIYAN, Richard; [ed.]. *African history and culture.* Ikeja-Lagos, Longman Nigeria,
        82, ix-259 p.

978   PAGES LARRAYA, Fernando. *Irracional en la cultura* (The irrational in culture). Buenos
        Aires, Fecic, 83, 1640 p.

979   PEILLON, Michel. *Contemporary Irish society: an introduction.* Dublin, Gill and Macmillan,
        82, 231 p.

980   PELOILLE, Bernard. "Retour à une sociologie de la nation française", *Cahiers internationaux
        de Sociologie* 75, 83 : 239-261.

981   PELOILLE, Bernard. "Le vocabulaire des notions 'nation', 'État', 'patrie'. Quelques résultats
        d'enquête", *Revue française de Science politique* 33(1), feb 83 : 65-108. [résumé en anglais.]

982   POSPISZYL, Kazimierz. "Charakter narodowy w świetle międzykulturowych badań
        kwestionariuszami Eysencków" (National character in the light of inter-cultural research
        by means of the Eysencks questionnaire), *Studia Socjologiczne* 89(2), 83 : 309-333.

983   RABOW, Jerome; BERKMAN, Sherry L.; KESSLER, Ronald. "The culture of poverty
        and learned helplessness: a social psychological perspective", *Sociological Inquiry* 53(4),
        83 : 419-434. [USA]

984   RAY, Baren. *India: nature of society and present crisis.* New Delhi, Intellectual, 83, 203 p.

985   ROBEL, Léon; [et al.]. "La place de la culture dans la vie socialiste", *Recherches internationales*
        (9), sep 83 : 233-251.

986   ROCCA, Jean-Louis. "Aspects de la vie quotidienne en Chine", *Économie et Humanisme* 272, aug 83 : 58-65.

987   SAŁUDA, Bronisław. "Nowe elementy stylu życia na wsi" (New elements of the life style in the country), *Wieś Współczesna* 311(1), 83 : 56-63.

988   SATO, Tomoo. "Simmel shakaigaku no kihon mondai: Iwayuru 'Kogi no shakai' to 'Kyogi no shakai' ni tsuite" (The fundamental problems of Simmel's sociology: reflection on what is called 'the society in a narrow sense' and 'the society in a broad sense'), *Chuo daigaku bungakubu kiyo* 109, 83 : 1-38.

989   SEEWANN, Gerhard; SITZLER, Kathrin. "Ungarisches Nationalbewusstsein heute. Zur historisch-politischen Selbstinterpretation einer sozialistischen Gesellschaft" (Hungarian national conscousness today. On the historico-political self-interpretation of a socialist society), *Südosteuropa — Zeitschrift für Gegenwartsforschung* 32(2), 83 : 91-106.

990   ŠESTAKOV, V. P. "'Iskusstvo trivializacii' nekotorye teoretičeskie problemy massovoj kul'tury" (The art of 'trivialization': some theoretical problems of mass culture), *Voprosy Filosofii* 35(10), 82 : 64-75.

991   SICIŃSKI, Andrzej; [ed.]. *Styl życia, obyczaje, ethos w Polsce lat siedemziesiątych — z perspektywy roku 1981* (The life style, customs, ethos in Poland of the seventies — from the perspective of 1981 year). Warszawa, Polska Akademia Nauk Instytut Filozofi i Socjologii, 83, 126 p.

992   SIERADZKI, Maciej. "Naród a klasy społeczne. Wybrane problemy socjologii narodu w świetle pism społeczno-politycznych Kazimierza Kelles-Krauza" (Nation and social classes. Selected problems of sociology of nation in the light of Kazimierz Kelles-Krauz's socio-political writings), *Kultura i Społeczeństwo* 27(3), 83 : 101-117.

993   SIMUS, P. I. "Nekotorye problemy izučenija obraza žizni sovetskoj derevni" (Problems concerning the study of the way of life in Soviet villages), *Istorija SSSR* 26(3), 83 : 3-19.

994   SMOLIN, O. N. "Obraz žizni i kul'tura: k voprosu o sootnošenii kategorij" (The way of life and culture: question on the categories correlation),, 1982 : 95-105.

995   SORJ, Bernard; TAVARES DE ALMEIDA, Maria Hermínia; [eds.]. *Sociedade e política no Brasil pós-64* (Society and politics in Brazil after 1964). São Paulo, Brasiliense, 83, 261 p.

996   TAMURA, Kenji. "Keizai o chushin toshita Nihon no shorai" (Future of Japanese society on the economic basis), *Musashi daigaku junbungakukkai zasshi* 15(2), 83 : 17-32.

997   TARMAHANOV, É. D. "Internationalizacija socialističeskogo obraza žizni" (Internationalization of the socialist way of life), *in: Razvitie XXVI s'ezdom KPSS teorii naučnogo kommunizma.*

998   THOMAS, Louis-Vincent. "Mort et vie quotidienne. La logique de la vie", *Cahiers internationaux de Sociologie* 74, 83 : 83-96.

999   TYSZKA, Andrzej. "Policentryzm i pluralizm kultury" (Cultural polycentrism and pluralism), *Kultura i Społeczeństwo* 27(1), 83 : 49-60.

1000   USPENSKIJ, V. N. "Socialističeskij obraz žizni: vzaimosvjaz' obščestvennyh uslovij i dejatel'nost' ličnosti" (The socialist way of life: interrelation of the social conditions and the personality activity), *Filosofskie Nauki* 24(4), 82 : 5-12.

1001   VIANU, Tudor. *Studii de filozofia culturii* (Studies of cultural philosophy). Bucureşti, Editura Eminescu, 82, 470 p. [Edited by Gelu IONESCU and George GANĂ]

1002   VOZ'MITEL', A. A.; POKROVSKAJA, M. V. "Sovetskij obraz žizni — realizacija principov social'noj spravedlivnosti" (The Soviet way of life is the realization of the social justice principles), *in: Social'naja spravedlivost' i puti eě realizacii v social'noj prolitike. I.* Moskva, 1982 : 30-43.

1003   WACHTEL, Paul L. *The poverty of affluence: a psychological portrait of the American way of life.* New York, NY, Macmillan, Free Press; London, Collier Macmillan, 83, xvi-316 p.

1004   WYKA, Anna. "On some avant-garde and alternative milieux in Poland", *Polish Sociological Bulletin* 53(1), 81 : 47-58.

1005   ZEA, Leopoldo. *Latinoamérica, un nuevo humanismo* (Latin America: a new humanism). Tunja-Boyacá, Editorial Bolivariana Internacional, 82, 175 p.

1006   ZUEV, S. É. "K voprosu o hronologičeskih ramkah massovoj kul'tury: na materiale kul'tury Anglii XVIII v." (Questions on the chronological limits of mass culture: with England cultural materials in the XVIIIth century), *in: K voprosy social'nogo funkcionirovanija iskusstva: teoretičeskie i ěmpiričeskie aspekty.* Moskva, 1982 : 118-138.

1007   ZVORYKIN, A. A. "Iz istorii razvitija teorii kul'tury na Zapade" (History of the culture theory development in the West), *Voprosy Filosofii* 35(10), 82 : 99-104.

13130   Cultural dynamics. Cultural relations
Dynamique culturelle. Relations culturelles

1008   "Cultural policy in India", *Pacific Affairs* 56(1), spr 83 : 5-50. [with contributions by Lloyd I. RUDOLPH, Susanne Hoeber RUDOLPH, Robert S. ANDERSON]

1009   "Politiques culturelles: du modèle à la réalité du marché", *Cultures* 9(33), 83 : 9-215. [with
        contributions by Makaminan MAKAGIANSAR, Odhiambo ANACETI, Melina
        MERCOURI]

1010   BOCHNER, Stephen; [ed.]. *Cultures in contact: studies in cross-cultural interaction.* Oxford-
        New York, NY, Pergamon Press, 82, xiv-232 p.

1011   BOGOV, V. I. "O pokazateljah razvitija kul'tury" (On the indexes of cultural development),
        Sociologičeskie Issledovanija (Moskva) (1), 83 : 129-133.

1012   DISKIN, I. "Social'no-èkonomičeskie problemy razvitija infrastruktury kul'tury" (Socio-
        economic problems of developing culture infrastructure), *Voprosy Èkonomiki* 53(12),
        82 : 117-128. [USSR]

1013   ERENC, Janusz. "Dziedzictwo minionych pokoleń a kultura państwa" (Heritage of the
        past generations and the culture of a socialist state), *Zeszyty Naukowe Wydziału Humanistycznego
        Uniwersytetu Gdańskiego* 7, 83 : 7-20. [Spec. No Filozofia i Socjologia]

1014   FELSON, Marcus. "Unobtensive indicators of cultural change: neckties, girdles, marijuana,
        garbage, magazines and urban sprawl", *American Behavioral Scientist* 26(4), mar-apr
        83 : 534-542. [USA]

1015   FORSTNER, Martin. "Die kulturelle und nationale Identität Tunesiens angesichts der
        Reislamisierungsbestrebungen" (Cultural and national identity of Tunisian in the light
        of re-islamization efforts), *Orient* 24(1), mar 83 : 43-63.

1016   FUSE, Toyomasa. "Cultural values and social behaviour of the Japanese: a comparative
        analysis", *Civilisations* 33(1), 82 : 97-139.

1017   GARCÍA CANCLINI, Néstor. "Políticas culturais na América latina" (Cultural policy in
        Latin America), *Novos estudos CEBRAP* 2(2), jul 83 : 39-51.

1018   INOUE, Shun. "Bunka no 'Nichijoka' ni tsuite" (Contemporary cultural change in Japan),
        Shakaigaku hyoron 34(2), 83 : 30-37.

1019   KLEVCOV, A. I.; IVANOVA, M. K. "Problemy kul'tury v svete rešenij XVI s'ezda
        KPSS" (Cultural problems in the light of the CPSU XXVIth Congress decisions),
        Problemy Filosofii 55, 82 : 3-15. [USSR]

1020   KŁOSKOWSKA, Antonina. "Wartości i wybory kulturalne" (Values and cultural choices),
        Kultura i Społeczeństwo 27(1), 83 : 67-72.

1021   KOGAN, L. N. "K voprosu o sozdanii kompleksnoj naučnoj programmy razvitija
        kul'tury" (Question on the creation of a complex scientific program of cultural development),
        Naučnye Trudy (Tjumenskij Universitet) 91, 81 : 69-72.

1022   KONARE, Alpha Oumar. "Politiques culturelles en Afrique occidentale", *Cultures* 9(33),
        83 : 110-124.

1023   KREISER, Klaus. "Gesichtspunkte der türkischen Kulturpolitik. Polarisation und Konsensus"
        (Aspects of cultural policy in Turkey. Polarization and consensus), *Orient* 23(4), dec
        82 : 557-569.

1024   LE GOFF, Jacques; KOPECZI, Béla; [eds.]. *Objet et méthodes de l'histoire de la culture: actes du
        Colloque franco-hongrois de Tihany (Hongrie), 10-14 octobre 1977.* Paris, Éditions du CNRS;
        Budapest, Akadémiai Kiadó, 82, 247 p.

1025   MARTINIÈRE, Guy. *La coopération franco-brésilienne. Transplantation culturelle et stratégie de la
        modernité.* Paris, Maison des sciences de l'Homme-Presses Universitaires de Grenoble,
        82, 223 p.

1026   NEGROTTI, Massimo. "Dinamica della 'complessità' culturale. Discussione sull'informatica"
        (The dynamics of cultural 'complexity'. Discussion on informatics), *Studi di Sociologia*
        20(3-4), jul-dec 82 : 315-332.

1027   ORY, Pascal. *L'entre-deux-mai: histoire culturelle de la France, mai 1968-mai 1981.* Paris, Éditions
        du Seuil, 83, 282 p.

1028   PETERSON, Richard A.; [ed.]. "Patterns of cultural choice", *American Behavioral Scientist*
        26(4), mar-apr 83 : 419-552. [USA]

1029   PIGANIOL, Pierre. "Culture et développement", *Revue des Sciences morales et politiques* 137(4),
        82 : 655-672.

1030   QIAN XUESEN. "Culturology study of the creation of socialist spiritual wealth", *Social
        Sciences in China* 4(1), mar 83 : 17-26.

1031   RITAINE, Evelyne. *Les stratèges de la culture.* Paris, Presses de la Fondation Nationale des
        Sciences Politiques, 83, 189 p.

1032   SÁGI, Mária. *Transmission of cultural values through the family in the conditions of the scientific-technical
        revolution.* Budapest, Institute for Culture, 82, 14 p.

1033   ŠEVELEV, V. N. "Kul'turnye preobrazovanija v stranah socialističeskoj orientacii:
        nekotorye teoretičeskie aspekty" (Cultural change in the socialist-orientated countries:
        some theoretical aspects), *Izvestija Severo-Kavkazskogo Naučnogo Centra Vysšej Školy. Obščestvennye
        Nauki* (2), 82 : 50-55.

1034   SYNAK, Brunon. "Identyfikacja kulturowa jako istotny element adaptacji osoby starszej w
        nowym środowisku" (Cultural identification of elderly people in a new environment),
        Zeszyty Naukowe Wydziału Humanistycznego Uniwersytetu Gdańskiego 7, 83 : 53-80. [Spec.
        No Filozofia i Socjologia.]
1035   VITÁNYI, Iván. *The goals, methods and achievements of cultural policies as reflected in the social
        development of countries.* Budapest, Müvelődéskutató Intézet, 83, 59 p.
1036   VITÁNYI, Iván; SÁGI, Mária; LIPP, Márta. *A kultúra közvetítése a családban* (The transmission
        of culture through the family). Budapest, Müvelődéskutató Intézet, 82, 129 p.
1037   YU, Lucy C.; HARBURG, Ernest. "Acculturation and stress among Chinese Americans
        in a university town", *International Journal of Group Tensions* 10(1-4), 80 : 99-119.

13140   Social norms. Social control. Value systems
           Normes sociales. Régulation sociale. Systèmes de valeurs

1038   "Répression — emprise — violence", *Homme et Société* 67-68, jan-jun 83 : 5-195.
1039   "Sociologie de la création institutionnelle", *Année sociologique* 33, 83 : 9-20.
1040   BORISTUK, V. I.; BUNIN, I. M. "Cennostnye orientacii sovremennoj buržuazii:
        preemstvennost' i razryv?" (Value orientation of present-day bourgeoisie: continuity
        or break?), *Voprosy Filosofii* 35(9), 82 : 95-106.
1041   BOVONE, Laura. "Vita composita e nuovi valori: ipotesi sulla generazione de mezzo"
        (Composite life and new values: some hypotheses on the adult generation), *Studi di
        Sociologia* 21(3), jul-sep 83 : 281-292.
1042   CHENAL, Odile. "Les sociologues et les institutions: le cas des Pays-Bas", *Année sociologique*
        33, 83 : 37-65.
1043   CHONG, Dennis; [et al.]. "Patterns of support for democratic and capitalist values in the
        United States", *British Journal of Political Science* 13(4), oct 83 : 401-440.
1044   CIMINO, Enrico. "Consistenza e sviluppo di alcuni valori sociali: ricerca preliminare"
        (Constancy and development of some social values: preliminary research), *Bolletino di
        psicologia applicata* (166), jun 83 : 23-31. [Italy]
1045   DJAIT, Hichem. "Une quête pour les valeurs en Islam", *Diogène* 124, dec 83 : 95-111.
1046   FELLING, A.; PETERS, J.; SCHREUDER, Osmund. *Burgerlijk en onburgerlijk Nederland:
        een nationaal onderzoek naar waardenoriëntaties op de drempel van de jaren tachtig* (Bourgeois and
        non-bourgeois Netherlands: a national survey of value orientations at the threshold of
        the eighties). Deventer, Van Loghum Slaterus, 83, 216 p.
1047   FELLING, Albert; PETERS, Jan; SCHREUDER, Osmund. "Bürgerliche und alternative
        Wertorientierungen in den Niederlanden" (Bourgeois and alternative value orientations
        in the Netherlands), *Kölner Zeitschrift für Soziologie und Sozialpsychologie* 35(1), mar 83 : 83-107.
1048   FLORIAN, Victor. "The impact of social environment and sex on adolescent social values:
        a comparison of the kibbutz and the city in Israel", *European Journal of Social Psychology*
        13(3), jul-sep 83 : 281-286.
1049   GALILEA W., Carmen. *Valores en el Chile de hoy* (Values in Chile today). Santiago, Centro
        Bellarmino, Departamento de Investigaciones Sociológicas, 83, 131 p.
1050   GRASMICK, Harold G.; JACOBS, Darlene; MCCOLLOM, Carol B. "Social class and
        social control: an application of deterrence theory", *Social Forces* 62(2), dec 83 : 359-374.
1051   GUARINO GHEZZI, Susan. "A private network of social control: insurance investigation
        units", *Social Problems* 30(5), jun 83 : 521-531.
1052   JERSCHINA, Jan. "System wartości młodych robotników i inteligentów w procesie przemian"
        (Value system of young workers and white-collar workers in the process of changes),
        Kultura i Społeczeństwo 27(2), 83 : 5-39.
1053   LEONARDI, Franco. "Valori o stereotipie eticosociali? Riflessioni sulla 'nuova sinistra'
        di Ronald Inglehart" (Values or ethico-social stereotypes? Reflections on Ronald
        Inglehart's 'new left'), *Sociologia (Roma)* 17(1), jan-apr 83 : 3-39.
1054   MASTEKAASA, Arne. "Post-materialist values and subjective satisfaction: testing Ronald
        Inglehart's hypotheses", *Acta Sociologica* 26(2), 83 : 141-159.
1055   MEULEMANN, Heiner. "Value change in West Germany, 1950-1980: integrating the
        empirical evidence", *Social Science Information* 22(4-5), 83 : 777-800.
1056   MEYER, Ruth. "Value change in the Swiss population", *Revue internationale de Sociologie*
        17(1), apr 81 : 48-64.
1057   MEYER, Thomas. "Wertwandel, industrielle Gesellschaft und Demokratischer Sozialismus"
        (Value change, industrial society and democratic socialism), *Jahrbuch für Theorie und Praxis
        des Demokratischen Sozialismus*, 81 : 59-95.
1058   MÜLLER, Hans-Peter. *Wertkrise und Gesellschaftsreform: Emile Durkheims Schriften zur Politik* (Value
        crisis and social reform: Emile Durkheim's writings on politics). Stuttgart, Enke, 83, 247 p.

1059 ORTEGA, V. "El cambio de valores en España" (Change of values in Spain), *Revista de Fomento social* 37(152), oct-dec 83 : 363-378.

1060 PLAHOV, V. D. "Voprosy dialektiki v sistemnom issledovanii social'nyh norm" (Questions of dialectics in the systemic research of social norms), *Problemy Dialektiki* (10), 82 : 140-145.

1061 PLATT, John. "Reflections on the approach of 1984: recent developments in social control in the UK", *International Journal of the Sociology of Law* 11(4), nov 83 : 339-360.

1062 POPKOV, V. D. "Povyšenie roli prava i morali v razvitii socialističeskih obščestvennyh otnošenij" (Elevation of the law and ethics role in the development of the socialist social relations), *Vestnik Moskovskogo Universiteta. Serija Pravo* 37(3), 83 : 3-12.

1063 RAES, J. "¿Hacia un nuevo sistema de valores?" (Towards a new system of values?), *Revista de Fomento social* 37(152), oct-dec 83 : 341-348. [Spain]

1064 ROLSTON, Holmes III. "Values gone wild", *Inquiry* 26(2), jun 83 : 181-207.

1065 ŠERKOVIN, Ju. A. "Problemy eennostnoj orientacii i massovye informacionnye processy" (Problem of value orientation and mass communication processes), *Psichologičeskij Žurnal* (3-5), 82 : 135-145.

1066 SHEARING, Clifford D.; STENNING, Philip C. "Private security: implications for social control", *Social Problems* 30(5), jun 83 : 493-506.

1067 SOPUCH, Kazimierz. *Postawy wobec życia i wybór wartości a struktura społeczna* (Attitudes towards life and a choice of values and social structure). Gdańsk, Uniwersytet Gdański, 83, 206 p.

1068 SPATES, James L. "The sociology of values", *Annual Review of Sociology* (9), 83 : 27-49.

1069 SPITZER, Steven; SIMON, Rita J.; [eds.]. *Research in law, deviance and social control.* Greenwich, CT-London, JAI Press, 82, xv-299 p.

1070 STOETZEL, Jean. *Les valeurs du temps présent: une enquête européenne.* Paris, Presses Universitaires de France, 83, 309 p.

1071 SUŁEK, Antoni. "Wartości życiowe dwóch pokoleń. 'Dokument lat siedemdziesiątych'" (Life values of two generations. 'Document of 1970s'), *Kultura i Społeczeństwo* 27(2), 83 : 73-87.

1072 SZAKOLCZAI, Árpád. "A cigányság értékrendjének sajátosságai" (The characteristics of the value system of Gypsies), *Szociológia* 11(4), 82 : 521-533.

1073 TESSER, Abraham; CAMPBELL, Jennifer; MICKLER, Susan. "The role of social pressure, attention to the stimulus, and self-doubt in conformity", *European Journal of Social Psychology* 13(3), jul-sep 83 : 217-233.

1074 TOHARIA, José-Juan. *Valores básicos de los adolescentes españoles* (Basic values of Spanish adolescents). Madrid, Ministerio de Cultura, Dirección General de Juventud y Promoción Socio-Cultural, 82, 182 p. bibliogr.

1075 TUOMELA, Raimo. *The components of social control.* Helsinki, University of Helsinki, Department of Social Psychology, 82, 43-12 p.

1076 WISNIEWSKI, Wiesław. "Power, welfare and education in the Polish value system", *Polish Sociological Bulletin* 53(1), 81 : 37-46.

13150   Alienation. Socialization. Social conformity
Aliénation. Socialisation. Conformité sociale

1077 "Political violence and civil disobedience in Western Europe 1982", *Conflict Studies* (145), 82 : 1-31.

1078 "Terorizam, militarizacija, teror" (Terrorism, militarization, terror), *Gledišta* 22(12), dec 81 : 3-107. [with contributions by Katarina TOMAŠEVSKI]

1079 "Women and violence", *Signs* 8(3), spr 83 : 397-592. [with contributions by Sara RUDDICK, Wini BREINES, Linda GORDON, Irene HANSON FREIZE, Pauline W. GEE]

1080 ÁGÓ, Erzsébet. "A társadalmi normáktól eltérő magatartásformák néhány kérdése" (Some questions in connection with the attitudes deviating from the social norms), *Területi Statisztika* 33(3), 83 : 220-241.

1081 AKERS, Ronald L.; [et al.]. "Are self-reports of adolescent deviance valid? Biochemical measures, randomized response, and the bogus pipeline in smoking behavior", *Social Forces* 62(1), sep 83 : 234-251.

1082 AYUKAWA, Jun. " 'Kateinai boryoku': Satsujin jiken o maneita 3 case o chushin nishite" ('Violence in the family': a study of three murder cases), *Matsuyama shoka daigaku Matsuyama shodai ronshu* 34(3), 83 : 69-118.

1083 BARBANO, Filippo. "Marginalità versus complessità" (Marginality versus complexity), *Studi di Sociologia* 21(4), oct-dec 83 : 336-355.

1084 BARNES, Barry. "Social life as bootstrapped induction", *Sociology (London)* 17(4), nov 83 : 524-545.

1085 BATSON, C. Daniel. "Sociobiology and the role of religion in promoting prosocial behavior: an alternative view", *Journal of Personality and Social Psychology* 45(6), dec 83 : 1380-1385.

1086   BELOV, G. A. "O social'noj osnove SSSR: vzaimosvjaz' social'nyh, nacional'nyh i
        političeskih otnošenij" (On the USSR social basis: interrelations of social, national and
        political relations), *Vestnik Moskovskogo Universiteta. Serija Teorija naučnogo Kommunizma*
        (6), 82 : 12-19.

1087   BENVENUTI, Leonardo; [et al.]. *Disadattamento sociale: teoria e ricerca* (Social maladjustment:
        theory and research). Milano, F. Angeli, 83, 193 p.

1088   BESNARD, Philippe. "Le destin de l'anomie dans la sociologie du suicide", *Revue française
        de Sociologie* 24(4), oct-dec 83 : 605-629.

1089   BONANATE, Luigi. "Terrorismo e governabilità" (Terrorism and governability), *Revista
        italiana di scienza politica* 13(1), apr 83 : 37-64.

1090   BRUNETTA, Giuseppe. "Atti di terrorismo in Italia (1968-1982)" (Terrorism acts in Italy,
        1968-1982), *Aggiornamenti sociali* 34(6), jun 83 : 455-473.

1091   BUONO, Anthony F.; KAMM, Judith B. "Marginality and the organizational socialization
        of female managers", *Human Relations* 36(12), dec 83 : 1125-1140.

1092   BURKART, Günter. "Zur Mikroanalyse universitärer Sozialisation im Medizinstudium:
        eine Anwendung der Methode der objektiv-hermeneutischen Textinterpretation"
        (Microanalysis of academic socialization in medical studies: an application of the method
        of objective-hermeneutical text interpretation), *Zeitschrift für Soziologie* 12(1), jan 83 : 24-48.

1093   CAMERINI, Massimo. "Condizione marginale e communicazione" (Marginal condition
        and communication), *Studi di Sociologia* 21(4), oct-dec 83 : 370-377.

1094   CAPPADOCIA, Ezio. "Terrorism in Italy — a commentary", *Queen's Quarterly* 89(4),
        wint 82 : 770-782.

1095   CARMAN, Roderick S.; FITZGERALD, B. J.; HOLMGREN, Charles. "Alienation
        and drinking motivations among adolescent females", *Journal of Personality and Social
        Psychology* 44(5), mai 83 : 1021-1024.

1096   CREMER, Günter. *Sozialisations- und Jugendforschung 1970-1982: eine Literaturdokumentation*
        (Socialization and youth research 1970-1982: a literature documentation). München,
        Verlag Deutsches Jugendinstitut, 83, 245 p. [Germany FR]

1097   DAL FERRO, Giuseppe. "Emarginazione e auto-emarginazione" (Marginalization and
        self-marginalization), *Studi di Sociologia* 21(4), oct-dec 83 : 378-391.

1098   DAVISON, James D.; KNUDSEN, Dean D.; LERCH, Stephen H. "Involvement in
        family, religion, education, work, and politics", *Sociological Focus* 16(1), jan 83 : 13-36.
        [USA]

1099   DIDORČUK, L. S. "Metodologičeskie problemy issledovanija struktury obščestvennyh
        otnošenij v svete rešenij XXVI s'ezda KPSS" (Methodological problems of research
        on the social relations structure in the light of the XXVIth Congress of the CPSU
        decisions), *Vestnik Harkovskogo Universiteta* 233, 82 : 3-7. [USSR]

1100   DIMITRIJEVIĆ, Vojin. *Terorizam* (Terrorism). Beograd, Radnička Štampa, 82, 272 p.

1101   DONOGHUE, Edwin. *The illusion of the absolute: a critical study of the Marxian concept of alienation
        and its Hegelian foundation*. Göteborg, Sociologiska Institutionen, Göteborgs Universitet,
        82, ii-201 p.

1102   DUMA, Andrzej. *Świadomość demokracji w społeczeństwie polskim* (Consciousness of democracy
        in the Polisy society). Warszawa, Wydawnictwa Radia i Telewizji, 83, 173 p.

1103   DZIĘCIELSKA-MACHNIKOWSKA, Stefania. "Problemy świadomości społecznej w
        Polsce" (Problems of social consciousness in Poland), *Nowe Drogi* 413(10), 83 : 143-152.

1104   FERRAROTTI, Franco. "Riflessioni preliminari su 'cinema, letteratura e contesto sociale'"
        (Preliminary reflections on cinema, literature and social protest), *Critica sociologica* 67,
        83 : 147-157.

1105   FLIS, Andrzej. "Karol Marks a teoria alienacji" (Marx and the theory of alienation),
        Studia Socjologiczne 89(2), 83 : 65-84.

1106   FUSE, Toyomasa. "Cultural values and social behaviour of the Japanese: a comparative
        analysis", *Cultures et développement* 14(2-3), 82 : 227-257.

1107   GEAMANU, Grigore. "Origine et causes du terrorisme", *Revue roumaine des Sciences sociales.
        Série des Sciences juridiques* 27(2), dec 83 : 133-137.

1108   GIBBONS, Don C. "Deviance, crime, and the greying of America", *Sociological Perspectives*
        26(3), jul 83 : 235-252.

1109   GIORDANO, Peggy C. "Sanctioning the high-status deviant: an attributional analysis",
        Social Psychology Quarterly 46(4), dec 83 : 329-342.

1110   GREENWOOD, John D. "On the relation between laboratory experiments and social
        behaviour: causal explanation and generalization", *Journal for the Theory of Social Behaviour*
        12(3), oct 82 : 225-250.

1111   HAMILTON, Lawrence C.; HAMILTON, James D. "Dynamics of terrorism", *International
        Studies Quarterly* 27(1), mar 83 : 39-54.

1112 HANDMAN, Marie-Elisabeth. *La violence et la ruse: hommes et femmes dans un village grec.* Aix-en-Provence, Edisud, 83, 209 p.

1113 HANKISS, Elemér; [et al.]. *Interactions between socioeconomic factors, ways of life, and value orientations.* Budapest, Hungarian Academy of Sciences, Institute of Sociology, 83, 159 p.

1114 HATANAKA, Munekazu. "Shakai funsō no dōtai ni kansuru kisoteki kenkyū: Nagoyashi ni okeru Shinkansen kogai hantai undo no jirei o chushin toshite" (A basic study of dynamics in social conflicts: centering on the Nagoya Movement against noise pollution generated by the New Tokaido Train Lines), *Okinawa Kirisutokyo tanki daigaku kiyo* 11, 83 : 33-45.

1115 HELLSBRUNN, Richard. *Pathologie de la violence: pour une stratégie thérapeutique.* Paris, Éditions Réseaux, 82, 195 p.

1116 HOMANS, George C. "Steps to a theory of social behaviour: an autobiographical account", *Theory and Society* 12(1), jan 83 : 1-45.

1117 HORN, Michael. *Sozialpsychologie des Terrorismus* (Social psychology of terrorism). Frankfurt-am-Main-New York, NY, Campus Verlag, 82, 196 p. [Germany FR]

1118 IKEDA, Yoshisuke. "Shakaigaku ni okeru shakai kankeiron no tenkai" (The history of sociological studies on social relationship), *Ohtani gakuho* 63(1), 83 : 1-13.

1119 JANSEN, Harrie. "Klasse- en sekse-specificiteit in de waardering van conformiteit en selfbepaling. Enkele ervaringen met de schaal van Kohn" (Class and sex specificity in evaluation of conformity and self-management. Some experiments with the Kohn's scale), *Sociologische Gids* 30(1), jan-feb 83 : 37-44. [Netherlands]

1120 JASIEWICZ, Krzysztof. "Evolution de la conscience sociale (1979-1981)", *Temps modernes* 40(445-446), sep 83 : 232-240.

1121 JOHNSON, Jeffrey C.; MILLER, Marc L. "Deviant social positions in small groups: the relation between role and individual", *Social Networks* 5(1), mar 83 : 51-69.

1122 JONES, Gareth R. "Organizational socialization as information processing activity: a life history analysis", *Human Organization* 42(4), 83 : 314-320.

1123 KIRK, Richard M. "Political terrorism and the size of government: a positive institutional analysis of violent political activity", *Public Choice* 40(1), 83 : 41-52.

1124 KWAŚNIEWSKI, Jerzy. "Determinanty postaw wobec dewiacji. 'Rekapitulacja wyników polskich badań empirycznych'" (Determinants of attitudes to deviation. 'Recapitulation of the results of Polish empirical studies'), *Studia Socjologiczne* 88(1), 83 : 147-171.

1125 LE BOT, Yvon. "Violence sociale: sens ou non-sens. Sur quelques interprétations de la violence dans les sociétés latino-américaines", *Homme et Société* 67-68, jan-jun 83 : 59-74.

1126 LITTLE, Craig B. *Understanding deviance and control: theory, research, and social policy.* Itasca, IL, F. E. Peacock Publishers, 83, xiv-285 p.

1127 LONG, Sharon K.; WITTE, Anne D.; KARR, Patrice. "Family violence: a microeconomic approach", *Social Science Research* 12(4), dec 83 : 363-392.

1128 MARIE, Alain. "Marginalité et conditions sociales du prolétariat urbain en Afrique. Les approches du concept de marginalité et son évaluation critique", *Cahiers d'Études africaines* 21(1-3), 81 : 347-374.

1129 MARKOWSKI, Daniel. "Polityczne i strukturalne determinanty kryzysu świadomości społecznej w Polsce" (Political and structural determinants of the social consciousness crisis in Poland), *Problemy Marksizmu-Leninizmu* 3-4, 83 : 15-29.

1130 MARTIN, Harry J.; GREENSTEIN, Theodore N. "Individual differences in status generalization: effects of need for social approval, anticipated interpersonal contact, and instrumental task abilities", *Journal of Personality and Social Psychology* 45(3), sep 83 : 641-662.

1131 MAUGER, Gérard; FOSSÉ-POLIAK, Claude. "Les loubards", *Actes de la Recherche en Sciences sociales* 50, nov 83 : 49-67. [résumés en anglais et en allemand]

1132 MCLUNG LEE, Alfred. "Terrorism's social-historical context in Northern Ireland", *Research in Social Movements, Conflicts and Change* (5), 83 : 99-131.

1133 MILLS, Edgar W. Jr. "Sociological ambivalence and social order: the constructive uses of normative dissonance", *Sociology and Social Research* 67(3), apr 83 : 279-287.

1134 MIYAJIMA, Takashi. *Gendai shakai ishikiron* (Contemporary social consciousness). Tokyo, Nihon Hyōronsha, 83, 249 p.

1135 MONTI, Daniel J.; [ed.]. *Impact of desegregation.* San Francisco, CA, Jossey-Bass, 82, 108 p. [USA]

1136 MOURA, Clóvis. *Brasil: raízes do protesto negro* (Brazil: roots of Black protest). São Paulo, Global Editora, 83, 173 p.

1137 MOWON-BROWNE, Edward. "Terrorism in France", *Conflict Studies* (144), 83 : 1-26.

1138 MUNČAEV, R. "O metodologičeskom principe opredeljaemosti obščestvennogo soznanija obščestvennym bytiem" (On the methodological principle of determination of the social consciousness of social existence), *Problemy Filosofii* 55, 82 : 32-36.

1139   NARSKIJ, I. S. *Otčuždenie intrud: po stranicam proizvedenij K. Marksa* (Alienation and labour in the K. Marx's works). Moskva, Mysl', 83, 114 p.
1140   OBRADOVIĆ, Josip; GARDUN, Jasna. "Socializacija: jedan pokušaj integrativnog pristupa" (Socialization: an effort in integrated approach), *Sociologija* 24(1), 82 : 57-68.
1141   OISHI, Yutaka. "Shakai undo toshiteno terorizumu" (Terrorism as social movement), *Keio gijuku daigaku shinbun kenkyujo nenpo* 21, 83 : 45-64.
1142   ORCUTT, James D. *Analyzing deviance.* Homewood IL, Dorsey Press, 83, xi-416 p.
1143   ORRU, Marco. "The ethics of anomie: Jean Marie Guyau and Emile Durkheim", *British Journal of Sociology* 34(4), dec 83 : 499-518.
1144   ORRU, Marco. "L'anomie come concetto morale: Jean Marie Guyau ed Émile Durkheim" (Anomie as moral concept: Jean Marie Guyau and Émile Durkheim), *Rassegna italiana di Sociologia* 24(3), jul-sep 83 : 429-451.
1145   ORZECHOWSKI, Marian. "Świadomość historyczna jako płaszczyzna walki ideologicznej i politycznej" (Historical consciousness as an area of the ideological and political struggle), *Edukacja polityczna* 1, 82 : 13-33.
1146   PICAT, Jean. *Violences meurtrières et sexuelles: essai d'approche psychopathologique.* Paris, Presses Universitaires de France, 82, 123 p.
1147   PRASAD, R. C. "Electoral and political violence", *Indian Journal of Politics* 15(3), dec 81 : 1-13. [India]
1148   QUINNEY, Richard. *Social existence: metaphysics, marxism and the social sciences.* Beverly Hills, CA, Sage Publications, 82, 193 p.
1149   RAUFER, Xavier. *Sur la violence sociale.* Paris, Alésia, 83, 224 p. [France]
1150   REIMANIS, Gunars. "Anomie and interest in education", *Journal of Social Psychology* 119(2), apr 83 : 243-248.
1151   ROES, F. L. "Laws to explain any social behaviour", *Sociologia internationalis* 21(1-2), 83 : 7-16.
1152   ROSENBERG, M. Michael; STEBBINS, Robert A.; TUROWETZ, Allan; [eds.]. *The sociology of deviance.* New York, St. Martin's Press, 82, ix-369 p.
1153   ROTTGER-HOGAN, Elizabeth. "Insurrection...or ostracism: a study of the Santal rebellion of 1855", *Contributions to Indian Sociology* 16(1), jan-jun 82 : 79-96. [India]
1154   RUS, Veljko. "Funkcionalna, socijalna i ekosistemska integracija" (Functional, social, and ecosystemic integration), *Sociologija* 25(2-3), 83 : 185-208. [Yugoslavia]
1155   SADOWSKI, Jerzy Z. "Świadomość społeczna — świadomość polityczna — świadomość historyczna. Próba ujęcia modelowego" (Social consciousness — political consciousness — historical consciousness: an attempt at the model approach), *Edukacja polityczna* 1, 82 : 125-144.
1156   SANDLER, Todd; [et al.]. "A theoretical analysis of transnational terrorism", *American Political Science Review* 77(1), mar 83 : 36-53.
1157   SCHERMER, Klaas; WIJN, Marcel. *Vergaderen en onderhandelen* (To meet and to bargain). Alphen aan den Rijn, Samsom, 83, 183 p.
1158   SEEMAN, Melvin. "Alienation motifs in contemporary theorizing: the hidden continuity of the classic themes", *Social Psychology Quarterly* 46(3), sep 83 : 171-184.
1159   SEEMAN, Melvin; ANDERSON, Carolyn S. "Alienation and alcohol: the role of work, mastery, and community in drinking behavior", *American Sociological Review* 48(1), feb 83 : 60-77.
1160   SERGEJEV, Dimitrije. "Procesi društvene integracije i pitanja sistematizacije ljudskog razvoja" (Social integration processes and questions of systematization of human development), *Sociologija* 25(2-3), 83 : 209-220. [Yugoslavia]
1161   SHEPHERD, John C. "Conflict in patterns of socialization: the role of the classroom music teacher", *Canadian Review of Sociology and Anthropology* 20(1), feb 83 : 22-43.
1162   SILVA, Ludovico. *La alienación como sistema: la teoría de la alienación en la obra de Marx* (Alienation as a system: the theory of alienation in Marx's works). Caracas, Alfadil Ediciones, 83, 389 p.
1163   SOLIVETTI, Luigi M. "Violenza e controllo sociale: il problema della antisocialità diffusa" (Violence and social control: the problem of latent antisocial behaviour), *Revue internationale de Sociologie* 18(1-2-3), apr-aug-sep 82 : 315-322.
1164   STEPANOV, I. G. "Kategorija 'obščestvennye otnošenija' i eě mesto v istoričeskom materializme" (The 'social relations' category and its place in historical materialism), *Naučnye Trudy (Tjumenskij Universitet)* 91, 81 : 15-26.
1165   SUGIMOTO, Atsuo. "Sport shūdan ni okeru itsudatsu kodo no bunseki model" (The analysis model of deviant behavior in sport groups), *Hiroshima taiikugaku kenkyu* 9, 83 : 1-10.
1166   SUPEK, Rudi. "Integracijski i dezintegracijski procesi u društvu 'prelaznog perioda'" (Integration and disintegration processes in the social period of transition), *Sociologija* 25(2-3), 83 : 145-183. [Yugoslavia]

1167 SVALASTOGA, Kaara. "Integration: a seven nation comparison", *International Journal of Comparative Sociology (Leiden)* 23(3-4), sep-dec 82 : 190-203.

1168 TAKAHARA, Masaoki. "Itsudatsu no tōgōriron no tameno ichi-kōsatsu" (A study for the integrated theory on deviance), *Kagoshima joshi-daigaku kenkyu kiyo* 4(1), 83 : 57-75.

1169 TELUNC, A. A. "Problema istoričeskoj zakonomernosti i social'nogo poznanija v 'Filosofii istorii' G. Rikkerta" (The historical law and social consciousness problem in the H. Rickert's 'Philosophy of history'), *Voprosy Filosofii (Ėrevan)* (2), 82 : 45-56.

1170 THOITS, Peggy A. "Multiple identities and psychological well-being: a reformulation and test of the social isolation hypothesis", *American Sociological Review* 48(2), apr 83 : 174-187.

1171 TITTENBRUN, Jacek. *Interakcjonizm we współczesnej socjologii amerykańskiej* (Interactionism in contemporary American sociology). Poznań, Wydawnictwo Naukowe Uniwersytetu im. Adama Mickiewicza, 83, 277 p.

1172 TITTENBRUN, Jacek. "Życie społeczne jako teatr" (Social life as a theatre), *Przegląd Humanistyczny* 210(3), 83 : 29-40.

1173 VAN DER WESTHUIZEN, J.; [ed.]. *Crimes of violence in South Africa.* Pretoria, University of South Africa, 82, 323 p.

1174 VAN RAALTEN, F. *Eenzaamheid & communicatie* (Alienation and communication). Bossum, Wereldvenster, 82, 167 p.

1175 WARBRICK, Colin. "The European Convention on human rights and the prevention of terrorism", *International and Comparative Law Quarterly* 32(1), jan 83 : 82-119.

1176 WAY, Frank; BURT, Barbara J. "Religious marginality and the free exercise clause", *American Political Science Review* 77(3), sep 83 : 652-665. [USA]

1177 WEIMANN, Gabriel. "On the importance of marginality: one more step into the two-step flow of communication", *American Sociological Review* 47(6), dec 82 : 764-773.

1178 WEINRICH, Peter H. *Social protest from the left in Canada, 1870-1970.* Toronto-Buffalo, University of Toronto Press, 82, xxiii-627 p.

1179 WIGGINS, James A. "Family violence as a case of interpersonal aggression: a situational analysis", *Social Forces* 62(1), sep 83 : 102-123.

1180 WIJGAERTS, Dany. "Politiek terrorisme en massa-media: een causaal verband?" (Political terrorism and mass media: a causal relation?), *Mens en Maatschappij* 58(2), mai 83 : 167-180.

1181 WILLIAMS, Thomas Rhys. *Socialization.* Englewood Cliffs, NJ, Prentice-Hall, 83, xx-476 p.

1182 YARKIN-LEVIN, Kerry. "Anticipated interaction, attribution, and social interaction", *Social Psychology Quarterly* 46(4), dec 83 : 302-311.

1183 ZAKRZEWSKI, Stanisław. "Wpływ polityki społecznej na zmiany w świadomości mięszkańców wsi" (Impact of social policies on social consciousness of rural population), *Ruch prawniczy, ekonomiczny i socjologiczny* 45(2), 83 : 254-263.

13200 CUSTOMS. TRADITIONS
COUTUMES. TRADITIONS

1184 "Fêtes (Les) dans le monde hindou", *Homme* 22(3), sep 82 : 5-120. [with contributions by Marc GABORTEAU, Olivier HERRENSCHMIDT, Gérard TOFFIN, Véronique BOUILLIER, Michel VERDON]

1185 "Quotidien et imaginaire de la cuisine", *Temps modernes* 39(438), jan 83 : 1250-1359. [with contributions by Françoise KERLEROUX, Michèle FERRAND, Sonia DAYAN BERZBRUN, Maîté CLAVEL]

1186 ARISUE, Ken. "Minzoku no toshika: Minzoku no sai-seisan" (Urbanization of folk culture: reproduction of Japanese folk culture), *Rekishi koron* 92, 83 : 46-51.

1187 ARISUE, Ken. "Toshi sairei no jusoteki kozo: Tsukuda-Tsukishima no saishi soshiki no jirei kenkyu" (Multi-layered structure of the urban festival: a case study of ritual organization), *Shakaigaku hyoron* 33(4), 83 : 37-62. [Japan]

1188 BAHLOUL, Joëlle. "Nourritures de l'altérité: le double langage des juifs algériens en France", *Annales-Économies, Sociétés, Civilisations* 38(2), apr 83 : 325-340. [résumé en anglais]

1189 BEJARANO, Ramón César. *Caraí vosá: elementos para el estudio del folklore paraguayo* (Caraí vosá: materials for the study of Paraguayan folklore). Asunción, Editorial Toledo, 82, rev., 144 p.

1190 CALHOUN, Craig Jackson. "The radicalism of tradition: community strength or venerable disguise and borrowed language?", *American Journal of Sociology* 88(5), mar 83 : 886-914.

1191 CHARTIER, Roger. "La culture populaire en question", *H Histoire* 8, apr-jun 81 : 85-96.

1192 CURCIO, Anna Maria. "Moda e fenomeno culturale" (Fashion and cultural phenomenon), *Revue internationale de Sociologie* 18(1-2-3), apr-aug-sep 82 : 136-144.

1193 DELAPORTE, Yves. "Teddies, rockers, punks et cie: quelques codes vestimentaires urbains", *Homme* 22(4), dec 82 : 49-62. [France] [résumé en anglais]

1194   GLYNN, Prudence. *Skin to skin: eroticism in dress*. New York, NY, Oxford University
        Press, 82, 157-24 p.
1195   HEERS, Jacques. *Fêtes des fous et carnavals*. Paris, Fayard, 83, 315 p.
1196   HOFFMANN, Márta D.; SZILÁGYI, Erzsébet; [eds.]. *Ünnepek a mai magyar társadalomban*
        (Feasts in present Hungarian society). Budapest, Tömegkommunikációs Kutatóközpont,
        82, 194 p.
1197   KLANICZAY, Gábor; NAGY, Katalin S.; [eds.]. *Divatszociológia* (Fashion sociology).
        Budapest, Tömegkommunikációs Kutatóközpont, 82, 172p; 247 p. [2 vols.]
1198   MACIOTI, Maria I. "La festa della SS. Trinità a Vallepietra" (The feast of the Holy
        Trinity in Vallepietra), *Critica sociologica* 68, 83-84 : 170-173. [Italy]
1199   MATSUDAIRA, Makoto. *Matsuri no bunka: toshi ga tsukuru seikatsu bunka no katashi* (Culture
        of the feasts in Japan: the forms of life culture in Japanese cities). Tokyo, Yuhikaku,
        83, 309 p.
1200   MERFEA, Mihai. "La culture populaire et la valorisation critique des traditions et des
        coutumes", *Revue roumaine des sciences sociales. Série de sociologie* 27(2), 83 : 115-126.
        [Romania]
1201   MEYER, Fernand. "Pratiques alimentaires et diététique médicale en milieu tibétain",
        Social Science Information 22(2), 83 : 283-309.
1202   MURCOTT, Anne; [ed.]. *The sociology of food and eating: essays on the sociological significance of
        food*. Aldershot, Hants, Gower, 83, viii-195 p.
1203   NUMATA, Kenya. "'Ryuko'-ron" (On 'fashion'), *Momoyama gakuin daigaku shakaigaku
        ronshu* 17(1), 83 : 27-59.
1204   SUZUKI, Masataka. "Un'nansho minsoku note" (Notes on the folklore in Yunnan Province
        of China), *Kikan jinruigaku* 14(3), 83 : 202-252.
1205   TANAKA, Shigeyoshi; [et al.]. "Hirosaki Neputa-matsuri no kenkyu" (A study of urban
        festival in Hirosaki city), *Hirosaki daigaku jinbungakubu bunkei ronso* 18(3), 83 : 33-72. [Japan]
1206   TERADA, Atsuhiro. "Kako shokuhin to gaishoku no riyo ga kazoku kankei ni oyobosu
        eikyo" (The impact of processed food and fast food on family relationships), *Nihon daigaku
        Mishima gakuen seikatsukagaku kenkyujo hokoku* 6, 83 : 87-96.
1207   TURIM, Maureen. "Fashion shapes: film, the fashion industry and the image of women",
        Socialist Review 13(71), oct 83 : 79-96.
1208   YANAGI, Yōko. *Fashion-ka shakaishi* (History of fashion). Tokyo, Gyosei, 83, 345 p.
1209   ZABARAH, Mohammed Ahmad. *Yemen, traditionalism vs. modernity*. New York, NY,
        Praeger, 82, xxi-154 p.

        **13300   ETHICS. MORALS
                   ÉTHIQUE. MORALE**

1210   ABBOTT, Andrew. "Professional ethics", *American Journal of Sociology* 88(5), mar 83 : 855-885.
1211   ANTES, Peter. *Ethik und Politik im Islam* (Ethics and politics in Islam). Stuttgart, W. Kohl-
        hammer, 82, 112 p.
1212   ARHANGEL'SKIJ, L. M. "Sociologičeskie issledovanija nravstvennogo razvitija ličnosti"
        (Sociological research on the personality moral development), *Sociologičeskie Issledovanija
        (Moskva)* (1), 83 : 197-201.
1213   BERGHAUS, Margot. "Moral, Erziehung, gerechte Gesellschaft. Soziologische Anmerkungen
        zu Piaget, Kohlberg und der 'Moral-Education' -Bewegung" (Ethics, education, fair
        society. Sociological comments on Piaget, Kohlberg and the 'Moral-Education' move-
        ment), *Kölner Zeitschrift für Soziologie und Sozialpsychologie* 35(1), mar 83 : 121-132.
1214   BRODY, Baruch A. *Ethics and its applications*. New York, NY, Harcourt Brace Jovanovich,
        83, vii-200 p. [Edited by Robert J. FOGELIN]
1215   COMMERS, Ronald. *De overbodigheid en de noodzakelijkheid van de moraal* (The inutility and
        necessity of morals). Bussum, Wereldvenster, 83, x-275 p.
1216   DASZKOWSKI, Julian. "Społeczna psychologia odpowiedzialności" (Social psychology of
        responsibility), *Studia Socjologiczne* 89(2), 83 : 291-307.
1217   DOWD, James J.; LAROSSA, Ralph. "Primary group contact and elderly morale: an
        exchange power analysis", *Sociology and Social Research* 66(2), jan 82 : 184-197.
1218   FEDOTOVA, A. V. "Social'naja otvetstvennost' kak faktor naučnoj dejatel'nosti sovetskogo
        učenogo" (Social responsibility as a factor of the Soviet scientist's scientific activity),
        Problemy Filosofii 56, 82 : 108-114.
1219   FLANDRIN, Jean-Louis. *Un temps pour embrasser: aux origines de la morale sexuelle occidentale,
        VIe-XIe siècles*. Paris, Éditions du Seuil, 83, 249 p.
1220   FRIEDRICHS, Robert W. "Ethics in social research. A review essay", *Sociological Quarterly*
        24(3), sum 83 : 453-462.

1221   GEORGESCU, Florin. "Specificul moralei religioase" (Specific features of religious morals), *Revista de filozofie* 29(6), dec 82 : 592-596.

1222   GORSUCH, Richard L.; ORTBERG, John. "Moral obligation and attitudes: their relation to behavioral intentions", *Journal of Personality and Social Psychology* 44(5), mai 83 : 1025-1028.

1223   HOLZER, Jerzy Z.; MIJAKOWSKA, Jadwiga. "Zróżnicowanie umieralności według płci w europejskich krajach socjalistycznych" (Differentiation of morality by sex in European socialist countries), *Studia demograficzne* 20(4), 82 : 3-25.

1224   HUSZÁR, Tibor. *Erkölcs és társadalom. Erkölcsiség és erkölcsösség* (Ethics and society. Morality and moral behaviour). Budapest, Kossuth Kiadó, 83, 528 p.

1225   KOYANO, Wataru. "Morale ni taisuru shakaiteki katsudo no eikyo: Katsudo riron to ridatsu riron no kensho" (Effect of social activity upon morals in the elderly), *Shakai ronengaku* 17, 83 : 36-49.

1226   KUDINOVA, A. A. "Social'naja otvetstvennost' — harakternaja černa socialisticeskoj ličnosti" (Social responsibility is a characteristic feature of the socialist personality), *Problemy Filosofii* 55, 82 : 85-89.

1227   LAMO DE ESPINOSA, E.; CARABAÑA MORALES, J. "Vicios privados y virtudes públicas. Consideraciones sobre ética, marginación social y derecho penal" (Private vices and public virtues. Considerations on ethics, social marginality and penal law), *Sistema* (53), mar 83 : 3-28.

1228   LONG, Gary L.; DORN, Dean S. "Sociologist' attitudes toward ethical issues: the management of an impression", *Sociology and Social Research* 67(3), apr 83 : 288-300.

1229   LOVIBOND, Sabina. *Realism and imagination in ethics.* Minneapolis, MN, University of Minnesota Press, 83, 238 p.

1230   MICHEL, Patrick. "Morale et société en Pologne: le discours de l'Eglise", *Revue d'Études comparatives Est-Ouest* 14(1), mar 83 : 121-132.

1231   MILJOVSKI, Kiril. "Privreda i etika" (Economy and ethics), *Sociologija* 25(1), 83 : 93-99. [Yugoslavia]

1232   MUNRO, Jocelyn. "Religion, age, sex and moral issues: some relationships", *Political Science* 34(2), dec 82 : 214-220. [New Zealand]

1233   NATSUKARI, Yasuo. "Durkheim no dotokuteki kojinshugi shiso" (A study of moral individualism of E. Durkheim), *Shakaigaku-shi kenkyu* 5, 83 : 12-30.

1234   PAŠAEV, S. Š. "Rol' nauki v nravstvennom vospitanii studenčeskoj molodeži" (Role of the science in the student youth moral education), *Naučnye Doklady vysšej Školy. Naučnyj Kommunizma* (4), 82 : 74-80.

1235   POPESCU, Vasile. "Morala socialistă şi valoarea omului" (Socialist morals and human value), *Revista de filozofie* 30(4), aug 83 : 293-299.

1236   REAMER, Frederic G. *Ethical dilemmas in social service.* New York, NY, Columbia University Press, 82, xiii-280 p.

1237   REEDER, Glenn D.; SPORES, John M. "The attribution of morality", *Journal of Personality and Social Psychology* 44(4), apr 83 : 736-745.

1238   SIEGAL, Michael. *Fairness in children: a social-cognitive approach to the study of moral development.* London-New York, NY, Academic Press, 82, 207 p.

1239   ŠIHARDINA, T. N. "Évoljucija cennostej buržuaznogo moral'nogo soznanija i koncepcija 'vospitanija dlja vyživanija'" (Evolution of bourgeois moral consciousness values and conception of 'education for survival'), *in:* Sovremennaja civilizacija i moral'nye cennosti. Moskva, 1982 : 42-52.

1240   SNOEYENBOS, Milton; ALMEDER, Robert; HUMBER, James; [eds.]. *Business ethics: corporate values and society.* Buffalo, NY, Prometheus Books, 83, 502 p.

1241   SOUTO, Claudio. "Ethisches Faktum und soziologische Theorie" (Ethical fact and sociological theory), *Archiv für Rechts- und Sozialphilosophie* 68(4), 82 : 482-502.

1242   SVARCMAN, K. A. *Sovremennaja buržuaznaja ètika: illjuzii i real'nost'* (Contemporary bourgeois ethics: illusions and reality). Moskva, Mysl', 83, 215 p.

1243   TOLSTOVA, O. I.; STORIŽKO, A. I. "Nravstvennaja otvetstvennost' učenogo" (The scientist's moral responsibility), *Problemy Filosofii* 56, 82 : 114-122.

1244   TORNEY, Judith Purta; SCHWILLE, John. "The trend toward more directive moral education in the United States", *International Journal of Political Education* 6(2), aug 83 : 101-111.

1245   VAUGHAN, Judith. *Sociality, ethics, and social change: a critical appraisal of Reinhold Niebuhr's ethic in the light of Rosemary Radford Ruether's works.* Lanham, MD, University Press of America, 83, vii-220 p.

1246   YOSHIDA, Mitsukuni; TANAKA, Ikkō; SESOKO, Tsune; [eds.]. *The compact culture: the ethos of Japanese life.* Hiroshima, Toyo Kogyo Co., 82, 118 p.

13400   LAW. REGULATION
LOI. RÉGLEMENTATION

1247   "Débat: les noyés du lac Lagoda?'', *Déviance et Société* 7(2), jun 83 : 153-191. [droit pénal et justice criminelle en France; with contributions by André VARINARD, Ursula CASSANI, Françoise TULKENS]

1248   "Perspectives on regulation: law, discretion and bureaucratic behavior'', *Law and Policy Quarterly* 5(1), jan 83 : 3-152. [with contributions by Barry B. BOYER, Keith HAWKINS, Cento G. VELJANOVSKI, D. R. HARRIS, Kenneth VOGEL]

1249   "Réflexions sur le droit'', *Esprit* (3), mar 83 : 20-90. [with contributions by Luc FERRY, Alain RENAUT, Paul THIBAUD]

1250   "Special issue: psychology and law'', *Law and Society Review* 17(1), 82 : 3-228. [USA] [with contributions by Shari SEIDMAN DIAMOND, Tom R. TYLER, Renee WEBER, Martin S. GREENBERG, Benjamin KLEINMUNTZ, Julian J. SZUCKO, David A. SCHUM, Anne W. MARTIN]

1251   ALEKSEEV, S. S. "Pravo: metodologičeskie podhody k issledovaniju'' (Law: methodological approach of research), *Voprosy Filosofii* 36(3), 83 : 116-119.

1252   AUBERT, Vilhelm. *Rettssosiologi* (Sociology of law). Oslo, Universitetsforlaget, 82, 171 p.

1253   BELLEY, Jean-Guy. "Les sociologues, les juristes et la sociologie du droit'', *Recherches sociographiques* 24(2), mai-aug 83 : 263-282.

1254   BENNEY, Mark. "Gramsci on law, morality, and power'', *International Journal of the Sociology of Law* 11(2), mai 83 : 191-208.

1255   BUTLER, Kenneth G. "Esquisse d'une théorie de la justice et du bon droit. Dans le cadre de la théorie des systèmes généraux'', *Diogène* 122, apr-jun 83 : 111-129.

1256   CARBONNIER, Jean; TERRÉ, François. "Sociologie juridique'', *Année sociologique* 32, 82 : 361-378. [Compte rendu bibliographique]

1257   CARBONNIER, Jean; TERRE, François. "Sociologic juridique'', *Année sociologique* 33, 83 : 509-518. [Compte rendu bibliographique]

1258   CHIBA, Masaji. "Hogaku ni okeru kanshuho no gainen'' (The concept of customary law in jurisprudence), *Kokuritsu minzokugaku hakubutsukan kenkyu hokoku* 8(1), 83 : 1-17.

1259   CHOI, Chong-Ko. "The traditional and Western law in Korea: a historical analysis'', *Social Science Journal (Seoul)* 9, 82 : 96-120.

1260   DAMICO, Alfonso J. "The sociology of justice: Kohlberg and Milgram'', *Political Theory* 10(3), aug 82 : 409-434.

1261   GEISTLINGER, Michael. "Zur Traditionalität sozialistischer Rechtsquellen'' (On the traditional character of the sources of socialist law), *Recht in Ost und West* 27(4), jul 83 : 137-146.

1262   GOFF, Edwin L. "Justice as fairness: the practice of social science in a Rawlsian model'', *Social Research* 50(1), 83 : 81-97.

1263   HASSLER, Théo. "La solidarité familiale confrontée aux obligations de collaborer à la justice pénale'', *Revue de Science criminelle et de Droit pénal comparé* (3), sep 83 : 437-461.

1264   HEYNITZ, Jobst v. "Überwindung des Positivismus im Recht'' (Victory of positivism in law), *Fragen der Freiheit* 160, 83 : 18-44.

1265   HIDAY, Virginia Aldige. "Sociology of mental health law'', *Sociology and Social Research* 67(2), jan 83 : 111-128. [USA]

1266   ITSCHERENSKA, Ilse; NOROUZI, David. "Zur Islamisierung des iranischen Rechtswesens'' (On the islamization of the Iranian legal system), *Staat und Recht* 32(9), 83 : 705-712.

1267   KAZMER, M. É. *Sociologičeskie napravlenie v russkoj dorevoljucionnoj pravovoj mysli* (The sociological direction in the Russian pre-revolutionary legal thought). Riga, Zinatne, 83, 130 p.

1268   KILLIAS, Martin. "Conflits politiques et législation en matière de droit pénal. L'exemple d'une révision partielle du code pénal suisse'', *Déviance et Société* 7(3), sep 83 : 219-236.

1269   KOUDRIAVTSEV, Vladimir. "Le système juridique de la société nouvelle'', *Sciences sociales — Académie des Sciences de l'URSS* (4), 82 : 46-59.

1270   KRONMAN, Anthony T. *Max Weber*. Stanford, CA, Stanford University Press, 83, 214 p. [A profile in legal theory]

1271   LANG, Gerhardus. "Die Idee des Rechts und die soziale Dreigliederung von Kultur, Staat und Wirtschaft'' (The concept of law and the triple chaining of culture, state and economy), *Fragen der Freiheit* 160, 83 : 45-57.

1272   LIN, Xin. "Criminal jurisdiction in international law, and the minimal law of the People's Republic of China'', *Social Sciences in China* 4(2), jun 83 : 155-166.

1273   LOS, Maria. "Law and order in contemporary Poland'', *Canadian Slavonic Papers* 25(3), sep 83 : 392-410. [résumé en français]

1274   LUHMANN, Niklas. "Bürgerliche Rechtssoziologie. Eine Theorie des 18. Jahrhunderts" (Bourgeois sociology of law. An eighteenth century theory), *Archiv für Rechts- und Sozialphilosophie* 69(4), 83 : 431-445.

1275   MATUZOV, N. I. "Pravovaja sistema razvitogo socializma" (Legal system of developed socialism), *Sovetskoe Gosudarstvo i Pravo* 56(1), 83 : 18-26.

1276   NELKEN, David. "Is there a crisis in law and legal ideology?", *Journal of Law and Society* 9(2), wint 82 : 177-189.

1277   NUVOLONE, Pietro. "La legislation pénale italienne récente et la politique criminelle bipolaire", *Revue de Science criminelle et de Droit pénal comparé* (4), dec 82 : 733-740.

1278   O'MALLEY, Michael N. "Interpersonal and intrapersonal justice: the effect of subject and confederate outcomes on evaluations of fairness", *European Journal of Social Psychology* 13(2), apr-jun 83 : 121-128.

1279   O'MALLEY, Pat. *Law, capitalism, and democracy: a sociology of Australian legal order.* Sydney-Boston, MA, Allen and Unwin, 83, viii-204 p.

1280   ROGOVIN, V. Z. Spravedlivost', kak social'no-filosofskaja i social'noěkonomičeskaja kategorija (Justice as a socio-philosophical and socio-economic category). Moskva, 82 : 7-18.

1281   SCHMID, Walter. *Zur sozialen Wirklichkeit des Vertrages* (On the social reality of contracts). Berlin, Duncker und Humblot, 83, 219 p.

1282   SMAUS, Gerlinda. "Les recherches KOL au service de la légitimation du droit pénal", *Déviance et Société* 7(2), jun 83 : 131-152. [Knowledge and Opinion about Law]

1283   SPITZER, Steven. "Marxist perspectives in the sociology of law", *Annual Review of Sociology* (9), 83 : 103-124.

1284   ŠVEKOV, G. V. "Progress i preemstvennost' v prave" (Progress and continuity in law), *Sovetskoe Gosudarstvo i Pravo* 56(1), 83 : 37-46.

1285   TAMMELO, Ilmar. *Zur Philosophie der Gerechtigkeit* (On the philosophy of justice). Frankfurt-am-Main, P. Lang, 82, 149 p.

1286   TIHOMIROV, Ju. "Zakon: social'noe javlenie i sistema kategorij" (The law: social event and categories system), *Obščestvennye Nauki* (1), 83 : 120-132.

1287   TOBOLKIN, P. S. *Social'naja obuslovlennost' ugolovno-pravovyh norm* (Social conditionality of penal and legal norms). Sverdlovsk, Sredno-Ural'skoe Knižnoe Izdatel'stvo, 83, 177 p.

1288   TREVES, Renato. *La sociologia del diritto in Italia oggi* (Sociology of law in Italy today). Napoli, Guida, 82, 71 p.

1289   TULKENS, Françoise. "La réforme du code pénal en Belgigue. Question critique", *Déviance et Société* 7(3), sep 83 : 197-218.

1290   WILLEN, Richard S. "Rationalization of Anglo-legal culture: the testimonial oath", *British Journal of Sociology* 24(1), mar 83 : 109-128.

13500   MAGIC. MYTHOLOGY. RELIGION
MAGIE. MYTHOLOGIE. RELIGION

13510   Religion. Sociology of religion
Religion. Sociologie religieuse

1291   "Religion and politics", *Journal of International Affairs* 36(2), wint 83 : 187-328. [with contributions by Fred HALLIDAY, Tommie Sue MONTGOMERY, Paul BEW, Henry PATTERSON, Steven L. SPIEGEL, Dennis J. DUNN, Abraham ASHKENASI]

1292   "Religione e societa" (Religion and society), *IDOC internazionale* 14(2-3), mar 83 : 11-56. [with contributions by Franco GARELLI, Cesare MARTINO]

1293   "Symposium (A) on religion and politics", *Teaching Political Science* 10(1), aut 82 : 4-61. [with contributions by George W. CAREY, Donald W. BRANDON, John W. COOPER, James V. SCHALL]

1294   AUGÉ, Marc. *Génie du paganisme.* Paris, Gallimard, 82, 336 p.

1295   BECFORD, James A. "The restoration of 'power' to the sociology of religion", *Sociological Analysis* 44(1), spr 83 : 11-31.

1296   BOCK, E. Wilbur; BEEGHLEY, Leonard; MIXON, Anthony J. "Religion, socioeconomic status, and sexual morality: an application of reference group theory", *Sociological Quarterly* 24(4), 83 : 545-559.

1297   BOERO VARGAS, M. "Materiales informales para un análisis sobre el cambio religioso y eclesial en España" (Informal materials for an analysis of religious and ecclesiastical change in Spain), *Documentación Social* (50), jan-mar 83 : 201-214.

1298   BOERO VARGAS, Mario. "Religion y sociedad en Iberoamérica" (Religion and society in Latin America), *Cuadernos hispanoamericanos* (395), mai 83 : 257-289.

1299   BOULARD, Fernand; [ed.]. *Matériaux pour l'histoire religieuse du peuple français: XIXᵉ-XXᵉ siècle. I. Région de Paris, Haute Normandie, Pays de Loire, Centre.* Paris, Éditions EHESS, FNSP, CNRS, 82, 635 p.

1300   CALDAROLA, Carlo; [ed.]. *Religions and societies, Asia and the Middle East.* The Hague-New York, NY-Berlin, Mouton, 82, viii-688 p.

1301   CIPRIANI, Roberto. "Religione e politica. Il caso italiano: la religione diffusa" (Religion and politics. The Italian case: diffused religion), *Studi di Sociologia* 21(3), jul-sep 83 : 245-271.

1302   DERICQUEBOURG, Régis. "Religion et thérapie", *Archives de Sciences sociales des Religions* 55(2), apr-jun 83 : 169-173.

1303   ELIADE, Mircea. *Histoire des croyances et des idées religieuses. III. De Mahomet à l'âge des réformes.* Paris, Payot, 83, 361 p.

1304   FERRAROTTI, Franco. "Religione e rapporti sociali in K. Marx" (Religion and social relations in K. Marx), *Critica sociologica* 65, 83 : 50-59.

1305   IKADO, Fujio. "Gendai shakai to shukyo" (Contemporary Japan and religion), *Shumu jiho* 64, 83 : 18-42.

1306   KONYA, Istvan. "Értékfelfogás a mai protestáns teologiában" (The notion of value in the current Protestant theology), *Acta marxista leninistica. Filozofiai Tanulmányok* 28, 82 : 5-20. [Hungary]

1307   MADURO, Otto. *La cuestión religiosa en el Engels pre-marxista: estudio sobre la génesis de un punto de vista en sociología de las religiones* (The religious question in pre-Marxist Engels: study in the genesis of a point of view in religious sociology). Caracas, Monte Avila Editores, 82, 324 p.

1308   MAEYAMA, Takashi. "Japanese religions in Southern Brazil: change and syncretism", *Tsukuba daigaku Latin American Studies* 6, 83 : 181-238.

1309   MAEYAMA, Takashi; SMITH, Robert J. "Omoto: a Japanese 'New Religion' in Brazil", *Tsukuba daigaku Latin American Studies* 5, 83 : 83-102.

1310   MATTHES, Joachim. "Religion als Thema komparativer Sozialforschung — Erfahrungen mit einem Forschungsprojekt zum religiösen Wandel in einer Entwicklungsgesellschaft" (Religion as a theme of comparative social research. Lessons from a research project in religious evolution in a developing society), *Soziale Welt* 34(1), 83 : 3-21. [Singapore] [résumé en anglais]

1311   MCEDLOV, M. O. *Religija i sovremennost'* (Religion and present day). Moskva, Politizdat, 82, 272 p.

1312   MCGUIRE, Meredith B. "Discovering religious power", *Sociological Analysis* 44(1), spr 83 : 1-10. [see also pp. 11-31 by James A. BECFORD]

1313   MEYER, Charles Robert. *Religious belief in a scientific age.* Chicago, IL, Thomas More Press, 83, 290 p.

1314   MICHEL, Marc. *La théologie aux prises avec la culture: de Schleiermacher à Tillich.* Paris, Cerf, 82, 341 p.

1315   MOL, J. J. *The fixed and the fickle: religion and identity in New Zealand.* Waterloo, ON, Wilfrid Laurier University Press, 82, viii-109 p.

1316   MORGAN, S. Philip. "A research note on religion and morality: are religious people nice people?", *Social Forces* 61(3), mar 83 : 683-692.

1317   NAITO, Kanji. "Durkheim ni okeru shukyogainen no keisei" (On Durkheim's notion of 'Religion'), *Rissho daigaku bungakubu ronso* 77, 83 : 61-82.

1318   PLONGERON, Bernard. *Religion et sociétés en Occident, XVIe-XXe siécles: recherches françaises et tendances internationales, 1973-1981.* Paris, CNRS, Centre de Documentation Sciences Humaines, 82, 319 p.

1319   POULAT, Emile. "Sociologie des religions", *Année sociologique* 33, 83 : 381-431. [Compte rendu bibliographique]

1320   POULAT, Emile. "Sociologie religieuse", *Année sociologique* 32, 82 : 225-284. [Compte rendu bibliographique]

1321   ROBERTSON, Roland; [ed.]. "Talcott Parsons on religion", *Sociological Analysis* 43(4), 82 : 283-373. [with a bibliography of Talcott Parsons' writings on religion: 369-374]

1322   RONDOT, Pierre. "Chrétiens et musulmans au Soudan", *Études* 358(1), jan 83 : 23-38.

1323   SKLEDAR, Nikola. "Kritika marxove kritike religije" (Criticism of Marx's criticism of religion), *Sociologija* 24(4), 82 : 397-407.

1324   UGRINOVIČ, D. "Religija kak social'noe javlenie" (Religion as a social event), *Nauka i Religija* (8), 82 : 17-21.

13520   Magic. Primitive religion
Magie. Religion primitive

1325   "Colloquium on the occult, magic and witchcraft in American culture", *Social Science Information* 22(6), 83 : 941-1004.

1326   BANNERMAN-RICHTER, Gabriel. *The practice of witchcraft in Ghana*. Winona, MN, Apollo Books, 82, iii-149 p.

1327   GATTO TROCCHI, Cecilia. *Magia e medicina popolare in Italia* (Magic and popular medicine in Italy). Roma, Newton Compton Editori, 83, 322 p.

1328   LE ROY LADURIE, Emmanuel. *La sorcière de Jasmin*. Paris, Éditions du Seuil, 83, 281 p.

1329   OFFIONG, Daniel. "The social context of Ibibio witch beliefs", *Africa (London)* 53(3), 83 : 73-82. [Nigeria] [résumé en français]

1330   OFFIONG, Daniel A. "Witchcraft among the Ibibio of Nigeria", *African Studies Review* 26(1), mar 83 : 107-124.

1331   TURNER, Ronny E.; EDGLEY, Charles. "From witchcraft to drugcraft: biochemistry as mythology", *Social Science Journal (Fort Collins)* 20(4), oct 83 : 1-12.

1332   ZAMITI, Khalil. *Sociologie de la folie; introduction au shamanism maghrébin: Sidi Hammadi Soltane el Jaane*. Tunis, Université de Tunis, Centre d'Études et de Recherches Économiques et Sociales, 82, 205 p.

13530   Buddhism. Christianity
Bouddhisme. Christianisme

1333   "Islamisme (L') en effervescence", *Peuples Méditerranéens / Mediterranean Peoples* (21), dec 82 : 3-213. [with contributions by Hassan HANAFI, Krichen ZYED, Tarek EL BECHERI, Abol-Hassan BANI-SADR, Ahmed BEN BELLA]

1334   "L'Islam et ses métamorphoses", *Esprit* (5-6), jun 83 : 161-206. [Pierre-Jean LUIZARD, Amr Helmy IBRAHIM, Jean-François CLEMENT]

1335   "Modern Korean buddhism", *Korea Journal* 23(9), sep 83 : 4-46. [with contributions by Ki-Yong RHI, Ik-jin KOH, Chong-bae MOK, Young-ja LEE, Sun-young PARK]

1336   "Protestantismos y sociedades latinoamericanas" (Protestantism and Latin American societies), *Cristianismo y sociedad* 21(76), 83 : 5-59. [with contributions by Jorge V. PIXLEY, Jean-Pierre BASTIAN, Carlos GARMA NAVARRO, Pedro Enrique CARRASCO, Ely Eser B. CESAR]

1337   AHMED, Akbar S. *Religion and politics in Muslim society*. Cambridge-London-New York, NY-New Rochelle-Melbourne-Sydney, Cambridge University Press, 83, xiii-215 p.

1338   AKHAVI, Shahrough. "The ideology and praxis of shiism in the Iranian revolution", *Comparative Studies in Society and History* 25(2), apr 83 : 195-221.

1339   ANDEZIAN, Sossie. "Pratiques féminines de l'Islam en France", *Archives de Sciences sociales des Religions* 55(1), jan-mar 83 : 53-66.

1340   ASHRAF, Mujeeb. *Muslim attitudes towards British rule and Western culture in India in the first half of the nineteenth century*. Delhi, Idarah-i Adabiyat-i Delli, 82, x-326 p.

1341   AVNI, Haim. *Argentina y la historia de la inmigración judía, 1810-1950* (Argentina and the history of Jewish immigration, 1810-1950). Buenos Aires, Universitaria, 83, 593 p.

1342   AZIZ, Philippe; BRUNEAU, Florence. *Les sectes secrètes de l'Islam: de l'Ordre des assassins aux Frères musulmans*. Paris, R. Laffont, 83, 358 p.

1343   BABALOLA, E. O. *The advent and growth of Islam in West Africa*. Ondo State, Bamgboye and Co. Press, 82, rev. and enl., vii-188 p.

1344   BADRUL, A. H. "Islam v narodnoj Respublike Bangladeš" (Islam in the People's Republic of Bangladesh), *in: Filosofskaja i obščestvennaja mysl' stran Azii i Afriki*. Moskva, 1981 : 142-154.

1345   BARRACLOUGH, Simon. "Managing the challenges of Islamic revival in Malaysia: a regime perspective", *Asian Survey* 23(8), aug 83 : 958-975.

1346   BARRON, Milton L. "The Jews of California's Middle town: ethic vs. secular social services", *Jewish Social Studies* 44(3-4), aut 82 : 239-254.

1347   BERG, Eïnar. *Islam: fra conflikt til dialog* (Islam: from conflict to dialogue). Oslo, Universitetsforlaget, 82, 115-1 p.

1348   BIBBY, Reginald W. "Regionless Christianity: a profile of religion in the Canadian 80s", *Social Indicators Research* 13(1), jul 83 : 1-16.

1349   BONE, David S. "Islam in Malawi", *Journal of Religion in Africa* 13(2), 82 : 126-138.

1350   BOULARES, Habib. *L'Islam: la peur et l'espérance*. Paris, J. C. Lattès, 83, 245 p.

1351   BOUTEILLER, Georges de. "L'arabisation de l'Islam contemporain", *Défense nationale* 39, oct 83 : 77-91.

1352   BRÄKER, Hans. *Der Buddhismus in der Sowjetunion im Spannungsfeld zwischen Vernichtung und Überleben* (Buddhism in Soviet Union in the tense situation between extermination and survival). Köln, Bundesinstitut für Ostwissenschaftliche und Internationale Studien, 82, iv-94 p.

1353   BUSS, Andreas. "Buddhism and national economic activity", *Internationales Asien Forum* 13(3-4), nov 82 : 211-230.

1354   CHAOUAT, Bernard. "Le retour de la diaspora", *Esprit* (4), apr 83 : 16-27. [France]

1355   CHISWICK, Barry R. "The earnings and human capital of American Jews", *Journal of Human Resources* 18(3), sum 83 : 313-336.

1356   COULON, Christian. "Le réseau islamique", *Politique africaine* (9), mar 83 : 68-83.

1357   DE, Amalendu. *Islam in modern India.* Calcutta, Maya Prakashan, 82, 248-iv-vii p.

1358   DHAVAMONY, Mariasusai. *Classical Hinduism.* Roma, Università Gregoriana Editrice, 82, vii-525 p.

1359   DOBBELAERE, K.; BILLIET, J. "Les changements internes au pilier catholique en Flandre: d'un catholicisme d'église à une chrétienté socioculturelle", *Recherches sociologiques* 14(2), 83 : 141-184.

1360   DONOHUE, John J.; ESPOSITO, John L.; [eds.]. *Islam in transition: Muslim perspectives.* New York, NY, Oxford University Press, 82, xii-322 p.

1361   DROULERS, Paul. *Cattolicesimo sociale nei secoli XIX e XX: saggi di storia e sociologia* (Social catholicism in the XXth and XXth centuries: essays on history and sociology). Roma, Edizioni di Storia e Letteratura, 82, xv-539 p.

1362   ERTEL, Rachel. *Le Shtetl: la bourgade juive de Pologne, de la tradition à la modernité.* Paris, Payot, 82, 321 p.

1363   ÉTIENNE, Bruno. "La möelle de la prédication: essai sur le prône politique dans l'Islam contemporain", *Revue française de Science politique* 33(4), aug 83 : 706-720. [résumé en anglais]

1364   FESTIVAL INTERNATIONAL DE LA CULTURE JUIVE. I. *Tradition et modernité dans la pensée juive.* Paris, FICJ, 83, 152 p. [Paris, April 26-May 25, 1981]

1365   FIRBOVSI, Zubaid Ahmed. "Conflict in Islamism and nationalism in Pakistan", *Political Science Review* 21(1), mar 82 : 97-107.

1366   FISHMAN, Aryei. "Judaism and modernization: the case of the religious kibbutzim", *Social Forces* 62(1), sep 83 : 9-31.

1367   GUPTA, Dipankar. "Racism without colour: the catholic ethic and ethnicity in Quebec", *Race and Class* 25(1), sum 83 : 23-44.

1368   HERBERT, Jean. *L'Hindouisme vivant.* Paris, Dervy-Livres, 83, 258 p.

1369   HOFMEYR, J. "Homogeneity and South African Hinduism", *Journal of Religion in Africa* 13(2), 82 : 139-149.

1370   IMTIAZ, Ahmad; [ed.]. *Modernization and social change among Muslims in India.* New Delhi, Manohar, 83, 281 p.

1371   ISRAELI, Raphael; [ed.]. *The crescent in the East: Islam in Asia Major.* London, Curzon Press; Atlantic Highlands, NJ, Humanities Press, 82, 245 p.

1372   KURZ, Lester R. "The politics of heresy", *American Journal of Sociology* 88(6), mai 83 : 1085-1115. ['Modernist controversy' in Roman Catholicism]

1373   KUZNETSOV, Edward. "Jewish emigration from the USSR", *Crossroads* (9), aut 82 : 169-190.

1374   LEWIN, Boleslao. *Cómo fue la inmigración judía en la Argentina* (How Jewish immigration developed in Argentina). Buenos Aires, Plus Ultra, 83, 336 p.

1375   LUBECK, Paul M. "Islamic networks and urban capitalism: an instance of articulation from Northern Nigeria", *Cahiers d'Études africaines* 21(1-3), 81 : 67-78.

1376   MARMUR, Dow. *Beyond survival: reflections on the future of Judaism.* London, Darton Longman and Todd, 82, xviii-218 p.

1377   MEHL, Roger. *Le protestantisme français dans la société actuelle, 1945-1980.* Genève, Labor et Fides, 82, 253 p.

1378   MIDDLETON, John. "One hundred and fifty years of Christianity in a Ghanaian town", *Africa (London)* 53(3), 83 : 2-19. [résumé en français]

1379   MILELLA, Giovanna. "La storia del cristianesimo in Polonia" (History of christianity in Poland), *Sociologia (Roma)* 17(1), jan-apr 83 : 249-270.

1380   MONTEIL, Vincent. *Les musulmans soviétiques.* Paris, Seuil, 82, 253-8 p.

1381   NICOLAS, Guy. "Dieu, Marx et les modèles de la 'Guerre sainte', et du sacrifice au Nigéria", *Archives de Sciences sociales des Religions* 56(1), jul-sep 83 : 123-146.

1382   NORTON, Augustus Richard. "Militant protest and political violence under the banner of Islam", *Armed Forces and Society* 9(1), aut 82 : 3-19.

1383   PANDEY, S. V. "Crisis of identity among the Muslim minority", *Indian Journal of Social Research* 23(1), apr 82 : 80-89.

1384   PANGBORN, Cyrus R. *Zoroastrianism, a beleaguered faith*. New Delhi, Vikas, 82, xvi-162-4 p.
1385   PARASURAM, T. V. *India's Jewish heritage*. New Delhi, Sagar Publications, 82, xi-136-8 p.
1386   PICKEN, Stuart D. B. *Christianity and Japan: meeting, conflict, hope*. Tokyo-New York, NY,
        Kodansha International, 83, 80 p.
1387   ROES, Jan. "A crippled emancipation? The shortfall of Dutch Catholics in scholarship
        and science since the end of the 19th century", *Netherlands Journal of Sociology* 19(1), apr
        83 : 1-28.
1388   RÖSEL, Jakob. *Die Hinduismusthese Max Webers: Folgen eines kolonialen Indienbildes in einem
        relgionssoziologischen Gedankengang* (Max Weber's Hinduism thesis: results of a colonial
        picture of India in a religious-sociological evolving of thought). München, Weltforum,
        82, iv-102 p.
1389   SANSON, Henri. *Laïcité islamique en Algérie*. Paris, Éditions du CNRS, 83, 174 p.
1390   SCHIPPER, Kristofer Marinus. *Le corps taoïste: corps physique, corps social*. Paris, Fayard,
        82, 339 p.
1391   SCHNAPPER, Dominique. "Les jeunes générations juives dans la société française",
        Études 358(3), mar 83 : 323-337.
1392   SHARMA, Keshav Dev. "Hinduism and modernization of India", *Indian Journal of Social
        Research* 24(2), aug 83 : 161-176.
1393   SHINAR, Pessah. *Essai de bibliographie sélective et annotée sur l'Islam maghrébin contemporain:
        Maroc, Algérie, Tunisie, Libye: 1830-1978*. Paris, Éditions du CNRS, 83, xxi-506 p.
1394   SIMAKIN, S. A. "K voprosu o specifike birmanskogo buddizma" (On the specificity of
        Burmese Buddhism), *in: Aktual'nye problemy ideologii i kul'tury stran Vostoka*. Moskva,
        1982 : 91-100.
1395   SNG, Bobby Ewe Kong; YOU, Poh Seng. *Religious trends in Singapore: with special reference
        to Christianity*. Singapore, Graduates' Christian Fellowship, Fellowship of Evangelical
        Students, 82, 86 p.
1396   SPIRO, Melford E. *Buddhism and society: a great tradition and its burmese vicissitudes*. Berkeley, CA-
        London, University of California Press, 82, 2nd expande, xxiv-510 p.
1397   SUBRAMANIAM, V. *Glimpses of Buddhist culture in India including four dance dramas*. New
        Delhi, Ashish, 83, 122 p.
1398   SZLEK MILLER, Stefania. "Catholic personalism and pluralist democracy in Poland",
        Canadian Slavonic Papers 25(3), sep 83 : 425-439. [résumé en français]
1399   THEISSEN, Gerd. *Studien zur Soziologie des Urschristentums* (Studies on sociology of early
        Christian Church). Tübingen, Mohr, 83, vi-364 p.
1400   TRANVOUEZ, Yvon. "Résistance au pouvoir dans le catholicisme. La Quinzaine face à
        l'ACA (1952-1954)", *Archives de Sciences sociales des Religions* 56(1), jul-sep 83 : 3-35. [action
        catholique, France]
1401   WALDENFELS, Hans. *Faszination des Buddhismus: zum christlichbuddhistischen Dialog* (Fascination
        of Buddhism: to Christian Buddhist dialogue). Mainz, M. Grünewald Verlag, 82, 194 p.
1402   WEIL, Shalva. "Symmetry between Christians and Jews in India: the Cnanite Christians
        and the Cochin Jews of Kerala", *Contributions to Indian Sociology* 16(2), jul-dec 82 : 175-196.
1403   YAMAMOTO, J. Isamu. *Beyond Buddhism: a basic introduction to the Buddhist tradition*. Downers
        Grove, IL, Inter-Varsity Press, 82, 141 p.

13540   Churches. Religious communities. Sects
        Églises. Communautés religieuses. Sectes

1404   "Chiese (La) in Cina dopo Mao" (The Church in China after Mao), *IDOC internazionale*
        14(4), apr 83 : 15-38.
1405   "Églises populaires en Amérique centrale" (Popular Churches in Central America), *Estudios
        sociales centroamericanos* 11(33), dec 82 : 9-310. [with contributions by Andrés OPAZO
        BERNALES, Oscar Rolando SIERRA POP, Jorge CACERES PRENDES, Rosa Maria
        POCHET CORONADO, Luis SAMANDU]
1406   "Iglesias (Las) en la crisis centroamericana" (Church in Central American crisis),
        Cristianismo y sociedad 20(4), 82 : 5-88. [with contributions by Tommie Sue MONTGOMERY,
        Enrique DUSSEL, Raúl VIDALES, Arturo ARIAS, Eduardo GALEANO]
1407   "Social and economic bases of communalism", *Social Action* 33(4), dec 83 : 363-452. [Relations
        between religious communities in India; with contributions by Victor D'SOUZA,
        Surindar SURI, Joseph VELACHERRY, Ahmad IMTIAZ]
1408   BALCH, Robert W.; FARNSWORTH, Gwen; WILKINS, Sue. "When the bombs drop:
        reactions to disconfirmed prophecy in a millennial sect", *Sociological Perspectives* 26(2),
        apr 83 : 137-158. [USA]

1409   BAR, Luc-Henri de. *Les communautés confessionnelles du Liban.* Paris, Recherche sur les
        Civilisations, 83, 238 p.
1410   BAYARD, Jean Pierre. *La spiritualité de la Franc-Maçonnerie: de l'ordre initiatique traditionnel
        aux obédiences.* St. Jean de Braye, Éditions Dangles, 82, 430 p.
1411   BOINOT, Patrick. "Sectes religieuses et droit pénal", *Revue de Science criminelle et de Droit
        pénal comparé* (3), sep 83 : 409-436.
1412   BRUCE, Steve. "The persistence of religion: conservative Protestantism in the United
        Kingdom", *Sociological Review* 31(3), aug 83 : 453-470.
1413   DE CARVALHO AZEVEDO, Marcello. "Sécularisation et évangélisation en Amérique
        latine", *Études* 358(2), feb 83 : 255-262.
1414   GELDENHUYS, E. O'Brien. "The dilemma of the Dutch reformed Church in South
        Africa", *Optima* 31(3), 83 : 148-158.
1415   GLÄSSGEN, Heinz. *Katholische Kirche und Rundfunk in der Bundesrepublik Deutschland, 1945-1962*
        (Catholic Church and broadcasting in the Federal Republic of Germany, 1945-1962).
        Berlin, Spiess, 83, 329 p.
1416   GOLDSCHLAGER, Alain. "Quelques objections de Simone Weil à l'Eglise catholique",
        Revue de l'Institut de Sociologie (3-4), 82 : 509-525.
1417   HAMÈS, Constant. "Cheikh Hamallah ou qu'est-ce qu'une confrérie islamique (Tarîqa)?",
        Archives de Sciences sociales des Religions 55(1), jan-mar 83 : 67-83. [Western Africa]
1418   HAMPSHIRE, Annette P.; BECKFORD, James A. "Religious sects and the concept of
        deviance: the Mormons and the Moonies", *British Journal of Sociology* 24(2), jun 83 : 208-229.
1419   HURBON, Laënnec. "Les Témoins de Jéhovah en Guadeloupe", *Temps modernes* 40(447),
        oct 83 : 711-727.
1420   IKOR, Roger. *La tête du poisson: les sectes; un mal de civilisation.* Paris, Albin Michel, 83, 233 p.
1421   KINKEL, R. John. "Roman Catholic Church structure and the issue of women's ordination",
        Social Science Journal (Fort Collins) 20(1), jan 83 : 17-29.
1422   LESBAUPIN, Ivo. "As mudanças na Igreja católica no Brasil, 1960-1982" (The evolution
        of the Catholic Church in Brazil), *Vozes* 76(10), dec 82 : 56-60.
1423   LEVINE, Edward M. "Religious cults: their implications for society and the democratic
        process", *Political Psychology* 3(3-4), wint 82 : 34-49.
1424   MANSUKHANI, Gobind Singh. *Aspects of Sikhism.* New Delhi, Punjabi Writers Cooperative
        Industrial Society, 82, 247 p. [India]
1425   MARTINEZ TERRERO, José. "Igreja e comunicação popular" (Church and popular
        communication), *Vozes* 77(4), mai 83 : 5-17.
1426   MAT-HASQUIN, Michèle. *Les sectes contemporaines.* Bruxelles, Éditions de l'Université de
        Bruxelles, 82, 112 p.
1427   MICHEL, Patrick. "Église et religion en Pologne", *Archives de Sciences sociales des Religions*
        55(2), apr-jun 83 : 149-162.
1428   MONTUCLARD, Maurice. "Limites épistémologiques du système orthodoxe", *Archives de
        Sciences sociales des Religions* 56(1), jul-sep 83 : 107-121.
1429   MORIOKA, Kiyomi. "Kyodan soshiki no bunka no kata" (Religious organizations and
        cultural patterns), *Bungaku* 51(11), 83 : 102-111.
1430   NICOLAS, Guy. "Communautés islamiques et collectivité nationale dans trois États
        d'Afrique occidentale", *Revue française d'Histoire d'Outre-mer* 68(250-253), 81 : 156-194.
1431   RÖSEL, Jakob. "The economy of an Indian temple. Landed endowment and sacred food",
        Archives européennes de Sociologie 24(1), 83 : 44-59. [Jagannath temple of Puri, Orissa]
1432   ROSNY, Eric de. "Les Eglises indépendantes africaines. Fonction sociale et originalité
        culturelle", *Études* 358(1), jan 83 : 93-107.
1433   ROUX, Rodolfo Ramón de. *Una iglesia en estado de alerta: funciones sociales y funcionamiento
        del catolicismo colombiano, 1930-1980* (The standing by Church: social function and
        functioning of the Colombia catholicism, 1930-1980). Bogotá, Servicio Colombiano de
        Comunicación Social, 83, 190 p.
1434   RÜEGG, Walter. "Die Kirche im Spannungsfeld von Religion und Politik. Ergebnisse
        einer Schweizer Wertuntersuchung" (Church in the conflictoral field of religion and
        politics. Results of a Swiss research in values), *Hamburger Jahrbuch für Wirtschafts- und
        Gesellschaftspolitik* 27, 82 : 233-250.
1435   SOSA, Enrique. *Los ñáñigos: ensayo* (The 'ñáñigos': an essay). Ciudad de La Habana,
        Casa de las Américas, 82, 464-44 p. [Cuba]
1436   STROTHMANN, Dietrich. "Camarade Luther: une Église en régime socialiste", *Documents*
        38(3), jun 83 : 26-41. [German DR]
1437   SWATOS, William H. Jr. "Sects and success: 'Missverstehen' in Mt. Airy", *Sociological
        Analysis* 43(4), 82 : 375-380. [USA]
1438   URRY, James. "Who are the Mennonites?", *Archives européennes de Sociologie* 24(2), 83 : 241-262.

1439 YEO, Richard. *The structure and content of monastic profession: a juridical study, with particular regard to the practice of the English Benedictine Congregation since the French Revolution.* Roma, Edizioni Abbazia S. Paolo, 82, 360 p.

13550 Clergy. Religious authority
Clergé. Autorité religieuse

1440 GABORIEAU, Marc. "Typologie des spécialistes religieux chez les musulmans du sous-continent indien. Les limites de l'islamisation", *Archives de Sciences sociales des Religions* 55(1), jan-mar 83 : 29-51.

1441 RICHARD, Yann. "Le rôle du clergé: tendances contradictoires du chi'isme iranien contemporain", *Archives de Sciences sociales des Religions* 55(1), jan-mar 83 : 5-27.

1442 UNIVERSITÉ DES SCIENCES HUMAINES DE STRASBOURG. CENTRE DE SOCIOLOGIE DU PROTESTANTISME. *Prêtres, pasteurs et rabbins dans la société contemporaine.* Paris, Éditions du Cerf, 82, 260 p.

13560 Cults. Rites
Cultes. Rites

1443 ASAD, Talal. "Notes on body pain and truth in medieval Christian ritual", *Economy and Society* 12(3), 83 : 287-327.

1444 DOROGUNCOVA, N. S. "Social'nye funkcii sovetskoj obrjadnosti" (Social functions of Soviet ceremonial rites), *Voprosy Ateizma* (18), 82 : 72-78.

1445 FUJII, Masao. "Maintenance and change in Japanese traditional funerals and death-related behavior", *Japanese Journal of Religious Studies* 10(1), 83 : 39-64.

1446 JUNKER, Louis. "The conflict between the scientific-technological process and malignant ceremonialism", *American Journal of Economics and Sociology* 42(3), jul 83 : 341-352.

1447 KNOTTNERUS, J. David. "The Melanesian cargo cults: a test of the value-added theory of collective behavior", *Sociological Inquiry* 53(4), 83 : 389-403.

1448 NAGASAWA, Toshiaki. "Kumejima no senkotsu shuzoku kara" (Custom of Bone and Ash Purification in Kumejima, Okinawa Prefecture), *Nihon minzokugaku* 149, 83 : 1-16.

1449 RIVIÈRE, Claude. "Pour une approche des rituels séculiers", *Cahiers internationaux de Sociologie* 74, 83 : 97-117.

1450 WAEFELAER, Carine. "Rites du mariage dans une tribu berbère en Tunisie: les Frechich", *Civilisations* 33(1), 83 : 187-208.

1451 WIERZBICKI, M. Z. "Rites et pratiques dans un village polonais. L'exemple du village de Zacisze", *Archives de Sciences sociales des Religions* 56(1), jul-sep 83 : 77-96.

13570 Myths. Religious doctrines
Mythes. Doctrines religieuses

1452 BARTRA, Agustí. *Diccionario de mitología* (Dictionary of mythology). Barcelona, Grijalbo, 82, 209 p.

1453 BELTZ, Walter. *Die Mythen der Ägypter* (Egyptian's myths). Düsseldorf, Claassen, 82, 268 p.

1454 DECONCHY, Jean-Pierre. "Un vieux stéréotype épistémologique: les 'deux' religions", *Archives de Sciences Sociales de Religions* 55(2), apr-jun 83 : 175-181. [A propos de C. Daniel BATSON and W. Larry VENTIS, 'The religious experience. A socio-psychological perspective', New York, NY-Oxford, Oxford University Press, 1982, vii-356]

1455 GANE, Mike. "Durkheim: the sacred language", *Economy and Society* 12(1), 83 : 1-47.

1456 IONS, Veronica. *Egyptian mythology.* New York, NY, P. Bedrick Books, 83, 144 p.

1457 MAÎTRE, Jacques. "Entre femmes. Notes sur une filière du mysticisme catholique", *Archives de Sciences sociales des Religions* 55(1), jan-mar 83 : 105-137.

1458 PAOLUCCI, Gabrielle; [ed.]. *Bibliografia su religioni e società nel Centro America (1976-1981)* (Bibliography on religion and society in Central America (1976-1981)). Pisa, Giardini, 82, 121 p.

1459 RAYMAEKERS, Paul; DESROCHE, Henri. *L'administration et le sacré: discours religieux et parcours politiques en Afrique centrale (1921-1957).* Bruxelles, Académie Royale des Sciences d'Outre-Mer, 83, 399 p.

1460 RUTIGLIANO, Enzo. "Sul concetto di destino in Max Weber" (On the concept of fate in Max Weber), *Critica sociologica* 67, 83 : 85-89.

1461 SAVONNET-GUYOT, Claudette. "La force du destin: anthropologie et politique", *Revue française de Science politique* 33(4), aug 83 : 721-735. [résumé en anglais]

1462   WADSWORTH, M. E. J.; FREEMAN, S. R. "Generation differences in beliefs: a cohort
          study of stability and change in religious beliefs", *British Journal of Sociology* 24(3), sep
          83 : 416-437. [UK]

          13580   Religious behaviour
          Comportement religieux

1463   ABRAHAM, Gary. "The Protestant ethic and the spirit of utilitarianism", *Theory and Society*
          12(6), nov 83 : 739-773.
1464   ALONSO BAQUER, Miguel. "La religiosidad del militar español" (Religiosity of the
          Spanish military), *Razón y Fe* 208(1021), oct 83 : 162-172.
1465   BAHR, Howard M. "Youth and the church in Middletown", *Tocqueville Review* 4(1),
          sum 82 : 31-63.
1466   DICKSON, Tony; MCLACHLAN, Hugh. "Scottish capitalism and Weber's protestant
          ethic theses", *Sociology (London)* 17(4), nov 83 : 560-568.
1467   KENT, Stephen A. "The Quaker ethic and the fiscal price policy: Max Weber and beyond",
          Sociological Inquiry 53(1), 83 : 16-32.
1468   MARTIN, Jack; STACK, Steven. "The effect of religiosity on alienation: a multivariate
          analysis of normlessness", *Sociological Focus* 16(1), jan 83 : 65-76.
1469   MILANESI, G. "La domanda di religione dei giovani tra 'eclissi' e 'ritorno' del sacro"
          (Youth demand for religion between eclipse and return of the sacred), *Sociologia (Roma)*
          17(1), jan-apr 83 : 283-296. [Italy]
1470   PADOVANI, Giuseppe; RAHO, Giovanni. "Religiosità e immagine di Chiesa" (Religiosity
          and the image of the Church), *Studi di Sociologia* 21(1), mar 83 : 65-78. [Italy]
1471   PIWOWARSKI, Władisław; [ed.]. *Religijność ludowa: ciągłość i zmiana* (Folk religiosity:
          continuity and change). Wrocław, Wydawnictwo Wrocławskiej Księgarni Archidjecezjalnej,
          83, 367 p. [Poland]
1472   TITTLE, Charles R.; WELCH, Michael R. "Religiosity and deviance: toward a contingency
          theory of constraining effects", *Social Forces* 61(3), mar 83 : 653-682.

          13590   Church and State. Religious practice
          Église et État. Pratique religieuse

1473   "Intégrisme religieux", *Schweizerische Zeitschrift für Soziologie / Revue suisse de Sociologie* 9(3),
          83 : 473-823.
1474   "Symposium on religious awakenings", *Sociological Analysis* 44(2), sum 83 : 81-122. [USA]
          [with contributions by R. C. GORDON-McCUTCHAN, Timothy L. SMITH, William
          G. McLOUGHLIN, John L. HAMMOND]
1475   BARKER, Eileen. "New religious movements in Britain: the context and the membership",
          Social Compass 30(1), 83 : 33-48. [résumé en français; see also James A. BECKFORD:
          pp. 49-62]
1476   BECKFORD, James A. "The public response to new religious movements in Britain",
          Social Compass 30(1), 83 : 49-62.
1477   BEIDELMAN, T. O. *Colonial evangelism. A socio-historical study of an East African mission at the
          grassroots.* Bloomington, IN, Indiana University Press, 82, xix-274 p.
1478   BÖCKENFÖRDE, Ernst-Wolfgang. "Bemerkungen zum Verhältnis von Staat und Religion
          bei Hegel" (Remarks on the relations between State and religion in Hegel), *Staat* 21(4),
          82 : 481-503.
1479   BRUCE, Steve. "Ideology and isolation: a failed Scots Protestant movement", *Archives
          de Sciences sociales des Religions* 56(1), jul-sep 83 : 147-159.
1480   CLÉMENT, Jean-François. "Journalistes et chercheurs des sciences sociales face aux
          mouvements islamistes", *Archives de Sciences sociales des Religions* 55(1), jan-mar 83 : 85-104.
1481   CURLEY, Richard. "Dreams of power: social process in a West African religious movement",
          Africa (London) 53(3), 83 : 20-38. [Cameroon] [résumé en français]
1482   DAVIS, Winston. "Japanese religious affiliations: motives and obligations", *Sociological
          Analysis* 44(2), sum 83 : 131-146.
1483   FINKLER, Kaja. "Dissident sectarian movements, the Catholic Church, and social class
          in Mexico", *Comparative Studies in Society and History* 25(2), apr 83 : 277-305.
1484   FRIGOLE REIXACH, Joan. "Religión y política en un pueblo murciano entre 1966-1976:
          la crisis del nacionalcatolicismo desde la perspectiva local" (Religion and politics in a
          Murcian village between 1966 and 1976: crisis of the national catholicism from the local
          perspective), *Revista Española de Investigaciones Sociológicas* 23, jul-sep 83 : 77-126. [Spain]

1485   HARDIN, Bert. "Quelques aspects du phénomène des nouveaux mouvements religieux en
         République fédérale d'Allemagne", *Social Compass* 30(1), 83 : 13-32. [résumé en anglais]
1486   HOUGLAND, James G. Jr.; CHRISTENSON, James A. "Religion and politics: the
         relationship of religious participation to political efficacy and involvement", *Sociology
         and social Research* 67(4), jul 83 : 404-420. [USA]
1487   JACKSON, Hugh. "The late Victorian decline in churchgoing: some New Zealand
         evidence", *Archives de Sciences sociales des Religions* 56(1), jul-sep 83 : 97-106.
1488   LEE, Raymond L. M. "Sai Baba, salvation and syncretism: religious change in a Hindu
         movement in urban Malaysia", *Contributions to Indian Sociology* 16(1), jan-jun 82 : 125-140.
1489   MICHEL, Patrick. "L'Église et le mouvement social", *Temps modernes* 40(445-446),
         sep 83 : 469-481.
1490   O'HEARN, Denis. "Catholic grievances, catholic nationalism: a comment", *British Journal
         of Sociology* 24(3), sep 83 : 438-445.
1491   OSCHLIES, Wolf. *Kirchen und religiöses Leben in Bulgarien* (Churches and religious life in
         Bulgaria). Köln, Bundesinstitut für Ostwissenschaftliche und Internationale Studien,
         83, 37 p.
1492   PEROUAS, Louis. "Le Grand Retour de Notre-Dame-de-Boulogne à travers la France
         (1943-1948). Essai d'interpretation", *Archives de Sciences sociales des Religions* 56(1), jul-
         sep 83 : 37 57.
1493   RICHARDSON, James T. "New religious movements in the United States: a review",
         Social Compass 30(1), 83 : 85-110. [résumé en français]
1494   ROMEH, Aida K. "Fundamentalism and status concern: a study in cross-cultures",
         International Social Science Review 58(4), 83 : 211-221.
1495   SCHNABEL, Paul. *Tussen stigma en charisma: nieuwe religieuze bewegingen en geestelijke volksgezondheid*
         (Between stigma and charisma: new religious movements and spiritual health). Deventer,
         Van Loghum Slaterus, 82, 372 p.
1496   SCHRODER, P. "Secularización y cambio de valores en Alemania" (Secularization and
         change of values in Germany), *Revista de Fomento social* 37(152), oct-dec 83 : 349-361.
1497   ŠEVCOVA, L. F. *Socializm i katolicizm: vzaimootnošenija gosudarstva i katoličeskoj cerkvi v
         socialističeskih stranah* (Socialism and catholicism: interrelations between the State and
         the Catholic Church in the socialist countries). Moskva, Nauka, 82, 215 p.
1498   SHARMA, Sattish Kumar. "Shuddhi: a case study of role of a religious movement in the
         status improvement of untouchables", *Indian Journal of Social Research* 24(1), apr 83 : 70-77.
         [India]
1499   SIIKALA, Jukka. *Cult and conflict in tropical Polynesia: a study of traditional religion, Christianity
         and nativistic movements.* Helsinki, Suomalainen Tiedeakatemia, 82, 308 p.
1500   TROFIMOVA, Z. P. "Evangelizacija kak popytka preodvlenija krizisa religii v sovremennom
         amerikanskom obščestve" (Evangelization as an attempt at curing religious crisis in
         American society today), *Vestnik Moskovskogo Universiteta. Serija Filosofija* 37(5), 83 : 85-91.
1501   VAN DER LANS, Jan M.; DERKS, Frans. "Les nouvelles religions aux Pays-Bas.
         Contexte, appartenance et réactions", *Social Compass* 30(1), 83 : 63-83.
1502   VAN DORP, P. Patricia. *Grupos juveniles en parroquias* (Youth groups in parishes). Santiago,
         Centro Bellarmino, Departamento de Investigaciones Sociológicas, 82, 303 p. [Chile]
1503   VILLIERS, Bruckner de. "A crisis of Christian conscience. The interaction between Church
         and State in South Africa", *Internationales Afrika Forum* 19(1), trim. 1, 83 : 59-76.

**13600   SCIENCE. SOCIOLOGY OF KNOWLEDGE
         SCIENCE. SOCIOLOGIE DE LA CONNAISSANCE**

1504   "Fonctions (Les) sociales de la science", *Sciences sociales — Académie des Sciences de l'URSS* (4),
         82 : 74-87.
1505   "Physique, philosophie, concepts, catégories", *La pensée* (235), oct 83 : 49-124. [with
         contributions by Pierre JAEGLE, Pierre ROUBAUD, Bernard MICHAUX, Giles
         COHEN-TANNOUDJI, N. P. KONOPLEVA, V. N. POPOV]
1506   "'Wissenschaft in unserer Gesellschaft" (Sciences in our society), *Einheit* 38(2), 83 : 129-160.
         [German DR] [résumés en anglais, russe, français et espagnol, with contributions by
         Haunes HÖRNIG, Herbert WEIZ, Bernhard LARISCH]
1507   ALEK-KOWALSKI, Tadeusz. "Problem przedmiotu i zadań socjologii poznania" (The
         problem of scope and tasks of the sociology of knowledge), *Rozprawy z filozofii i socjologii*,
         83 : 155-170.
1508   ARIMOTO, Akira. "Kagaku shakaigaku ni okeru 'Matai kōka'-ron no keisei to tenkai"
         (The formation and development of 'Matthew Effect' theory in the sociology of science),
         Daigaku-shi kenkyu 3, 83 : 1-10.

1509   BARNES, Barry; EDGE, David; [eds.]. *Science in context: readings in the sociology of science.*
        Cambridge, MA, MIT Press, 82, xi-371 p.

1510   BRIDGSTOCK, Martin. "A sociological approach to fraud in science", *Australian and New
        Zealand Journal of Sociology* 18(3), nov 82 : 364-383.

1511   COLE, Stephen. "The hierarchy of the sciences?", *American Journal of Sociology* 89(1), jul
        83 : 111-139.

1512   COLLINS, H. M. "The sociology of scientific knowledge: studies of contemporary science",
        Annual Review of Sociology (9), 83 : 265-285.

1513   COLLINS, Randall; RESTIVO, Sal. "Development, diversity, and conflict in the sociology
        of science", *Sociological Quarterly* 24(2), spr 83 : 185-200. [USA]

1514   FEDOTOVA, V. G. "Issledovanija v oblasti metodologii social'nogo poznanija: obzor
        sovremennoj literatury" (Research in the field of the social knowledge methodology:
        a review of present-day literature), *Filosofskie Nauki* 24(4), 82 : 41-53.

1515   FRANKLIN, Richard L. "Libre arbitre, déterminisme et pensée scientifique", *Diogène* 123,
        jul-sep 83 : 53-75.

1516   FRISBY, David. *The alienated mind: the sociology of knowledge in Germany, 1918-1933.* London,
        Heinemann Education Books; Atlantic Highlands, NJ, Humanities Press, 83, ix-270 p.

1517   FROLOV, I. T. "Sociologija i ètika poznanija žizni i čeloveka" (Sociology and ethics of
        knowledge on life and man), *Priroda* (9), 82 : 29-37.

1518   GRAHAM, Loren; LEPENIES, Wolf; WEINGART, Peter; [eds.]. "Functions and uses of
        disciplinary histories", *Sociology of the Sciences* 7, 83 : 3-307. [with contributions by Rachel
        LAUDAN, Rolf WINAU]

1519   HELLER, Agnes. "The power of knowledge", *Revue internationale de Sociologie* 17(1),
        apr 81 : 3-21.

1520   KALINIČENKO, V. V.; [ed.]. "Nauka v sisteme kul'tury: aspekty kul'turnoj determinacii
        nauki" (Science in the culture system and aspects of cultural determination of science),
        Obščie Problemy Kul'tury i kul'turnogo Stroitel'stva-naučno-referativnyj Sbornik (1), 82 : 1-40.

1521   KAPLAN, Marcos. "Estado, cultura y ciencia en América latina" (State, culture and science
        in Latin America), *Desarrollo indoamericano* 17(77-78), sep 83 : 13-31.

1522   KARAMYŠEV, G. V. "Kritika èklektiki v social'nom poznanii" (Critics on eclecticism in
        social knowledge), *Vestnik Moskovskogo Universiteta. Serija Filosofija* 36(4), 82 : 35-42.

1523   KNORR-CETINA, K. D. "New developments in science studies: the ethnographic
        challenge", *Canadian Journal of Sociology / Cahiers canadiens de Sociologie* 8(2), 83 : 153-177.

1524   KOBAYASHI, Shuichi. "Yakuwari renkan to kashisei: Yakuwari no chishiki shakaigaku e
        mukete" (Role reference and visibility: toward a sociology of knowledge), *Hosei daigaku
        kyoyobu kiyo shakai-kaguku-hen* 47, 83 : 45-59.

1525   KUKLICK, Henrika. "The sociology of knowledge: retrospect and prospect", *Annual Review
        of Sociology* (9), 83 : 287-310.

1526   LÉCUYER, Bernard-Pierre. "Sociologie des sciences et des techniques", *Année sociologique*
        33, 83 : 301-342. [Compte rendu bibliographique]

1527   LITVÁN, György; BAK, János M.; [eds.]. *Socialism and social science. Selected writings of Ervin
        Szabó, 1877-1918.* London, Routledge and Kegan Paul, 82, vii-215 p.

1528   MEJA, Volker; STEHR, Nico; [eds.]. *Der Streit um die Wissenssoziologie. I. Die Entwicklung der
        deutschen Wissenssoziologie. II. Rezeption und Kritik der Wissenssoziologie* (The controversy
        on the sociology of knowledge. I. The development of the German sociology of knowledge.
        II. Reception and critique of the sociology of knowledge). Frankfurt-am-Main,
        Suhrkamp, 82, 973 p.

1529   MIKULINSKI, S. R.; RICHTA, Radovan; [eds.]. *Socialism and science.* Prague, Czechoslovak
        Academy of Sciences, Institute of Philosophy and Sociology, 83, 455 p.

1530   NAKAJIMA, Michio. "Kagaku shakaigaku no atarashii tenkai o mezashite" (Toward a new
        sociology of science), *Soshioroji* 28(1), 83 : 139-156.

1531   NAMER, Gérard. "Sociologie de la connaissance", *Année sociologique* 33, 83 : 343-354.
        [Compte rendu bibliographique]

1532   ROMERO, José L. *Desarrollo de las ideas en la sociedad argentina del siglo XX* (Development of
        ideas in the Argentine society of the XXth century). Buenos Aires, Solar, 83, 230 p.

1533   ROTTER, Frank. "Wissenssoziologie und Rechtstheorie" (Sociology of knowledge and
        theory of law), *Archiv für Rechts- und Sozialphilosophie* 68(4), 82 : 463-481.

1534   SNIZEK, W. E.; HUGHES, M. "An empirical assessment of the validity of Mullins' theory
        group classifications", *Scientometrics* 5(3), 83 : 155-162.

1535   ŠOŠKIC, Branislav. "Položaj i problemi nauke u našem društvu" (Situation and problems
        of science in our society), *Socijalizam* 26(2), 83 : 195-211. [Yugoslavia]

1536   STEWART, John. "Génétique et schizophrénie: une étude dans le domaine de la sociologie
        de la connaissance", *Social Science Information* 22(1), 83 : 149-163.

1537   UMEZAWA, Sei. "Durkheim ni okeru genshogakuteki shiten no tsuikyu: Kagakukan to shizenkan o megutte" (Inquisition of the phenomenological view in Durkheim's sociology: on his conceptions of science and nature), *Soka daigaku daigakuin kiyo* 4, 83 : 201-215.

1538   UVAROVA, L. I. *Nauka kak proizvoditel'naja sila obščestva* (Science as a productive force of the society). Moskva, Nauka, 82, 168 p.

1539   VISNEVŠKIJ, M. I. "Vozdejstvie nauki na social'nye potrebnosti razvitogo socialistićeskogo obšćestva" (The influence of science on the social needs of the developed socialist society), *Filosofija i Naučnyj Kommunizm* (9), 82 : 47-56.

1540   WETTERSTEN, John. "The sociology of knowledge vs. the sociology of science: a conundrum and an alternative", *Philosophy of the Social Sciences* 13(3), sep 83 : 325-333.

1541   WOLFF, Kurt H. "The sociology of knowledge and surrender-and-catch", *Canadian Journal of Sociology / Cahiers canadiens de Sociologie* 8(4), 83 : 421-453.

1542   ZENTNER, Henry. "Durkheim's conception of time, space, and the theory of knowledge as a theory of change", *Indian Journal of Social Research* 23(3), dec 82 : 212-223.

1543   ZINEVIČ, Ju. A.; FEDOTOVA, V. G. "Rol' social'nokul'turnyh faktorov v issledovanii nauk" (Role of socio-cultural factors in scientific research), *Voprosy Filosofii* 35(9), 82 : 67-77.

1544   ŽOG, V. I.; KANKE, V. A. "Mesto i rol' kategorii vremeni v social'nom poznanii" (Place and role of the time category in social knowledge), *in: Problemy social'nogo poznanija: voprosy formirovanija social'noj aktivnosti.* Moskva, 1981 : 121-134.

13700   COMMUNICATION. LANGUAGE
COMMUNICATION. LANGAGE

13710   Linguistics. Semiotics
Linguistique. Sémiotique

1545   "Sociolinguistics today", *Society* 20(4), jun 83 : 32-81. [with contributions by Roef KJOLSETH, Brenda DANET, Shirley BRICE HEATH, Ron SCOLLON, Suzanne SCOLLON]

1546   AEBISCHER, Verena; [et al.]. *Parlers masculins, parlers féminins?.* Paris, Delachaux et Niestlé, 83, 197 p.

1547   ASMAH, Omar. *Language and society in Malaysia.* Kuala Lumpur, Dewan Bahasa dan Pusytaka, Kementerian Pelajaran, 82, xiii-205 p.

1548   BYRNES, Heidi; [ed.]. *Contemporary perceptions of language: interdisciplinary dimensions.* Washington, DC, Georgetown University Press, 82, xvii-245 p.

1549   CARON, Jean. *Les régulations du discours: psycholinguistique et pragmatique du langage.* Paris, Presses Universitaires de France, 83, 255 p.

1550   COOPER, Robert L.; [ed.]. "Sociolinguistic perspective on Israeli Hebrew", *International Journal of the Sociology of Language* 41, 83 : 5-130.

1551   DATTA, Ansu. *Sociolinguistic behaviour and social change: as illustrated by the Swahili and Bengali speech communities: a comparative study.* Calcutta, Indian Publications, 82, xii-108 p.

1552   ENCREVÉ, Pierre; BOURDIEU, Pierre. "Le changement linguistique. Entretien avec William Labov", *Actes de la Recherche en Sciences sociales* 46, mar 83 : 67-71.

1553   FISHMAN, Joshua A.; [ed.]. "Levels of analysis in sociolinguistic explanation", *International Journal of the Sociology of Language* 39, 83 : 5-177.

1554   HELBO, André. *Sémiologie des messages sociaux: du texte à l'image.* Paris, Edilig, 83, 126 p.

1555   HOVDHAUGEN, Even. *Foundations of Western linguistics: from the beginning to the end of the first millennium A.D.* Oslo, Universitetsforlaget , 82, 156 p.

1555   JULIÀ, Pere. *Explanatory models in linguistics: a behavioral perspective.* Princeton, NJ, Princeton University Press, 83, xv-227 p.

1555   LAMIZET, Bernard. "La Sémiotique et les communications de masse: problèmes théoriques", *International Journal of the Sociology of Language* 40, 83 : 9-28.

1555   MAINGUENEAU, Dominique. *Sémantique de la polémique; discours religieux et ruptures idéologiques au XVIIᵉ siècle.* Lausanne, L'Âge d'Homme, 83, 206 p.

1559   MALMBERG, Bertil. *Analyse du langage au XXᵉ siècle: théories et méthodes.* Paris, Presses Universitaires de France, 83, 348 p.

1560   MEYER, Michel. *Logique, langage et argumentation.* Paris, Classiques Hachette, 83, 142 p.

1561   PORTER, Michael J. "Applying semiotics to the study of selected prime television programs", *Journal of Broadcasting* 27(1), wint 83 : 69-75.

1562   ROMAINE, Suzanne. *Socio-historical linguistics: its status and methodology.* Cambridge, Cambridgeshire-New York, NY, Cambridge University Press, 82, xi-315 p.

1563   SINGH, Jaspal; [ed.]. *Semiosis and semiotics: explorations in the theory of signs.* Chandigarh, Lokayat Prakashan, 82, 178 p.

1564   SOEFFNER, Hans-Georg; [ed.]. *Beiträge zu einer empirischen Sprachsoziologie* (Essays on an
        empirical sociology of language). Tübingen, Narr, 82, 220 p.
1565   TRUDGILL, Peter. *Sociolinguistics: an introduction to language and society.* Harmondsworth,
        Middlesex-New York, NY, Penguin, 83, 204 p.
1566   VAN DIJK, Teun A. "Discourse analysis: its development and application to the structure
        of news", *Journal of Communication* 33(2), spr 83 : 20-43.
1567   VIDENOV, Michail. *Sotsiolingvistika: osnovni tezisi, bulgarski sotiolingvisticheski problemi*
        (Sociolinguistics: main theses, Bulgarian sociolinguistic problems). Sofiia, Izdvo Nauka
        i Izkustvo, 82, 213 p.

13720   Communication. Signs
             Communication. Signes

1568   "Communication (La) locale", *Communications (Sankt Augustin)* 8-9(3), 82 : 179-295. [with
        contributions by Hannes LEOPOLDSEDER, Rolf T. WIGAND, Gian Piero ORSELLO,
        Matthias F. STEINMANN]
1569   "Communication: East and West", *Communication* 8(1), 83 : 1-132. [with contributions by
        Bernard GLASSMAN, Wimal DISSANAYAKE, Tulsi L. SARAL, Jan MILLS]
1570   "Énonciation et cinéma", *Communications* 38, 83 : 1-255.
1571   "Humor y comunicación" (Humour and communication), *Communicación* (38), jun 82 : 3-98.
        [Venezuela] [with contributions by Jesús M. AGUIRRE, Rafael E. CARIAS, Jesús
        ROSAS MARCANO, Ricardo MARTINEZ, Maria E. RAMOS, José SANTOS
        URRIOLA, Francisco TREMONTTI, G. EDUARDO]
1572   "Information, technology and development", *Information Society* 2(1), 1983 : 1-89. [with
        contributions by Robert A. WHITE, James M. McDONNELL, Donald McLEAN
        LAMBERTON, Harry EAST, R. NARASHIMHAN]
1573   BARBIČ, Ana. "Komunikacijski procesi u okviru društvenog sistema informisanja"
        (Processes of communication in the frame of societal information system), *Sociologija*
        24(1), 82 : 69-79.
1574   BERGER, Charles R.; BRADAC, James J. *Language and social knowledge: uncertainty in
        interpersonal relations.* London, E. Arnold, 82, viii-151 p.
1575   BOKSZAŃSKI, Zbigniew. "Komunikowanie zniekształcone" (Deformed communication),
        Przegląd Humanistyczny 210(3), 83 : 15-27.
1576   BRANNIGAN, Augustine; WANNER, Richard A. "Multiple discoveries in science: a test
        of the communication theory", *Canadian Journal of Sociology / Cahiers canadiens de Sociologie*
        8(2), 83 : 135-151.
1577   CARPENTIER, Jean-Baptiste. "Enseigner l'audio-visuel à l'université", *Humanisme et
        Entreprise* 137, feb 83 : 17. [France]
1578   CERTEAU, Michel de; GIARD, Luce. *L'ordinaire de la communication.* Paris, Dalloz, 83, 167 p.
1579   CHEBAT, Jean-Charles; ILLE, Bilgert. "Recherche empirique sur la sociologie de la
        communication familiale. Le cas des francophones de Montréal", *Revue de l'Institut de
        Sociologie* (3-4), 83 : 327-360.
1580   COURVOISIER, C. "Le Tiers-Monde et l'information", *Annuaire du Tiers-Monde* 6,
        80 : 289-299.
1581   CRESPI, Franco. *Mediazione simbolica e società* (Symbolic mediation and society). Milano,
        F. Angeli, 82, 169 p.
1582   CURRIEN, Nicolas; PERIN, Pascal. "La communication des ménages. Une cartographie
        socio-économique", *Futuribles* 65, apr 83 : 35-58. [France]
1583   DAVISON, W. Phillips. "The third-person effect in communication", *Public Opinion Quarterly*
        47(1), 83 : 1-15.
1584   DRÖSE, Peter W. *Kommunikative Kompetenz und Persönlichkeit: theoretische Analysen und
        empirische Untersuchungen* (Communication skills and personality: theoretical analyses and
        empirical researches). Köln, Studienverlag Hayit, 82, v-236 p.
1585   DUCATTE, Jean-Claude. "Le point sur les stratégies de communication sociale",
        Cahiers de la Communication 3(3), 83 : 172-183. [France]
1586   FISHMAN, Joshua A.; [ed.]. "Face-to-face interaction", *International Journal of the Sociology
        of Language* 43, 83 : 5-164.
1587   FLAHAUT, François. "Sur le rôle des représentations supposées partagées dans la
        communication", *Connexions* 38, 82 : 31-37.
1588   FREITAG, Barbara. "Theorie des Kommunikativen Handelns und genetische Psychologie.
        Ein Dialog zwischen Jürgen Habermas und Jean Piaget" (Theory of communicative
        behaviour and genetic psychology. A dialogue between Jürgen Habermas and Jean
        Piaget), *Kölner Zeitschrift für Soziologie und Sozialpsychologie* 35(3), sep 83 : 555-576.

1589   GOFFMAN, Erving. "Felicity's condition", *American Journal of Sociology* 89(1), jul 83 : 1-53.

1590   GREWLICH, Klaus W. "Transnationale Informations- und Datenkommunikation" (Transnational information and data communication), *Aussenpolitik* 34(1), trim. 1, 83 : 67-79.

1591   HAIKEN, Shelly; EAGLY, Alice H. "Communication modality as a determinant of persuasion: the role of communicator salience", *Journal of Personality and Social Psychology* 45(2), aug 83 : 241-256.

1592   HUISMAN, Denis. *Le dire et le faire: pour comprendre la persuasion; propagande, publicité, relations publiques; essai sur la communication efficace*. Paris, Éditions CDU-Sedes, 83, 201 p.

1593   JAVEAU, Claude. "Les symboles de la banalisation", *Cahiers internationaux de Sociologie* 75, 83 : 343-353.

1594   KŁOSKOWSKA, Antonina. "The autotelic character of symbolic culture", *Dialectics and Humanism* 10(1), wint 83 : 153-162.

1595   KOCH-WESER AMMASSARI, Elke. "Comunicazione simbolica e costruzione sociale della realtà" (Symbolic communication and social construction of reality), *Sociologia (Roma)* 17(1), jan-apr 83 : 115-124.

1596   KYLE, James; WOLL, Bernice; [eds.]. *Language in sign: an international perspective on sign language*. London, Croom Helm, 83, 288 p.

1597   LINOWES, David F. "The U.S. privacy protection commission: a retrospective view from the chair", *American Behavioral Scientist* 26(5), mai-jun 83 : 577-590.

1598   MANZI, Gianluca. "La comunicazione è incomunicabile" (Communication is incommunicable), *Critica sociologica* 66, 83 : 79-83.

1599   MARTIN, Jésus. "Retos a la investigación de comunicación en América latina" (Challenges to communication research in Latin America), *Comunicación y cultura* (9), 83 : 99-113.

1600   MOND, Georges H. *Histoire et systèmes actuels de l'information à l'étranger: pays socialistes. I. URSS*. Paris, Institut Français de Presse et de l'Information, 83, 101 p.

1601   OKADA, Naoyuki. "Mass communication kenkyu niokeru 3-tsu no chiteki paradigm" (Three paradigms for mass communication research), *Seijo daigaku communication kiyo* 1, 83 : 23-35.

1602   PIÑUEL RAIGADA, Jose Luis. "Verificación de la dialéctica 'acción/comunicación' en el análisis de mensajes. Producción de expresiones y reproducción social" (Verification of the 'action/communication' dialectics in message analysis. Production of expressions and social reproduction), *Revista española de Investigaciones sociológicas* 22, apr-jun 83 : 119-136.

1603   PIOTROWSKI, Andrzej. "Reguły mówienia według etnometodologicznej odmiany analizy konwersacji" (Speaking rules according to ethnomethodological version of conversational analysis), *Kultura i Społeczeństwo* 27(1), 83 : 7-33.

1604   QUÉRÉ, Louis. *Des miroirs équivoques: aux origines de la communication moderne*. Paris, Aubier Montaigne, 82, 214 p.

1605   SANTACRUZ, Adriana; ERAZO, Viviana. "La comunicación alternativa de la mujer" (The alternative communication for women), *Revista de Ciencias Sociales de la Universidad de Costa Rica* 25(1), 83 : 85-90.

1606   STRONG, John R. *Creating closeness: the communication puzzle*. Ames, IA, Human Communication Institute, 83, 340 p.

1607   TANAKA, Norichika. "Mass Communication kenkyu ni okeru 'Riyo to manzoku' no genjo to kongo no kadai" (The present and future problems of 'Uses and gratifications' in mass communication research), *Waseda daigaku kotogakuin kenkyu nenshi* 27, 83 : 153-167.

1608   USUI, Takashi. "Soshiki communication no katei bunseki: soshiki no ishi kettei kozo (sono 9)" (Sociological analysis of organizational communication), *Kinjo gakuin daigaku ronshu shakai-kagaku-hen* 25, 83 : 25-56.

1609   VAN BOL, J. "Communication locale et sciences de la communication. Le cas de la Belgique", *Communications (Sankt Augustin)* 8-9(3), 82 : 277-278.

1610   WEISS, Johannes. "Verständigungsorienticrung und Kritik. Zur Theorie des kommunikativen Handelns' von Jürgen Habermas" (Communication orientation and critique. On Jürgen Habermas' theory of communicative behaviour), *Kölner Zeitschrift für Soziologie und Sozialpsychologie* 35(1), mar 83 : 108-120.

13730   Language
       Langage

1611   "Langage en situation: pratiques sociales et interaction", *Connexions* 38, 82 : 5-121.

1612   "Plurilinguisme (Le) dans les structures d'une société", *Recherches sociologiques* 14(1), 83 : 3-102.

1613   "Symposium: the economics of language planning", *Language Problems and Language Planning* 7(2), sum 83 : 135-178. [with contributions by Toussaint HOČEVAR, Timothy REAGAN, François VAILLANCOURT]

1614   BAETENS BEARDSMORE, Hugo. *Bilingualism: basic principles*. Clevedon, Avon, Tieto, 82, viii-172 p.

1615   BARTSCH, Renate; VENNEMANN, Theo. *Grundzüge der Sprachtheorie: eine linguistische Einführung* (Essential features of the theory of language: a linguistic introduction). Tübingen, Niemeyer, 82, viii-204 p.

1616   BASDEVANT, Claire. "Questions sur le bilinguisme d'enfants de migrants", *Annales de Vaucresson* 20, 83 : 103-130. [France]

1617   BOURDIEU, Pierre. "Vous avez dit 'populaire?' ", *Actes de la Recherche en Sciences sociales* 46, mar 83 : 98-105. [critique de la notion de 'language populaire', résumés en anglais et en allemand]

1618   BOUTON, Charles. "La situation du Français dans les provinces de l'Ouest du Canada", *Zeitschrift der Gesellschaft für Kanada-Studien* (1), 82 : 103-116.

1619   BRAUNER, Siegmund; OCHOTINA, Natalia Veniaminovna. *Studien zur nationalsprachlichen Entwicklung in Afrika: soziolinguistische und sprachpolitische Probleme* (Studies on national language development in Africa: sociolinguistic and language political problems). Berlin, Akademie-Verlag, 82, 284 p.

1620   BRÉDART, Serge; RONDAL, Jean-Adolphe. *L'analyse du langage chez l'enfant: les activités métalinguistiques*. Bruxelles, P. Mardaga, 82, 146 p.

1621   CAPO, Hounkpatin C. "Le Gbe est une langue unique", *Africa (London)* 53(2), 83 : 47-57. [résumé in English]

1622   CHARAUDEAU, Patrick. "Eléments de sémiolinguistique d'une théorie du langage à une analyse du discours", *Connexions* 38, 82 : 7-30.

1623   COLLEYN, Jean-Paul. "La couleur des mots", *Revue de l'Institut de Sociologie* (3-4), 83 : 467-479.

1624   D'ALESSANDRO, Paolo. *Linguaggio e comprensione* (Language and understanding). Napoli, Guida, 82, 161 p.

1625   ENCREVÉ, Pierre. "La liaison sans enchaînement", *Actes de la Recherche en Sciences sociales* 46, mar 83 : 39-66. [résumés en anglais et en allemand]

1626   ENCREVÉ, Pierre; FORNEL, Michel de. "Le sens en pratique. Construction de la référence et structure sociale de l'interaction dans le couple question/résponse", *Actes de la Recherche en Sciences sociales* 46, mar 83 : 3-30.

1627   FELIX, Sascha W.; WODE, Henning; [eds.]. *Language development at the crossroads: papers from the Interdisciplinary Conference on Language Acquisition at Passau, 1981*. Tübingen, G. Narr, 83, 242 p.

1628   FORNEL, Michel de. "Légitimité et actes de langage", *Actes de la Recherche en Sciences sociales* 46, mar 83 : 31-38.

1629   FRANÇOIS, Frédéric. "Ebauches d'une dialogique", *Connexions* 38, 82 : 61-87.

1630   GALLAIS-HAMONNO, Janine. *Langage, langue et discours économiques*. Metz, Centre d'Analyse Syntaxique de l'Université de Metz, 82, 306 p.

1631   GALTUNG, Johan; NISHIMURA, Fumiko. "Structure, culture and languages: an essay comparing the Indo-European, Chinese and Japanese languages", *Social Science Information* 22(6), 83 : 895-925.

1632   GHIGLIONE, R.; BEAUVOIS, J. L. "Language attitudes and social influence", *Journal of Social Psychology* 121(1), oct 83 : 97-109.

1633   GHIGLIONE, Rodolphe. "Analyse proportionnelle et modèles argumentatifs", *Connexions* 38, 82 : 89-106.

1634   GOULD, Lawrence V. Jr. "Against trivialization: a brief commentary on dependency and epistemology", *Social Science Information* 22(6), 83 : 867-894.

1635   GROSSE, Rudolf; NEUBERT, Albrecht. *Soziolinguistische Aspekte der Theorie des Sprachwandels* (Sociolinguistic aspects of the theory of language transformation). Berlin, Akademie-Verlag, 82, 43 p.

1636   HAGLUND, L. *'Bokmål' or 'nynorsk' — some data on language preferences in Norway 1979 and 1981*. s.l., Bedriftsökonomisk Institutt, Working Paper Series No 2, 83, 13 p.

1637   HARDT-DHATT, Karin. *Les attitudes face à l'utilisation de l'anglais et du français chez les travailleurs francophones dans trois entreprises de production à Québec*. Québec, PQ, Gouvernement du Québec, Office de la Langue Française, 82, 305 p.

1638   HARGRAVE, Susanne; [ed.]. *Language and culture*. Darwin, Summer Institute of Linguistics, Australian Aborigines Branch, 82, x-226 p.

1639   KELEMEN, János. "Language, action and society", *Annales Universitatis Scientiarum budapestiensis de Rolando Eötvös nominatae. Sectio philosophica et sociologica* 16, 82 : 149-156.

1640   LABAHN, Thomas. *Sprache und Staat: Sprachpolitik in Somalia* (Language and State: language policy in Somalia). Hamburg, Buske, 82, ii-297 p.

1641   LAKS, Bernard. "Langage et pratiques sociales. Étude sociolinguistique d'un groupe d'adolescents", *Actes de la Recherche en Sciences sociales* 46, mar 83 : 73-97. [résumés en anglais et en allemand]

1642   LAVOIE, Marc. "Bilinguisme, langue dominante et réseaux d'information", *Actualité économique* 59(1), mar 83 : 38-62. [Canada]

1643   LEITNER, Gerhard; [ed.]. "Language and mass media", *International Journal of the Sociology of Language* 40, 83 : 5-120.

1644   LÉVY, André. "Organisation et discours", *Connexions* 39, 83 : 21-45.

1645   MILLETT, David. "The social context of bilingualism in Eastern Ontario", *American Review of Canadian Studies* 13(1), spr 83 : 1-12. [Canada]

1646   OLSON, Paul; BURNS, Georges. "Politics, class and happenstance: French immersion in a Canadian context", *Interchange* 14(1), 83 : 1-16. [see also ibid. pp. 17-22 by Mary Alice JULIUS GUTTMAN]

1647   ORLANDI, Eni Pulcinelli. *A linguagem e seu funcionamento: as formas do discurso* (The language and its functioning: the forms of speech). São Paulo, Brasiliense, 83, 23 p.

1648   OYELARAN, Olasope O. "Langage et nationalisme en Afrique noire", *Revue française d'Histoire d'Outre-mer* 68(250-253), 81 : 268-273.

1649   PECHEUX, Michel. *Language, semantics and ideology.* New York, NY, St. Martin's Press, 82, 244 p.

1650   PRADHAN, R. C. *Language and experience: an interpretation of the later philosophy of Wittgenstein.* Meerut, Anu Prakashan, 81, 258 p.

1651   PUBUSA, Andrea. "Considerazioni sulle tutela delle lingua in Sardegna" (Language policy considerations in Sardinia), *Rivista trimestrale di Diritto pubblico* (2), 83 : 552-599.

1652   QUATTROCCHI, Enrico. "Il linguaggio come comportamento sociale" (Language as social behaviour), *Critica sociologica* 60, 82 : 67-73.

1653   RICHER. STEPHEN. "French immersion and classroom behavior", *Canadian Journal of Sociology / Cahiers canadiens de Sociologie* 8(4), 83 : 377-393. [Canada]

1654   ROSSIER, Robert E. "Bilingual education: training for ghetto", *Policy Review* (25), sum 83 : 36-45.

1655   RYAN, Ellen Bouchard; GILES, Howard; [eds.]. *Attitudes towards language variation: social and applied contexts.* London, E. Arnold, 82, xiv-286 p.

1656   SHAFIR, Gershon. "Organic intellectuals and the renaissance of the Hebrew language", *Sociologia internationalis* 21(1-2), 83 : 215-242.

1657   SILVA DE BONILLA, Ruth. "El lenguaje como mediación ideológica entre la experiencia y la conciencia de las mujeres trabajadoras en Puerto Rico" (The language as ideological mediation between women workers' experience and consciousness in Puerto Rico), *Revista de Ciencias sociales* 23(1-2), jun 81 : 23-50.

1658   TOMELLINI, Paola. *Linguaggio e percezione* (Language and perception). Roma, Ianua, 83, 195 p.

1659   TROGNON, Alain. "Analyse interlocutoire", *Connexions* 38, 82 : 39-59.

1660   VELTMAN, Calvin. "L'évolution de la ségrégation linguistique à Montréal, 1961-1981", *Recherches sociographiques* 24(3), sep-dec 83 : 379-390.

1661   WANG, William S.-Y. *Human communication: language and its psychobiological bases.* San Francisco, CA, W. H. Freeman, 82, 186 p.

1662   YALDEN, Max F. "Language and the state. A Canadian perspective", *Zeitschrift der Gesellschaft für Kanada-Studien* (1), 82 : 95-101.

13740   **Audience**
         Public

13750   **Advertising. Propaganda**
         Publicité. Propagande

1663   "Publicité-propagande (La)", *Travaux de l'Association Henri Capitant* 32, 81 : 2-614. [with contributions by Arnaud LYON-CAEN, Francisco PEREIRA COELHO, Yvette MERCHIERS, Oscar BARRETO FILHO]

1664   BASQUE, Michelle; DIONNE, Guy; GIRARD, Sylvie. *Publicité / Banque de terminologie du Québec. État terminologique. Bibliographie.* Québec, PQ, Gouvernement du Québec, Office de la Langue Française, 82, 201 p.

1665   BRODY, Charles J. "Advertising campaigns as arms races: a test of a mathematical model", *Sociological Perspectives* 26(3), jul 83 : 323-339.

1666   DEGON, Renaud. "L'impact du changement social sur la publicité", *Revue française du Marketing* (2), apr 83 : 49-61.

1667   PIQUET, Sylvère; [ed.]. *La publicité: nerf de la communication.* Paris, Éditions d'Organisation, 83, 227 p.
1668   ROTH, Paul. "Die Propaganda in der UdSSR" (Propaganda in the USSR), *Europäische Rundschau* 10(4), 82 : 77-86.

13760   **Mass communication**
         Communication de masse

1669   "After the Frankfurt school", *Media, Culture and Society* 5(1), jan 83 : 7-116. [with contributions by Burkhard HOFFMANN, Franz DROCE, Wulf D. HUND, Horst HOLZER]
1670   "Broadcasting rituals", *Media, Culture and Society* 5(2), apr 83 : 117-228. [with contributions by David CHANEY, Philip ELLIOTT, Emile G. McANANY]
1671   "Éducation (L') aux médias", *Perspectives (UNESCO)* 13(2), 83 : 203-264. [with contributions by Sirkka MINKKINEN, Kaarle NORDENSTRENG, Gérald BERGER, Evelyne PIERRE]
1672   "Individuals in mass media organization: creativity and constraint", *Sage Annual Reviews of Communications Research* 10, 82 : 7-254. [with contributions by Walter W. POWELL, Anne K. PETERS, Muriel G. CANTOR, Horace M. NEWCOMB, Robert S. ALLEY]
1673   "Mass media", *Pakistan Year Book* (10), 83 : 73-91. [Pakistan]
1674   "Medias et criminalité", *Schweizerische Zeitschrift für Soziologie / Revue suisse de Sociologie* 9(2), 83 : 407-436.
1675   "Neue Medien — Verkabelung" (New media — cabling), *Gewerkschaftliche Monatshefte* 34(6), jun 83 : 329-399. [Germany FR] [with contributions by Axel ZERDICK, Rüdiger LUTZ]
1676   "Nuevo periodismo" (New journalism), *Comunicación* (37), mar 82 : 4-84. [Venezuela] [with contributions by Luis ANGULO, Sebastian de la NUEZ, Jesús SANIJA HERNANDEZ]
1677   "Presse und Kultur" (Press and culture), *Deutsche Studien* 20(79), sep 82 : 277-301. [Germany FR] [with contributions by Wilmont HAACKE, Walter HILDEBRANDT]
1678   "Psychology in the public forum. The role of television in our lives", *American Psychologist* 38(7), jul 83 : 815-848. [USA] [with contributions by Eli A. RUBINSTEIN, Jerome L. SINGER, Dorothy G. SINGER]
1679   "Radio-télévision: la fin du monopole? La loi du 29 juillet 1982", *Cahiers de la Communication* 3(1-2), 83 : 5-115. [résumés en anglais, with contributions by Jean d'ARCY, Jacques ROBERT, Roland DRAGO, Jean-Jacques ISRAEL, Francis BALLE]
1680   "Technology and cable", *Journal of Broadcasting* 27(2), spr 83 : 119-183. [USA] [with contributions by James G. WEBSTER, Lee B. BECKER, Ted BOLTON]
1681   ABDULGANI, H. Roeslen. "Mass communication in Indonesia and its perception on cultural exchange", *Indonesian Quarterly* 11(2), apr 83 : 56-75.
1682   ALBRECHT, Richard. "La télévision en RFA. Approche empirique et théorique", *Allemagnes d'aujourd'hui* (85), sep 83 : 6-27.
1683   AMORIN, José Salomao David. "La radiodifusión en Brésil, 1974-1981" (Broadcasting in Brazil, 1974-81), *Comunicación y cultura* (9), 83 : 151-171.
1684   BAXTER, Lesli A.; KAPLAN, Stuart J. "Context factors in the analysis of prosocial and antisocial behavior on prime time television", *Journal of Broadcasting* 27(1), wint 83 : 25-36. [USA]
1685   BECHELLONI, Giovanni; [ed.]. *Il mestiere di giornalista: sguardo sociologico sulla pratica e sulla ideologia della professione giornalistica* (The profession of journalist: a sociological consideration of practice and ideology of journalism). Napoli, Liguori, 82, 308 p.
1686   BELBASE, Subhadra; MURPHY, James E. "Press performance in Nepal during two political climates", *Journalism Quarterly* 60(1), spr 83 : 61-66.
1687   BENIGER, James R. "Does television enhance the shared symbolic environment? Trends in labeling of editorial cartoons, 1948-1980", *American Sociological Review* 48(1), feb 83 : 103-111.
1688   BESOZZI, Elena. "Mass media e cultura di massa: alcune considerazioni generali e una rivisitazione del contributo di E. Morin" (Mass media and mass culture: some general considerations and a reappraisal of E. Morin's contribution), *Studi di Sociologia* 21(2), apr-jun 83 : 181-189.
1689   BLACK, Jay; WHITNEY, Frederick C. *Introduction to mass communication.* Dubuque, IA, W. C. Brown Co. Publishers, 83, xi-473 p.
1690   BOVENTER, Hermann. "Journalistenmoral als 'Media Ethics'. Kodifizierte Pressemoral und Medienethik in den Vereinigten Staaten von Amerika" (Journalists' morals as 'media ethics'. Codified press morals and media ethics in the USA), *Publizistik* 28(1), 83 : 19-39.

1691   BOYD, Douglas A. "Broadcasting between the two Germanies", *Journalism Quarterly* 60(2), sum 83 : 232-239.

1692   BRIMMER, Karl W. "US telecommunications common carrier policy", *Annual Review of Information Science and Technology* 17, 82 : 33-82.

1693   BURG, Paul. "La presse de l'Ordre Nouveau: sa diffusion et son public", *Archipel* (25), 83 : 7-22. [Indonesia]

1694   BURNS, John P. "Democracy, the rule of law, and human rights in Beijin's unofficial journals, 1978-1979", *Internationales Asien Forum* 14(1), mar 83 : 35-53.

1695   CLARK, Paul. "Film-making in China: from the cultural Revolution to 1981", *China Quarterly* (94), jun 83 : 304-322.

1696   COOK, Thomas D.; KENDZIERSKI, Deborah A.; THOMAS, Stephen H. "The implicit assumptions of television research: an analysis of the 1982 NIMH report on television and behavior", *Public Opinion Quarterly* 47(2), sum 83 : 161-201.

1697   DANIELS, Douglas J. "Socializing the socialists: French politics and the US press", *Contemporary French Civilization* 7(2), aut 82 : 63-73.

1698   DI BELLA, Maria Pia. "Mythe et histoire dans l'élaboration du fait divers: le cas Franca Viola", *Annales-Économies, Sociétés, Civilisations* 38(4), aug 83 : 827-841.

1699   DUARTE, Celina Rabello. "Imprensa e redemocratização no Brasil" (The press and the new democratization of Brazil), *Dados* 26(2), 83 : 181 195. [résumé en français]

1700   EGBON, Mike. "Western Nigeria television service: oldest in tropical Africa", *Journalism Quarterly* 60(2), sum 83 : 329-334.

1701   FERNÁNDEZ CHRISTLIEB, Fátima. *Los medios de difusión masiva en México* (Mass media in Mexico). México, J. Pablos, 82, 330 p.

1702   FLORES, Lupita; GARDELA, Ana Isabel. "Origen, desarrollo y actualidad de la radio-difusion" (Origin, development and present-day status of radio broadcasting), *Revista de Ciencias Sociales de la Universidad de Costa Rica* 26(2), 83 : 17-26.

1703   FUKUOKA, Yasunori. "Masukomi to sabetsu mondai' no skahaigaku-teki bunseki: Masukomijin no 'Sabetsu yogo kisei' eno taido o megutte" (The problem of discrimination in Japanese journalism: a sociological analysis), *Chiba kenritsu eisei tanki daigaku kiyo* 1(1), 83 : 45-70.

1704   FURRER, Hans-Peter. "Medien und Völkerrecht" (Media and international law), *Archiv des Völkerrechts* 21(1), 83 : 37-59.

1705   GALUŠKO, R. I. "Televidenie v Latinskoj Amerike" (Television in Latin America), *Latinskaja Amerika* 14(10), 83 : 48-61.

1706   GAY, Daniel. "L'information sur l'Amérique latine et les silences de la presse québécoise", *Études internationales* 13(4), dec 82 : 679-690.

1707   GERBER, Raquel. *O cinema brasileiro e o processo político e cultural (de 1950 a 1978)* (Brazilian cinema and the political and cultural process (1950-1978)). Rio de Janeiro, EMBRA-FILME, 82, 290 p.

1708   GREENBERG, Bradley S.; [et al.]. *Mexican Americans and the mass media.* Norwood, NJ, Ablex, 83, 304 p.

1709   GUTTO, S. B. O. "Captivity of the press", *Monthly Review* 34(8), jan 83 : 31-41.

1710   HAGLUND, L. *Media classification, segmentation and selection on the Norwegian market — empirical findings from media surveys in Norway.* s.l., Bedriftsökonomisk Institutt, Working Paper Series No 5, 83, 31 p.

1711   HESS-LÜTTICH, Ernest W. "Jugendpresse und Sprachwandel" (Youth press and language change), *International Journal of the Sociology of Language* 40, 83 : 93-105.

1712   HOUIDI, Fethi; NAJAR, Ridha. "Les rôle des médias en Tunisie: conception et pratiques", *Revue tunisienne de communication* (2), dec 82 : 53-72.

1713   HOWE, Michael J. A.; [eds.]. *Learning from television: psychological and educational research.* London-New York, NY, Academic Press, 83, xvi-226 p.

1714   JAIBI, Hatim. "Les médias et leur message en Tunisie", *Revue tunisienne de communication* 2, dec 82 : 5-51.

1715   JYRKIÄINEN, Hyrki; [comp.]. *Social role of mass communication: report of the 2nd Finnish-Soviet seminar.* Tampere, Tampereen Yliopisto, Tiedotusopin Laitos, 82, vi-226 p.

1716   KARIEL, Herbert; ROSENVALL, Lynn A. "United States news flows to Canadian newspapers", *American Review of Canadian Studies* 13(1), spr 83 : 44-64.

1717   KIRSCH, Jeffrey W. "The ethics of going public: communicating through mass media", *American Behavioral Scientist* 26(2), nov-dec 82 : 251-264.

1718   KIYOHARA, Keiko. "New media to ningen: Shutaiteki media riyo no kanosei" (New media and people: from the mass audience toward the independent audience), *Senden kaigi* 30(1), 83 : 114-119.

1719   KOROBEJNIKOV, V. S.; [ed.]. *Metody issledovanija sredstv massovoj informacii* (Methods of research on the mass media). Moskva, Institut Sociologičeskih Issledovanij, Akademija Nauk SSSR, 82, 104 p.

1720   KORZENNY, Felipe; ARMSTRONG, G. Blake; GALVAN, Tatiana. "Mass communication, cosmopolite channels, and family planning among villagers in Mexico", *Development and Change* 14(2), apr 83 : 237-253.

1721   LA ROCHE, Walther von. *Massenmedien* (Mass-media). Heidelberg, Müller, 83, 119 p. [Germany FR]

1722   LEON, Patricia; OVARES, Isabel. "La prensa llama a la guerra. Un caso de parcialidad informativa" (Press calls for war. A case of informative bias), *Revista de Ciencias Sociales de la Universidad de Costa Rica* 26(2), 83 : 55-77.

1723   LUKAČ, Sergije. "Dnevni listovi" (Daily newspapers), *Jugoslovenski pregled* 27(4), apr 83 : 161-166. [Yugoslavia]

1724   LULL, James. "How families select television programmes: a mass observational study", *Journal of Broadcasting* 26(4), aut 82 : 801-811.

1725   MAIRE, Paul. "Information, culture, communication, sous le règne des médias", *Masses ouvrières* (383), mar 83 : 21-37.

1726   MARTÍN SERRANO, Manuel. *El uso de la comunicación social por los españoles* (Social communication utilization by Spanish people). Madrid, Centro de Investigaciones Sociológicas, 82, 383 p.

1727   MARTIN-GODBOUT, Johannes. "Les medias d'information ou le pouvoir insolite des boucs émissaires", *Optimum* 13(3), 82 : 20-30. [résumé en anglais]

1728   MCQUAIL, Denis. *Mass communication theory: an introduction.* London-Beverly Hills, CA, Sage Publications, 83, 245 p.

1729   MEYN, Hermann. "Ungeahnte Vielfalt: die Presse der Bundesrepublik" (Unsuspected multiplicity: the press in the Federal Republic), *Neue Politische Literatur* 27(4), dec 82 : 463-480.

1730   MICKIEWICZ, Ellen. "Feedback, surveys, and Soviet communication theory", *Journal of Communication* 33(2), spr 83 : 97-110.

1731   MIKUŁOWSKI POMORSKI, Jerzy. "Wartość a społeczna użyteczność badań nad masowym komunikowaniem" (Value and social utility of investigations on mass communication), *Prakseologia* 85-86(1-2), 83 : 133-144.

1732   MISSIKA, Jean-Louis; WOLTON, Dominique. *La folle du logis: la télévision dans les sociétés démocratiques.* Paris, Gallimard, 83, 338 p.

1733   NAWAZ, Shuja. "The mass-media and development in Pakistan", *Asian Survey* 23(8), aug 83 : 934-957.

1734   NOELLE-NEUMANN, Elisabeth. "Die Legitimation der Massenmedien" (The legitimation of mass media), *Hamburger Jahrbuch für Wirtschafts- und Gesellschaftspolitik* 27, 82 : 215-231. [Germany FR]

1735   NÚÑEZ LADEVEZE, Luis. "Para un tratamiento autónomo de la noción y las funciones del medio de comunicación de masas" (For a specific consideration of the concept and functions of the mass communication medium), *Revista española de Investigaciones sociológicas* 22, apr-jun 83 : 101-118.

1736   PARASCHOS, Manny. "Legal constraints on the press in post-junta Greece, 1974-77", *Journalism Quarterly* 60(1), spr 83 : 48-53.

1737   PENNACHIONI, Irène. *La nostalgie en images: une sociologie du récit dessiné.* Paris, Librairie des Méridiens, 82, 197 p. [France]

1738   PEREZ VILARIÑO, José. "Campo religioso y espacio político en los periódicos españoles a comienzos de los años setenta" (Religious field and political space in Spanish newspapers at the beginning of the 70s), *Revista de estudios políticos* (29), oct 82 : 253-271.

1739   PHILLIPS, David P. "The behavioral impact of violence in the mass media: a review of the evidence from laboratory and nonlaboratory investigations", *Sociology and Social Research* 66(4), jul 82 : 387-398. [USA]

1740   PHILLIPS, David P. "The impact of mass media violence on US homicide", *American Sociological Review* 48(4), aug 83 : 560-568.

1741   PILLI, Arja. *The Finnish-language press in Canada, 1901-1939: a study in the history of ethnic journalism.* Turku, Institute of Migration, 82, 328 p.

1742   PLENKOVIĆ, Mario. "Podruštvljavanje masovnih medija u samoupravnom socijalističkom društvu" (Socialization of mass media in self-managed socialist society), *Sociologija* 24(1), 82 : 109-118. [Yugoslavia]

1743   PONCEYRI, Robert. "L'information locale interdite", *Annales de l'Université des Sciences sociales de Toulouse* 30, 82 : 319-375. [France]

1744   RALLE, Francis. "La liberté d'expression et les nouvelles techniques de communication", *Revue des Sciences morales et politiques* 138(1), 83 : 41-57.

1745 RAZLOGOV, K. É. "Katolicizm i kinematograf" (Catholicism and cinema), *Voprosy Filosofii* 35(10), 82 : 135-144.

1746 REIMANN, Helga. "Der Einfluss der Massenmedien auf die Frauen in Entwicklungsregionen" (Influence of mass media on women in developing regions), *Communications (Sankt Augustin)* 7(2-3), 81 : 215-225. [résumés en français et anglais]

1747 RICHARDS, Jeffery; ALDGATE, Anthony. *Best of British: cinema and society, 1930-1970.* Oxford, B. Blackwell, 83, 170 p.

1748 RIEFFEL, Rémy. "Analyse de l'éthique des journalistes: questions de méthode", *Revue française de Science politique* 33(3), jun 83 : 455-479. [résumé en anglais]

1749 ROEH, Itzhak. *The rhetoric of news in the Israel radio: some implications of language and style for newstelling.* Bochum, Studienveralg N. Brockmeyer, 82, vii-202 p.

1750 RONCI, Donatella. "Le televisione nel Mediterranea" (Television in the Mediterranean countries), *Affari sociali internazionali* 11(3), 83 : 23-31.

1751 ROSENFELD, Shalom. "Newspaper editor's dilemmas", *Jerusalem Quarterly* (25), aut 82 : 100-115. [Israel]

1752 RUBIN, Alan H. "Television uses and gratifications: the interactions of viewing patterns and motivations", *Journal of Broadcasting* 27(1), wint 83 : 37-51. [USA]

1753 RUDOLF, Walter; ABMEIER, Klaus. "Satellitendirektfunk und Informationsfreiheit" (Satellite direct broadcasting and freedom of information), *Archiv des Völkerrechts* 21(1), 83 : 1-36.

1754 SATO, Tomoo; [ed.]. *Journalism to mass media* (Journalism and mass media). Tokyo, Obunsha, 83, 214 p.

1755 SCHURMANN, Leo. "Die Verantwortung der Medium" (The responsibility of the media), *Schweizer Monatshefte* 63(3), mar 83 : 207-213.

1756 SILBERMANN, Alfons. "Les médias et notre perception du monde actuel", *Revue des Sciences morales et politiques* 138(1), 83 : 97-107.

1757 SOLEY, Lawrence C. "The political context of clandestine radio braodcasting in 1981", *Journal of Broadcasting* 27(3), sum 83 : 233-250.

1758 STAPPERS, J. G.; REIJNDERS, A. D.; MÖLLER, W. A. J. *De werking van massamedia: een overzicht van inzichten* (The effect of mass media: an opinion survey). 's-Gravenhage, Staatsuitgeverij, 83, 219 p.

1759 SZECSKÖ, Tamás; [ed.]. *Studying social communications in Hungary.* Kecskemét, Petőfi Nyomda, 82, 293 p.

1760 TAMURA, Norio; KODAMA, Miiko. "Colorado nikkei shinbun shoshi" (A brief history of Japanese American newspapers in Colorado), *Tokyo keizai daigaku jinbun shizen kagaku ronshu* 64, 83 : 101-157.

1761 TAMURA, Norio; SHIMPO, Mitsuru. "Senzen Canada no nikkeishi (jo)" (A short history of Japanese Canadian newspapers), *Tokyo keizai daigaku kaishi* 133, 83 : 317-343.

1762 TAMURA, Norio; YAMAMOTO, Taketoshi. "Kashu nikkeishi no shinbun kokoku to keiei: 1910-1940" (Japanese American's newspapers and business in California, 1910-1940), *Tokyo keizai daigaku kaishi* 132, 83 : 187-238.

1763 TRAORE, Biny. "Cinéma africain et développement", *Peuples Noirs — Peuples Africains* 6(33), jun 83 : 51-62.

1764 VAN CUILENBURG, J. J.; MCQUAIL, Denis. *Media en pluriformiteit* (Media and pluralism). 's-Gravenhage, Staatsuitgeverij, 82, 187 p.

1765 VAN DER VOORT, T. H. A. *Kinderen en TV-geweld* (Children and violence in TV). Lisse, Swets en Zeitlinger, 82, ix-349 p. [Netherlands]

1766 VYTLAČIL, Josef. "Sledování relevize v ČSSR" (Television audience in Czechoslovakia), *Statistika* (7), 83 : 319-324.

1767 WAGNER, Joseph. "Media do make a difference: the differential impact of mass media in the 1976 presidential race", *American Journal of Political Science* 27(3), aug 83 : 407-430. [USA]

1768 WEATHERFORD, M. Stephen. "Judging politicians' management of the economy: the role of the media", *American Politics Quarterly* 11(1), jan 83 : 31-48. [USA]

1769 WEIMANN, Gabriel. "The theater of terror: effects of press coverage", *Journal of Communication* 33(1), wint 83 : 38-45. [Israel]

1770 WESTERSTAHL, Jörgen. "Dagspressen och den politiska opinionsbildningen" (Daily press and political opinion formation), *Statsvetenskaplig tidskrift* 85(4), 82 : 221-248. [Sweden]

1771 WOLF, Michelle A.; [et al.]. "A rules-based study of television's role in the construction of social reality", *Journal of Broadcasting* 26(4), aut 82 : 813-829.

1772 YGLESIAS, Mariana; CISNEROS, Pilar. "Periodismo científico: un motor que aceleraría el desarrollo" (Scientific journalism: an engine that would accelerate development), *Revista de Ciencias Sociales de la Universidad de Costa Rica* 26(2), 83 : 7-15.

1773   ZEFF, Eleanor E. "The Ghanaian press as a translator of public policy", *Journal of African Studies* 10(2), sum 83 : 50-65.

1774   ZIRES, Margarita. "El discuro de la televisión y los juegos infantiles" (Television discourse and children's games), *Comunicación y cultura* (10), aug 83 : 109-136. [Mexico]

13800   ART
         ART

13810   Aesthetics. Artists. Museums
         Esthétique. Artistes. Musées

1775   "Arts (The) in education", *Educational Analysis* 5(2), 83 : 1-116. [UK] [with contributions by Peter BRINSON, Peter HULTON, Christopher SMALL, Fraser SMITH, Ralph A. SMITH]

1776   ARNOLD, Bruce. "Politics and the arts: the Dail debates", *Administration (Dublin)* 30(2-3), 82 : 281-297. [Ireland]

1777   BECKER, Howard S. "Mondes de l'art et types sociaux", *Sociologie du Travail* 25(4), oct-dec 83 : 404-417.

1778   DUBOST, Françoise. "Les paysagistes et l'invention du paysage", *Sociologie du Travail* 25(4), oct-dec 83 : 432-445. [résumé en anglais]

1779   DUNCAN, Carol. "Who rules the art world?", *Socialist Review* 13(70), aug 83 : 99-119.

1780   FIELD, Karen L. "Artists in Liberia and the United States: a comparative view", *Journal of Modern African Studies* 20(4), dec 82 : 713-730.

1781   GAMBONI, Dario. "Méprises et mépris. Eléments pour une étude de l'iconoclasme contemporain", *Actes de la Recherche en Sciences sociales* 49, sep 83 : 2-28.

1782   GROMYKO, A. A. "O tradicionnom iskusstve Tropičeskoj Afriki" (Traditional art of tropical Africa), *Narody Azii i Afriki* (3), jun 83 : 40-49.

1783   HASKELL, Francis. "Les musées et leurs ennemis", *Actes de la Recherche en Sciences sociales* 49, sep 83 : 103-106.

1784   HEINICH, Nathalie. "L'aura de Walter Benjamin. Note sur l'oeuvre d'art à l'ère de sa reproductibilité technique", *Actes de la Recherche en Sciences sociales* 49, sep 83 : 107-109.

1785   HENNION, Antoine. "Une sociologie de l'intermédiaire: le cas du directeur artistique de variétés", *Sociologie du Travail* 25(4), oct-dec 83 : 459-474.

1786   KIRÁLY, Jenő. "A tömegművészet a társadalmi kommunikációban" (Mass art in the social communication), *Kultúra és Közösség* 10(5), 83 : 91-108. [see also 10 (6), 1983: 91-108]

1787   LEVŠINA, I. S. "Vosprijatie iskusstva v massovoj auditorii" (The art perception in a mass audience), in: *K voprosu social'nogo funkcionirovanija iskusstva: teoretičeskie i ėmpiričeskie aspekty.* Moskva, 1982 : 6-52.

1788   MOULIN, Raymonde. "De l'artisan au professionnel: l'artiste", *Sociologie du Travail* 25(4), oct-dec 83 : 388-403. [France]

1789   NOGUCHI, Takashi. *Geijutsu shakaigaku non riron* (Studies on the theories of aesthetic sociology). Hiroshima, Hiroshima Shudo Daigaku Sogo Kenkyujo, 83, 144 p.

1790   PARENT, Claude. *L'architecte, bouffon social.* Tournai, Casterman, 82, 179 p.

1791   PASQUIER, Dominique. "Carrières de femmes: l'art et la manière", *Sociologie du Travail* 25(4), oct-dec 83 : 418-431. [résumé en anglais]

1792   SALAKHOV, Tahir. "Les conditions de travail des artistes en Union soviétique", *Cultures* 9(33), 83 : 188-196.

1793   SHIBATA, Shingo; [ed.]. *Geijutsuteki rodo no riron: geijutsuteki rodo no shakaigaku* (Theory of artistic work: sociology of artistic labor). Tokyo, Aoki Shoten, 83, 459 p.

1794   VITÁNYI, Iván; SÁGI, Mária. "Rediscovery and reanimation of folk-art in modern industrial societies", *International Social Science Journal* 35(1), 83 : 201-211.

1795   WENK, Silke. *Zur gesellschaftlichen Funktion der Kunst: historische Analyse und empirische Untersuchung in Betrieben der Bundesrepublik* (The social function of art: historical analyses and empirical research in enterprises of the Federal Republic). Köln, Pahl-Rugenstein, 82, 235 p.

1796   ZOLBERG, Vera. "Le musée d'art américain: des optiques contradictoires", *Sociologie du Travail* 25(4), oct-dec 83 : 446-458. [résumé en anglais]

1797   ZUKIN, Sharon. "Art in the arms of power: market relations and collective patronage in the capitalist state", *Theory and Society* 11(4), jul 82 : 423-451.

13820   Literature
         Littérature

1798   "Roman (Le) policier", *Littérature* (49), feb 83 : 3-127. [with contributions by Uri EISENZWEIG, Alain ROBBE-GRILLET, Shoshona FELMAN, Roger DADOUN, Michel KORINMAN, Fredric JAMESON]

1799   AARON, Daniel. "The 'Inky curse': miscegenation in the white American literary imagination", *Social Science Information* 22(2), 83 : 169-190.

1800   BALAN, Jars; [ed.]. *Identifications: ethnicity and the writer in Canada.* Edmonton, Canadian Institute of Ukrainian Studies, University of Alberta, 82, xii-158 p.

1801   BALMIR, Guy-Claude. *Du chant au poème: essai de littérature sur le chant et la poésie populaires des noirs américains.* Paris, Payot, 82, 376 p.

1802   BARBE, Jean-Paul. "RDA: tendances du roman, depuis 1975", *Allemagnes d'aujourd'hui* (85), sep 83 : 102-118.

1803   BECK, Brenda E. F. "Indian minstrels as sociologists: political strategies depicted in a local epic", *Contributions to Indian Sociology* 16(1), jan-jun 82 : 35-57.

1804   BOULLATA, Issa J. "Contemporary arab writers and the literary heritage", *International Journal of Middle East Studies* 15(1), feb 83 : 111-119.

1805   CASALI, Elide. *Letteratura e cultura popolare* (Literature and popular culture). Bologna, Zanichelli, 82, vi-237 p.

1806   CORSINI, Gianfranco. "Sociologia della letteratura e studi culturali: la scuola inglese" (Sociology of literature and cultural studies: the English school), *Critica sociologica* 68, 83-84 : 32-38.

1807   DAILLY, Christophe. "The novelist as a cultural policy-maker", *Présence africaine* (125), trim. 1, 83 : 202-213.

1808   DAIYUN, Yue; WAKEMAN, Carolyn. "Women in recent Chinese fiction. A review article", *Journal of Asian Studies* 42(4), aug 83 : 879-888.

1809   FEDJAKIN, I. A.; [ed.]. *Sredstva massovoj informacii i propagandy. Sovetskaja literatura 1980 g.* (Mass information and propaganda media. The Soviet literature of the year 1980). Moskva, INION Akademija Nauk SSSR, 82, 318 p.

1810   GENTILI, Bruno. "Oralità e cultura archaica" (Oral expression and ancient culture), *Critica sociologica* 68, 83-84 : 16-31.

1811   GOURAGE, Ghislain. *Histoire de la littérature haïtienne (de l'indépendance à nos jours).* Port-au-Prince, Éditions de l'Action Sociale, 82, 507 p.

1812   GRAYSON, J. Paul. "Male hegemony and the English Canadian novel", *Canadian Review of Sociology and Anthropology* 20(1), feb 83 : 1-21.

1813   JUDD, Ellen. "China's amateur drama: the movement to popularize the revolutionary mode operas", *Bulletin of Concerned Asian Scholars* 15(1), feb 83 : 26-35.

1814   KARLINGER, Felix; [ed.]. *Rumänische Märchen ausserhalb Rumäniens* (Romanian fairy-tales outside Romania). Kassel, Röth, 82, 128 p.

1815   LIKHATCHEV, Dmitri; ANDREEV, Youri. "Les sources et le caractère de la communauté des littératures soeurs", *Sciences sociales — Académie des Sciences de l'URSS* (4), 82 : 88-96.

1816   MOELLER, Hans-Bernhard; [ed.]. *Latin America and the literature of exile: a comparative view of the 20th-century European refugee writers in the New World.* Heidelberg, C. Winter, 83, 473 p.

1817   RUPEL, Dimitrij. *Literarna sociologya* (Sociology of literature). Ljubljana, Državna Založba Slovenije, 82, 115 p.

1818   SACCÀ, Antonio. "Sul concetto di rappresentatività del personaggio letterario" (On the concept of representativeness of literary personage), *Critica sociologica* 60, 82 : 80-91.

1819   SCHWARZ, Roberto. "The form of the novel on the periphery of capitalism", *Social Science Information* 22(1), 83 : 51-60.

1820   ȘERBAN, Ion Vasile. *Literatură și societate: repere pentru interpretarea sociologica a literaturii* (Literature and society: guidelines for a sociological interpretation of literature). BucureSti, Editura Eminescu, 83, 423 p.

1821   WOJCIECHOWSKI, Jacek. *Funkcje prozy literackiej* (Functions of the literary prose). Kraków, Miejska Biblioteka Publiczna, 83, 134 p.

13830   **Fine arts**
         Beaux-arts

1822   "Architecture et sciences humaines", *Recherches sociologiques* 14(3), 83 : 247-363.

1823   "Peinture (La) et son public", *Actes de la Recherche en Sciences sociales* 49, sep 83 : 2-113.

1824   ALPERS, Svetlana. "L'oeil de l'histoire. L'effet cartographique dans la peinture hollandaise au 17e siècle", *Actes de la Recherche en Sciences sociales* 49, sep 83 : 71-101.

1825   HEINICH, Nathalie. "La perspective académique. Peinture et tradition lettrée: la référence aux mathématiques dans les théories de l'art du 17e siècle", *Actes de la Recherche en Sciences sociales* 49, sep 83 : 47-70.

1826   INAGA, Shigemi. "La réinterprétation de la perspective linéaire au Japon (1740-1830) et son retour en France (1860-1910)", *Actes de la Recherche en Sciences sociales* 49, sep 83 : 29-45.

1827   KRAUSS, André. *Vincent van Gogh: studies in the social aspects of his work*. Göteborg, Acta
          Universitatis Gothoburgensis, 83, 205 p.
1828   NOVIKOV, Félix. "Propos d'un architecte", *Diogène* 121, mar 83 : 73-85. [URSS]

13840   Music
          Musique

1829   "Aspects de la musique", *Diogène* 122, apr-jun 83 : 3-94.
1830   BARSAMIAN, Jacques. *L'âge d'or de la popmusic*. Paris, Ramsay, 82, 243 p.
1831   BONNERY, Bernard. "Bilan de la chanson en RFA", *Allemagnes d'aujourd'hui* (83),
          mar 83 : 143-154.
1832   DE VELDE, P. A. *Popmuziek: een christelijke visie op populaire muziek* (Pop music: a Christian
          outlook on popular music). Groningen, Vuurbaak, 82, 128 p.
1833   FABREGAT, Aquiles; DABEZEIS, Antonio. *Canto popular uruguayo* (Uruguayan popular
          song). Buenos Aires, Juglar, 83, 175 p.
1834   FALCK, Robert; RICE, Timothy; [eds.]. *Cross-cultural perspectives on music*. Toronto-Buffalo,
          University of Toronto Press, 82, xxiv-189 p.
1835   KOIZUMI, Fumio. "Problèmes des musiciens au Japon", *Cultures* 9(33), 83 : 176-187.
1836   MENGER, Pierre-Michel. "De la division du travail musical", *Sociologie du Travail* 25(4),
          oct-dec 83 : 475-488.
1837   MENGER, Pierre-Michel. *Le paradoxe du musicien: le compositeur, le mélomane et l'État dans la
          société contemporaine*. Paris, Flammarion, 83, 395 p.
1838   MOORE, Carlos. *Fela Fela*. Paris, Karthala, 82, 307 p.
1839   STRATTON, Jon. "What is 'popular music'?", *Sociological Review* 31(2), mai 83 : 293-309.
1840   STRÉM, Kálmán. *Ifjúsági hangversenyek hatása* (The impact of concerts for youth). Budapest,
          Müvelődéskutató Intézet, 82, 72 p.
1841   VILLARAN, Carlos A. *Sociología de la música* (Sociology of music). Buenos Aires, Droit,
          83, 155 p.

13850   Dramatic art
          Art dramatique

1842   "Théâtre (La) par ceux qui le font", *Europe* 61(648), apr 83 : 3-135. [France] [with
          contributions by Raymonde TEMKINE, Georges LAVAUDANT, Roger PLANCHON,
          Philippe ADRIEN, Gildas BOURDET, Daniel MESGUISCH]
1843   CHONG, Chin-Su. "Le théâtre coréen en 1982", *Revue de Corée* 15(1), spr 83 : 94-103.
1844   COLLINS, J. A. *Contemporary theater in Puerto Rico: the decade of the seventies*. Río Piedras,
          Editorial Universitaria, Universidad de Puerto Rico, 82, xxiii-261 p.
1845   DELDIME, Roger. "Théâtre, public, perception", *Revue de l'Institut de Sociologie* (3-4),
          83 : 493-496.
1846   DELDIME, Roger; [ed.]. "Le théâtre belge de langue française", *Revue de l'Institut de Sociologie*
          (1-2), 83 : 7-254. [with contributions by Jeanne PIGEON]
1847   FABRE, Geneviève. *Le théâtre noir aux États-Unis*. Paris, Éditions du CNRS, 82, 354 p.
1848   HRENOV, N. A.; [ed.]. *Voprosy sociologii teatra* (Questions on the sociology of theatre).
          Moskva, Vserossijskoe Teatral'noe Obščestvo, 82, 296 p.
1849   JAUMAIN, Michel. "Quelques aspects économiques des arts du spectacle vivant", *Revue de
          l'Institut de Sociologie* (3-4), 82 : 539-571.
1850   NGUGI WA THIONG'O. "Women in cultural work: the fate of Kamiríthu people's theatre
          in Kenya", *Development Dialogue* (1-2), 82 : 115-133.
1851   PAVIS, Patrice. *Voix et images de la scène: essais de sémiologie théâtrale*. Lille, Presses Universitaires
          de Lille, 82, 225-16 p.
1852   RAZ, Jacob. *Audience and actors: a study of their interaction in the Japanese traditional theatre*. Leiden,
          E. J. Brill, 83, xii-307 p.

13860   Folk art
          Art populaire

13900   EDUCATION
          ÉDUCATION

13910   Educational sociology
          Sociologie de l'éducation

1853   "Education and personhood", *Teachers College Record* 84(2), wint 82 : 283-390. [with
        contributions by Philip H. PHENIX, Iona H. GINSBURG, Peter A. BERTOCCI]
1854   "Education and training", *Pakistan Year Book* (10), 83 : 284-302. [Pakistan]
1855   "Éducation en Amérique latine: entre la reproduction et l'invention", *Amérique latine* (14),
        jun 83 : 22-78. [with contributions by German W. RAMA; Juan Carlos TEDESCO,
        Jean Eduardo GARCIA-HUIDOBRO, Roberto SANTANA, Iván NUÑEZ]
1856   "Minority education in comparative perspective", *Comparative Education Review* 27(2),
        jun 83 : 165-245. [with contributions by John U. OGBU, Bee-lan CHAN WANG,
        John N. HAWKINS, Brian M. BULLIVANT]
1857   ABROSOLI, Luigi. *La scuola in Italia dal dopoguerra ad oggi* (School in Italy from afterwar
        to nowadays). Bologna, Il Mulino, 82, 525 p.
1858   ALONSO HINOJAL, Isidoro. "Centro y periferia en sociología de la educación: su desigual
        e incierto proceso de institucionalización" (Centre and periphery in educational sociology:
        its unequal and uncertain process of institutionalization), *Revista Española de Investigaciones
        Sociológicas* 24, oct-dec 83 : 163-181. [Spain]
1859   ALTBACH, Philip G.; ARNOVE, Robert F.; KELLY, Gail P.; [eds.]. *Comparative education.*
        New York, NY, Macmillan, 82, ix-533 p.
1860   ANWEILER, Oskar; [ed.]. *Bildung und Erziehung in Osteuropa im 20. Jahrhundert: ausgewählte
        Beiträge zum Zweiten Weltkongress für Sowjet- und Osteuropastudien* (Training and education
        in Eastern Europe in the 20th century: selected contributions to the 2nd World Congress
        for Soviet and East European studies). Berlin, Berlin Verlag, 82, 216 p.
1861   ARCHER, Margaret Scotford; [ed.]. *The sociology of educational expansion: take-off, growth and
        inflation in educational systems.* Beverly Hills, CA, Sage Publications, 82, 313 p.
1862   BARÓTI, F. *Nevelésszociológia. Iskolai és társadalmi mobilitás* (Sociology of education. School
        and social mobility). Budapest, National Pedagogical Library and Museum, 82, 99 p.
1863   BARTOLOMÉ, Margarita; [et al.]. *Modelos de investigación educativa* (Educational research
        models). Barcelona, Publicación del Instituto de Ciencias de la Educación de la Universidad
        de Barcelona, 82, 354 p.
1864   BARTON, Leo; WALKER, Stephen; [eds.]. *Race, class, and education.* London, Croom
        Helm, 83, 235 p. [UK]
1865   BASTIDA, F.; LARA, F. "Educación y cambio" (Education and change), *Documentación
        Social* (50), jan-mar 83 : 185-200. [Spain]
1866   BASU, Aparna. *Essays in the history of Indian education.* New Delhi, Concept, 82, x-105 p.
1867   BEILLEROT, Jacky. *La société pédagogique: action pédagogique et contrôle social.* Paris, Presses
        Universitaires de France, 82, 223 p.
1868   BELLOUNI, Ahmed. "Analyse du système éducatif en Tunisie depuis l'indépendance",
        Conjoncture (Tunis) (70), aug 82 : 1-13.
1869   BESOZZI, Elena. "Concetti weberiani nella sociologia dell'educazione" (Weberian concepts
        in the sociology of education), *Studi di Sociologia* 21(1), mar 83 : 3-13.
1870   BLAT GIMENO, José. *Education in Latin America and the Caribbean: trends and prospects,
        1970-2000.* Paris, UNESCO, 83, 190 p. [Regional Conference of Ministers of Education
        and Those Responsible for Economic Planning of Member States in Latin America
        and the Caribbean, organized by UNESCO, Mexico City, 1979]
1871   BLISS, Joan; [et al.]. *Qualitative data analysis for educational research: a guide to uses of systemic
        networks.* London, Croom Helm, 83, 215 p.
1872   BROWNHILL, Robert J. *Education and the nature of knowledge.* London, Croom Helm, 83, 135 p.
1873   BUSCH, Adelheid. *Die vergleichende Pädagogik in der DDR: eine disziplingeschichtliche Untersuchung*
        (Comparative education in the GDR: a discipline historical research). München,
        Berchman, 83, 263 p.
1874   CAMBRE MARIÑO, Jesus. "Puerto Rico: educación a la deriva" (Puerto Rico: education
        adrift), *Cuadernos americanos* 42(4), aug 83 : 43-57.
1875   COBALTI, Antonio. "Alcune riflessioni sull'insegnamento della sociologia dell'educazione
        nelle università italiane" (The teaching of educational sociology in Italian universities:
        some considerations), *Studi di Sociologia* 21(3), jul-sep 83 : 293-297.
1876   COHEN, Louis; THOMAS, John Bernard; MANION, Lawrence; [eds.]. *Educational research
        and development in Britain, 1970-1980.* Windsor, Berks., NFER-Nelson, 82, xxi-567 p.
1877   COLE, Mike. "Contradictions in the educational theory of Gintis and Bowles", *Sociological
        Review* 31(3), aug 83 : 471-488. [About Samuel BOWLES, Herbert GINTIS. 'Schooling
        in Capitalist America', London, Routledge and Kegan Paul, 1976]

1878   COX, Caroline; MARKS, John; [eds.]. *The right to learn: purpose, professionalism, and accountability in State education*. London, Centre for Policy Studies, 82, 222 p. [UK]

1879   DELÁNCER, Víctor Hugo. *Planeamiento, educación y política: enfoques para una sociología de la educación dominicana* (Planning, education and policy: focal points for a sociology of the Dominican education). Santo Domingo, DN, Taller, 83, 145 p.

1880   EGGINTON, Everett. "Educational research in Latin America: a twelve-year perspective", *Comparative Education Review* 27(1), feb 83 : 119-127.

1881   EPSTEIN, Erwin H. "Currents left and right: ideology in comparative education", *Comparative Education Review* 27(1), feb 83 : 3-45.

1882   EZEWU, Edward. *Sociology of education*. London, Longman, 83, vii-152 p.

1883   GIOVANNINI, Graziella. "La ricerca in sociologia dell'educazione: due nodi di riflessione e un problema" (Research in the sociology of education: two reflection points and one problem), *Studi di Sociologia* 21(3), jul-sep 83 : 298-302. [Italy]

1884   GOODNOW, Wilma Elizabeth. "The contingency theory of education", *International Journal of Lifelong Education* 1(4), 82 : 341-352.

1885   HEYNEMAN, Stephen P. "Education during a period of austerity: Uganda, 1971-1981", *Comparative Education Review* 27(3), oct 83 : 403-413.

1886   JOHNSTONE, James N.; JIYONO, J. "Out-of-school factors and educational achievement in Indonesia", *Comparative Education Review* 27(2), jun 83 : 278-295.

1887   KIKUCHI, Sachiko; SENZAKI, Takeshi; [eds.]. *Ningen keisei no shakaigaku* (Sociology of education). Tokyo, Fukumura Shuppan, 83, 238 p.

1888   KITA KYANKENGE MASANDI. *Colonisation et enseignement: cas du Zaïre avant 1960*. Bukavu, Éditions du CERUKI, 82, 287 p.

1889   KLOPOV, É. V. "Problemy obrazovanija v SSSR i povyšenie obrazovatel'nogo urovnja rabočego klassa: istoriko-sociologičeskij analiz" (Education problems in the USSR and the elevation of the working class educational level: an historical and sociological analysis), in: *K izučeniju rabočego klassa i rabočego dviženija*. Moskva, 1982 : 328-346.

1890   LANDSHEERE, Gilbert de. *Empirical research in education*. Paris, UNESCO, 82, 113 p.

1891   LÉON, Antoine. *Histoire de l'éducation populaire en France*. Paris, F. Nathan, 83, 207 p.

1892   LERENA ALESÓN, Carlos. *Reprimir y liberar: crítica sociológica de la educación y de la cultura contemporáneas* (Repression and liberation: sociological critique of contemporary education and culture). Madrid, Akal, 83, 643 p.

1893   LIM, Chong-Yah. *Education and national development*. Singapore, Federal Publications, 83, vi-122 p. [Singapore]

1894   MARTIN, Michel. *Sémiologie de l'image et pédagogie: pour une pédagogie de la recherche*. Paris, Presses Universitaires de France, 82, 267 p.

1895   MAYDELL, Jost von; [ed.]. *Bildungsforschung und Gesellschaftspolitik* (Educational research and social policy). Oldenburg, H. Holzberg, 82, 243 p. [Germany FR]

1896   MERANI, Alberto L. *La educación en Latinoamérica: mito y realidad* (Education in Latin America: myth and reality). México, DF, Editorial Grijalbo, 83, 203 p.

1897   METELICA, L. V. "Internationalistskoe i patriotičeskoe vospitanie v zrelom socialističeskom obščestve" (Internationalist and patriotic education in the mature socialist society), *Naucnye Doklady vysšej Školy. Naučnyj Kommunizma* (6), 82 : 56-65.

1898   MIFFLEN, Frank James; MIFFLEN, Sydney C. *The sociology of education: Canada and beyond*. Calgary, AB, Detselig Enterprises, 82, 407 p.

1899   MÍGUEZ, Francisco. *Metodología de la educación comparada* (Methodology of comparative education). Buenos Aires, Ediciones Centro Cultural Corregidor, 83, 169 p.

1900   MONCADA, Alberto. "Los usos de la sociología de la educación" (Uses of educational sociology), *Revista internacional de Sociología (Madrid)* 40(43), sep 82 : 399-411. [Spain]

1901   MORI, Shigeo. "Weber no kyoiku shakaigaku" (Sociology of education in Max Weber), *Kyoiku shakaigaku kenkyu* 38, 83 : 185-197.

1902   NAKAJIMA, Akinori. "L'Annee Sociologique to kyoiku shakaigaku" ('L'Année sociologique' and sociology of education), *Aichi kyoiku daigaku Aikyodai kenpo, kyoiku-kagaku-hen* 32, 83 : 41-60.

1903   NELLO, Guiomar N. de. *Educación y proceso de democratización en Brasil* (Education and democratization process in Brazil). Buenos Aires, FLACSO, 83, s.p.

1904   NESTVOGEL, Renate. "Lernen von der Dritten Welt: Traditionelle afrikanische Erziehungsmuster" (Learning from the Third World: Africa's traditional educative schemes), *Afrika Spectrum* 18(1), 83 : 27-47. [résumés in French and English]

1905   PANTELEDIS, Veronica S. *Arab education, 1956-1978: a bibliography*. London, Mansell Publications, 82, xvii-552 p.

1906   PATAKI, Ferenc. *Nevelés és társadalom. Válogatott tanulmányok* (Education and society. Selected studies). Budapest, Tankönyvkiadó, 82, 351 p.

1907   RIBOLZI, Luisa. "Problemi e prospettive di sociologia dell'educazione. Note in margine ad un incontro di studio" (Problems and prospects of educational sociology. Notes about a working meeting), *Studi di Sociologia* 21(2), apr-jun 83 : 221-232.
1908   RODRIGUES, Neidson. *Estado, educação e desenvolvimento econômico* (State, education and economic development). São Paulo-SP, Editora Autores Associados, Cortez Editora, 82, 158 p. [Brazil]
1909   ROUQUAIROL, Pierre. "L'enseignement en Guinée équatoriale avant août 1979", *Mois en Afrique* 18(203-204), jan 83 : 129-143.
1910   SEIFERT, Kelvin. *Educational psychology.* Boston, MA, Houghton Mifflin, 83, xi-453 p.
1911   SIROTNIK, Kenneth A. "What you see is what you get: consistency, persistency, and mediocrity in classrooms", *Harvard Educational Review* 53(1), feb 83 : 16-31. [USA]
1912   TYLER, William. *The sociology of the school: a review.* Herne Bay Kent, the author, 82, 77 p.
1913   WIŚNIEWSKI, Wiesław. "Wykształcenie a przemiany niektoórych aspiracji i potrzeb społecznych" (Education and transformation of some social needs and aspirations), *Problemy Marksizmu-Leninizmu* 3-4, 83 : 36-48.
1914   WOODRING, Paul. *The persistent problems of education.* Bloomington, IN, Phi Delta Kappa Educational Foundation, 83, 123 p. [USA]
1915   WOSKOWSKI, Jan. *Socjologia wychowania* (Sociology of education). Warszawa, Wydawnictwa Szkolne i Pedagogiczne, 83, 168 p.
1916   YADAV, S. K. *Harijan awareness of educational schemes: antecedents and consequences.* Gurgaon, Academic Press, 83, 96 p.

13920   Educational systems. Educational policy
Systèmes d'enseignement. Politique de l'éducation

1917   "Apprendre et travailler", *Perspectives (UNESCO)* 12(4), 82 : 477-550. [with contributions by Andri ISAKSSON, Stephen CASTLES, Dimitar TZVETKOV, Carlos ORNELAS, Amara FOFANA]
1918   "Éducation-formation", *Recherches économiques et sociales* (5), trim. 1, 83 : 3-154. [France] [with contributions by Robert FRAISSE, Pierre-Yves DUWOYE, Michel de VIRVILLE, Pascale GRUSON, Hélène DEBROUSSES]
1919   "Orientación (La) escolar" (Educational guidance), *Revista de educación* 30(270), aug 82 : 5-210. [Spain] [with contributions by Zacaría RAMO TRAVER, José Antonio RIOS GONZALEZ, Adelicio CABALERRO CABALLERO, Serafín SANCHEZ SANCHEZ, Mario de MIGUEL DIAZ]
1920   "Politique (Une) de l'éducation pour l'Europe", *Documentation européenne* (4), 82 : 3-33.
1921   "Ressources du non-formel", *Perspectives (UNESCO)* 13(1), 83 : 37-117. [with contributions by Manzoor AHMED, Harbans S. BHOLA, Chitras NAIK, David BROCKINGTON, Roger WHITE]
1922   "School desegregation", *Journal of Black Studies* 13(2), dec 82 : 139-252. [USA] [with contributions by Frank BROWN, J. John HARRIS, Gail E. THOMAS]
1923   "Schulpolitik in Österreich" (School policy in Austria), *Österreichische Zeitschrift für Politikwissenschaft* 12(1), 83 : 5-120. [résumés en anglais; with contributions by Susanne DERMUTZ]
1924   AGGARWAL, J. C. *Development and planning of modern education: with special reference to India.* New Delhi, Vikas Publishing House, 82, 424 p.
1925   AIKARA, J.; KURRIEN, J. "Mass education for development in India: evolution and new strategies", *Indian Journal of Social Work* 43(4), jan 83 : 439-454.
1926   ALLIE, Robert. "L'évolution de la scolarisation du Québec, 1951-1976", *Cahiers québécois de Démographie* 11(3), dec 82 : 295-322.
1927   BASDEVANT, Claire. "Les carrières scolaires. Étude comparative de la trajectoire scolaire d'adolescents français et immigrés", *Annales de Vaucresson* 20, 83 : 89-101. [France]
1928   BEHRMAN, Jere R.; BIRDSALL, Nancy. "The quality of schooling: quantity alone is misleading", *American Economic Review* 73(5), dec 83 : 928-946.
1929   BENČO, Jozef. "Niektoré aspekty prognózovania a plánovania výchovy a vzdelávania" (Some aspects of projection and planning of education), *Ekonomický Časopis* 31(8), 83 : 769-781. [Czechoslovakia]
1930   BLAUG, Mark; DOUGHERTY, Christopher; PSACHAROPOULOS, George. "The distribution of schooling and the distribution of earnings: raising the school leaving age in 1972", *Manchester School of Economic and Social Studies* 50(1), mar 82 : 24-40. [UK]
1931   BOUSQUET, Pierre; [et al.]. *Histoire de l'administration de l'enseignement en France, 1789-1981.* Genéve, Droz, 83, 154 p.

1932   CAO GARCIA, Ramon. "Educación privada y desigualdad: un análisis económico" (Private education and inequality: an economic analysis), *Revista de Ciencias sociales* 23(1-2), jun 81 : 53-69. [Puerto Rico]

1933   CRAIN, Robert L.; MAHARD, Rita E. "The consequences of controversy accompanying institutional change: the case of school desegregation", *American Sociological Review* 47(6), dec 82 : 697-708.

1934   DEBLÉ, Isabelle. "Population et besoins scolaires", *Tiers-Monde* 24(94), jun 83 : 349-366.

1935   DRONKERS, Jaap. "Have unequalities in educational opportunity changed in the Netherlands? A review of empirical evidence", *Netherlands Journal of Sociology* 19(2), oct 83 : 133-150.

1936   DUCLAUD-WILLIAMS, Roger. "Centralization and incremental change in France: the case of the Haby educational reform", *British Journal of Political Science* 13(1), jan 83 : 71-91.

1937   EVERHART, Robert B.; [ed.]. *The public school monopoly: a critical analysis of education and the state of American society.* San Francisco, CA, Pacific Institute for Public Policy Research; Cambridge, MA, Harper and Row, Ballinger, 82, xxi-583 p.

1938   FORRAY R., Katalin. "Iskolázási tendenciák Budapesten" (Trends of schooling in Budapest), *Szociológia* 11(3), 82 : 399-415.

1939   FRY, Gerald W. "Empirical indicators of educational equity and equality: a Thai case study", *Social Indicators Research* 12(2), feb 83 : 199-215.

1940   GARNIER, Maurice A. "Equality of educational opportunities in Western Europe", *Comparative Social Research* 5, 82 : 221-243.

1941   GAVRILENKO, I. N. "Selektivnaja funkcija školy v buržuaznoj obščestve" (The school selective functions in the bourgeois society), *Sovetskaja Pedagogika* (1), 83 : 126-129.

1942   GEISSLER, Rainer. "Bildungschancen und Statusvererbung in der DDR" (Educational opportunities and status attainment in the German DR), *Kölner Zeitschrift für Soziologie und Sozialpsychologie* 35(4), dec 83 : 755-770.

1943   GEORGEOFF, Peter John. *The educational system of Yugoslavia.* Washington, DC, United States Department of Education, International Education Programs, 82, 116 p.

1944   HANSON, E. Mark. "Administrative development in the Colombian Ministry of Education: a case analysis in the 1970's", *Comparative Education Review* 27(1), feb 83 : 89-107.

1945   HEBERER, Thomas. "Das Erziehungswesen der nationalen Minderheiten in China" (The education of national minorities in China), *Asien* (6), 83 : 67-89.

1946   HEYNEMAN, Stephen P.; LOXLEY, William A. "The effect of primary-school quality on academic achievement across twenty-nine high and low income countries", *American Journal of Sociology* 88(6), mai 83 : 1162-1194.

1947   HOGGART, Keith. "Changes in education outputs in English local authorities, 1949-1974", *Public Administration* 61(2), sum 83 : 169-178.

1948   HORII, Kishio. "Bunka chitei no kasetsu saikō" (Reflection on the hypothesis of cultural lag), *Yahata daigaku ronshu* 34(2), 83 : 26-41.

1949   HOWELL, David Antony; BROWN, Roger. *Educational policy making: an analysis.* London, Heinemann Education Books for the Institute of Education, University of London, 83, 135 p. [UK]

1950   HUNTER, Howard O. "The Constitutional status of academic freedom in the United States", *Minerva* 19(4), wint 81 : 519-568.

1951   INKELES, Alex; SIROWY, Larry. "Convergent and divergent trends in national education systems", *Social Forces* 62(2), dec 83 : 303-333.

1952   KALMUSS, Debra; [et al.]. "Political conflict in applied scholarship: expert witnesses in school desegregation litigation", *Social Problems* 30(2), dec 82 : 168-178.

1953   KAMENS, David H.; ROSS, R. Danforth. "Chartering national educational systems: the institutionalization of education for elite recruitment and its consequences", *International Journal of Comparative Sociology (Leiden)* 24(3-4), sep-dec 83 : 176-186.

1954   KARYPKULOV, A. K. "Razvitie sistemy narodnogo obrazovanija — važnyj faktor ukreplenija internacional'nogo ėdinstva sovetskogo naroda" (Development of the people's education system is an essential factor of reinforcement of the Soviet people's unity), *Voprosy Filosofii* 35(10), 82 : 30-41.

1955   KASSAM, Yusuf. "Nyerere, philosophy and educational experiment in Tanzania", *Interchange* 14(1), 83 : 56-68.

1956   KORPOROWICZ, Leszek. "Kompetencja kulturowa jako problem badawczy" (Cultural competence as a research problem), *Kultura i Społeczeństwo* 27(1), 83 : 35-47.

1957   KUČERA, Milan. "Le niveau d'éducation de la population", *Demosta* 15(4), 82 : 18-23. [Czechoslovakia]

1958   LODGE, Paul. *Educational policy and educational inequality.* Oxford, M. Robertson, 82, xiii-256 p. [UK]

1959   MACHADO, Lia Zanotta. *Estado, escola e ideologia* (State, school and ideology). São Paulo, Brasiliense, 83, 242 p. [Brazil]

1960   MAUGER, Peter. "Changing policy and practice in Chinese rural education", *China Quarterly* (93), mar 83 : 138-148.

1961   MCCLENDON, McKee J.; PESTELLO, Fred P. "Self-interest and public policy attitude formation: busing for school desegregation", *Sociological Focus* 16(1), jan 83 : 1-12. [USA]

1962   MEESTERS, M.; DRONKERS, J.; SCHIJF, H. "Veranderende onderwijskansen? Een derde voorbeeld en afrondende conclusies" (Changing educational opportunities? A third example and conclusions), *Mens en Maatschappij* 58(1), feb 83 : 5-27. [Netherlands]

1963   MONCADA, Alberto. *La crisis de la planificación educativa en América Latina* (Educational planning crisis in Latin America). Madrid, Tecnos, 82, 221 p.

1964   MORINIS, E. A. "Levels of culture in Hinduism: a case study of dream incubation at a Bengali pilgrimage centre", *Contributions to Indian Sociology* 16(2), jul-dec 82 : 255-270. [Tarakeswar, India]

1965   MUZAMMIL, Mohd. "Education and economic equality", *Indian Journal of Economics* 63(249), oct 82 : 239-247.

1966   NAJDUCHOWSKA, Halina. "Droga na studia i wartość studiów" (A way to higher schools and value of studies), *Studia Socjologiczne* 89(2), 83 : 335-359.

1967   NISKANEN, Erkki A.; [et al.]. *Research project on educational aims*. Helsinki, Department of Education, University of Helsinki, 82, 105 p.

1968   OPOLSKI, Krzysztof. "Oświata i demokracja: dialektyka rozwoju" (Education and democracy: dialectics of development), *Studia Socjologiczne* 88(1), 83 : 107-122.

1969   ORGANISATION DE COOPÉRATION ET DE DÉVELOPPEMENT ÉCONOMIQUES. *Examens des politiques nationales d'éducation: Nouvelle-Zélande*. Paris, OCDE, 83, 161 p.

1970   ORGANISATION DE COOPÉRATION ET DE DÉVELOPPEMENT ÉCONOMIQUES. *L'enseignement obligatoire face à l'évolution de la société*. Paris, OCDE, 83, 167 p.

1971   ORGANISATION DE COOPÉRATION ET DE DÉVELOPPEMENT ÉCONOMIQUES. *La planification de l'enseignement: vers une réévaluation*. Paris, OCDE, 83, 438 p.

1972   RAMA, Germán W. *Unidad y diferenciación de los sistemas educativos latinoamericanos* (Unity and differentiation of Latin American educational systems). Buenos Aires, FLACSO, 83, 24 p.

1973   REGUZZONI, Mario. "Riforma della scuola e sistema 'policentrico' di formazione" (School reform and 'polycentric' system of formation), *Aggiornamenti sociali* 33(11), nov 82 : 661-676. [Italy]

1974   ROSS, Kenneth Norman. *Social area indicators of educational need: a study of the use of census descriptions of school neighbourhoods in guiding decisions concerning the allocation of resources to educationally disadvantaged schools in Australia*. Hawthorn, Vic., Australian Council for Educational Research, 83, xiv-213 p.

1975   ROSSELL, Christine H.; CRAIN, Robert L. "The importance of political factors in explaining Northern school desegregation", *American Journal of Political Science* 26(4), nov 82 : 772-796. [USA]

1976   ROWLAND, D. T. *Population and educational planning*. Canberra, Australian Government Publishing Service, 83, viii-211 p.

1977   RUSSO, Cosimo P. "Developing educational policies for traditionally oriented aborigenes", *Interchange* 14(2), 83 : 1-13. [Australia]

1978   SAMOFF, Joel. "Schooling and socialism: educational reform in Tanzania", *Genève-Afrique* 21(1), 83 : 55-72.

1979   SCHIEFELBEIN, Ernesto. *Educational networks in Latin America: their role in the production, diffusion, and use of educational knowledge*. Ottawa, International Development Research Centre, 82, 44 p.

1980   SCHIFF, Michel. *L'intelligence gaspillée: inégalité sociale, injustice scolaire*. Paris, Seuil, 82, 225 p.

1981   SHAPIRO, H. Svi. "Class, ideology and basic skills movement: a study in the sociology of educational reform", *Interchange* 14(2), 83 : 14-24. [USA]

1982   SINGH, Nirmal. *Education under siege: a sociological study of private colleges*. New Delhi, Concept, 83, xiii-238 p.

1983   SMITH WILTSHIRE, David. "Modela de desarrollo y políticas educativas en Panamá, 1970-1980" (Development model and educational policy in Panama, 1970-1980), *Estudios sociales centroamericanos* 12(34), apr 83 : 59-84.

1984   SOBHE, Khosrow. "Educational planning for engineering schools: a study of Iran between 1962 and 1982", *Higher Education* 12(1), jan 83 : 61-76.

1985   TIMMONS, G. "The dilemma of selection in education", *New Universities Quarterly* 36(4), aut 82 : 375-387.

1986   TOMES, Nigel. "Religion and the rate of return on human capital: evidence from Canada", *Canadian Journal of Economics / Revue canadienne d'Économique* 16(1), feb 83 : 122-138.

1987   URWICK, James. "Politics and professionalism in Nigerian educational planning", *Comparative Education Review* 27(3), oct 83 : 323-340.

1988   VAN SCHALKWYK, Ockert Johannes. *Focus on the education system.* Durban, Butterworths, 82, 241 p.

1989   WALTERS, Pamela Barnhouse; RUBINSON, Richard. "Educational expansion and economic output in the United States, 1890-1969: a production function analysis", *American Sociological Review* 48(4), aug 83 : 480-493.

1990   WIRT, Frederick M.; KIRST, Michael W. *Schools in conflict: the politics of education.* Berkeley, CA, McCutchan Publishing Corporation, 82, xii-322 p. [USA]

1991   WOODSIDE, Alexander. "The triumphs and failures of mass education in Vietnam", *Pacific Affairs* 56(3), aut 83 : 401-427.

13930   Primary education. Secondary education
Enseignement primaire. Enseignement secondaire

1992   "Arts (The) and humanities in America's schools", *Daedalus* 112(3), sum 83 : 1-247. [with contributions by William G. DURDEN and Jon J. MURRAY]

1993   "Reforma (La) de las ensenanzas medias" (Reform of secondary education), *Revista de educación* 30(271), dec 82 : 3-171. [Spain] [with contributions by Manuel UTANDE IGUALADA, José V. BEVIA PASTOR, Matilde VAZQUEZ]

1994   BISSON, Antonio; LAVIGNE, Jacques. "Départs et abandons scolaires au niveau secondaire selon la langue d'enseignement, Québec, 1972-73 à 1977-78", *Cahiers québécois de Démographie* 11(2), aug 82 : 167-194. [Canada]

1995   BROWN, Janet F.; [ed.]. *Curriculum planning for young children.* Washington, DC, National Association for the Education of Young Children, 82, 267 p.

1996   CADWALLADER, Mervyn L. "The destruction of the College and the collapse of general education", *Teachers College Record* 84(4), sum 83 : 909-916.

1997   CSAPO, Marg. "Universal primary education in Nigeria: its problems and implications", *African Studies Review* 26(1), mar 83 : 91-106.

1998   ELCHARDUS, M. "Kinderopvang en Onafhankelijkheidsverwerving" (Day care of school-age children), *Bevolking en Gezin* (2), 82 : 205-213. [Belgium]

1999   HEYNEMAN, Stephen P.; LOXLEY, William A. "The distribution of primary school quality within high and low income countries", *Comparative Education Review* 27(1), feb 83 : 108-118.

2000   ISANGO, Idi Wanzila. "Quelle réforme pour l'enseignement secondaire au Zaïre?", *Zaïre-Afrique* 22(170), dec 82 : 603-616.

2001   MAHEU, Robert; MAISONNEUVE, Daniel. "La progression des élèves au secondaire supérieur", *Cahiers québécois de Démographie* 11(2), aug 82 : 139-166. [Canada]

2002   MOUALLEM, Antoinette Safa. *L'école maternelle au Liban et en France.* Beyrouth, Université libanaise, 83, 273 p.

2003   OKABE, Shigeru; TANAKA, Yukitane; [eds.]. *Jissen hoiku genri no kenkyu* (Studies of practical principles in early childhood education). Tokyo, Gakujutsu Tosho Shuppansha, 83, 199 p. [Japan]

2004   ORTEGA RUIZ, P. "La escuela entre la reproducción y el cambio" (School between reproduction and change), *Cuadernos de Realidades Sociales* (22), jan 83 : 73-94.

2005   RAMSAY, Peter; [et al.]. "Successful and unsuccessful schools: a study in Southern Auckland", *Australian and New Zealand Journal of Sociology* 19(2), jul 83 : 272-304. [New Zealand]

2006   RICHARDS, Colin; [ed.]. *New directions in primary education.* Lewes, Sussex, Falmer Press, 82, 319 p. [UK]

2007   SIQUET, Marie-Jeanne. "Bilan de l'enseignement secondaire rénové", *Wallonie* 10(5), 83 : 151-163.

2008   TANGUY, Lucie. "Savoirs et rapports sociaux dans l'enseignement secondaire en France", *Revue française de Sociologie* 24(2), apr-jun 83 : 227-254. [résumés en anglais, allemand et espagnol]

2009   VIÑAO FRAGO, Antonio. *Política y educación en los orígenes de la España contemporánea: examen especial de sus relaciones en la enseñanza secundaria* (Politics and education in the origins of the contemporary Spain: special examination of their relationships in secondary education). Madrid, Siglo Veintiuno de España, 82, viii-516 p.

2010   WESTHUES, Kenneth. "Defensiveness and social structure: the ideology of Catholic school trustees", *Canadian Review of Sociology and Anthropology* 20(1), feb 83 : 59-78. [Canada]

13940 School environment
Milieu scolaire

2011 BENADUSI, Luciano. *Governo e programmazione della scuola: analisi sociologiche e ipotesi progettuali* (School management and programming: sociological analyses and projective assumptions). Venezia, Marsilio, 82, 238 p. [Italy]

2012 MILLER, Paul W. "The determinants of school participation rates: a cross-sectional analysis for New South Wales and Victoria", *Economic Record* 59(164), mar 83 : 43-56.

2013 OXENHAM, John. *Paper qualification syndrome (PQS) and unemployment of school leavers: a comparative sub-regional study.* Addis Ababa, Jobs and Skills Programme for Africa, 82, viii-227 p.

2014 SHUKLA, P. D. *Administration of education in India.* New Delhi, Vikas, 83, viii-216 p.

2015 TAKEYA, Tetsuhiro; TAKEI, Makiji. "Kosen gakusei no gakko tekio ni kansuru tsuiseki kenkyu: Tokuni hattatsusa, sedaiṭeki-sa o tegakarinishite" (A follow-up study on the adjustment of technical college students to school-life: from the viewpoint of development and age segregation), *Tsuruoka kogyo koto senmon gakko kenkyu kiyo* 18, 83 : 95-120. [Japan]

2016 WILES, Jon; BONDI, Joseph. *Principles of school administration: the real world of leadership in schools.* Columbus, OH, Merrill, 83, x-355 p.

2017 ZERCHYKOV, Ross; OWEN, Helen; WEAVER, W. Timothy. *A review of the literature and an annotated bibliography on managing decline in school systems.* Boston, MA, Institute for Responsive Education, 82, xv-276 p.

13950 Higher education
Enseignement supérieur

2018 "Education (The) of talented students", *Minerva* 19(3), aut 81 : 480-497. [Germany FR]

2019 "Enseignement supérieur et université", *Études* 358(4), apr 83 : 465-485. [France] [with contributions by Claude JEANTET, Marcel MERLE]

2020 AL-SHAMI, Ibrahim. "The need for Saudi faculty and the media for instruction in Saudi Arabian universities", *Higher Education* 12(3), jun 83 : 285-296.

2021 ALCANDRE, Jean-Jacques. "La politique universitaire de la coalition sociale-libérale", *Allemagnes d'aujourd'hui* (83), mar 83 : 74-80. [Germany FR]

2022 ALMARCHA BARBADO, María Amparo. *Autoridad y privilegio en la universidad española* (Authority and privilege in Spanish university). Madrid, Centro de Investigaciones Sociológicas, 82, 376 p.

2023 ALMARCHA, Amparo. "Poder y participación en el sistema de enseñanza superior" (Power and participation in the higher education system), *Revista Española de Investigaciones Sociológicas* 24, oct-dec 83 : 185-198. [Spain]

2024 ALTBACH, Philip G. *Higher education in the Third World: themes and variations.* Singapore, Maruzen Asia, Regional Institute of Higher Education and Development, 82, 228 p.

2025 ALUDAAT, K. "Les étudiants jordaniens à l'étranger de 1975 à 1981: relations culturelles et relations économiques", *Cahiers de l'Analyse des Données* 8(3), 83 : 293-310. [résumés en anglais et en arabe]

2026 ANNAN. "British higher education, 1960-80: a personal retrospect", *Minerva* 20(1-2), sum 82 : 1-24.

2027 AUSTIN, Dennis. "Ivory towers? Universities in Sri Lanka", *Minerva* 19(2), sum 81 : 203-235.

2028 BARDIS, Panos D. "Student attitudes toward world government, universal peace, and international law", *Sociologia internationalis* 21(1-2), 83 : 261-274. [USA]

2029 BARMAR, Geneviève; DULIOUST, Nicole. *Étudiants-ouvriers chinois en France, 1920-1940: catalogue des archives conservées au Centre de recherches et de documentation sur la Chine contemporaine de l'École des hautes études en sciences sociales.* Paris, Éditions de l'EHESS, 81, xviii-160 p.

2030 BERNALES, B. Enrique. "Universidad, política e identidad nacional" (University, politics and national identity), *Cuadernos americanos* 42(3), jun 83 : 31-43. [Latin America]

2031 BETEILLE, André. "The Indian university: academic standards and the pursuit of equality", *Minerva* 19(2), sum 81 : 282-310.

2032 BROADED, Montgomery. "Higher education policy changes and stratification in China", *China Quarterly* (93), mar 83 : 125-137.

2033 CAMARERO GONZÁLEZ, Arturo. "La expansión del movimiento estudiantil en Madrid. Formas de movilización y organización. Solidaridad con los estudiantes" (Expansion of the student movement in Madrid. Forms of mobilization and organization. Solidarity with the students), *Revista internacional de Sociología (Madrid)* 40(43), sep 82 : 349-395.

2034 CANCIAN, Francesca M. "Rapid social change: women students in business schools", *Sociology and Social Research* 66(2), jan 82 : 169-183. [USA]

2035   CARABAÑA, Julio; ARANGO, Joaquin. "La demanda de educación universitaria en España, 1960-2000" (Demand for higher education in Spain, 1960-2000), *Revista Española de Investigaciones Sociológicas* 24, oct-dec 83 : 47-88.

2036   CARPENTER, Peter; WESTERN, John. "The facilitation of attainment aspirations", *Australian and New Zealand Journal of Sociology* 19(2), jul 83 : 305-318. [Restructuring higher education in Australia]

2037   CHUPRUNOV, D.; [et al.]. *Enseignement supérieur, emploi et progrès technique en URSS.* Paris, Presses de l'UNESCO, Institut International de Planification de l'Éducation, 82, 266 p.

2038   FIELDING, Anthony J.; CAVANAGH, Darol M.; [eds.]. *Curriculum priorities in Australian higher education.* Canberra, Croom Helm Australia, 83, ix-195 p.

2039   FULLER, Winship C.; [et al.]. "New evidence on the economic determinants of post secondary schooling choices", *Journal of Human Resources* 17(4), aut 82 : 477-498. [USA]

2040   GANESH, S. R.; SARUPRIA, Dalpat. "Explorations in helplessness of higher education institutions in the Third World", *Higher Education* 12(2), apr 83 : 191-204. [India]

2041   GHOSH, D. K. *University system in India.* Jabalpur, M. P. Rahul Publications, 83, xiii-474 p.

2042   GORELICK, Sherry. "Boom and bust in higher education: economic and social causes of the current crisis", *Insurgent Sociologist* 11(4), 83 : 77-90. [USA]

2043   GRACIANI, Maria Stela Santos. *O ensino superior no Brasil a estrutura de poder na universidade em questão* (Higher education in Brazil: the questioned power structure in the university). Petrópolis, Vozes, 82, 164 p.

2044   GRUSON, Pascale. "L'enseignement supérieur", *Recherches économiques et sociales* (5), trim. 1, 83 : 61-108. [France]

2045   HEREDIA SORIANO, A. "¿Forma hoy la universidad española europeos?" (Does Spanish university train Europeans?), *Cuadernos de Realidades Sociales* (22), jan 83 : 115-119.

2046   IVANOVIĆ, Stanoje. "Staffing tertiary education", *Yugoslav Survey* 24(1), feb 83 : 83-90.

2047   JOHNSTON, Lloyd; BACHMAN, Jerald G.; O'MALLEY, Patrick M. *Student drug use, attitudes, and beliefs: national trends, 1975-1982.* Rockville, MD, National Institute on Drug Abuse, US Department of Health and Human Service; Washington, DC, US GPO, 82, vi-134 p. [USA]

2048   JOLIVET, Muriel. "Le mythe de l'université au Japon et l'emploi", *Critique* 39(428-429), feb 83 : 82-92.

2049   KUBKA, Janina; PAWLAK, Adam; STĄPOREK, Bolesław. "Z badań nad światopoglądowymi postawami młodzieży akademickiej" (For investigations on attitudes connected with university students' philosophy of life), *Życie Szkoły Wyższej* 4, 83 : 45-58.

2050   KWIATKOWSKI, Stefan; [ed.]. *Integracja szkół wyższych z gospodarka i struktura organizacyjna uczelni* (Higher school integration with the economy and organizing structure of the colleges). Warszawa, Państwowe Wydawnictwo Naukowe, 83, 167 p. [Poland]

2051   LANDINELLI, Jorge. *El movimiento estudiantil universitario en el Uruguay* (The movement of university students in Uruguay). México, FLACSO, 83, 209 p.

2052   LÁSZLÓ, Tivadamé. "Felsöoktajási reformok — felsöoktatasi törvényhozas az evropai szocialista országokban" (Higher education reforms: legislation concerning higher education in the European socialist countries), *Jogtudományi Közlöny* 37(9), sep 82 : 706-718.

2053   LÓPEZ LUBIAN, Francisco J. "La demanda social de educación superior" (Social demand of higher education), *Cuadernos de economía* 10(27), apr 82 : 119-143. [Spain]

2054   MALIYAMKONO, T. L.; ISHUMI, Abel G. M.; WELLS, Stuart J. *Higher education and development in Eastern Africa: an Eastern African Universities Research Project report on the impact of overseas training on development.* London-Exeter, NH, Heinemann, 82, xii-312 p.

2055   MARCZUK, Stanisław. *Wartości i ideały młodego pokolenia: z badań nad studentami i młodymi robotnikami Rzeszowa* (Values and ideals of the young generation: a research on students and young workers in Rzeszów). Rzeszów, Wydawnictwo Uczelniane Wyższej Szkoły Pedagogicznej, 83, 217 p.

2056   MARUYAMA, Tetsuo. "Nihon ni okeru koto kyoiku no chiiki bunpu" (The regional distribution of the institutions of higher education in Japan), *Kinjo gakuin daigaku ronshu shakai-kagaku-hen* 25, 83 : 157-217.

2057   MONCHABLON, Alain. *Histoire de l'UNEF de 1956 à 1968.* Paris, Presses Universitaires de France, 83, 205 p. [Union nationale des étudiants de France]

2058   MONTORO ROMERO, Ricardo. "Universidad y paro: reflexiones críticas sobre el desempleo de licenciados universitarios" (University and unemployment: cricital reflections on graduate unemployment), *Revista Española de Investigaciones Sociológicas* 24, oct-dec 83 : 89-112.

2059   MOORE, Peter G. "Higher education: the next decade", *Journal of the Royal Statistical Society. Series A* 146(3), 83 : 213-229.

2060   NISHIKAWA, Miki; [et al.]. "Chugakusei to kazoku kankei: Kansai-chiku no baai" (Junior-High School students and their family relationships: in the case of Kansai District), *Otemae joshi tanki-daigaku Otemae bunka gakuin kenkyu shuroku* 5, 83 : 57-93.

2061   NOGUEIRA, H. "L'université dans la société latino-américaine", *Documents CEPESS* 21(5-6), 82 : 177-190.

2062   PALMIER, Leslie. "Occupations of Indonesian graduates", *Higher Education* 11(6), nov 82 : 685-712.

2063   PEAUCELLE, Irma. "Les étudiants salariés: enseignement de quelques enquêtes", *Education et Formations* (1), dec 82 : 81-97. [France]

2064   PELLE, János. "A diplomák inflációja" (The inflation of academic degrees), *Kultúra és Közösség* 10(2), 83 : 52-69. [Hungary]

2065   PHILLIPSON, Nicholas; [ed.]. *Universities, society, and the future: a conference held on the 400th anniversary of the University of Edinburgh.* Edinburgh, Edinburgh University Press, 83, xiv-319 p. [UK]

2066   PONDE, Lafayette. "Considerações sobre o sistema universitário" (Considerations on the university system), *Revista de Direito administrativo* (146), dec 81 : 26-43. [Brazil]

2067   RANKOVIĆ, Miodrag. "Glavne nesrazmere i problemi našeg visokog školstva" (Essential discrepancies and problems of university education), *Sociologija* 25(2-3), 83 : 247-260. [Yugoslavia]

2068   REUTERBERG, Sven-Eric; SVENSSON, Allan. "The importance of financial aid: the case of higher education in Sweden", *Higher Education* 12(1), jan 83 : 89-100.

2069   REZENDE, Antônio Muniz de. *O saber e o poder na universidade: dominação ou serviço?* (Knowledge and power in the university: domination or service?). São Paulo, SP, Editora Autores Associados, Cortez Editora, 82, 88 p. [Brazil]

2070   SADOWSKI, Andrzej. "Białostockie środowisko studenckie na tle środowiska społecznego miasta w opinii studentów Białegostoku" (The student environment in the city of Białystok against a background of social environment of the city), *Zeszyty Naukowe Filii UW. Humanistyka* 6(34), 83 : 31-79.

2071   SAKAKI, Hirobumi; [et al.]. "Taibei nihonjin gakusei no tekio katei ni kansuru kenkyu: Taibei gakusei no tokusei to tekio katei" (A study on Japanese students' adjustment process to the life in the United States: characteristics of Japanese students and their adjustment process), *Nihon daigaku seisan kogakubu hokoku B.* 16(1), 83 : 59-77.

2072   SETHI, Jai Dev. *The crisis and collapse of higher education in India.* New Delhi, Vikas Publishing House, 83, xiii-255 p.

2073   SIBAJACH, Luis Fernando; GUTIÉRREZ ESPELETA, Nelson. "Crisis económica y educación superior en Costa Rica" (Economic crisis and higher education in Costa Rica), *Estudios sociales centroamericanos* 12(34), apr 83 : 31-42. [see also pp. 43-58 by R. Ana Cecilia HERNANDEZ]

2074   SIDEL, Mark. "Graduate education in the People's Republic of China: new step, new challenges", *Higher Education* 12(2), apr 83 : 155-170.

2075   SILVA, Adroaldo Moura de; [et al.]. *Para onde vai a universidade brasileira?* (Where is the Brazilian university going?). Fortaleza, Universidade Federal do Ceará, 83, 301 p.

2076   TAMURA, Kiyo. "Gendai seinen no shohi kodo to katei seikatsukan" (Modern students' consuming behaviour and their attitude toward family life), *Tokyo gakugei daigaku kiyo* 6(35), 83 : 79-120. [Japan]

2077   TEICHLER, Ulrich; SANYAL, Bikas C. *Higher education and the labour market in the Federal Republic of Germany.* Paris, UNESCO, 82, 178 p.

2078   THELIN, John R. *Higher education and its useful past: applied history in research and planning.* Cambridge, MA, Schenkman Publishing Co., 82, x-215 p.

2079   TROYON, Marie-Dominique. "Une approche particulière d'adéquation des formations universitaires aux finalités professionnelles: la fonction information-communication", *Humanisme et Entreprise* 141, oct 83 : 73-93. [France]

2080   WESLEY PERKINS, H.; SPATES, James L. "American and English student values", *Comparative Social Research* 5, 82 : 245-265.

2081   WILLIAMS, Peter. "Look West? Asian attitudes to study abroad and Britain's response", *Asian Affairs (London)* 14(1), feb 83 : 15-26.

2082   WISNIEWSKI, Jean. "Étudiants étrangers en grandes écoles et écoles spécialisées", *Hommes et Migrations* 35(1044), 15 jan 83 : 3-22. [France] [Documents]

2083   WITKOWSKI, Janusz. "Losy zawodowe i warunki socjalnobytowe absolwentów Wydziału Ekonomiczno-Społecznego SGPiS" (Professional careers and social living conditions of graduates from the socio-economic faculty of the Central School of Planning and Statistics), *Biuletyn Instytutu Gospodarstwa Społecznego* 25(3), 82 : 104-130.

2084   ZAKIDALSKA, Irena. "Aktywność kulturalna młodzieży studenckiej a działalność klubów studenckich" (The cultural activity of the academic youth and the activity of the students' clubs), *Zeszyty Naukowe Wydziału Humanistycznego Uniwersytetu Gdańskiego* 7, 83 : 81-93.

2085   ZYCH, Adam. *Metodologiczne problemy badań światopoglądu młodzieży akademickiej* (Methodological problems of research on the university students' philosophy of life). Kielce, Wyższa Szkoła Pedagogiczna, 83, 168 p.

**13960   Adult education
Éducation des adultes**

2086   "Adult learners, learning and public libraries", *Library Trends* 31(4), spr 83 : 513-686. [USA] [with contributions by D. Roby KIDD, Alan B. KNOX, David CARR, Robert L. CLARK Jr.]

2087   "Educación bilingüe e intercultural" (Bilingual and intercultural education), *América indígena* 42(2), jun 82 : 197-361. [Latin America] [with contributions by Salomón NAHMAD SITTON, Fernando MIÑO-GARCES, Aleida GIMENEZ, Miguel URIOSTE F. DE C.]

2088   "Educations permanentes en mouvement?", *Revue internationale d'action communautaire* (9), spr 83 : 3-235. [résumés en anglias et en espagnol; with contributions by Georges PETERS, Serge NOEL, Catherine MOUGENOT, Claire PIERPONT, Jean-Pierre KOROLITSKI]

2089   AMARATUNGA, C. A.; SHUTE, J. C. M. "Extension and adult learning in a Ghanaian community", *Canadian Journal of African Studies* 16(3), 82 : 549-566. [résumé en français]

2090   BECKER, Hellmut; [et al.]. *Wissenschaftliche Perspektiven zur Erwachsenenbildung* (Scientific perspectives on adult education). Braunschweig, Westermann, 82, 317 p.

2091   BERCOVITZ, Alain; [et al.]. *Education et alternance.* Paris, Edilig, 82, 287 p. [France]

2092   CONSEIL INTERNATIONAL POUR L'ÉDUCATION DES ADULTES. *Le monde de l'alphabétisation. Politique, recherche et action.* Ottawa, Centre de Recherches pour le Développement International, 83, 159 p. [Also published in English]

2093   DUKE, Chris. "Evolutions of the recurrent education concept", *International Journal of Lifelong Education* 1(4), 82 : 323-340.

2094   ELLIS, C. S. *The promotion of literacy in South Africa: numbers and distribution of literate Black adults.* Pretoria, Human Sciences Research Council, 82, xii-74 p.

2095   FLITNER, Wilhelm. *Erwachsenenbildung* (Adult education). Paderborn, F. Schöningh, 82, 372 p.

2096   FRENCH, Edward. *The promotion of literacy in South Africa: a multi-faceted survey at the start of the eighties.* Pretoria, Human Sciences Research Council, Institute for Research into Language and the Arts, 82, xvii-133 p.

2097   GIESECKE, Michael; ELWERT, Georg. "Literacy and emancipation: the literacy process in two cultural revolutionary movements (16th century Germany and 20th century Bénin)", *Development and Change* 14(2), apr 83 : 255-276.

2098   GRIFFIN, Colin. "Social control, social policy and adult education", *International Journal of Lifelong Education* 2(3), 83 : 217-244.

2099   HANNAM, Will G. "A foot behind the door: an historical analysis of adult education in prisons", *International Journal of Lifelong Education* 1(4), 82 : 361-372.

2100   HILTON, William J. "US project on enhancing the quality of state-level services to adult learners", *Convergence* 16(2), 83 : 48-59. [résumés en français et espagnol]

2101   ISLAMI, Hivzi. "Nepismenost u današnjem kosovskom selu" (Illiteracy in Kosovo villages today), *Sociologija sela* 20(77-78), 83 : 219-232. [Yugoslavia]

2102   LEITE, Sérgio Antonio da Silva. *Alfabetização: um projeto bem sucedido* (Literacy: a successful project). São Paulo, EDICON, 82, 184 p. [Brazil]

2103   MATZKE, Peter. *Funktionaler Analphabetismus in en USA: zur Bildungsbenachteiligung in Industriegesellschaften* (Functional literacy in the USA: on educational disadvantage in industrial societies). München, Minerva Publikation, 82, viii-125 p.

2104   MENSON, Betty; [ed.]. *Building on experiences in adult development.* San Francisco, CA, Jossey-Bass, 82, 129 p. [USA]

2105   MEUELER, Erhard. *Erwachsene lernen: Beschreibung, Anstösse, Erfahrungen* (Teaching adults: description, stimulations, experiments). Stuttgart, Klett-Cotta, 82, 186 p.

2106   NADEAU, Jean-Réal. *L'éducation permanente dans une 'cité éducative': approche systèmique.* Québec, PQ, Presses de l'Université Laval, 82, xiv-358 p.

2107   NAKAYAMA, Shigeru; [et al.]. *Jitsugaku no susume* (The reconsideration of 'practical' education). Tokyo, Yuhikaku, 83, 220 p.

2108   PERESSON T., Mario; MARIÑO S., Germán; CENDALES G., Lola. *Educación popular y alfabetización en América Latina* (Popular education and literacy in Latin America). Bogotá, Dimensión Educativa, 83, 415 p.

2109 PETTRUCCI, Armando. "Alfabetismo e rivolta sociale" (Literary and social revolt), *Critica sociologica* 67, 83 : 22-27.

2110 PLA I MOLINS, Maria. *El bilinguisme escolar a Barcelona* (School bilingualism in Barcelona). Barcelona, Edicions de la Magrana, 83, 258 p.

2111 RIVERA, William M. "International strategies for the development of adult education: a review and critique", *International Journal of Lifelong Education* 2(2), jun 83 : 111-132.

2112 SANTANA, Roberto. "Cultures indigènes et politique en Equateur", *Amérique latine* (14), jun 83 : 47-52.

2113 SHOR, Francis. "Innovation and ideology in adult education: American and Italian working class experiences", *Insurgent Sociologist* 11(4), 83 : 91-96.

2114 SOMRATY STONE, Helene. "Nonformal adult education: case studies from India", *International Journal of Lifelong Education* 2(3), 83 : 297-304.

2115 TABELLINI, Maria. *La lutte contre l'alphabétisme dans le monde: quelques expériences positives et perspectives d'avenir de 1971 à 1980.* Paris, UNESCO, 82, 95 p.

2116 TORRES, Carlos Alberto. "Adult education policy, capitalist development and class alliance: Latin America and Mexico", *International Journal of Political Education* 6(2), aug 83 : 157-173.

2117 UESUGI, Takamichi. "Shogai kyoiku no doko: igirisu no jirei o chushin ni" (Trends in lifelong education: the case of the United Kingdom), *Nihon joseigaku kenkyu* 2, 83 : 3-12.

2118 WAGNER, Daniel A.; [ed.]. "Literacy and ethnicity", *International Journal of the Sociology of Language* 42, 83 : 5-121.

13970 Civic education. Technical education
Instruction civique. Enseignement technique

2119 "Educación (La) compensatoria" (Compensatory education), *Revista de educación* 31(272), apr 83 : 5-157. [Spain] [with contributions by Angel Lázaro J. MARTINEZ, Quintina MARTIN-MORENO CERRILLO, Manuel MARTINEZ LOPEZ, Pablo GUZMAN CEBRAIN]

2120 "Formation (La) civique et sociale", *Humanisme* 153, sep 83 : 2-74. [France]

2121 BOOTH, Tony; POTTS, Patricia; [eds.]. *Integrating special education.* Oxford, B. Blackwell, 83, viii-230 p.

2122 CONLEY, Marshall Won; OSBORNE, Kenneth. "Political education in Canadian school: as assessment of social studies and political science courses and pedagogy", *International Journal of Political Education* 6(1), apr 83 : 65-85.

2123 HOWELL, David L.; [et al.]. *Elements of the structure of agricultural education in the United States of America.* Paris, UNESCO, 83, 72 p.

2124 LANE, Robert E. "Political education in a market society", *Micropolitics* 3(1), 83 : 39-65. [USA]

2125 NEAL, David. "The right to education: the case of special education", *Australian Quarterly* 54(2), wint 82 : 147-160.

2126 O'CONNOR, Sile. "Mild mental handicap and special educational need: a social process perspective", *Economic and Social Review* 14(3), apr 83 : 203-224. [Ireland]

2127 PRILLAMAN, Douglas; ABBOTT, John C. *Educational diagnosis and prescriptive teaching: a practical approach to special education in the least restrictive environment.* Belmont, CA, Fearon Education, Pitman Learning, 83, ix-285 p.

13980 Academic success. School failure
Réussite dans les études. Échec scolaire

2128 "Assessing educational achievement", *Educational Analysis* 4(3), 82 : 1-134. [with contributions by Henry G. MACINTOSH, Graeme WITHERS, Roy H. FORBES, Les D. MCLEAN]

2129 BORSOTTI, Carlos; BRASLAVSKY, Cecilia. *Fracaso escolar y actividades infantiles en familias de estratos populares* (Schooling failure and child activities in popular strata families). Buenos Aires, FLACSO, 83, 74 p. [Latin America]

2130 CLIFTON, Rodney A. "Socioeconomic status and educational performances: a comparison of students in England and New Zealand", *International Journal of Comparative Sociology (Leiden)* 24(3-4), sep-dec 83 : 187-199.

2131 MARSHALL, Harvey; PERRUCCI, Robert. "The structure of academic fields and rewards in academia", *Sociology and Social Research* 66(2), jan 82 : 127-146.

2132 OAKES, Jeannie. "Tracking and ability grouping in American schools: some constitutional questions", *Teachers College Record* 84(4), sum 83 : 801-819.

2133 SAHA, Lawrence J. "Social structure and teacher effects on academic achievement: a comparative analysis", *Comparative Education Review* 27(1), feb 83 : 69-88.

2134   SIMKUS, Albert; ANDORKA, Rudolf. "Inequalities in educational attainment in
        Hungary, 1923-1973", *American Sociological Review* 47(6), dec 82 : 740-751.
2135   TURRITTIN, Anton H.; ANISEF, Paul; MACKINNON, Neil J. "Gender differences
        in educational achievement: a study of social inequality", *Canadian Journal of Sociology /*
        Cahiers canadiens de Sociologie 8(4), 83 : 395-419. [Canada]

        13990   Pedagogy. Teaching. Teachers
        Pédagogie. Enseignement. Enseignants

2136   "Computers, education, and public policy", *Journal of Communication* 33(1), wint 83 : 92-173.
        [USA] [with contributions by Carolyn MARVIN, Mark WINTHER, Timothy R.
        HAIGHT, Robert M. RUBINYI, Marc S. TUCKER, Ronald E. RICE, Donald CASE]
2137   "Passions (Les) pédagogiques", *Autogestions* (12-13), wint 83 : 3-172. [France] [with
        contributions by Marie-France GUILLOT, Georges LAPASSADE, Michel LOBROT,
        Anne-Marie BONNISSEAU, Marie Noëlle BONNISSEAU]
2138   BAIRD, Lloyd; SCHNEIER, Craig Eric; LAIRD, Dugan; [eds.]. *The training and development*
        sourcebook. Amherst, MA, Human Resource Development Press, 83, xvi-381 p.
2139   BONILAURI, Bernard. *La désinformation scolaire. Essai sur les manuels d'enseignement.* Paris,
        Presses Universitaires de France, 83, 151 p. [France]
2140   BORKOWSKI, Tadeusz. "Wpływ wykształcenia na funkcje biologiczne i ekonomiczne
        rodzin pozarolniczych" (Effect of education on biological and economic functions of
        non-farmer families), *Studia Socjologiczne* 88(1), 83 : 123-145.
2141   BORKOWSKI, Tadeusz. "Wpływ wykształcenia rodziców na pełnienie przez rodzinę jej
        funkcji socjalizacyjnowychowawczej" (Effect of parents' education on the fulfilment by
        the family: its socialized and educational functions), *Studia Socjologiczne* 90 (3), 83 : 163-182.
2142   CANNON, Robert A. "The professional development of Australian university teachers:
        an act of faith?", *Higher Education* 12(1), jan 83 : 19-33.
2143   CHARLE, Christophe. "Le champ universitaire parisien à la fin du 19ᵉ siècle", *Actes de la*
        Recherche en Sciences sociales 47-48, jun 83 : 77-89.
2144   CRITTENDEN, Brian. *Cultural pluralism and common curriculum.* Carlton, Vic., Melbourne
        University Press, 82, v-103 p. [Australia]
2145   DELORME, Charles. *De l'animation pédagogique à la recherche-action: perspectives pour l'innovation*
        scolaire. Lyon, Chronique Sociale, 82, 239 p. [France]
2146   DESBROUSSES, Hélène. "Les enseignants en crise d'identité", *Recherches économiques et*
        sociales (5), trim. 1, 83 : 109-154. [France]
2147   FENSTERMACHER, Gary D.; GOODLAD, John I.; [eds.]. *Individual differences and the*
        common curriculum. Chicago, IL, National Society for the Study of Education, 83, xii-339 p.
2148   GÁBOR, László; HÁBER, Judit. "Tanító- és tanárképző főiskolák végzős hallgatóinak
        munkahelyválasztása" (Young teachers after graduating: their choice of jobs), *Szociológia*
        11(2), 82 : 265-282. [Hungary]
2149   HIREMATH, Siddalingaswami Gurulingashastrigalu. *Sociology of academics in India and abroad.*
        Delhi, Sundeep Prakashan, 83, 10-294 p.
2150   IKADO, Fujio. "Daigaku kyoiku to curriculum" (Principles of curriculum innovations:
        mainly at college levels), *Hiroshima daigaku ronshu* 12, 83 : 139-161.
2151   ITO, Nobuhiro. "Shoto gakko kyoshoku ni okeru semi-profession-sei" (Semi-professionality
        in elementary school teaching), *Shizuoka joshi tanki-daigaku kenkyu kiyo* 31, 83 : 90-107.
        [Japan]
2152   JULIA, Dominique. "Une réforme impossible. Le changement du cursus dans la France
        du 18ᵉ siècle", *Actes de la Recherche en Sciences sociales* 47-48, jun 83 : 53-76.
2153   KARADY, Victor. "Les professeurs de la République. Le marché scolaire, les réformes
        universitaires et les transformations de la fonction professorale à la fin du 19ᵉ siècle",
        Actes de la Recherche en Sciences sociales 47-48, jun 83 : 90-112. [France]
2154   LANGOUET, Gabriel. *Technologie de l'éducation et démocratisation de l'enseignement: méthodes*
        pédagogiques et classes sociales. Paris, Presses Universitaires de France, 82, 185 p. [France]
2155   LEITHWOOD, Kenneth A.; [ed.]. *Studies in curriculum decision making.* Toronto, ON, OISE
        Press/Ontario Institute for Studies on Education, 82, 310 p.
2156   MÄKINEN, Raimo. *Teachers' work, well-being, and health.* Jyväskylä, Jyväskylän Yliopisto,
        82, 232 p. [Finland]
2157   MARTIN, Roger. *Les instituteurs de l'entre-deux guerres: idéologie et action syndicale.* Lyon, Presses
        Universitaires de Lyon, 82, 448 p. [France]
2158   MELEZINEK, Adolf. *Unterrichtstechnologie: Einführung in die Medienverwendung im Bildungswesen*
        (Educational technology: introduction to the use of media in educational system). Wien-
        New York, NY, Springer-Verlag, 82, xi-226 p.

2159   MEYLAN, Jean-Pierre. *Evaluation von Innovation im Bereich der Primarschule / Évaluation d'innovations dans l'école primaire.* Bern, P. Haupt, 83, 465 p.

2160   MORRILL, Paul H.; SPEES, Emil R. *The academic profession: teaching in higher education.* New York, NY, Human Sciences Press, 82, xiv-363 p.

2161   MOYNE, Albert. *Le travail autonome: vers une autre pédagogiqe?.* Paris, Fleurus, 82, xv-395 p. [France]

2162   NADANER, Dan. "Toward an analysis of the educational value of film and television", *Interchange* 14(1), 83 : 43-55. [Canada]

2163   ODEDE, Esther A. *The role of the teachers advisory centres in the qualitative improvement of teacher education in Kenya.* Nairobi, ACO Project, 82, 55-1 p.

2164   POWELL, J. P.; [et al.]. "How academics view their work", *Higher Education* 12(3), jun 83 : 297-313. [Australia]

2165   PRITCHARD, Rosalind M. O. "The status of teachers in Germany and Ireland", *Comparative Education Review* 27(3), oct 83 : 341-350.

2166   SZAFRAN, Robert F. "A note on the recruitment and reward equity of organizations: US universities before affirmative action", *Social Forces* 61(4), jun 83 : 1109-1118.

2167   VEIRA VEIRA, S. L. *Análisis sociológico del profesorado universitario: entre la participación y el retraimiento* (Sociological analysis of academic professors: between participation and withdrawal). Santiago de Compostela, Universidad de Santiago de Compostela, 83, 243 p.

2168   VIAL, Jean. *Histoire et actualité des méthodes pédagogiques.* Paris, Editions ESF, 82, 206 p.

2169   WHITE, R. D. "Teacher militancy, idelology and politics", *Australian and New Zealand Journal of Sociology* 19(2), jul 83 : 253-271.

14100   SOCIAL SYSTEM
SYSTÈME SOCIAL

2170   "Methodologies for the study of social systems", *Behavioral Science* 28(2), apr 83 : 91-186. [with contributions by Richard M. CYERT, Herbert A. SIMON, Clark GLYMOUR, Stephen A. FIENBERG, Judith M. TANUR]

2171   ALYMOV, A. N.; [et al.]. *Social'naja infrastruktura: voprosy teorii i praktiki* (Social infrastructure: theoretical and practical questions). Kiev, Naukova Dumka, 82, 335 p.

2172   AROUTUNIAN, Youri; DROBIJEVA, Leokadia. "La structure sociale des nations soviétiques", *Sciences sociales — Académie des Sciences de l'URSS* (3), 83 : 132-148.

2173   BAKARIC, Vladimir. "La reproduction sociale dans le système socialiste", *Questions actuelles du Socialisme* 33(1), jan 83 : 36-90.

2174   BENETON, Philippe. "Logique et prégnance du social. A propos de 'Effets pervers et ordre social' et 'La logique du social' de Raymond Boudon", *Tocqueville Review* 3(1), wint 81 : 119-136.

2175   CATANZARO, Raimondo. "Struttura sociale, sistema politico e azione collettiva nel Mezzogiorno" (Social structure, political system and collective action in Southern Italy), *Stato e Mercato* (8), aug 83 : 271-315. [Italy] [résumé en anglais]

2176   DEMARCHI, Franco. "La struttura sociale della popolazione europea nelle opere di Frederic Le Play, ripensata cent'anni dopo" (The social structure of European population in the works of Frederic Le Play re-examined a hundred years later), *Studi di Sociologia* 20(3-4), jul-dec 82 : 297-314.

2177   ESCALA, Alberto. *Argentina, estructura social y sectores intermedios* (Argentina, social structure and intermediate sectors). Buenos Aires, Ediciones Estudio, 82, 136 p.

2178   FAUBLÉE, Jacques; STAMM, Anne; AUBIN, Françoise. "Systèmes sociaux et civilisation", *Année sociologique* 32, 82 : 285-360. [Compte rendu bibliographique]

2179   FUKADA, Hiroshi. "J. S. Mill to shakaiyukitai-setsu" (Social organismic theory on J. S. Mill), *Shakaigaku ronso* 86, 83 : 59-77.

2180   GRAFSTEIN, Robert. "The search for social strucjture", *Social Science Quarterly* 63(4), dec 82 : 640-642.

2181   HARAYAMA, Tetsu. "Shakaiteki ketteiron to shakaiteki sogo koi no paradigm: R. Boudon no shosetsu o tegakari toshite" (Social determinism and the paradigm of social interaction: a review of R. Boudon's theory), *Seiroka kango daigaku kiyo* 9, 83 : 49-56.

2182   KOLM, Serge-Christophe. "Introduction à la réciprocité générale", *Social Science Information* 22(4-5), 83 : 569-630.

2183   KRYSMANSKI, Hans Jürgen. *Gesellschaftsstruktur der Bundesrepublik* (Social structure of the Federal Republic). Köln, Pahl-Rugenstein, 82, 242 p.

2184   LECHNER, Norbert. *La lucha por el orden en Chile* (The struggle for social order in Chile). Santiago, FLACSO, 83, 28 p.

2185   MILECKIJ, V. P. "O social'noj strukture razvitogo socializma" (On the social structure of developed socialism), *Vestnik Leningradskogo Universiteta. Serija Ėkonomika, Filosofija Pravo* 36(4), 82 : 120-123.

2186   MLINAR, Zdravko. "Teoretski i metodološki trendovi u sociološkom iztraživanju (prostorno) društvenih struktura i procesa razvoja" (Theoretical and methodological trends of sociological research on spatial social structure and development processes), *Sociologija* 25(1), 83 : 21-38. [Yugoslavia] [continued in ibid. 25 (2-3), 1983: 311-324]

2187   MOLM, Linda D. "Changes in reinforcement contingencies and the disruption of social exchange", *Social Science Research* 12(4), dec 83 : 330-352.

2188   NIEBRZYDOWSKI, Leon. "Interpersonalne aspekty wymiany społecznej" (Interpersonal aspects of social exchange), *Studia Socjologiczne* 88(1), 83 : 89-105.

2189   OLIVIER, G.; DEVIGNE, G. "Biology and social structure", *Journal of Biosocial Science* 15(4), oct 83 : 379-389. [France]

2190   PACI, Massimo. *La struttura sociale italiana: costanti storiche e trasformazioni recenti* (The Italian social structure: historical constantes and recent transformations). Bologna, Il Mulino, 82, 277 p.

2191   PEROV, Ju. V. "Social'nyj determinizm v duhovnoj žizni obščestva" (Social determinism in the society intellectual life), *in: Social'nyj determinizm i naučno-tehničeskij progress.* Moskva, 1982 : 146-157.

2192   PIGROV, K. S. "O masštabe social'nyh sistem" (On the scale of social systems), *Problemy Dialektiki* (10), 82 : 131-139.
2193   POPOVIĆ, Mihailo V. "Društveni sistem, komuniciranje i društveni konsensus" (Social system, communication and social consensus), *Sociologija* 24(4), 82 : 369-380.
2194   PORPORA, Douglas V. "On the prospects for a nomothetic theory of social structure", *Journal for the Theory of Social Behaviour* 13(3), oct 83 : 243-264. [with comments by Peter M. BLAU: 265-308, and a rejoinder by the author: 309-329]
2195   ROSENBAUM, Heidi. "Die Konzeption der Sozialstruktur in der schichtenspezifischen Sozialisationsforschung" (Conception of social structure in the class specific socialization research), *Kölner Zeitschrift für Soziologie und Sozialpsychologie* 35(1), mar 83 : 41-58.
2196   ROTTMAN, David; O'CONNELL, Philip. "The changing structure of Ireland", *Administration (Dublin)* 30(2-3), 82 : 63-88.
2197   SCHULEIN, Johann August. "Normalität und Opposition. Über Ursachen und gesellschaftliche Funktion der 'Alternativbewegung'" (Normality and opposition. Causes and social function of the alternative movement), *Leviathan* 11(2), 83 : 252-274.
2198   SEKULIĆ, Duško. "O pristupima izučavanju stratifikacione strukture jugoslavenskog društva" (On approaches to the study of structure of Yugoslav society's strata), *Sociologija* 25(1), 83 : 1-20.
2199   SMITH, Charles X.; [ed.]. "Special topic papers: the duality of social structures, structuration, and the intentionality of human action", *Journal for the Theory of Social Behaviour* 13(1), mar 83 : 1-95.
2200   STAME, Nicoletta. "Poland: the logic of two anti-systemic movements", *Review (F. Braudel Center)* 7(1), sum 83 : 15-51.
2201   STEZKO, Z. V. "Filosofsko-sociologičeskij analiz kategorii 'social'nyj determinizm'" (Philosophical and sociological analysis of the 'social determinism' category), *Problemy Filosofii* 55, 82 : 36-41.
2202   SZTOMPKA, Piotr. "Zmiana strukturalna społeczeństwa: szkic teorii" (Structural change of the society: an outline of the theory), *Studia Socjologiczne* 89(2), 83 : 125-151.
2203   TYSZKA, Andrzej. "Studies of the structure of Polish society", *Polish Sociological Bulletin* 54(2), 81 : 5-14.
2204   VICKERS, Geoffrey. *Human systems are different.* London-New York, NY, Harper and Row, 83, xxviii-188 p.

14200   SOCIAL STRATIFICATION
STRATIFICATION SOCIALE

14210   Social differentiation
Différenciation sociale

2205   "Soziale Ungleichheiten" (Social inequalities), *Soziale Welt* (2), 83 : 3-408. [a special issue, with contributions by Reinhard KRECKEL, Anthony GIDDENS]
2206   BERNIK, Ivan. "Sociološki pojan društvene nejednakosti" (Social inequality as a sociological concept), *Sociologija* 25(2-3), 83 : 287-310.
2207   BÉTEILLE, André; [ed.]. *Equality and inequality: theory and practice.* Delhi-New York, NY, Oxford University Press, 83, xii-302 p.
2208   BETEILLE, André; [ed]. *Equality and inequality: theory and practice.* Delhi, Oxford University Press, 83, 302 p.
2209   BLUCHE, François; SOLNON, Jean-François. *La véritable hiérarchie sociale de l'ancienne France: le tarif de la premiére capitation (1695).* Genéve, Droz, 83, 210 p.
2210   BÖHM, Antal; KOLOSI, Tamás; [eds.]. *Structure and stratification in Hungary.* Budapest, Tempo, 82, 449 p.
2211   CLAEYS, Paul; MAWHOOD, Philip; [eds.]. "Le gouvernement des sociétés plurales d'Afrique noire", *Civilisations* 32-33(2-1), 82-83 : 3-309.
2212   DEMERATH, J. N. III. "Past and future in Anglo-American stratification: a note on prospective vs. retrospective ideologies", *Sociology and Social Research* 67(4), jul 83 : 363-373.
2213   DOMAŃSKI, Henryk. "Klasyfikacja zawodów jako narzędzie analizy systemu uwarstwienia społecznego" (Classification of occupations as an instrument of system analysis of social stratification), *Studia Socjologiczne* 89(2), 83 : 251-269.
2214   HOLMWOOD, J. M.; STEWART, A. "The role of contradictions in modern theories of social stratificatioon", *Sociology (London)* 17(2), mai 83 : 234-254.
2215   KILIBARDA, Risto. "O socijalnoj hijerarhiji u jugoslovenskom društvu" (On social hierarchy in Yugoslav society), *Sociologija* 25(2-3), 83 : 221-245.

2216   KING, Mervyn A. "An index of inequality: with applications to horizontal equity and
         social mobility", *Econometrica* 51(1), jan 83 : 99-115.

2217   KNIGHTS, David; WILLMOTT, Hugh. "Dualism and domination: an analysis of
         Marxian, Weberian and existentialist perspectives", *Australian and New Zealand Journal
         of Sociology* 19(1), mar 83 : 33-49.

2218   KORALEWICZ-ZEBIK, Jadwiga. "Potoczna percepcja nierówności w Polsce w latach
         1960-1980" (Everyday perception of inequalities in Poland between 1960-1980), *Studia
         Socjologiczne* 90 (3), 83 : 143-162.

2219   KORDASZEWSKI, Jan. "Egalitaryzm w świetle motywacji pracy" (Egalitarianism in the
         light of the theory of motivation), *Biuletyn Instytutu Gospodarstwa Społecznego* 25(3), 82 : 6-26.

2220   KOSTOWSKA, Elżbieta. *Idea równości społecznej* (The idea of social equality). Warszawa,
         Wiedza Powszechna, 83, 301 p. [Poland]

2221   KUMAR, Awadhesh. "Religion, politics and social stratification: a case study of Satnamis
         of Chhattisgarh", *Indian Journal of Social Research* 24(1), apr 83 : 63-69. [India]

2222   LEE, Gloria. "Implementing equal opportunity: a training perspective", *Equal Opportunities
         International* 2(1), 83 : 25-36. [UK]

2223   NEELSEN, John P.; [ed.]. *Social inequality and political structures: studies in class formations and
         interest articulation in an Indian coalfield and its rural hinterland.* New Delhi, Manohar, 83, 285 p.

2224   PANDE, S. V. "Social stratification, elites and Indian society", *Indian Journal of Social Research*
         23(2), aug 82 : 170-176.

2225   PANDEY, Rajendra. *Social inequality: features, forms, and functions.* Lucknow, Anuj Publications,
         82, viii-317 p. [India]

2226   PETERSEN, Larry R.; WILKINSON, Karen. "Sex role conventionality, race inequality,
         and despair: evidence concerning a personal consequence of change", *Sociology and Social
         Research* 67(2), jan 83 : 190-203.

2227   REUSCH, Jürgen. *Pluralismus und Klassenkampf* (Pluralism and class struggle). Frankfurt-
         am-Main, Verlag Marxistische Blätter, 82, 226 p.

2228   ROBINSON, Robert V. "Explaining perceptions of class and racial inequality", *British
         Journal of Sociology* 24(3), sep 83 : 344-366.

2229   STEWART, Joseph Jr.; BULLOCK, Charles S. III. "Implementing equal education
         opportunity policy: a comparison of the outcome of HEW and justice department efforts",
         Evaluation Studies 7, 82 : 665-684. [USA]

2230   SUFIN, Zbigniew. "Egalitaryzm i sprawiedliwość w świadomości społecznej" (Egalitarianism
         and justice in the social consciousness), *Problemy Marksizmu-Leninizmu* 1, 83 : 62-72.

2231   TÖRNBLOM, Kjell Y.; FOA, Uriel G. "Choice of a distribution principle: crosscultural
         evidence on the effects of resources", *Acta Sociologica* 26(2), 83 : 161-173.

2232   VINKLER, G. "Vlijanie social'noj politiki na umen'šenie social'nyh različij" (Influence
         of social policy on the social differences diminution), *in: Social'naja spravdlivost' i puti
         eě realizacii v social'noj politike. I.* Moskva, 1982 : 72-81.

2233   VIR, Dharam. "Education and social stratification in Nepal", *Indian Journal of Social Work*
         43(3), oct 82 : 321-326.

2234   WESTERN, John S. *Social inequality in Australian society.* South Melbourne, Macmillan Co.
         of Australia, 83, vi-385 p.

2235   WOODBURN, James. "Egalitarian societies", *Man* 17(3), 82 : 431-451.

2236   ZABOROWSKI, Zbigniew. "Teoria równości" (Theory of equality), *Studia Socjologiczne*
         89(2), 83 : 271-290.

14220   Castes. Slavery
**   Castes. Esclavage**

2237   BANAC, Ivo; BUSHKOVITCH, Paul; [eds.]. *The nobility in Russia and Eastern Europe.* New
         Haven, CT, Yale Concilium on International and Area Studies, 83, 220 p.

2238   CARDOSO, Ciro Flamarion Santana. *A Afro-América: a escravidão no novo mundo* (Afro-
         America: slavery in the new world). São Paulo, Brasiliense, 82, 120 p.

2239   DESHPANDE, Vasant. *The Mhaisal untouchables.* Pune, Dastane Ramchandra, 83, 168 p.

2240   HALCROW, Elizabeth M. *Canes and chains: a study of sugar and slavery.* Kingston, Heinemann,
         82, viii-88 p.

2241   INIKORI, J. E. *Forced migration: the impact of the export slave trade on African societies.* London,
         Hutchinson, 82, 349 p.

2242   KAMBLE, N. D. *Deprived castes and their struggle for equality.* New Delhi, Ashish, 83, 364 p.

2243   KOILPARAMPIL, George. *Caste in the Catholic community in Kerala: a study of caste elements
         in the inter rite relationships of Syrians and Latins.* Cochin, Department of Sociology, St.
         Teresa's College, 82, x-289 p.

2244   MERCER, John. "Slavery in Mauritania today", *Plural Societies* 12(3-4), wint 81 : 125-130.

2245   MISRA, L. S.; AGNIHOTRI, U. S. "Role of factions in the status mobility of Harijans in rural social organization", *Indian Journal of Social Research* 24(2), aug 83 : 132-144. [India]

2246   PFAFFENBERGER, Bryan. *Caste in Tamil culture: the religious foundations of sudra domination in Tamil Sri Lanka.* Syracuse, NY, Maxwell School of Citizenship and Public Affairs, Syracuse University, 82, xii-257 p.

2247   SANTHAKUMARI, R. *Scheduled caste and welfare measures.* New Delhi, Classical Publishing Co., 82, 219 p.

2248   SHAH, A. M. "Division and hierarchy: an overview of caste in Gujarat", *Contributions to Indian Sociology* 16(1), jan-jun 82 : 1-33. [India]

2249   SINGH, Parmanand. *Equality, reservation, and discrimination in India: a constitutional study of scheduled castes, scheduled tribes, and other backward classes.* New Delhi, Deep and Deep, 82, 248 p.

2250   UNIYAL, M. P.; SHAH, Beena. "Caste and vocational mobility among graduates of Humaun Mills", *Indian Journal of Social Research* 23(3), dec 82 : 269-276. [India]

2251   WALVIN, James; [ed.]. *Slavery and British society, 1776-1846.* Baton Rouge, LA, Louisiana State University Press, 82, 272 p.

2252   WHITE, Deborah G. "Female slaves: sex roles and status in the antebellum plantation South", *Journal of Family History* 8(3), 83 : 248-261. [USA]

14230   **Social classes**
         Classes sociale

2253   "Class formation and struggle. Social classes in Latin America", *Latin American Perspectives* 10(2-3), sum 83 : 2-184.

2254   "Évolutions dans la classe ouvrière", *Projet* (177), aug 83 : 679-710. [France] [with contributions by André GORZ, Daniel MOTHE, Michel VERRET, Albert MERCIER]

2255   "Origen de las burguesías" (Origin of the bourgeoisies), *Revista mexicana de Sociología* 44(4), oct-dec 82 : 1279-1378. [Latin America]

2256   AHRNE, Göran; WRIGHT, Erik Olin. "Classes in the United States and Sweden: a comparison", *Acta Sociologica* 26(3-4), 83 : 211-235.

2257   APKARIAN-LACOUT, Arlette; VERGÈS, Pierrette. "L'irrésistible ascension des couches moyennes face à l'hégémonie communiste: Martigues", *Sociologie du Travail* 25(2), apr-jun 83 : 206-225. [France] [résumé en anglais]

2258   ARMSTRONG, Peter. "Class relationships at the point of production: a case study", *Sociology (London)* 17(3), aug 83 : 339-358.

2259   BAMAT, Thomas. "Peru's Velasco regime and class domination after 1968", *Latin American Perspectives* 10(2-3), sum 83 : 128-150.

2260   BARROW, Andrew. *International gossip: a history of high society, 1970-1980.* London, H. Hamilton, 83, 288 p.

2261   BARTSCH, Volker. *Liberalismus und arbeitende Klassen: zur Gesellschaftstheorie John Stuart Mills* (Liberalism and working classes: on John Stuart Mill's theory of society). Opladen, Westdeutschland Verlag, 82, 313 p.

2262   BAUER, Michel; [et al.]. "Couches moyennes et 'cadres' ", *Revue française de Sociologie* 24(2), apr-jun 83 : 285-338. [France] [continued in ibid. 24 (4), oct-dec 83: 679-733]

2263   BETTELHEIM, Charles. *Les luttes de classes en URSS. III. Troisième période 1930-1941. 2. Les dominants.* Paris, Maspéro, Seuil, 83, 340 p.

2264   BRADLEY, Ian C. *The English middle classes are alive and kicking.* London, Collins, 82, 240 p.

2265   CALVERT, Peter. *The concept of class: an historical introduction.* London, Hutchinson, 82, 254 p.

2266   CESTARO, Antonio. "Mezzogiorno e classi sociali" (Southern Italy and social classes), *Sociologia (Roma)* 17(2), mai-aug 83 : 3-29.

2267   CHAMBERLAIN, Chris. *Class consciousness in Australia.* Sydney-Boston, MA, Allen and Unwin, 83, xi-174 p.

2268   CHENU, Alain. "La classe ouvrière en mouvement: repères statistiques", *La pensée* (233), jun 83 : 22-36.

2269   COLEMAN, Kenneth M.; DAVIS, Charles L. "Preemptive reform and the Mexican working class", *Latin American Research Review* 18(1), 83 : 3-31.

2270   COLMENARES, Francisco. *Petróleo y lucha de clases en México, 1864-1982* (Petroleum and class struggle in Mexico, 1864-1982). México, DF, Ediciones El Caballito, 82, 235 p.

2271   COPANS, Jean. "Les classes ouvrières d'Afrique noire. Bibliographie sélectionnée, classée et commentée", *Cahiers d'Études africaines* 21(1-3), 81 : 405-429.

2272   DATTA RAY, B.; [ed.]. *The emergence and role of middle class in North-East India.* New Delhi, Uppal, 83, xvi-284 p.

2273   DILIGENSKIJ, G. G. "Problemy klassovogo soznanija v istorii i sociologii rabočego klassa" (Problems of class consciousness in history and sociology of the working class), *in: K izučeniju rabočego klassa i rabočego dvizenija.* Moskva, 1982 : 276-286.

2274   DRIVER, Edwin D. "Class, caste, and 'status summation' in urban South India", *Contributions to Indian Sociology* 16(2), jul-dec 82 : 225-253.

2275   DRIVER, Edwin D. "Social class in South India: a cognitive approach", *Journal of Asian and African Studies* 16(3-4), oct 81 : 238-260.

2276   ERBE, Günther. *Arbeiterklasse und Intelligenz in der DDR* (Working class and managers in the GDR). Opladen, Westdeutscher Verlag, 82, 224 p.

2277   EYERMAN, Ron. "Some recent studies in class consciousness", *Theory and Society* 11(4), jul 82 : 541-553.

2278   FARJOUN, Emmanuel. "Class divisions in Israeli society", *Khamsin* (10), 83 : 29-39.

2279   FEHÉR, Ferenc; HELLER, Agnes. "Class, democracy, modernity", *Theory and Society* 12(2), mar 83 : 211-244.

2280   FEHÉR, Ferenc; HELLER, Ágnes. "Classe, modernità, democrazie" (Class, modernity, democracy), *Critica sociologica* 63-64, 82-83 : 6-14. [continued in ibid. 65, 1983: 6-34]

2281   FORM, William. "Sociological research and the American working class", *Sociological Quarterly* 24(2), spr 83 : 163-184.

2282   FRICKER, Yves. "La classe ouvrière des années quatre-vingts", *Travail et Société* 8(4), oct-dec 83 : 431-443.

2283   GALKIN, A. A.; [ed.]. *Rabocij klass v stranah Zapadnoj Évropy* (The working class in the West European countries). Moskva, Nauka, 82, 375 p.

2284   GARZON VALDES, E. "La paradoja de Johnson. Acerca del papel político-económico de las clases medias" (The Johnson's paradox. On the political and economic role of the middle classes), *Sistema* (56), sep 83 : 131-147.

2285   GRAETZ, Brian R. "Images of class in modern society: structure, sentiment and social location", *Sociology (London)* 17(1), feb 83 : 79-96. [Australia]

2286   GRANT, Geraldine. "The State and the formation of a middle class: a Chilean example", *Latin American Perspectives* 10(2-3), sum 83 : 151-171.

2287   GUIBERT, Joël. *La vieillesse ouvrière.* Nantes, Laboratoire d'Études et de Recherches Sociologiques sur la Classe Ouvrière, 83, 95-xii p. [France]

2288   HOLLINGSWORTH, J. Rogers; HANNEMAW, Robert A. "Working class power and the political economy of Western capitalist societies", *Comparative Social Research* 5, 82 : 61-80.

2289   HONG, Doo-Seung. "Class stratification in contemporary Korea: a preliminary observation", *Social Science Journal (Seoul)* 9, 82 : 7-15.

2290   HORVAT, Branko. "Prilog teoriji klasne stratifikacije s analizom klasa u suvremenom kapitalizmu" (A contribution to the theory of class stratification), *Sociologija* 24(1), 82 : 25-43.

2291   HRYNIEWICZ, Janusz T. "Metodologiczne aspekty analizy struktury klasowej w Polsce. Stosunki produkcji, władza, klasy społeczne" (Methodological aspects of the analysis of class structure in Poland. Production relations, power, social class), *Studia Socjologiczne* 88(1), 83 : 43-73.

2292   HUNT, Ian; STARRS, Chris. "The dynamics of class and the 'new middle class' ", *Social Theory and Practice* 9(1), spr 83 : 85-114.

2293   ICHIYO, Muto. "Class struggle in postwar Japan. Its past, present and future", *Ampo* 14(3), 82 : 19-27.

2294   JÄRVELÄ, Marja. "The permanency of social classes and intergenerational mobility in Finland", *Acta Sociologica* 26(3-4), 83 : 287-298.

2295   JAYAWARDENA, Kumari. "Aspects of class and ethnic consciousness in Sri Lanka", *Development and Change* 14(1), jan 83 : 1-18.

2296   JONES, Gareth Stedman. *Languages of class: studies in English working class history, 1832-1982.* Cambridge-New York, NY, Cambridge University Press, 83, viii-260 p.

2297   JOVANOVIĆ, Radiša. "Izmedu autokratskog i anarhističkog modela socijalnog uticaja radničke klase" (Between autocratic and anarchist model of the working class social influence), *Sociologija* 24(4), 82 : 409-420.

2298   KAMADA, Toshiko; KAMADA, Tetsuhiro. *Shakai sho-kaiso to gendai kazoku: jukagaku kogyo toshi ni okeru rodosha kaikyu no jotai* (Social stratification and family: the conditions of the working class in industrial city). Tokyo, Ochanomizu Shobo, 83, 514 p. [Japan]

2299   KIURANOV, Chavdar. "Social classes and social stratification", *International Journal of Sociology* 12(3), 82 : 3-100. [Bulgaria]

2300   KONINGS, Piet. "Riziculteurs capitalistes et petits paysans: la naissance d'un conflit de classe au Ghana", *Politique africaine* (11), sep 83 : 77-94.

2301   KOZLOVA, G. P.; FAJNBORG, Z. I. "Rabočij klass i obrazovanie: problemy i al'ternativy" (The working class and education: problems and alternatives), *in: Social'noe i kul'turnoe razvitie rabočesgo klassa v socialističeskom obščestve*. Moskva, 1982 : 73-113.

2302   KRUHMALEV, A. E.; SERGEJCIK, S. I. "Rol'social'noj i nacional noj politiki KPSS v razvitii rabočego klassa" (The role of the social policy and national policy carried out by the CPSU for the working class development), *Voprosy istorii KPSS* 26(12), dec 83 : 3-16.

2303   KUMAR, Krishan. "Class and political action in nineteenth-century England: the theoretical and comparative perspectives", *Archives européennes de Sociologie* 24(1), 83 : 3-43.

2304   LARSON, Oscar W. III; GILLESPIE, Gilbert W. Jr.; BUTTEL, Frederick H. "Sources of social class identification among farmers", *Rural Sociology* 48(1), spr 83 : 82-103.

2305   LEE, Chong-Jae. "Social class and distribution of educational opportunity", *Social Science Journal (Seoul)* 9, 82 : 27-36.

2306   LEE, Jung-Bock. "Social classes and political culture in Korea", *Social Science Journal (Seoul)* 9, 82 : 66-75.

2307   LOAEZA, Soledad. "El papel político de las clases medias en el México contemporáneo" (The political role of middle classes in contemporary Mexico), *Revista mexicana de Sociología* 45(2), apr-jun 83 : 407-439.

2308   LOJKINE, Jean. "Classe operária e Estado: a experiência francesa das municipalidades socialistas e comunistas" (Working class and State: the French experience of socialist and communist municipalities), *Dados* 26(2), 83 : 197-212.

2309   LOJKINE, Jean. "La classe ouvrière et l'automation", *Pensée* (233), jun 83 : 9-21.

2310   LUEBKE, Paul; ZIPP, John F. "Social class and attitudes toward big business in the United States", *Journal of Political and Military Sociology* 11(2), spr 83 : 251-264.

2311   MARCUS, Alfred A. "Whatever happened to the 'new class'?", *Sage Yearbooks in Politics and Public Policy* (10), 82 : 93-114. [USA]

2312   MBWILIZA, J. F. "Classes, class struggle and the State during the transition to socialism in Tanzania", *Taamuli* 12, dec 82 : 11-28.

2313   MCNAMEE, Stephen J.; VANNEMAN, Reeve. "The perception of class. Social and technical relations of production", *Work and Occupations* 10(4), nov 83 : 437-469.

2314   MJØSET, Lars; PETERSEN, Trond. "Class and gender: a note on class structure in Norway and USA", *Acta Sociologica* 26(1), 83 : 49-60.

2315   MUNSON, J. Michael; SPIVEY, W. Austin. "Relation between social class and three aspects of self-concept: actual, ideal, and egocentric self", *Journal of Social Psychology* 119(1), feb 83 : 85-94.

2316   NEALE, R. S.; [ed.]. *History and class: essential readings in theory and interpretation.* Oxford, B. Blackwell, 83, x-318 p. [UK]

2317   NEUFELD, Maurice F.; LEAB, Daniel J.; SWANSON, Dorothy. *American working class history: a representative bibliography.* New York, NY-London, Bowker, 83, xi-356 p.

2318   NOVE, Alec. "The class nature of the Soviet Union revisited", *Soviet Studies* 35(3), jul 83 : 298-312.

2319   O'BRIEN, Robert M.; BURRIS, Val. "Comparing models of class structure", *Social Science Quarterly* 64(3), sep 83 : 445-459.

2320   PALMER, Bryan D. *Working-class experience: the rise and reconstitution of Canadian labour, 1800-1980.* Toronto, ON-Boston, MA, Butterworth, 83, 347 p.

2321   PENN, R. D. "Theories of skill and class structure", *Sociological Review* 31(1), feb 83 : 22-38.

2322   PENN, R. D.; DAWKINS, D. C. "Structural transformations in the British class structure: a log linear analysis of marital endogamy in Rochdale 1856-1964", *Sociology (London)* 17(4), nov 83 : 506-523.

2323   PETRAS, James. "Class formation and politics in Greece", *Journal of Political and Military Sociology* 11(2), spr 83 : 241-250.

2324   PINEO, Peter C.; LOOKER, E. Dianne. "Class conformity in the Canadian setting", *Canadian Journal of Sociology / Cahiers canadiens de Sociologie* 8(3), 83 : 293-317.

2325   POLJAKOV, Ju. S. "Polnoe uničtoženie klassovsteržnevaja social'no-ėkonomičeskaja problema kommunističeskogo stroitel'stva" (The complete elimination of classes is the essential socio-economic problem of the communism edification), *Vestnik Leningradskogo Universiteta. Serija Ėkonomika, Filosofija Pravo* 36(3), 82 : 10-17.

2326   POPOV, S. V. "Rabočij klass i umstvennyj trud" (The working class and intellectual work), *in: K izučeniju rabočego klassa i rabočego dvizenija.* Moskva, 1982 : 385-402.

2327   PRAVDA, Alex. "Is there a Soviet working class?", *Problems of Communism* 31(6), dec 82 : 1-24.

2328   ROUX, Alain. "La classe ouvrière chinoise et la question de son rôle dirigeant", *Recherches internationales* (9), sep 83 : 95-112.

2329   RUSSELL, Raymond. "Class formation in the workplace: the role of sources of income",
        Work and Occupations 10(3), aug 83 : 349-372. [USA]

2330   SEN, Anupam. *The state, industrialization, and class formation in India: a neo-Marxist perspective
        on colonialism, underdevelopment, and development.* London-Boston, MA, Routledge and Kegan
        Paul, 82, xii-289 p.

2331   SHIN, Dong-Wook. "The significance of social class in literature", *Social Science Journal
        (Seoul)* 9, 82 : 76-95.

2332   SPOORMANS, H. "Burgerij, liberalen en democratie. Kanttekeningen bij een toetsing
        van de bourgeoisie-these" (Bourgeoisie, liberals and democracy. Remarks on a test of
        the bourgeoisie-thesis), *Sociologische Gids* 30(6), nov-dec 83 : 414-428. [see also A. T.
        DERKSEN, ibid. 29, 1982: 386-409]

2333   STARSKI, Stanislaw. *Class struggle in classless Poland.* Boston, MA, South End Press, 82,
        xiv-253-6 p.

2334   STEVEN, Rob. *Classes in contemporary Japan.* Cambridge-New York, NY-Sydney, Cambridge
        University Press, 83, xvi-357 p.

2335   TATUR, Melanie. *Zu Wandlungen der Sozialstruktur in der polnischen Arbeiterschaft* (Social structure
        changes in Polish labour force). Köln, Bundesinstitut für Ostwissenschaftliche und
        Internationale Studien, 82, ii-55 p.

2336   THÉVENOT, Laurent. "À propos d'une définition des couches moyennes et de la nouvelle
        nomenclature des professions et catégories socioprofessionnelles", *Revue française de
        Sociologie* 24(2), apr-jun 83 : 317-326.

2337   TITTENBRUN, Jacek. "Kryzysy w Polsce Ludowej — analiza klasowa" (Crisis in People's
        Poland — class analysis), *Problemy Marksizmu-Leninizmu* 1, 83 : 116-132.

2338   TSUDA, Masumi. "Class consciousness of Japanese workers", *Rivista internazionale di Scienze
        economiche e commerciali* 29(12), dec 82 : 1169-1183.

2339   UZNAŃSKI, Andrzej. "Badania nad identyfikacjami klasowymi" (Studies on class
        identification), *Studia Socjologiczne* 89(2), 83 : 171-195.

2340   VASIL'ČUK, Ju. A. "O dialektika razvitija rabočego klassa" (On dialectics of the working
        class development), *in: K izučeniju rabočego klassa i rabočego dviženija.* Moskva, 1982 : 402-420.

2341   VERGÈS, Pierre. "Approche des classes sociales dans l'analyse localisée", *Sociologie du Travail*
        25(2), apr-jun 83 : 226-232. [France] [résumé en anglais]

2342   VERRET, Michel; NUGUES, Paul. *Le travail ouvrier.* Paris, A. Colin, 82, 238 p. bibliogr.
        [France]

2343   VISHER, Mary G. "Perception of class conflict in Scandinavia", *Acta Sociologica* 26(3-4),
        83 : 237-245. [Data from the Scandinavian Welfare Study, 1972]

2344   WAISMAN, Carlos Horacio. *Modernization and the working class. The politics of legitimacy.*
        Austin, TX, University of Texas Press, 82, xii-244 p.

2345   WINTER, J.; [ed.]. *The working class in modern British history.* Cambridge, Cambridge
        University Press, 83, xii-315 p.

2346   WINTER, Lothar. *Das Proletariat der Welt von heute: Wesen, Umfang, Strukturveränderungen* (The pro-
        letariat of today's world: nature, extent, evolutions in its structure). Berlin, Dietz, 82, 256 p.

2347   WITTE, Eberhard. "Klassenkampf und Gruppenkampf im Unternehmen. Abschied von
        der Konfliktideologie" (Class struggle and group conflict in enterprises. The end of
        conflict ideology), *Hamburger Jahrbuch für Wirtschafts- und Gesellschaftspolitik* 27, 82 : 167-182.
        [Germany FR]

2348   WITTEN, Samuel M. "'Compensatory discrimination' in India: affirmative action as a
        means of combatting class inequality", *Columbia Journal of Transnational Law* 21(2), 83 : 353-387.

2349   WRIGHT, Erik Olin; [et al.]. "The American class structure", *American Sociological Review*
        47(6), dec 82 : 709-726.

2350   ZAJMIST, G. I.; ZAJMIST, F. L. "Političeskie interesy rabočego klassa i kolhoznogo
        krest'janstva v razvitom socialističeskom obščestve" (The working class and collective
        farmers political interests in the developed socialist society), *Filosofija i Naučnyj Kommunizm*
        (9), 82 : 22-30.

2351   ZIÓŁKOWSKI, Marek. "Świadomość klasowa. Kształt — uwarunkowania — funkcje —
        dynamika" (Class consciousness. Form — determinants — functions — dynamics),
        Kultura i Społeczeństwo 27(3), 83 : 73-99.

14240   **Social status**
        Statut social

2352   CAMPBELL, Richard T.; PARKER, Robert Nash. "Substantive and statistical considerations
        in the interpretation of multiple measures of SES", *Social Forces* 62(2), dec 83 : 450-466.
        [socioeconomic status]

2353 GRAY, Lois C.; [et al.]. "Individual and contextual social status. Contributions to psychological well-being", *Sociology and Social Research* 68(1), oct 83 : 78-95.

2354 KESSLER, Ronald C. "A disaggregation of the relationship between socioeconomic status and psychological distress", *American Sociological Review* 47(6), dec 82 : 752-764.

2355 KWONG, Julia. "Is everyone equal before the system of grades: social background and opportunities in China", *British Journal of Sociology* 24(1), mar 83 : 93-108.

2356 LOOKER, E. Dianne; PINEO, Peter C. "Social psychological variables and their relevance to the status attainment of teenagers", *American Journal of Sociology* 88(6), mai 83 : 1195-1219.

2357 MERLLIÉ, Dominique. "Une nomenclature et sa mise en oeuvre: les statistiques sur l'origine sociale des étudiants", *Actes de la Recherche en Sciences sociales* 50, nov 83 : 3-47. [résumés en anglais et en allemand]

2358 RUMBERGER, Russell W. "The influence of family background on education, earnings and wealth", *Social Forces* 61(3), mar 83 : 755-773.

2359 SØRENSEN, Aage B. "Processes of allocation to open and closed positions in social structure", *Zeitschrift für Soziologie* 12(3), jul 83 : 203-224.

2360 TAYLOR, Robert Joseph; TAYLOR, Willie H. "The social and economic status of the Black eldery", *Phylon* 43(4), dec 82 : 295-306.

2361 WEBSTER, Murray Jr.; DRISKELL, James E. Jr. "Beauty as status", *American Journal of Sociology* 89(1), jul 83 : 140-165.

2362 WHITT, Hugh P. "Status inconsistency: a body of negative evidence or a statistical artifact?", *Social Forces* 62(1), sep 83 : 201-233.

14250   Elite. Intellectuals
Élite. Intellectuels

2363 "Intellectuels (Les) aux États-Unis", *Revue française d'études américaines* 8(16), feb 83 : 7-185. [with contributions by Norman BOWEN, Jeanine BRUN-ROYET, Christopher LASCH, Morris DICKSTEIN, Pierre BESSES; résumés en français et en anglais]

2364 AŠIN, G. K. "Élita i gospodstvujuščij ěkspluatatorskij klass" (Elite and the ruling exploiter class), *Voprosy Filosofii* 36(2), 83 : 74-84.

2365 AŠIN, G. K. "'Pljuralističeskja demokratija' ili vselastie monopolističeskoj ělity" ('Pluralist democracy' or the all-power of the monopolist elite), *SŠA* 13(4), 83 : 18-29. [USA]

2366 BELKHIR, Jean; [et al.]; [eds.]. *L'intellectuel: l'intelligentsia et les manuels*. Paris, Anthropos, 83, 233 p.

2367 BOSSLE, Lothar. "Von der Zirkulation zur Polarisierung der Eliten" (On the circulation and polarization of elite), *Hamburger Jahrbuch für Wirtschafts- und Gesellschaftspolitik* 27, 82 : 183-195. [Germany FR]

2368 BRUNNER, José J.; FLISFISCH, Angel. *Los intelectuales y las instituciones de la cultura* (The intellectuals and the institutions of culture). Santiago de Chile, FLACSO, 83, 390 p. [Chile]

2369 BRYK, Andrzej; ROTHENBERG, Lawrance. "Elitarne i pluralistyczne koncepcje władzy — próba krytyki immanentnej" (Elite and pluralistic conceptions of power — an attempt at immanent critique), *Studia Nauk Politycznych* 1, jan-feb 82 : 81-99.

2370 CHEN, Guuying. "The reform movement among intellectuals in Taiwan since 1970", *Bulletin of Concerned Asian Scholars* 14(3), sep 82 : 32-47.

2371 DAGNAUD, Monique; MEHL, Dominique. "Elite, sub-elite, counter-elite", *Social Science Information* 22(6), 83 : 817-865.

2372 ELERT, Claes-Christian; ERIKSSON, Gunnar; [eds.]. *Suppression, struggle, and success: studies on three representatives of cultural life in Sweden: Fredrika Bremer, Andreas Kempe, and Linnaeus*. Umeå, Universitetet i Umeå, 82, 195 p.

2373 GRAF, William D. "Nigerian elite consolidation and African elite theories: towards an explanation of African liberal democracy", *Verfassung und Recht in Übersee* 16(2), sem. 2, 83 : 119-138.

2374 HOLLANDER, Paul. "Intellectuals, estrangement and wish fulfillment", *Society* 20(5), aug 83 : 16-24.

2375 JANOVSKIJ, R. G.; [ed.]. *Idejno-političeskoe vospitanie naučno-tehničeskoj intelligencii: opyt i problemy* (Ideological and political education of scientific and technical intellectuals: experiment and problems). Moskva, Nauka, 82, 184 p.

2376 JEREZ, M. *Elites políticas y centros de extracción en España, 1938-1957* (Political elite and centres of origin in Spain, 1938-1957). Madrid, Centro de Investigaciones Sociológicas, 82, 499 p.

2377 KAPCIA, Antoni. "Revolution, the intellectual and a Cuban identity: the long tradition", *Bulletin of Latin American Research* 1(2), mai 82 : 63-78.

2378   KOSTRUBIEC, Stanisława; KOWALSKA, Grażyna. "Warszawskie rodziny inteligenckie osób z wyższym wykształceniem" (Families of the intelligentsia of people with higher education in Warsaw), *Biuletyn Instytutu Gospodarstwa Społecznego* 25(3), 82 : 146-166.

2379   LENGYEL, György. *Gazdasági elit* (Economic elite). Budapest, Magyar Tudományos Akadémia Szociológiai Kutatóintézete, 82, 49 p. [Hungary]

2380   LEW, Roland. "L'intelligentsia chinoise et la révolution, 1898-1927", *Revue de l'Institut de Sociologie* (3-4), 82 : 367-420.

2381   LIBBY, Ronald T. "Transnational class alliances in Zambia", *Comparative Politics* 15(4), jul 83 : 379-400.

2382   MAZURKIEWICZ, Wojciech. "Pozycja społeczna inteligencji wiejskiej" (Social status of rural intelligentsia), *Wieś Współczesna* 316(6), 83 : 72-82.

2383   MBOUKOU, Alexandre. "The rise of anti-intellectualism among the modern African elite", *Journal of African Studies* 9(4), wint 82-83 : 180-186.

2384   MENYHÁRT, Lajos; ULLAGA, József. "Debrecen város értelmisége az 1980-as évek elején" (The intellectuals of the town of Debrecen at the beginning of the eighties), *Debreceni Szemle* 2(1), 83 : 29-48. [Hungary]

2385   MITCHELL, Judson R. "Immobilism, depoliticization and the emerging Soviet elite", *Orbis* 26(3), aut 82 : 591-610.

2386   MORAN, M. L. "El problema de la ideología en los teóricos de la élite" (The problem of ideology among the theoreticians of the elite), *Sistema* (52), jan 83 : 85-100.

2387   OPELLO, Walter C. "Portugal's administrative elite: social origins and political attitudes", *West European Politics* 6(1), jan 83 : 63-74.

2388   OSTAPENKO, L. V.; SUSOKOLOV, A. A. "Étnosocial'nye osobennosti vosproizvodstva intelligencii" (Ethno-social features of the intellectuals reproduction), *Sociologičeskie Issledovanija (Moskva)* (1), 83 : 10-16.

2389   OTAKPOR, Kneonye. "The Nigerian power elite (a theoretical critique)", *International Review of History and Political Science* 19(4), nov 82 : 1-16.

2390   OTAKPOR, Nkeonye. "The Nigerian power elite: a critique", *Indian Journal of Social Research* 23(3), dec 82 : 253-264.

2391   PAIK, Wan-Ki. "The formation of the governing elite in Korean society", *Social Science Journal (Seoul)* 9, 82 : 49-65.

2392   PAKULSKI, Jan. *Elite recruitment in Australia: a comparative study.* Canberra, Department of Sociology, Research School of Social Sciences, Australian National University, 82, 228 p.

2393   PELLE, János. "Az értelmiség autonómiája vagy egy illúzió realitása" (The autonomy of intellectuals or the reality of an illusion), *Szociológia* 11(3), 82 : 416-446. [Hungary]

2394   PEREIRA REIS, Elisa Maria. "Elites agrárias, 'state-building' e autoritarismo" (Agrarian elite, state building, and authoritarianism), *Dados* 25(3), 82 : 331-348.

2395   SAINZ, Enrique. "Hipotesis para el estudio del intellectual en España" (Assumptions for the study of the intellectual in Spain), *Revista internacional de Sociología (Madrid)* 40(43), sep 82 : 413-422.

2396   SAKURAI, Tetsuo. *Chishikijin no unmei* (The destiny of intellectuals). Tokyo, San'ichi Shobo, 83, 254 p.

2397   SOLYMÁR, Magda. *Az elit. Az elitizmustól a technokratikus hatalomig. Műhelytanulmány* (The elite. From elitism to technocratic power. Workshop paper). Budapest, Magyar Szocialista Munkáspárt KB Társadalomtudományi Intézete, 82, 292 p.

2398   SZTUMSKI, Janusz. "Uwagi w sprawie inteligencji w Polsce Ludowej" (Observations on intelligentsia in People's Poland), *Nowe Drogi* 405(2), 83 : 127-137.

2399   TOLSTYH, V. I. "Ob intelligencii i intelligentnosti: kul'turno-ličnostnyj aspekt" (On the intellectuals and culture: the cultural and personal aspect), *Voprosy Filosofii* 35(10), 82 : 83-98.

2400   VAJPEYI, Dhirendra K. "Modernity and industrial culture of Indian elites", *Journal of Asian and African Studies* 17(1-2), jan-apr 82 : 74-97.

2401   WIDERSZPIL, Stanisław. "Inteligencja — uwarunkowania klasowe" (Intelligentsia — class determinants), *Nowe Drogi* 405(2), 83 : 121-126.

2402   ZIMMERMAN, Carle C. "The nature of the intelligentsia", *Indian Journal of Social Research* 24(3), dec 83 : 209-226.

        14260   Social mobility
        Mobilité sociale

2403   ANZALONE, Pasquale. "Aspetti strutturali della riuscità sociale in Italia" (Structural aspects of social success in Italy), *Revue internationale de Sociologie* 18(1-2-3), apr-aug-sep 82 : 181-192.

2404   BIANCO, Maria Luisa. "Ipotesi di ricerca sui problemi della mobilità sociale. Comparazione fra paesi industrializzati" (Research hypotheses on social mobility. Some comparisons among industrial countries), *Rassegna italiana di Sociologia* 24(4), oct-dec 83 : 503-552.

2405   COLCLOUGH, Glenna; HORAN, Patrick M. "The status attainment paradigm: an application of a Kuhnian perspective", *Sociological Quarterly* 24(1), 83 : 25-42.

2406   ERIKSON, Robert; GOLDTHORPE, John H.; PORTOCARERO, Lucienne. "Intergenerational class mobility and the convergence thesis: England, France and Sweden", *British Journal of Sociology* 24(3), sep 83 : 303-343.

2407   GIBSON, J. B.; [et al.]. "Social mobility and psychometric variation in a group of Oxfordshire villages", *Journal of Biosocial Science* 15(2), apr 83 : 193-205.

2408   JURA, Michel; KAMÍNSKI, Philippe. "Mobilité sociale des ménages et évolution économique", *Consommation* 30(1), mar 83 : 93-123. [France] [résumé en anglais]

2409   LAKI, László. "A társadalom, a gazdaság és a társadalmi mobilitás néhány összefüggése a hatvanas és a hetvenes években" (Some relations of society and social mobility in the 1960s and 1970s), *Társadalomtudományi Közlemények* 13(4), 83 : 616-631.

2410   LE BRAS, Hervé. "Les origines d'une promotion de Polytechniciens", *Population* 38(3), mai-jun 83 : 491-502. [France]

2411   PAYNE, Geoff; PAYNE, Judy. "Occupational and industrial transition in social mobility", *British Journal of Sociology* 24(1), mar 83 : 72-92.

2412   PÖNTINEN, Seppo. *Social mobility and social structure: a comparison of Scandinavian countries.* Helsinki, Finnish Society of Sciences and Letters, 83, 195 p.

2413   PORTOCARERO, Lucienne. "Social mobility in industrial nations: women in France and Sweden", *Sociological Review* 31(1), feb 83 : 56-82.

2414   TOLBERT, Charles M. II. "Industrial segmentation and men's intergenerational mobility", *Social Forces* 61(4), jun 83 : 1119-1137.

2415   YAMANOI, Atsunori. "Nihon no daigaku kyoju no shakai ido ni kansuru kenkyu shiryo" (Data for the study of social mobility of college professors in Japan), *Toyama daigaku kyoikugakubu kiyo* 31, 83 : 167-176.

14300   SOCIAL CHANGE
CHANGEMENT SOCIAL

14310   History
Histoire

2416   "Historians and movies: the state of the art", *Journal of Contemporary History* 18(3), jul 83 : 357-531. [with contributions by Marc FERRO, Nicholas PRONAY, Wolfgang ERNST, R. C. RAACK]

2417   "Military history", *Journal of Contemporary History* 18(4), oct 83 : 533-744. [with contributions by Walter LAQUEUR, Martin VAN CREVELD, Stephen P. GLICK, L. Ian CHARTERS, Dennis E. SHOWALTER, Mira Beth LANSKY, Amnon SELLA]

2418   BARG, M. A. "Istoričeskoe soznanie kak problema istoriografii" (Historical consciousness as an historiographical problem), *Voprosy Istorii* 56(12), 82 : 49-66.

2419   BEZOUCHA, Robert J. "The French Revolution of 1848 and the social history of work", *Theory and Society* 12(4), jul 83 : 469-484.

2420   BRIGGS, Asa. *A social history of England.* London, Weidenfeld and Nicolson, 83, 320 p.

2421   CONZE, Werner; LEPSIUS, Mario Rainer; [eds.]. *Sozialgeschichte der Bundesrepublik Deutschland: Beiträge zum Kontinuitätsproblem* (Social history of the Federal Republic of Germany: contributions on the problem of continuity). Stuttgart, Klett-Cotta, 83, 467 p.

2422   FERRAROTTI, Franco. "Note su storia e sociologia" (Notes on history and sociology), *Critica sociologica* 60, 82 : 60-66.

2423   GOULDNER, Alwin W. "Artisans and intellectuals in the German revolution of 1848", *Theory and Society* 12(4), jul 83 : 521-532.

2424   HANDA, M. L. "India historiography: writing and rewriting Indian history", *Journal of Asian and African Studies* 17(3-4), oct 82 : 218-234.

2425   KAYE, Harvey J. "History and social theory: notes on the contribution of British Marxist historiography to our understanding of class", *Canadian Review of Sociology and Anthropology* 20(2), mai 83 : 167-192.

2426   MANCHIN, Róbert; [et al.]. *Kényszerpályán? A magyar társadalom alakulása 1930 és 1980 között* (On a forced way? The formation of the Hungarian society between 1930 and 1980). Budapest, Magyar Tudományos Akadémia Szociológiai Kutató Intézete, 82, xxii-240 p. [2 vols.]

2427   POLLAK, Michaël. "Historisation des sciences sociales et sollicitation sociale de l'histoire", *Bulletin de l'Institut d'Histoire du Temps présent* 13, sep 83 : 5-13.

2428   SANTARELLI, Enzo. *Storia sociale del mondo contemporaneo: dalla Comune di Parigi ai nostri
        giorni* (Social history of the contemporary world: from the Commune of Paris to the
        present time). Milano, Feltrinelli, 82, 638 p.
2429   STUART-FOX, Martin. "On theory of history and its context of discovery", *Philosophy of
        the Social Sciences* 13(4), 83 : 401-424.
2430   TROJANO, Paolo Raffaello. *La storia come scienza sociale* (History as a social science). Napoli,
        Giannini, 83, xxiv-197 p.

        14320   Future
        Futur

2431   MAINES, David R.; SUGRUE, Noreen M.; KATOVICH, Michael A. "The sociological
        import of G. H. Mead's theory of the past", *American Sociological Review* 48(2), apr 83 : 161-173.
2432   MRÁČEK, Karel; SUŠA, Oleg. "K soudobým tendencím buržoazního výzkumu budoucnosti"
        (Contemporary tendencies of bourgeois futurology), *Ekonomický Časopis* 31(9), 83 : 840-858.
2433   VAN STEENBERGEN, Bart. "The sociologist as social architect. A new taste for macro-
        sociology", *Futures* 15(5), oct 83 : 376-386.
2434   WILCOX, Larry D. "Futurology and the social sciences. Bloom and gloom or gloom and
        doom?", *International Social Science Review* 58(4), 83 : 202-210.

        14330   Social change
        Changement social

2435   *Obščestvennye razvitie i NTR: očerki metodologičeskih issledovanij* (Social development and the
        scientific and technical revolution: aspects of methodological research). Leningrad, Nauka,
        82, 268 p.
2436   "Social development and social policy in the third world", *Development and Peace* 3(2),
        aut 82 : 5-108. [with contributions by V. LI, C. K. BROWN, C. B. CHIDEBE]
2437   "Transição social e democracia" (Social transition and democracy), *Dados* 26(1), 83 : 5-115.
        [Latin America]
2438   "Wandel und Beharrung in der Frühen Neuzeit" (Change and permanence in the early
        new time), *Geschichte und Gesellschaft* 8(4), 82 : 435-553.
2439   ALSTON, Jon P. "Japan as number one? Social problems of the next decades", *Futures*
        15(5), oct 83 : 342-356.
2440   ARZANOV, O. S.; [et al.]. "Sistemnyj podhod, protivorečija, zakony obščestvennogo
        razvitija" (Systemic approach, contradictions, laws of the social development), *Problemy
        Dialektiki* (10), 82 : 75-83.
2441   ASPLUND, Gunnar. "Menjajuščajasja struktura finskogo obščestva" (The changing
        structure of Finnish society), *Kommunist (Moskva)* 59(2), jan 83 : 83-93.
2442   BALOYRA, Herp; ENRIQUE; LÓPEZ-PINTOR, Rafael; [comps.]. *Iberoamérica en los
        años 80: perspectivas de cambio social y político* (Latin America in the eighties: social and
        political change prospects). Madrid, Centro de Investigaciones Sociológicas, 82, 210 p.
2443   BECHER, Berthold. "Gesellschaftlicher Wandel und neue Funktionsbedingungen kommunaler
        Sozialpolitik" (Social change and new conditions of the communal social policy), *Sociologia
        internationalis* 20(1-2), 82 : 87-115. [Germany FR] [résumé en anglais]
2444   BOUDON, Raymond. "Individual action and social change: a no-theory of social change",
        British Journal of Sociology 24(1), mar 83 : 1-18.
2445   BOUDON, Raymond. "Why theories of social change fail: some methodological thoughts",
        Public Opinion Quarterly 47(2), 83 : 143-160.
2446   BRÓDY, András. "A társadalmi folyamatok időszükségletéről" (Time scales of social
        processes), *Társadalomkutatás* 1(3), 83 : 30-41.
2447   BRUCE, Steve. "Social change and collective behaviour: the revival in eighteenth-century
        Ross-shire", *British Journal of Sociology* 34(4), dec 83 : 554-572. [UK: Scottish Highlands]
2448   CHAMPAGNE, Duane. "Social structure, revitalization movements and state building:
        social change in four Native American societies", *American Sociological Review* 48(6), dec
        83 : 754-763.
2449   COHEN, Francis. "Mutations sociales et contradictions", *Recherches internationales* (9),
        sep 83 : 77-94.
2450   D'AGOSTINO, Federico. *La dinamica del razionale e non razionale nel processo del mutamento
        sociale: un'analisi teorica di Durkheim, Weber, Marx e un modello di sintesi* (Dynamics of the
        rational and non-rational in the process of social change: a theoretical analysis of
        Durkheim, Weber, Marx and a model of synthesis). Milano, F. Angeli, 83, 171 p.

2451 EKPO, Monday U. "Karl Marx's theory of revolution and the world historical development of capitalism: a critique", *Indian Journal of Social Research* 23(3), dec 82 : 277-288.

2452 FEATHERMAN, David L.; SØRENSEN, Annemette. "Societal transformation in Norway and change in the life course transition into adulthood", *Acta Sociologica* 26(2), 83 : 105-126.

2453 FORSE, Michel. "Observations locales du changement social", *Futuribles* 62, jan 83 : 44-60. [France]

2454 GADOUREK, Ivan. *Social change as redefinition of roles: a study of structural and causal relationships in the Netherlands of the 'seventies'*. Assen, Van Gorcum, 82, x-522 p.

2455 GAJDA, A. V. "Materialistiĉeskoe ponimanie istorii i 'teorija socialnoj ėvoljucii' Ju. Habermas" (The materialist conception of history and the J. Habermas 'theory of social evolution'), *Filosofskie Nauki* 25(1), 83 : 85-95.

2456 GRATH, Joseph E.; [ed.]. "Social issues and social change: some views from the past", *Journal of Social Issues* 39(4), 83 : 1-239. [USA]

2457 GRUNFELD, F. "De rol ruimtelijke factoren bij maatschappelijke veranderingsprocessen" (The role of spatial factors in social change processes), *Mens en Maatschappij* 58(3), aug 83 : 221-239.

2458 HOROWITZ, Irving Louis. "Military origins of Third World dictatorship and democracy", *Research in Social Movements, Conflicts and Change* (5), 83 : 295-307.

2459 JONAS, Friedrich. *Soziologische Betrachtungen zur Französischen Revolution* (Sociological reflections on the French Revolution). Stuttgart, Enke, 82, 178 p. [Edited by Manfred HENNEN, Walter G. RÖDEL]

2460 KAMAT, A. R. *Essays on social change in India*. Bombay, Somaiya, 83, 121 p.

2461 KATARIA, M. S. "Infrastructure for a stable white revolution in India", *Asian Profile* 11(3), jun 83 : 279-292.

2462 KULCSÁR, Kálmán. "A társadalmi változások és a modernizáció Magyarországon. Kísérlet az utolsó három évtized tapasztalatainak elemzésére" (Social change and modernization in Hungary. An attempt to analize the experiences observed during the last three decades), *Társadalomkutatás* 1(1), 83 : 7-28.

2463 LEW, Roland. "Économie, classes sociales et révolution: Chine, 1900-1925. Les sources modernes de la crise chinoise du XXᵉ siècle", *Revue de l'Institut de Sociologie* (3-4), 83 : 387-422.

2464 LEWIS, Vaughan A. "The political feasibility of social development", *Planning Bulletin* 9, 82 : 3-16.

2465 LUKE, Timothy W. "Angola and Mozambique: institutionalizing social revolution in Africa", *Review of Politics* 44(3), jul 82 : 413-436.

2466 NAG, Moni. "Modernization affects fertility", *Populi* 10(1), 83 : 56-77.

2467 NEDELEA, Marin. "The present stage and development prospects of the Romanian society", *Revue roumaine des sciences sociales. Série de sociologie* 27(2), 83 : 107-114.

2468 NOVOPAŠIN, Ju. S. "Vozdejstvie real'nogo socializma na mirovoj revoljucionnyj process: metodologiĉeskie aspekty" (Influence of real socialism on the world revolutionary process: methodological aspects), *Voprosy Filosofii* 35(8), 82 : 3-16.

2469 ONDRČKA, Pavol. "Metodologické prístupy k vymedzeniu cel'ov sociálneho rozvoja" (Methodological approaches to defining social development goals), *Plánované Hospodářství* 40(6), 83 : 69-76.

2470 ORZECHOWSKI, Marian. "Spór o marksistowską teorię rewolucji" (Dispute about Marxist theory of revolution), *Nowe Drogi* (8), 83 : 5-28.

2471 PARYS, Jan. *Ghana. Problemy rozwoju społecznego* (Ghana. Social development problems). Wrocław, Ossolineum, 83, 142 p.

2472 PASTORE, José; ZYLBERSTAJN, Hélio; PAGOTTO, Carmen Silvia. *Mudança social e pobreza no Brasil, 1970-1980: o que ocoreu com a família brasileira?* (Social change and poverty in Brazil, 1970-1980: or what is happening with the Brazilian family?). São Paulo, Fundação Instituto de Pesquisas Econômicas, Livraria Pioneira Editora, 83, 152 p.

2473 PETROV, I. I. "Social'nyj progress i vyživanie: novye tendencii v buržuaznoj ideologii" (Social progress and survival, new tendencies in bourgeois ideology), *Voprosy Filosofii* 36(2), 83 : 125-131.

2474 RODRÍGUEZ IBÁÑEZ, José Enrique. *El sueño de la razón: la modernidad y sus paradojas a la luz de la teoría social* (The sleep of the reason: modernity and its paradoxes in the light of social theory). Madrid, Taurus, 82, 254 p.

2476 ROY, Girish Chandra. *Value conflict in study of social change in India*. New Delhi, S. Chand, 83, viii-272 p.

2477 RUBENSTEIN, Richard L.; [ed.]. *Modernization: the humanist response to its promise and problems: selected readings from the proceedings of the International Conferences on the Unity of the Sciences*. Washington, DC, Paragon House, 82, 393 p.

2478   RUEDA ORTIZ, Juan. *Los factores del cambio* (The factors of change). México, DF, Federación Editorial Mexicana, Federación Mexicana de Escritores, 83, 233 p. [Mexico]

2479   RUNCIMAN, W. G. "Unnecessary revolution: the case of France", *Archives européennes de Sociologie* 24(2), 83 : 291-318.

2480   RUTKEVIČ, M. N. "O roli torgovli v social'nom razvitii sovetskogo obščestva" (On the role of trade in the social development of Soviet society), *Sociologičeskie Issledovanija (Moskva)* (1), 83 : 16-28.

2481   SACHCHIDANANDA; VERMA, K. K. *Electricity and social change.* Patna, Janaki Prakashan, 83, 264 p. [India]

2482   SAFAROV, R. A. "Vzaimodesjtvie gosudarstva i social'nogo progressa: k metodologiju analiza mehanizma vzaimodejstvija gosudarstva i progressa" (Interaction of the state and social progress: analysis methodology of the mechanism of interaction between the state and social progress), *in: Socialističeskoe gosudarstvo i obščestvennyj progress.* Moskva, 1982 : 22-31.

2483   SCHABERT, Tilo. "Modernité et histoire", *Diogène* 123, jul-sep 83 : 121-137.

2484   SIVOKON', P.; [et al.]. "Smysl i napravlenie obščestvenno-istoričeskogo razvitija" (Sense and direction of the socio-historical development), *in: O gumanizme v nauke i kul'ture.* Moskva, 1982 : 145-169.

2485   SOLOV'EV, O. M. "Obščestvennyj progress i socialističeskaja demokratija" (Social progress and socialist democracy), *Vestnik Leningradskogo Universiteta. Serija Ėkonomika, Filosofija Pravo* 36(3), 82 : 41-47.

2486   SRUBAR, Ilja. "Diskursive und dialektische Vernunft: das Konzept der gesellschaftlichen Rationalisierung bei Marx und Weber" (Discursive and dialectical reason: the concept of social rationalization in Marx and Weber), *Zeitschrift für Soziologie* 12(1), jan 83 : 7-23.

2487   SUJATOZEL'KAJA, A. V. "Metodologičeskie aspekty issledovanija ob'ektivnogo i sub'ektivnogo v social'nyh processah" (Methodological aspects of research on the subjective and the objective in social processes), *in: Marksistsko-leninskoe obrazovanie i naučnoe tvorčestvo.* Minsk, 1982 : 88-102.

2488   TAKAHATA, Masato; SANUKI, Koji; SUMIOKA, Hidetake; [eds.]. *Ningen hattatsu no shakaigaku* (The sociology of human development). Kyoto Academia shuppankai, 83, 299 p.

2489   VÁRDY, Steven Béla; VÁRDY-HUSZÁR, Agnes. *Society in change: studies in honour of Béla K. Király.* Boulder, CO-New York, NY, Columbia University Press, 83, xii-680 p.

2490   VAZJULIN, V. A. "Voprosy teorii obščestvenno-ėkonomičeskih formacij v trudah K. Marksa: istoričeskij aspekt" (Question on the theory of socio-economic formation in K. Marx's works: the historical aspect), *Vestnik Moskovskogo Universiteta. Serija Filosofija* 37(2), 83 : 14-24.

2491   VOLGYES, Ivan. "Social change in communist Eastern Europe: Hungary in a comparative perspective", *Südosteuropa — Zeitschrift für Gegenwartsforschung* 32(5), 83 : 254-267. [see also ibid. 32 (6), 83: 334-343]

2492   VOLGYES, Ivan. "Soziale Wandlungen in Osteuropa: Ungarn im Vergleich zu anderen" (Social changes in Eastern Europe: Hungary compared to other countries), *Europäische Rundschau* 11(3), 83 : 71-97.

2493   WEISBROT, David; PALIWALA, Abdul; SAWYERR, Akilagpa; [eds.]. *Law and social change in Papua New Guinea.* Sydney, Butterworths, 82, xxiv-319 p.

2494   WIATR, Jerzy J. *Marksistowska teoria rozwoju społecznego* (Marxist theory of social development). Warszawa, Państwowe Wydawnictwo Naukowe, 83, 567 p.

2495   ZARUBIN, A. G. "Social'noe razvitie i teorii vremeni v obščestvoznanii" (Social development and time theory in the social sciences), *Vestnik Moskovskogo Universiteta. Serija Filosofija* 36(6), 82 : 19-27.

2496   ŽIVOTIĆ, Miladin. *Revolucija i kultura* (Revolution and culture). Beograd, Filozofsko Društvo Srbije, 82, 195 p.

14340   Changing society
Société en transformation

2497   BÜHL, Walter L. "Die 'postindustrielle Gesellschaft': eine verfrühte Utopie?" (The 'post industrial society': a refreshed utopia?), *Kölner Zeitschrift für Soziologie und Sozialpsychologie* 35(4), dec 83 : 771-780.

2498   CAKUNOV, V. V. "Nekotorye metodologičeskie aspekty ėdinstva ėkonomčeskogo i social'nogo razvitija obščestva" (Some methodological aspects of the unity of economic and social development of society), *Naučnoe Upravlenie Obščestvom* 15, 82 : 35-39.

2499   HETTNE, Björn. "The development of development theory", *Acta Sociologica* 26(3-4), 83 : 247-266. [From its early economistic and eurocentric phase to the present ('dependency school')]

2500   KENT, George. "Meanings of development", *Human Systems Management* 3(3), sep 82 : 188-194.

2501   MEYER, Thomas. "Grundlagen einer neuen Theorie der westlichen Industriegesellschaft: Fred Hirschs 'Die sozialen Grenzen des Wachstums' " (Foundations of a new theory of Western industrial society: Fred Hirsch's 'The social limits of growth'), *Zeitschrift für Soziologie* 12(1), jan 83 : 74-85.

2502   PRESTON, P. W. *Theories of development.* Boston, MA-London-Melbourne, Routledge and Kegan Paul, 82, xiii-296 p.

2503   SATYANĀRAYĀNA, P.; SURYANARAYANA RAO, T.; [eds.]. *Perspectives on national integration.* Hyderabad, Prakasam Institute of Development Studies, 82, 218 p.

2504   SEDAS NUNES, A.; MARINHO ANTUNES, Manuel L.; VILLAVERDE CABRAL, Manuel; [eds.]. "A formação de Portugal contemporâneo: 1900-1980" (The formation of contemporary Portugal, 1900-1980), *Análise social* 18(3-4-5), 82 : 639-1500. [continued in ibid. 19(3-4-5), 1983 : 415-1260]

2505   TSUBOUHI, Yoshihiro. "Tonan asia ni okeru jinko to dentoteki kiso shakai no seikaku: Toyobu o chusin toshite" (The population and character of traditional communities in insular Southeastern Asia), *Tonan Asia kenkyu* 21(1), 83 : 6-16.

2506   YOUNG, Grawford. "Nationalizing the Third-World State: categorical imperative or mission impossible?", *Polity* 15(2), wint 82 : 161-181.

2507   ZIMMERMAN, Carle C. "The sociology of change in the underdeveloped lands", *Indian Journal of Social Research* 24(2), aug 83 : 176-196.

15100   DEMOGRAPHY. GENETICS
DÉMOGRAPHIE. GÉNÉTIQUE

15110   Population research
Recherche démographique

2508   "France: recensement 1982. Évolutions régionales de population", *Futuribles* 69, sep 83 : 48-66.

2509   "Malthus our contemporary", *History of European Ideas* 4(2), 83 : 121-214. [with contributions by Kurt W. BACK, E. R. WEISS-ALTANER, Linda GORDON]

2510   "Perspectives démographiques", *Futuribles* 67, jun 83 : 7-105. [with contributions by Gérard CALOT, Louis ROUSSEL, Paul PAILLAT, Alain PARANT, Jean BOURGEOIS-PICHAT]

2511   "Population", *Australian Foreign Affairs Record* 53(12), dec 82 : 755-769. [with contributions by A. STRUIK, David LUCAS, Gavin JONES, D. T. ROWLAND]

2512   "Sociología de la población" (Sociology of the population), *Revista mexicana de Sociología* 45(1), jan-mar 83 : 233-308.

2513   ARCE, Wilfredo F.; ALVAREZ, Gabriel C.; [eds.]. *Population change in Southeast Asia.* Singapore, Southeast Asia Population Research Awards Program, Institute of Southeast Asian Studies, 83, 499 p.

2514   ASSOCIATION INTERNATIONALE DES DÉMOGRAPHES DE LANGUE FRANÇAISE. *Démographie et destin des sous-populations; colloque de Liège 21-23 septembre 1981.* Paris, AIDELF, 83, xiii-452 p.

2515   BAKER, Theodore Cardwell; DRAKE, Michael; [eds.]. *Population and society in Britain, 1850-1980.* London, Batsford Academic and Educational, 82, 221 p.

2516   BOLDYREV, V. A. *Narodonaselenie v razvitom socialističeskom obščestve: teorija i politika* (Population in the developed socialist society: theory and politics). Moskva, Finansy i Statistika, 83, 231 p.

2517   CAPUTO, Cataldo. *Malthus et Ricardo: le pessimisme démographique et économique à l'époque de la révolution industrielle.* Bologna, Editrice Club, 82, 120 p.

2518   CHARMES, Jacques. "Principales tendances de la démographie tunisienne au cours des deux décennies 1960-1980 et perspectives pour la décennie 1980-1990", *Cahiers ORSTOM. Série Sciences humaines* 18(3), 82 : 341-346.

2519   CRISOSTOMO, Rosemarie. *The demographic dilemma of the Soviet Union.* Washington, DC, United States Department of Commerce, Bureau of the Census, 83, 15 p.

2520   DE CANDIA, Michele. "Migrazioni e recente evoluzione della popolazione delle regioni italiane" (Migrations and recent evolution of the population in the Italian regions), *Affari sociali internazionali* 11(4), 83 : 115-129.

2521   DOMENACH, Hervé; GUENGANT, Jean-Pierre. "Continuité et changements de la démographie de la Guadeloupe", *Bulletin d'Information du CENADDOM* 12(68), dec 82 : 45-57.

2522   DUPUIS, Jacques. *L'Inde et ses populations.* Bruxelles, Éditions Complexe, 82, 278 p.

2523   DURAND, Jean Pierre; TENGOUR, H. *L'Algérie et ses populations.* Bruxelles, Éditions Complexe, 82, 301 p.

2524   ESENWEIN-ROTHE, Ingeborg. *Einführung in die Demographie: Bevölkerungsstruktur und Bevölkerungsprozess aus der Sicht der Statistik* (Introduction to demography: population structure and population process from the statistical viewpoint). Wiesbaden, Steiner, 82, xix-400 p.

2525   HODGSON, Dennis. "Demography as social sciences and policy science", *Population and Development Review* 9(1), mar 83 : 1-34.

2526   HOLZER, Jerzy Z. "Ludność Chińskiej Republiki Ludowej. Stan strukturalny, polityka ludnościowa, perspektywy" (The population of the People's Republic of China. Present situation, population policy, perspectives), *Studia demograficzne* 21(2), 83 : 21-32.

2527   INSTITUTO NACIONAL DE ESTADÍSTICA Y CENSOS; CENTRO LATINO-AMERICANO DE DEMOGRAFÍA. *Estimaciones y proyecciones de población, 1950-2025* (Population estimates and forecasts, 1950-2025). Buenos Aires, INEC, CELADE, 82, 132 p. [Argentina]

2528   JOHNSON, Peter David; CAMPBELL, Paul R. *Detailed statistics on the population of South Africa, by race and urban/rural residence, 1950 to 2010.* Washington, DC, International Demographic Data Center, United States Bureau of the Census, 82, vii-455 p.

2529   KOSTEN, M.; WILLIAMS, J.; MITCHELL, R. J. "Historical population structure of two Tasmanian communities using surname analyses", *Journal of Biosocial Science* 15(3), jul 83 : 367-376.

2530   KPEDEKPO, G. M. K. *Essentials of demographic analysis for Africa.* London-Exeter, NH, Heinemann, 82, xii-210 p.

2531   LEVITS, Egil. "Die demographische Situation in der UdSSR und in den baltischen Staaten unter besonderer Berücksichtigung von nationalen und sprachsoziologischen Aspekten" (The demographic situation in the USSR and the Baltic States under special consideration of national and linguistic sociological aspects), *Acta Baltica* 21, 81 : 18-142.

2532   LÉVY, Michel Louis. *La population de la France des années 80.* Paris, Hatier, 82, 80 p.

2533   LIPPMANN, Lorna. "Land rights and the Aboriginal situation in Australia", *Patterns of Prejudice* 17(2), apr 83 : 31-35.

2534   LORENTE ARENAS, S. "El cambio demográfico en España" (Demographic change in Spain), *Documentación Social* (50), jan-mar 83 : 35-47.

2535   MIGUEL, Armando de. *Ensayo sobre la población de México* (Essay on the population of Mexico). Madrid, Centro de Investigaciones Sociológicas, 83, 216 p.

2536   MIRANDA, Armindo. *The demography of Bangladesh: data and issues.* Fantoft-Bergen, Chr. Michelsen Institute, Development Research and Action Programme, 82, ii-x-268 p.

2537   MOSS, Jennifer. "Population projections for Third World countries: how to circumvent inadequate data", *Third World Planning Review* 5(2), mai 83 : 115-135.

2538   NATIONS UNIES. DÉPARTEMENT DES AFFAIRES ÉCONOMIQUES ET SOCIALES INTERNATIONALES. *Les perspectives d'avenir de la population mondiale évaluées en 1980.* New York, NY, UN, 82, vi-101 p.

2539   PONS, Xavier. *L'Australie et ses populations.* Bruxelles, Éditions Complexe, 83, 220 p.

2540   POPULATION RESEARCH INSTITUTE, HELSINKI. *Yearbook of population research in Finland, 1983.* Helsinki, PRI, 83, 184 p.

2541   PREMI, M. K.; [et al.]. *An introduction to social demography.* New Delhi, Vikas, 83, 214 p.

2542   RJABUŠKIN, T. V.; GALECKAJA, P. A. *Naselenie i socialističeskoe obščestvo* (Population and the socialist society). Moskva, Statistika, 83, 247 p.

2543   RUPP, Sabine; SCHWARZ, Karl; [eds.]. *Beiträge aus der bevölkerungswissenschaftlichen Forschung* (Contributions from demographic research). Wiesbaden, Boldt Verlag, 83, 592 p.

2544   SANCHEZ CORDERO DE GARCIA VILLEGAS, Olga. "Sociologia de la población y de los grupos sociales" (Sociology of population and social groups), *Revista de la Facultad de derecho de México* 31(119), aug 81 : 519-566. [Mexico]

2545   ŠELESTOV, D. K. *Demografija: istorija insovremennost'* (Demography: history and the contemporary era). Moskva, Finansy i Statistika, 83, 271 p.

2546   STRZELECKI, Zbigniew. "O korzystne perspektywy demograficzne Polski" (About favourable demographic perspectives for Poland), *Studia demograficzne* 21(2), 83 : 95-112.

2547   TABAH, Léon. "Les perspectives démographiques mondiales", *Tiers-Monde* 24(94), jun 83 : 305-324.

2548   THIBAULT, Normand. "Présentation des perspectives provisoires de la population du Québec, 1981-2001", *Cahiers québécois de Démographie* 11(3), dec 82 : 277-322.

2549   THOMAS, Armand C. *The population of Sierra Leone.* Freetown, Demographic Research and Training Unit, Fourah Bay College, 83, xvii-229 p.

2550   UNITED NATIONS. *Population of Papua New Guinea.* New York, NY, UN; Noumea, South Pacific Commission, 82, xv-285 p.

2551   VIKTOROVNA ZVEREVA, Natalie. "Současný stav sovětské demografie" (Present state of the Soviet demography), *Demografie* 24(4), 82 : 292-301.

2552   VOLLMAR, Rainer. "Bevölkerungsgeographische und soziale Veränderungen in den USA. Der Census von 1980" (Population geography and social change in the USA. The 1980 census), *Geographische Rundschau* 35(4), 83 : 152-160.

15120   Households. Men. Women
          Ménages. Hommes. Femmes

2553   "Frauen und Kultur" (Women and culture), *Argument* 25(138), apr 83 : 189-229. [Germany FR] [with contributions by Silke WENK, Emily HICKS, Biddy MARTIN, Inge BAXMANN]

2554   "Sexisme et loi anti-sexiste: contributions au débat", *Temps modernes* 40(444), jul 83 : 1-61. [France] [with contributions by Marie-Jo DHAVERNAS, Liliane KANDEL, Béatrice SLAMA]

2555   ALLEN, Sheila. "Production and reproduction: the lives of women homeworkers", *Sociological Review* 31(4), nov 83 : 649-665.

2556   ANTILL, John K. "Sex role complementarity versus similarity in married couples",
            Journal of Personality and Social Psychology 45(1), jul 83 : 145-155.

2557   BAHR, Howard M.; CHADWICK, Bruce. "Sex and social change in Middletown",
            Tocqueville Review 3(1), wint 81 : 5-41.

2558   BAINBRIDGE, William Sims; CRUTCHFIELD, Robert D. "Sex role ideology and
            delinquency", *Sociological Perspectives* 26(3), jul 83 : 253-274.

2559   BAUCOM, Donald H. "Sex role identity and the decision to regain control among women:
            a learned helplessness investigation", *Journal of Personality and Social Psychology* 44(2), feb
            83 : 334-343.

2560   BERNSTEIN, Marianne E. "Sex distribution in sibships according to occupation of
            parents", *Genus* 37(3-4), jul-dec 81 : 179-188. [Finland]

2561   BERTHELOT, Jean-Michel. "Corps et société. Problèmes méthodologiques posés par une
            approche sociologique du corps", *Cahiers internationaux de Sociologie* 74, 83 : 119-131.

2562   CARR, Shirley G. E. "L'emploi et la discrimination fondée sur le sexe: problèmes et progrès
            au Canada", *Revue internationale du Travail* 122(6), dec 83 : 819-829.

2563   CHECK, James V. P.; MALAMUTH, Neil M. "Sex role stereotyping and reactions to
            depictions of stranger versus acquaintance rape", *Journal of Personality and Social Psychology*
            45(2), aug 83 : 344-356.

2564   CHESTER, Nia Lane. "Sex differentiation in two high school environments: implications
            for career development among black adolescent females", *Journal of Social Issues* 39(3),
            83 : 29-40. [USA]

2565   CHIPLIN, Brian; SLOANE, Peter J. *Tackling discrimination at the workplace: an analysis of
            sex discrimination in Britain.* Cambridge-New York, NY-Sydney, Cambridge University
            Press, 82, vii-156 p.

2566   EDWARDS, Anne R. "Sex roles: a problem for sociology and for women", *Australian and
            New Zealand Journal of Sociology* 19(3), nov 83 : 385-412.

2567   ELMENDORF, Mary L.; ISELY, Raymond B. "Public and private roles of women in
            water supply and sanitation programs", *Human Organization* 42(3), 83 : 195-204.

2568   GANE, Mike. "Durkheim: woman as outsider", *Economy and Society* 12(2), 83 : 227-270.

2569   GARCÍA DE LEÓN, María Antonia. *Las elites femeninas españolas* (Spanish feminine elite).
            Madrid, Queimada, 82, 301 p.

2570   GOLDTHORPE, John H. "Women and class analysis: in defence of the conventional
            view", *Sociology (London)* 17(4), nov 83 : 465-488.

2571   GONZÁLEZ, Mirta. "Aproximaciones al estudio de la diferenciación conductual entre
            hombres y mujeres" (An approach to the studies of behavioral differentiation between
            men and women), *Revista de Ciencias Sociales de la Universidad de Costa Rica* 25(1), 83 : 75-84.

2572   GUNDERSON, Morley; REID, Frank. *Sex discrimination in the Canadian labour market: theories,
            data, and evidence.* Ottawa, Labour Canada, 83, 77 p.

2573   GUTEK, Barbara A.; [ed.]. *Sex role stereotyping and affirmative action policy.* Los Angeles, CA,
            Institute of Industrial Relations, University of California, Los Angeles, 82, 227 p.

2574   HAUSEN, Karin; [ed.]. *Frauen suchen ihre Geschichte* (Women looking for their history).
            München, C. H. Beck, 83, 278 p. [Germany]

2575   HOLMSTROM, Nancy. "Do women have a distinct nature?", *Philosophical Forum* 14(1),
            aut 82 : 25-42.

2576   HOPE, Keith. "On defining normative consistency: the case of sex-stereotyping", *Sociological
            Methods and Research* 12(1), aug 83 : 95-111.

2577   HOWELL-MARTINEZ, Vicky. "The influence of gender roles on political socialization:
            an experimental study of Mexican-American children", *Women & Politics* 2(3), aut 82 : 33-46.

2578   ISMAIL, Ellen T. *Social environment and daily routine of Sudanese women: a case study of urban
            middle class housewives.* Berlin, Reimer, 82, 224-1 p.

2579   JAMES, Kerry E. "Women on Australian farms: a conceptual scheme", *Australian and
            New Zealand Journal of Sociology* 18(3), nov 82 : 302-319.

2580   JONES, F. L. "Sources of gender inequality in income: what the Australian census says",
            Social Forces 62(1), sep 83 : 134-152.

2581   KAHN, Arnold S.; JEAN, Paula J. "Integration and elimination or separation and
            redefinition: the future of the psychology of women", *Signs* 8(4), sum 83 : 652-671.

2582   KANDIYOTI, Deniz. "Economie monétaire et rôles des sexes: le cas de la Turquie", *Current
            Sociology / Sociologie contemporaine* 31(1), 83 : 213-228.

2583   KAWAMURA, Nozomu. "The transition of the household system in modernizing Japan",
            Tokyo toritsu daigaku jinbungaku-ho 159, 83 : 1-18.

2584   KOESOEBJONO, Santo. *Trends of one-person households in the Netherlands, 1960-1978: a
            demographic analysis.* Voorburg, Netherlands Interuniversity Demographic Institute,
            83, viii-100 p.

2585   KRAMPEN, Günter. "Eine Kurzform der Skala zur Messung normativer Geschlechtsrollen-Orientierung" (A short version of the scale for measuring normative sex roles orientation), *Zeitschrift für Soziologie* 12(2), apr 83 : 152-156.

2586   KUČERA, Milan. "Vývoj počtu a složeni domácností v letech 1970-1980" (Development of numbers and structure of households in 1970-1980), *Demografie* 25(1), 83 : 34-47. [Czechoslovakia]

2587   KYNCH, Jocelyn; SEN, Amartya. "Indian women: well-being and survival", *Cambridge Journal of Economics* 7(3-4), sep-dec 83 : 363-380.

2588   LANE, Christel. "Women in socialist society with special reference to the German Democratic Republic", *Sociology (London)* 17(4), nov 83 : 489-505.

2589   LEONARD, Candice J. "Women and depression: reintegrating the diagnosis", *Sociologia internationalis* 21(1-2), 83 : 175-188.

2590   LOETERS, Alice. *Vrouwen van Nicaragua* (Women of Nicaragua). Amsterdam, Pegasus, 82, 104-16 p.

2591   MACKIE, Marlene. *Exploring gender relations: a Canadian perspective.* Toronto, ON, Butterworths, 83, vi-358 p.

2592   MARGUERYE, Colette de. "Les juges français et la discrimination sexuelle", *Droit social* (2), feb 83 : 119-130. [France]

2593   MARSHALL, Ian; MORRIS, Cecilia. *Crosstalk: women, partners, and children in the eighties.* Sydney, Fontana/Collins, 83, 253 p. [Australia]

2594   MCCARTHY, Florence; FELDMAN, Shelley. "Rural women discovered: new sources of capital and labour in Bangladesh", *Development and Change* 14(2), apr 83 : 211-236.

2595   MEI, Ida Lee. *Chinese womanhood.* Taipei, Taiwan, China Academy, 82, xiii-146 p. [Based on: Lieh nü chuan, by Liu Hsiang (77-76? B.C.)]

2596   MOOR, Ed de; [et al.]. *Vrouwen in het Midden-Oosten* (Women of the Middle East). Bussum, Wereldvenster, 82, 277-12 p.

2597   MUSALLAM, B. F. *Sex and society in Islam.* Cambridge-New York, NY-New Rochelle-Melbourne-Sydney, Cambridge University Press, 83, x-176 p.

2598   NAPP-PETERS, Anneke. "Geschlechtsrollenstereotypen und ihr Einfluss auf Einstellungen zur Ein-Elternteil-Situation" (Sex-role stereotypes and their influence on attitudes towards one-parent situation), *Kölner Zeitschrift für Soziologie und Sozialpsychologie* 35(2), jun 83 : 321-334.

2599   NETTLES, Elizabeth Jane; LOEVINGER, Jane. "Sex role expectations and ego level in relation to problem marriages", *Journal of Personality and Social Psychology* 45(3), sep 83 : 676-687.

2600   OHDE, Harue. "Kosodateki sengyo shufu no fuan" (Anxiety of young housewives: a case study), *Kazoku kenkyu nenpo* 9, 83 : 52-64.

2601   OPPONG, C. *Female and male in West Africa.* London, George Allen and Unwin, 83, xix-402 p.

2602   PICARD, Dominique. *Du code au désir: le corps dans la relation sociale.* Paris, Dunod, 83, xi-226 p.

2603   PONGY, Mireille. *La part des sexes.* Grenoble, Presses Universitaires de Grenoble, 83, 158 p.

2604   PUGH, M. D.; WAHRMAN, Ralph. "Neutralizaing sexism in mixed sex-groups: do women have to be better than men?", *American Journal of Sociology* 88(4), jan 83 : 746-762. [USA]

2605   QUARM, Daisy. "The effect of gender on sex-role attitudes", *Sociological Focus* 16(4), oct 83 : 285-303.

2606   REID, Ivan; WORMALD, Eileen; [eds.]. *Sex differences in Britain.* London, Grant McIntyre, 82, x-277 p.

2607   ROMERO, Carmen Ma.; RAMIREZ, Mario; TANZI, Geanina. "La investigación de los problemas de la mujer rural" (The research of rural women's problems), *Revista de Ciencias Sociales de la Universidad de Costa Rica* 25(1), 83 : 47-58.

2608   ROSENFELD, Rachel A. "Sex segregation and sectors: an analysis of gender differences in returns from employer changes", *American Sociological Review* 48(5), oct 83 : 637-655. [USA]

2609   ROTHSCHILD, Joan; [ed.]. *Women, technology, and innovation.* Oxford-New York, NY, Pergamon Press, 82, vii-289-382 p. [Published also as volume IV No 3 of Women's Studies International Quarterly]

2610   SARDE, Michèle. *Regard sur les Françaises: Xe siècle-XXe siécle.* Paris, Stock, 83, 667 p.

2611   SELLARI, Maricla. "La donna, la comunicazione e lo sviluppo in America Latina" (Woman, communication and development in Latin America), *Critica sociologica* 68, 83-84 : 157-162.

2612   SIMPONS, Donita Vasiti; YEE, Sin Joan; [eds.]. *Women in the South Pacific: a bibliography.* Suva, University of the South Pacific, Library, 82, vi-124 p.

2613   SJÖHOLM, Tommy. "Women in the Swedish class structure, 1910-1975", *Acta Sociologica* 26(3-4), 83 : 299-311.

2614   SKRĘTOWICZ, Biruta; BODYCH, Grażyna. "Małżeństwo i rodzina w ocenie kobiet wiejskich" (Marriage and family as appreciated by rural females), *Studia demograficzne* 21(1), 83 : 125-140.

2615   SMITH, Robert John; WISWELL, Ella Lury. *The women of Suye-mura*. Chicago, IL-London, University of Chicago Press, 82, xxxvii-253 p.

2616   STIDHAM, Ronald. "Women's rights before the Federal Courts, 1971-1977", *American Politics Quarterly* 11(2), apr 83 : 205-218. [USA]

2617   THORNTON, Arland; ALWIN, Duane F.; CAMBURN, Donald. "Causes and consequences of sex-role attitudes and attitude change", *American Sociological Review* 48(2), apr 83 : 211-227.

2618   THORNTON, Margaret. "Sex discrimination legislation in Australia", *Australian Quarterly* 54(4), sum 82 : 393-403.

2619   THORNTON, Merle. "Psychoanalysis and feminist social theory of gender", *Politics* 17(2), nov 82 : 52-64.

2620   TOMEH, Aida K. "Correlation of sex role attitudes in a Korean student population", *Journal of Asian and African Studies* 16(3-4), oct 81 : 169-185.

2621   WHITLEY, Bernard E. Jr. "Sex role orientation and self-esteem: a critical meta-analytic review", *Journal of Personality and Social Psychology* 44(4), apr 83 : 765-778.

2622   WISTRAND, Birgitta. "Le mythe de l'égalité des sexes en Suède: la lutte continue", *Cultures* (4), 82 : 69-90.

2623   WONG, Herbert Y.; SANDERS, Jimy M. "Gender differences in the attainment of doctorates", *Sociological Perspectives* 26(1), jan 83 : 29-50. [USA]

2624   YOHDA, Hiroe. "Josei alcohl-sho-sha no keisei katei to shogu ni truite" (Life-careers of alcoholic women: rethinking sex-role stereotyping and reconstructing supportive system), *Osaka shiritsu daigaku shakai fukushi ronshu* 19(20), 83 : 167-209.

2625   YOSHIOKA, Masamitsu. "Shakai hendo to josei no ishiki no kindaika: aru chiho toshi no chosa kara" (Social change and modernization of women's consciousness: through a social research in a local city), *Chuo daigaku daigakuin kenkyu nenpo* 12(IV), 83 : 55-72.

2626   YOSHIZUMI, Kyoko. "Sei kihan ni miru josei sabetsu: Wakamono no ishiki chosa o chushin toshite" (Discrimination against women in sexual standards: a study of the sexual attitudes of college students), *Nihon joseigaku kenkyukai Joseigaku nenpo* 4, 83 : 63-76.

15130   **Eugenism. Heredity**
         Eugénisme. Hérédité

15200   **AGE GROUPS**
         GROUPES D'ÂGE

15210   **Age. Cohorts. Generations**
         Âge. Cohortes. Générations

2627   BAKER, Carolyn. "The 'age of consent' controversy: age and gender as social practice", *Australian and New Zealand Journal of Sociology* 19(1), mar 83 : 96-112.

2628   CORNELL, Laurel L. "Retirement inheritance, and intergenerational conflict in preindustrial Japan", *Journal of Family History* 8(1), 83 : 55-69.

2629   GAREWICZ, Jan. "Pokolenie jako kategoria socjofilozoficzna" (Generation as a socio-philosophical category), *Studia Socjologiczne* 88(1), 83 : 75-87.

2630   KERTZER, David I. "Generation as a sociological problem", *Annual Review of Sociology* (9), 83 : 125-149.

2631   LAMBIRI-DIMAKI, Jane. "Abstand und Problem der Generationen. Unveränderliche Elemente und zeitgenössische Merkmale mit besonderem Bezug auf den Fall Griechenland" (Distance and problem of generations. Unchangeable elements and contemporary character-istics with a special reference to the case of Greece), *Sociologia internationalis* 21(1-2), 83 : 189-213.

2632   LATYŠEV, I. A. "'Duhovnyj razryv' pokolenij: po materialam issledovanij japonskih sociologov" ('Intellectual gap' of the generations: with Japanese sociologists' research materials), *Sociologičeskie Issledovanija* (3), 82 : 175-181.

2633   PFEFFER, Georg. "Generation and marriage in Middle India: the evolutionary potential of 'restricted exchange'", *Contributions to Indian Sociology* 17(1), jan-jun 83 : 87-121.

2634   RODGERS, Willard L. "Estimable functions of age, period, and cohort effects", *American Sociological Review* 47(6), dec 82 : 774-787. [USA] [With a comment by Herbert SMITH, William M. MASON, and Stephen E. FIENBERG, 787-793, and a reply by the author, 793-796]

2635   WIDMER, Jean. "Remarques sur les classements d'âge", *Schweizerische Zeitschrift für Soziologie / Revue suisse de Sociologie* 9(2), 83 : 337-363.

15220   Childhood
Enfance

2636   "Neuen (Die) Kinder" (The new children), *Kursbuch* (72), jun 83 : 1-180. [with contributions by Yvonne SCHÜTZE, Wolfgang MERTEN]

2637   BRYAN, James H.; BRYAN, Tanis H. *Exceptional children*. Palo Alto, CA, Mayfield Publishing Co., 82, xiii-424 p.

2638   CALLAN, Victor. "How do Australians value children?: a review and research update using the perceptions of parents and voluntarily childless adults", *Australian and New Zealand Journal of Sociology* 18(3), nov 82 : 384-398.

2639   CHOQUET, M.; DAVIDSON, F. "Le mode de garde et le développement physique et psycho-affectif du jeune enfant", *Enfance* (5), dec 82 : 323-334. [France]

2640   FISCHER, Kurt W.; [ed.]. *Levels and transitions in children's development*. San Francisco, CA, Jossey-Bass, 83, 114 p.

2641   FLAKE-HOBSON, Carol; ROBINSON, Bryan E.; SKEEN, Patsy. *Child development and relationships*. Reading, MA, Addison-Wesley Publishing Co., 83, 581 p.

2642   HAYASHI, Masataka. "Chugoku no jido shakai gaisetsu" (An introduction to child society in communist China), *Yamaguchi joshi daigaku kenkyu hokoku* 8, 83 : 1-9.

2643   HOLOWINSKY, Ivan Z. *Psychology and education of exceptional children and adolescents: United States and international perspectives*. Princeton, NJ, Princeton Book Co., 83, xiii-359 p.

2644   JENKS, Chris; [ed.]. *The sociology of childhood: essential readings*. London, Batsford Academic and Educational, 82, 299 p.

2645   KAGITÇIBASI, Çiğdem. *The changing value of children in Turkey*. Honolulu, HI, East-West Center, 82, viii-100 p.

2646   KOHN, Igor. "L'ethnographie de l'enfance", *Sciences sociales — Académie des Sciences de l'URSS* (4), 82 : 204-214.

2647   LAHTI, Janet. "A follow-up study of foster children in permanent placements", *Social Service Review* 56(4), dec 82 : 556-571.

2648   LIPSITZBEM, Sandra. "Gender schema theory and its implication for child development: raising gender-aschematic children in a gender-schematic society", *Signs* 8(4), sum 83 : 598-616.

2649   MORTON, Miriam. *Growing up in the Soviet Union: from the cradle to coming of age*. Moscow, Progress Publishers, 82, 212-64 p.

2650   ODOM, Mildred; CLARK, Diane. *The exceptional child in a regular classroom*. Manhattan, KS, Master Teacher, 83, 117 p. [USA]

2651   PAGE, H. J.; LESTHAEGHE, R. J.; SHAH, I. H. *Illustrative analysis: breastfeeding in Pakistan*. Voorburg, International Statistical Institute, 82, 84 p.

2652   PARR, Joy; [ed.]. *Childhood and family in Canadian history*. Toronto, ON, McClelland and Stewart, 82, 221 p.

2653   RIEBEN, Laurence; RIBAUPIERRE, Anik; LAUTREY, Jacques. *Le développement opératoire de l'enfant entre 6 et 12 ans: élaboration d'un instrument d'évaluation*. Paris, Éditions du CNRS, 83, 187 p.

2654   SASAKI, Atsunobu. "Gendai shakai to kodomono skahaika" (Modern society and children's socialization), *Aizu tanki daigaku gakuho* 40, 83 : 1-12.

2655   SEABROOK, Jeremy. *Working-class childhood*. London, Gollancz, 82, 251 p.

2656   SUTTON, John R. "Social structure, institutions, and the legal status of children in the United States", *American Journal of Sociology* 88(5), mar 83 : 915-947.

2657   TEASDALE, T. W. "Educational attainment and social class in adoptees: genetic and environmental contributions", *Journal of Biosocial Science* 15(4), oct 83 : 509-518. [Denmark]

2658   YOSHIZUMI, Kyoko. "Nihon ni okeru hichakushutsushi no shussei, yoiku katei no kosatsu; jido sodanjo sato-oya itaku jirei o toshite" (Birth and rearing of illegitimate children: an analysis of foster child cases field at a child guidance clinic), *Soshioroji* 27(3), 83 : 45-73.

2659   YUZAWA, Yasuhiko. "Nihon ni okeru yoshi engumi no tokeiteki taisei" (Statistical trend of the adopted child in Japan), *Atarashii kazoku* 3, 83 : 21-29.

15230   Youth
Jeunesse

2660   "Plan de sauvetage des jeunes?", *Contradictions* (36-37), aut 83 : 1-185. [France] [with contributions by Jacques HEDOUX, Alain FALIU, Gérard MLEKUZ, Marie-Geo DELEDICQUE, Vincent VAL DELIEVRE]

2661   ALVAREZ, Vladimir. "Políticas nacionales de juventud en América Latina" (National
        youth policies in Latin America), *Juventud* 9, mar 83 : 53-71.
2662   ANDERSON, D. S.; BLAKERS, Catherina; [eds.]. *Youth, transition, and social research.*
        Canberra-New York, NY, Australian National University Press, 83, xvii-204 p.
2663   BAER, Max Frank. *Dealing in futures: the story of a Jewish youth movement.* Washington, DC,
        B'nai B'rith International, 83, v-378 p. [USA]
2664   BCHIR, Badra. "Les présupposés idéologiques liés à la notion de jeune appliquée à la
        société pré-industrielle", *Revue tunisienne des Sciences sociales* 19(68-69), 82 : 11-24. [Tunisia]
2665   BIANCHI, Letizia. "Giovani, famiglia e classe sociale" (Youth, family and social class),
        Rassegna italiana di Sociologia 24(2), apr-jun 83 : 160-210.
2666   BLINOV, Nikolai. "Sociologie de la jeunesse: acquis, perspectives", *Sciences sociales —
        Académie des Sciences de l'URSS* 52(2), 83 : 233-245. [USSR]
2667   BOBERACH, Heinz. *Jugend unter Hitler.* Düsseldorf, Droste, 82, 173 p.
2668   CZARKOWSKI, Heinz. "Die Jugend in der Dritten Welt und ihre gegenwärtige Lage"
        (Youth in the Third World and their present problems), *Universitas* 36(5), 81 : 457-466.
2669   DAVIDOW, Mike. *Third Soviet generation.* Moscow, Progress Publishers, 83, 220-40 p.
2670   DIAMENT, M.; HUMBLET, C.; SAND, E. A. "Présentation d'une recherche: la situation
        sociale des adolescents", *Population et Famille* 55(1), 82 : 79-100. [Belgique]
2671   FRANCIS, Leslie J. *Youth in transit: a profile of 16-25 year olds.* Aldershot, Hampshire, Gower,
        82, vii-189 p. [UK]
2672   FULLER, Bruce. "Educational evaluation and shifting youth policy", *Evaluation Studies* 7,
        82 : 551-572. [USA]
2673   GANDHI, Praveen Kumar. *Rural youth in urban India.* Delhi, Seema Publications, 83, xx-256 p.
2674   GAWDA, Witold; KOWALCZYK, Tomasz; RYCHARD, Andrzej. "Social context of
        the organizational heterogeneity. Examplified by an analysis of values and attitudes of
        youth organization activists", *Polish Sociological Bulletin* 53(1), 81 : 71-84.
2675   GAZSÓ, Ferenc. "Az ifjúság társadalmunk szerkezetében" (Youth in the Hungarian social
        structure), *Társadalomtudományi Közlemények* 12(4), 82 : 579-589.
2676   GOŁBIOWSKI, Bronisław. "Awans społeczny młodzieży w Polsce Ludowej. 'Próba zarysu
        problematyki i efektów'" (Social rise of young people in People's Poland), *Kultura i
        Społeczeństwo* 27(2), 83 : 41-54.
2677   GROTEVANT, Harold D.; COOPER, Catherine R.; [eds.]. *Adolescent development in the
        family.* San Francisco, CA, Jossey-Bass, 83, 116 p.
2678   HERR, Theodor. "Jugendprotest und Familie" (Youth revolt and family), *Jahrbuch für
        Christliche Sozialwissenschaften* 24, 83 : 175-191. [Germany FR]
2679   JOSHI, Gopa. "Channellization of youth energies for economic development in India and
        China 1950-80", *China Report* 19(1), feb 83 : 21-33.
2680   MISRA, V. D. "Youth and dissent in Indian society: an overview", *Eastern Anthropologist*
        35(1), mar 82 : 37-48.
2681   MITEV, Petŭr-Emil. *Sociology facing the problems of youth.* Sofiĭa, s.n., 82, 222 p.
2682   MUSHABEN, Joyce M. "New dimensions of youth protest in Western Europe", *Journal of
        Political and Military Sociology* 11(1), spr 83 : 123-144.
2683   PAWLUCZUK, Włodzimierz. "Wokół aspiracji młodzieży wiejskiej" (Aspirations of rural
        youth), *Wieś Współczesna* 313(3), 83 : 51-58.
2684   ROMEIJN, J. W. "Het verlaten van het ouderlijk huis" (Starting from the family home),
        Bevolking en Gezin (2), 83 : 273-290.
2685   SEKI, Kiyohide; ODA, Toshikatsu. *Seinen no seikatsu to ishiki* (Life and consciousness of
        the youth). Hokkaido, Ishikari-cho, 83, 131 p. [Japan]

        15240   Adulthood
        **   Âge adulte**

2686   VAN HOOSE, William H.; WORTH, Maureen R. *Adulthood in the life cycle.* Dubuque, IA,
        W. C. Brown Co. Publishers, 82, xii-384 p.

        15250   Old age
        **   Vieillesse**

2687   "America in transition: an aging society", *Current Population Reports. Special Studies* (128),
        sep 83 : 1-28.
2688   "Researching the elderly", *Journal of the Market Research Society* 25(3), jul 83 : 215-286. [UK]
        [with contributions by Mark ABRAMS, Joyce EPSTEIN, David TAYLOR; Jonathan
        BARKER]

2689 "Travailleurs vieillissants, vieillissement dans le travail et cessations anticipées d'activité", *Travail et Emploi* (15), mar 83 : 5-84. [with contributions by Jennifer BUÉ and Anne-Françoise MOLINIÉ]

2690 "Vieillesses (Les) en 1983", *Projet* (176), jun 83 : 563-602. [France] [with contributions by Jean LESTAVEL, Raymonde GRUMBACH, Yvon SCHLERET, Georges CAUSSANEL]

2691 "Women's retirement. Policy implications of recent research", *Sage Yearbook in Women's Policy Studies* (6), 82 : 1-271. [USA] [with contributions by Timothy H. BRUBAKER, Charles B. HENNON]

2692 BHATIA, H. S. *Ageing and society: a sociological study of retired public servants*. Udaipur, Arya's Book Centre, 83, 212 p.

2694 BORKOWSKI, Jean-Louis. "Trois dimensions de la vie des personnes âgées", *Économie et Statistique* 158, sep 83 : 37-49. [France]

2695 BRÖSCHEN, Elisabeth; HIMMIGHOFEN, Wilbert. "The aged in the countryside. Implications for social planning", *Sociologia ruralis* 23(3-4), 83 : 261-275. [Germany FR]

2696 BURGALASSI, Silvano. "La condizione anziana: problemi e prospettive" (Ageing: problems and prospects), *Studi di Sociologia* 21(4), oct-dec 83 : 356-369. [Italy]

2697 CASALS, Ignasi. *Sociología de la ancianidad en España* (Sociology of the old age in Spain). Madrid, Editorial Mezquita, 82, 136 p.

2698 DELISLE, Marc-André. "Loisir et structuration du temps chez les personnes âgées", *Loisir et société* 5(2), aut 82 : 387-413. [Canada] [résumés en anglais, en espagnol et en allemand]

2699 DESAI, K. G.; [ed.]. *Ageing in India*. Bombay, Tata Institute of Social Sciences, 82, viii-179 p.

2700 FLOSS, Franziska. *Soziale Ungleichheit im Alter* (Social inequality in old age). Wien, VWGÖ, 82, ii-204-iv p. [Austria]

2701 GENNARO, Giovanni. "Anziani e società rurale. Risultati di una ricerca" (Aged and rural society. Results of a research), *Sociologia (Roma)* 17(3), sep-dec 83 : 125-153. [Italy]

2702 HAGA, Hiroshi; [et al.]. "Rojin ni okeru itami no uttae to kanren yoin" (Complaints of pain and associated factors in the elderly), *Ronen shakai-kagaku* 5, 1983 : 158-167.

2703 HAMPSON, Joe. *Old age: a study of ageing in Zimbabwe*. Gweru, Mambo Press, 82, 96 p.

2704 HATCHUEL, G.; MANNONI, P. *Les retraités et leurs ressources*. Paris, Centre de Recherche pour l'Étude et l'Observation des Conditions de Vie, 83, iii-149 p. [France]

2705 KLINGER, András. "Az öregedés demográfiai vonatkozásai" (The demographical aspects of the elderly), *Demográfia* 26(1), 83 : 9-49.

2706 KOYANO, Wataru. "Morale scale, seikatsu manzoku shakudo oyobi kofukudo shakudo no kyotsu jigen to shakudokan no kanrensei (sono 2)" (Common dimensions and inter-relationships of the measures of morale, life satisfaction and happiness of the aged: a re-examination), *Ronen shakai-kagaku* 5, 1983 : 129-142.

2707 KURODA, Toshio. "Nenrei kozo-ron to korei-ka jinkogaku" (On the demography of ageing: transition in age compositon), *Ronen shakai-kagaku* 5, 1983 : 71-84.

2708 LA ROSA, Michele. "Anziani e realtà sociale: considerazioni sociologiche" (Aged and social reality: sociological considerations), *Sociologia (Roma)* 17(1), jan-apr 83 : 125-141. [Italy]

2709 LALIVE D'EPINAY, Christian; KELLERHALS, Jean; MODAK, Marianne. "L'hédonisme stoïque de la culture populaire. Le prolétaire retraité", *Schweizerische Zeitschrift für Soziologie / Revue suisse de Sociologie* 9(1), 83 : 169-185.

2710 LÉVY, Raymond; POST, Felix; [eds.]. *The psychiatry of late life*. Oxford-Boston, MA, Blackwell Scientific Publications, 82, viii-297 p.

2711 MEANS, Robin; SMITH, Randall. "From public assistance institutions to 'Sunshine Hotels': changing State perceptions about residential care for elderly people", *Ageing and Society* 3(2), jul 83 : 157-182. [UK]

2712 MIZRUCHI, Ephraim H.; GLASSNER, Barry; PASTORELLO, Thomas; [eds.]. *Time and ageing: conceptualization and application in sociological and gerontological research*. Bayside, NY, General Hall, 82, 186 p.

2713 MORSE, Dean W.; DUTKA, Anna B.; GRAY, Susan H. *Life after early retirement: the experiences of lower-level workers*. Totowa, NJ, Littlefield, Adams, Rowman and Allanheld, 83, xiv-192 p.

2714 PAILLAT, Paul. "Les pays du monde face au vieillissement de leurs populations", *Futuribles* 67, jun 83 : 45-58.

2715 PAILLAT, Paul M.; PARANT, Alain. *Conditions de vie et ressources des retrait202es agricoles*. Paris, Presses Universitaires de France, 83, 208 p. [France]

2716 PAPP, Gabor. "The aged in Hungary", *New Hungarian Quarterly* 24(89), spr 83 : 130-139.

2717 RONZE, Bernard. "Vieillesse et développement", *Études* 358(11), nov 83 : 457-469.

2718   SRIVASTAVA, R. S. *The aged and the society.* New Delhi, Citizenship Development Study, 83, x-89 p. [India]

2719   SYNAK, Brunon. "Zróżnicowanie adaptacji osób starszych do nowego środowiska" (Differentiation of adaptation of elderly people to a new environment), *Studia Socjologiczne* 88(1), 83 : 245-265.

2720   SZALAI, Alexander. *Hungarian national report on aging and the situation of the aged population.* Budapest, Hungarian Academy of Sciences, 82, 23 p.

2721   TAYLOR, Red; FORD, Graeme. "Inequalities in old age: an examination of age, sex and class differences in a sample of community elderly", *Ageing and Society* 3(2), jul 83 : 183-208. [UK]

2722   THIJSSEN, L. "Sociale relaties en eenzaamheid bij ouderen" (Social relations and loneliness among aged), *Mens en Maatschappij* 58(3), aug 83 : 271-284. [Netherlands]

2723   THOMSON, David. "Workhouse to nursing home: residential care of elderly people in England since 1840", *Ageing and Society* 3(1), mar 83 : 43-69.

2724   YASUI, Koji; AMANO, Katsuyuki; SAKATA, Shuichi. "Korei fujin no shuro mondai ni kansuru ishiki to genjo: Nagano-ken no jirei kenkyu" (Labor and life of aged women: a case study of Nagano Prefecture), *Nagano daigaku kiyo* 5(1), 83 : 79-118.

**15300   POPULATION EVOLUTION. POPULATION POLICY
          ÉVOLUTION DE LA POPULATION. POLITIQUE DÉMOGRAPHIQUE**

**15310   Population growth
          Accroissement de la population**

2725   "Growth (The) of urban population in the Philippines: 1975-1980", *Journal of Philippine Statistics* 33(3), trim. 3, 82 : 1-21.

2726   "Sexual harassment as a social issue: historical, legal, and organizational perspectives", *Journal of Social Issues* 38(4), 82 : 5-74. [USA]

2727   ALEŠ, Milan. "L'évolution de la population en Tchécoslovaquie en 1982", *Demosta* 16(1-2), 83 : 6-8.

2728   ALPEROVICH, Gershon. "Determinants of urban population density function", *Regional Science and Urban Economics* 13(2), mai 83 : 287-295.

2729   ANKER, Richard; KNOWLES, James C. *Population growth, employment and economic-demographic interactions in Kenya: Bachue-Kenya.* New York, NY, St. Martin's Press; Aldershot, Gower, 83, xix-735 p.

2730   BANGUERO, Harold; GUERRERO, Bernardo. "La transición demográfica en Colombia: determinantes e impactos económicos y sociales" (Demographic transition in Colombia: factors and economic and social effects), *Revista de Planeación y Desarrollo* 15(1), apr 83 : 119-213.

2731   BONVALET, Catherine; LEFEBVRE, Monique. "Le dépeuplement de Paris, 1968-1975. Quelques éléments d'explication", *Population* 38(6), nov-dec 83 : 941-958.

2732   BRENEZ, Jacques; SELTZER, William. "La collecte des informations démographiques dans les pays du Tiers-Monde: recensements et enquêtes dans les années 70 et 80", *Tiers-Monde* 24(94), jun 83 : 245-260.

2733   BROUK, Solomon; KABOUZAN, Vladimir. "Le mouvement général de la population russe après la révolution", *Sciences sociales — Académie des Sciences de l'URSS* (3), 83 : 114-131.

2734   CARTIER, Michel. "Le sous-développement chinois. Un effet de la croissance démographique?", *Tiers-Monde* 24(94), jun 83 : 451-462.

2735   CHAUDHYRY, Mahinder D. "The demographic transition in India", *Economic Development and Cultural Change* 31(2), jan 83 : 397-404.

2736   CONROY, John D. "Demographic change and population policy in four Asian nations: Japan, Korea, Singapore and Thailand", *Majalah Demografie Indonesia* 8(16), dec 81 : 74-104.

2737   CORREA, Hector; EL TORKY, Mohamed Ali. *The biological and social determinants of the demographic transition.* Washington, DC, University Press of America, 82, v-290 p.

2738   COUSSY, Jean. "Croissance démographique et dynamique de la spécialisation du Tiers-Monde", *Tiers-Monde* 24(94), jun 83 : 377-398.

2739   DE SOUZA, Aída Laura Ferreira. "Observações sobre a evolucão da população rural e urbana do Brasil no período 1940 a 1980" (Observation on the development of rural and urban population of Brazil in the period 1940-1980), *Revista brasileira de Estatística* 42(167), sep 81 : 197-217.

2740   DEERE, Carmen Diana. "La mujer rural y las reformas agrarias en Perú, Chile y Cuba" (Rural women and land reforms in Peru, Chile and Cuba), *Revista de Ciencias Sociales de la Universidad de Costa Rica* 25(1), 83 : 59-74.

2741 DZIENIO, Kazimierz; WASILEWSKA-TRENKNER, Halina. "Zagrożenie rozwoju demograficznego Polski w wyniku kryzysu społeczno-gospodarczego i politcznego" (Threat to Poland's demographic development resulting fromn the socio-economic and political crisis), *Studia demograficzne* 20(4), 82 : 35-58.

2742 ÉTIENNE, Gilbert. "La population de l'Inde et les niveaux de vie", *Tiers-Monde* 24(94), jun 83 : 463-471.

2743 FEENEY, G. "Population dynamics based on birth intervals and parity progression", *Population Studies* 37(1), mar 83 : 75-90. [China]

2744 FRANCART, Gabriel. "Le rééquilibrage démographique de la France", *Économie et Statistique* 153, mar 83 : 35-46.

2745 GIDWITZ, Betsy. "Demographic trends in the Soviet Union", *World Today* 39(6), jun 83 : 224-230.

2746 GINZBURG, Lev R. *Theory of natural selection and population growth.* London, Addison-Wesley; Menlo Park, MA, Benjamin/Cummings Publishing Co., 83, xv-160 p.

2747 GURUNG, Harka B. *Population increase in Nepal, 1971-1981.* Kathmandu, New ERA, 82, 18 p.

2748 GUTKIND, Peter C. W. "Change and consciousness in urban Africa: African workers in transition", *Cahiers d'Études africaines* 21(1-3), 81 : 289-346.

2749 HUGO, Graeme J. *Population mobility and health transfers in Indonesia and other Third World societies.* Honolulu, HI, East-West Center, 83, v-50 p.

2750 HUGON, Philippe. "Pression démographique, 'secteur informel' et choix technologiques dans les pays du Tiers-Monde", *Tiers-Monde* 24(94), jun 83 : 399-408.

2751 HUSSMANNS, Ralf; MAMMEY, Ullrich; SCHULZ, Reiner. "Die demographische Lage in der Bundesrepublik Deutschland" (The demographic situation in the Federal Republic of Germany), *Zeitschrift für Bevölkerungswissenschaft* 9(3), 83 : 291-362.

2752 KOZLOV, V. I. "Dinamika nacional'nogo sostava naselenija SSSR i problemy demografičeskoj politiki" (Dynamics of the Soviet population composition and population policy problems), *Istorija SSSR* 26(4), 83 : 20-30.

2753 KUGLER, Jacek; [et al.]. "Political determinants of population dynamics", *Comparative Political Studies* 16(1), apr 83 : 3-36.

2754 LESTHAEGE, Ron. "A century of demographic and cultural change in Western Europe: an exploration of underlying dimensions", *Population and Development Review* 9(3), sep 83 : 411-435.

2755 LOMBARDO, Enzo. "Alcune questioni sulla demografia della Somalia" (Some questions on demography of Somalia), *Genus* 38(1-2), jan-jun 82 : 159-176.

2756 MACALPIN, Michelle B. "Famines, epidemics, and population growth: the case of India", *Journal of Interdisciplinary History* 14(2), aut 83 : 351-366. [cont. in ibid. pp. 367-370 by Santhebachahalli G. SRIRANTIA]

2757 MAJUMDAR, Tapan K. *Urbanising poor: a sociological study of low-income migrant communities in the metropolitan city of Delhi.* New Delhi, Lancers Publishers, 83, xix-278-6 p.

2758 MISIAK, Władysław. "O stylach życia społeczności wsi" (The country people's life styles), *Wieś Współczesna* 320(10), 83 : 92-101.

2759 MORRISON, Peter A.; [ed.]. *Population movements: their forms and functions in urbanization and development.* Liège, Ordina Éditions, 83, iv-351 p.

2760 NAZARETH, J. Manuel. *Explosão demográfica e planeamento familiar* (Demographic explosion and family planning). Lisboa, Editorial Presença, Gabinete de Investigaçoes Sociais, 82, 235 p. [Portugal]

2761 NOIN, Daniel. *La transition démographique dans le monde.* Paris, Presses Universitaires de France, 83, 214 p.

2762 ODA, Toshikatsu. "Population distribution changes and redistribution policy in recent Japan", *Hokkaido daigaku Environmental Science* 6(1), 83 : 67-94.

2763 OKÓLSKI, Marek. "Demographic transition in Poland: the present phase", *Oeconomica polona* 10(2), 83 : 185-232.

2764 ORLOVOVÁ, Nina. "Sčítání lidu v SSSR v roce 1979" (Population census in the Soviet Union in 1979), *Demografie* 24(4), 82 : 317-325.

2765 OUELLET, Fernand. "L'accroissement naturel de la population catholique québécoise avant 1850: aperçus historiographiques et quantitatifs", *Actualité économique* 59(3), sep 83 : 402-422. [Canada]

2766 PANT, Yadav Prasad. *Population growth and employment opportunities in Nepal.* New Delhi, Oxford and IBH, 83, viii-131 p.

2767 PANTELIDES, Edith Alejandra. "La transición demográfica argentina" (Argentina's demographic transition), *Desarrollo económico* 22(88), mar 83 : 511-534.

2768 PANTELIDES, Edith Alejandra. "La transición demográfica argentina: un modelo no ortodoxo" (Demographic transition in Argentina: a non-orthodox model), *Desarrollo económico* 22(88), jan-mar 83 : 511-534.

2769 PETROVIC, Ruza. "Nacionalni sastav stanovnistva" (Population national composition), *Jugoslovenski Pregled* 27(3), mar 83 : 97-104. [Yugoslavia]

2770 POFFENBERGER, M. "Toward a new understanding of population change in Bali", *Population Studies* 37(1), mar 83 : 43-59.

2771 RICHARD, J.; [et al.]. *Demographic transition in metropolitan Sudan.* Canberra, Department of Demography, Australian National University, 82, xv-197 p.

2772 RICHARDSON, Harry W. "Population distribution policies", *Population Bulletin of the United Nations* 15, 83 : 35-49.

2773 RJABUŠKIN, T. V.; RYBAKOVSKIJ, L. L.; [eds.]. *Demografičeskie processy v SSSR* (Demographic processes in the USSR). Moskva, Institut Sociologičeskih Issledovanij Akademii Nauk SSSR, 83, 137 p.

2774 RODGERS, Gerry. "Croissance démographique, inégalité et pauvreté", *Revue internationale du Travail* 122(4), aug 83 : 469-489.

2775 ROSENBERG, Gerhard. "High population densities in relation to social behaviour", *Ekistics* 49(296), sep 82 : 400-405.

2776 ROTOVA, R. S.; [et al.]. *Osobennosti demografičeskogo razvitija v SSSR* (Characteristics of demographic development in the USSR). Moskva, Finansy i Statistika, 82, 232 p.

2777 SAGRERA, Martin. *El problema pobliacinal: demasiados Españoles* (The population problem: too many Spaniards). Madrid, Editorial Fundamentos, 83, 247 p.

2778 SENKER, Wienfried. "Demographische Lage und Bevölkerungspolitik in der CSSR" (Demographic situation and population policy in the PRC), *Zeitschrift für Bevölkerungswissenschaft* 9(4), 83 : 497-512. [Czechoslovakia]

2779 SIKORSKA, Alina. "Ludność bezrolna we wsiach podmiejskich" (Landless population in villages adjoining cities), *Zagadnienia Ekonomiki rolnej* (3), 83 : 39-52.

2780 SIMON, J. L. "The present value of population growth in the Western world", *Population Studies* 37(1), mar 83 : 5-22.

2781 SINHA, Debasish; PAL, Bikas Chandra. "Population dynamics among the Totos of West Bengal: a positive response to culture contact", *Journal of Biosocial Science* 15(2), apr 83 : 237-245.

2782 SMITH, W. Randy; [et al.]. "Population concentration in an urban system: Korea 1949-1980", *Urban Geography* 4(1), mar 83 : 63-79.

2783 SRB, Vladimír. "L'urbanisation de la population en Tchécoslovaquie durant les années 1970-1980", *Demosta* 15(3), 82 : 7-11.

2784 STEHLÍK, Jiří. "Problém početního maxima lidské populace světa — konfrontace názorů" (Problem of numerical maximum of world population — confrontation of opinions), *Demografie* 25(2), 83 : 109-119.

2785 STESZENKO, Walentyna S. "Reprodukcja ludności jako proces społeczny i przedmiot badań demograficznych" (Reproduction of the population as social process and object of demographic enquiries), *Studia demograficzne* 21(1), 83 : 85-99.

2786 UMEZAWA, Takashi. "Nihon shakai no koreika to kaikyu, kaiso kozo no hendo: Koyo kanko hendo shikaku karano bunseki" (Aging of the population composition and change of the class-stratum structure in Japan: an analysis from the angle of the change of the practice of employment), *Nihon daigaku shakaigaku ronso* 87, 83 : 28-57. [cont. in ibid. 88, 1983 : 1-19]

2787 VAZQUEZ CALZADA, José L. "La distribución geografica de la población de Puerto Rico" (Geographical distribution of population in Puerto Rico), *Revista de Ciencias sociales* 23(1-2), jun 81 : 93-123.

2788 VEYS, Dion. "Waarheen met de volkstelling? Verslag studiedag van de Vereniging voor Demografie, Brussel, 23 april 1982" (What about the future of population censuses? Report on a seminar of the Flemish demographic association, Brussels 23 apr 1982), *Bevolking en Gezin* (3), 82 : 329-338.

2789 VOLKOF, A. G.; [et al.]. *Vosproizvodstvo naselenija SSSR* (Reproduction of the USSR population). Moskva, Finansy i Statistika, 83, 303 p.

2790 ZEEDYK-RYAN, Janice; SMITH, Gene F. "The effects of crowding on hostility, anxiety, and desire for social interaction", *Journal of Social Psychology* 120(2), aug 83 : 245-252.

15320   Morbidity
Morbidité

2791 "Études épidémiologiques et approches géographiques des maladies en Afrique tropicale. Mélanges pour un dialogue", *Cahiers d'Études africaines* 22(1-2), 82 : 7-168.

2792 "Folie (La)", *Esprit* (11), nov 83 : 77-111. [with contributions by Marcel GAUCHET, Gladys SWAIN, François AZOUVI, Philippe RAYNAUD]

2793   "Images of the disabled/disabling images", *Social Policy* 13(2), aut 82 : 15-35. [with contributions by Alan GARTNER, Leonard KRIEGEL, Leonard QUART, Albert AUSTER, Robert BOGDAN]

2794   DODIER, Nicolas. "La maladie et le lieu de travail", *Revue française de Sociologie* 24(2), apr-jun 83 : 255-270. [résumés en anglais, allemand et espagnol]

2795   ELLENA, Guy. "La bilharziose en Egypte: une approche micro-économique", *Bulletin du Centre de Documentation d'Études juridiques, économiques et sociales* 11(14), jul 82 : 131-152.

2796   FRANKEL, B. Gail; TURNER, R. Jay. "Psychological adjustment in chronic disability: the role of social support in the case of the hearing impaired", *Canadian Journal of Sociology / Cahiers canadiens de Sociologie* 8(3), 83 : 273-291. [Canada]

2797   HEGARTY, Seamus; POCKLINGTON, Keith; LUCAS, Dorothy. *Integration in action: case studies in the integration of pupils with special needs.* Windsor, Berks, NFER-Nelson, 82, viii-294 p.

2798   JOŃCZYK, Jan. "O sytuacji ludzi niepełnosprawnych i stanie rehabilitacji w PRL" (Situation of disabled persons and rehabilitation conditions in Poland), *Polityka społeczna* 10(7), 83 : 1-4.

2799   KINABLE, J. "Le psychopathe: un sujet en actes?", *Déviance et Société* 7(4), dec 83 : 317-338.

2800   MACNEIL, John M. "Labor force status and other characteristics of persons with a work disability: 1982", *Current Population Reports. Special Studies* (127), jul 83 : 1-76. [USA]

2801   MAJEWSKA, Anna. "O sytuacji ludzi niepełnosprawnych w Polsce" (The situation of the handicapped in Poland), *Praca i Zabezpieczenie społeczne* 25(1), jan 83 : 23-31.

2802   MASSON, Gérard. "Aide aux handicapés et changement de société", *Recherche sociale* (85), mar 83 : 55-65.

2803   MIROWSKY, John; ROSS, Catherine E. "Paranoia and the structure of powerlessness", *American Sociological Review* 48(2), apr 83 : 228-239.

2804   MITTLER, Peter; MCCONACHIE, Helen; [eds.]. *Parents, professionals, and mentally handicapped people: approaches to partnership.* London, Croom Helm, 83, xi-243 p.

2805   MOLLO, Suzanne. *Construire Fabrice: l'insertion sociale d'un enfant handicapé.* Paris, Edilig, 82, 109 p.

2806   MURPHY, Henry B. M. *Comparative psychiatry: the international and intercultural distribution of mental illness.* Berlin, Springer-Verlag, 82, 327 p.

2807   NIETO, José A. "Algunos aspectos culturales de las enfermedades y de la medicina" (Some cultural aspects of diseases and medicine), *Revista española de Investigaciones sociológicas* 22, apr-jun 83 : 137-146.

2808   ORGANISATION DE COOPÉRATION ET DE DÉVELOPPEMENT ÉCONOMIQUES. *L'éducation des adolescents handicapés: le passage de l'école à la vie active.* Paris, OCDE, 83, 222 p.

2809   ORSINI, Gabriele. "L'integrazione sociale dei soggetti portatori di 'handicaps'" (The social integration of the handicapped), *Sociologia (Roma)* 17(2), mai-aug 83 : 65-95. [Italy]

2810   RAO, Vidya. "Services for the handicapped persons — organisation and policy implications", *Indian Journal of Social Work* 43(4), jan 83 : 351-368. [India]

2811   RICOSSÉ, Jean-Henri; HUSSER, Jean-Alain. "Bilan et avenir de la lutte contre les grandes endémies en Afrique occidentale francophone", *Cahiers d'Études africaines* 22(1-2), 82 : 145-168.

2812   ROSE-ACKERMAN, Susan. "Mental retardation and society: the ethics and politics of normalization", *Ethics* 93(1), oct 82 : 81-101.

2813   SMITH, Christopher J.; HANHAM, Robert Q. "Disinstitutionalization and community acceptance of the mentally ill in the USA", *Ekistics* 49(296), sep 82 : 358-368.

2814   TABONE, B. "Aspects socio-culturels de la folie en Tunisie", *Ibla* 45(2), 82 : 259-279.

2815   VILLEVAL, Marie-Claire. "Politique sociale et emploi des personnes handicapées", *Revue française des Affaires sociales* 37(3), sep 83 : 7-32.

15330   Mortality
Mortalité

2816   "Life tables, fertility and mortality", *American Statistical Association. Proceedings of the Social Statistics Section*, 82 : 316-345. [USA]

2817   ADAMCHAK, Donald J.; FLINT, William C. "Socioeconomic status and infant mortality: evidence from a rural agricultural state", *Sociological Focus* 16(1), jan 83 : 77-89. [USA]

2818   BENNETT, Neil G.; GARSON, Lea Keil. "The centenarian question and old-age mortality in the Soviet Union, 1959-1970", *Demography* 20(4), nov 83 : 581-606.

2819   BOURBEAU, Robert; LÉGARÉ, Jacques. *Évolution de la mortalité au Canada et au Québec, 1831-1931: essai de mesure par génération.* Montréal, PQ, Presses de l'Université de Montréal, 82, 140 p.

2820   BOURGEOIS-PICHAT, Jean. "L'évolution de la mortalité dans les pays industrialisés",
        Futuribles 67, jun 83 : 63-74.

2821   BOUVIER-COLLE, Marie-Hélène. "Mortalité et activité professionnelle chez les femmes",
        Population 38(1), jan-feb 83 : 107-135. [résumés en anglais et espagnol]

2822   CALDWELL, J. C.; REDDY, P. H.; CALDWELL, Pat. "The social component of
        mortality decline: an investiagation in South India employing alternative methodologies",
        Population Studies 37(2), jul 83 : 185-205.

2823   CASELLI, Graziella; EGIDI, Viviana. "Analyse des données multidimensionnelles dans
        l'étude des relations entre la mortalité et les variables socioéconomiques d'environnement
        et de comportement individuel", *Genus* 37(3-4), jul-dec 81 : 57-91.

2824   CHESNAIS, Jean-Claude. "La durée de la vie dans les pays industrialisés", *Recherche* (147),
        sep 83 : 1040-1048.

2825   EDMONSTON, Barry. "Demographic and maternal correlates of infant and child mortality
        in Bangladesh", *Journal of Biosocial Science* 15(2), apr 83 : 183-192.

2826   FLEGG, A. T. "On the determinants of infant mortality in underdeveloped countries",
        International Journal of Social Economics 10(5), 83 : 38-51.

2827   FLORIAN, Victor; KRAVETZ, Shlomo. "Fear of personal death: attribution, structure,
        and relation to religious belief", *Journal of Personality and Social Psychology* 44(3), mar
        83 : 600-607.

2828   GATZWEILER, Hans-Peter; STIENS, Gerhard. "Regionale Mortalitätsunterschiede in
        der Bundesrepublik Deutschland. Daten und Hypothesen" (Regional differences of
        mortality in the Federal Republic of Germany. Data and assumptions), *Jahrbuch für
        Regionalwissenschaft* 3, 82 : 36-63.

2829   GREEMAN, John; CARROLL, Glenn R.; HANNAN, Michael T. "The liability of
        newness: age dependence in organization death rates", *American Sociological Review* 48(5),
        oct 83 : 692-710. [USA]

2830   GROSSMAN, Michael; JACOBOWITZ, Steven. "Variations in infant mortality rates
        among counties of the United States: the roles of public policies and programs",
        Demography 18(4), nov 81 : 695-713. [USA]

2831   HABERMAN, Steven; [et al.]. "Mortality patterns of British Jewry 1975-79: insights and
        applications for the size and structure of British Jewry", *Journal of the Royal Statistical
        Society.* 146(3), 83 : 294-310. [Series A]

2832   HAINES, Michael R. "Differentials in infant and child mortality and their change over time:
        Guatemala, 1959-1973", *Demography* 20(4), nov 83 : 607-621.

2833   HEDDERSON, John; DAUDISTEL, Howard C. "Infant mortality of the Spanish surname
        population", *Social Science Journal (Fort Collins)* 19(4), oct 82 : 67-78. [USA]

2834   IKANEM, Ita I. "Estimation of infant and child mortality trends from reported and
        surviving children", *Genus* 38(1-2), jan-jun 82 : 185-197. [Nigeria]

2835   JONES, Ellen; GRUPP, Fred W. "Infant mortality trends in the Soviet Union", *Population
        and Development Review* 9(2), jun 83 : 213-246.

2836   KEARL, Michael C.; RINALDI, Anoel. "The political uses of the dead as symbols in
        contemporary civil religions", *Social Forces* 61(3), mar 83 : 693-708.

2837   KĘDELSKI, Mieczysław. "Ewolucja trwania życia ludności w Polsce w przekroju miasto-
        wieś w latach 1950-1979" (Evolution of life expectancy of Poland's population in towns
        and villages 1950-1979), *Studia demograficzne* 20(4), 82 : 59-79.

2838   KĘDELSKI, Mieczysław. *Szacowanie potencjału zyciowego ludności w Polsce* (Estimate of life
        potential in Poland). Poznań, Akademie Ekonomiczna w Poznaniu, 82, 198 p.

2839   KĘDELSKI, Mieczysław. "Zróżnicowanie średniego trwania życia ludności w przekroju
        wielkich miast w Polsce" (Differentiation of average duration of life in large towns in
        Poland), *Studia demograficzne* 21(1), 83 : 69-84.

2840   KOHLI, K. L.; AL-OMAIM, Musa'ad. "Infant and child mortality in Kuwait", *Journal of
        Biosocial Science* 15(3), jul 83 : 339-348.

2841   LANGSTEN, Ray. "The effects of crises on differential mortality by sex in Bangladesh",
        Bangladesh Development Studies 9(2), sum 81 : 75-96.

2842   LÓPEZ, Alan D.; RUZICKA, Lado T.; [eds.]. *Sex differentials in mortality: trends, determinants
        and consequences.* Canberra, Department of Demography, Australian National University,
        83, viii-498 p.

2843   MARTIN, Linda G. "Mortality decline and Japanese family structure", *Population and
        Development Review* 9(4), dec 83 : 633-649.

2844   MASUY-STROOBANT, G. *Les déterminants de la mortalité infantile. La Belgique d'hier et
        d'aujourd'hui.* Bruxelles, CIACO Éditeur, 83, 540 p.

2845   MASUY-STROOBANT, Godeliève; TABUTIN, Dominique. "L'approche explicative en
        matière de mortalité des enfants. Réflexions et perspectives", *Genus* 18(3-4), jul-dec 82 : 19-37.

2846   MIJAKOWSKA, Jadwiga. "Zmiany i zróżnicowanie trwania życia w Polsce w przekroju wojewódzkim" (Changes and differentiation of duration of life by voivodships), *Studia demograficzne* 21(1), 83 : 113-123.

2847   MINA V., Alejandro. "Estimaciones de los niveles, tendencias y diferenciales de la mortalidad infantil y en los primeros años de vida en México, 1940-1977" (Estimations of infant and child mortality levels, trends and differentials in Mexico, 1940-1977), *Demografía y Economía* 15(1), 81 : 85-142.

2848   MOTT, Frank L. *Infant mortality in Kenya: evidence from the Kenya fertility survey.* Voorburg, International Statistical Institute; London, World Fertility Survey, 82, 27 p.

2849   MUNIR, Rozy; DASVARMA, Gour. *Studi mortalitas di Indonesia: catatan bibliografi* (Mortality studies in Indonesia: a bibliographic note). Jakarta, Lembaga Demografi, Fakultas Ekonomi, Universitas Indonesia, 82, iv-57 p.

2850   NATIONS UNIES. DÉPARTEMENT DES AFFAIRES ÉCONOMIQUES ET SOCIALES INTERNATIONALES-ORGANISATION MONDIALE DE LA SANTÉ. *Niveaux et tendances de la mortalité depuis 1950.* New York, NY, UN, 83, xiv-203 p.

2851   OKÓLSKI, Marek; PUŁASKA, Beata. "Trendy i wzorce umieralności w Polsce w okresie powojennym" (Trends and patterns of mortality in post-war Poland), *Studia demograficzne* 21(2), 83 : 49-74.

2852   OLSEN, Randall J.; WOLPIN, Kenneth I. "The impact of exogenous child mortality on fertility: a waiting time regression with dynamic regressors", *Econometrica* 51(3), mai 83 : 731-749. [Malaysia]

2853   PARLANGE, J. Y.; GUILFOYLE, M. J.; RICKSON, R. E. "Mortality levels and family fertility goals", *Demography* 20(4), nov 83 : 535-540.

2854   PITKANEN, Kari. "Infant mortality decline in a changing society", *Yearbook of Population Research in Finland* 21, 1983 : 46-74. [Finland]

2855   RAZZAQUE RUKANUDDIN, Abdul. "Infant-child mortality and son preference as factors influencing fertility in Pakistan", *Pakistan Development Review* 21(4), wint 82 : 297-328.

2856   RILEY, John W. Jr. "Dying and the meanings of death: sociological inquiries", *Annual Review of Sociology* (9), 83 : 191-216.

2857   SEMBAJWE, Israel S. L. "Socio-economic factors affecting mortality in rural Tanzania", *Journal of Biosocial Science* 15(4), oct 83 : 487-500.

2858   STERN, Jon. "Social mobility and the interpretation of social class mortality differentials", *Journal of Social Policy* 12(1), jan 83 : 27-49.

2859   SYROVÁTKA, A.; MACHKOVÁ, B. "Les décès des nouveaux-nés dus à 'une cause extérieure' ou au 'syndrome du décès subit?", *Demosta* 14(4), 81 : 116-121. [Czechoslovakia]

2860   TRUSSEL, James; OLSEN, Randall. "Evaluation of the Olsen technique for estimating the fertility response to child mortality", *Demography* 20(3), aug 83 : 391-405.

2861   TRUSSELL, James; HAMMERSLOUGH, Charles. "A hazards-model analysis of the covariates of infant and child mortality in Sri Lanka", *Demography* 20(1), feb 83 : 1-26.

2862   VALLIN, Jacques. "Tendances récentes de la mortalité française", *Population* 38(1), jan-feb 83 : 77-105. [résumés en anglais et espagnol]

2863   VAN DEN BROEKE, C. "Differentiele sterfte tijdens de negentiende eeuw. Het sterfterisico van medici" (Differential mortality in the 19th century. A test case: the death risk for physicians), *Bevolking en Gezin* (2), 82 : 133-145.

2864   VOVELLE, Michel. *La mort et l'Occident de 1300 à nos jours.* Paris, Gallimard, 83, 793 p.

2865   WEATHERBY, Norman L.; NAM, Charles B.; ISAAC, Larry W. "Development, inequality, health care, and mortality at the older ages: a cross-national analysis", *Demography* 20(1), feb 83 : 27-43.

2866   WILKINS, Russell. "La distribution de l'espérance de vie parmi les différents états de santé: composantes, méthodes de calcul et résultats pour le Québec, 1978", *Cahiers québécois de Démographie* 11(2), aug 82 : 253-276.

2867   WUNSCH, Guillaume. "Life-styles and death-styles: differentials and consequences of mortality trends", *Genus* 37(3-4), jul-dec 81 : 41-56.

2868   YOUNG, Frank W.; EDMONSTON, Barry; ANDES, Nancy. "Community-level determinants of infant and child mortality in Peru", *Social Indicators Research* 12(1), jan 83 : 65-81.

2869   ZAMPONI, Simonetta Falasca. "La maschera e il tabù: contributo a un'interpretazione della ideologia della morte" (Mask and tabu: contribution to an interpretation of the ideology of death), *Critica sociologica* 67, 83 : 128-146.

15340　　Fertility. Natality
**　　　　　Fécondité. Natalité**

2870　　"Economics of fertility", *American Economic Review* 73(2), mai 83 : 29-42. [Papers and Proceedings, with contributions by Randall J. OLSEN, John L. NEWMAN, Mark R. ROSENZWEIG, T. Paul SCHULTZ]

2871　　ATOH, Makoto; OHTANI, Kenji. "Wagakuni fufu no shussei ishiki to shussei kodo: Dai-8-ji shussanryoku chosa no kekka kara" (Ideal intended and achieved fertility for the Japanese married couples), *Jinko mondai kenkyu* 166, 83 : 1-34.

2872　　BEAN, Frank D. "The baby boom and its explanations", *Sociological Quarterly* 24(3), sum 83 : 353-365. [USA] [1940's and 1950's]

2873　　BECKMAN, Linda J.; [et al.]. "A theoretical analysis of antecedents of young couples' fertility decisions and outcomes", *Demography* 20(4), nov 83 : 519-534.

2874　　BONGAARTS, J.; POTTER, R. G. *Fertility, biology and behaviour: an analysis of the proximate determinants.* New York, NY-London, Academic Press, 83, xi-230 p.

2875　　BRECKENRIDGE, Mary B. *Age, time and fertility.* New York, NY-London, Academic Press, 83, xxiii-317 p.

2876　　BULATO, Rodolfo A.; FAWCETT, James T. *Influence on childbearing intentions across the fertility career: demographic and socio-economic factors and the values of children.* Honolulu, HI, East-West Institute, East-West Center, 83, iX-152 p.

2877　　CARLSON, Elwood. "Dispersion of childbearing outside marriage", *Sociology and Social Research* 66(3), apr 82 : 335-347.

2878　　CHERNICHOVSKY, Dov. "Fertility behaviour in rural and urban Indonesia", *Majalah Demografie Indonesia* 9(17), jun 82 : 1-21.

2879　　CHOWDHURY, Tawfiq-E-Elahi. "Fertility behaviour under uncertainty: a mathematical model", *Bangladesh Development Studies* 9(2), 81 : 97-101.

2880　　COLLINS, Jane L. "Fertility determinants in a high Andes community", *Population and Development Review* 9(1), mar 83 : 61-75.

2881　　COMMITTEE ON POPULATION AND DEMOGRAPHY. *The estimation of recent trends in fertility and mortality in Egypt.* Washington, DC, National Academy Press, 82, xviii-144 p.

2882　　COSTA, Manoel Augusto. "Fecundidade e desenvolvimento no Brasil. Uma análise com regressão em etapas" (Fertility and development in Brazil. A regression analysis by steps), *Revista brasileira de Estatística* 42(168), dec 81 : 315-330.

2883　　DA GRAÇA MORAIS, Maria. "A substituição das gerações em Portugal: análise regional, 1930-1975" (The replacement of generations in Portugal: a regional analysis, 1930-1975), *Análise social* 19(1), mar 83 : 79-99.

2884　　DOW, Thomas E. Jr.; WERNER, Linda H. "Prospects for fertility decline in rural Kenya", *Population and Development Review* 9(1), mar 83 : 77-97.

2885　　EKPO, Monday U. "Birth order and attitude towards marriage", *Indian Journal of Social Research* 24(3), dec 83 : 234-244.

2886　　EVERSLEY, David Edward Charles; KÖLLMANN, Wolfgang; [eds.]. *Population change and social planning: social and economic implications of the recent decline in fertility in the United Kingdom and the Federal Republic of Germany.* London, Arnold, 82, ix-485 p.

2887　　FRANCOME, Colin. "Unwanted pregnancies amongst teenagers", *Journal of Biosocial Science* 15(2), apr 83 : 139-143.

2888　　GHETAU, Vasile. "Évolution de la fécondité en Roumanie. Une approche longitudinale", *Population* 38(2), mar-apr 83 : 247-265. [résumés en anglais et espagnol]

2889　　JAGIELSKI, Andrzej. "Zróżnicowanie zachowań prokreacyjnych migrantów" (Differentiation of procreative attitudes of migrants), *Biuletyn Instytutu Gospodarstwa Społecznego* 25(3), 82 : 75-103.

2890　　JOHANSSON, Leif; FINNÄS, Fjalar. *Fertility of Swedish women born 1927-1960.* Stockholm, Statistika Centralbyrån, 83, 217 p.

2891　　KABIR, Mohammad; HOWLADER, Ali Ahmed. "Regional differences of fertility in Bangladesh estimated from the relational Compertz model", *Genus* 37(3-4), jul-dec 81 : 189-200.

2892　　KELLY, William R.; POSTON, Dudley L. Jr.; CUTRIGHT, Phillips. "Determinants of fertility levels and change among developed countries: 1958-1978", *Social Science Research* 12(2), jun 83 : 87-108.

2893　　KOO, Helen P.; JANOWITZ, Barbara K. "Interrelationships between fertility and marital dissolution: results of a simultaneous logit model", *Demography* 20(2), mai 83 : 129-145. [USA]

2894　　KOVÁŘ, Jiří. "Plodnost žen v oblastech ČSR 1961-1976" (Woman's fertility in regions of the Czech Socialist Republic in 1961-1976), *Demografie* 25(2), 83 : 120-129.

2895   KUCZYNSKI, Robert René. *Fertility and reproduction.* Berlin, Akademie Verlag, 82, 147 p.

2896   LAMBRECHTS, E. "De sociaal-culturele determinanten van de vruchtbaarheid in longitudinal perspectief" (Socio-cultural factors of fertility in a longitudinal prospect), *Bevolking en Gezin* (1), 83 : 55-76.

2897   LERIDON, Henri. "Tendances récentes de la fécondité et de la mortalité dans les pays du Tiers-Monde", *Tiers-Monde* 24(94), jun 83 : 261-276.

2898   LESNY, Yvan. "La fécondité des générations tchèques et slovaques nées depuis 1930", *Population* 38(2), mar-apr 83 : 267-282. [résumés en anglais et espagnol]

2899   LOCKRIDGE, Kenneth A. *The fertility transition in Sweden: a preliminary look at smaller geographic units, 1855-1980.* Umeå, Demographic Data Base, Umeå University, 83, 135 p.

2900   MASITAH MOHD, Yatim. *Evaluation of the Malaysian fertility and family survey, 1974.* Voorburg, International Statistical Institute; London, World Fertility Survey, 82, 34 p.

2901   MCINTOSH, James. "Reproductive behaviour in peasant societies: a theoretical and empirical analysis", *Review of Economic Studies* 50(1), jan 83 : 133-142. [Bangladesh]

2902   MCNICOLL, Geoffrey; SINGARIMBUN, Masri. *Fertility decline in Indonesia.* New York, NY, Population Council, 82, s. p. [2 vols.]

2903   MOEN, Bjørg; SEVALDSON, Per. *Fødselstallene i Norge 1950-1975: endringsfaktorer* (Births in Norway 1950-1975: components). Oslo-Kongsvinger, Statistisk Sentralbyrå, 82, 81 p.

2904   MOSHER, William D. "Fertility and family planning in the 1970's: the National Survey of Family Growth", *Family Planning Perspectives* 14(5), nov-dec 82 : 314-320. [USA]

2905   NELISSEN, J.; VOSSEN, A. "Een korte termijn model voor de prognose van geboorten" (A short-term model for birth projections), *Bevolking en Gezin* (1), 83 : 77-105.

2906   NOVAES, Simone. "La procréation par insémination artificielle: vers une analyse de la dynamique sociale", *Social Science Information* 22(1), 83 : 139-148.

2907   O'CONNELL, Martin; ROGERS, Carolyn C. "Differential fertility in the United States: 1976-1980", *Family Planning Perspectives* 14(5), sep-oct 82 : 281-286.

2908   PAKRASI, Kanti; HALDER, Ajit. "Fertility in contemporary Calcutta: a biosocial profile", *Genus* 37(3-4), jul-dec 81 : 201-219. [India]

2909   PATHAK, K. B.; MURTY, P. K. "Socio-economic determinants of fertility in some countries of Asia", *Artha Vijnana* 24(2), jul 82 : 163-178.

2910   PATHAK, K. B.; SASTRY, V. S. "A modified stochastic model for closed birth interval", *Journal of Mathematical Sociology* 9(2), 83 : 155-163.

2911   PEERASIT, Kamnuansilpa; APHICHAT, Chamrathithirong. *A new decade of fertility and family planning in Thailand: 1981 contraceptive prevalence survey.* Bangkok, Westinghouse Health Systems, 82, xi-132 p.

2912   POTTS, M.; JANOWITZ, B. S.; FORTNEY, J. A.; [eds.]. *Childbirth in developing countries.* Boston, MA-The Hague-Dordrecht-Lancaster, MTP Press Ltd., 83, xxi-162 p.

2913   RALLU, Jean-Louis. "Permanence des disparités de la fécondité en Italie?", *Population* 38(1), jan-feb 83 : 29-59. [résumés en anglais et espagnol]

2914   RYDER, N. B. "A time series of instrumental fertility variables", *Demography* 18(4), nov 81 : 487-510.

2915   RYDER, Norman B. "Fertility and family structure", *Population Bulletin of the United Nations* 15, 83 : 15-34.

2916   SHIELDS, Michael P.; TSUI, Steve W. "The probability of another child in Costa Rica", *Economic Development and Cultural Change* 31(4), jul 83 : 787-807.

2917   SMOLIŃSKI, Zbigniew. *Reprodukcja ludności w świetle postaw prokreacyjnych nowożeńców* (Reproduction of the population in the light of procreative attitudes of young married couples). Warszawa, Szkoła Planowania i Statystyki, 82, 105 p. [Poland]

2918   SUPRAPTILAH, Bondan. *Evaluation of the Indonesian fertility survey 1976.* Voorburg, International Statistical Insitute; London, World Fertility Survey, 82, 43 p.

2919   TAUCHER, Erica. "Fertility and mortality in Latin America", *Populi* 10(3), 83 : 31-40.

2920   WESTOFF, Charles F.; CALOT, Gérard; FOSTER, Andrew D. "Teenage fertility in developed nations, 1971-1980", *Family Planning Perspectives* 15(3), mai-jun 83 : 105-110.

2921   WILSON-DAVIS, K. "Components of period fertility in the Irish Republic, 1962-1977", *Journal of Biosocial Science* 15(1), jan 83 : 95-105.

2922   WOODS, R.; SMITH, C. W. "The decline of marital fertility in the late nineteenth century: the case of England and Wales", *Population Studies* 37(2), jul 83 : 207-225.

15350   Family planning
Planification de la famille

2923   ALBERDI, Ines. "El destino y la libertad. Notas sobre la interrupción del embarazo en las
        sociedades occidentales" (Fate and freedom. Notes on abortion in Western societies),
        Revista Española de Investigaciones Sociológicas 21, jan-mar 83 : 135-150.

2924   BASSEN, Paul. "Present stakes and future prospects: the status of early abortion", *Philosophy
        and Public Affairs* 11(4), aut 82 : 314-337.

2925   BUDI, Suradji; HATMADJI, Sri Harijati. *Contraceptive use in Jaya-Bali: a multivariate analysis
        of the determinants of contraceptive use.* Voorburg, International Statistical Institute; London,
        World Feritility Survey, 82, 24 p.

2926   CAGIANO DE AZEVEDO, Raimondo. "Possibilités d'une coopération démographique
        européenne", *Affari sociali internazionali* 10(4), 82 : 19-46.

2927   CALLAN, Victor J. "Repeat abortion-seeking behaviour in Queensland, Australia:
        knowledge and use of contraception and reasons for terminating the pregnancy", *Journal
        of Biosocial Science* 15(1), jan 83 : 1-8.

2928   CALLAN, Victor J. "Repeat and first abortion seekers: single women in Brisbane,
        Australia", *Journal of Biosocial Science* 15(2), apr 83 : 217-222.

2929   CHASAJEV, Habib; KOUBEK, Josef. "Populační politika v Sovětském svazu" (Population
        policy in the Soviet Union), *Demografie* 24(4), 82 : 302-310.

2930   CHASTELAND, Jean Claude. "Les politiques de population dans le Tiers-Monde huit ans
        après Bucarest: espoirs et réalités", *Tiers-Monde* 24(94), jun 83 : 277-304.

2931   CHEN, Peter S. J.; KUO, Eddie C. Y.; CHUNG, Betty Jamie. *The dilemma of parenthood:
        a study of the value of children in Singapore.* Singapore, Maruzen Asia, 82, 120 p.

2932   CHUNG, Chin Sik; [et al.]. *The effects of induced abortion on subsequent reproductive function and
        pregnancy outcome: Hawaii.* Honolulu, HI, East-West Population Institute, East-West
        Center, 83, xi-144 p.

2933   COLEMAN, Samuel. *Family planning in Japanese society.* Princeton, NJ, Princeton University
        Press, 83, x-269 p.

2934   COOK, Rebecca J.; DICKENS, Bernard M. "Abortion laws in African Commonwealth
        countries", *Journal of African Law* 25(2), aut 81 : 60-79.

2935   DÜRR, Heiner. "Bevölkerungsfragen in der Volksrepublik China" (Population problems
        in the People's Republic of China), *Geographische Rundschau* 35(4), 83 : 1-8.

2936   EARNHARDT, Kent C. *Development planning and population policy in Puerto Rico: from historical
        evolution towards a plan for population stabilization.* Río Piedras, Editorial de la Universidad
        de Puerto Rico, 82, xiv-214 p.

2937   FORREST, Jacqueline Darroch; HENSHAW, Stanley K. "What US women think and
        do about contraception", *Family Planning Perspectives* 15(4), jul-aug 83 : 157-166.

2938   FUCHS, Roland J. *Population distribution policies in Asia and the Pacific: current status and future
        prospects.* Honolulu, HI, East-West Center, 83, vii-40 p.

2939   FUCHS, Roland J.; DEMKO, George S. "Rethinking population policies", *Population
        Research and Policy Review* 2(2), mai 83 : 161-187.

2940   GOLDBERG, H. I. "Contraception, marital fertility, and breast-feeding in Yemen Arab
        Republic", *Journal of Biosocial Science* 15(1), jan 83 : 67-82.

2941   GRANBERG, Donald; BURLISON, James. "The abortion issue in the 1980 elections",
        Family Planning Perspectives 15(5), sep-oct 83 : 231-243. [USA]

2942   HEBERER, Thomas. "Die Bevölkerungspolitik gegenüber den ethnischen Minoritäten
        in der Volksrepublik China" (Population policy as regards ethnic minorities in the
        People's Republic of China), *Zeitschrift für Bevölkerungswissenschaft* 9(2), 83 : 259-273.

2943   HEMBLET, Jean-Emile. "Wallonie an 2000. Une politique de population?", *Wallonie*
        10(1), 83 : 3-13.

2944   HENSHAW, Stanley K. "Characteristics of abortion patients in the United States, 1979
        and 1980", *Family Planning Perspectives* 15(1), jan-feb 83 : 5-16.

2945   HERDERSHOT, Gerry E. "Family planning services from multiple provider types: an
        assessment for the United States", *Studies in Family Planning* 14(8-9), aug-sep 83 : 218-227.

2946   HERNANDEZ, Donald J. "A note on measuring the independent impact of family planning
        programs on fertility declines", *Demography* 18(4), nov 81 : 627-634. [in developing
        countries]

2947   HOGAN, Dennis P.; FRENZEN, Paul D. "Antecedents to contraceptive innovation:
        evidence from rural Northern Thailand", *Demography* 18(4), nov 81 : 597-614.

2948   JOHNSON, Charles A.; BOND, Jon R. "Policy implementation and responsiveness in
        nongovernmental institutions: hospital abortion services after Roe v Wade", *Western
        Political Quarterly* 35(3), sep 82 : 285-405.

2949   KAUFMAN, Joan. *A billion and counting: family planning campaigns and policies in the People's Republic of China.* San Francisco, CA, San Francisco Press, 83, viii-63-4 p.

2950   KELLY, William R.; CUTRIGHT, Philipps. "Determinants of national family planning effort", *Population Research and Policy Review* 2(2), mai 83 : 111-130. [84 developing countries]

2951   KELLY, William R.; CUTRIGHT, Phillips. "A time series analysis of Swedish illegitimacy rates, 1911-1974", *Sociological Focus* 16(2), apr 83 : 117-127.

2952   KHALIFA, Atef M.; [et al.]. *Family planning in rural Egypt 1980.* Cairo, Population and Family Planning Board, 83, xxii-221 p.

2953   KIKASSA, Mwanalessa. "Le planning familial et le concept de Naissances désirables au Zaïre", *Zaïre-Afrique* 23(174), apr 83 : 221-238.

2954   KURIAN, George. "Social change in the Third World in the context of family planning", *Indian Journal of Social Research* 24(3), dec 83 : 290-299.

2955   LAING, John. *Demographic evaluation of family planning programs.* Canberra, Australian National University, 82, viii-157 p.

2956   LEEUW, F. L.; KREFT, G. G. "Opinies over het bevolkingsvraag stuk en daarop gericht beleid: een beschouwing en resultaten uit een Nederlands, regional onderzoek" (Public opinion on population problems and policy orientations: results of a Dutch regional survey), *Bevolking en Gezin* (2), 83 : 227-254.

2957   LEHTO, Markku. "Population policy and policy measures", *Yearbook of Population Research in Finland* 21, 1983 : 40-45. [Finland]

2958   LUCAS, David. "Australian family planning surveys: some problems of comparability", *Journal of Biosocial Science* 15(3), jul 83 : 357-366.

2959   MARINI, Margaret Mooney; HODSDON, Peter J. "Effects of the timing of marriage and first birth on the spacing of subsequent births", *Demography* 18(4), nov 81 : 529-548. [USA]

2960   MCINTOSH, C. Alison. "Population policy in Western Europe: responses to low fertility in France, Sweden and Western Germany", *International Journal of Politics* 12(3), aug 82 : 3-100.

2961   MISRA, Bhasker D.; [et al.]. *Organization for change. A systems analysis of family planning in rural India.* Ann Arbor, MI, University of Michigan-Family Planning Foundation of India, 82, xxiv-444 p.

2962   MOSLEY, Wiley Henry; WERNER, Linda H.; BECKER, Stan. *The dynamics of birth spacing and marital fertility in Kenya.* Voorburg, International Statistical Institute; London, World Fertility Survey, 82, 30 p.

2963   MUKHERJI, Shekhar. *The demographic field theory: population policies and demographic behaviour in India.* Allahabad, Thinker's Library, 83, 156 p.

2964   MUKHERJI, Shekhar. *The demographic field theory: population policies and demographic behaviour in India.* Allahabad, Thinker's Library, 83, xii-156 p.

2965   NARAIN, Vatsala; PRAKASHAN, C. P.; [eds.]. *Population policy perspectives in developing countries.* Bombay, Himalaya Publishing House, 83, xxxii-470 p.

2966   NARYANA, Vatsala; PRAKASHAN, C. P.; [eds.]. *Population policy perspectives in developing countries.* Bombay, Himalaya, 83, 470 p.

2967   OKOLSKI, Marek. "Abortion and contraception in Poland", *Studies in Family Planning* 14(11), nov 83 : 263-274.

2968   PAI PANANDIKER, V. A.; [et al.]. *Organisational policy for family planning.* New Delhi, Uppal, 83, ix-227 p. [India]

2969   PERRY, Paul; TRLIN, Andrew. "Attitudes toward abortion in a provincial area of New Zealand: differentials and determinants", *Australian and New Zealand Journal of Sociology* 18(3), nov 82 : 399-416.

2970   PRESL, Jiří. "Rizika a perspektivy kontracepce" (Risks and prospects of contraception), *Demografie* 24(4), 82 : 336-342.

2971   QIAN XINZHONG. "China's population policy: theory and methods", *Studies in Family Planning* 14(12), dec 83 : 295-301.

2972   RAMIREZ DEARELLANO, Annette B.; SEIPP, Conrad. *Colonialism, Catholicism and contraception: a history of birth control in Puerto Rico.* Chapel Hill, NC-London, University of North Carolina Press, 83, xii-219 p.

2973   RAMOS, Ramón. "Informe-resumen de los resultados de una investigación sociológica sobre el avorto mediante discusiones de grupo" (Review of a sociological research on abortion through group discussions), *Revista Española de Investigaciones Sociológicas* 21, jan-mar 83 : 243-254. [Spain] [see also pp. 255-302 by Maria Pilar ALCOBENSAS TIRADO]

2974   REED, Fred W. "Family planning communication research possibilities in Indonesia", *Majalah Demografie Indonesia* 9(17), jun 82 : 53-63.

2975   REQUILLART, Marie-Alix. "Une enquête sur le recours des adolescents à la contraception",
        Revue française de Sociologie 24(1), jan-mar 83 : 81-95. [France]
2976   ROSENHOUSE-PERSSON, Sandra; SABAGH, Georges. "Attitudes toward abortion
        among Catholic Mexican women: the effects of religiosity and education", *Demography*
        20(1), feb 83 : 87-98.
2977   ROSSET, Edward. "Regionalizacja polityki demograficznej" (Regionalization of demographic
        policy), *Studia demograficzne* 21(1), 83 : 3-23. [Poland] [continued in ibid. 21 (2), 1983 : 3-19]
2978   ROWLANDS, Sam; GUILLEBAUD, John; BOOTH, Margaret. "Behavioural patterns
        in women requesting post-coital contraception", *Journal of Biosocial Science* 15(2), apr
        83 : 145-152. [UK]
2979   SCHRIJVERS, Joke. "Manipulated motherhood. The marginalization of peasant women
        in the North Central Province of Sri Lanka", *Development and Change* 14(2), apr 83 : 185-209.
2980   SENKER, Wienfried. "Demographische Lage und Bevölkerungspolitik in Ungarn"
        (Demographic situation and population policy in Hungary), *Zeitschrift für Bevölkerungs-
        wissenschaft* 8(4), 82 : 589-605.
2981   SLOAN, Douglas G. "The extent of contraceptive use and the social paradigm of modern
        demography", *Sociology (London)* 17(3), aug 83 : 380-387.
2982   SRIKANTAN, K. S.; BALASUBRAMANIAN, K. "Demographic evolution of India's
        family planning", *Artha Vijnana* 25(3), sep 83 : 205-230.
2983   STEINER, Gibert Y.; [ed.]. *The abortion dispute and the American system.* Washington, DC,
        Brookings Institution, 83, x-103 p.
2984   STEŠENKO, V. S.; PIROŽKOV, S. I.; [eds.]. *Problemy demografičeskoj politiki v socialističeskom
        obščestve* (Population policy problems in the socialist society). Kiev, Institut Ėkonomiki
        Akademii Nauk USSR, 82, 170 p.
2985   TEACHMAN, Jay D.; [et al.]. "Perceived availability of contraceptives and family limitation",
        Human Organization 42(2), sum 83 : 123-131. [Korea R; Mexico]
2986   VARELA, Amelia P. "The Philippine family planning program: organizational correlates
        of performance", *Philippine Journal of Public Administration* 26(1), jan 82 : 19-46.
2987   VAZQUEZ, J. M. *La vida a debate: el aborto en la prensa* (Life as a discussion matter: abortion
        through the press). Madrid, Instituto de Sociologia Aplicada, 83, 200 p. [Spain]
2988   VEKEMANS, Marcel; DOHMEN, Brigitte. "Induced abortion in Belgium: clinical experience
        and psychosocial observation", *Studies in Family Planning* 13(12), dec 82 : 355-364.
2989   VICZIANY, Marika. "Coercion in a soft State: the family-planning program of India",
        Pacific Affairs 55(3), aut 82 : 373-402. [continued in ibid. 55 (4), wint 83 : 557-592]
2990   WARHURST, John; MERRILL, Vance. "The abortion issue in Australia: pressure politics
        and policy", *Australian Quarterly* 54(2), wint 82 : 119-135.
2991   WASSERMAN, Ira M. "A cross-national comparison of contraception and abortion laws",
        Social Indicators Research 13(3), oct 83 : 281-309.
2992   WASSERMAN, Ira M.; USUI, Chikako. "Indicators of contraceptive policy for nations
        at three levels of development", *Social Indicators Research* 12(2), feb 83 : 153-168.
2993   WILTGEN, Richard; HERSCHEDE, Fred. "Marxism and Chinese population policies",
        Review of Radical Political Economics 14(4), wint 82 : 18-28.

15400   **MARRIAGE. FAMILY**
        MARIAGE. FAMILLE

15410   **Sexual behaviour**
        Comportement sexuel

2994   "Sexual harassment in the university", *Signs* 8(2), wint 82 : 296-336. [USA] [with contributions
        by Bernice LOTT, Judith BERMAN BRANDERBURG]
2995   "Social (The) psychology of sexual harassment: perceptions, attitudes and attributions",
        Journal of Social Issues 38(4), 82 : 75-157. [USA]
2996   ALDRICH, Robert. "Homosexuality in France", *Contemporary French Civilization* 7(1),
        aut 82 : 1-19.
2997   AUFFRET, Séverine. *Des couteaux contre des femmes:* [de l'excision]. Paris, Des Femmes,
        82, xiii-297 p.
2998   BAKWESEGHA, Christopher James. *Profiles of urban prostitution: a case study from Uganda.*
        Nairobi, Kenya Literature Bureau, 82, xxiv-125 p.
2999   BARGON, Michael. *Prostitution und Zuhälterei: zur kriminologischen und strafrechtlichen Problematik
        mit einem geschichtlichen und rechtsvergleichenden Überblick* (Prostitution and pimping: on
        criminological and criminal law problem with a historical and comparative legal overview).
        Lübeck, Schmidt-Römhild, 82, 330 p.

3000   BAUDRY, André. *La condition des homosexuels.* Toulouse, Privat, 82, 238 p.

3001   BIBBY, Reginald W. "The moral mosaic: sexuality in the Canadian 80s", *Social Indicators Research* 13(2), aug 83 : 171-184.

3002   BOUHDIBA, Abdelwahab. *La sexualité en Islam.* Paris, Presses Universitaires de France, 82, 320 p.

3003   BRYANT, Clifton D. *Sexual deviancy and social proscription: the social context of carnal behavior.* New York, NY, Human Sciences Press, 82, 432 p.

3004   CROCKER, Phyllis L. "An analysis of university definitions of sexual harassment", *Signs* 8(4), sum 83 : 696-707. [USA]

3005   IGLESIAS DE USSEL, Julio. "La sociología de la sexualidad en España: notas introductorias" (Sociology of sexuality in Spain: introductory notes), *Revista Española de Investigaciones Sociológicas* 21, jan-mar 83 : 103-133.

3006   ISHIKAWA, Yoshiyuki. "Insesuto tabū-kō" (Some considerations on the incest taboo), *Tokushima daigaku gakugei kiyo (shakai-kagaku)* 32, 83 : 57-69.

3007   MATARAGNON, Rita H. "Sex and the Filipino adolescent: a review", *Philippine Studies* (30), trim. 3, 82 : 311-334.

3008   OSBORNE, R. "La pornografía como 'delito sin victima' y la crítica feminista" (Pornography as 'crime without victim' and the feminist criticism), *Sistema* (57), nov 83 : 97-106.

3009   PASUK PHONGPAICHIT. *From peasant girls to Bangkok masseuses.* Geneva, International Labour Office, 82, ix-80 p.

3010   PILLAI, T. Vikraman. "Prostitution in India", *Indian Journal of Social Work* 43(3), oct 82 : 313-320.

3011   ROSSI, Peter H.; WEBER-BURDIN, Eleanor. "Sexual harassment on the campus", *Social Science Research* 12(2), jun 83 : 131-158. [USA]

3012   SHOHAM, S. Gione; [et al.]. "Family variables and stigma among prostitutes in Israël", *Journal of Social Psychology* 120(1), jun 83 : 57-62.

3013   STEIN GREENBLAT, Cathy. "The satience of sexuality in the early years of marriage", *Journal of Marriage and the Family* 45(2), mai 83 : 289-299. [USA]

3014   THEVENOT, Xavier. "Les homosexualités. Éléments de réflexion éthique", *Études* 358(3), mar 83 : 339-354.

15420   Marriage. Nuptiality
Mariage. Nuptialité

3015   "Children and marriage", *International Journal of Sociology and Social Policy* 2(3), 82 : 1-94. [with contributions by Robert CHESTER, Penny MANSFIELD, Frances BAUM, David CLARK, G. D. MITCHELL]

3016   ADLER, Laure. *Secrets d'alcôve: histoire du couple de 1830 à 1930.* Paris, Hachette, 83, 238 p.

3017   ALLERS, Robert D. *Divorce, children, and the school.* Princeton, NJ, Princeton Book Co., 82, xi-158 p.

3018   ATOH, Makoto. "Rikon no bunseki" (Trends in Japanese divorce), *Tokei* 34(4), 83 : 12-17.

3019   ATOH, Makoto; KOJIMA, Hiroshi. "Gendai seinen no kekkonkan: Dai-8-ji shussanryoku chosa'Dokushin chosa' no kekka kara" (Attitudes toward marriage among the unmarried Japanese youth), *Jinko mondai kenkyu* 168, 83 : 31-59.

3020   AULT, James M. Jr. "Making 'modern' marriage 'traditional': state power and the regulation of marriage in colonial Zambia", *Theory and Society* 12(2), mar 83 : 181-210.

3021   BAKIC, Vojislav. "Brak i porodicni odnosi" (Marriage and relationships in family), *Jugoslovenski pregled* 26(11), nov 82 : 379-396. [Yugoslavia]

3022   BORSCHEID, Peter. "Partnerwahl und Ehenzyklus in einer württembergischen Industriestadt im 19. Jahrundert" (Mate selection and marriage cycle in a Worttemberg industrial town in the 19th century), *Archiv für Sozialgeschichte* 22, 82 : 227-262.

3023   BOYD, Donald A.; NUNN, Gerald D.; PARISH, Thomas S. "Effects of marital status and parents' marital status on evaluation of self and parents", *Journal of Social Psychology* 119(2), apr 83 : 229-234.

3024   CARABAÑA, Julio. "Homogamia y movilidad social" (Homogamy and social mobility), *Revista Española de Investigaciones Sociológicas* 21, jan-mar 83 : 61-81.

3025   CHOWDHURY, A. K. M. Alauddin. "Applications of marriage in rural Bangladesh", *Journal of Biosocial Science* 15(3), jul 83 : 281-287.

3026   COMMAILLE, Jacques; [et al.]. *Le divorce en Europe occidentale: la loi et le nombre.* Paris, Éditions de l'Institut National d'Études Démographiques, 83, 242 p.

3027   CULPAN, Oya; MARZOTTO, Toni. "Changing attitudes toward work and marriage: Turkey in transition", *Signs* 8(2), wint 82 : 337-351.

3028   DONAHUE, Charles Jr. "The canon law on the formation of marriage and social practice in the later middle ages", *Journal of Family History* 8(2), 83 : 144-158.

3029   DOOLEY, Martin D. "Labor supply and fertility of married women: an analysis with grouped and individual data from the 1970 U.S. census", *Journal of Human Resources* 17(4), aut 82 : 499-532.

3030   EDWARDS, Meredith. "Financial arrangements made by husbands and wives: findings of a survey", *Australian and New Zealand Journal of Sociology* 18(3), nov 82 : 320-338.

3031   FIRASAT, Ali; FURQAN, Ahmed. *Divorce in Mohammedan law: the law of triple divorce.* New Delhi, Deep and Deep, 83, 324 p.

3032   FLETCHER, Ben C. "Marital relationships as a cause of death: an anlysis of occupational mortality and hidden consequences of marriage — some UK data", *Human Relations* 36(2), feb 83 : 123-133.

3033   FÖLDESINÉ SZABÓ, Gyöngyi. "Élsportolónők párválasztási esélyeinek szociológiai elemzése" (What chances do female sport stars have in choosing a spouse: a sociological investigation), *Testnevelés és Sporttudomány* 14(1), 83 : 21-25.

3034   FREEMAN, Michael D. E.; LYON, Christiana M. *Cohabitation without marriage: an essay in law and social policy.* Aldershot, Hants, Gower, 83, vii-228 p.

3035   FURSTENBERG, Frank F.; [et al.]. "The life course of children of divorce: marital disruption and parental contact", *American Sociological Review* 48(5), oct 83 : 656-668. [USA]

3036   GLOS, George E. "The Spanish divorce law of 1981", *International and Comparative Law Quarterly* 32(3), jul 83 : 667-688.

3037   GOLDMAN, Noreen. "Dissolution of first unions in Colombia, Panama, and Peru", *Demography* 18(4), nov 81 : 659-679.

3038   GOLDMAN, Noreen; LORD, Graham. "Sex differences in life cycle measures of widowhood", *Demography* 20(2), mai 83 : 177-195. [USA]

3039   GRECO, Mario; CARRANNANTE, Leonarda Roveri. "Separazioni e divorzi in Italia secondo l'età dei coniugi e la durata del matrimonio, 1969-1978" (Separations and divorces in Italy according to the spouses' age and the length of the marriage, 1969-1978), *Genus* 37(3-4), jul-dec 81 : 125-164.

3040   HASKEY, John. "Remarriage of the divorced in England and Wales — a contemporary phenomenon", *Journal of Biosocial Science* 15(3), jul 83 : 253-271. [UK]

3041   HUSSAIN, S. Jaffer. *Marriage breakdown and divorce law reform in contemporary society: a comparative study of USA, UK and India.* New Delhi, Concept, 83, 240 p.

3042   ISHWARAN, Karigoudar; [ed.]. *Marriage and divorce in Canada.* Toronto, ON-New York, NY, Methuen, 83, vii-341 p.

3043   JANSEN, Clifford. "Inter-ethnic marriages", *International Journal of Comparative Sociology (Leiden)* 23(3-4), sep-dec 82 : 225-235. [Canada]

3044   KAMARÁS, Ferenc. "A házasságok stabilitása és a családnagyság" (The stability of marriages and the size of the family), *Demográfia* 26(1), 83 : 50-93. [Hungary]

3045   KELLERHALS, Jean; [et al.]. *Mariages au quotidien: inégalités sociales, tensions culturelles et organisation familiale.* Lausanne, P.-M. Favre, 82, 285 p. [Switzerland]

3046   KOJIMA, Hiroshi. "Nihon-jin no kekkon" (Marriage in Japan), *Tokei* 34(4), 83 : 1-6.

3047   KUMAGAI, Fumie. "Changing divorce in Japan", *Journal of Family History* 8(1), 83 : 85-107.

3048   LATTEN, J. J. "Over trouwen en samenwonen onder jongeren" (Marriage and cohabitation among youth), *Bevolking en Gezin* (1), 83 : 5-26. [Netherlands]

3049   LEUPHOLD, Andrea. "Liebe und Partnerschaft: Formen der Codierung von Ehen" (Love and partnership: a comparison of marital codes), *Zeitschrift für Soziologie* 12(4), oct 83 : 297-327.

3050   LEVANDE, Diane I.; KOCH, Joanne B.; KOCH, Lewis Z. *Marriage and the family.* Boston, MA, Houghton Mifflin Co., 83, xix-515-39 p.

3051   LEVENSON, Robert W.; GOTTMAN, John M. "Marital interaction: physiological linkage and affective exchange", *Journal of Personality and Social Psychology* 45(3), sep 83 : 587-597.

3052   LIKER, Jeffrey K.; ELDER, Glen H. Jr. "Economic hardship and marital relations in the 1930's", *American Sociological Review* 48(3), jun 83 : 343-359. [USA]

3053   LOVAS, Šandor; KAPOR-STANULOVIĆ, Nila. "Stavovi braku kod mladih pre sklapanja bračne zajednice" (Youth's attitudes towards marriage before marriage), *Sociologija* 24(1), 82 : 99-107. [Novi Sad, Yugoslavia]

3054   LUTHRA, Arati. "Dowry among the urban poor: perception and practice", *Social Action* 33(2), apr-jun 83 : 194-217. [India]

3055   MALAKER, Chitta Ranjan. "Evaluation of widowhood data in Indian censuses: a life table investigation", *Genus* 37(3-4), jul-dec 81 : 165-177.

3056   MALINA, Robert M.; [et al.]. "Assortative mating for phenotypic characteristics in a Zapotec community in Oaxaca, Mexico", *Journal of Biosocial Science* 15(3), jul 83 : 273-280.

3057   MARMIER-CHAMPENOIS, Marie Pierre; FAUCHEUX, Madeleine. *Le mariage et l'argent.* Paris, Presses Universitaires de France, 82, 226 p.

3058   MAYER, Egon. *Children of intermarriage: a study in patterns of identification and family life.* New York, NY, American Jewish Committee, Institute of Human Relations, 83, x-45 p. [USA]

3059   MEYER, Sibylle; SCHULZE, Eva. "Nichteheliche Lebensgemeinschaften — Alternativen zur Ehe? Eine internationale Datenübersicht" (Consensual unions — alternatives for marriage? An international data survey), *Kölner Zeitschrift für Soziologie und Sozialpsychologie* 35(4), dec 83 : 735-754.

3060   MOKWENY, C. "La polygamie et la révolte de la femme africaine", *Peuples Noirs — Peuples Africains* (31), feb 83 : 86-94.

3061   MOSKOFF, William. "Divorce in the USSR", *Journal of Marriage and the Family* 45(2), mai 83 : 419-425.

3062   NAKAMURA, Alice; NAKAMURA, Masao. "Part-time and full-time work behaviour of married women: a model with a double truncated dependent variable", *Canadian Journal of Economics / Revue canadienne d'Économique* 16(2), mai 83 : 229-257.

3063   PAHL, Jan. "The allocation of money and the structuring of inequality within marriage", *Sociological Review* 31(2), mai 83 : 237-262.

3064   PONNAMBALAM, Shirani. *Law and the marriage relationship in Sri Lanka.* Colombo, the author, 82, xviii-508 p.

3065   PROKOPEC, Jiří; DYTRYCH, Zdeněk; SCHÜLLER, Vratislav. "Řešení manželské krize: návrhy na rozvod vzaté zpět" (Resolution of matrimonial crisis: withdrawn divorce proposals), *Demografie* 25(2), 83 : 138-143. [Czechoslovakia]

3066   RAKIĆ, Vojislav. "Marriage and family relations", *Yugoslav Survey* 24(2), mai 83 : 3-28.

3067   RIVIERE, Claude. "Le divorce chez les Evé du Togo. Note ethno-sociolgique", *Mois en Afrique* 18(203-204), jan 83 : 118-128.

3068   ROGERS, John; [ed.]. *Marriage and fertility: local patterns in preindustrial Sweden, Finland, and Norway.* Uppsala, University of Uppsala, Department of History, 82, 95 p.

3069   ROSS, Catherine E.; MIROWSKY, John; HUBER, Joan. "Dividing work, sharing work, and in-between: marriage patterns and depression", *American Sociological Review* 48(6), dec 83 : 809-823. [USA]

3070   ROSS, Patricia A. "Marriage and women's occupational attainment in cross-cultural perspective", *American Sociological Review* 48(6), dec 83 : 852-864.

3071   SCHAAP, Cas. *Communication and adjustment in marriage.* Lisse, Swets en Zeitlinger, 82, xviii-281 p.

3072   SCHOEN, Robert. "Measuring the tightness of a marriage squeeze", *Demography* 20(1), feb 83 : 61-78.

3073   SIXMA, Herman; ULTEE, W. C. "Trouwpatronen en de openheid van een samenleving. De samenhang tussen de opleidingsniveaus van (huwelijks) partners in Nederland tussen 1959 en 1977" (Marriage patterns and tolerance of a society. The correlation between the training levels of partners in the Netherlands over the 1959-1977 period), *Mens en Maatschappij* 58(2), mai 83 : 109-131. [résumé en anglais]

3074   SOLOMON, Norman. "Jewish divorce law and contemporary society", *Jewish Journal of Sociology* 24(2), dec 83 : 131-139.

3075   SPANIER, Graham B. "Married and unmarried cohabitation in the United States: 1980", *Journal of Marriage and the Family* 45(2), mai 83 : 277-288. [USA]

3076   SZKLUT, Jay. "Bride wealth, an alternate view", *Behavior Science Research* 16(3-4), 81 : 225-247.

3077   UPRETI, H. C.; UPRETI, Nandini. "Parental authority and attitude of women students toward marriage and dowry", *Indian Journal of Social Work* 43(3), oct 82 : 247-252. [India]

3078   VAN DORPE, H.; NIJS, P. "Partnerrelatie en seksualiteit tijdens de zwangerschap" (Partners relationship and sexuality during pregnancy), *Bevolking en Gezin* (2), 82 : 215-233.

3079   VEENHOVEN, Ruut. "The growing impact of marriage", *Social Indicators Research* 12(1), jan 83 : 49-63.

3080   VERGATI, Anne. "Social consequences of marrying Viṣṇu Nārāyaṇa: primary marriage among the Newars of Kathmandu valley", *Contributions to Indian Sociology* 16(2), jul-dec 82 : 271-287.

3081   WIJEWICKREMA, Stanley; [et al.]. *Marital status trends in Belgium (1961-1977): application of multi-state analysis.* Brussels, Interuniversity Programme in Demography, Vrije Universiteit, 83, 39 p.

3082   YAMAMOTO, Fumio. "Haigu kankei no nenjibetsu hendo no shakaiteki bunkateki yoin" (Socio-cultural factors of changes by year in marital status), *Nakamura gakuen kenkyu kiyo* 15, 83 : 97-108.

3083   YUANTIEN, H. "Age at marriage in the People's Republic of China", *China Quarterly* (93), mar 83 : 90-107.

        15430   Family
        Famille

3084   "Famille (La)", *Contrepoint* (46), 83 : 13-100. [France] [with contributions by Alfred SAUVY, Jean-Yves LE GALLOU, Gérard-François DUMONT, Joseph VEBRET, Fernand LAFARGUE]
3085   "Functiile sociale educative şi responsabilitateă socialǎ a familiei" (Social education function and social responsibility of the family), *Viitorul social* 75(5), oct 82 : 638-645.
3086   ALMEIDA, Maria Suely Kofes de; [et al.]. *Colcha de retalhos: estudos sobre a família no Brasil* (Patchwork: studies on the family in Brazil). São Paulo, Brasiliense, 82, 204 p.
3087   ALVAREZ, María de la Luz. *Deprivación y familia* (Deprivation and family). Santiago de Chile, Editorial Universitaria, 82, 158 p.
3088   ANDORKA, Rudolf; KULCSÁR, Rózsa. "Az anya társadalmi helyzetének és iskolai végzettségének hatása a gyermekek társadalmi mobilitására" (The influence of mothers' social status and education on the mobility of children), *Szociológia* 11(4), 82 : 577-588.
3089   ARIOTI, Maria. "Sistema di parentela e scambi matrimoniali in una comunità contadina dell'Umbria" (Kinship and marriage in an Umbrian community), *Rassegna italiana di Sociologia* 24(2), apr-jun 83 : 253-288. [Italy]
3090   BALCERZAK-PARADOWSKA, Bożena; KONWERSKA, Barbara. *Sytuacja społeczna i materkalna matek niezamężnych* (Social and economical situation of unmarried mothers). Warszawa, Instytut Pracy i Spraw Socjalnych, 83, 207 p.
3091   BARRETT, Michèle; MCINTOSH, Mary. *The anti-social family.* London, NLB, 82, 164 p.
3092   BENCHENEB, Ali. "Le droit algérien de la famille entre la tradition et la modernité", *Revue algérienne des Sciences juridiques, économiques et politiques* 19(1), mar 82 : 23-33.
3093   BENDIXEN, Ernst Otto. *Die Situation landwirtschaftlicher Familien mit Hilfebedürftigen* (The situation of agricultural families with dependent persons). Göttingen, Agrarsoziale Gesellschaft, 82, xx-160 p.
3094   BENDOTTI, Grazia. "La famiglia: aspetti demografici ed economici connessi alla sua evoluzione" (The family: demographic and economic aspects related to its evolution), *Rivista internazionale di Scienze sociali* 91(2-3), apr-sep 83 : 193-210. [Italy]
3095   BERK, Richard A.; BERK, Sarah Fenstermaker. "Supply-side sociology of the family: the challenge of the New Home Economics", *Annual Review of Sociology* (9), 83 : 375-395. [USA]
3096   BISHOP, Libby. "The family: prison, haven or vanguard?", *Berkeley Journal of Sociology* 28, 83 : 19-38.
3097   BONTEMPS, C. "L'influence française dans le projet de code de la famille algérienne", *Revue algérienne des Sciences juridiques, économiques et politiques* 19(4), dec 82 : 625-645.
3098   BRODIN, Eric. "The family in Sweden", *Journal of Social, Political and Economic Studies* 7(4), wint 82 : 357-367.
3099   CAPLOW, Theodore. "The sociological myth of family decline", *Tocqueville Review* 3(2), aut 81 : 349-369.
3100   CHARTIER, Jean-Pierre; CHARTIER, Laetitia. *Les parents martyrs: passions, haines et vengeances d'adolescents.* Toulouse, Privat, 82, 248 p.
3101   CHERLIN, Andrew. "Changing family and household: contemporary lessons from historical research", *Annual Review of Sociology* (9), 83 : 51-66.
3102   CHRISMAN, Miriam. "Family and religion in two noble families: French Catholic and English Puritan", *Journal of Family History* 8(2), 83 : 190-210.
3103   CONDE, Rosa. "Tendencias de cambio en la estructura familiar" (Trends of change in family structure), *Revista Española de Investigaciones Sociológicas* 21, jan-mar 83 : 33-60.
3104   CONDE, Rosa; [comp.]. *Familia y cambio social en España* (Family and social change in Spain). Madrid, Centro de Investigaciones Sociológicas, 82, 351 p.
3105   CUPIA, Luciano. *Famiglia oggi: sociologia della famiglia e psicologia della coppia* (Family today: sociology of the family and psychology of the couple). Roma, Edizioni Paoline, 83, 154-6 p. [Italy]
3106   DAHLSTRÖM, Edmund; LILJESTRÖM, Rita. "The patriarchal heritage and the working-class women", *Acta Sociologica* 26(1), 83 : 3-20. [Sweden]
3107   DE BERNARDIS, Alessandra. "La famiglia in Italia nella ricerca sociologica recente" (The Italian family in recent sociological research), *Vita e pensiero* 66(9), sep 83 : 34-40.
3108   DE OLIVEIRA, Graziela. "O abandono de crianças e a criminalidade infantil no Brasil" (Child neglect and juvenile delinquency in Brazil), *Vozes* 77(6), aug 83 : 60-63.

3109   DEL CAMPO URBANO, Salustiano. *La evolución de la familia española en el siglo XX* (Spanish family evolution in the XXth century). Madrid, Alianza, 82, 251 p.

3110   DIETL, L. Kay; NEFF, Marsha J. *Single parent families: choice or change?*. New York, NY-London, Columbia University, Teachers College Press, 83, ix-110 p.

3111   DOW, Thomas E. Jr.; WERNER, Linda H. "Perceptions of family among rural Kenyan women", *Studies in Family Planning* 14(2), feb 83 : 35-43.

3112   DYSON, Tim; MOORE, Mick. "On kinship structure, female autonomy and demographic behavior in India", *Population and Development Review* 9(1), mar 83 : 35-60.

3113   ENGLISH, Brian A.; KING, Raymond J. *Families in Australia.* Kensington, NSW, Family Research Unit, University of New South Wales, 83, ix-377 p.

3114   ESPENSHADE, Thomas J.; TURCHI, Boone A.; KAMENSKI, Gloria. "Family size and economic welfare", *Family Planning Perspectives* 16(6), nov-dec 83 : 289-294. [USA]

3115   FERGUSSON, D. M.; HORWOOD, L. J. "A Markovian model of childhood family history", *Journal of Mathematical Sociology* 9(2), 83 : 139-154.

3116   FREED, S. A.; FREED, R. S. "Changing family types in India", *Ethnology* 21(3), 82 : 189-202.

3117   GRAHAM, James Q. Jr. "Family and fertility in rural Ohio: Wood County, Ohio in 1869", *Journal of Family History* 8(3), 83 : 262-279.

3118   GRAY, Elizabeth Dodson. *Patriarchy as a conceptual trap.* Wellesley, MA, Roundtable Press, 82, 142 p.

3119   GROSS, Friederike. "La réforme de la puissance parentale en droit allemand", *Annales de l'Université des Sciences sociales de Toulouse* 29, 81 : 343-363.

3120   GUPTA, Kuntesh. "Female sociologists and family sociology in India: theoretical and empirical concerns", *Indian Journal of Social Research* 23(3), dec 82 : 229-244.

3121   GYÁNI, Gábor. *Család, háztartás és a városi cselédség* (Family, household and the domestic workers). Budapest, Magvető, 83, 251 p.

3122   HALLA, Klaus. *Yksinhuoltajien asema ja ongelmat* (The position and problems of single parents in Finland). Helsinki, Sosiaali- ja Terveysministeriö, Tutkimusosasto, Myy Valtion Painatuskeskus, 82, 168 p.

3123   HALLEN, G. C. "Family theory in India: some strategies", *Indian Journal of Social Research* 23(2), aug 82 : 98-106.

3124   HANSON, Sandra L.; SPANIER, Graham B. "Family development and adjustment to marital separation", *Sociology and Social Research* 68(1), oct 83 : 19-40.

3125   HARČEV, A. G.; [ed.]. *Sem'ja i obščestvo* (Family and society). Moskva, Nauka, 82, 128 p.

3126   HERLIHY, David. "The making of the medieval family: symmetry, structure, and sentiment", *Journal of Family History* 8(2), 83 : 116-130.

3127   HOFFERTH, Sandra L. "Childbearing decision making and family well-being: a dynamic, sequential model", *American Sociological Review* 48(4), aug 83 : 533-545.

3128   HOYT, Danny R.; BABCHUK, Nicholas. "Adult kinship networks: the selective formation of intimate ties with kin", *Social Forces* 62(1), sep 83 : 84-101.

3129   IIDA, Tetsuya. "Kazoku shakaigaku no rironteki sho-mondai: Kazoku mondai o chushin ni" (Theoretical problems to the family sociology: especially on the viewpoint of family problem), *Ritsumeikan daigaku Sangyo shakai ronshu* 36, 83 : 1-34.

3130   ISHIKAWA, Yasuko. "Nihon shakai no 'gisei fukeiteki' kōzō: shakaishiteki kosatsu" (Pseudo-patrilineal structure of Japanese society: an essay from a socio-historical viewpoint), *Soka daigaku Soshiorojika* 8(1), 83 : 100-125.

3131   ISHWARAN, Karigoudar; [ed.]. *The Canadian family.* Toronto, ON, Gage, 83, xi-380 p.

3132   JALLINOJA, Riitta; HAAVIO-MANNILA, Elina. "State intervention and privatization in family life", *Yearbook of Population Research in Finland* 21, 1983 : 7-25. [Finland]

3133   JENSEN, Thyra Buus; KRAFT, Birgit; WAMMEN, Ingelise Kamp. *Den danske kernefamilie* (The Danish nuclear family). København, Danmarks Biblioteksskole, 82, 141 p.

3134   KALIA, Narendra Nath. "Family analysis: a class project in the application of sociology to personal life", *Indian Journal of Social Research* 24(2), aug 83 : 101-110. [India]

3135   KAPUR, Promilla. *Conflict between adolescent girls and their parents in India.* New Delhi, Vision Books, 82, xi-128 p.

3136   KAUFMANN, Franz-Xavier; [et al.]. "Familienentwicklung — generatives Verhalten im familialen Kontext" (Family development. Procreative behaviour in the family context), *Zeitschrift für Bevölkerungswissenschaft* 8(4), 82 : 523-545.

3137   KLOEHN, Ekkehard. *Die neue Familie: zeitgemässe Formen menschlichen Zusammenlebens* (The new family: present forms of human living together). Hamburg, Hoffmann und Campe, 82, 244 p.

3138   KODANDA RAO, M. "Kinship and marriage among the Jalari of coastal Andhra: a study of Dravidian kinship terminology", *Contributions to Indian Sociology* 16(2), jul-dec 82 : 197-223. [India]

3139   KUROSU, Nobuyuki. "'Kōkan riron' niyoru kazoku no bunseki: kazoku o kōseisuru itsutsu no kōkan yōso" (An analysis for family by exchange theory: five exchange elements to constitute family), _Nihon daigaku Soshiorojikusu_ 6, 83 : 43-61.

3140   LATYSEV, I. A. "Vzaimo-otnošenija vzroslyh japoncev s požilymi roditeljami" (Adults and aged parents relations), _Narody Azii i Afriki_ (3), jun 83 : 50-60. [Japan]

3141   LAYISH, Aharon. _Marriage, divorce and succession in the Druze family: a study based on decisions of Druze arbitrators and religious courts in Israel and the Golan heights._ Leyden, Brill, 82, ccv-474 p.

3142   LEE, Hung-Tak. _Causes of son preference in Korea._ Geneva, World Health Organization, 82, vi-404 p.

3143   LEHNING, James R. "Nuptiality and rural industry: families and labor in French countryside", _Journal of Family History_ 8(4), 83 : 333-345.

3144   LEHR, Ursula. _Familie in der Krise? Ein Plädoyer für mehr Partnerschaft in Ehe, Familie und Beruf_ (Family in crisis? A demand for increased partnership in marriage, family and occupation). München, G. Olzog, 82, 134 p.

3145   LESTHAEGHE, R.; WILLEMS, P. "Gezinsvorming en -uitbouw in België: onderzoek naar de economische en culturele achtergronden van een transformatie" (Formation of the family, disintegration and procreation in Belgium: economic and cultural factors of change), _Bevolking en Gezin_ (2), 83 : 191-226.

3146   LINZER, Norman. "The Jewish family: authority and tradition in modern perspective", _Journal of Jewish Communal Service_ 59(2), wint 82 : 132-143.

3147   LOČSEI, Pál. "A tradicionális magyar család sorsa századunk második felében" (The destiny of traditional Hungarian family in the second half of our century), _Mozgó Világ_ 8(3), 83 : 105-113.

3148   LUPRI, Eugen; SYMONS, Gladys. "The emerging symmetrical family: fact or fiction?", _International Journal of Comparative Sociology (Leiden)_ 23(3-4), sep-dec 82 : 166-189.

3149   MAŁEK, Ewa. "Potrzeby młodych rodzin miejskich" (Needs of young urban families), _Biuletyn Instytutu Gospodarstwa Społecznego_ 25(3), 82 : 167-199.

3150   MCNALL, Scott G.; MCNALL, Sally Allen. _Plains families: exploring sociology through social history._ New York, NY, St. Martin's Press, 83, xiii-328 p. [USA]

3151   MIKAMI, Katsuya. "Kazoku to shinrui network" (Family and kindred), _Soshioroji_ 28(1), 83 : 57-75.

3152   MLADENOVIĆ, Marko. "Idejno-političke i sociološke osnove zakona o braku i porodičnim odnosima SR Srbije" (Ideological-political and sociological principles of family relations law in Serbia), _Sociologija_ 24(1), 82 : 81-98.

3153   MORGAN, S. Philip; HIROSIMA, Kiyosi. "The persistence of extended family residence in Japan. Anachronism or alternative strategy?", _American Sociological Review_ 48(2), apr 83 : 269-281.

3154   MORIOKA, Kiyomi; MOCHIZUKI, Takashi. _Atarashii kazoku shakaigaku_ (A new sociology of family). Tokyo, Baifukan, 83, 219 p.

3155   MOSK, Carl. _Patriarchy and fertility: Japan and Sweden, 1880-1960._ New York, NY-London-Paris-San Diego, CA-San Francisco, CA-São Paulo-Tokyo-Toronto, Academic Press, 83, XXII-320 p.

3156   MOŽNY, Ivo. "Ekonomika rodiny jako sociálního mikrosystému" (Family economy as a social micro-system), _Sborník prací filozofické Fakulty Brněnské University_ 31(26), 82 : 43-67. [Czechoslovakia] [résumés en russe et en anglais]

3157   NISHIMURA, Hiroko. "Shutoken kenko noson ni okeru roshin dokyo kazoku no seikatsu kozo: Saitama-ken Ohsato-mura no baai" (The life-structure of three generation family of the rural area of Tokyo metropolis), _Soka daigaku Soshiorojika_ 8(1), 83 : 104-124.

3158   NONOYAMA, Hisaya. "America kazoku no kenkyu: rinen to genjitsu" (A sociological study of the American family: an ideal and reality), _Momoyama gakuin daigaku shakaigaku ronshu_ 16(2), 83 : 89-123.

3159   NORTON, Arthur J. "Family life cycle: 1980", _Journal of Marriage and the Family_ 45(2), mai 83 : 267-275. [USA]

3160   O'DONNELL, Carol; CRANEY, Jan; [eds.]. _Family violence in Australia._ Melbourne, Longman Cheshire, 82, xii-204 p.

3161   OSMONT, Annik. "Stratégies familiales, stratégies résidentielles en milieu urbain", _Cahiers d'Études africaines_ 21(1-3), 81 : 175-195. [résumé en anglais]

3162   OZMENT, Steven. "The family in Reformation Germany: the bearing and rearing of children", _Journal of Family History_ 8(2), 83 : 159-176.

3163   PAILLAT, Paul; DELBES, Christiane. "La famille des salariés du secteur privé à la veille de la retraite", _Population_ 38(3), mai-jun 83 : 527-552. [continued in ibid. 38 (6), nov-dec 83: 959-974]

3164 PARK, Chai Bin. "Preference for sons, family size, and sex ratio: an empirical study in Korea", *Demography* 20(3), aug 83 : 333-352.

3165 PEREVEDENTSEV, Viktor Ivanovich. "The Soviet family today", *Sociology and Social Research* 67(3), apr 83 : 245-259.

3166 POLANSKY, Norman A.; GAUDIN, James M. Jr. "Social distancing of the neglectful family", *Social Service Review* 57(2), jun 83 : 196-208.

3167 QUERE, France. "La famille à l'épreuve du temps", *Études* 358(9), sep 83 : 185-196. [France]

3168 RAPPING, Elayne. "The view from Hollywood: the American family and the American dream", *Socialist Review* (67), feb 83 : 71-92.

3169 RECIO ADRADOS, J. L. "Los cambios en la familia española" (Spanish family's changes), *Documentación Social* (50), jan-mar 83 : 85-103.

3170 RENDLOVÁ, Eliška. "Proměny rodiny a sociální aspekty nároku na samostatnou domácnost" (Family changes and social aspects of right to an independent household), *Demografie* 25(2), 83 : 130-137. [Czechoslovakia]

3171 RETTIG, Kathryn D.; BUBOLZ, Margaret M. "Perceptual indicators of family well-being", *Social Indicators Research* 12(4), mai 83 : 417-438. [USA]

3172 ROSEN, Bernard Carl. *The industrial connection: achievement and the family in developing societies.* New York, NY, Aldine Publishing Co., 82, viii-359 p.

3173 ROUSSEL, Louis. "Familles d'aujourd'hui et familles de demain", *Futuribles* 67, jun 83 : 29-43.

3174 RUBELLIN-DEVICHI, Jacqueline. *L'évolution civile de la famille depuis 1945.* Lyon-Paris, Éditions du CNRS, 83, 134 p.

3175 RUŽŽE, V. L.; [et al.]. *Struktura i funkcii semejnyh grupp* (Structure and functions of the family group). Moskva, Finansy i Statistika, 83, 160 p. [USSR]

3176 SAATY, Thomas L.; WONG, Molly M. "Projecting average family size in rural India by the analytic hierarchy process", *Journal of Mathematical Sociology* 9(3), 83 : 181-209.

3177 SAITO, Osamu. "Population and the peasant family economy in proto-industrial Japan. A note on household size in a Japanese proto-industrial region: Suwa County in the 19th century", *Journal of Family History* 8(1), 83 : 30-54.

3178 SCHNEEWIND, Klaus A.; [et al.]. *Eltern und Kinder: Umwelteinflüsse auf das familiäre Verhalten* (Aged and children: environmental impacts on family behaviour). Stuttgart, Kohlhammer, 83, 229 p. [Germany FR]

3179 SHIMIZU, Shinji. "Gendai kazoku no mondai jokyo to sono kaikei: Kazoku byorigaku-teki sekkin" (The emergent family pathology in the current Japan: fact or fiction?), *Osaka shiritsu daigaku shakai fukushi ronshu* 19(20), 83 : 121-166.

3180 SHIMIZU, Yoshifumi. "Kazoku to shinzoku soshiki" (Family and kinship organization), *Soshioroji* 28(1), 83 : 33-55.

3181 SMITH, A. Wade. "Old fashioned families as an endangered species", *Social Indicators Research* 13(1), jul 83 : 17-38. [USA]

3182 SMITH, Allen G.; ROBBINS, Albert E. "Structured ethnography. The study of parental involvement", *American Behavioral Scientist* 26(1), sep-oct 82 : 45-61.

3183 SOMLAI, Péter. "A családi stabilitás kapcsolati szemlélete" (The interaction aspects of family stability), *Szociológia* 11(4), 82 : 503-520.

3184 SOTA, Carmen; ABALLEA, François. "La famille monoparentale: une marginalité en mutation", *Recherche sociale* (85), mar 83 : 3-53.

3185 STEFANILE, Claudio. "La famiglia tra continuita e mutamento: un'analisi del ruolo feminile" (Family between continuity and change: an anlysis of women's role), *Bolletino di psicologia applicata* (167), sep 83 : 13-23. [Italy]

3186 STOKES, C. Shannon; SCHUTJER, Wayne A.; POINDEXTER, John R. "A note on desired family size and contraceptive use in rural Egypt", *Journal of Biosocial Science* 15(1), jan 83 : 59-65.

3187 STRAUTYN', A.; JURCINJA, A. "Sem'ja v socialističeskom obščestve" (Family in the socialist society), *Naučnye Doklady vysšej Školy. Naučnyj Kommunizma* (1), 83 : 149-150.

3188 SUGAYA, Yoshiko. "Sedaikan kankei to life course bunseki: Noson sansedai kazoku chosa (sono 1)" (Intergenerational relations and life course analysis), *Miyagigakuin joshi daigaku kenkyu ronbunshu* 59, 83 : 1-20.

3189 TAKEUCHI, Takao. "Shoki hon-byakusho no kazoku kōzō to dōsokudan no hensei katei" (The family structure of the peasant in the early Tokugawa Era and the formation of Dozoku), *Kinjo gakuin daigaku ronshu* 101, 83 : 129-155.

3190 TAŠTEMIROV, V. *Sovremennaja socialističeskaja sem'ja i tendencii eě razvitija: iz opyta respublik Srednej Azii* (The contemporary socialist family and tendencies of its development: from the Central Asian republics experiment). Taškent, Fan, 82, 99 p.

3191 THRALL, Charles A. "Legal images of the family in the United States: an exercise in using law as data", *Population Research and Policy Review* 2(1), feb 83 : 53-65.

3192   TODD, Emmanuel. *La troisième planète: structures familiales et systèmes idéologiques*. Paris, Seuil, 83, 251 p.

3193   TOSCANO, Roberto. "Crisi della famiglia e ruolo delle donne in URSS" (Family crisis and women's role in USSR), *IDOC internazionale* 14(8-9), sep 83 : 22-30.

3194   TOTANI, Osamu. "Tonan Asia ni okeru kazoku Shinzoku no kozo" (Family and kinship structures in South East Asia), *Kinki daigaku Kindai fudo* 19, 83 : 84-92.

3195   TROVATO, Franck; HALLI, S. S. "Regional differences in family size: the case of the Atlantic provinces in Canada", *Rural Sociology* 48(2), sum 83 : 271-290.

3196   UMEZAWA, Sei. "Durkheim no kazokuron: Dotoku to kojin-shugi no kantenkara" (Durkheim's theory of families: from viewpoints of morals and individualism), *Shakaigaku-shi kenkyu* 5, 83 : 31-48.

3197   VILLAC, Michel. "Les structures familiales se transforment profondément", *Économie et Statistique* 152, feb 83 : 39-53. [France]

3198   VLASSOFF, Carol; VLASSOFF, Michael. "Family type and fertility in rural India: a critical analysis", *Journal of Biosocial Science* 15(4), oct 83 : 407-419.

3199   VORONINA, O. A. "Kritičeskij analiz metodologičeskih osnov sovremennoj amerikanskoj sociologii sem'i" (Critical analysis of methodological bases of the contemporary American sociology of the family), *in: Voprosy teorii i metodov sociologičeskih issledovanij*. Moskva, 1981 : 89-94.

3200   WATKINS, Carol R. *Victims, aggressors, and the family secret: an exploration into family violence*. S.l., MN, Minnesota Department of Public Welfare, 82, vi-148 p.

3201   WEINER, Nella Fermi. "Baby bust and baby boom: a study of family size in a group of University of Chicago Faculty wives born 1900-1934", *Journal of Family History* 8(3), 83 : 279-291. [USA]

3202   WEISS, Wolfgang W. *Familienstruktur und Selbständigkeitserziehung: ein empirischer Beitrag zur latenten politischen Sozialisation in der Familie* (Family structure and education of autonomy: an empirical contribution to latent political socialization in the family). Göttingen, Hogrefe, 82, xi-249 p.

3203   YAMAMOTO, Takeo. "Nichijo kosai kara mita social network" (Social network in family), *Soshioroji* 28(1), 83 : 77-95.

3204   YAMAMURA, Yoshiaki. *Nihon no oya, Nihon no katei* (Japanese parents, Japanese family). Tokyo, Kaneko Shobo, 83, 248 p.

3205   YUZAWA, Yasuhiko. "Hendosuru kazoku no kon'nichiteki tokushitsu" (Characteristics today of changing family), *Kateika kyoiku* 57(9), 83 : 5-14. [Japan]

3206   ZBIEG, Krystyna. "Badania ankietowe rodzin we Władysławowie" (Surveys on families in Władysławowo), *Biuletyn Instytutu Gospodarstwa Społecznego* 25(4), 82 : 154-169.

3207   ZIMMERMANN, Klaus F. "Humankapital, Kinderwunsch und Familiengrösse" (Human capital, desired children and family size), *Zeitschrift für Bevölkerungswissenschaft* 8(4), 82 : 547-558.

15440   Women's status
        Statut de la femme

3208   "Femme (La): des éléments pour un débat", *Cultures* 8(3), 82 : 101-169. [with contributions by Amal RASSAM, Leela DUBE, Scilla McLEAN]

3209   "Femmes (Les): quelavenir?", *Cultures* 8(4), 82 : 7-150. [with contributions by Amadou-Mahtar M'BOW, A. K. H. WEINRICH, Birgitta WISTRAND, Josefina Zoraida VASQUEZ, Christine FAURÉ]

3210   "Femmes de la Méditerranée", *Peuples Méditerranéens / Mediterranean Peoples* (22-23), jun 83 : 3-305. [with contributions by Khaoula MOKHTAR, Pepita CARPENA, Nicole BEAURAIN]

3211   "Passé et présent de la femme au Mexique", *Cultures* 8(3), 82 : 59-97. [with contributions by José AGUSTIN MAHIEU]

3212   "Weiblichkeit als soziales Konstrukt" (Femininity as a social construct), *Das Argument* 25(141), oct 83 : 653-696. [with contributions by Frigga HAUG, Jutta BRÜCKNER, Elizabeth FOX-GENOVESE]

3213   "Women and Blacks in literature and society", *Phylon* 44(1), mar 83 : 1-91. [with contributions by Leota S. LAWRENCE, Noel A. CAZENAVE]

3214   "Women in developing countries: a policy focus", *Women and Politics* 2(4), wint 82 : 1-128. [with contributions by Kathleen A. STAUDT, Jane S. JAQUETTE, T. BACHRACH EHLERS, Susan G. ROGERS, Rae LESSER BLUMBERE, Cara HINDERSTEIN]

3215   "Women in power spheres. Politics, the economy, social movements", *International Social Science Journal* 35(4), 83 : 569-755.

3216   "Women in Southern Africa", *Africa Report* 28(2), apr 83 : 4-19. [with contributions by Olivia MUCHENA, Ivy MATSEPE-CASABURIRI, Gwendoline KONIE, Eddison ZVOBGO, Gayle COOK ISAACS; continued in ibid. 45-55]

3217   ALEGRÍA, Juana Armanda. *Emancipación femenina en el subdesarrollo* (Women's emancipation in underdevelopment). México, Editorial Diana, 82, 213 p. [Latin America]

3218   ALIBAR, France; LEMBEYE-BOY, Pierrette; [et al.]. *'Le couteau seul sonde le fond des choses': la condition féminine aux Antilles / 'Sé kouto sèl ki sav sa ini an ké a jiromon'. I. Enfance et adolescence. II. Vies de femmes.* Paris, Éditions Caribéennes, 82, 199 p; 283 p.

3219   ALLEN, Michael; MUKHERJEE, S. N.; [eds.]. *Women in India and Nepal.* Canberra, Australian National University, 82, xiii-297 p.

3220   AMANO, Masako. "Josei no shakai sanka: 'Tsukau-gawa' kara 'Tsukuru-gawa' e" (Social participation of woman: from 'Consumer' to 'Creator'), *Toshi mondai kenkyu* 35(3), 83 : 72-87.

3221   ANDORS, Phyllis. *The unfinished liberation of Chinese women, 1949-1980.* Bloomington, IN, Indiana University Press; Brighton, Harvester Press, Wheatsheaf Books, 83, ix-212 p.

3222   ARIZPE, Lourdes. "Women and development in Latin America and the Caribbean: lessons from the seventies and hopes for the future", *Development Dialogue* (1-2), 82 : 74-84.

3223   ATSUMI, Ikuto. "Women's movements in contemporary Japan", *Equal Opportunities International* 2(1), 83 : 9-13.

3224   AUDIBERT, A. "La place et le rôle de la femme dans la famille et la société paysanne en Basse-Bretagne et particulièrement dans le Léon", *Recherches sociologiques* 14(2), 83 : 229-242.

3225   BACA ZINN, Maxine. "Mexican-American women in the social sciences", *Signs* 8(2), wint 82 : 259-272.

3226   BEHAINE DE CENDALES, Gladys. "La mujer colombiana: projección social de un determinismo" (The Colombian woman: social projection of a determinism), *Revista javeriana* 99(492), mar 83 : 145-151.

3227   BENALLÈGUE, Nora. "Algerian women in the struggle for independence and reconstruction", *International Social Science Journal* 35(4), 83 : 703-717.

3228   BHANDARI, R. K. *Educational development of women in India.* New Delhi, Ministry of Education and Culture, Government of India, 83, ii-109 p.

3229   BISILLIAT, Jeanne; FIELOUX, Michèle. *Femmes du Tiers-Monde: travail et quotidien.* Paris, Le Sycomore, 83, 122 p.

3230   BRENNER, Johanna; HOLMSTROM, Nancy. "Women's self organization: theory and strategy", *Monthly Review* 34(11), apr 83 : 34-46.

3231   BURGMANN, Meredith. "Black sisterhood: the situation of urban aboriginal women and their relationship to the White Women's Movement", *Politics* 17(2), nov 82 : 23-37.

3232   CARTWRIGHT, Rosalind L.; [et al.]. "The traditional-liberated woman dimension: social stereotype and self-concept", *Journal of Personality and Social Psychology* 44(3), mar 83 : 581-588.

3233   CESARE, Bianca Maria. "The woman in the Italian family in the light of socio-cultural conditioning", *Revue internationale de Sociologie* 18(1-2-3), apr-aug-sep 82 : 376-382.

3234   CHITNIS, Suma. "Women and development — not by constitutional guarantees or legal provisions alone", *Indian Journal of Social Work* 43(4), jan 83 : 401-417. [India]

3235   CLARKE, Jocelyn. "Losing the numbers game: women, tokenism and power", *Politics* 17(2), nov 82 : 45-51.

3236   COOK, Terrence E. " 'Misbegotten males'? Innate differences and stratified choice in the subjection of women", *Western Political Quarterly* 36(2), jun 83 : 194-220.

3237   CORBETT, Patricia. "Australian women and voting patterns: stability and change in the Ms Age", *Politics* 17(2), nov 82 : 70-77.

3238   COUTINHO-WIGGELENDAM, Anneke. "Women's emancipation around the turn of the century and the opposition to it. A comparative study of feminism and anti-feminism in the Netherlands from 1870 to 1919", *Netherlands Journal of Sociology* 19(2), oct 83 : 113-131.

3239   CURTIN, Leslie B. *Status of women: a comparative analysis of twenty developing countries.* Washington, DC, Population Reference Bureau, 82, 60 p.

3240   D'LIMA, Hazel. *Women in local government: a study of Maharashtra.* New Delhi, Concept, 83, 211 p.

3241   DI CRISTOFARO LONGO, Gioia. "Mouvements des femmes et partis politiques en Italie du XXᵉ siècle", *Cultures* 8(4), 82 : 131-150.

3242   DIXON, Marlène; [et al.]. "Chicanas and Mexicanas within a transnational working-class: theoretical perspectives", *Review (F. Braudel Center)* 7(1), sum 83 : 109-150.

3243   DOWSE, Sara. "The women's movement's Fandango with the State: some thoughts on the movement's role in public policy since 1972", *Australian Quarterly* 54(4), sum 82 : 324-345. [Australia]

3244   DUARTE, Isis; CORTEN, André. "Procesos de proletarización de mujeres en la República Dominica" (Women's proletarianization process in the Dominican Republic), *Archipelago* (2), nov 82 : 9-43. [résumés en anglais et en français]

3245   DUBE, Leela. "La recherche sur la femme en Indonésie", *Cultures* 8(3), 82 : 145-157.

3246   DUNAYEVSKAYA, Raya. *Rosa Luxemburg, women's liberation, and Marx's philosophy of revolution*. Atlantic Highlands, NJ, Humanities Press; Brighton, Sussex, Harvester Press, 82, xii-234 p.

3247   FERDOWS, Adele K. "Women and the islamic revolution", *International Journal of Middle East Studies* 15(2), mai 83 : 283-298.

3248   FITZGERALD, Maureen; GUBERMAN, Connie; WOLFE, Margie; [eds.]. *Still ain't satisfied! Canadian feminism today*. Toronto, ON, Women's Press, 82, 318 p.

3249   FLICK, Rachel. "The new feminism and the world of work", *Public Interest* (71), spr 83 : 33-44. [USA]

3250   GEIGER, Susan. "U moja wa wanawake wa Tanzania and the needs of the rural poor", *African Studies Review* 25(2-3), sep 82 : 45-65.

3251   GONZÁLEZ, Vinicio. "Diferencia e igualdad en la situación de la mujer: una aproximación a su estudio en Costa Rica" (Difference and equality in the situation of women: an approach to its study in Costa Rica), *Revista de Ciencias Sociales de la Universidad de Costa Rica* 25(1), 83 : 91-106.

3252   HERVÉ, Florence; [ed.]. *Geschichte der deutschen Frauenbewegung* (History of German women's movement). Köln, Pahl-Rugenstein, 82, 277 p.

3253   HOWARD, Rhoda. "Human rights and personal law: women in sub-saharan Africa", *Issue* 12(1-2), sum 82 : 45-52.

3254   IKEDA, Hideo. "Fujin no gakushu kikai no kakuju hosaku: Hiroshimaken Fukuyamashi ni okeru jkken kenkyu jigyo no chukan hokoku" (Experimental study to extend and improve the learning opportunities for young women in a community), *Shakai kyoiku* 38, 83 : 93-115. [Japan]

3255   INDERJEET, Kaur. *Status of the Hindu women in India*. Allahabad, Chugh Publications, 83, 116 p.

3256   JENSON, Jane. "The modern women's movement in Italy, France and Great Britain: differences in life cycles", *Comparative Social Research* 5, 82 : 341-375.

3257   KANDA, Michiko. "Kokuren-fujin no junen kohanki ni okeru fujin kyoiku no kadai" (Problems of women's education in the second half of the UN decade for women), *Toshi mondai kenkyu* 35(3), 83 : 58-71.

3258   KARIM, Wazir-jahan. "Malay women's movements: leadership and processes of change", *International Social Science Journal* 35(4), 83 : 719-731.

3259   KELLY, Gail P.; ELLIOTT, Carolyn M.; [eds.]. *Women's education in the Third World: comparative perspectives*. Albany, NY, University of New York Press, 82, ix-406 p.

3260   KIRKWOOD, Julieta. *La política del feminismo en Chile* (The politics of Chilean feminism). Santiago de Chile, FLACSO, 83, 24 p.

3261   LAWRENCE, Leota S. "Women in Caribbean literature: the African presence", *Phylon* 44(1), mar 83 : 1-11.

3262   LEWIS, J.; [ed.]. *Women's welfare, women's rights*. London, Croom Helm, 83, 225 p. [UK]

3263   MACAULEY, W. A. "Female representations on State grand juries: a case study with application of minority representation standards", *Women & Politics* 2(3), aut 82 : 23-32.

3264   MAJUPURIA, Indra. *Nepalese women: a vivid account of the status and role of Nepalese women in the total spectrum of life, religious, social, economic, political, and legal*. Kathmandu, M. Devi, 82, 304-64 p.

3265   MANOHAR, K. Murali; [ed.]. *Socio-economic status of Indian women*. Delhi, Seema, 83, 137 p.

3266   MARTIN, Patricia Yancey; HARRISON, Dianne; DINITTO, Diana. Advancement for women in hierarchical organizations: a multilevel analysis of problems and prospects. *Journal of Applied Behavioral Science* 19(1), 83 : 19-33. [USA]

3267   MASSIAH, Joycelin. *Les femmes chefs de ménage dans les Caraïbes: structures familiales et conditions de la femme*. Paris, UNESCO, 83, 65 p.

3268   MCALLISTER, Pam; [ed.]. *Reweaving the web of life: feminism and nonviolence*. Philadelphia, PA, New Society Publishers, 82, viii-440 p. [USA]

3269   MCDONAGH, Eileen L. "Profiles of achievement: women's entry into the professions, the arts, and social reform", *Sociological Inquiry* 53(4), 83 : 343-367. [USA]

3270   MCDONALD, Flora. "The status and economic prospects of women in Canada", *Queen's Quarterly* 90(3), aug 83 : 655-662.

3271   MCELROY, Wendy; [eds.]. *Freedom, feminism, and the state: an overview of individualist feminism*. Washington, DC, Cato Institute, 82, xi-357 p.

3272   MEHTA, Sushila. *Revolution and the status of women in India*. New Delhi, Metropolitan, 82, vi-278 p.

3273   MENGOLI, Giovanna. "Collocazione della donna nell'ambiente marocchino contemporaneo" (Woman's place in present-day Morocco), *Studi di Sociologia* 21(2), apr-jun 83 : 190-197.

3274   MISZTAL, Barbara A. "Perspektywa feministyczna w socjologii amerykańskiej" (Feministic perspective in the American sociology), *Studia Socjologiczne* 90 (3), 83 : 195-208.

3275   MOSSUZ-LAVAU, Janine; SINEAU, Mariette. *Enquête sur les femmes et la politique en France.* Paris, Presses Universitaires de France, 83, 280 p.

3276   MOTROSHILOVA, Nelya V. "Soviet women in the life of society: achievements and problems", *International Social Science Journal* 35(4), 83 : 733-746.

3277   MUELLER, Carol. "Feminism and the new women in public office", *Women and Politics* 2(3), aut 82 : 7-21.

3278   MUKHERJEE, S. N.; [ed.]. *Women in India and Nepal.* Canberra, Australian National University, 82, xii-297 p.

3279   MURALI MANOHAR, K.; [ed.]. *Socio-economic status of Indian women.* Delhi, Seema Publications, 83, xii-137 p.

3280   MUTWE-KARWERA, Spérancie. "Problèmes de la femme et de la famille dans la société actuelle en Afrique", *Cahiers européens* (46), jun 82 : 65-77.

3281   NAVE-HERZ, Rosemarie. *Die Geschichte der Frauenbewegung in Deutschland* (The history of women movement in Germany). Hannover, Niedersächsische Landeszentrale für Politische Bildung, 82, 80 p.

3282   NELSON, Margaret K. "Working class women, middle-class women, and models of childbirth", *Social Problems* 30(3), feb 83 : 284-297.

3283   OLSEN, Frances E. "The family and the market: a study of ideology and legal reform", *Harvard Law Review* 96(7), mai 83 : 1497-1578.

3284   ORGANISATION DES FEMMES DE L'UNION NATIONALE DU CAMEROUN. *Intégration de la femme camerounaise dans le processus de développement économique* (Integration of the Cameroon women in the economic development processus). Yaoundé, OFUNC, 82, 151 p.

3285   OTTO, Ingeborg; SCHMIDT-DUMONT, Marianne. *Frauenfragen im Modernen Orient: eine Auswahlbibliographie* (Women in the Middle East and North Africa: a selected bibliography). Hamburg, Deutsches Orient-Institut, Dokumentations-Leitstelle Moderner Orient, 82, xv-247 p.

3286   PAGLIARI, Marcella Pompili. "Condizione femminile e organizzazione familiare nell'Italia meridionale. Ipotesi per une ricerca sulla soggettivitá della donna nel lavoro" (Women's status and family organization in Southern Italy. Assumptions for a research on Women's subjectivity in work), *Revue internationale de Sociologie* 18(1-2-3), apr-aug-sep 82 : 396-410.

3287   PAQUOT, Elisabeth; [ed.]. *Terre des femmes: panorama de la situation des femmes dans le monde.* Paris, la Découverte-Maspéro, 83, 448 p.

3288   PONOMARENKO, N. P. "Kul'turno-nravstvennye aspekty ženskogo ravnopravlja" (Cultural and moral aspects of the women's equality of rights), *Sbornik Naučnyh Trudov (Leningradskij Institut Kultury)* 57, 81 : 75-88. [USSR]

3289   RANSFORD, H. Edward; MILLER, Jon. "Race, sex and feminist outlooks", *American Sociological Review* 48(1), feb 83 : 46-59.

3290   RAO, N. J. Usha. *Women in a developing society.* New Delhi, Ashish, 83, 180 p. [India]

3291   RASHEDI, Khorram. *Les femmes en Iran avant et après la révolution.* Paris, Nouvelles Éditions Rupture, 83, 198 p.

3292   RASSAM, Amal. "Vers l'élaboration d'un cadre théorique pour l'étude de la condition féminine dans le monde arabe", *Cultures* 8(3), 82 : 127-144.

3293   RIZZA, Carolyn. "Women's status and fertility in Finland", *Yearbook of Population Research in Finland* 21, 1983 : 130-141.

3294   ROSEMBERG, Fúlvia; PINTO, Regiona P.; NEGRÃO, Esmeralda Vailati. *A educação da mulher no Brasil* (Women's education in Brazil). São Paulo, SP, Global Editora, 82, 112 p.

3295   SAHA, S. C. "Roles and status of women in a traditional African setting: a study of women in Liberia", *Africa Quarterly* 22(1), 82 : 25-33.

3296   SAPIRO, Virginia. *The political integration fo women: roles, socialization, and politics.* Urbana, IL, University of Illinois Press, 82, 205 p.

3297   SCHWARZENBERG, Claudio. *Condizione della donna e lavoro femminile in Italia* (Women's status and female labour in Italy). Milano, Giuffrè, 82, 164 p.

3298   SHARMA, Arvind. "Hindu religious reformers as feminists: paradox or hypocrisy?", *Asian Profile* 11(2), apr 83 : 195-199.

3299   SHAUL, Mernie S. "The status of women in local governments: an international assessment", *Public Administration Review* 42(6), dec 82 : 491-500.

3300   SHOEMAKER, Susan. "The status of women in the rural USSR", *Population Research and Policy Review* 2(1), feb 83 : 35-51.

3301   SIEVERS, Sharon L. *Flowers in salt: the beginnings of feminist consciousness in modern Japan.* Stanford, CA, Stanford University Press, 83, xiv-240 p.

3302   SMITH, Robert J. "Making village women into 'good wives and wise mothers' in prewar Japan", *Journal of Family History* 8(1), 83 : 70-84.

3303   TABARI, Azar. "The rise of Islam: what did happen to women?", *Khamsin* (10), 83 : 59-72.
3304   THIAM, Awa. "Women's fight for the abolition of sexual mutilation", *International Social Science Journal* 35(4), 83 : 747-756.
3305   VAN DOORNE-HUISKES, J.; VAN DOORNE-HUISKES, Anneke. *De sociale positie van vrouwen* (The social position of women). Deventer, Van Loghum slaterus, 82, 94 p. [Netherlands]
3306   VASQUEZ, Josefina Zoraida. "L'émancipation des femmes en Amérique latine: pour une histoire du présent", *Cultures* 8(4), 82 : 91-111.
3307   VINCI, Elena. "La donna nella Pubblica Amministrazione: l'impiego del tempo libero" (Woman in public administration: leisure utilization), *Revue internationale de Sociologie* 18(1-2-3), apr-aug-sep 82 : 411-442. [Italy]
3308   WALMSLEY, Robyn. "Women, feminism and the political process", *Politics* 17(2), nov 82 : 65-69.
3309   WARD, Kathryn B. "The economic status of women in the world-system: a hidden crisis in development", *Political Economy of the World System Annuals* 6, 83 : 117-139.
3310   WARD, Margaret. *Unmanageable revolutionaries: women and Irish nationalism.* London, Pluto Press, 83, ix-296 p.
3311   WEINBERG, Martin S.; [et al.]. "Sexual autonomy and the status of women: models of female sexuality in U.S. sex manuals form 1950 t0 1980", *Social Problems* 30(3), feb 83 : 312-324.
3312   WEINRICH, A. K. H. "Evolution du rôle politique et économique de la femme au Zimbabwe depuis l'indépendance", *Cultures* 8(4), 82 : 47-68.
3313   WHIP, Rosemary. "The parliamentary wife: participant in the 'two-person single career' ", *Politics* 17(2), nov 82 : 38-44.
3314   YOUNG, Sheila; SMITH, Sheila. "Women's disadvantage: capitalist development and socialist alternatives in Britain", *Development Dialogue* (1-2), 82 : 85-100.
3315   ZEPHIR, Jacques J. "Néo-féminisme et socialisme selon Simone de Beauvoir", *Contemporary French Civilization* 7(3), spr 83 : 293-315.

15500   **ETHNIC GROUPS**
         GROUPES ETHNIQUES

15510   **Ethnicity. Tribes**
         Ethnicité. Tribus

3316   "Black experience in the United States", *Social Problems* 30(4), apr 83 : 369-409. [with contributions by Sharon M. COLLINS, William H. EXUM, Richard E. BALL]
3317   "Cuestión (La) étnica en America latina" (The ethnic question in Latin America), *Revista mexicana de ciencias politicas y sociales* 27(103), mar 81 : 5-260. [with contributions by Miguel Alberto BARTOLOME, Darcy RIBEIRO, Georg GRUNBERG, Alicia M. BARABAS, Eva SALVADOR HERNANDEZ, Víctor TOLEDO]
3318   "Étrangers (Les) qui sont aussi la France", *Projet* (171-172), feb 83 : 1-155. [with contributions by Jean-Louis SCHLEGEL, Antonio PEROTTI, Abel JEANNIÈRE, Michel SERAIN, Pierre EWENCZYK, Jean-Pierre GARSON, Yves DUEL]
3319   "Gli stranieri in Svizzera" (Foreigners in Switzerland), *Affari sociali internazionali* 11(2), 83 : 101-132. [with contributions by Silvana RAFFAEL, Franco PITTAU, Benedetto PETRIS, Aldo VALEO, Vittorio GAZZERO]
3320   "Minorités, ethnicité, mouvements nationalitaires", *Pluriel* (32-33), 83 : 3-149. [with contributions by Pierre-Jean SIMON, Louis QUERE, Wanda DRESSLER-HOLOHAN]
3321   "Nacionalidades (Las) indígenas en México" (Indigenous nationalities in Mexico), *Revista mexicana de ciencias politicas y sociales* 25(97), sep 79 : 5-193. [with contributions by Alicia M. BARABAS, Miguel A. BARTOLOME, Franco Gabriel HERNANDEZ, Laura COLLINS, Felix BAEZ JORGE, Gabina Aurora PEREZ JIMENEZ, M. Arten E. R. G. N. JANSEN]
3322   *North and north-eastern frontier tribes of India.* Delhi, Cultural Publishing House, 83, iv-249 p.
3323   AGHAJANIAN, Akbar. "Ethnic inequality in Iran: an overview", *International Journal of Middle East Studies* 15(2), mai 83 : 211-224.
3324   ALBA, Richard D.; CHAMLIN, Mitchell B. "A preliminary explanation of ethnic identification among Whites", *American Sociological Review* 48(2), apr 83 : 241-247. [USA]
3325   ANDERSON, Barbara A. "Estimating russification of ethnic identity among non-Russians in the USSR", *Demography* 20(4), nov 83 : 461-490.
3326   ANESHENSEL, Carol S.; [et al.]. "Race, ethnicity, and depression: a confirmatory analysis", *Journal of Personality and Social Psychology* 44(2), feb 83 : 385-398.

3327   ANTHIAS, Floya; AYRES, Ron. "Ethnicity and class in Cyprus", *Race and Class* 25(1), sum 83 : 59-76.

3328   BERNDT, Ronald Murray; [ed.]. *Aboriginal sites, rights, and resource development*. Perth, University of Western Australia Press, 82, xii-256 p.

3329   BRAUEN, Martin; KANTOWSKY, Detlef; [eds.]. *Junge Tibeter in der Schweiz: Studien zum Prozess kultureller Identifikation: Gemeinschaftsprojekt der Universität Konstanz und des Völkerkundemuseums der Universität Zürich* (Young Tibetans in Switzerland: studies on the process of cultural identification: collective project of the University of Constance and the Ethnology Museum of the University of Zurich). Diessenhofen, Rüegger, 82, 259-23-8 p.

3330   BROMLEI, Youlian. "Les processus ethniques dans le monde contemporain", *Sciences sociales — Académie des Sciences de l'URSS* 51(1), 83 : 104-120.

3331   BROMLEJ, Ju. "Ětničeskie processy SSSR" (Ethnic processes in the USSR), *Kommunist (Moskva)* 59(5), mar 83 : 56-64.

3332   BULIMAR, M. "Înşemnări despre rasă si cultură" (Considerations on race and culture), *Revista de filozofie* 30(3), jun 83 : 203-209.

3333   CASHMORE, Ernest. "The champions of failure: black sportsmen", *Ethnic and Racial Studies* 6(1), jan 83 : 90-102. [UK]

3334   CAZEMAJOU, Jean; MARTIN, Jean-Pierre. *La crise du melting-pot: ethnicité et identité aux États-Unis de Kennedy á Reagan*. Paris, Aubier Montaigne, 83, 189 p.

3335   COHEN, Percy S. "Ethnicity, class and political alignment in Israel", *Jewish Journal of Sociology* 24(2), dec 83 : 119-130.

3336   DRAKAKIS-SMITH, David. "Des villes comme Alice... conflit de races, conflit de classes en Australie aborigène", *Espace géographique* 12(1), mar 83 : 5-17.

3337   DUBET, François. "Le populisme occitan, rapports entre militants et sociologues", *Pluriel* (32-33), 83 : 113-118.

3338   DUMON, Wilfried A. *Het profiel van de vreemdelingen in België* (Foreigners' profile in Belgium). Leuven, Davidsfonds, 82, 144 p.

3339   EIPPER, Chris. "The magician's hat: a critique of the concept of ethnicity", *Australian and New Zealand Journal of Sociology* 19(3), nov 83 : 427-446.

3340   ESSER, Elke. *Ausländerinnen in der Bundesrepublik Deutschland: eine soziologische Analyse des Eingliederungsverhaltens ausländischer Frauen* (Foreign women in the Federal Republic of Germany: a sociological analysis of their integration behaviour). Frankfurt-am-Main, R. G. Fischer, 82, 229 p.

3341   FEATHERMAN, Sandra. "Ethnicity and ethnic candidates: vote advantages in local elections", *Polity* 15(3), spr 83 : 397-415. [USA]

3342   FEDOSEEV, P. N. "Real'nyj socializm i ukreplenie družby narodov: k 60-letiju Sojuza SSR" (Real socialism and the reinforcement of people's friendship: to the 60th anniversary of the USSR),, 1982 : 131-166.

3343   FILLA, Wilhelm; [et al.]. *Am Rande Österreichs: ein Beitrag zur Soziologie der österreichischen Volksgruppen* (At the edge of Austria: an essay on the sociology of Austrian ethnic groups). Wien, W. Braunmüller, 82, viii-126 p.

3344   FILLA, Willa; [et al.]. "Soziologie der nationalen Minderheiten in Österreich" (Sociology of national minorities in Austria), *Journal für Sozialforschung* 22(4), 82 : 462-469.

3345   FLORES, Maegarita; LEÓN, Arturo. "Los indígenas hoy" (Indigenes today), *Investigación económica* 42(163), jan-mar 83 : 27-64. [Mexico]

3346   GUPTA, R. K. "The tribals in India", *Eastern Anthropologist* 35(4), oct-dec 82 : 309-318.

3347   GUZMAN BOCKLER, Carlos. "Memoria colectiva, identidad histórica y conciencia étnica en Guatemala" (Collective memory, historical identity and ethnic consciousness in Guatemala), *Revista mexicana de ciencias politicas y sociales* 27(103), mar 81 : 193-208.

3348   HERAUD, Guy. "Les Slovènes d'Autriche et d'Italie", *Plural Societies* 13(1-4), 82 : 127-141.

3349   HINTON, Peter. "Where have the new ethnicists gone wrong?", *Australian and New Zealand Journal of Sociology* 17(3), nov 81 : 14-19.

3350   HIRSCHMAN, Charles. "America's melting pot reconsidered", *Annual Review of Sociology* (9), 83 : 397-423.

3351   HRABA, Joseph; HOIBERG, Eric. "Ideational origins of modern theories of ethnicity: individual freedom vs. organizational growth", *Sociological Quarterly* 24(3), sum 83 : 381-391.

3352   JUTEAU-LEE, Danielle; [ed.]. "Enjeux ethniques. Production de nouveaux rapports sociaux", *Sociologie et Sociétés* 15(2), oct 83 : 3-174. [Canada]

3353   KIM, Eung-Ryul. "Zaikan nihonjin-zuma no hinkon to seikatsu fuan" (Poverty and anxiety of the Japanese minority in Korea), *Shakai ronengaku* 17, 83 : 67-82.

3354   KOENS, M. J. C. *Jeugdige vreemdelingen in Nederland* (Young foreigners in the Netherlands). Arnhem, Gouda Quint, 83, xix-373 p.

3355   KRAUS, Vered. "Ethnic origin as a hierarchical dimension of social status, and its correlates", *Sociology and Social Research* 66(4), jul 82 : 452-466. [Israel]

3356   LEMARCHAND, René. "The politics of Sara ethnicity: a note on the origins of the civil war in Chad", *Cahiers d'Études africaines* 20(4), 80 : 449-471.

3357   LIEBERMAN, Leonard; [et al.]. "Institutional and socio-cultural influences on the debate over Race", *Catalyst* (15), 83 : 45-63. [USA]

3358   LIEGEOIS, Jean-Pierre. "Associationnisme et gestion des minorités. En France, le 'Bureau des Affaires tsiganes' et ses associations adhérentes", *Pluriel* (31), 82 : 65-88.

3359   MAEYAMA, Takashi. "Religion, kinship, and the middle classes of the Japanese in Urban Brazil", *Tsukuba daigaku Latin American Studies* 5, 83 : 57-82.

3360   MCCORQUODALE, John. "Aborigines in the High Court", *Australian Quarterly* 55(1), aut 83 : 104-113. [Australia]

3361   MEDINA, Manuel. "Minority problems in democratic Spain", *Plural Societies* 13(1-4), 82 : 41-46.

3362   MOMENI, Jamshid A. *Demography of the Black population in the United States: an annotated bibliography with a review essay.* Westport, CT-London, Greenwood Press, 83, xxi-354 p.

3363   MOODLEY, Kogila. "Canadian multiculturalism as idelogy", *Ethnic and Racial Studies* 6(3), jul 83 : 320-331.

3364   MORRISON, Minion K. C. "Ethnicity and integration: dynamics of change and resilience in contemporary Ghana", *Comparative Political Studies* 15(4), jan 83 : 445-468.

3365   NAGEL, Joane; OLZAK, Susan. "Ethnic mobilization in new and old States: an extension of the competition model", *Social Problems* 30(2), dec 82 : 127-143.

3366   NELSON, Dale C. "Assimilation, acculturation and political participation", *Polity* 15(1), aut 82 : 26-47. [ethnic minorities in the USA]

3367   OLZAK, Susan. "Contemporary ethnic mobilization", *Annual Review of Sociology* (9), 83 : 355-374.

3368   PATHY, Jaganath. "Politics of tribal welfare: some reflections", *Eastern Anthropologist* 35(4), oct-dec 82 : 285-300. [India]

3369   PAVLENKO, Ju. K. "K voprosu ob uslovijah formirovanija ětnosa i ětničeskih svojstv" (Question on conditions of the 'ethnos' formation and ethnical characteristics), *in: Metodologičeskie i metodičeskie voprosy arheologii.* Kiev, 1982 : 75-85.

3370   PETROVIĆ, Ruža. "The national composition of the population", *Yugoslav Survey* 24(3), aug 83 : 21-34.

3371   PRUNIER, Gérard A. "Structures ethniques et système politique en Ouganda", *Cultures et développement* 14(2-3), 82 : 365-391.

3372   REITERER, Albert F. "Die Ethnie als Problem der Nationenbildung. Entwicklungstheoretische Überlegungen" (Ethnicity as a problem of nation formation. Thoughts on development theories), *Dritte Welt* 9(3-4), 81 : 410-419.

3373   ROBERTS, H. J. R. "The economics of Berberism: the material basis of the Kabyle question in contemporary Algeria", *Government and Opposition* 18(2), spr 82 : 218-235.

3374   SELINTAR, Ofira. "National integration of a minority in an acute conflict situation: the case of Israeli Arabs", *Plural Societies* 12(3-4), wint 81 : 25-40.

3375   SERBIN, Andrés. "Estado, indigenismo e indianidad en Venezuela 1946-1979" (State, indigenism and indianism in Venezuela, 1946-1979), *Boletín de Estudios latinoamericanos y del Caribe* (34), jun 83 : 17-40.

3376   SHAMSH, Shamsuddin. *Meos of India: their customs and laws.* New Delhi, Deep and Deep, 83, 211 p.

3377   SIDMU, Manjit S. "Sikhs in peninsular Malaysia: their distribution and occupations", *Asian Profile* 11(3), jun 83 : 293-307.

3378   SKIDMORE, Thomas E. "Race and class in Brazil: historical perspectives", *Luso-Brazilian Review* 20(1), sum 83 : 104-118.

3379   SMOOHA, Sammy. "Minority responses in a plural society: a typology of the Arabs in Israel", *Sociology and Social Research* 67(4), jul 83 : 436-456.

3380   VAN DEN BERGHE, Pierre L. "Australia, Canada and the United States: ethnic melting pots or plural societies?", *Australian and New Zealand Journal of Sociology* 19(2), jul 83 : 238-252.

3381   VAN DER BERGHE, Pierre L. "Class, race and ethnicity in Africa", *Ethnic and Racial Studies* 6(2), apr 83 : 221-236.

3382   VAN DIJK, Teun Adrianus. *Minderheden in de media: een analyse van de berichtgeving over etnische minderheden in de dagbladpers* (Minorities in the media: an analysis of articles on ethnic minorities in daily press). Amsterdam, SUA, 83, 168 p. [Netherlands]

3383   WEIMANN, Gabriel. "The not-so-small world: ethnicity and acquaintance networks in Israel", *Social Networks* 5(3), sep 83 : 289-302.

3384   WU, David Y. H.; [ed.]. *Etnicity and interpersonal interaction: a cross cultural study.* S.l., Maruzen Asia, 82, 307 p.

3385   YOSHINO, I. Roger. "The Buraku minority of Japan", *Patterns of Prejudice* 17(1), jan 83 : 39-47.

3386   YOUNG, Crawford. "The temple of ethnicity", *World Politics* 35(4), jul 83 : 652-662.

15520   Interethnic relations. Racism
Relations interethniques. Racisme

3387   "Antisemitism today: a symposium", *Patterns of Prejudice* 16(4), oct 82 : 3-52.

3388   "Antisémitisme (L')", *Conscience et liberté* (24), sem. 2, 82 : 24-175. [with contributions by Jean HALPERIN, M. Th. HOCH, Jacob M. LANDAU]

3389   "Current research on racial and ethnic segregation", *Social Science Quarterly* 63(4), dec 82 : 674-770. [with contributions by Douglas LONGSHORE, David R. MORGAN, Robert E. ENGLAND, Guadalupe SAN MIGUEL Jr., Louis G. POL]

3390   ADAM, Heribert. "Combatting racism", *Queen's Quarterly* 89(4), wint 82 : 785-793.

3391   BANTON, Michael. "The influence of colonial status upon black-white relations in England, 1948-1958", *Sociology (London)* 17(4), nov 83 : 546-559.

3392   BOLCE, Louis. "Why people riot", *Policy Review* (22), oct 82 : 119-140.

3393   BONACICH, Edna. "Capitalism and race relations in South Africa: a split labor market analysis", *Political Power and Social Theory* 2, 81 : 239-277.

3394   BROWN, Paula. "Chimbu disorder: tribal fighting in newly independent New Guinea", *Pacific Viewpoint* 23(1), mai 82 : 1-21.

3395   BURAWOY, Michael. "The capitalist State in South Africa: marxist and sociological perspectives on race and class", *Political Power and Social Theory* 2, 81 : 279-335.

3396   BUTLER, Richard J. "Direct estimates of the demand for race and sex discrimination", *Southern Economic Journal* 49(4), apr 83 : 975-990. [USA]

3397   CHAHNAZARIAN, Anouch; MEYER, Jean-Luc de. "Le racisme, mythe et sciences", *Revue de l'Institut de Sociologie* (3-4), 82 : 527-540.

3398   COMBS, Micheal W.; COMER, John C. "Race and capital punishment: a longitudinal analysis", *Phylon* 43(4), dec 82 : 350-359.

3399   DEBROEY, Steven. *Zuid-Afrika naar de bronnen van de apartheid* (The roots of Apartheid in South Africa). Kasterlee, De Vroente, 82, 620 p.

3400   DENEMARK, Robert A.; LEHMAN, Howard P. "The political economy of repression and reform in South Africa", *Africa Today* 29(3), trim. 3, 82 : 5-31.

3401   DU TOIT, André. "Facing up to the future: some personal reflections on the predicament of Afrikaner intellectuals in the legitimation crisis of Afrikaner nationalism and the apartheid state", *Social Dynamics* 7(2), dec 81 : 1-27.

3402   FENDRICH, James Max. "Race and ethnic relations: the elite policy response in capitalist societies", *American Behavioral Scientist* 26(6), jul-aug 83 : 757-772.

3403   FILSON, Glen. "Class and ethnic differences in Canadians' attitudes to native people's rights and immigration", *Canadian Review of Sociology and Anthropology* 20(4), nov 83 : 454-482.

3404   GABEL, Joseph. "Racisme et aliénation", *Praxis International* 2(4), jan 83 : 421-437. [résumé en anglais]

3405   GAERTNER, Samuel L.; MCLAUGHLIN, John P. "Racial stereotypes: associations and acriptions of positive and negative characteristics", *Social Psychology Quarterly* 46(1), mar 83 : 23-30.

3406   GALE, Thomas S. "Segregation in British West Africa", *Cahiers d'Études africaines* 20(4), 80 : 495-507.

3407   GORDON, Leonard. "Aftermath of a race riot: the emergent norm process among Black and White community leaders", *Sociological Perspectives* 26(2), apr 83 : 115-135.

3408   GREENBERG, Stanley B. "Race and business enterprise in Alabama", *Political Power and Social Theory* 2, 81 : 203-238.

3409   HACK, H. "Land problems in the Paraguayan Chaco", *Boletín de Estudios latinoamericanos y del Caribe* (34), jun 83 : 99-115.

3410   HILL, Richard J. "Minorities, women, and institutional change: some administrative concerns", *Sociological Perspectives* 26(1), jan 83 : 17-28. [USA]

3411   INSKO, Chester A.; NACOSTE, Rupert W.; MOE, Jeffrey L. "Belief congruence and racial discrimination: review of the evidence and critical evaluation", *European Journal of Social Psychology* 13(2), apr-jun 83 : 153-174.

3412   IRIS, Mark. "American urban riots revisited", *American Behavioral Scientist* 26(3), jan-feb 83 : 333-352. [USA]

3413   KAWE-BERMAN, John. "Population removal, displacement and divestment in South Africa", *Social Dynamics* 7(2), dec 81 : 28-46.

3414   KLINAR, Peter. "Sociološki prilog razotkrivanju i prerastanju kriznih pojava u među-
        nacionalnim odnosima" (A sociological contribution to the identification and overcoming
        of crises in inter-ethnic relations), *Revija za Sociologiju* 11(3-4), 81 : 153-166. [résumé
        en anglais]

3415   KLUEGEL, James R.; SMITH, Eliot R. "Affirmative action attitudes: effects of self-
        interest, racial affect, and stratification beliefs on whites' views", *Social Forces* 61(3),
        mar 83 : 797-824.

3416   LEVIN, Michael. "Is racial discrimination special?", *Policy Review* (22), oct 82 : 85-95.

3417   LUNDAHL, Mats. "The rationale of apartheid", *American Economic Review* 72(5), dec
        82 : 1169-1179.

3418   MARIN, Bernd. "Antisemitismus in Österreich 1968-1982" (Antisemitism in Austria
        1968-1982), *Journal für Sozialforschung* 23(1), 83 : 75-106. [cont. in ibid. 23 (2), 1983 : 205-244]

3419   MARINOVA, V. M. "'JOAR': cvetnoj bar'er" (South Africa: barrier of colour), *Narody
        Azii i Afriki* (1), jan-feb 83 : 19-29.

3420   MARRUS, Michael R. "French antisemitism in the 1980s", *Patterns of Prejudice* 17(2),
        apr 83 : 3-20.

3421   MARTY, Michel. "Les relations inter-raciales dans les quartiers à forte densité d'immigrés",
        Hommes et Migrations 34(1052), 15 jun 83 : 14-26. Documents

3422   NEWBURY, Catherine M. "Colonialism, ethnicity, and rural political protest: Rwanda
        and Zanzibar in comparative perspective", *Comparative Politics* 15(3), apr 83 : 253-280.

3423   NITOBURG, É. L. "Rasizm v SŠA" (Racism in the USA), *in: Rasy i obščestvo*. Moskva,
        1982 : 220-244.

3424   NIXON, Jaqi. "The Home Office and race relations policy: coordinator and initiator",
        Journal of Public Policy 2(4), oct 82 : 365-378. [UK]

3425   ORBACH, William W. "Major themes of Soviet antisemitism", *Crossroads* (10), spr 83 : 217-243.

3426   ORLOVÁ, Helena. "Onderzoek naar etnische segregatie in Rotterdam: een ritiek"
        (Research on ethnic segregation in Rotterdam: a review), *Sociologische Gids* 30(2), mar-apr
        83 : 131-143.

3427   PATCHEN, Martin. "Students' own racial attitudes and those of peers of both races, as
        related to interracial behaviors", *Sociology and Social Research* 68(1), oct 83 : 59-77. [USA]

3428   PERLMUTTER, Nate; PERLMUTTER, Ruth Ann. *The real anti-Semitism in America*.
        New York, NY, Arbor House, 82, 303 p.

3429   PRIOR, Andrew; [ed.]. *Catholics in apartheid society*. Cape Town, D. Philip, 82, x-197 p.

3430   PUSHKIN, Isidore; NORBURN, Veronica. "Ethnic preferences in young children and
        in their adolescence in three London districts", *Human Relations* 36(4), apr 83 : 309-344.

3431   RAY, John J. "Racial attitudes and the contact hypothesis", *Journal of Social Psychology* 119(1),
        feb 83 : 3-10.

3432   RECORD, Wilson. "Race and ethnic relations: the conflict continues. A review essay",
        Sociological Quarterly 24(1), wint 83 : 137-149. [USA]

3433   RICH, Paul. "Landscape, social darwinism and the cultural roots of South-African racial
        ideology", *Patterns of Prejudice* 17(3), jul 83 : 9-16.

3434   RUBENS, Monique. "Combating apartheid", *Africa Report* 28(4), aug 83 : 47-52.

3435   RUDDER, Véronique de; TABOADA-LEONETTI, Isabelle. "La cohabitation pluri-
        ethnique: espace collectif, phénomènes minoritaires et relations sociales", *Pluriel* (31),
        82 : 37-54.

3436   SAADI, Mustapha. "Cohabitation et relations intertehniques: la Goutte d'Or à Paris",
        Pluriel (31), 82 : 55-64.

3437   SCHNAPPER, Eric. "Perpetuation of past discrimination", *Harvard Law Review* 96(4),
        feb 83 : 828-864. [USA]

3438   SCHUMAN, Edward; [et al.]. "Discriminatory behavior in New York restaurants: 1950
        and 1981", *Social Indicators Research* 13(1), jul 83 : 69-83.

3439   SEKELJ, Laslo. "Antisemitizam u Jugoslaviji (1918-1945)" (Antisemitism in Yugoslavia,
        1919-1945), *Revija za Sociologiju* 11(3-4), 81 : 179-189.

3440   SELIGSON, Mitchell A.; CASPI, Dan. "Arabs in Israel: political tolerance and ethnic
        conflict", *Journal of Applied Behavioral Science* 19(1), 83 : 55-66.

3441   SMITH, Althea; STEWART, Abigail J.; [eds.]. "Racism, sexism in black women's lives",
        Journal of Social Issues 39(3), 83 : 1-139. [USA]

3442   STEWART, Mark B. "Racial discrimination and occupational attainment in Britain",
        Economic Journal 93(371), sep 83 : 521-541.

3443   SZUPEJKO, Magorzata. "The contemporary State and the traditions of tribal State system:
        case study of Uganda and Buganda", *Revue française d'Histoire d'Outre-mer* 68(250-253),
        81 : 430-435. [résumé en français]

3444   TERGEIST, Peter. *Schwarze Bewegung und Gettoaustände: Strukturen rassischer Gewalt in den USA* (The Black movement and the ghetto rebellions: structures of the racial force in the USA). Frankfurt-am-Main, R. G. Fischer, 82, v-319 p.

3445   TOKAREV, S. A. "Rasistskie teorii XIX-načala XX v." (Racist theories in the XIXth century and the beginning of the XXth century), *in: Rasy i obščestvo.* Moskva, 1982 : 21-33.

3446   TRLIN, Andrew D. "The New Zealand race relations Act: conciliators, conciliation and complaints (1972-1981)", *Political Science* 34(2), dec 82 : 170-193.

3447   UNESCO. *Racisme, science et pseudo-science.* Paris, UNESCO, 83, 162 p. [Colloque réuni en vue de l'examen des différentes théories pseudo-scientifiques invoquées pour justifier le racisme et la discrimination raciale, Athènes, 30 mars-3 avril 1981]

3448   VAN HARTESVELDT, Fred R. "Race and political parties in Britain, 1954-1965", *Phylon* 44(2), jun 83 : 126-134.

3449   VOGT, Hermann. *Apartheid und Unterentwicklung: Möglichkeiten und Strategien gesellschaftlicher Veränderung in Südafrika* (Apartheid and underdevelopment: social change possibilities and strategies in South Africa). Frankfurt-am-Main, Campus, 82, 331 p.

3450   WARD, Russell A. "The stability of racial differences across age strata", *Sociology and Social Research* 67(3), apr 83 : 312-323.

3451   WILSON, Stephen. *Ideology and experience: antisemitism in France at the time of the Dreyfus affair.* Rutherford, NJ, Fairleigh Dickinson University Press; London, Associated University Press, 82, xviii-812 p.

3452   WILSON, Thomas C. "White response to neighborhood racial change", *Sociological Focus* 16(4), oct 83 : 305-318. [USA]

15600   MIGRATION
MIGRATION

15610   Migrants. Migration policy
Migrants. Politique migratoire

3453   "Donna (La) nei fenomeni migratori" (Woman in migratory phenomena), *Studi Emigrazione* 20(70), jun 83 : 130-247. [with contributions by Mirjana MOROKVASIC, Catherine WIHTOL DE WENDEN, Gioyanna BRUNETTA]

3454   "Femmes (Les) migrantes: bibliographie internationale (1965-1982)", *Studi Emigrazione* 19(68), dec 82 : 451-512.

3455   BAYDAR, Nazli. *Analysis of the temporal stability of migration patterns in the context of multiregional forecasting.* Voorburg, Netherlands International Demographic Institute, 83, xiv-155 p.

3456   CALDERON, R. "Inbreeding, migration and age at marriage in rural Toledo, Spain", *Journal of Biosocial Science* 15(1), jan 83 : 47-57.

3457   CASTRO, Luis J.; ROGERS, Andrei. "What the age composition of migrants can tell us", *Population Bulletin of the United Nations* 15, 83 : 63-79.

3458   FERREIRA DE PAIVA, Amadeu. "Portuguese migration: a critical survey of Portuguese studies on the economic aspects of the phenomenon since 1973", *International Migration Review* 17(61), 83 : 138-147.

3459   FLIGSTEIN, Neil. "The transformation of southern agriculture and the migration of blacks and whites, 1930-1940", *International Migration Review* 17(62), 83 : 268-290. [USA]

3460   HEDLUND, Hans; LUNDAHL, Mats. *Migration and change in rural Zambia.* Uppsala, Scandinavian Institute of African Studies, 83, 107 p.

3461   KOZIEŁ, Romuald. "Preferencje migracyjne ludności na Dolnym Śląsku w drugiej połowie lat siedemdziesiątych" (Migration preferences of the population in Lower Silesia in the late 1970's), *Biuletyn Instytutu Gospodarstwa Społecznego* 25(4), 82 : 114-127.

3462   MARGER, Martin N.; OBERMILLER, Phillip J. "Urban Appalachians and Canadian maritime migrants: a comparative study of emergent ethnicity", *International Journal of Comparative Sociology (Leiden)* 24(3-4), sep-dec 83 : 229-243.

3463   MARKHAM, William T.; [et al.]. "A note on sex, geographic mobility and career advancement", *Social Forces* 61(4), jun 83 : 1138-1146.

3464   MARTIN, Jack K.; LICHTER, Daniel T. "Geographic mobility and satisfaction with life and work", *Social Science Quarterly* 64(3), sep 83 : 524-535.

3465   MOISEENKO, U. "Vlijanie migracii na formirovanie naselenija" (Impact of migration on population formation), *Vestnik Statistiki* 64(7), 83 : 8-14. [USSR]

3466   OCHOCKI, Andrzej. "Metodologia badań migracji ludności" (Methodology of enquiries concerning migration of population), *Biuletyn Instytutu Gospodarstwa Społecznego* 25(4), 82 : 84-113.

3467   OCQUETEAU, Frédérique. "Contribution à une sociologie de l'expulsion", *Déviance et Société* 7(1), mar 83 : 3-21.

3468   ROUCLOUX, Jean Claude; DECLERCQ-TIJTGAT, Annie. "Les migrations du 3e âge.
        Importance et impact sur la structure par âge de la population des agglomérations de
        Bruxelles, Leège, Charleroi, Verviers et Namur", *Population et Famille* 55(1), 82 : 35-78.
        [Belgique]
3469   SAINTE-ROSE, Pierre-Leval. *Le jeune Antillais face à la migration: analyse du couple attrait-
        répulsion dans le phénomène migratoire.* Paris, Éditions Caribéennes, 83, 158 p. FRE
3470   SELL, Ralph R. "Analyzing migration decisions: the first step — whose decisions?",
        Demography 20(3), aug 83 : 299-311.
3471   SIVAMURTHY, M. *Growth and structure of human population in the presence of migration.* London-
        New York, NY, Academic Press, 82, xvii-227 p. [Australia]
3472   STIER, Frances. "Modeling migration: analyzing migration histories from a San Blas Cuna
        community", *Human Organization* 42(1), 83 : 9-22. [Panama]
3473   TROVATO, Frank; HALLI, S. S. "Ethnicity and migration in Canada", *International
        Migration Review* 17(62), 83 : 245-267.
3474   VINING, Daniel R. "Migration between the core and the periphery", *Scientific American*
        247(6), dec 82 : 36-45.
3475   WATSON, Hilbourne A. "Theoretical and methodological problems in Commonwealth
        Caribbean migration research: conditions and casuality", *Social and Economic Studies* 31(1),
        82 : 165-206.
3476   WATTS, Susan J. "Marriage migration, a neglected form of long-term mobility: a case
        study from Ilorin, Nigeria", *International Migration Review* 17(64), 83 : 682-698.
3477   WIJEWICKREMA, Stanley; RIK, Bulte. *Migration impact on population growth in Belgium:
        a multiregional investigation with detailed projection results for the period 1976-2001.* Brussels,
        Interuniversity Programme in Demography, Vrije Universiteit, 83, 75 p.
3478   ZAGRABOVSKAJA, A. F. *Migracija, vosproizvodstvo i uroven' obrazovanija naselenija* (Migration,
        reproduction and educational level of the population). Kiev, Naukova Dumka, 82, 178 p.
        [USSR]

        **15620   External migration
                   Migration externe**

3479   "African refugees", *Issue* 12(1-2), sum 82 : 2-44. [with contributions by Richard LAPCHICK,
        Paul HARTLING, Aderanti ADEPOJU, Robert F. GORMAN]
3480   "Einwanderungsland: Bundesrepublik Deutschland" (Immigration country: Federal
        Republic of Germany), *Liberal (Bonn)* 25(2), feb 83 : 103-135. [with contributions by
        Liselotte FUNCKE, Ludger DIEKAMP, Sybille UKEN]
3481   "Emigrazione (L') di ritorno: rassegna bibliografica" (Return migration: bibliographical
        review), *Studi Emigrazione* 20(72), dec 83 : 459-519.
3482   "Gli italiani in Australia" (Italians in Australia), *Studi Emigrazione* 20(69), mar 83 : 2-114.
        [with contributions by Charles A. PRICE, Luigi FAVERO, Graziano TASSELLO,
        Lidio BERTELLI]
3483   "Immigrant assimilation", *Research in Race and Ethnic Relations* 3, 82 : 3-225. [with contributions
        by Michel LaFERRIERE, Sally TOMLINSON, Sherry ROSEN, Ting CHEWPEH]
3484   "Immigration policy and the rights of aliens", *Harvard Law Review* 96(6), apr 83 : 1286-1465.
        [USA]
3485   "Immigrazione (L') straniera in Italia" (Foreign immigration in Italy), *Studi Emigrazione*
        20(71), sep 83 : 257-457. [with contributions by Marcello NATALE, Nora FEDERICI;
        résumés en anglais et en français]
3486   "International migration and development", *International Migration Review* 16(60), 82 : 732-899.
3487   "Međunarodni okrugli sto — metodološki pristup izučavanju srpskog iseljeništva u SAD
        i Kanadi" (International round-table on study of the Serb emigration to USA and
        Canada), *Medunarodni Problemi* 34(3-4), mar 83 : 347-482. [with contributions by Mihailo
        PETROVIC]
3488   AGAR CORBINOS, Lorenzo. "El comportamiento urbano de los migrantes árabes en
        Chile" (Urban behaviour of Arab migrants in Chile), *EURE* 9(27), apr 83 : 73-84.
3489   ASHMUN, Lawrence F. *Resettlement of Indochinese refugees in the United States: a selective and
        annotated bibliography.* DeKalb, IL, Northern Illinois University, Center for Southeast
        Asian Studies,, 83, v-212 p.
3490   BARAN, Alina; JÓŹWIAK, Janina. "Próba oszacowania liczebności i struktury Polonii
        w USA w 1980 r" (Tentative estimation of the size and structure of the population of
        Polish origin in the USA in 1980), *Studia demograficzne* 20(4), 82 : 81-93.
3491   BASTIDE, Henri. *Les enfants d'immigrés et l'enseignement français: enquête dans les établissements
        du premier et du second degré.* Paris, Presses Universitaires de France, 82, viii-280 p.

3492   BEAN, Frank D.; KING, Allan G.; PASSEL, Jeffrey S. "The number of illegal migrants of Mexican origin in the United States: sex ratio-based estimates for 1980", *Demography* 20(1), feb 83 : 99-109.

3493   BEHREND, Manfred. "Ausländerpolitik und Fremdenfeindlichkeit in der BRD" (Immigration policy and hostility towards foreigners in Germany FR), *IPW Berichte* 12(5), mai 83 : 21-26 & 65.

3494   BORJAS, George J. "The labor supply of male Hispanic immigrants in the United States", *International Migration Review* 17(64), 83 : 653-671.

3495   BOUBEKER, Ahmed. "Quartier cousin, les immigrés de la deuxième génération", *Esprit* (4), apr 83 : 28-47. [France]

3496   BOYER, Jean-Pierre. "Processus d'installation d'une communauté turque à Terrasson, ville du Périgord", *Hommes et Migrations* 34(1049), 15 apr 83 : 3-29. [Documents]

3497   BURNLEY, J. H. "Immigration et ethnicité en Australie", *Espace géographique* 12(2), jun 83 : 81-89.

3498   BUSTAMANTE, Jorge A. "The Mexicans are coming: from ideology to labor relations", *International Migration Review* 17(62), 83 : 323-341. [USA]

3499   CEALIS, Roza; [et al.]. "Immigration clandestine: la régularisation des travailleurs 'sans papiers' (1981-1982)", *Statistiques du travail. Supplément au bulletin mensuel* (106), 83 : 5-61.

3500   CHISNICK, Barry R. "An alternative approach to immigration policy: rationing by skill", *Population Research and Policy Review* 2(1), feb 83 : 21-33. [USA]

3501   COLEMAN, D. A.; [ed.]. *Demography of immigrants and minority groups in the United Kingdom: proceedings of the 18th annual symposium of the Eugenics Society, London 1981.* London-New York, NY, Academic Press, 82, xvi-270 p.

3502   CONDOMINAS, George; POTTIER, Richard; [eds.]. *Les réfugiés originaires de l'Asie du sud-est: arrière plan historique et culturel, les motivations de départ; rapport.* Paris, La Documentation Française, 82, 227 p.

3503   COX, David. "Refugee settlement in Australia: review of an era", *International Migration* 21(3), 83 : 332-344.

3504   DE LEY, Margo. "French immigration policy since May 1981", *International Migration Review* 17(61), 83 : 196-211.

3505   DIAZ-BRIQUETS, Sergio. "Demographic and related determinants of recent Cuban emigration", *International Migration Review* 17(61), 83 : 95-119.

3506   DUFFIELD, Mark. "Change among West African settlers in Northern Sudan", *Review of African Political Economy* (26), 83 : 45-59.

3507   EDER, Wiestawa. "Polonia belgijska w latach 1945-1980" (Poles in Belgium in the years 1945-1980), *Przeglad zachodni* 39(1), 83 : 79-98.

3508   FALLOWS, James. "Immigration: how it's affecting us", *Atlantic* 252(5), nov 83 : 45-68, 85-106. [USA]

3509   GAUTIER, Xavier. "L'Allemagne fédérale et ses Turcs", *Documents* 38(3), jun 83 : 59-72.

3510   GENIZI, Haim. *American apathy: the plight of Christian refugees from Nazism.* Ramat-Gan, Bar-Ilan University Press, 83, 411 p.

3511   GMELCH, George. "Who returns and why: return migration behavior in two North Atlantic societies", *Human Organization* 42(1), 83 : 46-54. [Ireland; Newfoundland]

3512   GRAHL-MADSEN, Atle. "International refugee law today and tomorrow", *Archiv des Völkerrechts* 20(4), 82 : 411-467.

3513   HABERL, Othmar Nikola. "Die jugoslawische Gastarbeiterpolitik während der westeuropäischen Krise der 70er Jahre" (The policy toward Yugoslavian immigrant workers during the crisis of the seventies in Western Europe), *AWR-Bulletin* 21(1), 83 : 3-26.

3514   HARWOOD, Edwin. "Alienation: American attitudes toward immigration", *Public Opinion* 6(3), jul 83 : 49-56.

3515   HARWOOD, Edwin. "Can immigration laws be enforced?", *Public Interest* (72), sum 83 : 107-123. [USA]

3516   HOSKIN, Marilyn; MISHLER, William. "Public opinion toward new migrants: a comparative", *International Migration* 21(4), 83 : 440-462.

3517   HOUSTOUN, Marion F. "Aliens in irregular status in the United States: a review of their numbers, characteristics, and role in the US labor market", *International Migration* 21(3), 83 : 372-414.

3518   INTERGOVERNMENTAL COMMITTEE FOR MIGRATION. "Undocumented migrants or migrants in an irregular situation", *International Migration* 21(2), 83 : 91-308. [6th Seminar]

3519   JAAKKOLA, M. *Finnish immigrants in Sweden: networks and life styles.* Helsinki, University of Helsinki, Research Group F, No 30, 83, 146 p.

3520   KATS, Rachel. "Occupational mobility of immigrants and their job satisfaction", *International Migration* 21(3), 83 : 345-357.

3521   KELLY, Deirdre. "Guatemala's refugees: victims and shapers of government policies", *Fletcher Forum* 7(2), sum 83 : 323-353.

3522   KHANDRICHE, Mohamed. *Développement et réinsertion: l'exemple de l'émigration algérienne.* Paris, Éditions Publisud, 82, 402-5 p.

3523   KIRKLAND, James R. "The social adjustment of Armenian immigrants in Australia", *International Migration* 21(4), 83 : 515-539.

3524   KOERTVELYESSY, Tibor. "Demography and evolution in an immigrant ethnic community: Hungarian settlement, Louisiana, USA", *Journal of Biosocial Science* 15(2), apr 83 : 223-236.

3525   LANPHIER, G. Michael. "Refugee resettlement: models in action", *International Migration Review* 17(61), 83 : 4-33.

3526   LATER-CHODYŁOWA, Elżbieta. "Organizacja polskiego ruchu emigracyjnego do Danii w latach 1892-1929" (Organization of Polish emigration movement to Denmark in the years 1892-1929), *Przegląd zachodni* 39(1), 83 : 43-59.

3527   LAWLESS, Richard I.; FINDLAY, Allan M. "Algerian emigration to France and the Franco-Algerian accords of 1980", *Orient* 23(3), sep 82 : 454-467.

3528   LE CALLOC'H, Bernard. "La communauté vietnamienne de France", *Acta Geographica* (54), trim. 2, 83 : 1-14.

3529   LE MASNE, Henri. *Le retour des émigrés algériens: projets et contradictions.* El Djazair, Office des Publications Universitaires; Paris, Centre d'Information et d'Études sur les Migrations, 82, vii-215 p.

3530   LEBON, André. "Maintien des liens culturels et insertion des migrants: quelles relations?", *Revue française des Affaires sociales* 37(2), jun 83 : 89-114.

3531   LOESCHER, Gilburt D.; SCANLAN, John A.; [eds.]. "The global refugee problem: US and world response", *Annals of the American Academy of Political and Social Science* 467, mai 83 : 9-253.

3532   MAHMOUD, Maghoub El-Tigani. "Sudanese emigration to Saudi Arabia", *International Migration* 21(4), 83 : 500-514.

3533   MARIE, Claude-Valentin. "L'immigration clandestine en France", *Hommes et Migrations* 34(1059), 15 nov 83 : 3-19.

3534   MARIE, Claude-Valentin. "L'immigration clandestine en France", *Travail et Emploi* (17), sep 83 : 27-40. [résumés en anglais et en espagnol]

3535   MASSEY, Douglas S.; SCHNABEL, Kethleen M. "Recent trends in Hispanic immigration to the United States", *International Migration Review* 17(62), 83 : 212-244.

3536   MCKEE, David L. "Some specifics on the brain drain from the Andean region", *International Migration* 21(4), 83 : 488-499.

3537   MILLER, Jake C. "The homeless of Africa", *Africa Today* 29(2), trim. 2, 82 : 5-30.

3538   MONTICELLI, Giuseppe Lucrezio. "L'emigrazione femminile italiana" (Italian feminine emigration), *Affari sociali internazionali* 11(4), 83 : 95-113.

3539   PAQUET, Gilles; SMITH, Wayne R. "L'émigration des Canadiens français vers les États-Unis 1790-1940: problématique et coups de sonde", *Actualité économique* 59(3), sep 83 : 423-453.

3540   PASCUAL, A. "Connotaciones ideológicas en el concepto de retorno de emigrantes" (Ideological connotations in the concept of the return of emigrants), *Papers. Revista de Sociologia* (20), 83 : 61-71.

3541   PINKUS, Benjamin. "The emigration of national minorities from the USSR in the post-Stalin era", *Soviet Jewish Affairs* 13(1), feb 83 : 3-36.

3542   POINARD, Michel. "Emigrantes portugueses: o regresso" (Portuguese emigrants: the return), *Análise social* 19(1), mar 83 : 29-56.

3543   POITRAS, Guy. "Through the revolving door: central American manpower in the United States", *Inter-American Economic Affairs* 36(4), spr 83 : 63-78.

3544   PUSKÁS, Julianna. *From Hungary to the United States (1880-1914).* Budapest, Akadémiai Kiadó, 82, 225 p.

3545   RATH, Jan. "The enfranchisement of immigrants in practice: Turkish and Moroccan islands in the fairway of Dutch politics?", *Netherlands Journal of Sociology* 19(2), oct 83 : 151-179.

3546   ROCKETT, Ian R. H. "Ethnicity, immigration process and short-term occupational mobility", *International Migration* 21(3), 83 : 358-371.

3547   RODRÍGUEZ VILLAMIL, Silvia; SAPRIZA, Graciela. *La inmigración europea en el Uruguay: los italianos* (European immigration in Uruguay: the Italians). Montevideo, Ediciones de la Banda Oriental, 82, 144-8 p.

3548   ROSH WHITE, Naomi; WHITE, Peter B. "Evaluating the immigrant presence: press reporting of immigrants to Australia 1935-1977", *Ethnic and Racial Studies* 6(3), jul 83 : 284-307.

3549   SARPELLON, Giovanni. "Emigrazione e povertà: problemi di concettualizzazione e misura" (Emigration and poverty: conceptualization and measurement), *Studi di Sociologia* 21(4), oct-dec 83 : 392-406.

3550   SCHIERUP, Carl-Ulrik. "Povratne migracije i nova međunarodna podjela rada" (Return migration and the new international division of labour), *Revija za Sociologiju* 11(3-4), 81 : 131-142. [résumé en anglais]

3551   SCHMITTER, Barbara E. "Immigrant minorities in West Germany, some theoretical concerns", *Ethnic and Racial Studies* 6(3), jul 83 : 308-319.

3552   SHAH, Nasra M. "Pakistani workers in the Middle East: volume, trends and consequences", *International Migration Review* 17(63), 83 : 410-424.

3553   SIMON, Rita J.; SIMON, Julian L. "The Jewish dimension among recent Soviet immigrants to the United States", *Jewish Social Studies* 44(3-4), aut 82 : 283-290.

3554   SIMON, Rita J.; SIMON, Julian L. "Some aspects of the socio-cultural adjustment of recent Soviet immigrants to the United States", *Ethnic and Racial Studies* 5(4), oct 82 : 535-541.

3555   TABOADA-LEONETTI, Isabelle. "Les immigrés de la deuxième génération. Vers une France pluraliste?", *Études* 358(5), mai 83 : 607-621.

3556   TOMOVIĆ, Vladislav A. "Kanadska imigracijska politika i promjene u obrascu zapošljavanja imigranata 1950-1980. Studija jednog slučaja" (Canadian immigration policy and changes in the pattern of employment of immigrants 1950-1980. Case study), *Revija za Sociologiju* 11(3-4), 81 : 143-151. [résumé en anglais]

3557   VAN DER KROEF, Justus M. "Refugees and rebels: dimensions of the Thai-Kampuchean border conflict", *Asian Affairs*, spr 83 : 19-36.

3558   VEITER, Theodor. "Flüchtlings- und Wanderungsfragen in Marokko und in der West-sahara" (Refugees and immigrants in Morocco and Western Sahara), *AWR-Bulletin* 20(3), 82 : 168-176.

3559   VIDAURRETA, Alicia. "Spanish immigration to Argentina, 1870-1930", *Jahrbuch für Geschichte von Staat, Wirtschaft und Gesellschaft Lateinamerikas* (19), 82 : 285-319.

3560   WEIDACHER, Alois. "Policy with respect to aliens and migration research in the Federal Republic of Germany, 1973-1983", *International Migration* 21(4), 83 : 463-487.

3561   WEINTRAUB, Sidney. "US foreign economic policy and illegal immigration", *Population Research and Policy Review* 2(3), oct 83 : 211-231.

3562   ZENNER, Walter P. "Arabic-speaking immigrants in North America as middleman minorities", *Ethnic and Racial Studies* 5(4), oct 82 : 457-477.

15630   Internal migration
Migration interne

3563   "Population and migration", *Rural Sociology* 48(3), 83 : 421-491. [USA]

3564   ADAMCHAK, Donald J.; FOSTER, Gary S.; GILL, Duane A. "Population turnaround in Kansas: the non-metropolitan-adjacency effect", *Social Science Journal (Fort Collins)* 20(2), apr 83 : 17-28.

3565   AHMED, Akbar S. "Nomadism as ideological expression: the case of the Gomal nomads", *Contributions to Indian Sociology* 17(1), jan-jun 83 : 123-138.

3566   AHN, Byong Man; BOYER, William W. "Rural-to-urban migration in South Korea: a cognitive-behavioral approach", *Planning and Administration* 10(1), spr 83 : 57-70.

3567   ALTHAUS, Paul G.; SCHACHTER, Joseph. "Interstate migration and the New Federalism", *Social Science Quarterly* 64(1), mar 83 : 35-45. [USA]

3568   ARNDT, H. W. "Transmigration: achievements, problems, prospects", *Bulletin of Indonesian Economic Studies* 19(3), dec 83 : 50-73. [Indonesia]

3569   ATZEMA, O. A. L. C.; VERGOOSEN, Th. W. M. "De selectiviteit van heit binnenlands migratiepatroon en het migratiegedrag ven pensioenmigraten" (The selectivity of the internal migration pattern and attitudes towards retired persons' migration), *Bevolking en Gezin* (1), 83 : 117-140. [Netherlands]

3570   BARBICHON, Guy. "Migration et conscience d'identité régionale. L'ailleurs, l'autre et le soi", *Cahiers internationaux de Sociologie* 75, 83 : 321-342. [France]

3571   BONDARUK, Mikołaj. "Ruchliwość przestrzenna ludności w Polsce w latach 1970-1980" (Spatial mobility of the population in Poland in the years 1970-1980), *Biuletyn Instytutu Gospodarstwa Społecznego* 25(4), 82 : 128-140.

3572   CHANG, Ming-Cheng. *Migration and fertility in Taiwan.* Nankang-Taipei, Institute of Economics, Academia Sinica, 82, xiv-220 p.

3573   CHARLEMAGNE, Jacqueline. *Populations nomades et pauvreté.* Paris, Presses Universitaires
        de France, 83, x-85 p.
3574   ČTRNÁCT, Pavel. "Dojížďka do zaměstnání podle výsledků sčítání 1980" (Commuting
        to work, by the 1980 census results), *Demografie* 25(3), 83 : 221-233. [Czechoslovakia]
3575   FALUSSY, Béla. "Az ingázás és az életmód összefüggései" (The relationship between
        commuting and the way of life), *Szociológia* 11(4), 82 : 535-560.
3576   GUERIN, Jean-Paul. "L'exode urbain: nouvelles valeurs, nouvelles élites", *Revue de
        Géographie alpine* 71(3), 83 : 267-277. [résumé en anglais]
3577   HUGO, Graeme J. "Sources of internal migration data in Indonesia: their potential and
        limitations", *Majalah Demografie Indonesia* 9(17), jun 82 : 23-52.
3578   ISLAM, Muhammed N. "The efficiency of interprovinical migration in Canada, 1961-1978",
        Regional Science and Urban Economics 13(2), mai 83 : 231-249.
3579   JOHNSTONE, Michael. "Urban squatting and migration in peninsular Malaysia",
        International Migration Review 17(62), 83 : 291-322.
3580   KENNA, Margaret E. "Institutional and transformational migration and the politics of
        community: Greek internal migrants and their Migrants' Association in Athens", *Archives
        européennes de Sociologie* 24(2), 83 : 263-287. [Nisos, Cyclaes, 1840-1940, 1945-1950]
3581   KOO, Hagen; SMITH, Peter C. "Migration, the urban informal sector, and earnings
        in the Philippines", *Sociological Quarterly* 24(2), spr 83 : 219-232.
3582   LICHTER, Daniel T. "Socioeconomic returns to migration among married women", *Social
        Forces* 62(2), dec 83 : 487-503. [USA]
3583   MARGUERAT, Yves. "Des ethnies et des villes. Analyse des migrations vers les villes
        de Côte d'Ivoire", *Cahiers ORSTOM. Série Sciences humaines* 18(3), 82 : 303-340.
3584   MCQUILLAN, Kevin. "Moving to the city: migration to London and Paris in the nineteenth
        century", *Sociological Focus* 16(1), jan 83 : 49-64.
3585   MERCIER, Claude; SIMONA, Giovanni. "Le néo-ruralisme. Nouvelles approches pour
        un phénomène nouveau", *Revue de Géographie alpine* 71(3), 83 : 253-265. [résumés en
        anglais et en italien]
3586   MICHNIEWSKA-SZCZEPKOWSKA, Barbara. "Wpływ migracji do miasta Olsztyna na
        pozycję społeczno-zawodową i zmianę funkcji zawodowej imigrantów" (The impact of
        migration to Olsztyn town on the socio-professional position and change of professional
        function of migrants), *Biuletyn Instytutu Gospodarstwa Społecznego* 25(4), 82 : 141-153.
3587   MIOSSEC, Jean-Marie. "Migrations intérieures en Tunisie et croissance du grand Tunis",
        Revue tunisienne de Géographie (9), 82 : 43-88. [résumés en arabe et en anglais]
3588   MORRISON, Peter A.; ABRAHAMSE, Allan F. "Is population decentralization lengthening
        commuting distances?", *Population Research and Policy Review* 2(2), mai 83 : 189-206. [USA]
3589   NAROFF, Joel L.; LIRO, Joseph R. "Factors influencing the actions of recent movers
        into and within metropolitan areas", *Urban Geography* 3(4), dec 82 : 300-314.
3590   NIEMINEN, Mauri. "Internal migration in Finland in 1977-1978", *Yearbook of Population
        Research in Finland* 21, 1983 : 99-117.
3591   OLIVEIRA-ROCA, Maria. "Privremene migracije radnika iz drugih republika i pokrajina
        u SR Hrvatskoj — pokušaj primjene regresijske analize" (Temporary labour migration
        from other Yugoslav republics and autonomous provinces to SR Croatia), *Revija za
        Sociologiju* 11(3-4), 81 : 103-124.
3592   ORTIZ SARAVIA, Alvaro. *Migraciones internas y desarrollo desigual: Perú, 1940-1972* (Internal
        migration and inequal development: Peru, 1940-1972). La Molina, Lima, Centro de
        Investigaciones Socioeconómicas, Departamento de Ciencias Humanas, Universidad
        Nacional Agraria, 82, 135 p. [Edited by Ibico ROJAS ROJAS]
3593   PEJANOVIĆ, Radovan. "Ekonomski faktori ruralnog eksodusa u Jugoslaviji" (Economic
        factors of rural exodus in Yugoslavia), *Sociologija sela* 20(77-78), 83 : 153-167.
3594   RAPADO, José Ramon. "Migraciones regionales y evolución de la ocupación en España"
        (Regional migration and employment evolution in Spain), *Revista española de Investigaciones
        sociológicas* 22, apr-jun 83 : 77-100.
3595   RHODA, Richard. "Rural development and urban migration: can we keep them down
        on the farm?", *International Migration Review* 17(61), 83 : 34-64.
3596   ROSNER, Andrzej. "Migracje ludności w przekroju 'wieś-miasto' w latach siedemdziesiątych"
        (Population migrations at the cross-section of country and town in the seventies), *Wieś
        i Rolnictwo* 40(3), 83 : 57-74. [Poland]
3597   ROWLAND, Richard H. "Regional migration and ethnic Russian population change in
        the USSR (1959-79)", *Soviet Geography* 22(8), oct 82 : 557-583.
3598   SELL, Ralph R. "Market and direct allocation of labor through migration", *Sociological
        Quarterly* 24(1), wint 83 : 93-105.

3599   SINHA, D. N. "Rural-urban migration to India", *Indian Journal of Economics* 63(251), apr 83 : 495-504.

3600   ŠTAMBUK, Maja. "O pokretljivosti seoskog stanov-ništva" (On the mobility of the rural population), *Revija za Sociologiju* 11(3-4), 81 : 125-130. [résumé en anglais]

3601   SUWARNO, Bambang. "Analisa path dan penggunaannya dalam studi tentang transmigrasi" (Path analysis and its utilization for studying transmigrations), *Majalah Demografie Indonesia* 8(16), dec 81 : 28-73. [Indonesia]

3602   SYNAK, Brunon. "Motywacje i mechanizmy migracji osób starszych ze wsi do miast" (Motivations and mechanisms of the migration of elderly people from the country to the town), *Wieś i Rolnictwo* 39(2), 83 : 145-160. [Poland]

3603   TANI, Katsuhide. "Philippin no jinkō toshika to jinkō idō" (Migration and population urbanization in the Philippines), *Tohoku fukushi daigaku kiyo* 7(1), 83 : 168-187.

3604   THADANI, Veena N. *Social relations and geographic mobility: male and female migration in Kenya.* New York, NY, Population Council, 82, 33 p.

3605   WEISS-ALTANER, E. R. "Rural exodus in the Third World: a Malthusian crisis?", *History of European Ideas* 4(2), 83 : 183-201.

3606   WILLIAMS, R. G. A. "Kinship and migration strategies among settled Londoners: two responses to population pressure", *British Journal of Sociology* 24(3), sep 83 : 386-415.

3607   YAMAGUCHI, Sokō. "Hokuriku sanson no kyoka risonsha no seikatsu (1): Toyama-ken Higashi-tonami-gun Toga-mura no risonsha no tsuiseki chōsa o chūshin nishite" (A study on the life of rural emigrants from a depopulated mountain village in Hokuriku district (1)), *Okayama daigaku kyoikugakubu kenkyu shuroku* 64, 83 : 131-143.

3608   ZIÓŁKOWSKI, Marek. "Dojazdy do pracy w województwie stołecznym warszawskim" (Travels to work in Warsaw voivodship), *Biuletyn Instytutu Gospodarstwa Społecznego* 26(1), 83 : 143-160.

16100   ECOLOGY. GEOGRAPHY. HUMAN SETTLEMENTS.
ÉCOLOGIE. GÉOGRAPHIE. ÉTABLISSEMENTS HUMAINS

16110   Human geography
Géographie humaine

3609   "Environmental sociology", *Sociological Inquiry* 53(2-3), spr 83 : 113-288. [USA] [with contributions by Riley E. DUNLAP, William R. CATTON Jr., Eugene ROSA, Gary E. MACHLIS, Richard P. GALE, Denton E. MORRISON]
3610   ALTMAN, Irwin; WOHLWILL, Joachim F.; [eds.]. *Behavior and the natural environment.* New York, NY-London, Plenum Press, 83, xvi-346 p.
3611   ANDER-EGG, E. "Ecologismo y juventud" (Ecology and youth), *Juventud* 11, sep 83 : 49-64.
3612   BRUNET, Roger. "Rapport sur la géographie française", *Espace géographique* 11(3), sep 82 : 196-214.
3613   GAUTIER, Jean-Yves. *Socioécologie: l'animal social et son univers.* Toulouse, Privat, 82, 267 p.
3614   GUEST, Avery M.; LEE, Barrett A. "Sentiment and evaluation as ecological variables", *Sociological Perspectives* 26(2), apr 83 : 159-184. [USA]
3615   LÓPEZ LÓPEZ, A. "La Ecología: cambio de la sociedad" (Ecology: change of the society), *Documentación Social* (50), jan-mar 83 : 69-83.
3616   WOLAŃSKI, Napoleon; [ed.]. *Ekologia populacji ludzkich* (Ecology of human population). Wrocław, Zakład Narodowy im. Ossolińskich, 82, 738 p.

16120   Nature. Soils. Water
Nature. Sols. Eau

3617   "Question (La) régionale", *Espaces et Sociétés* (41), dec 82 : 71-165. [France] [with contributions by P. PELLEGRINO, Charles RICQ, Gérard MONEDIAIRE, Bernard POCHE]
3618   "Région et identité", *Espaces et Sociétés* (42), jun 83 : 3-78. [Western Europe] [with contributions by Bernard POCHE, Michel BASSAND, Silvio GUINDANI, Anne BALDASSARI]
3619   WEST, Patrick C. *Natural resource bureaucracy and rural poverty: a study in the political sociology of natural resources.* Ann Arbor, MI, University of Michigan, School of Natural Resources, Natural Resources Sociology Research Lab, 82, xiii-168 p.

16130   Citizens. Inhabitants
Citoyens. Habitants

3620   "Asentamientos humanos precarios en América latina" (Precarious human settlements in Latin America), *Revista interamericana de planificación* 17(65), mar 83 : 5-155. [with contributions by Alberto LOVERA, Arturo MIER Y TERAN, Lucio KOWARICH, Suzana PASTERNAK, Diego CARRION, Gaitam VILLAVICENCIO]
3621   "Établissements (Les) humains", *Diogène* 121, jan-mar 83 : 3-85.
3622   "Health and human settlements", *Ekistics* 49(296), sep 82 : 349-412. [with contributions by Christopher J. SMITH, Robert Q. HANHAM, Alexander B. LEMAN, P. J. LAWTHER, Gerhard ROSENBERG]
3623   ADAIR, Philippe. "Économie politique de l'habitat rural. Les 'villages socialistes' algériens", *Espaces et Sociétés* (41), dec 82 : 39-49.
3624   ETHRIDGE, Marcus E. "The policy impact of citizen participation procedures — a comparative state study", *American Politics Quarterly* 10(4), oct 82 : 489-509. [USA]
3625   NIEDERHAUSER, Emil. *The rise of nationality in Eastern Europe.* Budapest, Corvina, 82, 339 p.
3626   PIVOVAROV, Yu L. "Demographic characteristics of settlement and a demogeographic regionalization of the USSR", *Soviet Geography* 24(1), jan 83 : 1-17.

16200   COMMUNITY
COMMUNAUTÉ

3627   "Sociologie du 'local' et 'relocalisation' du social", *Sociologie du Travail* 25(2), apr-jun 83 : 121-256. [France]

3628   BARRAGÁN C., Germán. *La organización popular: mito o realidad?* (Popular organization: myth or reality?). Quito, Departamento de la CEDOC, FEPAT, 82, 78 p.

3629   BONFIGLIO, Giovanni. *Desarrollo de la comunidad y trabajo social: ensayo; bibliografía* (Community development and social work: essay; bibliography). Lima, Celats Ediciones, 82, 269 p. [Latin America]

3630   FRANCK, Karen A. "Community by design", *Sociological Inquiry* 53(2-3), spr 83 : 289-313. [USA]

3631   KRANNICH, Richard S.; HUMPHREY, Craig R. "Local mobilization and community growth: toward an assessment of the 'growth machine' hypothesis", *Rural Sociology* 48(1), spr 83 : 60-81.

3632   MAEDA, Seizo. "Chiiki jumin no shakai kankei to gyosei eno taio: jisshoteki C. O. kenkyu no kokoromi" (Inhabitants' social relations and their approaches to community administration: an experiment in positive C. O. study), *Rissho daigaku bungakubu ronso* 76, 83 : 13-34. [Japan]

3633   MARIE, Michel; TAMISIER, Christian. *Un territoire sans nom: pour une approche des sociétés locales.* Paris, Librairie des Méridiens, 82, 176 p.

3634   MCRAE, James A. Jr. "Changes in religious communalism desired by Protestants and Catholics", *Social Forces* 61(3), mar 83 : 709-730.

3635   NAKATA, Minoru. "Communi gyosei no kadai" (Administrative tasks of community development), *Toshi mondai* 74(6), 83 : 35-46. [Japan]

3636   OGAWA, Takeo; KOYAMA, Tomoshi; [eds.]. *Chicho toshi shuhen noson kankyo seibi suishin chosa hokokusho; Inazawa-shi tobu-chiku* (Toward the rural-urban community in Inazawa). Nagoya, Aichi-ken Nogyo Suisanbu Nokyo Noseika, 83, 315 p. [Japan]

3637   OKADA, Makoto. "'Chiho no jidai' to social planning" (Social plannings on recent Japanese Community Development), *Nihon toshi-gakkai nenpo* 16, 83 : 156-166.

3638   SCHANELY, Leon. *Developing community potential.* Dallas, TX, Summer Institute of Linguistics, 83, vii-40 p. [Papua New Guinea] [Edited by Larry YOST and Willa YOST]

3639   SEKI, Kiyohide; ODA, Toshikatsu. *Ishikari-cho kinko hattensei ni kansuru chosa kenkyu* (Social and economic development of a little community: a case study of Ishikari town). Hokkaido, Ishikari-cho, 83, 138 p.

3640   TAKAGI, Masao. "Kansei-gata model-community no keifu to tenkai" (A study in 'Model community' movement: community organization and administrative leadership), *Ritsumeikan daigaku Sangyo shakai ronshu* 37, 83 : 63-106.

3641   TROUNSTINE, Philip J.; CHRISTENSEN, Terry. *Movers and shakers: the study of community power.* New York, NY, St. Martin's Press, 82, x-201 p.

3642   WILD, Ronald. "Community, communion and the counterculture", *Australian and New Zealand Journal of Sociology* 17(3), nov 81 : 27-34.

3643   ŽUPANČIČ, Milan. "Lokalna zajednica u sociološkoj perspektivi" (The local community in sociological perspective), *Sociologija sela* 20(77-78), 83 : 117-126.

16300   RURAL. URBAN
RURAL. URBAIN

16310   Rural sociology
Sociologie rurale

3644   "Peasant strategies in Asian societies: moral and rational economic approaches: a symposium", *Journal of Asian Studies* 42(4), aug 83 : 753-868. [with contributions by Charles F. KEYES, David FEENY, Pierre BROCHEUX]

3645   "Rural development", *Pakistan Year Book* (10), 83 : 331-337. [Pakistan]

3646   ADEWUMI, J. B. "Strategies for rural development in Nigeria: problems and prospects", *Planning and Administration* 10(2), aut 83 : 54-63.

3647   ADHIKARI, Shyam Prasad. *Rural development in Nepal: problems and prospects.* Lalitpur, Sajha Prakashan, 82, iv-117 p.

3648   ANDORKA, Rudolf; HARCSA, István. "Changes in village society during the last ten years", *New Hungarian Quarterly* 24(92), sum 83 : 30-44.

3649   ARN, Ann-lisbet; MANNAN, M. A. *Lakshmipur Thana: a socio-economic study of two villages.* Copenhagen, Centre for Development Research; Dacca, Bangladesh Institute of Development Studies, 82, 84 p. [Bangladesh]

3650   BAGES, Robert; NEVERS, Jean-Yves. "L'organisation locale de la chasse. Auto-défense collective et régulation des conflits", *Études rurales* 87-88, jul-dec 82 : 209-221. [résumé en anglais]

3651   BARDHAN, Pranab. "Agrarian class formation in India", *Journal of Peasant Studies* 10(1), oct 82 : 73-94.

3652   BEALER, Robert C. "Old wine in old bottles: so what is wrong with that? Some observations
           on metatheory in rural sociology", *Rural Sociology* 48(1), spr 83 : 1-22.
3653   BELLONCLE, Guy. *La question paysanne en Afrique noire.* Paris, Éditions Karthala, 82, 110 p.
3654   BELUSZKY, Pál; SIKOS, Tamás. *Magyarország falutipusai* (The village types of Hungary).
           Budapest, Magyar Tudományos Akadémia Földrajztudomanyi Kutató Intézet, 82, 167 p.
3655   BENATTIG, Rachid. "Conditions d'emploi et de revenus et évolution des inégalités sociales
           et culturelles en milieu rural", *Notes, critiques et débats de l'Institut des Sciences économiques*
           (3-4), sep 82 : 177-197. [Algeria]
3656   BENGUERGOURA, Cherif. "Villages socialistes: aménagement de l'espace et rapports
           ville/campagne", *Notes, critiques et débats de l'Institut des Sciences économiques* (3-4), sep
           82 : 198-215. [Algeria]
3657   BHADURI, Amil; RAHMAN, Md. Anisur; [eds.]. *Studies in rural participation.* New Delhi,
           Oxford and IBH, 82, vii-229 p.
3658   BOZON, Michel. "Chasse, territoire, groupements de chasseurs", *Études rurales* 87-88,
           jul-dec 82 : 335-342. [résumé en anglais]
3659   BUCHER, Bernadette. "Rites et stratégies d'adaptation: la chasse à courre en bocage
           vendéen", *Études rurales* 87-88, jul-dec 82 : 269-286. [résumé en anglais]
3660   CAMBOREDON, Jean-Claude. "La diffusion de la chasse et la transformation des usages
           sociaux de l'espace rural", *Études rurales* 87-88, jul-dec 82 : 233-260.
3661   CASCO MONTOVA, Rosario. "Desarrollo rural integral" (Integral rural development),
           Revista interamericana de Planificación 17(66), jun 83 : 117-137. [Mexico]
3662   CHAO, Kang. "Tenure systems in traditional China", *Economic Development and Cultural
           Change* 31(2), jan 83 : 295-314.
3663   CHÁVEZ, Daniel Constantino. "Tenencia de la tierra y relaciones sociales de producción en
           México" (Land tenure and social relations of production in Mexico), *Investigación económica*
           42(163), jan-mar 83 : 65-88.
3664   CHRETIEN, Jean-Pierre; LE JEUNE, Gabriel. "Développement rural et démocratie
           paysanne, un dilemme? L'exemple du Burundi", *Politique africaine* (11), sep 83 : 45-76.
3665   CIFRIĆ, Ivan. "Komparativni pristup proučavanju seljaštva u socijalističkoj revoluciji"
           (Comparative approach to the study of the peasantry in the socialist revolution), *Sociologija
           sela* 20(75-76), jun 82 : 3-13. [résumés en anglais et en russe]
3666   CLAVEL-LÉVÊQUE, Monique; LORCIN, Mari-Thérèse; LEMARCHAND, Guy. *La
           campagne française: précis d'histoire rurale.* Paris, Éditions Sociales, 83, 311 p.
3667   CONSTANTINESCU, Virgil. "Mutations qualitatives dans la vie du village sous l'incidence
           de la nouvelle révolution agraire", *Revue roumaine des sciences sociales. Série de sociologie*
           27(1), jan-jun 83 : 47-53. [Romania]
3668   COX, Terry. "Inequality and class in research on peasant societies", *Sociologia ruralis* 23(3-4),
           83 : 211-228.
3669   DHAUAGARE, D. N. *Peasant movements in India, 1920-1950.* New Delhi, Oxford University
           Press, 83, xiii-254 p.
3670   DIAMOND, Norma. "Model villages and village realities", *Modern China* 9(2), apr 83 : 163-181.
3671   DIOUF, Made B. "Migration artisanale et solidarité villageoise: le cas de Kanèn Njob,
           au Sénégal", *Cahiers d'Études africaines* 21(4), 81 : 577-582.
3672   DOZON, Jean-Pierre. "Les métamorphoses urbaines d'un 'double' villageois", *Cahiers
           d'Études africaines* 21(1-3), 81 : 389-403. [Côte d'Ivoire]
3673   DUNLAP, Riley E.; MARTIN, Kenneth E. "Bringing environment into the study of
           agriculture: observations and suggestions regarding the sociology of agriculture", *Rural
           Sociology* 48(2), sum 83 : 201-218.
3674   EDMUNDSON, Wade; EDMUNDSON, Stella. "A decade of village development in East
           Java", *Bulletin of Indonesian Economic Studies* 19(2), aug 83 : 46-59.
3675   EIZNER, Nicole; LAMARCHE, Hugues. "Barre-des-Cévennes ou le sursaut d'une société
           locale", *Sociologie du Travail* 25(2), apr-jun 83 : 179-194. [France]
3676   ETIENNE, Gilbert. *Développement rural en Asie: les hommes, le grain et l'outil.* Paris, Presses
           Universitaires de France, 82, 269 p.
3677   ETIENNE, Gilbert. *India's changing rural scene, 1963-1979.* Delhi, Oxford University
           Press, 82, x-231-1 p.
3678   FERNANDO, Edgar. "Sri Lanka: new dimensions in rural development", *Planning and
           Administration* 10(1), spr 83 : 77-82.
3679   FREEMAN, David; AZADI, Hosein. "Education, power distribution and adoption of
           improved farm practices in Pakistan", *Community Development Journal* 18(1), jan 83 : 60-67.
3680   FRIEDLAND, William H. "The end of rural society and the future of rural sociology",
           Rural Sociology 47(4), wint 82 : 589-608.

3681   GILBERT, Jess. "Rural theory: the grounding of rural sociology", *Rural Sociology* 47(4), wint 82 : 609-633.

3682   GLAVANIS, Kathy R. G.; GLAVANIS, Pandeli M. "The sociology of agrarian relations in the Middle East: the persistence of household production", *Current Sociology* 31(2), 83 : 1-109.

3683   GUHA, Ranajit. *Elementary aspects of peasant insurgency in colonial India.* Delhi, Oxford, 83, viii-361 p.

3684   HAINARD, François. "Oú va donc la sociologie rurale nord-américaine?", *Sociologia ruralis* 23(2), 83 : 145-158. [résumés en anglais, français et allemand]

3685   HAMROUNI, Tahar. "La paupérisation d'une collectivité montagnarde du Tell: les Amdoun", *Revue tunisienne de Géographie* (8), 81 : 99-116.

3686   HANRAHAN, Patrick J.; CLOKE, Paul J. "Towards a critical appraisal of rural settlement planning in England and Wales", *Sociologia ruralis* 23(2), 83 : 109-129. [résumés en anglais, français et allemand]

3687   HOOKS, Gregory M. "A new deal for farmers and social scientists: the politics of rural sociology in the Depression era", *Rural Sociology* 48(3), 83 : 386-408. [USA]

3688   IGLESIAS, Gabriel U. "Managing integrated rural development: key issues and problems", *Philippine Journal of Public Administration* 26(1), jan 82 : 47-59.

3689   IRIARTE, Gregorio. "El sindicalismo campesino en Bolivia" (Peasant trade unionism in Bolivia), *Revista mexicana de ciencias políticas y sociales* 27(103), mar 81 : 127-181.

3690   JOLAS, Tina. "La part des hommes. Une société de chasse au bois", *Études rurales* 87-88, jul-dec 82 : 345-356. [Bourgogne, France]

3691   JORALEMON, Victoria Lockwood. "Collective land tenure and agricultural development: a Polynesian case", *Human Organization* 42(2), sum 83 : 95-105.

3692   JORION, Paul. "Effet attracteur de la performance économique moyenne dans un village de pêcheurs", *Revue de l'Institut de Sociologie* (3-4), 83 : 423-437. [île de Houat, France]

3693   KALETA, Andrzej. "Determinanty zadowolenia i niezadowolenia z życia w opiniach mieszkańców wsi" (Determinants of satisfaction and dissatisfaction from life in the opinion of the rural population), *Wieś Współczesna* 317(7), 83 : 89-97.

3694   KITAHARA, Atsushi. "70-nendai Tai noson shakai no henka" (Change of Thai rural society in the 1970s), *Kobe daigaku bunkagaku nenpo* 2, 83 : 1-57.

3695   KITAJIMA, Shigeru. "Chiiki shakai no hendo to chiiki soshiki no dotai (3)" (Changing of the rural society and dynamics of the organizations), *Asahikawa daigaku kiyo* 16, 83 : 27-41.

3696   KUCHIBA, Masuo. "Tohoku Thai, Don Daeng-mura no rekishi to sonraku soshiki ni kansuru kojutsu shiryo" (Field note for history and community organization of Don Daeng Village in northeast Thailand), *Ryukoku daigaku ronshu* 422, 83 : 59-78.

3697   KULCSÁR, Kálmán. "Rural development in post-war Hungary", *Sociologia ruralis* 23(3-4), 83 : 204-210.

3698   KURSANY, Ibrahim. "Peasants of the Nuba mountain region", *Review of African Political Economy* (26), 83 : 35-44.

3699   MADAN, G. R.; MADAN, Tara. *Village development in India: a sociological approach.* New Delhi, Allied, 83, 390 p.

3700   MAESTRE ALFONSO, J. "La cultura y el mundo rural" (Culture and rural environment), *Documentación Social* (51), apr-jun 83 : 159-174. [Spain]

3701   MAQSUD, Saleem; NAEEM, Naeem Akhtar; CHISHTI, Javed Ahmed. *Rural urban balance study, Pakistan.* Comilla, Center on Integrated Rural Development for Asia and the Pacific, 82, i-148 p.

3702   MENDRAS, Henri. "Plaidoyer pour une politique de développement rural", *Observations et diagnostics économiques* (4), jun 83 : 123-144. [résumé en anglais]

3703   MISHRA, S. N.; SHARMA, Kushal. *Problems and prospects of rural development in India.* New Delhi, Uppal Publishing House, 83, viii-172 p.

3704   MIZRAHI, Roberto. "Desarrollo rural: necesidad de un análisis estructural asentado en la consideración explícita de los sujetos sociales" (Rural development: need of a structural analysis based on explicit considerations of social subjects), *Revista de la Facultad de Ciencias Económicas de la Universidad de Cuyo* 87, jan-jun 83 : 23-45.

3705   MUKHERJI, Shekhar. *Essays on rural development.* Varanasi, Utsargo, 82, 192 p. [India]

3706   NAKAE, Yoshio. "Noson shakai hendo to nominso no soshikiteki undo" (A study on the change of rural society and the systematic movement of the peasants), *Shakaigaku hyoron* 34(3), 83 : 75-101. [Japan]

3707   NEWBY, Howard. "The sociology of agriculture: toward a new rural sociology", *Annual Review of Sociology* (9), 83 : 67-81.

3708   NICARAGUA. MINISTRY OF AGRICULTURAL DEVELOPMENT AND AGRARIAN REFORM. "Agrarian reform in Nicaragua: the first three years", *International Journal of Sociology* 23(2), 83 : 3-91.

3709   NOOIJ, Ad. "Rural development: comparative perspectives", *Sociologia ruralis* 23(3-4),
        83 : 199-203. [Eastern and Western Europe]
3710   O'LEARY, Greg; WATSON, Andrew. "The role of the people's commune in rural
        development in China", *Pacific Affairs* 55(4), wint 83 : 593-612.
3711   OGAWA, Takeo; [et al.]; [eds.]. *Noson shuraku kozo bunseki chosa hokokusho* (The structure of
        woodland village). Tokyo, Nosei Chosa Iinkai, 83, 223 p. [Japan]
3712   OOMEN-MYIN, Marie Antoinette. "The involvement of rural women in village development
        in Tanzania", *Convergence* 16(2), 83 : 59-69.
3713   OXBY, Clare. "'Farmers groups' in rural areas of the Third World", *Community Development
        Journal* 18(1), jan 83 : 50-59.
3714   PETRESCU, N. "Coordonnées du développement économique et social dans l'espace rural
        roumain", *Revue roumaine des sciences sociales. Série de sociologie* 27(1), jan-jun 83 : 55-66.
3715   PIEKARA, Andrzej. "Instytucje wiejskie a wartości społecznomoralne" (Rural institutions
        and socio-moral values), *Wieś Współczesna* 311(1), 83 : 20-30. [Poland]
3716   POPPINGA, Onno. "Les paysans en Allemagne Fédérale", *Nouvelles campagnes* (21-22),
        jan 83 : 34-50.
3717   PRADELLES DE LATOUR, Charles-Henry. "La passion de la chasse dans une commune
        cévenole", *Études rurales* 87-88, jul-dec 82 : 325-334. [résumé en anglais]
3718   RODRÍGUEZ MOLAS, Ricardo E. *Historia social del gaucho* (Social history of the gaucho).
        Buenos Aires, Centro Editor de América Latina, 82, 302 p. [Argentina]
3719   ROIZ, M. "La persistencia del campesinado en la estructura social española" (Persistence
        of peasantry in Spanish social structure), *Documentación Social* (51), apr-jun 83 : 55-77.
3720   SHAH, Ghanshyam; CHATURVEDI, H. R. *Gandhi and approach to rural development: the
        valued experiment.* Delhi, Ajanta Publications, 83, ix-130 p.
3721   SIGELMAN, Lee. "Politics, economics, and the American farmer: the case of 1980", *Rural
        Sociology* 48(3), 83 : 367-385.
3722   SIJAPATI, Binod. *Rural urban balance study, Nepal.* Comilla, Center on Integrated Rural
        Development for Asia and the Pacific, 82, 77 p.
3723   SIMÓ, Tibor. *A tardi társadalom az ezerkilencszázhetvenes években* (The society of Tard in the
        seventies). Budapest, Magyar Szocialista Munkáspárt KB Társadalomtudományi
        Intézete, 83, 208 p. [Hungary: a village revisited 40 years after]
3724   SINGH, R. G. "In-consistencies in rural modernization: a case of two villages of Eastern
        Uttar-Pradesh", *Indian Journal of Social Research* 24(2), aug 83 : 111-120. [India]
3725   SINHA, Murli M. *Modernizing and commnity power: comparative study of villages in India.* New
        Delhi, Vikas, 83, 206 p.
3726   SOARES, Glaucio Ary Dillon; COLLINS, Jane. "The idiocy of rural life", *Civilisations*
        32(1), 82 : 31-65. [Latin America]
3727   ŠTAMBUK, Maja. "Sociodemografske promjene i perspektive razvitka sela Biokova"
        (Socio-demographic aspects of change and perspectives of development in villages of
        the Biokovo region), *Sociologija sela* 20(77-78), 83 : 169-183. [Yugoslavia]
3728   STAROVEROV, V. I. "Zadači sel'skoj sociologii v svete majskogo (1982 g.) Plenuma
        CK KPSS" (The rural sociology objectives in the light of the May, 1982 Plenum of
        the CC of the CPSU), *Sociologičeskie Issledovanija (Moskva)* (1), 83 : 29-38. [USSR]
3729   STASIAK, Andrzej. "Wybrane problemy zagospodarowania wsi polskiej" (The chosen
        problems of Polish country development), *Miasto* 32(5), 82 : 1-9.
3730   SUCHOCKA, Renata. "Zmiany strukturalne wsi przyszłości w opiniach studentów"
        (Structural transformation of future villages in students' opinions), *Ruch prawniczy,
        ekonomiczny i socjologiczny* 45(2), 83 : 237-253. [Poland]
3731   SUGIOKA, Naoto; SUZUKI, Toshimasa; YAZAKI, Shunji. *Nogyo seinen chiiki jissen katsudo
        genchi jirei chosa kekka hokokusho* (A case study of young farmers' community activities).
        Hokkaido, Hokkaido Nogyo Kaigi, 83, 43 p. [Japan]
3732   SYMES, David; MARSDEN, Terry K. "Complementary roles and asymmetrical lives.
        Farmers' wives in a large farm environment", *Sociologia ruralis* 23(3-4), 83 : 228-241. [UK]
3733   TAKAGI, Masao. "Jukyo to kazoku: Sanriku gyoson chokkei kazoku no dento to hendo"
        (Dwelling and family: a case study of fishing village at the Sanriku Sea), *Ritsumeikan
        daigaku Sangyo shakai ronshu* 36, 83 : 35-85. [Japan]
3734   THEKKAMALAI, S. S. *Rural development and social change in India.* New Delhi, D. K.
        Publications, 83, 280 p.
3735   VANDEN, Harry E. "Marxism and the peasantry in Latin America: marginalization or
        mobilization?", *Latin American Perspectives* 9(4), aut 82 : 74-98.
3736   WALKER, S. Tjip; CARAPICO, Sheila; COHEN, John M. *Emerging rural patterns in the
        Yemen Arab Republic: results of a 21-community cross-sectional study.* Ithaca, NY, Rural Develop-

ment Committee, Yemen Research Program, Center for International Studies, Cornell University, 83, 202 p.

3737   WEBER, Florence. "Gens du pays, émigrés, étrangers: conflits autour d'une chasse en montagne", *Études rurales* 87-88, jul-dec 82 : 287-294. [résumé en anglais]

3738   ZAMAN, M. Q. "Change and continuity in the patron-client relations among peasants of Bangladesh", *Eastern Anthropologist* 35(4), 82 : 271-284.

3739   ZAMAN, M. Q. "Rural elite in modernizing societies: Bangladesh and India", *Asian Profile* 11(3), jun 83 : 243-260.

3740   ZINGERLE, Arnold. "Gesellschaft, Kultur und Natur in den Alpen. Eine Erinnerung an Adolf Günthers Buch 'Die Alpenländische Gesellschaft' " (Society, culture and nature in the Alps. A remembrance of Adolf Günther's book 'The Alpine Country Society'), *Sociologia internationalis* 21(1-2), 83 : 93-103.

16320   Urban sociology
Sociologie urbaine

3741   "Capital cities", *Ekistics* 50(299), apr 83 : 86-150. [with contributions by Jean GOTTMAN, Sten SPARRE NILSON, Ludwik STRASZEWICZ, Calogero MUSCARÀI, Yasuo MIYAKAWA, Alan J. HENRIKSON]

3742   "Cities in the 21st century", *Urban Affairs Annual Review* 23, 82 : 1-352. [USA] [with contributions by Gary GAPPERT, James F. RICHARDSON, Richard V. KNIGHT, Arthur SHOSTAK, Kathleen BUTLER, Ben CHINITZ]

3743   "Contributions au débat sur la recherche urbaine", *Espaces et Sociétés* (42), jun 83 : 79-127. [France] [with contributions by J. S. BORDREUIL, André SAUVAGE, Maurice BLANC, Pierre SANSOT, Guy LOINGER]

3744   "Gestalt und Entwicklung der modernen Stadt" (Form and development of the modern town), *Mitarbeit* 31(3), 82 : 201-306.

3745   "Great (The) housing experiment", *Urban Affairs Annual Review* 24, 83 : 1-287. [USA] [with contributions by William L. HAMILTON, William L. HOLSHOUSER Jr., Joseph FRIEDMAN, Daniel H. WEINBERG, Kevin F. McCARTHY]

3746   "Housing in neighborhoods", *Ekistics* 50(298), feb 83 : 2-84. [with contributions by Kazuo HAYAKAWA, Yoram BAR-GAL, Dennis A. RONDINELLI, Frank J. COSTA, Ahmed MOUSTAPHA]

3747   "Nouvel (Le) aménageur: savoir occuper le terrain", *H: revue de l'habitat social* 91, dec 83 : 13-68. [France] [with contributions by Gérard KLEIN]

3748   "Planning and the changing family", *Journal of the American Planning Association* 49(2), spr 83 : 131-183. [USA] [with contributions by Denise SCOTT BROWN, Kathleen GERSON, Rojean MADSEN, Edith M. NETTER, Ruth G. PRICE]

3749   "Problemas urbanos y regionales" (Urban and regional problems), *Revista mexicana de Sociología* 45(1), jan-mar 83 : 9-232. [Latin America]

3750   "Sociologie urbaine et politique urbaine", *Recherche sociale* (86), jun 83 : 3-64. [France] [with contributions by François ABALLEA, Isabelle BENJAMIN]

3751   "Squatter (The) movement in the Netherlands", *International Journal of Urban and Regional Research* 7(3), sep 83 : 405-427. [résumés en français, espagnol et allemand, with contributions by J. DRAASMA, P. VAN HOGGSTRATEN, Hugo PRIEMUS]

3752   "Stadtökologie und Stadtplanung" (Urban ecology and urban planning), *Informationen zur Raumentwicklung* (10), 82 : 753-881. [Germany FR]

3753   "Symposium: race and residential segregation", *Urban Affairs Quarterly* 18(3), mar 83 : 299-346. [with contributions by John L. GOODMAN Jr., Mary L. STREITWIESER, Richard R. SCOTT, John E. FARLEY, Morton D. WINSBERG, see also ibid.: 347-370]

3754   "Symposium: remolding the urban future", *Urban Affairs Quarterly* 18(4), jun 83 : 445-484. [with contributions by E. C. SAVAS, George STERNLIEB, James W. HUGHES, Harrison C. WHITE]

3755   "Toulouse", *Revue géographique des Pyrénées et du Sud-Ouest* 54(1), spr 83 : 7-175. [with contributions by Guy JALABERT, Jean-Yves NEVERS, Michel IDRAC; résumés en anglais]

3756   "Urban (The) underclass", *Society* 21(1), dec 83 : 34-86. [USA] [with contributions by Elijah ANDERSON, Diana M. PEARCE, and John OGBU]

3757   "Urban housing policy", *Policy Studies* 6, 82 : 655-734. [with contributions by Harriett TEE TAGGART, Kevin W. SMITH, David R. GOLDFIELD, C. Peter RYDELL, Mary K. FARMER, Ray BARRELL]

3758   "Urban social research: problems and prospects", *Sociological Review Monograph* 30, 83 : 1-194. [UK] [with contributions by Elizabeth LEBAS, Andrew COX, J. R. MELLOR, Ian PROCTOR]

3759 "Urbanization and social change in the Arab world", *Ekistics* 50(300), jun 83 : 154-239. [with contributions by Mustafa O. ATTIR, H. N. MISRA, Ishaq J. QUTUB, Lee L. BERN]

3760 "Villes et campagnes: problèmes du monde en développement", *Mondes en Développement* 40, 82 : 439-633. [résumés en anglais et espagnol]

3761 ABELES, Marc. "Entre ville et campagne. Pratique de l'anthropologie dans une zone de lotissements de la province de Séville", *Homme* 22(4), dec 82 : 87-100. [Spain] [résumé en anglais]

3762 AGAFONOV, N. T.; [et al.]. "On some faulty concepts in Soviet urban studies", *Soviet Geography* 24(3), mar 83 : 179-188.

3763 AKIBA, Setsuo. "Jumin jichi soshiki toshiteno chonaikai" ('Chonaikai' as a self-governmental neighbourhood organization), *Shakaigaku kenkyu* 46, 83 : 149-170. [Japan]

3764 ALLEN, Luther A. "British and French new towns programs", *Comparative Social Research* 5, 82 : 269-298.

3765 ALVAREZ REGUILLO, Lino; [et al.]. *'Plazas' et sociabilité en Europe et Amérique latine* . Paris, Diffusion de Boccard, 82, 184 p.

3766 ANGEL, Shlome. "Upgrading slum infrastructure: divergents objectives in search of a consensus", *Third World Planning Review* 5(1), feb 83 : 5-22.

3767 ANKERL, Guy. "Rapide urbanisation dans le tiers monde et plus particulièrement en Afrique tropicale. Répercussions sociales et perspectives", *Travail et Société* 8(3), jul-sep 83 : 299-310.

3768 BAHR, Howard M.; CAPLOW, Theodore; CHADWICK, Bruce A. "Middletown III: problems of replication, longitudinal measurement, and triangulation", *Annual Review of Sociology* (9), 83 : 243-264. [USA]

3769 BAIROCH, Paul. "Tendances et caractéristiques de l'urbanisation du Tiers-Monde d'avant hier et après-demain", *Tiers-Monde* 24(94), jun 83 : 325-348.

3770 BALDASSARE, Mark; [ed.]. *Cities and urban living.* New York, NY, Columbia University Press, 83, vi-381 p.

3771 BALLESTER ROS, Ignacio. "Le vivienda en España: su tipología y distribución geográfica según el censo de 1981 y su evolución numérica en el periodo 1970-1981" (Housing in Spain: typology and geographic distribution according to the 1981 census, and quantitative evolution in the 1970-1981 period), *Revista de Estudios de la Vida local* 42(219), sep 83 : 499-520.

3772 BARDO, John W.; HARTMAN, John J. *Urban sociology: a systematic introduction.* Itasca, IL, F. E. Peacock, 82, vii-401 p.

3773 BASSAND, Michel. *Villes, régions et sociétés: introduction à la sociologie des phénomènes urbains et régionaux.* Lausanne, Presses Polytechniques Romandes, 82, 295 p.

3774 BATTYE, Nicholas; STEELE-PERKINS, Chris; TREVOR, Paul. *Survival programmes in Britain's inner cities.* Milton Keynes, Open University, 82, 224 p.

3775 BEAUCAGE, Pierre. "Crise urbaine et movement urbain au Mexique", *Amérique latine* (15), sep 83 : 57-63.

3776 BJALKOVSKAJA, V.; NOVIKOV, V. "Urbanizacija i problemy ograničenija rosta krupnejših gorodov" (Urbanization and problems of limitation of the biggest towns growth), *Voprosy Ekonomiki* 53(11), 82 : 89-98. [USSR]

3777 BOAPEAM, Samuel N.; TIPPLE, A. Graham. "Estimating housing stock in a Third World city: a method used in Kumasi", *Third World Planning Review* 5(2), mai 83 : 177-188.

3778 BÖHME, Helmut. "Die Entwicklung der Stadt in Geschichte und Gegenwart" (Urban development in history and today), *Universitas* 37(12), 82 : 1303-1313.

3779 BONNES-DOBROWOLNY, Mirilia; SECCHIAROLI, Gianfranco. "Space and meaning of the city-center cognition: an interactional-transactional approach", *Human Relations* 36(1), jan 83 : 23-35. [Milan, Italy]

3780 BONNIN, Philippe. "L'observateur observé. A propos de l'ethnologie urbaine", *Revue de l'Institut de Sociologie* (3-4), 82 : 459-475.

3781 BRADBURY, Katharine L.; DOWNS, Anthony; SMALL, Kenneth A. *Urban decline and the future of urban cities.* Washington, DC, Brookings Institution, 82, xiii-309 p.

3782 BREMAEKER, François E. J. de. "Urbanização em marcha" (On-going urbanization), *Revista de Administração municipal* 30(166), mar 83 : 60-90. [Brazil]

3783 BREMAN, Jan. "The bottom of the urban order in Asia: impressions of Calcutta", *Development and Change* 14(2), apr 83 : 153-183. [India]

3784 BRUNEAU, Jean-Claude; MBUYU, Mwenge. "Passé, présent et avenir possible de l'urbanisme à Lubumbashi. Réflexions et propositions pour une meilleure maîtrise des processus d'urbanisation au Zaïre", *Zaïre-Afrique* 23(176), aug 83 : 373-390.

3785   BUCK, Gerhard. "Von der Partizipation zu Selbsthilfe. Aktuelle Tendenzen in der Stadterneuerung" (From participation to self-help. Present trends of urban renewal), *Neue Praxis* 12(4), trim. 4, 82 : 358-371. [Germany FR]

3786   BURGESS, Rod. "The politics of urban residence in Latin America", *International Journal of Urban and Regional Research* 6(4), dec 82 : 465-480. [résumés en français, espagnol et allemand]

3787   ČALDAROVIĆ, Ognjen. "Razvoj urbane sociologije u nekim evropskim zemljama i SAD u posledhjih desetak godina" (Development of urban sociology in some European countries and the USA in the past ten years), *Sociologija* 24(4), 82 : 381-396.

3788   CASTELLS, Manuel. *The city and the grassroots: a cross-cultural theory of urban social movements.* London, E. Arnold, 83, xxi-450 p.

3789   CHABBI, Morched. "Une nouvelle forme d'urbanisation dans le Grand Tunis: l'habitat spontané péri-urbain", *Revue tunisienne de Géographie* (8), 81 : 9-47. [résumés en arabe et en anglais]

3790   CHOU, Bih-Er; CRIDER, Donald M.; WILLITZ, Fern K. "Urbanization and changing rural norms", *Sociology and Social Research* 66(2), jan 82 : 198-210.

3791   CLARK, W. A. V.; ONAKA, Jun L. "Life cycle and housing adjustment as explanations of residential mobility", *Urban Studies* 20(1), feb 83 : 47-57.

3792   CONZEN, Michael P. "Amerikanische Städte im Wandel. Die neue Stadtgeographie der achtziger Jahre" (American towns in change. The new urban geography of the 1980's), *Geographische Rundschau* 35(4), 83 : 142-150.

3793   DAHL, Grete. *Boligforehold og boutgifter* (Housing conditions and housing expenditures). Oslo-Kongsvinger, Statistisk Sentralbyrå, H. Aschehoug, Universitetsforlaget, 82, 87 p.

3794   DAHLBERG, Sven. *Bostadspolitik* (Housing policy). Stockholm, Timo, 83, 473-8 p.

3795   DAHMANN, Donald C. "Subjective assessments of neighborhood quality by size of place", *Urban Studies* 20(1), feb 83 : 31-45.

3796   DÁVID, G. János. "The housing problem: market and norms", *Annales Universitatis Scientiarum budapestiensis de Rolando Eötvös nominatae. Sectio philosophica et sociologica* 16, 82 : 207-221.

3797   DAVIES, R. L.; CHAMPION, Anthony Gerard; [eds.]. *The future for the city centre.* London-New York, NY, Academic Press, 83, xvi-294 p.

3798   DE CASTRO, Ina Elias. "Conjunto habitacional: ampliando a controvérsia sobre a remoção de favelas" (Public housing: enlarging the controversy over the removal of squatter settlements), *Dados* 26(2), 83 : 213-231.

3799   DE SOUZA, Alfred; [ed.]. *Urban growth and urban planning: political context and people's priorities.* New Delhi, Indian Social Institute, 83, xi-163 p. [India]

3800   DEBLÉ, Isabelle; [et al.]. *Vivre et survivre dans les villes africaines.* Paris, Presses Universitaires de France, 82, 310 p.

3801   DREIER, Peter. "The status of tenants in the United States", *Social Problems* 30(2), dec 82 : 179-198.

3802   DUBY, Georges; [ed.]. *Histoire de la France urbaine. IV. La ville de l'âge industriel: le cycle haussmannien.* Dir. par Maurice Agulhon. Paris, Seuil, 83, 665 p.

3803   DUCZKOWSKA-MAŁYSZ, Katarzyna. "Główne nurty dyskusji o relacjach 'wieś-miasto'" (Main trends of discussion on town-country relations), *Wieś i Rolnictwo* 40(3), 83 : 141-150. [Poland]

3804   DUCZKOWSKA-MAŁYSZ, Katarzyna. "Stosunki między miastem a wsią. 'Wybrane kwestie teoretyczne w ujęciu marksowskim" (Relations between the town and the country. Selected theoretical problems in the Marxist approach), *Wieś i Rolnictwo* 40(3), 83 : 41-56.

3805   EBERHARDT, Piotr. "Procesy urbanizacyjne w Polsce Ludowej" (Urbanization processes in Poland), *Miasto* 32(6), 82 : 10-15.

3806   EBONG, Maurice O. "The perception of residential quality: a case study of Calabar, Nigeria", *Third World Planning Review* 5(3), aug 83 : 273-285.

3807   ECKERT, J. Kevin. "Dislocation and relocation of the urban elderly: social networks as mediators of relocation stress", *Human Organization* 42(1), 83 : 39-45. [USA]

3808   EDWARDS, Michael. "Residential mobility in a changing housing market: the case of Bucaramanga, Colombia", *Urban Studies* 20(2), mai 83 : 131-145.

3809   ELA, Jean-Marc. *La ville en Afrique noire.* Paris, Karthala, 83, 219 p.

3810   EVERS, Hans-Dieter. *Sosiologi perkotaan: urbanisasi dan sengketa tanah di Indonesia dan Malaysia* (Urban sociology: urbanization in Indonesia and Malaysia). Lembaga Penelitian, Pendidikan dan Penerangan Ekonomi dan Sosial, 82, viii-232 p.

3811   FERNÁNDEZ DURAN, Ramón. "El sistema de transportes en Madrid: evolución, situación actual y perspectivas futuras" (Transport system in Madrid: evolution, present situation and prospects), *Revista internacional de Sociología (Madrid)* 40(43), sep 82 : 277-325.

3812   FLÓREZ E., Luis Bernardo; GONZÁLEZ MUÑOZ, César. *Industria, regiones y urbanización en Colombia* (Industry, regions and urbanization in Colombia). Bogotá, FINES, Editorial Oveja Negra, 83, 232 p.

3813   FÜLLENKEMPER, Horst. *Wirkungsanalyse der Wohnungspolitik in der Bundesrepublik Deutschland* (Effect analysis of housing policy in the Federal Republic of Germany). Münster, Institut fur Siedlungs- und Wohnungswesen und Zentralinstitut für Raumplanung der Universität Münster, 82, xiii-286-14 p.

3814   FUSCH, Richard; FORD, Larry R. "Architecture and the geography of the American city", *Geographical Review* 73(3), jul 83 : 324-340.

3815   GAŁAJ, Dyzma. "Przenikanie wartości i wzorów zachowań-'urbanizacja wsi' i 'ruralizacja miasta' " (The infiltration of values and models of behaviour: 'the urbanization of the country' and 'the ruralization of the town'), *Wieś i Rolnictwo* 40(3), 83 : 99-108.

3816   GARDEN, Maurice; LEQUIN, Yves; [eds.]. *Construire la ville: XVIIIᵉ-XIXᵉ siècles.* Lyon, Presses Universitaires de Lyon, 83, iv-186 p.

3817   GASPARINI, Alberto. *Crisi della città e sua reimmaginazione: effetti simbolici e valori di progettazione nel recupero del centro storico e delle aree urbane* (Crisis of the city and urban renewal: symbolic effects and projection values in the recuperation of historical center and urban areas). Milano, F. Angeli, 82, 368 p.

3818   GELLEN, Martin. "Housing crisis in California", *California Management Review* 24(3), 82 : 51-59.

3819   GIBBAL, Jean-Marie; [et al.]; [eds.]. "Villes africaines au microscope", *Cahiers d'Études africaines* 21(1-3), 81 : 7-429.

3820   GILLESPIE, Fran. "Comprehending the slow pace of urbanization in Paraguay between 1950 and 1972", *Economic Development and Cultural Change* 31(2), jan 83 : 355-375.

3821   GILLIS, A. R. "Strangers next door: an anlysis of density, diversity, and scale in public housing projects", *Canadian Journal of Sociology* 8(1), 83 : 1-20.

3822   GILLIS, A. R.; HAGAN, John. "Bystander apathy and the territorial imperative", *Sociological Inquiry* 53(4), 83 : 449-460. [USA]

3823   GOOSSENS, L. "La politique du logement social en Belgique", *Recherches sociologiques* 14(2), 83 : 203-228.

3824   GORNOSTAEVA, G. A.; HANIN, S. Ė. "Goroda RSFSR: tendencii i perspektivy razvitija" (Towns of the RSFSR: tendencies and prospects of development), *Vestnik Moskovskogo Gosudarstvennogo Universiteta. Serija Geografija* (1), 83 : 14-20.

3825   GRAY, Thomas A. "Student housing and discrimination: an empirical approach", *American Economist* 27(1), 83 : 61-68.

3826   GUPTA, Giri Raj; [ed.]. *Urban India.* New Delhi, Vikas, 83, xiv-424 p.

3827   GUPTA, R. G. *Planning and development of towns.* New Delhi, Oxford & IBH Publishing Co., 83, xxiv-279 p. [India]

3828   HALAMSKA, Maria. "Stosunki 'wieś-miasto' w sytuacji kryzysowej: napięcie czy konflikt?" (Town-country relations in the crisis situation: tensions or conflict?), *Wieś i Rolnictwo* 40(3), 83 : 123-140. [Poland]

3829   HANSEN, Karen Tramberg. "Lusaka's squatters: past and present", *African Studies Review* 25(2-3), sep 82 : 117-136.

3830   HASHIMOTO, Yuko. "Tonan asia dai-toshi no suramu kaizen seisaku to sono mondaiten" (Slum improvement programs in three Asian cities), *Kokusai kirisutokyo daigaku shakai-kagaku journal* 21(2), 83 : 133-153.

3831   HEINEBERG, Heinz. "Münster. Entwicklung und Funktionen der westfälischen Metropole" (Münster. Development and functions of the Westphalian metropolis), *Geographische Rundschau* 35(5), 83 : 204-210.

3832   HEUER, Hans. "Wohnungspolitik" (Housing policy), *Archiv für Kommunalwissenschaften* 21(1), 82 : 48-68. [Germany FR]

3833   HEYMANN-DOAT, Arlette; [ed.]. *Politiques urbaines comparées.* Paris, Arbre Verdoyant, A. Colin, 83, 180 p.

3834   HODGE, Gerald. "Canadian small town renaissance: implications for settlement systems concepts", *Regional Studies* 17(1), feb 83 : 19-28. [résumés en français et allemand]

3835   HODGE, Gerald; QADEER, Mohammad A. *Towns and villages in Canada: the importance of being unimportant.* Toronto, ON, Butterworths, 83, xx-250 p.

3836   HOWELL, Frank M.; FRESE, Wolfgang. "Size of place, residential preferences and the life cycle: how people come to like where they live", *American Sociological Review* 48(4), aug 83 : 569-580.

3837   HWANG, Sean-Shong; MURDOCK, Steve H. "Residential segregation in Texas in 1980", *Social Science Quarterly* 63(4), dec 82 : 737-748.

3838   IGNAR, Marek. "Dysparytety w warunkach życia ludności rolniczej. Stosunki 'wieś-miasto'"
        (Disparities in the living conditions of the farming population. Relations between the
        country and the town), *Wieś i Rolnictwo* 39(2), 83 : 41-55. [Poland]

3839   IGNAR, Marek. "Kwestia dysparytetów socjalno-bytowych między miastem a wsią" (The
        question of social and living disparities between the town and the country), *Wieś i Rolnictwo*
        40(3), 83 : 87-98. [Poland]

3840   JAILLET, Marie-Christine; JALABERT, Guy. "Politique urbaine et logement: la production
        d'espace pavillon-naire", *Espace géographique* 11(4), dec 82 : 293-306. [France]

3841   JAŁOWIECKI, Bohdan. "Relacje 'miasto-wieś'. Zarys problematyki teoretycznej" (Town
        and country relations. Outline of theoretical problems), *Wieś i Rolnictwo* 40(3), 83 : 19-26.
        [Poland]

3842   JARET, Charles. "Recent neo-Marxist urban analysis", *Annual Review of Sociology* (9),
        83 : 499-525.

3843   JIMÉNEZ, Emmanuel. "The magnitude and determinants of home improvement in self-help
        housing: Manila's Tondo Project", *Land Economics* 59(1), feb 83 : 70-83.

3844   JOHNSON, E. H. "Community as an intermediary in sustaining the urban order",
        Annales internationales de criminologie 20(1-2), 83 : 103-112.

3845   JOHNSON, James H. Jr. "The role of community action in neighborhood revitalization",
        Urban Geography 4(1), mar 83 : 16-39.

3846   JOHNSTON, Ronald John. *The American urban system: a geographical perspective.* New York, NY,
        St. Martin's Press, 82, xii-348 p.

3847   JOHNSTONE, Michael. "Urban squatters in peninsular Malaysia: a marginal workforce
        of a Third World proletariat?", *Australian and New Zealand Journal of Sociology* 19(3), nov
        83 : 491-516.

3848   JOLY, Jacques. "La réhabilitation des quartiers anciens de Grenoble. Mode d'intervention
        et effets sociaux", *Revue de Géographie alpine* 71(1), 83 : 35-63. [résumé en anglais]

3849   KABAGAMBE, Denis; MOUGHTIN, Cliff. "Housing the poor: a case study in Nairobi",
        Third World Planning Review 5(3), aug 83 : 227-248.

3850   KALTENBERG-KWIATKOWSKA, Ewa; KRYCZKA, Piotr; MIROWSKI, Włodzimierz;
        [eds.]. *Teorie socjologii miasta a problemy społeczne miast polskich. Materiały Konferencji Socjologów
        Miasta Lublin, 9-10 grudnia 1980* (Theories of urban sociology and social problems of
        Polish towns. Materials for a Conference of Urban Sociologists, Lublin, 9-10 December
        1980). Wrocław, Ossolineum, 83, 300 p.

3851   KIRSCHENBAUM, Alan. "The impact of new towns in rural regions on population
        redistribution in Israël", *Rural Sociology* 47(4), wint 82 : 692-704.

3852   KLERK, L. A. de; [ed.]. *Stadsvernieuwing in Rotterdam* (Urban renewal in Rotterdam).
        's-Gravenhage, VUGA, 82, 196 p.

3853   KNAUDER, Stefanie. *Shacks and mansions: an analysis of the integrated housing policy in Zambia.*
        Lusaka, Multimedia Publications, 82, ii-167 p.

3854   KOBAYASHI, Kazuho. "Chonaikai katsudo no genjo to kadai" (An essay on the
        'Chonaikai'), *Shakaigaku kenkyu* 46, 83 : 81-95. [Japan]

3855   KOCH, Franz. *Innerregionale Wanderungen und Wohnungsmarkt* (Intraregional migrations and
        housing market). Frankfurt-am-Main-New York, NY, Campus, 83, 156 p.

3856   KWOK, R. Yin-Wang. "The role of small cities in Chinese urban development", *International
        Journal of Urban and Regional Research* 6(4), dec 82 : 549-565. [résumés en français, espagnol
        et allemand]

3857   LABASSE, Jean. "Manaus, ville fluviale", *Revue de géographie de Lyon* 58(3), 83 : 259-275.
        [résumé en anglais]

3858   LAVEDAN, Pierre; HUGUENEY, Jeanne; HENRAT, Philippe. *L'urbanisme à l'époque
        moderne: XVI-XVIIIᵉ siècles.* Genève, Droz, 82, 310-cclxxxiii p.

3859   LAWRENCE, Roderick J. "The comparative analyses of homes: research method and
        application", *Social Science Information* 22(3), 83 : 461-485.

3860   LE BRIS, Émile. "Contenu géographique et contenu social de la notion de résidence.
        Quelques réflexions à partir de résultats d'enquêtes biographiques effectuées à Lomé
        (Togo) et Accra (Ghana)", *Cahiers d'Études africaines* 21(1-3), 81 : 129-174.

3861   LEE, Barrett A.; GUEST, Avery M. "Determinants of neighborhood satisfaction: a
        metropolitan-level analysis", *Sociological Quarterly* 24(2), spr 83 : 287-303.

3862   LEE, Robin H. "Black housing in South Africa: problem or challenge?", *South Africa
        International* 13(3), jan 83 : 207-220.

3863   LEHMKUHL, Reiner. "Städtebau und Solidaritätsprinzip" (Urbanism and solidarity
        principles), *Jahrbuch für Christliche Sozialwissenschaften* 24, 83 : 127-161. [Germany FR]

3864   LEPS, A.; [et al.]. "Social'noe prostranstvo goroda kak ob'ekt ėmpiričeskogo issledovanija:
        problemy metodologii i metodiki po materialam Tallina" (The town social space as an

object of empirical research: methodological and methodic problems with the Tallin materials), *in: Sociologičeskie issledovanija v Sovetskoj Pribaltike.* Vil'njus, 1982 : 347-362.

3865 LERNER, Jaime. "A experiência de planejamento urbano de Curitiba" (Urban planning experiment of Curitiba), *Revista de Administração municipal* 30(168), sep 83 : 8-17.

3866 LILLO A., Alonso. *Noter om Latinamerikas urbaniseringsproces* (Notes on the urbanization process of Latin America). København, Institut IV, Kunstakademiets Arkitektskole, 83, 105 p.

3867 LITOVKA, O. P.; MEZHEVICH, M. N. "Characteristics and trends of urbanization in a developed socialist society", *Soviet Geography* 24(5), mai 83 : 354-360.

3868 LONG, Larry; DE ARE, Diana. "The slowing of urbanization in the US", *Scientific American* 249(1), jul 83 : 31-39.

3869 LUGAN, Jean-Claude. *La petite ville au présent et au futur.* Paris, Éditions du CNRS, 83, ix-336 p.

3870 MAGUIÑA LARCO, Alejandrino; MANRIQUE CASTRO, Manuel. *Pobreza urbana y políticas de vivienda: el trabajo social en la problemática habitacional* (Urban poverty and housing policies: social work on housing problems). Lima, Centro Latinoamericano de Trabajo Social, 83, 235 p.

3871 MARSHALL, Harvey; LEWIS, Bonnie L. "City-suburb competition for high status males: age and size as determinants", *Sociology and Social Research* 67(2), jan 83 : 129-145. [USA]

3872 MASON, Joseph B. *History of housing in the US, 1930-1980.* Houston, TX, Gulf Publishing Co., Book Division, 82, 187-16 p.

3873 MASSEY, Douglas S. "A research note on residential succession: the Hispanic case", *Social Forces* 61(3), mar 83 : 825-833.

3874 MATSUDAIRA, Makoto. "Toshi no shakai shudan: Fuchu sairei shudan ni miru machiuchi no jisshoteki kenkyu" (Social groups in Japanese cities), *Rikkyo daigaku oyo shakaigaku kenkyu* 24, 83 : 67-117.

3875 MATSUMOTO, Kazuyoshi; JIN, Masaaki. "Inshi bunsekiho ni yoru tohoku 84-shi no hikaku bunseki" (A comparative analysis of 84 cities in Tohoku District by the method of the multivariate analysis), *Tohoku toshi gakkai kaiho* 21, 82 : 1-21.

3876 MAY, Peter J. "Expectations and urban revitalization", *Social Science Quarterly* 63(2), jun 82 : 225-235. [USA]

3877 MCGREGOR, Alan. "Neighbourhood influence on job search and job finding methods", *British Journal of Industrial Relations* 31(1), mar 83 : 91-99. [UK]

3878 MEL'NIKOV, A. N. "Gorodskaja melkaja burzunazija SŠA: nekotorye ėkonomičeskie i social'no-političeskie aspekty" (The urban small bourgeoisie in the USA: some economic and socio-political aspects), *SŠA* 13(11), 83 : 47-59.

3879 MORROW-JONES, Hazel A. "Federal mortgage insurance and the characteristics of intraurban movers in the United States", *Population Research and Policy Review* 2(1), feb 83 : 85-103.

3880 MUHAEV, R. T. "Mesto i rol' socialistićeskogo goroda v social'nom razvitii sovetskogo obšćestva" (Place and role of the socialist town in the social development of Soviet society), *in: Razvitie XXVI s'ezdom KPSS teorii naučnogo kommunizma.* Moskva, 1982 : 29-35.

3881 MULLINS, Patrick. "Theoretical perspectives on Australian urbanisation. II. Social components in the reproduction of Australian labour power", *Australian and New Zealand Journal of Sociology* 17(3), nov 81 : 35-43. [see for the first part, ibid. 17 (2), jun 81: 65-76]

3882 MURIE, Alan. *Housing inequality and deprivation.* London, Heinemann Educational, 83, 250 p. [UK]

3883 NABI KHAN, Rahat. "Les villes nouvelles: spontanéité et adaptation", *Diogène* 121, mar 83 : 53-72.

3884 NAGPAUL, Hans. "The slum and squatter settlements in metropolitan India: review of some strategies for better urban environment", *Indian Journal of Social Research* 23(1), apr 82 : 1-28.

3885 NAKANO, Saburo. "Kinko noson no toshika to shinkyu jumin: Tokyo-to Nishi-tamagun Itsukaichi-machi no jirei" (Urbanization of the rural community in the suburb and the new and old inhabitants), *Soka daigaku Soshiorojika* 8(1), 83 : 72-103.

3886 NAKANO, Saburo. "Oku-tama chiiki no toshika to jumin no taio: Hinohara-mura, Kazuma-chiku no jirei" (Urbanization of Okutama-zone and attitudes of inhabitants toward it: case of Kazuma-district, Hino-hara-mura), *Soka daigaku Soshiorojika* 7(2), 83 : 42-59.

3887 NESPOR, Stefano. "Revolution in land use policy: la pianificazione urbanistica negli Stati Uniti" (Revolution in land use policy: town planning in the USA), *Rivista trimestrale di Diritto pubblico* (4), 82 : 1218-1248.

3888 NISHIMURA, Hiroko. "Shutoken shuhenbu ni okeru chiiki seikatsu kozo no jittai to sono kozo" (The recent trends of community life in the fringe area of Tokyo metropolis: on the case of Hinode-cho, Nishitamagun), *Soka daigaku Soshiorojika* 7(2), 83 : 60-83.

3889   NOLASCO ARMAS, Margarita. *Cuatro ciudades: el proceso de urbanización dependiente* (Four cities: the dependent urbanization process). México, Instituto Nacional de Antropología e Historia, 81, 343 p.

3890   NOSCHIS, Kaj. "Fonction symbolique du logement: une analyse de cas", *Social Science Information* 22(3), 83 : 435-460.

3891   O'LOUGHLIN, John. "Spatial inequalities in Western cities: a comparison of North American and German urban areas", *Social Indicators Research* 13(2), aug 83 : 185-212.

3892   ODA, Toshikatsu. "Daitoshi ni okeru kinrin kankei ni kansuru ichi-kosatsu: Sapporo shimin no kinrin kosairyo sokutek no kokoromi" (A measurement of the neighboring of metropolitan inhabitants: a case of Sapporo of 1.5 million population), *Hokkaido toshi* 18-19, 83 : 67-116.

3893   OKADA, Makoto. "Kokusaikan jinko ido to toshi shakaigaku, fukushigaku" (Demography of international population: movement and urban sociology, science of social work), *Komazawa shakaigaku kenkyu* 15, 83 : 1-28.

3894   OSTERLING, Jorge. "La problemática de la vivienda en Lima: algunas políticas de vivienda estatal" (Housing problems in Lima: some state housing policies), *Socialismo y participación* (19), sep 82 : 11-23.

3895   PÁCL, Pavel. "Sociologické aspekty urbanizačnich trendů v současné migraci čs. obyvatelstva" (Sociological aspects of urbanization and present immigration of Czechoslovak population), *Sborník prací filozofické Fakulty Brněnské University* 31(26), 82 : 69-82. [résumés en russe et en allemand]

3896   PAJONI, Raul. "Buenos Aires, 1976-1982 — La ségrégation compulsive", *Hérodote* 31, dec 83 : 38-60.

3897   PALISI, Bartolomeo J.; CANNING, Claire. "Urbanism and social psychological well-being: a cross-cultural test of three theories", *Sociological Quarterly* 24(4), 83 : 527-543.

3898   PANWALKAR, Pratima. "New houses for old — an analysis of experiences", *Indian Journal of Social Work* 43(4), jan 83 : 383-393. [India]

3899   PARCEL, Toby L. "Wealth accumulation of black and white men: the case of housing equity", *Social Problems* 30(2), dec 82 : 199-211.

3900   PÉTONNET, Colette. *Espaces habités: ethnologie des banlieues.* Paris, Éditions Galilée, 82, 174-11 p. [France]

3901   PEZEU-MASSABUAU, Jacques. *La maison, espace social.* Paris, Presses Universitaires de France, 83, 252 p.

3902   POLYAN, P. M. "Large urban agglomeration in the Soviet Union", *Soviet Geography* 23(10), dec 82 : 707-718.

3903   POLYDORIDES, Nicos. *The concept of centrality in urban form and structure.* Bern-New York, NY, P. Lang, 83, iv-184 p.

3904   POPENOE, David. "Urban scale and the quality of community life: a Swedish community comparison", *Sociological Inquiry* 53(4), 83 : 404-418. [Sätra and Vällingby]

3905   POTTER, Robert B. "Urban development planning and demographic change, 1970-80", *Caribbean Geography* 1, 83 : 3-12.

3906   POZO, Hernán. *La ciudad como espacio de segregación social* (The city as a space of social segregation). Santiago de Chile, FLACSO, 83, 20 p.

3907   PROTASH, William; BALDASSARE, Mark. "Growth policies and community status: a test and modification of Logan's theory", *Urban Affairs Quarterly* 18(3), mar 83 : 397-412.

3908   QADEER, Mohammad A. *Urban development in the Third World: internal dynamics of Lahore, Pakistan.* New York, NY, Praeger, 83, xiv-282 p.

3909   QUTUB, Ishaq Yacoub. *Small cities and national development in Arab studies.* S.l., s.n., 83, 103 p. [Paper prepared for the International Seminar on Small Cities and National Development held in New Delhi, 24-29 January, 1983]

3910   RAO, V. L. S. Prakasa. *Urbanization in India: spatial dimensions.* New Delhi, Concept, 83, 327 p.

3911   REITZES, Donald C. "Urban images: a social psychological approach", *Sociological Inquiry* 53(2-3), spr 83 : 314-332. [USA]

3912   RIMMER, Peter J.; DRAKAKIS-SMITH, David. "La gestion des capitales de l'Asie du Sud-Est depuis les années 1960", *Espace géographique* 11(4), dec 82 : 259-268.

3913   ROMERO, Luis A.; [ed.]. *Historia de ciudades: Buenos Aires criolla, 1820-1850* (History of cities: creole Buenos Aires, 1820-1850). Buenos Aires, Centro Editor de América Latina, 83, 94 p.

3914   RONDINELLI, Dennis A. *Secondary cities in developing countries: policies for diffusing urbanization.* Beverly Hills, CA-London-New Delhi, Sage, 83, 288 p.

3915   ROSS, Robert; TRACHTE, Kent. "Global cities and global classes: the peripheralization of labor in New York City", *Review (F. Braudel Center)* 6(3), wint 83 : 393-431.

3916   SACHS, Céline. "The growth of squatter settlements in São Paulo", *Social Science Information* 22(4-5), 83 : 751-775.

3917   SAITO, Yoshio. "Toshi shakaigaku ni okeru community-ron no yakuwari" (The role of community theory of urban sociology), *Shakaigaku kenkyu* 46, 83 : 1-19.

3918   SAITOH, Masao. *Toshi seikatsu to jichi no shakaigaku (zohoban)* (Sociology of urban life and autonomy). Tokyo, Bunka Shobo Hakubunsha, 83, 358 p.

3919   SANTOS, Milton. *Ensaios sobre a urbanização latino-americana* (Essays on Latin American urbanization). São Paulo, Editora HUCITEC, 82, 194 p.

3920   SARIN, Madhu. *Urban planning in the Third World: the Chandigarh experience.* London, Mansell Publishers, 82, v-266 p. [Chandigarh, India]

3921   SCHNEIDER, Karl-Günther; WIESE, Bernd. *Die Städte des südlichen Afrika* (Towns of South Africa). Berlin, Gebr. Borntraeger, 83, ix-175 p.

3922   SCHÜRKENS, Ulrike. "Konkurrierende theoretische Perspektiven in der urbanen Soziologie unter besonderer Berücksichtigung der machtsoziologischen Ansätze" (Competing theoretical perspectives in urban sociology with special consideration of power sociological approaches), *Sociologia internationalis* 21(1-2), 83 : 17-49.

3923   SCHWARZ, Alf. *Les dupes de la modernisation: développement urbain et sous-développement en Afrique.* Montréal, PQ, Nouvelle Optique, 83, 293 p.

3924   SCHWIRIAN, Kent P. "Models of neighborhood change", *Annual Review of Sociology* (9), 83 : 83-102.

3925   SCOTT, Ian. *Urban and spatial development in Mexico.* Baltimore, MD, Johns Hopkins University Press, 82, xii-328 p.

3926   SELIM, Monique. "Rapports sociaux dans un quartier anciennement industriel. Un isolat social", *Homme* 22(4), dec 82 : 77-86. [France] [résumé en anglais]

3927   SELL, Ralph R.; DE JONG, Gordon F. "Deciding whether to move: mobility, wishful thinking and adjustment", *Sociology and Social Research* 67(2), jan 83 : 146-165.

3928   SHU, Yi-Rong Ann; PANNELL, Clifton W. "Urbanisation and residential spatial structure in Taiwan", *Pacific Viewpoint* 23(1), mai 82 : 22-52.

3929   SIGOV, I. I.; [ed.]. *Planirovanie kompleksnogo razvitija krupnyh gorodov: opyt i puti soveršenstvovanija* (Planning of the complex development of big towns: the experiment and ways of improvement). Leningrad, Nauka, 82, 239 p. [USSR]

3930   SMITH, A. Wade. "Attitudes of Whites toward residential integration", *Phylon* 43(4), dec 82 : 368-384.

3931   SMITH, Wallace F.; [ed.]. "Housing America", *Annals of the American Academy of Political and Social Science* 465, jan 83 : 9-222. [with contributions by Mark J. RIEDY, Leo GREBLER, Ned EICHLER, Michael SUMICHRAST, Lawrence B. SMITH, Anthony DOWNS]

3932   SOSNOWSKI, Adam; WALKOWIAK, Jerzy. "Sasiedztwo i jego odzwierciedlenie w świadomości mieszkańców wielkomiejskich osiedli" (Neighbours and their image in the awareness of inhabitants of settlements in big cities), *Studia Socjologiczne* 88(1), 83 : 223-244.

3933   SOUTH, Scott J.; POSTON, Dudley L. Jr. "The US metropolitan system: regional change, 1950-1970", *Urban Affairs Quarterly* 18(2), dec 82 : 187-206.

3934   SPATES, James L.; MACIONIS, John J. *The sociology of cities.* New York, NY, St. Martin's Press, 82, xiii-574 p.

3935   SPENCE, Nigel; [et al.]. *British cities: an analysis of urban change.* Oxford-New York, NY, Pergamon Press, 82, xx-310 p.

3936   STAHURA, John M. "Determinants of change in the distribution of blacks across suburbs", *Sociological Quarterly* 24(3), sum 83 : 421-433.

3937   STASIAK, Andrzej. "Mieszkalnictwo jako istotny element zagospodarowania polskiej wsi" (Housing as a real element of Polish development), *Miasto* 32(6), 82 : 1-7.

3938   STIMSON, Robert John. *The Australian city: a welfare geography.* Melbourne, Longman Cheshire, 82, xviii-309 p.

3939   STREITWIESER, Mary L.; GOODMAN, John L. Jr. "A survey of recent research on race and residential location", *Population Research and Policy Review* 2(3), oct 83 : 253-283. [USA]

3940   STUART, Robert C. "Migration and the growth of Soviet cities", *Jahrbuch der Wirtschaft Osteuropas* 10(1), 82 : 253-271.

3941   SUSLOV, Ju. A.; LEBEDEV, P. N.; [eds.]. *Problemy social'nogo razvitija krupnyh gorodov* (Problems of social development of big towns). Leningrad, Izdatel'stvo Leningradskogo Universiteta, 82, 191 p.

3942   SZCZEPAŃSKI, Jan. "Treść stosunków zachodzących między wsią i miastem" (The substance of relations between the country and the town), *Wieś i Rolnictwo* 40(3), 83 : 9-18. [Poland]

3943   SZELÉNYI, Iván. *Urban inequalities under state socialism.* Oxford-New York, NY, Oxford
        University Press, 83, 158 p. [Eastern Europe]
3944   TALIA, Michele. "Maturità e declino dei sistemi metropolitani in Europa occidentale"
        (Maturity and decline of the urban systems in Western Europe), *Rivista internazionale
        di Scienze sociali* 91(1), jan-mar 83 : 39-62.
3945   TARRADELL, Miquel; [et al.]. *Evolució urbana de Catalunya* (Urban development of
        Catalonia). Barcelona, Edicions de la Magrana, Institut Municipal d'Història, 83, 127 p.
3946   TERZIĆ, Vesna. "Neke karakteristike procesa urbanizacija u nerazvijenim zemljama i
        u zemljama u razvoju" (Some characteristics of the process of urbanization in under-
        developed and developing countries), *Revija za Sociologiju* 11(1-2), 81 : 37-42.
3947   TIÉVANT, Sophie. "Les études de 'communauté' et la ville: héritage et problèmes",
        Sociologie du Travail 25(2), apr-jun 83 : 243-256.
3948   TÓTH, Pál. "Lakótelepi társadalom mint helyi társadalom" (The society of residential
        quarters as local societies), *Társadalomtudományi Közlemények* 13(1), 83 : 67-81. [Hungary]
3949   TUPPEN, J. N. "The development of French New Towns: an assessment of progress",
        Urban Studies 20(1), feb 83 : 11-30.
3950   TURNER, Mark Macdonald. "Urbanization and class in the Ilocos region", *Philippine
        Studies* (30), trim. 2, 82 : 204-230. [Philippines]
3951   TUROWSKI, Jan. "Miejskie środowiska mieszkalne w świetle ocen" (Urban residential
        communities in the light of estimates), *Studia Socjologiczne* 88(1), 83 : 209-222.
3952   TUROWSKI, Jan. "Teoretyczne koncepcje relacji 'wieś-miasto' w socjologii" (Theoretical
        concepts of the town-country relations in sociology), *Wieś i Rolnictwo* 40(3), 83 : 27-40.
3953   URANO, Masaki. "Daitoshi-ken no susei to jinko ido gensho" (The rise and fall of the
        metropolitan area and residential mobility), *Waseda daigaku shakai-kagaku tokyu* 28(3),
        83 : 69-106.
3954   VALDES, Teresa. *El problem de la vivienda. Políticas estatales y movilización popular* (The housing
        problem. Housing policies and popular mobilization). Santiago, FLACSO, 83, 82 p.
3955   VARADY, David P. "Determinants of residential mobility decisions", *Journal of the American
        Planning Association* 49(2), spr 8 : 184-199. [USA]
3956   WEGLEŃSKI, Jan. *Urbanizacja. Kontrowersje wokół pojęcia* (Urbanization. Controversy on
        the notion). Warszawa, Państwowe Wydawnictwo Naukowe, 83, 143 p. [Poland]
3957   WHYTE, Martin King. "Urbanism as a Chinese way of life", *International Journal of
        Comparative Sociology (Leiden)* 24(1-2), jan-apr 83 : 61-85.
3958   WILD, Trevor; [ed.]. *Urban and rural change in West Germany.* Totowa, NJ, Barnes and
        Noble Books; London-Canberra, Croom Helm, 83, 259 p.
3959   WINSBERG, Morton D. "Ethnic competition for residential space in Miami, Florida,
        1970-80", *American Journal of Economics and Sociology* 42(3), jul 83 : 305-314.
3960   YAMAMOTO, Kenji. "Toshi to komitsudo kyoju" (The city and high density residence),
        Kagoshima keizai daigaku shakaigakubu ronshu 1(3), 83 : 1-18. [Japan]
3961   YOKOYAMA, Katsuhide. "Hi-sabetsu buraku ni okeru seikatsu hogo: Nara-shi no baai"
        (Public assistance and unliberated communities in Nara City), *Ryukoku kiyo* 5(1),
        83 : 17-43. [Japan]
3962   YOSHIHARA, Naoki. *Toshi shakaigaku no kihon mondai: America toshiron no keifu to tokushitsu*
        (Quest for American urban sociology: a critical approach). Tokyo, Aoki Shoten, 83, 267 p.
3963   YOUNG, Ken; MILLS, Liz. *Managing the post-industrial city.* London-Exeter, NH,
        Heinemann, 83, viii-168 p. [UK]
3964   ZAIS, James P.; STRUYK, Raymond J.; THIBODEAU, Thomas. *Housing assistance for
        older Americans: the Reagan prescription.* Washington, DC, Urban Institute Press, 82, xv-125 p.
3965   ZAIS, James P.; THIBODEAU, Thomas G. *The elderly and urban housing.* Washington, DC,
        Urban Institute Press, 83, xv-107 p.
3966   ZASLAVSKAJA, T. I.; GORJAČENKO, È. E.; [eds.]. *Social'no-territorial'naja struktura
        goroda i sela* (The socio-territorial structure of a town and a village). Novosibirsk, Institut
        Èkonomiki i Organizacii Promyšlennogo Proizvodstva Sibirskogo Otdelenija Akademii
        Nauk SSSR, 82, 154 p.
3967   ZEVELEV, I. A. "Goroda Jugo — Vostočnoj Azii: problemy social'noj struktury" (South-
        East Asia towns: problems concerning the social structure), *Narody Azii i Afriki* (1), jan-feb
        83 : 56-64.
3968   ZIJDERVELD, Anton C. *Steden zonder stedelijkheid: cultuursociologische verkenning van een
        beleidsprobleem* (Cities without urban policy: cultural and sociological examination of a
        policy problem). Deventer, Van Loghum Slaterus, 83, 132 p. [Netherlands]
3969   ZUKIN, Sharon. *Loft living: culture and capital in urban change.* Baltimore, MD, Johns Hopkins
        University Press, 82, xi-212 p.

17100   ECONOMIC SOCIOLOGY
         SOCIOLOGIE ÉCONOMIQUE

3970   BRAUDEL, Fernand; LABROUSSE, Ernest; [eds.]. *Histoire économique et sociale de la France.*
        IV. L'ère industrielle et la sociéte d'aujourd'hui: siècle 1880-1980. Paris, Presses Universitaires
        de France, 82, 983-1837 p. [Années 1950 à nos jours, par Jean BOUVIER]
3971   FOSSIER, Robert. *Enfance de l'Europe: X^e-XIIe siècles; aspects économiques et sociaux. I. L'homme
        et son espace. II. Structures et problèmes.* Paris, Presses Universitaires de France, 82, 1125 p.
3972   LE VAN-LEMESLE, Lucette. "L'économie politique à la conquête d'une légitimité,
        1896-1937", *Actes de la Recherche en Sciences sociales* 47-48, jun 83 : 113-117. [France]
3973   STINCHCOMBE, Arthur L. *Economic sociology.* New York, NY-London-Toronto-Sydney,
        Harcourt Brace Jovanovich, Academic Press, 83, ix-269 p.

17200   ECONOMIC SYSTEMS
         SYSTÈMES ÉCONOMIQUES

17210   Economic doctrines
         Doctrines économiques

3974   ALESSI, Louis de. "Property rights and transaction costs: a new perspective in economic
        theory", *Social Science Journal (Fort Collins)* 20(3), jul 83 : 59-69.
3975   GLASBERG, Davita Silfen; SCHWARTZ, Michael. "Ownership and control of corporations",
        Annual Review of Sociology (9), 83 : 311-332.
3976   HODSON, Randy; KAUFMAN, Robert L. "Economic dualism: a critical review",
        American Sociological Review 47(6), dec 82 : 727-739. [USA] [Labour market segmentation]
3977   LAHORE, James. "Harmonization of design laws in the European communities: the
        copyright dilemma", *Common Market Law Review* 20(2), aug 83 : 233-268.
3978   SUŠARIN, A. S. "Logika istoričeskogo razvitija sobstvennosti" (Logic of the ownership
        historical development), *Izvestija Akademii Nauk SSSR. Serija Ėkonomičeskaja* 12(5), 82 : 92-102.

17220   Capitalism. Collectivism
         Capitalisme. Collectivisme

3979   "Capitalismo (El) en la crisis" (Capitalism in crisis), *Revista mexicana de Sociología* 44(3),
        jul-sep 82 : 783-926. [with contributions by Sergio de la PEÑA, Bob JESSOP, Daniel
        CATAIFE, James O'CONNOR, Elmar ALTVATER]
3980   BEZBAKH, Pierre. *La société féodo-marchande.* Paris, Anthropos, 83, 278 p.
3981   CASSÁ, Roberto. *Capitlismo y dictadura* (Capitalism and dictatorship). Santo Domingo,
        Editora de la Universidad Autónoma de Santo Domingo, 82, 794 p.
3982   DESLAURIERS, Jean-Pierre; [et al.]. "Nouvelles coopératives et changement social.
        Auscultation québécoise", *Communautés* (62), dec 82 : 73-107.
3983   DOKTÓR, Kazimiers; MIROWSKI, Włodzimierz; [eds.]. *Teorija i metodologija social'nogo
        prognozirovanija i ich rol' v razvitii socialistićeskogo obšćestva* (Theory and methodology of the
        social prognosis and their role in the development of the socialist society). Warszawa,
        Polska Akademia Nauk Instytut Filozofii i Socjologii, 83, 146 p.
3984   DORE, Ronald. "Goodwill and the spirit of market capitalism", *British Journal of Sociology*
        34(4), dec 83 : 459-482.
3985   DRATHSCHMIDT, Ursula. *Portugiesischer Kulturimperialismus in Angola: ein halbes Jahrtausend
        'christlichen Imperiums'* (Portuguese cultural imperialism in Angola: a half century of
        'Christian empire'). Saarbrücken-Fort Lauderdale, Breitenbach, 82, iii-120 p.
3986   GEFFRAY, Christian. "Nobles, bourgeois, Inquisition: les prémisses de l'expansion
        coloniale portugaise au XVIe siècle", *Cahiers d'Études Africaines* 21(4), 81 : 523-546.
3987   GOLDSTONE, Jack A. "Capitalist origins of the English Revolution: chasing a chimera",
        Theory and Society 12(2), mar 83 : 143-180.
3988   HOLLOS, Maria. "The effect of collectivization on village social organization in Hungary",
        East European Quarterly 17(1), mar 83 : 57-65.
3989   KOVALEV, A. M. "Razvitoj socializm i obrazovanie sovetskogo naroda-novoj social'noj
        i internacional'noj obšćnosti ljudej" (Developed socialism and formation of the Soviet

people as a new social and international human community), *Vestnik Moskovskogo Univer-siteta. Teorija naučnogo Kommunizma* (4), 82 : 16-21.

3990   MOL'DON, A. I. "Gosudarstvo razvitogo socializma: ĕdinstvo klassovogo i obščenarodnogo" (The state of the developed socialism: unity of the class and the all-people), *Političeskaja Organizacija Obščestva i Upravlenie pri Socializme* (3), 82 : 63-75.

3991   PATAKI, Ferenc. "A nemzedékváltás és a szocialista fejlődés folytonossága" (The change of generations and the continuity of socialist development), *Társadalomtudományi Közlemények* 12(4), 82 : 590-601. [Hungary]

3992   PEJOVICH, Svetozar; [ed.]. *Philosophical and economic foundations of capitalism.* Lexington, MA-Toronto, ON, Heath, Lexington Books, 83, xii-144 p.

3993   PLAISANCE, Eric. "Familles bourgeoises et scolarisation des jeunes enfants: la fréquentation des écoles maternelles publiques à Paris de 1945 à 1975", *Revue française de Sociologie* 24(1), jan-mar 83 : 31-60. [résumés en anglais, allemand, et espagnol]

3994   ROSENKO, M. N.; [ed.]. *Vozrastanie integrujuščej roli marksistko-leninskoj filosofii v razvitii socialističeskogo obščestva* (Elevation of the integrating role of the Marxist-Leninist philosophy in the socialist society development). Leningrad, Izdatel'stvo Leningradskogo Univer-siteta, 82, 125 p.

3995   RUNCIMAN, W. G. "Capitalism without classes: the case of classical Rome", *British Journal of Sociology* 21(2), jun 83 : 157-181.

3996   RUSSO, Tommaso. "Lealtà, bisogni e dominio politico nel capitalismo maturo" (Loyalty, needs, and political power in mature capitalism), *Critica sociologica* 65, 83 : 72-79.

3997   SAMI, Uddin; RAHMAN, Mahfoozur. *Cooperative sector in India after independence.* New Delhi, S. Chand, 83, vi-597 p.

3998   SIDOROV, V. A.; STOLJAROVA, L. I. "Ob ĕtapah razvitija socialističeskogo obščestva i nekotoryh problemah ĕffektivnosti obščestvennogo proizvodstva" (On the stages of the socialist society development and some problems of the social production efficien-cy), 1982 : 3-13.

3999   STAATZ, John M. "The cooperative as a coalition: a game-theoretic approach", *American Journal of Agricultural Economics* 65(5), dec 83 : 1084-1089. [Proceedings, with a discussion by Leon GAROYAN, 1096-1098]

4000   TOKARZEWSKI, Tadeusz. "Karola Marksa teoria spółdzielczości" (Karl Marx' theory of co-operatives), *Spółdzielczy Kwartalnik naukowy* 17(3), 83 : 57-68.

4001   VITALIANO, Peter. "Cooperative enterprise: an alternative conceptual basis for analyzing a complex institution", *American Journal of Agricultural Economics* 65(5), dec 83 : 1078-1083. [Proceedings, with a discussion by Leon GAROYAN, 1096-1098]

17300   ECONOMIC SITUATION. STANDARD OF LIVING
SITUATION ÉCONOMIQUE. NIVEAU DE VIE

17310   Economy. Economic development
Économie. Développement économique

4002   "Institutions (Les) des Communautés européennes: propositions de réforme et perspectives d'évolution", *Revue d'Intégration européenne* 6(2-3), spr 83 : 121-235. [with contributions by Jean-Paul JACQUE, Michael PALMER, Jean-Victor LOUIS]

4003   AGLIETTA, Michel. "Crisis y transformaciones sociales" (Crisis and social transformations), *Investigación económica* 42(163), jan-mar 83 : 11-25. [Mexico]

4004   ARDAGH, John. *France in the 1980s.* London, Secker and Warburg, 82, 672 p.

4005   GLENDAY, Daniel. "The 'dependencia' school in Canada: an examination and evaluation", *Canadian Review of Sociology and Anthropology* 20(3), aug 83 : 346-358.

4006   HAAS, Aim; STACK, Steven. "Economic development and strikes: a comparative analysis", *Sociological Quarterly* 24(1), wint 83 : 43-58.

4007   IBAÑEZ, J. "Hacia un concepto teórico de 'explotación' " (Towards a theoretical concept of 'exploitation'), *Sistema* (53), mar 83 : 39-56.

4008   SUH, Sang-Mok. "Economic growth and urban poverty in Korea", *Social Science Journal (Seoul)* 9, 82 : 37-48.

4009   TAMINIAUX, Pierre. "La consommation de la crise", *Revue de l'Institut de Sociologie* (3-4), 83 : 481-491.

17320   Income. Living conditions
Revenu. Conditions de vie

4010   "Conditions de vie et aspirations des français", *Futuribles* 63, feb 83 : 15-33.

4011   ABOWD, John M.; KILLINGSWORTH, Mark R. "Sex, discrimination, atrophy, and the
        male-female wage differential", *Industrial Relations* 22(3), aut 83 : 387-402.
4012   BAILLY, A. S.; CUNHA, A. "A propos de la qualité de la vie en France", *Revue d'Économie
        régionale et urbaine* (4), 82 : 487-502. [résumé en anglais]
4013   BORJAS, George J. "The measurement of race and gender wage differentials: evidence
        from the federal sector", *Industrial and Labor Relations Review* 37(1), oct 83 : 79-91. [USA]
4014   CONNIDIS, Ingrid. "Living arrangement choices of older residents: assessing quantitative
        results with qualitative data", *Canadian Journal of Sociology / Cahiers canadiens de Sociologie*
        8(4), 83 : 359-375. [Canada]
4015   DESAI, Meghnad; SHAH, Anup. "Bequest and inheritance in nuclear families and joint
        families", *Economica* 50(198), mai 83 : 193-202.
4016   DI ORIO, Fernando. "Ipotesi di un modello par la misurazione della 'qualità della vita'
        mediante indicatori sociali" (Suggestions for a model to measure the 'quality of life'
        through social indicators), *Studi di Sociologia* 21(1), mar 83 : 29-42.
4017   FOSSETT, Mark; SOUTH, Scott J. "The measurement of intergroup income inequality:
        a conceptual review", *Social Forces* 61(3), mar 83 : 855-871.
4018   GOLDING, Peter; MIDDLETON, Sue. *Images of welfare: press and public attitudes to poverty.*
        Oxford, M. Robertson, 82, vii-283 p. [UK]
4019   HANSEN, Erik Jørgen. *The distribution of the living conditions in Denmark.* København,
        Socialforskningsinstituttet, Teknisk Forlag, 82, 102 p.
4020   HSIEH, Chang-Tseh; LIU, Ben-Chieh. "The pursuance of better quality of life: in the
        long run, better quality of social life is the most important factor in migration", *American
        Journal of Economics and Sociology* 42(4), oct 83 : 431-440.
4021   KALETA, Andrzej. "Uwarunkowania opinii rodzin wiejskich o 'jakości życia'" (Opinions
        of rural families on 'quality of life'), *Wieś i Rolnictwo* 39(2), 83 : 219-232. [Poland]
4022   KOLODNY, Harvey; VAN BEINUM, Hans; [eds.]. *The quality of working life and the 1980s.*
        New York, NY, Praeger, 83, xi-177 p.
4023   KUKURUDZA, I. I. "O buržuaznyh koncepcijah 'kačestva žizni'" (On bourgeois
        conceptions of the 'quality of life'), *Voprosy političeskoj Ékonomii* 164, 82 : 68-76.
4024   OFFER, John. "Spencer's sociology of welfare", *Sociological Review* 31(4), nov 83 : 719-752.
4025   ORNSTEIN, Michael D. *Gender wage differentials in Canada: a review of previous research and
        theoretical framework.* Ottawa, Labour Canada, 82, 57 p.
4026   PARKER, Robert Nash; FENWICK, Rudy. "The Pareto curve and its utility for open-ended
        income distributions in survey research", *Social Forces* 61(3), mar 83 : 872-885. [USA]
4027   PHILLIPS, Derek L. "The normative standing of economic inequalities", *Sociologische Gids*
        30(5), sep-oct 83 : 318-350.
4028   RAGONE, Gerardo; SPANO, Antonella. "Teoria e ideologia della qualità della vita"
        (Theory and ideology of the quality of life), *Rassegna economica* 47(3), mai-jun 83 : 543-561.
4029   SHIN, Doh C.; [et al.]. "Environmental effects on perceptions of life quality in Korea",
        Social Indicators Research 12(4), mai 83 : 393-416.
4030   SŁABY, Teresa. "Pewne ustalenia dotyczące bieżących prac nad minimum socjalnym w
        Polsce" (Some results of the current work on social minimum in Poland), *Biuletyn Instytutu
        Gospodarstwa Społecznego* 25(4), 82 : 69-83.
4031   SZALAI, Sándor. "The meaning of comparative research on the quality of life", *New
        Hungarian Quarterly* 24(92), sum 83 : 75-87.
4032   TASAKA, Toshio. "Tai ni okeru sžoku kankō to shakuchi kankei" (The custom of in
        heritance and the tenant relation in Central Thailand), *Gekkan Asia-Africa kenkyu* 23(2),
        83 : 2-20.
4033   TERRA, Juan Pablo. *Distribución social del ingreso en Uruguay* (Social distribution of income
        in Uruguay). Montevideo, Centro Latinoamericano de Economía Humana, 83, 203 p.
4034   TIENDA, Marta. "Nationality and income attainment among native and immigrant
        Hispanic men in the United States", *Sociological Quarterly* 24(2), spr 83 : 253-272.
4035   TRYFAN, Barbara. "Dysparytety a egalitaryzm" (Disparities and egalitarianism), *Wieś
        i Rolnictwo* 39(2), 83 : 57-73. [Poland]
4036   WALTER-BUSCH, E. "Subjective and objective indicators of regional quality of life in
        Switzerland", *Social Indicators Research* 12(4), mai 83 : 337-391.
4037   WEEDE, Erich. "The effects of democracy and socialist strength on the size distribution
        of income", *International Journal of Comparative Sociology* 23(3-4), sep-dec 82 : 151-165.

17400 **ENTERPRISES. PRODUCTION**
ENTREPRISES. PRODUCTION

17410 **Business economics. Management**
Économie de l'entreprise. Gestion

4038 BENSON, John. *The penny capitalists: a study of nineteenth-century working class entrepreneurs.* New Brunswick, NJ, Rutgers University Press, 83, 172 p. [UK]

4039 BOLTANSKI, Luc. "Visions of American management in post-war France", *Theory and Society* 12(3), mai 83 : 375-403.

4040 CARDOSO, Fernando Henrique. "O papel dos empresários no processo del transição: o caso brasileiro" (The role of entrepreneurs in the process of transition: the case of Brasil), *Dados* 26(1), 83 : 9-27.

4041 CASELLA, Mario. *Impresa e società: cronache di diritto, di costume e di varia umanità, 1976-1983* (Enterprise and society: a chronique of law, customs and types of humanity, 1976-1983). Milano, A. Giuffrè, 83, iv-168 p.

4042 CLAYTON, S. "The images of the development of companies", *Sociological Review* 31(1), feb 83 : 83-104.

4043 CLAYTON, Susan. "Les représentations sociales du développement des entreprises", *Revue de l'Institut de Sociologie* (3-4), 83 : 361-385. [a travers la presse]

4044 CRESSEY, Donald R.; MOORE, Charles A. "Managerial values and corporate codes of ethics", *California Management Review* 25(4), 83 : 53-77. [USA]

4045 ETTINGER, Jean-Claude. "Le profil psychologique du créateur d'entreprise", *Revue française de Gestion* (41), aug 83 : 24-30.

4046 FARKAS, János; [ed.]. *Technikafejlesztés, társadalmi ellenszélben. (Empirikus vizsgálatok egy magyar nagyvállalatnál)* (Technical development in social counterblast. (Empirical investigations in a Hungarian big enterprise)). Budapest, Magyar Tudományos Akadémia Szociológiai Inrézete, 82, 315 p.

4047 GARCÍA ECHEVARRIA, S. *Responsabilidad social y balance social de la empresa* (Social responsibility and social balance-sheet of the enterprise). Madrid, Mapfre, 82, 341 p.

4048 GOFFEE, Robert; SCASE, Richard. "Business ownership and women's subordination: a preliminary study of female proprietors", *Sociological Review* 31(4), nov 83 : 625-648. [UK]

4049 HOGNER, Robert H. "Corporate social reporting: eight decades of development at U.S. Steel", *Research in Corporate Social Performance and Policy* 4, 82 : 243-250.

4050 KENT, Calvin. "The new entrepreneurs", *Journal of Social, Political and Economic Studies* 8(2), sum 83 : 161-171. [USA]

4051 KERBO, Harold R.; DELLA FAVE, L. Richard. "Corporate linkage and control of the corporate economy: new evidence and a reinterpretation", *Sociological Quarterly* 24(2), spr 83 : 201-218.

4052 MICHEL, Andrée. "Multinationales et inégalités de classe et de sexe", *Current Sociology* 31(1), 83 : 1-208. [Amérique latine]

4053 MORGAN, Gareth. "Rethinking corporate strategy: a cybernetic perspective", *Human Relations* 36(4), apr 83 : 345-360.

4054 RICHARD, Pierre; AROCENA, José. "La création d'entreprise: de l'idée au faire", *Année sociologique* 33, 83 : 139-157.

4055 ROSKIN, Rick; MARGERISON, Charles. "The effectiveness of some measures of managerial effectiveness", *Human Relations* 36(10), oct 83 : 865-882.

4056 VAN WAAS, Michael. "Multinational corporations and the politics of labor supply", *Insurgent Sociologist* 11(3), 82 : 49-57.

4057 WAGNER, Thomas A. *Kognitive Problemlösungsbarrieren bei Entscheidungsprozessen in der Unternehmung* (Cognitive problem solving barriers in decision processes in the enterprise). Frankfurt-am-Main, Lang, 82, vi-245 p.

4058 WILLIAMS, Allan P. O.; SILVERSTONE, Rosalie. "Effective in-house personnel research units. Findings from six U. K. case studies", *Organization Studies* 4(1), 83 : 39-54.

4059 WILLIAMS, Oliver F. "Business ethics: a Trojan horse?", *California Management Review* 24(4), 82 : 14-24. [USA]

4060 WRENN, Robert. "Management and work humanization", *Insurgent Sociologist* 11(3), 82 : 23-38.

4061 YAMAOKA, Hiroko. "Keiei soshiki no kanryoka to 'Rodo no imi' no henka" (Bureaucratization of business organization and the changes of 'the meaning of work'), *Tokyo toritsu shoka tanki-daigaku* 27, 83 : 27-41.

17420 Productivity. Technology
Productivité. Technologie

4062 "Automatisation et société", *Culture technique* (7), mar 82 : 17-94. [France] [with contributions by Olivier PASIRE, Francis GINSBOURGER, Charles HALARY, Yann de KERSRGUEN]

4063 "Démocratie (La) face au développement des technologies", *Esprit* (8-9), sep 83 : 29-120. [Georges THILL, Jean GREA, Alexandre NICOLON, Philippe BRETON, Jean-Marc LEVY-LEBLOND]

4064 "Economic productivity and the behavioral sciences", *American Psychologist* 38(4), apr 83 : 451-493. [USA] [with contributions by Dan QUAYLE, Peter E. NATHAN, Raymond A. KATZELL, Richard A. GUZZO]

4065 "Energija i društvo" (Energy and society), *Revija za Sociologiju* 12(1-4), 82 : 3-124.

4066 "Enjeux (Les) de la robotique", *Futuribles* 64, mar 83 : 3-88. [with contributions by Joël Le QUEMENT, Jean Hervé LORENZI, Georges CHAVANES, Philippe COIFFET, Yves LASFARGUE, Wcévolode VOISIN, Pierre MARGRAIN]

4067 "Progrès (Le) technologique", *Actualité économique* 58(3), sep 82 : 253-400. [with contributions by Louis SEGUIN DULUDE, Marcel SIMONEAU, Eckhard SIGGEL]

4068 ARGOTE, Linda; [et al.]. "The human side of robotics: how workers react to a robot", *Sloan Management Review* 24(3), spr 83 : 31-41.

4069 ARIMOTO, Akira. "Kagaku no seisansei to kaisō kōzō" (Scientific productivity and social stratification), *Osaka kyoiku daigaku kyoikugaku ronshu* 12, 83 : 51-60.

4070 AYRES, Robert U.; MILLER, Steven M. *Robotics: applications and social implications.* Cambridge, MA, Harper and Row, Ballinger, 83, xx-339 p.

4071 BARRIER-LYNN, Christiane. "Notes en marge de celle de Jean Lojkine à propos d'automation à la japonaise", *Sociologie du Travail* 25(1), jan-mar 83 : 63-78. [see ibid. 24(2), apr-jun 82 : 192-206]

4072 BEKEMANS, Léonce. "Technologische verandering en tewerkstelling: een uitdaging voor de toekomst" (Technological change and employment: a challenge to the future), *Economisch en Sociaal Tijdschrift* 37(1), feb 83 : 5-17.

4073 BENSON, Ian; LLOYD, John. *New technology and industrial change. The impact of the scientific-technical revolution on labour and industry.* London, Kogan Page, 83, 224 p.

4074 BEREZINA, Ju. I. "Social'nye posledstvija naučnotehničeskogo progressa v Japonii" (Social consequences of the scientific and technical progress in Japan), *Problemy Dal'nego Vostoka* (4), 82 : 106-113.

4075 BERGER, René. *L'effet des changements technologiques: en mutation, l'art, la ville, l'image, la culture, nous!.* Lausanne, Favre, 83, 231 p.

4076 BINET, Jacques. "La technologie face à la culture de l'Afrique noire", *Mois en Afrique* 18(203-204), jan 83 : 46-65.

4077 BOURMEYSTER, A. "Révolution scientifique et technique et société socialiste avancée", *Économies et Sociétés* 17(1), jan 83 : 179-201.

4078 COATES, Vary T.; FABIAN, Thecla. "Technology assessment in Europe and Japan", *Technological Forecasting and Social Change* 22(3-4), dec 82 : 343-361.

4079 ELSTER, Jon. *Explaining technical change: a case study in the philosophy of science.* Cambridge-New York, NY-Sydney, Cambridge University Press; Oslo, Universitetsforlaget; Paris, Éditions de la MSH, 83, 273 p.

4080 FARTHMANN, Friedhelm. "Sozialpolitische Konsequenzen neuer Technologien" (Socio-political consequences of new technologies), *Sozialer Fortschritt* 31(10), 82 : 222-230.

4081 GODET, Michel. "Crisis and opportunity: from technological to social change", *Futures* 15(4), aug 83 : 251-263.

4082 HILL, Ellen B.; [ed.]. "Innovative processes in social change of highly industrialized societies", *Revue internationale de Sociologie* 17(1), apr 81 : 22-111.

4083 IMAIZUMI, Reisuke. "Gijutsu to ningen sogai: Gendai shakai ni okeru technology keitai to rodo no imi o megutte" (Technology and human alienation), *Koriyama joshi daigaku kiyo* 19, 83 : 155-169.

4084 KORTAVA, V. V. "K voprosu o duhovnom stanovlcnii čcloveka v êpohu naučno-tehničeskoj revoljucii" (Question on the man's spirituual future in the era of the scientific and technical revolution), *Izvestija Akademii Nauk Gruzinskoj SSR. Serija Filosofii i Psihologii* (4), 82 : 76-85.

4085 LEJMAN, I. I.; [ed.]. *Obščestvennoe razvitie i NTR: očerki metodologii issledovanij* (Social development and the STR: aspects of the research methodology). Leningrad, Nauka, 82, 268 p. [USSR] [Scientific and Technical Revolution]

4086   LÓPEZ LÓPEZ, A. "Juventud y tecnología: la nueva sociedad ecológica" (Youth and technology: the new ecological society), *Juventud* 10, jun 83 : 119-138.

4087   MALIK, Yogendra K. "Attitudinal and political implications of diffusion of technology: the case of North India youth", *Journal of Asian and African Studies* 17(1-2), jan-apr 82 : 45-73.

4088   MARTIN DE NICOLAS, J. "El cambio tecnológico y su impacto sobre el hombre" (Technological change and its impact on man), *Revista de Fomento social* 37(152), oct-dec 83 : 387-398.

4089   MAYNES, J. P. "Technology and collective bargaining. A union view", *Work and People* 8(3), 82 : 29-36.

4090   MILLER, Robert J.; [ed.]. "Robotics: future factories, future workers", *Annals of the American Academy of Political and Social Science* 470, nov 83 : 9-179. [with contributions by Leonard LYNN, Robert U. AYRES, Steven M. MILLER, Warren G. GROFF]

4091   ORGANISATION DE COOPÉRATION ET DE DÉVELOPPEMENT ÉCONOMIQUES. *Évaluation des incidences sociales de la technologie.* Paris, OCDE, 83, 88 p.

4092   PARYGIN, B. D.; [ed.]. *Social'no-psihologičeskie problemy naučno-tehničeskogo progressa* (Socio-psychological problems of the scientific and technical progress). Leningrad, Nauka, 82, 189 p.

4093   RAMMERT, Werner. *Soziale Dynamik der technischen Entwicklung: theoretisch-analytische Überlegungen zu einer Soziologie der Technik am Beispiel der 'science-based industry'* (Social dynamics of technical development: theoretical-analytical considerations to a sociology of technique by the example of the 'science-based industry'). Opladen, Westdeutscher Verlag, 83, xi-248 p.

4094   RANDOLPH, Robert H.; KOPPEL, Bruce. "Technology assessment in Asia: status and prospects", *Technological Forecasting and Social Change* 22(3-4), dec 82 : 363-384.

4095   RJABUŠKIN, T. V.; [ed.]. *Social'nye i social'no-psihologičeskie aspekty povyšenija effektivnosti nauki: materialy simpoziuma 'Social'nye i ekonomičeskie aspekty povyšenija effektivnoksti sovetskoj nauki', Zvenigorod, 24-26 maja 1982 g* (Social and socio-psychological aspects of the elevation of science efficiency: materials of a symposium on 'Social and economic aspects of elevation of the Soviet science efficiency', Zvenigorod, 24th-26th May of the 1982nd year). Moskva, Institut Sociologičeskih Issledovanij Akademii Nauk SSSR, 82, 138 p.

4096   ROVATI, Giancarlo. "Questione energetica e study sul futuro. Alcune considerazioni metodologiche" (The energetic issue and futurology: some methodological considerations), *Studi di Sociologia* 21(2), apr-jun 83 : 198-210.

4097   SACHCHIDANANDA; VERMA, Krishna Kumar. *Electricity and social change.* Patna, Janaki Prakashan, 83, xii-264 p.

4098   SILVER, Harry R. "Scientific achievement and the concept of risk", *British Journal of Sociology* 24(1), mar 83 : 39-43.

4099   STANKIEWICZ, Janina; WALKOWIAK, Jerzy. "Aktywność innowacyjna w ujęciu socjologicznym" (Sociological approach to innovational activity), *Ruch prawniczy, ekonomiczny i socjologiczny* 45(3), 83 : 215-236.

4100   STRASSOLDO, Raimondo. "Energia e società" (Energy and society), *Studi di Sociologia* 21(2), apr-jun 83 : 160-180.

4101   TITTENBRUN, Jacek. "Formacja azjatycka: zarys teorii" (Asiatic formation: an outline of the theory), *Studia Socjologiczne* 89(2), 83 : 99-124.

4102   VAAGS, D. W.; WEMELSFELDER, J. *Techniek, innovatie en maatschappij* (Technology, innovations and society). Utrecht, Spectrum, 83, 472 p.

4103   WALLACE, Anthony F. C. *The social context of innovation: bureaucrats, families, and heroes in the early industrial revolution, as foreseen in Bacon's New Atlantis.* Princeton, NJ, Princeton University Press, 82, xiii-175 p.

4104   WOOD, Fred B. "The status of technology assessment: a view from the Congressional Office of Technology Assessment", *Technological Forecasting and Social Change* 22(3-4), dec 82 : 211-222.

17430   Agriculture. Trade. Industry
Agriculture. Commerce. Industrie

4105   "Chasse (La) et la cueillette aujourd'hui", *Études rurales* 87-88, jul-dec 82 : 7-421. [France]

4106   "Special issue on part time farming", *Sociologia ruralis* 23(1), 83 : 3-94. [with contributions by Anthony M. FULLER, Stane KRAŠOVEC, Walter FRANK; résumés en anglais, français et allemand]

4107   ABBRUZZESE, Salvatore. "La logique du développement industriel: le cas de Civitacastellana", *Année sociologique* 33, 83 : 221-247. [Latium, Italie]

4108   ADDI, Lahouari. *Approche historique et théorique de l'industrialisation dans les formations sociales dépendantes.* Oran, Centre de Documentation des Sciences Humaines, Université d'Oran, 82, 49 p.

4109   BORA, Gyula. "Industrie und Dorf. Beziehungen zwischen der Industrialisierung und der Entwicklung der Dörfer in Ungarn" (Industry and village. Relations between industrialization and village development in Hungary), *Osteuropa* 33(6), jun 83 : 485-492.

4110   BOURGEY, André; [et al.]. *Industrialisation et changements sociaux dans l'Orient arabe.* Beyrouth, Éditions du Centre d'Études et de Recherches sur le Moyen-Orient Contemporain, 82, 433 p.

4111   BUDDE, Harald. "Kuntshandwerk in der DDR" (Art handicraft in German DR), *Deutschland Archiv* 16(3), mar 83 : 283-288.

4112   CARLSON, John E.; DILLMAN, Don A. "Influence of kinship arrangements on farmer innovativeness", *Rural Sociology* 48(2), sum 83 : 183-200. [USA]

4113   CARRACEDO, Orlando. "Acción cooperativa agraria" (Agrarian cooperative action), *Revista de la Cooperación* 38(206), feb 83 : 9-29. [Argentina] [see also pp. 53-57 by Carlos J. CORBELLA]

4114   CHANDRA, S. "Développement des coopératives de pêche en Inde", *Revue de la Coopération internationale* 76(1), 83 : 29-38.

4115   DIX, M. C.; [et al.]. *Car use: a social and economic study.* Aldershot, Hampshire, Gower, 83, xxviii-267 p.

4116   FIALA, Robert. "Inequality and the service sector in less developed countries: a reanalysis and respecification", *American Sociological Review* 48(3), jun 83 : 421-428.

4117   FREMEAUX, Philippe. "Coopératives agricoles: les servantes maîtresses", *Revue des Études coopératives* (7), trim. 1, 83 : 23-28.

4118   GOLOB, Matija. "Neka sociologijska gladišta o nasledivanju na seljačkim gospodarstvima" (Some sociological views on inheritance in agricultural enterprises), *Sociologija sela* 20(75-76), jun 82 : 45-52. [résumés en anglais et en russe]

4119   GRUSKY, David B. "Industrialization and the status attainment process: the thesis of industrialism reconsidered", *American Sociological Review* 48(4), aug 83 : 494-506. [Japan]

4120   KLOPPENBURG, Jack R. Jr. "Group development in Botswana: the principles of collective farmer action", *Research in Economic Anthropology* 5, 83 : 311-333.

4121   KONING, Niek. "Family farms and industrial capitalism", *Netherlands Journal of Sociology* 19(1), apr 83 : 19-46.

4122   KWAŚNIEWSKI, Krzysztof. "Problematyka socjologiczna związków indywidualnej gospodarki chłopskiej z rolnictwem uspołecznióným" (The sociological problems of links between individual peasant farming and socialized agriculture), *Ruch prawniczy, ekonomiczny i socjologiczny* 45(2), 83 : 181-187. [Poland]

4123   LANZALAVI, Jean-Claude. "La coopérative agricole est-elle une structure d'organisation sociale?", *Connexions* 39, 83 : 79-94.

4124   LEAF, Murray J. "The green revolution and cultural change in a Punjab village, 1965-1978", *Economic Development and Cultural Change* 31(2), jan 83 : 227-270.

4125   LEE, Dong Wong. "Développement des coopératives de pêche en Corée", *Revue de la Coopération internationale* 76(1), 83 : 39-47.

4126   MARCHETTI, Cesare. "The automobile in a system context. The past 80 years and the next 20 years", *Technological Forecasting and Social Change* 23(1), mar 83 : 3-23.

4127   MCHENRY, Dean E. "Communal farming in Tanzania: a comparison of male and female participants", *African Studies Review* 25(4), dec 82 : 49-64.

4128   MOORHOUSE, H. F. "American automobiles and workers' dreams", *Sociological Review* 31(3), aug 83 : 403-426.

4129   OLAGNERO, Manuela. *Terziario e terziarizzazione nell'analisi sociologica: profili di analisi e ricerca* (Service industry and the growth of the tertiary sector in sociological analysis: analysis and research profiles). Milano, F. Angeli, 82, 302 p.

4130   PUTTERMAN, Louis. "Incentives and the kibbutz: toward an economics of communal work motivation", *Zeitschrift für Nationalökonomie* 43(2), 83 : 157-188. [Israel]

4131   RADOMIROVIĆ, Vojin. "Reprodukcija faktora proizvodnje u našoj poljoprivredi" (Reproduction of the production factors in our agriculture), *Sociologija Sela* 20(75-76), jun 82 : 15-25. [Yugoslavia] [résumés en anglais et en russe]

4132   RAMBAUD, Placide. "Organisation du travail agraire et identités alternatives", *Cahiers internationaux de Sociologie* 75, 83 : 305-320.

4133   REICHMAN, Shalom. *Les transports: servitude ou liberté?.* Paris, Presses Universitaires de France, 83, 197 p.

4134   ROY, William G. "The unfolding of the interlocking directorate structure of the United States", *American Sociological Review* 48(2), apr 83 : 248-257.

4135   SOTO SERULLA, Manuel; CABRERIZO PLAZA, Florencio. "El cooperativismo agricola: la libertad individual y la organización social" (Agricultural cooperativism:

individual freedom and social organization), *Revue internationale de Sociologie* 18(1-2-3), apr-aug-sep 82 : 40-46.

4136 STUKIN, Kazimierz. "Bariery społeczne występujące między pracownikami PGR a rolnikami indywidualnymi" (Social barriers observed between workers of state farms and individual farmers), *Ruch prawniczy, ekonomiczny i socjologiczny* 45(2), 83 : 203-223. [Poland]

4137 TAVČAR, Jože. "Individualni sektor u slovenskoj poljoprivredi" (The private sector in Slovenian agriculture), *Sociologija sela* 20(77-78), 83 : 127-139. [Yugoslavia]

4138 THIÉBAULT, Jean-Louis. "'Complexe militaro-industriel': notion critique ou théorique?", *Cahiers internationaux de Sociologie* 75, 83 : 215-237.

4139 VIGNES DE PHYLAROQUE, Hippolyte de. "Les relations entre les coopératives agricoles et la coopérations de consommation: espoirs et désillusions", *Revue des Études coopératives* (7), trim. 1, 83 : 5-22.

4140 WEI, Hsian-Chuen; REISCHL, Uwe. "Impact of industrialization on attitude towards parents and children in contemporary Taiwan", *Industry of Free China* 60(1), 25 jul 83 : 1-19.

4141 YAGO, Glenn. "The sociology of transportation", *Annual Review of Sociology* (9), 83 : 171-190. [USA]

17500 CONSUMPTION. MARKET. PRICES
CONSOMMATION. MARCHÉ. PRIX

17510 Consumer behaviour
Comportement du consommateur

4142 DUSSART, Christian. *Comportement du consommateur et stratégie de marketing.* Montréal, PQ, McGraw-Hill, 83, xiv-554 p.

4143 HASHIMOTO, Kazutaka. "Shakai chosa toshiteno shohisha chosa" (The study of consumers-problem research), *Kokumin seikatsu kenkyu* 22(4), 83 : 28-51.

4144 MAYER, Robert N.; BELK, Russell. "Acquisition of consumption stereotypes by children", *Journal of Consumer Affairs* 16(2), wint 82 : 307-321. [USA]

4145 OKUDA, Kazuhiko. "Mono, hito, soshiki" (Goods, man and organization), *Shakaigaku nenpo* 17, 83 : 185-234.

4146 PITTS, Robert E.; WOODSIDE, Arch G. "Personal value influences on consumer product class and brand preferences", *Journal of Social Psychology* 119(1), feb 83 : 37-53.

4147 SCARDIGLI, Victor. *La consommation, culture du quotidien.* Paris, Presses Universitaires de France, 83, 254 p.

4148 TAKAHASHI, Hidehiro. "Toshi shakaigaku to shakaiteki kyōdō shōhi shudan; toshi no kōzō bunseki to shutai bunseki ni tsuiteno ichi kōsatsu" (Urban sociology and social collective means of consumption), *Shakaigaku kenkyu* 46, 83 : 171-182.

4149 WIATR, Jerzy J. "Polityczne aspekty konsumpcji i systemów wartości" (Political aspects of consumption and value systems), *Problemy Marksizmu-Leninizmu* 1, 83 : 23-36.

17520 Demand. Supply
Demande. Offre

17600 CREDIT. FINANCING. MONEY
CRÉDIT. FINANCEMENT. MONNAIE

4150 ARUTJUNJAN, L-A.; KARAPETJAN, L. M. "Nekotorye metodologičeskie voprosy soveršenstvovanija social' nogo mehanizma soglasovanija interesov obščestva i ličnosti" (Methodological problems of improving social mechanisms for the concordance of social and individual interests), *Voprosy Filosofii* 36(10), oct 83 : 26-36.

4151 BERNHOLZ, Peter. "Inflation and monetary constitutions in historical perspective", *Kyklos* 36(3), 83 : 397-419.

4152 GASPARINI, Giovanni. *Banche e bancari: una analisi sociologica* (Banks and bank employees: a sociological analysis). Milano, F. Angeli, 82, 310 p. [Italy]

4153 JACOBS, David; WALDMAN, Don. "Toward a fiscal sociology: determinants of tax regressivity in the American states", *Social Science Quarterly* 64(3), sep 83 : 550-565.

4154 RECKTENWALD, Horst Claus. "Finanzföderalismus. Eine empirische Analyse im internationalen Vergleich" (Financial federalism. An empirical analysis in international comparison), *Verwaltung* 16(1), 83 : 1-15.

4155 SZEGÖ, Andrea. "Érdek és struktúra — érdekstruktúra" (Interests and structure — the structure of interests), *Társadalomtudományi Közlemények* 13(2), 83 : 270-297.

**17700   ECONOMIC POLICY. PLANNING
         POLITIQUE ÉCONOMIQUE. PLANIFICATION**

4156   "Canada (Le) atlantique. Actes du Colloque de Nantes (15-16 octobre 1982)", *Études canadiennes / Canadian Studies* 8(13), dec 82 : 3-228. [with contributions by Jean CHAUSSADE, André VIGARIE, Hugues WILHELM]

4157   BRABANDER, Guido L. de. *Regionale structuur en werkgelegenheid: een economische en geografische studie over de Belgische lange-termijn-ontwikkeling* (Regional structure and employment: an economic and geographic study on Belgian long-term development). Brussel, Koninklijke Academie voor Wetenschappen, Letteren en Schone Kunsten, 83, 222 p.

4158   BUNKER, S. G. "Dependency, inequality, and development policy: a case from Bugisu, Uganda", *British Journal of Sociology* 24(2), jun 83 : 182-207.

4159   CIECHOCIŃSKA, Maria. "Region jako teren badań socjologicznych" (Region as an area of sociological research), *Studia Socjologiczne* 90 (3), 83 : 61-76.

4160   CLUZEL, Jean. "Bilan actuel de la régionalisation", *Revue des Sciences morales et politiques* 138(3), 83 : 355-377.

4161   DUMAS, Jean. "Une évolution longtemps méconnue: l'apprentissage régional de la France depuis 1974", *Sociologia internationalis* 20(1-2), 82 : 159-188. [résumé en anglais]

4162   HODARA, Joseph. "La planeación económica observada por un sociólogo" (Economic planning observed by a sociologist), *Trimestre económico* 50(3), jul-sep 83 : 1425-1435. [Latin America]

4163   MINGUET, Guy. "A la recherche du développement économique local. L'analyse comparée de l'industrialisation de la région d'Angers et du Choletais", *Année sociologique* 33, 83 : 159-179.

4164   MITSUO, Ogura. "The sociology of development and issues surrounding late development", *International Studies Quarterly* 26(4), dec 82 : 596-622.

4165   SCHÖNING, Walter. "Einige Überlegungen zur Berücksichtigung struktureller Unterschiede bei interregionalen Vergleichen" (Some remarks on the consideration of structural differences in interregional comparison), *Vierteljahreshefte zur Wirtschaftsforschung* (3), 82 : 320-332.

4166   SIMON, Arthur; OLIVERA, Manuel Felipe. "Ordenación territorial y urbanismo" (Regional planning and urbanism), *Revista javeriana* 99(492), mar 83 : 113-126. [Colombia]

4167   VACCARINI, Italo. "Attegiamenti e comportamenti degli attori sociali della politica economica italiana" (Attitudes and behavior of the social actors of the Italian economic policy), *Studi di Sociologia* 20(3-4), jul-dec 82 : 395-414.

4168   VOOGD, Heuk. *Multicriteria evaluation for urban and regional planning.* London, Pion, 83, xiv-367 p.

18100   INDUSTRIAL SOCIOLOGY. SOCIOLOGY OF WORK
         SOCIOLOGIE INDUSTRIELLE. SOCIOLOGIE DU TRAVAIL

4169   CASTILLO ALONSO, Juan José; PRIETO, Carlos. *Condiciones de trabajo: hacia un enfoque renovador de la sociologia del trabajo* (Working conditions: towards a renewal focus of the sociology of work). Madrid, Centro de Investigaciones Sociológicas, 83, 385 p.

4170   COHEN, Steven R. "From industrial democracy to professional adjustment: the development of industrial sociology in the United States, 1900-1955", *Theory and Society* 12(1), jan 83 : 47-67.

4171   DESMAREZ, Pierre. "La sociologie industrielle fille de la thermodynamique d'équilibre?", *Sociologie du Travail* 25(2), apr-jun 83 : 261-274.

4172   GIORDANO, Maria Grazia. *La sociologia del lavoro e dell'organizzazione attraverso i suoi periodici (1968-1973)* (Sociology of work and organizations through its various stages (1968-1973)). Milano, F. Angeli, 82, 345 p.

4173   GROSSIN, William. "Sociologie du travail", *Année sociologique* 32, 82 : 439-513. [Compte rendu bibliographique]

4174   KOCHAN, Thomas A.; MITCHELL, Daniel J. B.; DYER, Lee; [eds.]. *Industrial relations research in the 1970s: review and appraisal.* Madison, WI, Industrial Relations Research Association, 82, iv-374 p.

4175   MUCHINSKY, Paul M. *Psychology applied to work: an introduction to industrial and organizational psychology.* Homewood, IL, Dorsey Press, 83, xxii-580 p.

4176   PETKOV, Krŭst'o; KOLEV, Blagoĭi. *Sotsiologiiâ na trudoviiâ kolektiv: vŭprosi na teoriiâta i praktikata* (Sociology of collective work: problems in theory and practice). Sofiiâ, Profizdat, 82, 184 p. [Bulgaria]

4177   RÜDDENKLAU, Eberhard. *Gesellschaftliche Arbeit oder Arbeit und Interaktion? Zum Stellenwert des Arbeitsbegriffes bei Habermas, Marx und Hegel* (Social work or work and interaction? On the value of work concept in Habermas, Marx and Hegel). Frankfurt-am-Main-Bern, Lang, 82, 422 p.

4178   ŠAPOVALOV, É. A.; BAJUKIN, A. Ju. "O zadačah sociologičeskogo issledovanija inženernoj dejatel'nosti" (On the objectives of sociological research on the engineering activity), *in: Sociologija vysšej školy: podgotovka specialistov dlja narodnogo hozjajstva.* Gor'kij, 1982 : 73-82.

4179   SCHELLHASE, Rolf. *Die industrie- und betriebssoziologischen Untersuchungen der Sozialforschungsstelle an der Universität Münster (Sitz Dortmund) in den 1950er Jahren: ein Beitrag zur Geschichte des institutionalisierten Sozialforschung* (The industrial and entrepreneurial sociological researches of the Social Research Office of the University of Münster (located in Dortmund) in the 50's: a contribution to the history of institutionalized social research). Münster, Lit, 82, vii-408 p.

4180   SCHMIEDE, Rudi. "Abstrakte Arbeit und Automation. Zum Verhältnis von Industriesoziologie und Gesellschaftstheorie" (Abstract work and automation. On the relations between industrial sociology and social theory), *Leviathan* 11(1), 83 : 55-78.

4181   VILMAR, Fritz; KISSLER, Leo. *Arbeitswelt: Grundriss einer kritischen Soziologie der Arbeit* (The world of work: basis of a critical sociology of work). Opladen, Leske und Budrich, 82, 256 p.

4182   WINCHESTER, David. "Industrial relations research in Britain", *British Journal of Industrial Relations* 31(1), mar 83 : 100-114.

4183   ZADROŻYŃSKA, Anna. *Homo faber i homo ludens. Etnologiczny szkic o pracy w kulturach tradycyjnej w współczesnej* (Homo faber and homo ludens. Ethnological sketch on the work in traditional and contemporary cultures). Warszawa, Państwowe Wydawnictwo Naukowe, 83, 359 p.

18200   EMPLOYMENT. LABOUR MARKET
         EMPLOI. MARCHÉ DU TRAVAIL

18210   Labour. Manpower
         Travail. Main-d'oeuvre

4184   "Herausforderungen an die Arbeitsmarkt- und Berufsforschung in den 80er Jahren" (Challenges to labour market and occupational research in the 1980 years), *Mitteilungen aus der Arbeitsmarkt- und Berufsforschung* 15(4), 82 : 387-516.

4185   "Labour market participation and mobility", *Social Science Quarterly* 64(3), sep 83 : 494-535. [USA]

4186   "Local labour markets: analysis and policies", *Regional Studies* 17(2), apr 83 : 73-133. [UK] [résumés en français et allemand; with contributions by Doreen MASSEY, S. P. CHAKRAVARTY, Jim TAYLOR, Steven BRADLEY]

4187   "Thirty-fifth year of independence. A kaleidoscopic view of labour activities", *Indian Labour Journal* 23(9), sep 82 : 1265-1290.

4188   BARBASH, Jack; [et al.]. *The work ethic — a critical analysis.* Madison, WI, Industrial Relations Research Association, 83, v-261 p.

4189   BERGER, Mark C. "Labor supply and spouse's health: the effects of illness, disability, and mortality", *Social Science Quarterly* 64(3), sep 83 : 494-509.

4190   BOJE, Thomas. *Arbejdsmarkedet i Danmark* (Labour market in Denmark). København, H. Reitzel, 82, 202 p.

4191   BRADSHAW, Benjamin S.; FRISBIE, W. Parker. "Potential labor force supply and replacement in Mexico and the States of the Mexican cession and Texas: 1980-2000", *International Migration Review* 17(63), 83 : 394-409.

4192   CARTER, Michael J. "Competition and segmentation in internal labor markets", *Journal of Economic Issues* 16(4), dec 82 : 1063-1077.

4193   CHOUBKINE, Vladimir. "Les besoins de main-d'oeuvre de la société. Penchants professionnels de la jeunesse et système de l'instruction publique", *Année sociologique* 32, 82 : 23-37.

4194   FINLAY, William. "One occupation, two labor markets: the case of longshore crane operators", *American Sociological Review* 48(3), jun 83 : 306-315. [USA]

4195   GUILLAUME, Michel. "Vers un nouveau marché du travail?", *Wallonie* 10(3), 83 : 197-205.

4196   HARIK, Bassam E.; HARIK, Salim E. "Effects of labor mobility: the case of Arab countries of the Middle East", *Search* 4(1-2), wint 83 : 44-60.

4197   HERMANN, Hayo; PESCHEL, Karin. *Sektorale Wirtschaftsstruktur und Qualität des Arbeitsplatzangebots* (Sectoral economy structure and quality of work place supply). München, Florentz, 82, xx-342 p. [Germany FR]

4198   JACOBY, Sanford M. "Industrial labor mobility in historical perspective", *Industrial Relations* 22(2), spr 83 : 261-282.

4199   JULIEN, Pierre-André; MOREL, Bernard. "Quelques conditions pour sortir de la crise du travail", *Économie et Humanisme* 270, apr 83 : 5-19. [France]

4200   KOZYR-KOWALSKI, Stanisław. "Siła robocza jako obiekt własności" (Labour force as a property object), *Studia Socjologiczne* 89(2), 83 : 85-97.

4201   KRAHN, Harvey; GARTRELL, John W. "Labour market segmentation and social mobility in a Canadian single-industry community", *Canadian Review of Sociology and Anthropology* 20(3), aug 83 : 322-345. [Fort McMurray, Alberta]

4202   LOVERIDGE, Ray. "Sources of diversity in internal labour markets", *Sociology (London)* 17(1), feb 83 : 44-62.

4203   LUNDBERG, Shelly J.; STARTZ, Richard. "Private discrimination and social intervention in competitive labor markets", *American Economic Review* 73(3), jun 83 : 340-347.

4204   MACAROV, D.; BAERWALD, Paul. "Work and prospect of social development: in the West and elsewhere", *International Journal of Sociology and Social Policy* 2(4), 82 : 12-30.

4205   MEMOLI, Rosanna. "Demande et offre de travail: premières hypothéses pour une interprétation sociologique", *Revue internationale de Sociologie* 18(1-2-3), apr-aug-sep 82 : 109-120.

4206   MIHAJLOV, S. V. "Obostrennie situacii na rynke truda SŠA: problemy zanjatosti i bezraboticy" (Worsening of the situation in the USA labour market: problems of employment and unemployment), *Rabočij Klass i sovremennyj Mir* 12(1), 83 : 106-113.

4207   PREDETTI, Adalberto. "Some aspects of the labour market in Italy", *Review of Economic Conditions in Italy* (3), oct 82 : 405-425.

4208   RED'KINA, Z. V. "Vlijanie vosproizvodstva rabočej sily na potrebnosti v obrazovanii" (Influence of the labour force reproduction on the educational needs), in: *Nauka-obrazovanie — proizvodstvo: problemy razvitija.* Tomsk, 1982 : 95-102.

4209   RIBEIRO, Sérgio. *A situação actual e os prospectos dos recursos humanos em Moçambique* (The present state and prospects of human resources in Mozambique). Addis-Abeba, Organização Internacional de Trabalho, PECTA, 82, 72-55 p.

4210   SØRENSON, Aage B. "Sociological research on the labor market: conceptual and methodological issues", *Work and Occupations* 10(3), aug 83 : 261-287.

4211   ŠUMRATOV, B. I. "Metodologičeskoe značenie sistemnogo podhoda v izučenii socialističeskoj obščestvennoj formy truda" (Methodological meaning of systemic approach in the study of the socialist social form of labour), *Nekotorye Problemy Sozdanija Material'no-Tehničeskoj Bazy Kommunizma v Uslovijah Naučno-Tehničeskoj Revoljucii* (4), 82 : 27-40.

4212   SUVOROVA, I. P. *Regional'nye osobennosti vosproizvodstva inispol'zovanija trudovyh resursov* (Regional characteristics of the reproduction and utilization of labour resources). Kiev, Naukova Dumka, 82, 169 p. [USSR]

4213   SZIRACZKI, G. "The development and functioning of an enterprise labour market in Hungary", *Économies et Sociétés* 17(3-4), mar-apr 83 : 517-547. [résumé en français]

4214   TAGGART, Robert. *Hardship: the welfare consequences of labor market problems: a policy discussion paper*. Kalamazoo, MI, Upjohn Institute for Employment Research, 82, vii-440 p.

4215   VOS, C. J. *Arbeidsbeleid en arbeidsverhoudingen: centralisering en fragmentering in het arbeidsbeleid* (Labour policy and labour relations: centralization and segmentation in labour policy). Deventer, Van Loghum Slaterus, 82, 265 p.

4216   WIDMAIER, Hans Peter; [ed.]. *Das Arbeitskräfteangebot zwischen Markt und Plan* (The labour supply between market and plan). Berlin, Duncker und Humblot, 83, 280 p.

18220   Employment. Unemployment
Emploi. Chômage

4217   "Crisis of unemployment", *Political Affairs* 62(2), feb 83 : 15-40. [USA] [with contributions by Scott MARSHALL, Michael PARENTI, Rick NAGIN, Rocco SCAVETTA]

4218   "École (De l') à l'emploi: différences et concurrences", *Cahiers du Centre d'études de l'emploi* (26), 83 : 1-437. [France] [with contributions by Jean ROUSSELET, Catherine MATHEY-PIERRE, Philippe LIDVAN]

4219   AMBROSINI, Maurizio. "Società 'flessibile' e lavoro 'part-time' " ('Flexible' society and part-time work), *Aggiornamenti sociali* 34(6), jun 83 : 413-426. [Italy]

4220   AMBROSINI, Maurizio. "Sulla 'qualità della vita di lavoro' " (On the 'quality of working life'), *Studi di Sociologia* 21(3), jul-sep 83 : 272-280.

4221   AZOUVI, Alain; [et al.]. *L'emploi: enjeux économiques et sociaux; colloque du Groupe de sociologie du travail, Dourdan, 10-12 décembre 1980.* Paris, Maspéro, 82, 446 p.

4222   BALÁZS, Gabrielle. "Les facteurs et les formes de l'expérience du chômage", *Actes de la Recherche en Sciences sociales* 50, nov 83 : 69-83. [résumés en anglais et en allemand]

4223   BEACH, Charles M.; KALISKI, S. F. "Measuring the duration of unemployment from gross flow data", *Canadian Journal of Economics / Revue canadienne d'Économique* 16(2), mai 83 : 258-263. [Canada]

4224   BLAU, Francine; KAHN, Lawrence M. "Job search and unionized employment", *Economic Inquiry* 21(3), jul 83 : 412-430. [USA]

4225   BRATHWAITE, Farley. *Unemployment and social life: a sociological study of the unemployed in Trinidad.* Bridgetown, Antilles Publications, 83, xiv-165 p.

4226   BROWN, Clair. "Unemployment theory and policy, 1946-1980", *Industrial Relations* 22(2), spr 83 : 164-185.

4227   BRUYN-HUNDT, Marga. *Deeltijdwerk* (Part-time employment). Deventer, Van Loghum Slaterus, 82, 98 p. [Netherlands]

4228   BUSS, Terry F.; HOFSTETTER, C. Richard. "Powerlessness, anomie, and cynicism: the personal consequences of mass unemployment in a steel town", *Micropolitics* 2(4), 83 : 349-377. [USA]

4229   CHARLIER, Jean-Emile. "La crise de l'emploi et les jeunes en Belgique", *Revue internationale d'action communautaire* 8(48), aut 82 : 43-48. [résumés en anglais et espagnol]

4230   GARCÍA, Philip. "An evaluation of unemployment and employment differences between Mexican American and Whites: the seventies", *Social Science Journal (Fort Collins)* 20(1), jan 83 : 51-62.

4231   GERME, Jean-François. "Il lavoro precario: il caso della Francia" (Temporary employment: the case of France), *Economia e Lavoro* 17(1), mar 83 : 101-116. [résumé in English]

4232   HOPE, Kempe R. "Note sur le problème du chômage aux Caraïbes", *Travail et Société* 8(3), jul-sep 83 : 293-298.

4233   JOHNSON, Janet L. "Sex differentials in unemployment rates: a case for non concern", *Journal of Political Economy* 91(2), apr 83 : 293-303. [USA]

4234   JONGMAN. "Chômage et (puis?) crime", *Déviance et Société* 7(4), dec 83 : 339-346.

4235   KRIKORIAN, G. T. "Youth and the economic crisis", *Political Affairs* 62(3), mar 83 : 32-36.

4236   LAGRAVE, Michel. "Les difficultés d'évaluation du chômage. Problèmes de méthodes", *Revue française des Affaires sociales* 37(1), mar 83 : 91-107.

4237   LESTRADE, Brigitte. "Le travail à temps partiel en RFA", *Allemagnes d'aujourd'hui* (83), mar 83 : 126-139. [continued in ibid. (85), sep 83 : 67-82]

4238   LÓPEZ CABALLERO, A. "El paro y el derecho al trabajo" (Unemployment and right to work), *Revista de Fomento social* 37(150), apr-jun 83 : 217-220.

4239   MALDONADO, I.; MERCIER, D. "Chômage des jeunes et répartition du revenu: une
        problématique", *Économies et Sociétés* 17(3-4), mar-apr 83 : 629-654. [Canada]
4240   OLSÉN, Peter. *Arbejdsløsenhedens socialpsykologi* (Social psychology of unemployment).
        København, Dansk Psykologisk Forlag, 82, 190 p.
4241   PARNES, Herbert S. *Unemployment experience of individuals over a decade: variations by sex, race
        and age.* Kalamazoo, MI, Upjohn Institute for Employment Research, 82, ix-99 p. [USA]
4242   REINARMAN, Craig. "Unemployment and economic crisis: could a jobs movement arise
        from poverty of policy", *Berkeley Journal of Sociology* 28, 83 : 69-95. [USA]
4243   SCHNEIDER, Lothar. "Sozioökonomische und sozialethische Überlegungen zum Problem
        der Arbeitslosigkeit" (Socio-economic and social ethic considerations on the unemployment
        problem), *Sozialer Fortschritt* 31(10), 82 : 217-222. [Germany FR]
4244   STERN, J. "The relationship between unemployment, morbidity and mortality in Britain",
        Population Studies 37(1), mar 83 : 61-74.
4245   STEVENSON, Wayne. "Youth employment status and subsequent labor market experience",
        Social Science Journal (Fort Collins) 19(4), oct 82 : 35-45. [USA]
4246   STURMTHAL, Adolf. "Unemployment, inflation and 'guest workers': comparative study
        of three European countries", *Relations industrielles* 37(4), 82 : 739-764. [Austria;
        Germany FR; Sweden]
4247   TACHON, Michel. "Seront-ils les vaincus de l'histoire?", *Revue internationale d'action
        communautaire* 8(48), aut 82 : 49-59. [résumés en anglais et espagnol; chômage des jeunes
        en France]
4248   TOGEBY, Lise. *Ung og arbejdløs* (Youth and unemployment). Århus, Institut for Stats-
        kundskab, Aarhus Universitet, 82, 147 p. [Denmark]
4249   TOMLINSON, Jim. "Does mass unemployment matter?", *Quarterly Review — National
        Westminister Bank*, feb 83 : 35-45.
4250   TREMBLAY, Diane; VAN SCHENDEL, Vincent. "Le chômage des jeunes au Québec:
        un petit tour d'horizon", *Revue internationale d'action communautaire* 8(48), aut 82 : 33-41.
        [résumés en anglais et espagnol]
4251   TRIVEDI, P. K.; BAKER, G. M. "Unemployment in Australia: duration and recurrent
        spells", *Economic Record* 59(165), jun 83 : 132-148.
4252   UNIVERSIDAD DE CHILE. DEPARTAMENTO DE ECONOMÍA. *Ocupación y
        desocupación. Encuesta nacional. Marzo 1983* (Employment and unemployment. National
        survey. March 1983). Santiago, the author, 83, xi-399 p.
4253   VAN LOON, Francis; PAUWELS, Koenraad; VAN HUMSKERKE, Herman. *Werkloosheid
        en gezin: een onderzoek naar de gevolgen van werkloosheid* (Unemployment and family: a research
        on the impact of unemployment). Antwerpen, Sikkel; Amsterdam, Nederlandsche
        Boekhandel, 82, 108 p.
4254   WARR, P.; JACKSON, P. "Self-esteem and unemployment among young workers",
        Travail humain 46(2), 83 : 355-366. [résumé en français]
4255   WEBBER, Douglas. "Combatting and acquiescing in unemployment? Economic crisis
        management in Sweden and West Germany", *West European Politics* 6(1), jan 83 : 23-43.

**18230   Employment services. Job evaluation
            Services d'emploi. Évaluation des emplois**

4256   BAILEY, Catherine T. *The measurement of job performance.* Aldershot, Hants, Gower, 83, ix-238 p.
4257   BROWN, Charles. "The federal attack on labor market discrimination: the mouse that
        roared?", *Research in Labor Economics* 5, 82 : 33-68. [USA]
4258   BURRIS, Val; WHARTON, Ann. "Sex segregation in the US labor force", *Review of
        Radical Political Economics* 14(3), aut 82 : 43-56.
4259   CAIRNCROSS, Alec. "Is employment policy a thing of the past?", *Three Banks Review*
        (139), sep 83 : 3-18. [UK]
4260   DELL'ARINGA, Carlo. "Italy's active manpower policy: between inefficiency and utopia",
        Review of Economic Conditions in Italy (3), oct 82 : 427-444.
4261   DRUMM, Hans Jürgen; SCHOLZ, Christian. *Personalplanung: Planungsmethoden und
        Methodenakzeptanz* (Manpower planning: planning methods and methods acceptance).
        Bern, Haupt, 83, 253 p.
4262   GHEORGHIU, Al.; [et al.]. "Rationalizarea folosirii forţei de muncă în întreprinderi
        factor de creştere a eficienţei economice" (Rationalization of manpower utilization in
        the enterprises: a factor of growing economic efficiency), *Revista de Statistică* (7), jul
        83 : 1-10. [Romania]

4263 HÜBLER, Olaf. *Arbeitsmarktpolitik und Beschäftigung: ökonometrische Methoden und Modelle* (Labour market policy and employment: econometric methods and models). Frankfurt-am-Main-New York, NY, Campus Verlag, 82, 280 p.

4264 LOOS, Jocelyne. "Accord de contenu ou accord de méthode? L'exemple de l'accord national interprofessionnel de 1969 sur la sécurité de l'emploi", *Sociologie du Travail* 25(1), jan-mar 83 : 15-31.

4265 ORTEGA, Victorino. "El gobierno socialista y la política del empleo" (Socialist government and employment policy), *Razón y Fe* 207(1018), mai 83 : 517-523. [Spain]

4266 PARADIS, François P. "La gestion des ressources humaines: défis et perspectives", *Optimum* 14(2), 83 : 18-28. [résumé en anglais]

4267 RUTHERGLEN, George. *Major issues in the federal law of employment discrimination.* Washington, DC, Federal Judicial Center, 83, iv-260 p.

4268 SIMARD, Carolle. "Les mesures égalitaristes tn emploi: le début ou la fin d'une illusion", *Canadian Journal of Political Science* 16(1), mar 83 : 103-114. [Canada]

4269 WONG, John. *Labour mobilization in the Chinese commune system: a perspective from Guangdong.* Bangkok, ILO-ARTEP, 82, 40 p.

4270 ZIMMER, Michael; SULLIVAN, Charles A.; RICHARDS, Richard F. *Cases and materials on employment discrimination.* Boston, MA, Little, Brown, 82, xxxvi-1039 p. [USA]

18240 Women workers. Young workers
Travailleuses. Jeunes travailleurs

4271 "Ghettos ou cohabitation? Le logement des immigrés en France", *Hommes et Migrations. Documents* 34(1047), 1 mar 83 : 3-18. [with contributions by Véronique de RUDDER, Andrée CHAZALETTE, Jean GRANE]

4272 "Problemi dell'emigrazione" (Emigration problems), *Affari sociali internazionali* 11(1), 83 : 89-192. [with contributions by Antonio d'HARMANT FRANÇOIS, Claudio CALVARUSO, Daniele ROSSINI, Franco PITTAU]

4273 ANKER, Richard. "L'activité de la main-d'oeuvre féminine dans les pays en développement. Examen critique des définitions et des méthodes de collecte des données", *Revue internationale du Travail* 122(6), dec 83 : 761-777.

4274 ANTUNIASSI, Maria Helena Rocha. *Trabalhador infantil e escolarização no meio rural* (Child labour and school attendance in rural areas). Rio de Janeiro, Zahar Editores, 83, 135 p. [Brazil]

4275 APFELBAUM, Erika; VASQUEZ, Ana. "Les réalités changeantes de l'identité", *Peuples Méditerranéens / Mediterranean Peoples* (24), sep 83 : 83-101.

4276 APPERT, M.; [et al.]. *Diversification de l'emploi féminin: insertion professionnelle des femmes formées dans les métiers traditionnellement masculins.* Paris, Centre d'Études de l'Emploi, 83, 226-24 p. [France]

4277 ARENI, A.; MANNETTI, L.; TANUCCI, G. "La condizione lavorativa della donna nella realtà rurale italiana" (Women's working conditions in the Italian rural reality), *Revue internationale de Sociologie* 18(1-2-3), apr-aug-sep 82 : 364-375.

4278 BARRERE-MAURISSON, Marie-Agnès; [et al.]. "Trajectoires professionnelles des femmes et vie familiale", *Consommation* 30(4), dec 83 : 23-53. [France] [résumé en anglais]

4279 BENENCIA, Roberto. "Notas acerca del trabajo femenino en el área Capital Federal — Gran Buenos Aires, en el quinquenio 1975-80" (Notes on female work in Federal Capital and Gran Buenos Aires, 1975-80), *Boletín CEIL* 9, 83 : 48-72. [Argentina]

4280 CAMPANI, Giovanna. "Les réseaux italiens en France et la famille", *Peuples Méditerranéens / Mediterranean Peoples* (24), sep 83 : 13-23. [résumé en anglais]

4281 CAPEL MARTÍNEZ, Rosa María. *El trabajo y la educación de la mujer en España (1900-1930)* (Women's work and education in Spain (1900-1930)). Madrid, Ministerio de Cultura, Dirección General de Juventud y Promoción Socio-Cultural, 82, 608 p.

4282 CHAISON, Gary N.; ANDIAPPAN, P. "Characteristics of female union officers in Canada", *Relations industrielles* 37(4), 82 : 765-779.

4283 CLARK, M. Gardner. "The Swiss experience with foreign workers: lessons for the United States", *Industrial and Labor Relations Review* 36(4), jul 83 : 606-623.

4284 COONEY, Rosemary Santana; ORTIZ, Vilma. "Nativity, national origin, and Hispanic female participation in labor force", *Social Science Quarterly* 64(3), sep 83 : 510-523. [USA]

4285 CORDEIRO, Albano. "Reproduction de la force de travail et modèles de rotation: citoyens et résidents", *Peuples Méditerranéens / Mediterranean Peoples* (24), sep 83 : 33-44. [résumé en anglais]

4286   CRINO, Michael D.; [et al.]. "Female participation rates and the occupational prestige of the professions: are they inverseley related?", *Journal of Vocational Behaviour* 22(2), apr 83 : 243-255. [USA]

4287   CUALES, Sonia M. "Accumulation and gender relations in the flower industry in Colombia", *Research in Political Economy* 5, 82 : 109-137.

4288   D'AMICO, Ronald. "Status maintenance or status competition? Wife's relative wages as a determinant of labor supply and marital instability", *Social Forces* 61(4), jun 83 : 1186-1205.

4289   DABROWSKI, Irene. "Working-class women and civic action: a case study of an innovatice community role", *Policy Studies Journal* 11(3), mar 83 : 427-435.

4290   DAHLSTRÖM, Edmund; LILJESTRÖM, Rita. *Working-class women and human reproduction.* Göteborg, Sociologiska Institutionen, Göteborgs Universitet, 82, 167 p. [Sweden]

4291   DEERE, Carmen Diana; LÓN DE LEAL, Magdalena. *Women in Andean agriculture: peasant production and rural wage employment in Colombia and Peru.* Geneva, International Labour Office, 82, xii-172 p.

4292   DEMESMAEKER-WILLEMS, M. L. "Problèmes belgo-néerlandais des travailleurs frontaliers", *Benelux* (3), 82 : 9-13. [texte en français et néerlandais]

4293   DEVI, D. Radha; RAVINDRAN, M. "Women's work in India", *International Social Science Journal* 35(4), 83 : 683-701.

4294   FERBER, Marianne A. "Women and work: issues of the 1980's", *Signs* 8(2), wint 82 : 273-295.

4295   FOX, Bonnie J.; FOX, John. "Effects of women's employment on wages", *Canadian Journal of Sociology* 8(3), 83 : 319-328. [Canada]

4296   GEERTSEN, Kirsten. *Arbejderkvinder i Danmark* (Women workers in Denmark). København, Selskabet til Forskning i Arbejderbevaegelsens Historie, 82, 398 p.

4297   GOLDIN, Claudia. "The changing economic role of women: a quantitative approach", *Journal of Interdisciplinary History* 13(4), spr 83 : 707-733.

4298   GÓMEZ JIMÉNEZ, Alcides; DÍAZ MESA, Luz Marina. *La moderna esclavitud: los indocumentados en Venezuela* (Modern slavery: illegal immigrants in Venezuela). Bogotá, Fines, Editorial Oveja Negra, 83, 348 p.

4299   GRUZDEVA, É. B.; ČERTIHINA, É. S. *Trud i byt sovetskih ženščin* (Labour and daylife of Soviet women). Moskva, Politizdat, 83, 222 p.

4300   HANSON, Sandra L. "A family life-cycle appproach to the socioeconomic attainment of working women", *Journal of Marriage and the Family* 45(2), mai 83 : 323-338. [USA]

4301   HILY, Marie-Antoinette. "A l'écoute des expressions de l'identité. Un protocole d'interview de groupe de jeunes Portugais en France", *Peuples Méditerranéens / Mediterranean Peoples* (24), sep 83 : 71-81.

4302   HOFF, Ernst; LAPPE, Lothar; LEMPERT, Wolfgang. *Methoden zur Untersuchung der Sozialisation junger Facharbeiter* (Methods of research on the socialization of young skill workers). Berlin, Max-Planck-Institut für Bildungsforschung, 83. [2 vols.]

4303   HÖHN, Charlotte. "Frauenerwerbstätigkeit und soziale Sicherheit" (Women employment and social security), *Zeitschrift für Bevölkerungswissenschaft* 9(4), 83 : 475-486. [Germany FR]

4304   HUMPHRIES, Jane. "The 'emancipation of women' in the 1970s and 1980s: from the latent to the floating", *Capital and Class* (20), sum 83 : 6-28. [USA]

4305   JACOBSEN, G. "Women's work and women's role: ideology and reality in Danish urban society, 1300-1550", *Scandinavian Economic History Review* 31(1), 83 : 3-20.

4306   KAROUI, Naïma. "La femme tunisienne et le phénomène 'bureau': étude sociologique sur les attitudes et conduites des jeunes femmes tunisiennes dans l'administration des PTT", *Revue tunisienne des Sciences sociales* 19(70-71), 82 : 75-109.

4307   KIRKWAN, F. X.; NAIRN, A. G. "Migrant employment and the recession: the case of the Irish in Britain", *International Migration Review* 17(64), 83 : 672-681.

4308   KONCZ, Katalin. "A nők foglalkoztatásának alakulása és a feminizálódás tendenciája Magyarországon 1890 és 1980 között" (The development of females' employment and the tendency of feminization in Hungary between 1890 and 1980), *Demográfia* 26(1), 83 : 140-154.

4309   LEVER-TRACY, Constance. "Immigrant workers and postwar capitalism: in reserve or core troops in the front line?", *Politics and Society* 12(2), 83 : 127-157.

4310   MASSIAH, Joycelin. "Female-headed households and employment in the Caribbean", *Women's Studies International* 2, 82 : 7-16.

4311   MILKMAN, Ruth. "Female factory labor and industrial structure: control and conflict over 'woman's place' in auto and electrical manufacturing", *Politics and Society* 12(2), 83 : 159-203.

4312   MOLYNEUX, Maxine. *State policies and the position of women workers in the People's Democratic Republic of Yemen, 1967-1977.* Geneva, International Labour Office, 82, viii-87 p.

4313   MOSKOFF, William. "Women and work in Israel and the Islamic Middle East", *Quarterly Review of Economics and Business* 22(4), 82 : 89-104.

4314   MUNTEMBA, Shimwaayi. "Women as food producers and suppliers in the twentieth century: the case of Zambia", *Development Dialogue* (1-2), 82 : 29-50.

4315   MURPHY, Richard Charles. *Guestworkers in the German Reich: a Polish community in Wilhelmian Germany.* Boulder, CO, East European Monographs, 83, xi-255 p.

4316   NERI, Fabio. "The supply of foreign labour in Italy: the case of Friuli Venezia Giulia", *Review of Economic Conditions in Italy* (3), oct 82 : 445-459.

4317   NETO, Felix; MULLET, Étienne. "Résultats d'une enquête sur les conditions de vie des migrants portugais", *Orientation scolaire et professionnelle* 11(4), dec 82 : 355-368.

4318   NEUFERT, Siegfried. "Ausländische Arbeiter in der Bundesrepublik" (Foreign workers in the Federal Republic), *Neue Politische Literatur* 28(1), mar 83 : 85-97.

4319   NUNDI-ISRAELI, Dafna. "Israeli women in the work force", *Jerusalem Quarterly* (27), spr 83 : 59-80.

4320   ÒHASHI, Terue. "Josei no rodo shijo shinshutsu to ishiki no henka" (Participation in the labour force helps women to undergo change), *Soshioroji* 27(3), 83 : 95-115. [Japan]

4321   ORIOL, Michel. "L'effet Antée ou les paradoxes de l'identité périodique", *Peuples Méditerranéens / Mediterranean Peoples* (24), sep 83 : 45-60. [résumé en anglais]

4322   PAMPEL, Fred C.; WEISS, Jane A. "Economic development, pension policies, and the labor force participation of aged males: a cross-national longitudinal approach", *American Journal of Sociology* 89(2), sep 83 : 350-372.

4323   PAPAIOANNOU, Skevos M. *Arbeitsorientierung und Gesellschaftsbewusstsein von Gastarbeitern in der Bundesrepublik Deutschland* (Labour orientation and social consciousness of foreign workers in the Federal Republic of Germany). Frankfurt-am-Main-New York, NY, P. Lang, 83, ix-570 p.

4324   PHILLIPS, Paul Arthur; PHILLIPS, Erin. *Women and work: inequality in the labour market.* Toronto, ON, J. Lorimer, 83, 205 p. [Canada]

4325   POWER, Marilyn. "From home production to wage labor: women as reserve army of labor", *Review of Radical Political Economics* 15(1), spr 83 : 71-91. [USA]

4326   PRZYBYŁA-PIWKO, Elżbieta. *Aspiracje i postawy społeczno-zawodowe młodych robotników przemysłowych* (Aspirations and socio-professional attitudes of young industrial workers). Warszawa, Państwowe Wydawnictwo Naukowe, 83, 113 p. [Poland]

4327   PRZYBYLSKA, Krystyna. "Społeczno-prawna sytuacja obcej siły roboczey w krajach EWG" (Social and legal status of the foreign labour force in the EEC countries), *Sprawy międzynarodnowe* 9, 83 : 121-130.

4328   REUBENS, Beatrice G.; [ed.]. *Youth at work: an international survey.* Totowa, NJ, Littlefield, Adams; Rowman and Allanheld, 83, xvi-347 p.

4329   RISKA, Elianne; RAITASALO, Raimo. "Sex segregation of the Finnish occupational structure: its implications for the psychosocial aspects of women's work", *Economic and Industrial Democracy* 3(4), nov 82 : 431-444.

4330   SAMMAN, Mouna Liliane. "Activité économique des femmes Tiers-Monde et perspectives de baisse de leur fécondité", *Tiers-Monde* 24(94), jun 83 : 367-376.

4331   SARTIN, P. "Les femmes dans la vie professionnelle", *Travail et Méthodes* (408), mai 83 : 41-52.

4332   SCHMID, Carol. "Gastarbeiter in West Germany and Switzerland: an assessment of host society-immigrant relations", *Population Research and Policy Review* 2(3), oct 83 : 233-252.

4333   SÉGURET, Marie-Claire. "Les femmes et les conditions de travail: quelles perspectives d'amélioration?", *Revue internationale du Travail* 122(3), jun 83 : 313-330.

4334   SILVA, Manuela. *O emprego das mulheres em Portugal: a 'mão invisível' na discriminação sexual no emprego* (The employment of women in Portugal: the 'invisible hand' in sex discrimination in employment). Porto, Afrontamento, 83, 149 p.

4335   SMITH, Vicki. "The circular trap: women and part-time work", *Berkeley Journal of Sociology* 28, 83 : 1-17. [USA]

4336   SØRENSEN, Annemette. "Children and their mother's career", *Social Science Research* 12(1), mar 83 : 26-43.

4337   SOUTH, Scott J.; [et al.]. "Female labor force participation and the organizational experiences of male workers", *Sociological Quarterly* 24(3), sum 83 : 367-380.

4338   STEADY, Filomina Chioma. "African women, industrialization and another development: a global perspective", *Development Dialogue* (1-2), 82 : 51-64.

4339   STEPHENSON, Stanley P. Jr. "A turnover analysis of joblessness for young women", *Research in Labor Economics* 5, 82 : 279-317.

4340   STREIFF-FENART, Jocelyne. "Choix du conjoint et identité sociale. Les mariages des immigrés maghrébins de la deuxième génération", *Peuples Méditerranéens / Mediterranean Peoples* (24), sep 83 : 103-116.

4341   TAAMALLAH, Lamouria. "Les femmes et l'emploi en Tunisie", *Revue tunisienne des Sciences sociales* 19(70-71), 82 : 143-166.

4342   TARANOV, É. V. "Adaptacija molodogo rabočego na promyšlennom predprijatii" (The young worker's adaptation in an industrial enterprise), *in: Problemy psihologii ličnosti: sovetsko-finnskij simpozium.* Moskva, 1982 : 83-88.

4343   TERRY, James L. "The political economy of migrant farm labor. Immigration, mechanization and unionization in the Midwest", *Insurgent Sociologist* 11(4), 83 : 63-75. [USA]

4344   TRAY, Dennis de. "Children's work activities in Malaysia", *Population and Development Review* 9(3), sep 83 : 437-455.

4345   UNESCO. *Vivre dans deux cultures: la condition socio-culturelle des travailleurs migrants et de leurs familles.* Paris, UNESCO, 83, 348 p.

4346   WELCH, Susan; [et al.]. "Correlates of women's employment in local governments", *Urban Affairs Quarterly* 18(4), jun 83 : 551-564.

4347   WHITE, Julie. *Women and part-time work.* Ottawa, Canadian Advisory Council on the Status of Women, 83, v-159 p. [Canada]

4348   WONG, Morrison G.; HIRSCHMAN, Charles. "Labor force participation and socio-economic attainment of Asian-American women", *Sociological Perspectives* 26(4), oct 83 : 423-446. [USA]

4349   YAMAOKA, Hiroko. "Joshi no shokuba shinshutsu no haigo joken toshiteno chiho jichitai no ishiki to shisaku: Tokyo oyobi Osaka ni okeru chiho jichitai no fujin gyosei chosa o kiban toshite" (Considerations of public administration on female labour increase: based on research of the local administration in Tokyo and Osaka), *Tokyo toritsu shoka tanki daigaku kenkyu ronso* 26, 83 : 39-75.

18300   PERSONNEL MANAGEMENT. WORKING CONDITIONS
ADMINISTRATION DU PERSONNEL. CONDITIONS DE TRAVAIL

18310   Work standards. Work study
Normes de travail. Étude du travail

4350   BAR-YOSEF, Rivka W.; WEISS, Yochanan. "La souplesse de l'organisation du travail: un moyen de rééducation", *Travail et Société* 8(2), jun 83 : 147-162.

4351   BOMBERA, Zdzisław. "Karola Marksa teoria produkcyjności pracy" (Karl Marx's theory of labour productivity), *Nowe Drogi* 406(3), 83 : 45-53.

4352   CHERRINGTON, David J. *Personnel management: the management of human resources.* Dubuque, IA, W. C. Brown Co., 83, xiv-706 p.

4353   HERMAN, Andrew. "Conceptualizing control: domination and hegemony in the capitalist labor process", *Insurgent Sociologist* 11(3), 82 : 7-22.

4354   JANICKA, Krystyna; KACPROWICZ, Grażyna; SŁOMCZYŃSKI, Kazimierz M. "Złożoność pracy jako zmienna socjologiczna: modele pomiaru i ich ocena" (Complexity of work as a sociological variable: measurement models and their estimation), *Studia Socjologiczne* 90(3), 83 : 5-33.

4355   JEDRUSZEK, J. "Policy implications of the development in productivity of labor in Tanzania", *Utafiti* 5(2), dec 80 : 237-248.

4356   KIESER, Alfred; [et al.]. "Die Eingliederung neuer Mitarbeiter in die Unternehmung" (The integration of new employees in the enterprise), *Schmalenbachs Zeitschrift für Betriebswirtschaftliche Forschung* 34(11), 82 : 941-958.

4357   MUSANEF. *Manajemen kepegawaian di Indonesia* (Personnel management in Indonesia). Jakarta, Gunung Agung, 83, xvii-278 p.

4358   ORSI BATTAGLINI, Andrea. *Gli accordi sindacali nel pubblico impiego* (Collective labour agreements in the public enterprise). Milano, A. Giuffrè, 82, vi-325 p. [Italy]

4359   PERETTI, J. M. "Les politiques de gestion de l'emploi", *Travail et Méthodes* (404), dec 82 : 13-22.

4360   PURCELL, John. "The management of industrial relations in the modern corporation: agenda for research", *British Journal of Industrial Relations* 31(1), mar 83 : 1-16.

4361   RAY, Charles M.; EISON, Charles L. *Supervision.* Chicago, IL, Dryden Press, 83, 376 p.

4362   ROŽKOVA, V. V.; [et al.]. "Metodologičeskie problemy upravlenija proizvoditel'nost'ju truda" (Methodological problems of the labour productivity management), *Social'no-Ēkonomičeskie Problemy Truda* (1), 81 : 87-123. [USSR]

4363   SANDBERG, Thomas. *Work organization and autonomous groups.* Lund, LiberFörlag, 82, viii-249 p.

4364   SCHLESINGER, Leonard A. *Quality of work life and the supervisor.* New York, NY, Praeger, 82, 202 p.

4365 SCHOLZ, Christian. "Zur Konzeption einer strategischen Personalplanung" (On the concept of a strategic personnel planning), *Schmalenbachs Zeitschrift für Betriebswirtschaftliche Forschung* 34(11), 82 : 979-994.

4366 SERGEEV, M. A.; [et al.]. *Social'no-ĕkonomičeskie problemy povyšenija ĕffektivnosti obščestvennogo truda: teorii i metodologii. Nardno-hozjajstvennyj i regional'nyj aspekt* (Socio-economic problems of elevation of the social labour efficiency: theoretical and methodological questions. The national economic and regional aspects). Moskva, Nauka, 83, 150 p. [USSR]

4367 UMEZAWA, Tadashi. *Koyo kanri* (Personnel management). Tokyo, Nihon Rodo Kyokai, 83, 143 p. [Japan]

4368 WHITE, Michael Reginald Maurice; TREVOR, Malcolm. *Under Japanese management: the experience of British workers.* London, Heinemann, 83, xiii-162 p.

18320 Working conditions
Conditions du travail

4369 "Dossier réduction du temps de travail", *Wallonie* 10(3), 83 : 206-246. [with contributions by Paul ARETS, Jacques MASSAUT, Christian PIRET, Luc HUJOEL, Ph. DEPHEYT]

4370 "Flexibilisierung der Arbeitszeit" (Flexibility of working time), *Schmalenbachs Zeitschrift für Betriebswirtschaftliche Forschung* 35(10), 83 : 858-901. [Germany FR]

4371 "Policing the environment", *Social Problems* 30(4), apr 83 : 410-448. [with contributions by Donna M. RANDALL, James F. SHORT Jr., John LYNXWILER, Kitty CALAVITA]

4372 "Umsetzungsprobleme bei Arbeitszeitverkürzungen" (Re-organization problems raised by working time arrangement), *WSI Mitteilungen* 36(4), apr 83 : 209-276. [Germany FR] [with contributions by Johann FRERICHS, Jürgen ULBER]

4373 "Usure (L') au travail", *Mouvement social* 124, sep 83 : 3-169. [with contributions by Alain COTTEREAU, Françoise CRIBIER, Bernard-Pierre LECUYER]

4374 AKAOKA, Isao. "Motivation of employees in Japan", *Kyoto University Economic Review* 53(1-2), apr-oct 83 : 25-50.

4375 BEAUMONT, P. B.; LEOPOLD, John W. "The state of workplace health and safety in Britain", *Yearbook of Social Policy in Britain*, 82 : 102-131.

4376 BISPINCK, Reinhard. "Probleme gewerkschaftlicher Arbeitszeitpolitik" (Problems of trade unions' working time policy), *Sozialer Fortschritt* 32(9), 83 : 210-215. [Germany FR]

4377 BLUNT, Peter. "Work alienation and adaptation in sub-Saharan Africa: some evidence from Kenya", *Civilisations* 32(1), 82 : 1-29.

4378 BURAWOY, Michael. "Between the labor process and the State: the changing face of factory regimes under advanced capitalism", *American Sociological Review* 48(5), oct 83 : 587-605.

4379 BURDETSKY, Ben; KATZMAN, Marvin S. "Alternative work patterns: is productivity the real issue?", *Work and People* 8(2), 82 : 31-34.

4380 BÜSSING, André. "Arbeitssituation und Arbeitszufriedenheit. Ein theoretischer und methodischer Beitrag zur Kontroverse um die Bedeutung der Arbeitssituation für die Arbeitszufriedenheit" (Job situation and job satisfaction. A theoretical and methodical essay on the controversy on the significance of job situation for job satisfaction), *Kölner Zeitschrift für Soziologie und Sozialpsychologie* 35(4), dec 83 : 680-708.

4381 CRUZ VILLALON, J.; GARCÍA MURCIA, J. "La regulación de las condiciones de trabajo en los convenios colectivos (1980-1982)" (Regulation of working conditions in the collective agreements, 1980-1982), *Revista de Política Social* (137), jan-mar 83 : 445-534. [Spain]

4382 DE LOURDES LIMA DOS SANTOS, M. "Os fabricantes dos gozos da inteligência' — alguns aspectos da organização do mercado de trabalho intelectual no Portugal de Oito-centos" (The makers of the intelligence pleasures — some aspects of the organization of the intellectual labour market in Portugal in the nineteenth century), *Analise social* 19(1), 83 : 7-28.

4383 DESAINTES, Joseph; MANDART, Colette. "Les enjeux de l'humanisation des conditions de travail", *Reflets et Perspectives de la Vie économique* 22(1), feb 83 : 41-57. [Belgium]

4384 DICKSON, John W. "Beliefs about work and rationales for participation", *Human Relations* 36(10), oct 83 : 911-931.

4385 DOBROWOLSKA, Danuta. *Zróżnicowanie społeczno-zawodowe a stosunek do pracy* (Socio-occupational differentiation and the attitude towards work). Warszawa, Polska Akademia Nauk Instytut Filozofi i Socjologii, 83, 120 p. [Poland]

4386 ERBÈS-SEGUIN, Sabine. "Le contrat de travail ou les avatars d'un concept", *Sociologie du Travail* 25(1), jan-mar 83 : 1-14.

4387   FARBER, Samuel. "Material and non-material work incentives as ideologies and practices of order", *Review of Radical Political Economics* 14(4), wint 82 : 29-39.

4388   FERNET, André. "Heur(t)s et malheurs de la réduction de la durée du travail", *Revue nouvelle* 39(4), apr 83 : 420-438.

4389   FREDLAND, J. Eric; LITTLE, Roger D. "Job satisfaction determinants: differences between servicemen and civilians", *Journal of Political and Military Sociology* 11(2), spr 83 : 265-280. [USA]

4390   HASSENCAMP, Alfred; BIENECK, Hans-Jürgen. "Les changements techniques et organisationnels et la conception des conditions de travail en République fédérale d'Allemagne", *Travail et Société* 8(1), mar 83 : 43-62.

4391   HELD, Leonore; KARG, Peter W. "Variable Arbeitszeit, Anspruch und Wirklichkeit" (Flexible hours of work, claiming and possibilities), *WSI Mitteilungen* 36(8), aug 83 : 469-480. [Germany FR]

4392   HIRSZEL, Krzysztof. *Robotnicy i inżenierowie. 'Postawy wobec pracy i wybranych wartości społecznych'* (Workers and engineers. 'Attitudes towards work and selected social values). Warszawa, Ksiąʹzka i Wiedza, 83, 264 p. [Poland]

4393   IL'JASOV, F. N. "Sravnitel'nyj analiz metodik izučenija udovletvorennosti trudom" (Commarative analysis of study methods on job satisfaction), *in: Metodologičeskie i metodičeskie problemy sravnitel'nogo analiza v sociologiceskih issledovanijah. I.* Moskva, 1982 : 105-127.

4394   JOLIVET, Thierry. "La réduction de la durée du travail est-elle créatrice d'emploi?", *Relations industrielles* 38(1), 83 : 142-154. [France]

4395   KALLEBERG, Anne L.; LOSCOCCO, Karyn A. "Tying, values, and rewards: explaining age differences in job satisfaction", *American Sociological Review* 48(1), feb 83 : 78-90.

4396   KAZIS, Richard; GROSSMAN, Richard L. *Fear at work: job blackmail, labor and the environment.* New York, NY, Pilgrim Press, 82, xi-306 p.

4397   KEMP, Nigel J.; COOK, John D. "Job longevity and growth need strength as joint moderators of the task design-job satisfaction relationship", *Human Relations* 36(10), oct 83 : 883-898.

4398   LACY, William B.; [et al.]. "Job attribute preferences and work commitment of men and women in the United States", *Personnel Psychology* 36(2), sum 83 : 315-329.

4399   LALITHA, N. V.; KOHLI, Madhu. *Status of voluntary effort in social welfare.* New Delhi, National Institute of Public Cooperation and Child Development, 82, vii-199 p. [India]

4400   LANGENDORF, Gudrun; NICK, Harry. "Tendenzen der qualitativen Veränderung der Arbeitsmittel" (Trends in the qualitative change of working conditions), *Wirtschafts-wissenschaft* 32(1), jan 83 : 15-30. [German DR]

4401   LANGER, Jörg. "Die neue Arbeitszeitordnung in Frankreich" (The new working time arrangement in France), *Recht der Internationalen Wirtschaft* 29(2), 83 : 102-103.

4402   LE CALONNEC, Joseph. "Le nouveau régime du temps de travail en agriculture", *Revue de droit rural* (110), dec 82 : 483-494.

4403   LEIGH, J. Paul. "Education, working conditions, and workers' health", *Social Science Journal (Fort Collins)* 20(2), apr 83 : 99-107.

4404   LEIGH, J. Paul. "Risk preference and the interindustry propensity to strike", *Industrial and Labor Relations Review* 36(2), jan 83 : 271-285.

4405   LIDVAN, Philippe. "Attitudes des jeunes face au travail: contributions à l'étude des représentations sociales du travail", *Cahiers du Centre d'études de l'emploi* (26), 83 : 233-341. [France]

4406   LÓPEZ JIMENEZ, Ma. Angeles. "Consideraciones sobre la actitud de los jóvenes en el trabajo" (Considerations about youth's attitude to work), *Juventud* 9, mar 83 : 73-91.

4407   MAGUIRE, Mary Ann. "The effects of context on attitude measurement: the case of job satisfaction", *Human Relations* 36(11), nov 83 : 1013-1030.

4408   MAGUIRE, Mary Ann; KROLICZAK, Alice. "Attitudes of Japanese and American workers: convergence or diversity?", *Sociological Quarterly* 24(1), wint 83 : 107-122.

4409   MAYERE, Anne. "Revalorisation qualitative des emplois et substitution de jeunes travailleurs français à des travailleurs immigrés. Le cas d'une entreprise de collecte des ordures", *Travail et Emploi* (17), sep 83 : 41-47.

4410   MEYER, Wolf-Hartwig. *Arbeitszufriedenheit: ein interessiertes Missverständnis* (Satisfaction in work: an interested misunderstanding). Opladen, Westdeutscher Verlag, 82, 215 p.

4411   MINTON, Michael H.; BLOCH, Jean Libman. *What is a wife worth? The leading expert places a high dollar value on homemaking.* New York, NY, Morrow, 83, 192 p.

4412   MØKEBERG, Henrik. *Holdninger til arbejdstidspolitik* (Attitudes to working-hours policy). København, Socialforskningsinstituttet, 82, 137 p. [Denmark]

4413   MUKASA, R. "Les conditions de travail au Japon, leur aspect global après la Seconde Guerre mondiale", *Économies et Sociétés* 17(3-4), mar-apr 83 : 481-516. [résumé en anglais]

4414 MÜLLER-ARMACK, Andreas. "Kann Arbeitszeitverkürzung die Arbeitslosigkeit abbauen helfen?" (Can working time reduction solve unemployment problem?), *Politische Studien* 34(269), jun 83 : 293-300.

4415 PENC, Józef. "Kształtowanie treści pracy a zachowania pracownicze" (Shaping of the work content and employees behaviour), *Studia Socjologiczne* 89(2), 83 : 227-249.

4416 PENC, Józef. "Motywacja pracy w systemie ekonomicznym przedsiębiorstwa" (Work motivation in the enterprise economic system), *Praca i Zabezpieczenie społeczne* 25(3), 83 : 16-24. [Poland]

4417 PIGANIOL, Claude; TORRENCE, William D. "Attitudes au travail d'opérateurs sur terminal informatique: comparison de deux groupes, américain et français", *Revue française des Affaires sociales* 37(3), sep 83 : 77-101.

4418 POUCHOL, Marlyse. *Travail domestique et pouvoir masculin.* Paris, Éditions du Cerf, 83, 107 p.

4419 PUEL, Hugues. "Travail et mode de vie: l'action des acteurs sociaux sur les transformations des formes d'emploi", *Travail et Emploi* (16), jun 83 : 37-45. [résumés en anglais et en espagnol]

4420 REEVE STEARNS, Lisa. "A priority for worker health and safety: lessons from the British coal mines", *Contemporary Crises* 7(3), jul 83 : 271-291.

4421 RICHARDSON, Virginia. "Social change in perceptions of work relations", *Social Service Review* 56(3), sep 82 : 438-447.

4422 RUIZ CASTILLO, Ma. M. "La duración del contrato de trabajo: estudio de su régimen legal y jurisprudencial" (The duration of labour contract: study on its legal and jurisprudential regime), *Revista de Política Social* (138), apr-jun 83 : 25-97. [Spain]

4423 RUPPERT, Wolfgang. *Die Fabrik: Geschichte von Arbeit und Industrialisierung in Deutschland* (The factory: history of labour and industrialization in Germany). München, C. H. Beck, 83, 311 p.

4424 SATO, Yoshiyuki. "Volunteer katsudo no honshitsu to rinen" (The essence and idea of voluntary work), *Volunteer katsudo kenkyu* 2, 83 : 35-42.

4425 STONE, Carl. *Work attitudes survey: a report to the Jamaican Government.* Brown's Town, Earle Publishers Ltd., 82, 38 p.

4426 TEZANOS, José Félix. "Satisfacción en el trabajo y sociedad industrial. Una aproximación al estudio de las actitudes hacia el trabajo de los obreros industriales Madrileños" (Job satisfaction and industrial society. A tentative study on attitudes to work among industrial workers in Madrid), *Revista Española de Investigaciones Sociológicas* 22, apr-jun 83 : 27-52. [Spain]

4427 THOMAS, Jean. "Emploi et mode de vie au travail", *Orientation scolaire et professionnelle* 11(4), dec 82 : 319-340.

4428 TOMODA, Shizue. "Les conditions de travail dans l'hôtellerie et la restauration au Japon", *Revue internationale du Travail* 122(2), apr 83 : 257-270.

4429 TOUPIN, Louis; [et al.]. "La satisfaction au travail chez les enseignantes et enseignants du Québec", *Relations industrielles* 37(4), 82 : 805-826.

4430 TREPO, Georges. "L'amélioration des conditions de travail: un concept dépassé?", *Personnel* (247), jan 83 : 28-33.

4431 UMEZAWA, Tadashi. *Noryoku kaihatsu to shokumu no jujitsu* (Human development and job satisfaction). Tokyo Sangyo Noritsu Tanki Daigaku, 83, 120 p.

4432 VAN BASTELAER, Aloïs; VAN BEERS, Wim. *Organisatiestress en de personeelfunktionaris* (Organization stress and personnel management). Lisse, Swets en Zeitlinger, 82, xiv-465 p. [Netherlands]

4433 VAN DEN BOER, Mark; POLLEFLIET, Eric. "Arbeidstijdverkorting: een poging tot objectivering" (Working time reduction: an attempt to objectivity), *Economisch en Sociaal Tijdschrift* 37(2), apr 83 : 119-133.

4434 VISCUSI, W. Kip. *Risk by choice: regulatory health and safety in the workplace.* Cambridge, MA-London, Harvard University Press, 83, vii-200 p.

4435 VORKÖTTER, Uwe. *Auswirkungen einer Verkürzung der Wochenarbeitszeit auf die Nachfrage der Unternehmen nach Arbeitskräften: eine wirtschaftspolitische, empirische Analyse* (Consequences of a reduction of weekly working time on the demand for manpower of the enterprise: a political-economic, empirical analysis). Frankfurt-am-Main, P. Lang, 82, 228 p.

4436 VOUE, André. "La réduction du temps de travail: solution ou illusion?", *Reflets et Perspectives de la Vie économique* 22(2), mai 83 : 101-125. [Belgium]

4437 WALTERS, Vivienne. "Occupational health and safety legislation in Ontario: an analysis of its origins and content", *Canadian Review of Sociology and Anthropology* 20(4), nov 83 : 413-434. [Canada]

4438 WEST, Edwin G. "Marx's hypotheses on the length of the working day", *Journal of Political Economy* 91(2), apr 83 : 266-281.

4439　WIESENTHAL, Helmut; [et al.]. "Arbeitszeitflexibilisierung und gewerkschaftliche Interessenvertretung" (Working time flexibility and trade union interests representation. Regulation problems and risks of individualized working time systems), *WSI Mitteilungen* 36(10), oct 83 : 585-595. [Germany FR]

4440　WILLIAMS, Claire. "The 'work ethic', non-work and leisure in an age of automation", *Australian and New Zealand Journal of Sociology* 19(2), jul 83 : 216-237.

4441　ZUCCHETTI, Eugenio. "Rigidità e flessibilità del tempo di lavoro: il caso del 'part-time'" (Rigidity and flexibility in working hours: the case of part-time), *Studi di Sociologia* 21(3), jul-sep 83 : 303-315.

18330　Labour turnover
　　　Renouvellement de la main-d'oeuvre

4442　BARDWICK, Judith M. "Plateauing and productivity", *Sloan Management Review* 24(3), spr 83 : 67-73. [USA]

4443　DOLAN, Simon L.; [et al.]. "L'absentéisme hospitalier au Québec: aspects culturels et socio-démographiques", *Relations industrielles* 38(1), 83 : 45-57.

4444　HENRETTA, John C.; O'RAND, Angela M. "Joint retirement in the dual worker family", *Social Forces* 62(2), dec 83 : 504-520.

4445　HERAS BORRERO, Francisco Manuel de las. "El absentismo laboral: sus causas y tratamiento jurídico" (Work absenteeism: its causes and legal remedies), *Revista de Política Social* (136), dec 82 : 191-199. [Spain]

4446　LAROCCO, James M. "Job attitudes, intentions, and turnover: an anlysis of effects using latent variables", *Human Relations* 36(9), sep 83 : 813-825. [USA]

4447　LEIGH, J. Paul. "Sex differences in absenteeism", *Industrial Relations* 22(3), aut 83 : 349-361.

4448　OLSON, Craig A.; BECKER, Brian E. "Sex discrimination in the promotion process", *Industrial and Labor Relations Review* 36(4), jul 83 : 624-641. [USA]

4449　PITAUD, Philippe. *La retraite au féminin.* Paris, Horay, 83, 222 p.

4450　SALOVSKY, Heinz. *Fehlzeiten: ein internationaler Vergleich* (Absenteeism: an international comparison). Köln, Deutscher Instituts-Verlag, 83, 232 p.

4451　SEYBOLT, John W. "Dealing with premature employee turnover", *California Management Review* 25(3), 83 : 107-117. [USA]

4452　SUNDBO, Jon; [et al.]. *Arbejdsfravaer* (Absenteeism). København, Socialforskningsinstituttet, 82, 182 p.

4453　THOMPSON, Kenneth R.; TERPENING, Willbann D. "Job-type variations and antecedents to intention to leave: a content approach to turnover", *Human Relations* 36(7), jul 83 : 655-681.

4454　UPEX, Robert V. *Termination of employment: the legal and financial implications.* London, Sweet and Maxwell, 83, 1-276 p. bibliogr., index. [UK]

4455　WHITE, Barbara Ann. "Optimal strategies for workers on temporary layoff", *Economic Inquiry* 21(4), dec 83 : 520-544. [USA]

18400　OCCUPATIONS. VOCATIONAL TRAINING
　　　PROFESSIONS. FORMATION PROFESSIONNELLE

18410　Occupational sociology
　　　Sociologie de la profession

4456　"Professions (Les) artistiques", *Sociologie du Travail* 25(4), oct-dec 83 : 383-487. [with contributions by Raymonde MOULIN, Howard BECKER, Dominique PASQUIER, Françoise DUBOST, Vera ZOLBERG, Antoine HENNION]

4457　BASZANGER, Isabelle. "La construction d'un monde professionnel: entrées des jeunes praticiens dans la médecine générale", *Sociologie du Travail* 25(3), jul-sep 83 : 275-294. [France]

4458　BENNELL, Paul. "The professions in Africa: a case study of the engineering profession in Kenya", *Development and Change* 14(1), jan 83 : 61-81.

4459　BENNELL, Paul; GODFREY, Martin. "The professions in Africa: some interactions between local and international markets", *Development and Change* 14(3), jul 83 : 373-402.

4460　BJÖRKMAN, James Warner. "Professionalism in the welfare State: sociological saviour or political pariah?", *European Journal of Political Research* 10(4), dec 82 : 407-428.

4461　CHILD, John; [et al.]. "A price to pay? Professionalism and work organization in Britain and West Germany", *Sociology (London)* 17(1), feb 83 : 63-78.

4462　DENIOT, Joëlle. "Métiers ouvriers", *Sociologie du Travail* 25(3), jul-sep 83 : 355-362. [France]

4463   HALL, Richard H. "Theoretical trends in the sociology of occupations", *Sociological Quarterly* 24(1), 83 : 5-23. [USA]

4464   MARTÍN MORENO, Jaime; DE MIGUEL, Amando. *Sociología de las profesiones en España* (Occupational sociology in Spain). Madrid, Centro de Investigaciones Sociológicas, 82, 200 p.

4465   NÉVAI, László. "The role and functions of legal professions in Hungary", *International Journal of the Sociology of Law* 11(2), mai 83 : 209-219.

4466   SAKS, Mike. "Removing the blinkers? A critique of recent contributions to the sociology of professions", *Sociological Review* 31(1), feb 83 : 1-21.

18420   Occupational life. Vocational guidance
Vie professionnelle. Orientation professionnelle

4467   AGUDELO MEJÍA, Santiago. *La orientación profesional en América Latina* (Vocational guidance in Latin America). Montevideo, CINTERFOR/OIT, 82, 70 p.

4468   AGULHON, Catherine. "Quelques aspects de l'enseignement professionnel en France (Niveau V de formation)", *Orientation scolaire et professionnelle* 11(4), dec 82 : 301-317.

4469   ANGLE, John; WISSMANN, David A. "Work experience, age, and gender discrimination", *Social Science Quarterly* 64(1), mar 83 : 66-84. [USA]

4470   AUSTER, Carol J. "The relationship between sex and occupational statuses: a neglected status discrepancy", *Sociology and Social Research* 67(4), jul 83 : 421-435. [USA]

4471   BARRIS, Roann; KIELHOFNER, Gary; WATTS, Janet Hawkins. *Psychosocial occupational therapy: practice in a pluralistic arena.* Laudel, MD, Ramsco Publishing Co., 83, vii-315 p.

4472   BATORSKI, Jan. "Motywy wyboru zawodoów górniczych" (Choice motives for mining occupations), *Kultura i Społeczeństwo* 27(2), 83 : 171-182.

4473   BECK, Scott H. "The role of other family members in intergenerational occupational mobility", *Sociological Quarterly* 24(2), spr 83 : 273-285.

4474   BOSE, Christine E.; ROSSI, Peter H. "Gender and jobs: prestige standings of occupations as affected by gender", *American Sociological Review* 48(3), jun 83 : 316-330.

4475   BURRIS, Val. "The social and political consequences of overeducation", *American Sociological Review* 48(4), aug 83 : 454-467.

4476   CAMUSI, Maria Pia. "I sistemi di qualificazione del lavoro: aspetti e problemi dell'esperienza italiana" (Occupational qualification systems: aspects and problems of the Italian experience), *Studi di Sociologia* 21(1), mar 83 : 55-64.

4477   CESÁKOVÁ, Dana. "La formation professionnelle des jeunes en République socialiste tchécoslovaque", *Demosta* 16(1-2), 83 : 9-12.

4478   COENEN-HUTHER, Jacques. "Les rôles professionnels du sociologue extra universitaire", *Revue de l'Institut de Sociologie* (3-4), 82 : 351-366.

4479   COUGHENOUR, C. Milton; SWANSON, Louis. "Work statuses and occupations of men and women in farm families and the structure of farms", *Rural Sociology* 48(1), spr 83 : 23-43.

4480   COXON, Tony. "The misconstruction of occupational judgment", *British Journal of Sociology* 34(4), dec 83 : 483-490. [UK] [with a reply by Ray PAWSON, ibid. 491-497]

4481   CSÁKÓ, Mihály; LISKÓ, Ilona. "A magyar szakmunkásképzés rendszere és társadalmi meghatározói" (The system and social determinants of Hungarian skilled workers' training), *Medvetánc* 2(2-3), 82 : 173-188.

4482   DANIEL, Ann E. *Power, privilege, and prestige: occupations in Australia.* Melbourne, Longman Cheshire, 83, ix-235 p.

4483   DOYLE, Daniel P. "Orientations and membership: a study of group occupational mobility", *Sociological Perspectives* 26(4), oct 83 : 447-472. [USA]

4484   ELLIS, Robert A.; HERRMAN, Margaret S. "Three dimensions of occupational choice: a research note on measuring the career intentions of college women", *Social Forces* 61(3), mar 83 : 893-903. [USA]

4485   ELLIS, Robert A.; HERRMAN, Margaret S. "Understanding career goals of college women: intradimensional variation in sex-typed occupational choice", *Sociology and Social Research* 68(1), oct 83 : 41-58. [USA]

4486   ENGLAND, Paula; CHASSIE, Marilyn; MCCORMACK, Linda. "Skill demands and earnings in female and male occupations", *Sociology and Social Research* 66(2), jan 82 : 147-168.

4487   FAGUER, Jean-Pierre. "Le baccalauréat E et le mythe du technicien", *Actes de la Recherche en Sciences sociales* 50, nov 83 : 85-96. [résumés en anglais et en allemand]

4488   FARBER, Henry S. "The determination of the union status of workers", *Econometrica* 51(5), sep 83 : 1417-1437. [USA]

4489   FLOAREŞ, Alecu Al. "Features and characteristics of socio-professional mobility in the area of Jassy, Romania", *Revue roumaine des sciences sociales. Série de sociologie* 27(1), jan-jun 83 : 35-45.

4490   GANZEBOOM, H.; DE GRAAF, P. "Beroepsmobiliteit tussen generaties in Nederland
          in 1954 en 1977" (Intergenerational occupational mobility in the Netherlands in 1954
          and 1977), *Mens en Maatschappij* 58(1), feb 83 : 28-52. [résumé en anglais]

4491   GORDON, L. A.; NAZIMOVA, A. K. "Social'no-professional'naja struktura sovremennogo
          sovetskogo obščestva: tipologija i statistika" (Socio-professional structure of the con-
          temporary Soviet society: typology and statistics), *Rabočij Klass i sovremennyj Mir* 12(2),
          83 : 61-74.

4492   GORDON, L. A.; [et al.]. "Tehniko-tehnologičeskie svdvigi i razvitie professional'noj
          struktury" (Technical and technological changes and development of occupational
          structure), *in: Social'noe i kul'turnoe razvitie rabočego klassa v socialističeskom obščestve*. Moskva,
          1982 : 6-72.

4493   GREENBERG, Ellen; STEINBERG, Laurence D. "Sex differences in early labor force
          experience: Harbinger of things to come", *Social Forces* 62(2), dec 83 : 467-486. [USA]

4494   HARVEY, Edward B.; KALWA, Richard. "Occupational status attainments of university
          graduates: individual attributes and labour market effects compared", *Canadian Review
          of Sociology and Anthropology* 20(4), nov 83 : 434-453. [Canada]

4495   HEMPHILL, Barbara J.; [ed.]. *The evaluative process in psychiatric occupational therapy.*
          Thorofare, NJ, C. B. Slack, 82, 401 p.

4496   IIJIMA, Nobuko; ISHIKAWA, Akihiro; YAMASAKI, Kihiko. *Sonenki danshi no shokugyo
          seikatsu to kenko ni kansuru chosa* (Research on occupational life and health of middle-aged
          men). Tokyo, Toritsu Rodo Kenkyuto, 83, 127 p. [Japan]

4497   JACOBS, Jerry. "Industrial sector and career mobility reconsidered", *American Sociological
          Review* 48(3), jun 83 : 415-421.

4498   JESCHEK, Wolfgang. "Berufsausbildung in der Bundesrepublik Deutschland unter
          besonderer Berücksichtigung des dualen Systems" (Vocational training in the Federal
          Republic of Germany from the specific point of view of the dual system), *Vierteljahreshefte
          zur Wirtschaftsforschung* (3), 82 : 349-357.

4499   LOGAN, John A. "A multivariate model for mobility tables", *American Journal of Sociology*
          89(2), sep 83 : 324-349.

4500   MAHFOUDH, Dorra. "Politique scolaire et mobilisation des compétences pour le système
          productif tunisien", *Revue tunisienne des Sciences sociales* 19(68-69), 82 : 35-80.

4501   MATUSEVIČ, V. A.; OSSOVSKIJ, V. L. *Social'naja microsreda i vybor professii* (Social micro-
          environment and the choice of a profession). Kiev, Naukova Dumka, 82, 140 p.

4502   METCALF, David; NICKELL, Stephen. "Occupational mobility in Great Britain",
          Research in Labor Economics 5, 82 : 319-357.

4503   MOHANTY, S. "Professional status group consciousness in the capital town of Orissa,
          Bhubaneswar", *Indian Journal of Social Research* 24(2), aug 83 : 155-160. [India]

4504   MONK-TURNER, Elizabeth. "Sex, educational differentiation, and occupational status:
          analyzing occupational differences for community and four-year college entrants",
          Sociological Quarterly 24(3), sum 83 : 393-404. [USA]

4505   ORTH, Bernhard; WEGENER, Bernd. "Scaling occupational prestige by magnitude
          estimation and category rating methods: a comparison with the sensory domain", *European
          Journal of Social Psychology* 13(4), oct-dec 83 : 417-431.

4506   PEARSON, Jessica. "Mothers and daughters: measuring occupational inheritance", *Sociology
          and Social Research* 67(2), jan 83 : 204-217.

4507   PENC, Józef. "Ruchliwość zawodowa a polityka racjonalnego zatrudnienia" (Occupational
          mobility and rational employment policy), *Ruch prawniczy, ekonomiczny i socjologiczny* 45(1),
          83 : 247-268.

4508   PERRY, William G. Jr. *How to develop competency-based vocational education.* Ann Arbor, MI,
          Prakken Publications, 82, vii-174 p.

4509   PIETSCH, Anna-Jutta. "Interactions between the educational and employment systems
          in the German Democratic Republic and the Soviet Union", *Organization Studies* 4(4),
          83 : 301-316.

4510   PLAN, Odile. "Les débuts d'une politique nationale de formation professionnelle pour
          les jeunes en France", *Revue internationale d'action communautaire* 8(48), aut 82 : 141-145.
          [résumés en anglais et espagnol]

4511·   PORTOCARERO, Lucienne. "Social fluidity in France and Sweden", *Acta Sociologica* 26(2),
          83 : 127-139. [Intergenerational occupational mobility net of direct structural effects]

4512   POWELL, Brian; JACOBS, Jerry A. "Sex and consensus in occupational prestige ratings",
          Sociology and Social Research 67(4), jul 83 : 392-404. [USA]

4513   POWERS, Mary G.; [ed.]. *Measures of socioeconomic status: current issues.* Boulder, CO,
          Westview Press, 82, x-205 p.

4514 PRAIS, S. J.; WAGNER, K. "Some practical aspects of human capital investment: training standards in five occupations in Britain and Germany", *National Institute Economic Review* (105), aug 83 : 46-65.

4515 RODGERS, Ronald C.; [ed.]. *Measurement trends in career and vocational education.* San Francisco, CA, Jossey-Bass, 83, 100 p.

4516 RYNES, Sara; ROSEN, Benson. "A comparison of male and female reactions to career advancement opportunities", *Journal of Vocational Behaviour* 22(1), feb 83 : 105-116.

4517 SEEDLAND, S. *Égalité des chances et formation professionnelle: une enquête sur les initiatives de formation professionnelle en faveur des femmes dans la Communauté européenne.* Berlin, CEDEFOP, 82, 107 p.

4518 SELL, Ralph R. "Transferred jobs. A neglected aspect of migration and occupational change", *Work and Occupations* 11(2), mai 83 : 179-206. [USA]

4519 SŁOMCZYŃSKI, Kazimierz M. *Pozycja zawodowa i jej związki z wykształceniem* (Occupational status and its connections with educational level). Warszawa, Polska Akademia Nauk Instytut Filozofii i Socjologii, 83, 158 p.

4520 SMITH, Randall D. "Mobility in professional occupational-internal labor markets: stratification, segmentation and vacancy chains", *American Sociological Review* 48(3), jun 83 : 289-305.

4521 SOUTAR, Geoffrey N.; CLARKE, Alexander W. "Examining business students' career preferences: a perceptual space approach", *Journal of Vocational Behaviour* 23(1), aug 83 : 11-21. [Australia]

4522 SPENNER, Kenneth I. "Deciphering Prometheus: temporal change in the skill level of work", *American Sociological Review* 48(6), dec 83 : 824-837. [USA]

4523 STEWMAN, Shelby; KONDA, Surech L. "Careers and organizational labor markets", *American Journal of Sociology* 88(4), jan 83 : 637-685.

4524 TAAMALLAH, Lamouria. "La scolarisation et la formation professionnelle des femmes en Tunisie", *Revue tunisienne des Sciences sociales* 19(68-69), 82 : 107-128.

4525 TANGUY, Lucie. "Les savoirs enseignés aux futurs ouvriers", *Sociologie du Travail* 25(3), jul-sep 83 : 336-354.

4526 TIŠKOV, V. A. "Status professii istorika v SŠA" (Historians' occupational status in the USA), *Voprosy Istorii* 57(1), 83 : 40-57.

4527 VERHAEGEN, Lydwin. "Les nouvelles technologies psychiatriques et la traditionnalité des rôles professionnels des médecins", *Schweizerische Zeitschrift für Soziologie / Revue suisse de Sociologie* 9(2), 83 : 289-312. [résumé en allemand]

4528 WICKHAM, Alexandre; PATTERSON, Marc. *Les carriéristes: les grandes manoeuvres des cadres.* Paris, Ramsay, 83, 358 p.

4529 YAMAGUCHI, Kazuo. "The structure of intergenerational occupational mobility: generality and specificity in resources, channels, and barriers", *American Journal of Sociology* 88(4), jan 83 : 718-745. [USA]

18500 EMPLOYEES. TECHNICIANS. WORKERS
EMPLOYÉS. TECHNICIENS. TRAVAILLEURS

18510 Workers
Travailleurs

4530 BOHDZIEWICZ, Piotr. "Robotnicy wielkoprzemysłowi: zróźnicowania w zakresie stylów życia i niektóre ich uwarunkowania" (Manufacturing industry workers: differentiations of styles of life and some of their conditionings), *Studia Socjologiczne* 88(1), 83 : 173-191.

4531 GRANDO, Jean Marc. "Industrie et gestion de la main-d'oeuvre", *Formation emploi* (1), mar 83 : 19-36. [résumés en anglais et allemand]

4532 HOUTAUD, A. d'; [et al.]. "Hétérogénéité de caractères socio-culturels dans la catégorie des travailleurs manuels", *Cahiers de Sociologie et de Démographie médicales* 23(3), sep 83 : 225-250.

4533 IWAMA, Tsuyoshi. "Seinen nyushoku keikaku ni okeru nogyo rodosha Ceylon no baai" (Agricultural labourers in youth settlement scheme: case of Ceylon), *Tamagawa daigaku bungaku-bu kiyo* 23, 83 : 89-103.

4534 MANNHEIM, Bilha. "Male and female industrial workers. Job satisfaction, work role centrality, and work place preference", *Work and Occupations* 10(4), nov 83 : 413-436. [Israel]

4535 MARSZAŁEK, Czesława. "Niektóre uwarunkowania społeczne działalności racjonalizatorskiej i wynalazczej pracowników państwowych gospodarstw rolnych" (Some aspects of social conditioning of inventive and efficiency increasing activities of state farm workers), *Ruch prawniczy, ekonomiczny i socjologiczny* 45(2), 83 : 225-235. [Poland]

4536   MASŁYK, Ewa. "Górnicy w obliczu kryzysu w kraju i w górnictwie węgla kamiennego"
        (Miners vis-à-vis the crisis in Poland and in hard coal mining), *Studia Socjologiczne* 89(2),
        83 : 360-386.

4537   MOUY, Philippe. "La formation professionnelle initiale des ouvriers et l'évolution du travail
        industriel", *Formation emploi* (1), mar 83 : 52-69. [résumés en anglais et allemand]

4538   O'BRIEN, Jay. "Formation of the agricultural labour force", *Review of African Political
        Economy* (26), 83 : 15-34. [Sudan]

4539   PANETTIERI, José. *Los trabajadores* (Workers). Buenos Aires, Centro Editor de América
        Latina, 82, 135 p. [Argentina]

4540   PERRY, Charles S. "The rationalization of US farm labor: trends between 1956 and 1979",
        Rural Sociology 47(4), wint 82 : 670-691. [USA]

4541   RAMASWAMY, Uma. *Work, union and community: industrial man in South India.* London-
        New York, NY-Toronto, ON, Oxford University Press, 83, xii-163 p.

4542   RAMU, G. N.; SIVAPRASAD, R. "Working couples in an Indian urban setting: a case
        study and its implications", *Journal of Asian and African Studies* 16(3-4), oct 81 : 186-195.

4543   RAY, J. J. "The workers are not authoritarian: attitude and personality data from six
        countries", *Sociology and Social Research* 67(2), jan 83 : 166-189.

4544   SIDDIQUE, C. Muhammad; TURK, James L. "Work and social participation in a
        contemporary urban-industrial society: a review of the literature and analysis of Canadian
        data", *Canadian Review of Sociology and Anthropology* 20(2), mai 83 : 123-149.

4545   SOSNOWSKI, Adam. "Autosterotypy marynarzy w ich środowisku społeczno-zawodowym"
        (Auto-stereotypes of sailors in their socio-occupational environment), *Kultura i Społeczeństwo*
        27(3), 83 : 199-217. [Poland]

4546   SOSNOWSKI, Adam. "Marynarska zbiorowość na statku" (Sailors' community on ship),
        Ruch prawniczy, ekonomiczny i socjologiczny 45(3), 83 : 237-253.

4547   TYMOWSKI, Janusz. *Problemy kadr wysoko kwalifikowanych* (Problems of highly skilled staff).
        Wrocław, Zakład Narodowy im. Ossolińskich, 82, 118 p. [Poland]

18520   Employees
**   Employés**

4548   AUGUSTINS, Georges. "Esquisse d'une comparaison des systèmes de perpétuation des
        groupes domestiques dans les sociétés paysannes européennes", *Archives européennes de
        Sociologie* 23(1), 82 : 39-69.

4549   HANEDA, Arata. "Gendai whitecollar no ishiki kozo" (On the structure of work consciousness
        of Japanese whitecollar worker today), *Chingin jutsumu* 476, 83 : 33-39.

18530   Managers. Technicians
**   Cadres. Techniciens**

4550   DERBER, Charles. "Managing professionals: ideological proletarianization and post-
        industrial labor", *Theory and Society* 12(3), mai 83 : 309-341.

4551   JAOUI, Hubert. "Aperçu sur les cadres", *Futuribles* 63, feb 83 : 34-46. [France]

4552   KEYS, Bernard; BELL, Robert. "Four faces of the fully functioning middle manager",
        California Management Review 24(4), 82 : 59-67. [USA]

4553   LENGYEL, György; PÁRTOS, Gyula. "A 'hagyományos vezetői tipus' felbomlása"
        (Disintegration of the 'traditional type of manager'), *Szociológia* 11(4), 82 : 561-576.

4554   THOMAS, Alan Berkeley. "Managerial careers and the problem of control", *Social Science
        Information* 22(1), 83 : 1-25.

18540   Liberal professions
**   Professions libérales**

4555   BARRET, Pierre; [et al.]. *Ils voyageaient la France: vie et traditions des Compagnons du Tour
        de France du XIXᵉ siècle.* Paris, Hachette, 82, 574 p.

4556   TOMASIC, Roman. "Social organisation amongst Australian lawyers", *Australian and New
        Zealand Journal of Sociology* 19(3), nov 83 : 447-475.

18600   LABOUR RELATIONS
**   RELATIONS DU TRAVAIL**

4557   "Droit (Le) d'expression des salariés", *Humanisme et Entreprise* 140, aug 83 : 1-110. [France]
        [with contributions by Jean-Louis SENTIN, Jacques SALZER, Dominique LECONTE,
        Patrick CHALNEL]

4558 "Trasformazioni del lavoro in America" (Changing labour relations in America), *Rassegna sindicale. Quaderni* 20(98-99), dec 82 : 3-133. [USA] [with contributions by Antonio LETTIERI, Paul BLUMBERG, David M. GORDON, Richard EDWARDS, James SMITH]

4559 AMBROSINI, Mario. "Relazioni industriali e Stato assistenziale: alcune osservazioni sull'esperienza italiana" (Industrial relations and Welfare State: the Italian case), *Studi di Sociologia* 21(1), mar 83 : 43-54. [résumé en anglais]

4560 AMJAD, Rashid; MAHMOOD, Khalid. *Industrial relations and the political process in Pakistan, 1947-1977.* Geneva, International Institute for Labour Studies, 82, vii-61-viii p.

4561 BAIN, George Sayers. *Industrial relations in Britain.* Oxford, B. Blackwell, 83, xii-516 p.

4562 BERNSTEIN, Paul. "The unraveling of labor-management relations in Sweden", *Personnel Journal* 62(6), jun 83 : 468-477.

4563 BOMERS, Gerard B. J.; PETERSON, Richard B.; [eds.]. *Conflict management and industrial relations.* Boston, MA, Kluwer-Nijhoff Publishers, 82, x-454 p.

4564 DAYAL, Sahab. "Cooperative labor-management relations in the American automobile industry: the quality of work life approach", *Indian Journal of Economics* 64(252), jul 83 : 79-90.

4565 ENDERWICK, Peter; BUCKLEY, Peter J. "Les relations professionnelles en Grande-Bretagne: analyse comparative des entreprises étrangères et des entreprises nationales", *Travail et Société* 8(4), oct-dec 83 : 339-357.

4566 GIDWITZ, Betsy. "Labor unrest in the Soviet Union", *Problems of Communism* 31(6), dec 82 : 25-42.

4567 JACOBY, Sanford M. "Union-management cooperation in the United States: lessons from the 1920s", *Industrial and Labor Relations Review* 37(1), oct 83 : 18-33.

4568 KATZ, Harry C.; KOCHAN, Thomas A.; GOBEILLE, Kenneth R. "Industrial relations performance, economic performance, and QWL programs: an interplant analysis", *Industrial and Labor Relations Review* 37(1), oct 83 : 3-17. [Quality of Working Life, USA.]

4569 LEWIN, David; FEUILLE, Peter; [eds.]. "Behavioral research in industrial relations: an Arden House symposium", *Industrial and Labor Relations Review* 36(3), apr 83 : 339-480. [USA]

4570 MCGOLDRICK, James. "Industrial relations and the division of labour in the shipbuilding industry since the war", *British Journal of Industrial Relations* 31(2), jun 83 : 197-220. [UK]

4571 MEMORIA, C. B. *Dynamics of industrial relations in India.* Bombay, Himalaya, 83, 760 p.

4572 MERLI BRANDINI, Pietro. *Le relazioni industriali: introduzione allo studio sistematico dei rapporti imprenditori-lavoratori* (Labour relations: introduction to the systematic study of entrepreneurs-workers relations). Milano, F. Angeli, 82, 3rd, 178 p.

4573 MONGA, M. L. *Industrial relations and labour laws in India: their implementation and awareness.* New Delhi, Deep and Deep, 83, 300 p.

4574 RAMANUJAM, G. *The Honey bee: towards a new concept in industrial relations.* New Delhi, Sterling Publishers, 83, xii-112 p.

4575 RANDLE, D. N. L. *Industrial relations in the public sector.* Wellington, Industrial Relations Centre, Victoria University of Wellington, 82, iv-81 p.

4576 SABEL, Charles F. *Work and politics. The division of labor in industry.* Cambridge, Cambridge University Press, 82, xiii-304 p.

4577 SCHREGLE, Johannes. *Negotiating development: labour relations in southern Asia.* Geneva, International Labour Office, 82, vi-186 p.

4578 SCHUSTER, Michael. "The impact of union-management cooperation on productivity and employment", *Industrial and Labor Relations Review* 36(3), apr 83 : 415-430.

4579 SRIVASTAVA, Suresh C. *Industrial relations machinery: structure, working, and the law.* New Delhi, Deep and Deep Publications, 83, 268 p. [India]

4580 STRINATI, Dominic. *Capitalism, the state, and industrial relations.* London, Croom Helm, 82, 241 p. [UK]

4581 SUZUKI, Tomihisa. "Sengo 10-nenkan Toyota roshi kankei no tenkai: chingin-to no kigyobetsu hensei to sentoteki roso no haiboku" (Development of the Toyota industrial relations for a decade after the World War II: the defeat of the militant labor union), *Atarashii shakaigaku no tameni* 9(3), 83 : 35-61.

4582 THURLEY, Keith; WOOD, Stephen; [eds.]. *Industrial relations and management strategy.* Cambridge, MA-New York, NY-Sydney, Cambridge University Press, 83, ix-242 p.

4583 VAN DER HAEGEN, H.; [ed.]. *West European settlement systems.* Leuven, Instituut voor Sociale en Economische Geografie, Katholieke Universiteit te Leuven, 82, 370-1 p.

4584 WASCHKE, Hildegard. *Japans Arbeitsbeziehungen zwischen Tradition und Moderne* (Japan's labour relations between tradition and modernity). Köln, Deutscher Instituts-Verlag, 82, 59 p.

4585   WIARDA, Howard J. "From corporatism to neo-syndicalism: the state, organized labor
        and the changing industrial relations sytems of Southern Europe", *Comparative Social
        Research* 5, 82 : 3-57.
4586   ZIEGER, Robert H. "Industrial relations and labor history in the eighties", *Industrial
        Relations* 22(1), wint 83 : 58-70.

18610   Labour law
             Droit du travail

4587   "Législation (La) du travail", *Revue fiduciaire* (675), oct 83 : 18-459.
4588   "Réformes (Les)", *Droit social* (7-8), aug 83 : 434-508. [with contributions by Nicolas
        ALVAREZ, Gilles BELIER, Bernard BOYER]
4589   CEBULA, Richard J. "Right-to-work laws and geographic differences in living costs: an
        analysis of effects of the 'union ship' ban for the years 1974, 1976, and 1978", *American
        Journal of Economics and Sociology* 42(3), jul 83 : 329-340. [USA]
4590   DORSEY, James E. *Canada Labour Relations Board: federal law and practice.* Toronto, ON,
        Carswell, 83, iv-454 p.
4591   DURAN LOPEZ, F. "Legislación de empleo y reconversionnes industriales" (Labour law
        and industrial reconversions), *Revista de Política Social* (137), jan-mar 83 : 31-56. [Spain]
4592   FLOREK, Ludwik. "Fragen des polnischen Arbeitsrechts" (Problems of Polish labour law),
        Recht der Arbeit 36(1), 83 : 37-40.
4593   JEAMMAUD, Antoine. "Les lois Auroux: plus de droit ou en autre droit?", *Critiques de
        l'Économie politique* (23-24), sep 83 : 223-243. [France]
4594   ORSELLO, Gian Piero. *Lavoro e politica sociale nella Comunità europea* (Labour and social
        policy in the European Community). Palermo, Palumbo, 83, 273 p.
4595   RAWSON, D. W. "British and Australian labour law: the background to the 1983 bills",
        British Journal of Industrial Relations 31(2), jul 83 : 161-180.
4596   SUMMERS, C. W. "Comparisons in labour law: Sweden and the United States", *Svensk
        Juristtidning* 68(9), 83 : 589-616.
4597   VENCHARD, L. E. *Labour laws of Mauritius.* Port Louis, Law Publishers Ltd., 83, x-555 p.

18620   Employers' organizations
             Organisations patronales

4598   MOREAU DE BELLAING, Louis. "Le paternalisme aujourd'hui", *Connexions* 39, 83 : 95-113.

18630   Trade unions
             Syndicats

4599   "Pouvoir (Le) syndical", *Pouvoirs* (26), 83 : 7-131. [France] [with contributions by Olivier
        FOUQUET, Alain BERGOUNIOUX, Marie-Geneviève DEZES]
4600   "Sindacato, politica e corporativismo in Europa (1970-1980)" (Unionism, politics and
        corporatism in Europe (1970-1980)), *Problemi del Socialismo* 23(24-25), dec 82 : 5-308.
        [with contributions by Mario TELO, Philippe SCHMITTER, Tiziano TREU, Bruno
        TRENTIN]
4601   "Trabajadores" (Workers), *Investigación económica* 41(161), sep 82 : 9-245. [labour movement
        in Mexico] [with contributions by B. Martha RIVERO TORRES, Javier AGUILAR
        GARCIA, Javier RODRIGUEZ LAGUNAS; labour movement in Mexico]
4602   ALBORNOZ PERALTA, Osvaldo. *Historia del movimeinto obrero ecuatoriano* (History of
        Ecuadorian labour movement). Quito, Editorial Letranueva, 83, 187 p.
4603   ALEXIS, Marion. "Neo-corporatism and industrial relations: the case of German trade
        unions", *West European Politics* 6(1), jan 83 : 75-92.
4604   ALTMANN, Norbert; [et al.]. *Grenzen neuer Arbeitsformen: betriebliche Arbeitsstrukturierung,
        Einschätzung durch Industriearbeiter, Beteiligung der Betriebsräte* (Limits of new work forms:
        entrepreneurial work structuration, estimation by industrial workers, participation of entre-
        preneurial committees). Frankfurt-am-Main-New York, NY, Campus Verlag, 82, 373 p.
4605   ARMINGEON, Klaus. "Cooperative unionism in Austria and the Federal Republic of
        Germany: a review of recent literature", *European Journal of Political Research* 11(3), sep
        83 : 333-344.
4606   BAGLIONI, Guido; SANTI, Ettore; [eds.]. *L'Europa sindacale agli inizi degli anni '80* (Trade
        unions in Europe at the beginning of the eighties). Bologna, Il Mulino, 82, 385 p.
4607   BAUMANN, Michael. "Die Entwicklung der Gewerkschaftsbewegung in Thailand" (The
        development of labour movement in Thailand), *Asien* (6), 83 : 50-66.

4608 BEAUMONT, P. B. "Third party conciliation and trade union recognition: some British evidence", *Relations industrielles* 37(4), 82 : 827-842.

4609 BERGE, Geir. "Latin-amerikansk fagbevegelse i internasjonalt lys" (Latin American trade unionism from an international point of view), *Internasjonal Politikk* (1), 83 : 55-78. [résumé en anglais]

4610 BILSKY, Edgardo. *Contribution à l'étude du mouvement ouvrier et social argentin: bibliographie et sources documentaires de la région parisienne.* Nanterre, Bibliothèque de Documentation Internationale Contemporaine; Paris, Éditions du CNRS, 83, xx-229 p.

4611 BIZBERG, Ilán. "Les perspectivas de la oposición sindical en México" (Perspectives of trade union's opposition in Mexico), *Foro internacional* 23(4), jun 83 : 331-358.

4612 BLUMBACH, Helmut. "Der Niedergang der organisierten Arbeiterbewegung in Ghana" (The decline of organized worker movement in Ghana), *Forschungsinstitut der Friedrich-Ebert-Stiftung* 93, 83 : 237-249.

4613 BOOTH, Alison. "A reconsideration of trade union growth in the United Kingdom", *British Journal of Industrial Relations* 31(3), nov 83 : 377-391.

4614 BRISKIN, Linda; YANZ, Lynda; [eds.]. *Union sisters: women in the labour movement.* Toronto, ON, Women's Press, 83, 421 p.

4615 CALHOUN, Craig. "Industrialization and social radicalism. British and French workers' movements and the mid-nineteenth-century crises", *Theory and Society* 12(4), jul 83 : 485-504.

4616 CHESNEAUX, Jean; KAGAN, Richard C. "The Chinese labor movement: 1915-1949", *International Social Science Review* 58(2), 83 : 67-87.

4617 CHRISTENSEN, Sandra; MAKI, Dennis. "The wage effect of compulsory union membership", *Industrial and Labor Relations Review* 36(2), jan 83 : 230-238.

4618 COLE, Kathryn; [ed.]. *Power, conflict, and control in Australian trade unions.* Victoria-New York, NY, Penguin Books, 82, ix-309 p.

4619 COOKE, William N. "Determinants of the outcomes of union certification elections", *Industrial and Labor Relations Review* 36(3), apr 83 : 402-414.

4620 DAMM, Diethelm. "Arbeiterbürokratie statt Arbeiterbewegung. Zur Krise gewerkschaftlicher Jugendarbeit" (Workers' bureaucracy instead of labour movement. On the crisis of youth work in trade unions), *Vorgänge* 21(5-6), 82 : 118-128.

4621 DEL CAMPO, Hugo. *Sindicalismo y peronismo: los comienzos de un vínculo perdurable* (Syndicalism and peronism: the start of a lasting link). Buenos Aires, Ciencias Sociales, 83, 273 p.

4622 EASTHAN, Byron. "Canadian union growth", *Relations industrielles* 38(1), 83 : 58-71.

4623 EYRAUD, François. "The principles of union action in the engineering industries in Great Britain and France. Towards a neo-institutional analysis of industrial relations", *British Journal of Industrial Relations* 31(3), nov 83 : 358-376.

4624 FOHRBECK, Sebastian. *Gewerkschaften und neue internationale Arbeitsteilung* (Trade unions and new international division of labour). Saarbrücken-Fort Lauderdale, FL, Breitenbach, 82, 334 p.

4625 GARCÍA, Gervasio Luis; QUINTERO RIVERA, Angel G. *Desafío y solidaridad: breve historia del movimiento obrero puertorriqueño* (Challenge and solidarity: short history of the labour movement in Puerto Rico). Río Piedras, Ediciones Huracán, 82, 172 p.

4626 GILEJKO, Leszek. "Nowa formuła związków zawodowych" (The new formula for trade unions), *Biuletyn Instytutu Gospodarstwa Społecznego* 25(2), 82 : 10-23. [Poland]

4627 GODIO, J. *Sindicalismo y politica en América latina* (Trade unionism and politics in Latin America). Caracas, Instituto Latinoaméricano de Investigaciones Sociales, 83, 315 p.

4628 GOSPEL, Howard F. "Trade unions and the legal obligation to bargain: an American, Swedish and British comparison", *British Journal of Industrial Relations* 31(3), nov 83 : 343-357.

4629 GROTTIAN, Peter; NELLES, Wilfried; [eds.]. *Grossstadt und neue soziale Bewegungen* (The city and new social movements). Basel-Boston, MA, Birkhäuser, 83, xii-297 p. [Germany FR]

4630 HAUCK, David. *Black trade unions in South Africa.* Washington, DC, Investor Responsibility Research Center, 82, ii-73 p.

4631 JAWAID, Sohail. *Trade union movement in India.* Delhi, Sundeep, 82, x-230 p.

4632 KAWANISHI, Hirosuke. "Nihon ni okeru rodo-kumiai kenkyu no kadai to genjo" (The present state and tasks of research on labor unions in Japan), *Chiba daigaku kyoyobu kenkyu hokoku* A(16-jo), 83 : 119-147.

4633 KOCH, Alain; GUINARD, Danielle. "Les sections syndicales", *Revue française des Affaires sociales* 37(1), mar 83 : 153-172.

4634 KOSTIN, A. A.; [ed.]. *Formirovanie političeskoj kul'tury trudjaščihsja, opyt, problemy* (Formation of the workers' political culture: experiment, problems). Čeljabinsk, 82, 101 p. [USSR]

4635 KRIESI, Hanspeter. "Überblick über den gegenwärtigen Stand der Korporatismus-Debatte" (Overview on the present state of the corporatism-controversy), *Schweizerische Zeitschrift für Soziologie / Revue suisse de Sociologie* 9(2), 83 : 235-256.

4636   KWOKA, John E. Jr. "Monopoly, plant, and union effects on worker wages", *Industrial and Labor Relations Review* 36(2), jan 83 : 251-257.

4637   LALOR, Stephen. "Corporatism in Ireland", *Administration (Dublin)* 30(4), 82 : 74-97.

4638   LANDIER, Hubert. "Le syndicalisme face au changement", *Tocqueville Review* 5(1), sum 83 : 191-201.

4639   LAZEAR, Edward P. "A competitive theory of monopoly unionism", *American Economic Review* 73(4), sep 83 : 631-643.

4640   LÓPEZ GONZÁLEZ, Juan Jaime; GARCÍA LASAOSA, José. *Orígenes del movimiento obrero en Aragón (1854-1890)* (Origins of the labour movement in Aragon (1854-1890)). Zaragoza, Diputación Provincial, Institución Fernando el Católico, Publicación No 846, 82, 478 p. [Edited by Juan Rivero LAMAS]

4641   MAKI, Dennis R. "Unions as 'gatekeepers' of occupational sex discrimination: Canadian evidence", *Applied Economics* 15(4), aug 83 : 469-477.

4642   MARTENS, George. "Révolution ou participation: syndicats et partis politiques au Sénégal", *Mois en Afrique* 18(205-206), mar 83 : 72-113. [see also ibid. 18 (209-10), jul 83 : 78-109; 18 (211-12), sep 83 : 54-68; 18 (213-14), nov 83 : 63-109]

4643   MARTIN, Ross M. "Pluralism and the new corporatism", *Political Studies* 31(1), mar 83 : 86-102.

4644   MATEJKO, Alexander J. "The phenomenon of Solidarity: an attempt of assessment", *Nationalities Papers* 11(1), spr 83 : 77-92. [Poland]

4645   MATSUSHITA, Hiroshi. *Movimiento obrero argentino, 1930-1945: sus proyecciones en los orígenes del peronismo* (Argentine labour movement, 1930-1945: its projections in the origins of Peronism). Buenos Aires, Ediciones Siglo Veinte, 83, 347 p.

4646   MCCOLLOCH, Mark. "White collar unionism, 1940-1950", *Science and Society* 46(4), wint 82-83 : 405-419.

4647   MIELKE, Siegfried. *Internationales Gewerkschaftshandbuch* (International trade-union manual). Opladen, Leske und Budrich, 83, x-1263 p.

4648   MOISES, José Alvaro. "What is the strategy of the 'new syndicalism'?", *Latin American Perspectives* 9(4), aut 82 : 55-73. [Latin America]

4649   MOURIAUX, René. *Les syndicats dans la société française*. Paris, Presses de la Fondation Nationale des Sciences Politiques, 83, 271 p.

4650   NAVARRO, J. "La empresa y los sindicatos. Participación y cambio" (Enterprise and trade unions. Participation and change), *Documentación Social* (50), jan-mar 83 : 121-136. [Spain]

4651   NEWELL, David. "The status of British and American trade unions as defendants in industrial dispute litigation", *International and Comparative Law Quarterly* 32(2), apr 83 : 380-398.

4652   OLEDZKI, Michał. "Zwiazki zawodowe jako podmiot i przedmiot polityki społecznej w Polsce współczesnej" (Trade unions as object and subject of social policy in contemporary Poland), *Biuletyn Instytutu Gospodarstwa Społecznego* 25(2), 82 : 24-45.

4653   ORTEGA, V. "Los sindicatos y la negociación colectiva" (Trade unions and collective bargaining), *Revista de Fomento social* 37(150), apr-jun 83 : 145-157. [Spain]

4654   ORTOLANI, Maurizio. "Aspects of the trade union phenomenon in Western Europe", *Revue internationale de Sociologie* 18(1-2-3), apr-aug-sep 82 : 121-127.

4655   PEGUŠEVA, L. V. "Nasuščnye problemy profsojuznogo dviženija v Latinskoj Amerike" (Vital problems of the labour movement in Latin America), *Rabočij Klass i sovremennyj Mir* 12(2), apr 83 : 121-135.

4656   PEITCHINIS, Stephen G. "The attitude of trade unions towards technological changes", *Relations industrielles* 38(1), 83 : 104-119.

4657   POBEDA, N. A. *Proizvodstvennyj kollektiv i kul'tura rabočego* (The production collectivity and the worker's culture). Kišinev, Štiinca, 82, 158 p. [USSR]

4658   PRICE, Robert; BAIN, George Sayers. "Union growth in Britain: retrospect and prospect", *British Journal of Industrial Relations* 31(1), mar 83 : 46-68.

4659   QUINTANILLA OBREGÓN, Lourdes. *Lombardismo y sindicatos en América Latina* (Lombardism and trade unions in Latin America). México, DF, Fontamara, Ediciones Nueva Sociología, 82, 358 p. [Lombardo Toledano, Vicente, 1894-1968]

4660   RAMDIN, Ron. *From chattel slave to wage earner: a history of trade unionism in Trinidad and Tobago*. London, M. Brian and O'Keeffe, 82, 314 p.

4661   REID, Joseph D. Jr.; [ed.]. *New approaches to labor unions*. Greenwich, CT-London, JAI Press, 83, xiii-353 p.

4662   ROBERTS, Ben. "Black trade unionism: a growing force in South African industrial relations", *South Africa International* 13(4), apr 83 : 290-298.

4663   ROJO TORRECILLA, E. "La formación sindical en los acuerdos internacionales y en la negociación colectiva" (Workers' education in international agreements and collective bargaining), *Revista de Fomento social* 37(149), jan-mar 83 : 77-91.

4664   RUBLE, Blair A. *The applicability of corporatist models to the study of Soviet politics: the case of trade unions.* Pittsburgh, PA, Russian and East European Studies Program, University of Pittsburgh, 83, 35 p.

4665   RUL-LAN BUADES, G. "El sindicalismo como motor de cambio" (Trade uinionism as a motor of change), *Revista de Fomento social* 37(151), jul-sep 83 : 309-319. [Spain]

4666   SAGARDOY BENGOECHEA, Juan Antonio; BLANCO, David Léon. *El poder sindical en España* (Trade union power in Spain). Barcelona, Instituto de Estudios Económicos, 82, 207 p.

4667   SARVAROV, R. M. "O suščnosti social'nyh otnošenij i ih roli v žiznedejatel'nosti proizvodstvennogo kollektiva" (On the nature of social relations and their role in the production collectivity activity), *in: XXVI s'ezd KPSS o problema soveršenstvovanija socialističeskogo obraza žizni.* Ufa, 1982 : 37-47.

4668   SCHÜLLER, Tom; ROBERTSON, Don. "How representatives allocate their time: shop steward activity and membership contact", *British Journal of Industrial Relations* 31(3), nov 83 : 330-342. [UK]

4669   SIRIANNI, Carmen. *Workers control and socialist democracy: the Soviet experience.* London, NLB, 82, viii-437 p.

4670   THOMPSON, Mark; BLUM, Albert A. "International unionism in Canada: the move to local control", *Industrial Relations* 22(1), wint 83 . 71-86.

4671   TURNER, Jorge. *Raíz, historia y perspectivas del movimiento obrero panameño* (Origin, history and prospects of the labour management of Panama). México, DF, Editorial Signos, 82, 90 p.

4672   ULLRICH, Volker. "Die deutsche Arbeiterbewegung im ersten Weltkrieg und in der Revolution von 1918-19. Anmerkungen zu neueren Veröffentlichungen" (The German labour movement in the first world war and in the revolution of 1918-1919. Remarks on new publications), *Neue Politische Literatur* 27(4), 82 : 446-462.

4673   VALENZUELA, J. Samuel. "Movimientos obreros y sistemas políticos: un análisis conceptual y tipológico" (Labour movements and political systems: a conceptual and typological analysis), *Desarrollo económico* 23(91), oct-dec 83 : 339-368.

4674   VAN VLIET, G. E. "Plan unionism as a means of promoting workers' interest", *Netherlands Journal of Sociology* 19(1), apr 83 : 79-93. [Netherlands]

4675   VOOS, Paula B. "Union organizing: costs and benefits", *Industrial and Labor Relations Review* 36(4), jul 83 : 576-591. [USA]

4676   WARNER, Malcolm. "Corporatism, participation and society", *Relations industrielles* 38(1), 83 : 28-44.

4677   WATERMAN, Peter. *Division and unity among Nigerian workers: Lagos Port unionism, 1940x-60s.* The Hague, Institute of Social Studies; Ibadan, Heinemann, 82, xviii-234 p.

4678   WATERMAN, Peter. "Seeing the straws: riding the whirl wind, reflections on unions and popular movements in India", *Journal of Contemporary Asia* 12(4), 82 : 464-483.

4679   WON, George; OH, In-Hwan. "Grass roots democracy: the case of the Korean labor movement", *Sociological Perspectives* 26(4), oct 83 : 399-422.

4680   WÜRTELE, Werner. *Auf dem Weg zu einer 'authentischen' Gewerkschaftsbewegung in Brasilien: Grenzen und Chancen der Entwicklung starker, unabhängiger und repräsentativer Gewerkschaften im peripheren Kapitalismus* (On the way to an 'authentic' union movement in Brazil: limits and chances of development of stronger, more independent and more representative unions in peripheric capitalism). Heidelberg, Esprint-Verlag, 82, xxvii-651 p.

18640   Labour disputes
Conflits du travail

4681   BARBOSA CANO, Fabop. "Las luchas obreras de 1958-1959 y la izquierda mexicana" (Labour disputes in 1958-1959 and the Mexican Left), *Investigación económica* 42(163), jan-mar 83 : 89-119.

4682   BORREL, Monique. "Relations entre les conflits du travail et la vie socio-économique en France de 1950-1982", *Revue française des Affaires sociales* 37(2), jun 83 : 115-137.

4683   CAIRE, Guy. "Procédures de règlement pacifique des conflits collectifs en France", *Relations industrielles* 38(1), 83 : 3-27.

4684   CARINCI, Franco. "La via italiana alla istituzionalizzazione del conflitto sindacale" (The Italian way towards institutionalization of labour conflicts), *Politica ed Economia* 14(12), dec 83 : 72-76.

4685   DASSA, Sami. "Conflits ou négociations? Les grèves, leurs résultats et la taille des entreprises", *Sociologie du Travail* 25(1), jan-mar 83 : 32-44.

4686   EDWARDS, P. K. "The end of American strike statistics", *British Journal of Industrial Relations*
        31(3), nov 83 : 392-394.
4687   EDWARDS, Paul K.; SCULLION, Hugh. *The social organization of industrial conflict: control
        and resistance in the workplace.* Oxford, Blackwell, 82, xiii-314 p.
4688   GANNE, Bernard. "Conflit du travail et changement urbain: transformation d'un rapport
        local", *Sociologie du Travail* 25(2), apr-jun 83 : 127-146. [résumé en anglais]
4689   JULLIARD, Jacques. "La grève dans la conscience ouvrière", *H Histoire* 8, apr-jun 81 : 53-62.
4690   KAUFMAN, Bruce E. "Interindustry trends in strike activity", *Industrial Relations* 22(1),
        wint 83 : 45-57.
4691   LECLERCQ, Robert Jean. "Les conflits du secteur bancaire français depuis 1974: de la
        revendication organisationnelle à l'action contestataire", *Sociologie du Travail* 25(1),
        jan-mar 83 : 79-92.
4692   MERCIER, Nicole; SEGRESTIN, Denis. "Des ouvriers sur leurs terres: deux études de
        cas comparées", *Sociologie du Travail* 25(2), apr-jun 83 : 147-159. [France: conflits de
        la Montefibre à Saint-Nabord et de l'Alsthom à Belfort]
4693   MERCIER, Nicole; SEGRESTIN, Denis. "L''effet territoire' dans la mobilisation ouvrière.
        Essai d'analyse de situation complexe", *Revue française de Sociologie* 24(1), jan-mar
        83 : 61-79. [résumés en anglais, allemand, et espagnol; la grève d'Alsthom à Belfort
        en 1979]
4694   RAVIER, Jean-Pierre. "La grève, maladie britannique: mythe ou réalité?", *Sociologie du
        Travail* 25(1), jan-mar 83 : 93-107.
4695   SAPSFORD, David; [et al.]. *Strikes, theory and activity.* Bradford, West Yorkshire;
        Birmingham, AL, PCB Publications, 82, 50 p. [UK]
4696   SCHÄUBLE, Paul B. *Widerrechtlicher Streik und Abwehrungssperrung: die Reaktionsmöglichkeiten
        des widerrechtlichen und unmittelbar bestreikten Arbeitgebers* (Illegal strike and protective lockout:
        reaction possibilities of the employer illegally and unconsequently striked). Frankfurt-
        am-Main-New York, NY, P. Lang, 83, xxxvii-257 p. [Germany FR]
4697   SPÖHRING, Walger. *Streiks im internationalen Vergleich: Merkmale und Bedingungen der Streikmuster
        in Frankreich, Italien, Grossbritannien und in der Bundesrepublik Deutschland* (Strikes in inter-
        national comparison: strike characteristics and conditions in France, Italy, Great Britain
        and in the Federal Republic of Germany). Köln, Bund-Verlag, 83, 274 p.
4698   VENTURINI, Alessandra. "Le determinanti degli scioperi: Francia, Italia e Gran Bretagna
        1950-1980" (Strike determinants. France, Italy, Great Britain, 1950-1980), *Economia
        e Lavoro* 17(1), mar 83 : 3-16. [résumé in English]
4699   WATERS, Malcolm. *Strikes in Australia: a sociological analysis of industrial conflict.* Sydney-
        Boston, MA, Allen and Unwin, 82, xii-239 p.

        **18650   Arbitration. Mediation
                    Arbitrage. Médiation**

4700   BRANDSMA, Andries S.; VAN DER WINDT, Nico. "Wage bargaining and the Phillips
        curve: a macroeconomic view", *Applied Economics* 15(1), feb 83 : 61-71.
4701   COLASANTO, Michele. "Il problema della contrattazione collettiva: orientamenti e
        tendenze recenti nel paesi CEE" (The problem of collective bargaining: directions and
        recent trends in EEC countries), *Studi di Sociologia* 21(2), apr-jun 83 : 113-125.
4702   CONSOLI, Francesco. "Contraddizione tra libertà individuale e libertà sociale nella
        contrattazione collettiva" (Contradictions between individual freedom and social freedom
        in collective bargaining), *Revue internationale de Sociologie* 18(1-2-3), apr-aug-sep 82 : 47-57.
4703   EYRAUD, François. "La négociation salariale dans la métallurgie", *Sociologie du Travail*
        25(3), jul-sep 83 : 295-312. [France]
4704   ISHIKAWA, Akihiro; SUZUKI, Takashi. "Roshi kyogisei no mokuteki to koka" (The
        aim and effects of the joint consultation system), *Chuo daigaku shakai-kagaku kenkyujo-ho*
        1, 83 : 79-94.
4705   KOLB, Deborah M. "Strategy and the tactics of mediation", *Human Relations* 36(3),
        mar 83 : 247-268.
4706   MAYER, Jean. "Bien-être des salariés et productivité: le rôle de la négociation", *Revue
        internationale du Travail* 122(3), jun 83 : 363-374.
4707   MITCHELL, Daniel J. B. "The 1982 union wage concessions: a turning point for collective
        bargaining?", *California Management Review* 25(4), 83 : 78-92. [USA]
4708   VALDES DAL-RE, F. "Crisis y continuidad en la estructura de la negociación colectiva"
        (Crisis and continuity in the structure of collective bargaining), *Revista de Política Social*
        (137), jan-mar 83 : 395-444. [Spain]

18660 Collective agreements. Workers' participation
Conventions collectives. Participation des travailleurs

4709 ARZENŠEK, Vladimir. "Samoupravljanje i struktura moći: stabilnost sistema dominacije" (Self-management and the structure of power: stability of the domination system), *Revija za Sociologiju* 11(1-2), 81 : 3-12. [Yugoslavia] [résumé en anglais]

4710 BRADLEY, Keith; HILL, Stephen. "'Afterjapan': the quality circle transplant and productive efficiency", *British Journal of Industrial Relations* 31(3), nov 83 : 291-311.

4711 CECEZ, Momir. "Le marxisme originel et la promulgation de la loi sur le transfert de la gestion des entreprises aux collectivités de travail en Yougoslavie", *Questions actuelles du Socialisme* 33(4), apr 83 : 68-85.

4712 DE NITISH, R. "Un bilan concernant la participation des travailleurs dans le secteur structuré des pays en développement", *Travail et Société* 8(3), jul-sep 83 : 241-259.

4713 DERBER, Charles; SCHWARTZ, William. "Toward a theory of worker participation", *Sociological Inquiry* 53(1), 83 : 61-78.

4714 DEUTSCH, Steven; ALBRECHT, Sandra. "La participation des travailleurs aux États-Unis: les efforts de démocratisation de l'industrie et de l'économie", *Travail et Société* 8(3), jul-sep 83 : 261-291.

4715 DOKTÓR, Kazimierz. "Samorząd pracowniczy, administracja zakładowa a reforma gospodarcza" (Workers' self-management, factory administration and economic reform), *Nowe Drogi* 412(9), 83 : 28-39.

4716 FLAHERTY, Sean. "Contract status and the economic determinants of strike activity", *Industrial Relations* 22(1), wint 83 : 20-33.

4717 GAUTRAT, Jacques. "Expérience de création institutionnelle du participatif", *Année sociologique* 33, 83 : 123-138.

4718 HÉTHY, Lajos. "Az üzemi demokrácia és az érdekérvényesítési képesség" (Industrial democracy and ability to assert interests), *Gazdaság és Jogtudomány* 16(1-4), 82 : 1-24.

4719 HUBER, Mária. *Betriebliche Sozialplanung und Partizipation in der UdSSR* (Corporate social planning and participation in the USSR). Frankfurt-am-Main-New York, NY, Campus Verlag, 83, 293 p.

4720 ISHIKAWA, Akihiro. "Keiei sanka to sangyo minshu-shugi" (Workers' participation and industrial democracy), *Chuo daigaku shakai-kagaku kenkyujo-ho* 1, 83 : 1-10.

4721 KOWALAK, Tadeusz. "Wybrane zagadnienia współczesnych systemów/współ/zarządzania przedsiębiorstwem przemysłowym przez pracowników" (Selected problems from contemporary systems of worker's participation in management of industrial enterprise), *Spółdzielczy Kwartalnik naukowy* 16(3-4), 82 : 93-107. [Poland]

4722 LANGA GARCIA, L. "Notas sobre convenios colectivos en finales de 1982" (Notes on collective agreements at the end of 1982), *Revista de Política Social* (138), apr-jun 83 : 115-123. [Spain]

4723 LINDENFELD, Frank; ROTHSCHILD-WHITT, Joyce; [eds.]. *Workplace democracy and social change.* Boston, MA, Porter Sargent Publishers, 82, vii-447 p. [USA]

4724 MARTIN, Dominique. "La participation à l'épreuve de la représentativité et de pouvoir", *Année sociologique* 33, 83 : 101-121.

4725 MAVROIDIS, Petros. "Réflexions sur l'autogestion yougoslave", *Revue des Pays de l'Est* 23(2), 82 : 27-56.

4726 MORAWSKI, Witold. "Samorząd pracowniczy a reforma gospodarcza" (Workers' self-management and economic reform), *Studia Socjologiczne* 89(2), 83 : 197-225.

4727 MORAWSKI, Witold. "Samorząd pracowniczy jako instytucja reprezentacji interesów pracowniczych" (Employees' self-government as an Institution representative of employees' interests), *Problemy Marksizmu-Leninizmu* 2, 83 : 77-90. [Poland]

4728 O'BRIEN, Gordon E. "The success and failure of employee participation: a longitudinal study", *Work and People* 8(2), 82 : 24-28.

4729 PAŠIĆ, Najdan; GROZDANIĆ, Stanislav; RADEVIĆ, Milorad; [eds.]. *Workers' management in Yugoslavia: recent developments and trends.* Geneva, International Labour Office, 82, viii-198 p.

4730 PRZEWOŹNIAK, Tomasz. "Typy uczestnictwa robotników w kulturze" (Types of workers' participation in culture), *Studia Socjologiczne* 88(1), 83 : 193-208.

4731 RUBENOWITZ, Sigvard. "Some social psychological effects of direct and indirect participation in ten Swedish companies", *Organization Studies* 4(3), 83 : 243-259.

4732 RUNGGALDIER, Ulrich. *Kollektivvertragliche Mitbestimmung bei Arbeitsorganisation und Rationalisierung* (Collective contractual agreement in organization of work and rationalization). Frankfurt-am-Main, A. Metzner Verlag, 83, 434 p. [Germany FR]

4733 SAINSAULIEU, Renaud; TIXIER, Pierre-Eric; MARTY, Marie-Odile. *La démocratien en organisation: vers des fonctionnements collectifs de travail.* Paris, Librairie des Méridiens, 83, 272 p.

4734   SCHOLL, Wolfgang; BLUMSCHEIN, Harro. "Mitbestimmung und Bedürfnisbefriedigung der Arbeitnehmer" (Joint management and workers' needs satisfaction), *Schmalenbachs Zeitschrift für Betriebswirtschaftliche Forschung* 34(11), 82 : 959-978. [Germany FR]

4735   SCHRANK, Robert; [ed.]. *Industrial democracy at sea: authority and democracy on a Norwegian freighter.* Cambridge, MA-London, MIT Press, 83, xviii-220 p.

4736   TANNENBAUM, Arnold S. "Employee-owned companies", *Research in Organizational Behaviour* (5), 83 : 235-268. [USA]

4737   TOSCANO, David J. "Toward a typology of employee ownership", *Human Relations* 36(7), jul 83 : 581-601.

4738   UCA, Mahmet Nezir. *Workers' participation and self-management in Turkey: an evaluation of attempts and experiences.* The Hague, Institute of Social Studies, Nijhoff Booksellers, 83, 253 p.

4739   VADALA, Titta. "Primi risultati italiani di una ricerca europea sulla democrazia industriale" (First Italian results of an European research on industrial democracy), *Revue internationale de Sociologie* 18(1-2-3), apr-aug-sep 82 : 262-285.

18700   LEISURE
LOISIR

4740   "Animation et cultures professionnelles", *Loisir et société* 5(1), spr 82 : 1-241. [France; Canada] [with contributions by Roger LEVASSEUR, Jacques ION, Geneviève POUJOL]

4741   FUJIMOTO, Nobuko. "Rō-fūfu kazoku no yoka katsudō" (Leisure activities in the family of the aged married couple), *Shakai ronengaku* 18, 83 : 68-79.

4742   GIEGLER, Helmut. *Dimensionen und Determinanten der Freizeit* (Dimensions and determinants of leisure). Opladen, Westdeutscher Verlag, 82, xvii-579 p.

4743   MARCELLINO, Nelson Carvalho. *Lazer a humanização* (Leisure and humanization). Campinas, Papirus, 83, 83 p. [Brazil]

4744   MUÑOZ MIRA, J. "Pedagogía del ocio y cultura de masas en una época de cambio" (Leisure pedagogy and mass culture in an era of change), *Cuadernos de Realidades sociales* (22), jan 83 : 29-48. [Spain]

4746   NAUCK, Bernhard. "Konkurrierende Freizeitdefinitionen und ihre Auswirkungen auf die Forschungspraxis der Freizeitsoziologie" (Competitive definitions of leisure and their impact on the research practice of sociology of leisure), *Kölner Zeitschrift für Soziologie und Sozialpsychologie* 35(2), jun 83 : 274-303.

4747   SÁGI, Mária. *Methodological problems of research in the sociology of leisure of workers.* Budapest, Institute for Culture, 82, 12 p.

4748   UENO, Mamoru. "Yoka katsudo to atarashii life style" (Leisure and new life styles), *Tokyo toritsu daigaku shakaigaku ronko* 4, 83 : 76-100. [Japan]

18710   Leisure time
Temps de loisir

4749   "Dossier: vacances et temps libre", *Revue politique et parlementaire* 85(904), jun 83 : 57-79. [France] [with contributions by Yves RAYNOUARD, Jean-Pierre SOISSON, Raymond VAILLANT, Pierre de PORET]

4750   "Temps libre au Canada", *Loisir et société* 5(2), aut 82 : 415-456. [with contributions by Yvon FERLAND, Gilles PRONOVOST, Monique OUELLETTE, Madeleine YERLES, Roger BOILEAU]

4751   GRANSOW, Bettina; GRANSOW, Volker. "Disponible Zeit und Lebensweise. Freizeitforschung und Freizeitverhalten in der DDR" (Free time and way of life. Research on leisure and leisure behaviour in GDR), *Deutschland Archiv* 16(7), jul 83 : 729-749.

4752   JASTRZĘBSKA-SMOLAGA, Halina. "Rola czasu wolnego w życiu człowieka" (The role of leisure time in men's life), *Biuletyn Instytutu Gospodarstwa Społecznego* 25(1), 83 : 99-111.

4753   MUCHNICKA-DJAKOW, Iza. *Czas wolny w klubie seniora* (Leisure time in a club for elderly people). Warszawa, Instytut Wydawniczy Związków Zawodowych, 83, 94 p. [Poland]

4754   ZORINA, V. V. "K voprosu o sootnošeni ob'ektivnyh i sub'ektivnyh faktorov v formirovanii struktury svobodnogo vremeni" (Question on the correlation of the objective and subjective factors in the formation of the leisure time structure), *in: Voprosy teori i metodov sociologičeskih issledovanij.* Moskva, 1981 : 56-63.

4755   ŻYGULSKI, Kazimierz; HOFFMAN, Ilona; BURDOWICZ-NOWICKA, Maria. *Święta w środowisku robotniczym* (Holidays in work environment). S.l., Polska Akademia Nauk Instytut Filozofii i Socjologii, 83, 138 p.

18720 Leisure utilization
Utilisation des loisirs

4756   "Playing games. A symposium on some problems of sport in our country", *Seminar* (279), nov 82 : 11-40. [India] [with contributions by Ranjit BHATIA, Novy KAPADIA, K. R. WADHWANEY, R. N. MIRDHA, Ashwini KUMAR, Pankay BUTALIA, George THOMAS]

4757   ALLCOCK, John B. "Tourism and social change in Dalmatia", *Journal of Development Studies* 20(1), oct 83 : 34-55. [Yugoslavia]

4758   BAKER, William J.; ROG, James A.; [eds.]. *Sports and the humanities: a symposium.* Orono, ME, University of Maine at Orono Press, 83, 126 p.

4759   BRYSON, Lois. "Sport and the oppression of women", *Australian and New Zealand Journal of Sociology* 19(3), nov 83 : 413-426.

4760   CAGIGAL, J. M. "El cuerpo y el deporte en la sociedad moderna" (Body and sport in modern society), *Papers. Revista de Sociologia* (20), 83 : 145-156.

4761   COSPER, Ronald; NEWMANN, Brigitte; OKRAKU, Ishmael O. "Public drinking in Canada and the United States", *International Journal of Comparative Sociology (Leiden)* 23(3-4), sep-dec 82 : 204-215.

4762   FABIANI, Jean-Louis. "Quand la chasse populaire devient un sport. La redéfinition sociale d'un loisir traditionnel", *Études rurales* 87-88, jul-dec 82 : 309-323. [résumé en anglais]

4763   FREMBGEN, Jürgen. "Tourismus in Hunza: Beziehungen zwischen Gästen und Gastgebern" (Tourism in Hunza: relations between guests and hosts), *Sociologus* 32(2), 83 : 174-185. [North Pakistan]

4764   GREENBERG, Marshall G.; FRANK, Ronald E. "Leisure lifestyles: segmentation by interests, needs, demographics, and television viewing", *American Behavioral Scientist* 26(4), mar-apr 83 : 439-458.

4765   GREENBLAT, Cathy Stein; GAGNON, John H. "Temporary strangers: travel and tourism from a sociological perspective", *Sociological Perspectives* 26(1), jan 83 : 89-110.

4766   HARRIS, Janet C.; PARK, Roberta J. *Play, games and sports in cultural contexts.* Champaign, IL, Human Kinetics Publishers, 83, xi-521 p.

4767   KEMPF, Hervé. "L'enjeu du jeu vidéo", *Études* 358(8), aug 83 : 37-48.

4768   LOTZ, Roy; REGOLI, Robert M. "Aspects of traditionalism in modern sport organizations", *Social Science Journal (Fort Collins)* 19(4), oct 82 : 8-19. [USA] [baseball]

4769   MACHLIS, Garry E.; BURCH, William R. Jr. "Relations between strangers: cycles of structure and meaning in tourist systems", *Sociological Review* 31(4), nov 83 : 666-692.

4770   MOUSTARD, René. *Le sport populaire.* Paris, Éditions Sociales, 83, 223 p.

4771   PREGLAU, Max. "Grenzen des Massentourismus?" (Limits of mass tourism?), *Journal für Sozialforschung* 23(3), 83 : 325-349.

4772   SCHOFIELD, J. A. "The demand for cricket: the case of the John Player League", *Applied Economics* 15(3), jun 83 : 283-296. [UK]

4773   SLEPIČKA, Pavel. *Sociální interakce ve sportovní činnosti* (Social interaction in sport competition). Praha, Univerzita Karlova, 82, 127 p.

4774   SMITH, Michael A. "Social usages of the public drinking house: changing aspects of class and leisure", *British Journal of Sociology* 24(3), sep 83 : 367-385. [UK]

4775   SZCZEPANIAK, Marian. "The role of sports in international relations", *Indian Journal of Politics* 15(1-2), 81 : 48-60.

19100   POLITICAL SCIENCE. POLITICAL SOCIOLOGY
SCIENCE POLITIQUE. SOCIOLOGIE POLITIQUE

4776   "Political dimensions of psychology", *International Social Science Journal* 35(2), 83 : 221-351.
4777   "Special issue, part I: the utilization of organizational research", *Administrative Science Quarterly*
27(4), dec 82 : 588-685. [USA] [continued in ibid. 28(1), mar 83 : 65-144; with contributions by Janice M. BEYER, Harisson M. TRICE, Ronald G. CORWIN, Karen
SEASHORE LOUIS, Craig C. PINDER, V. Warren BOURGEOIS]
4778   CHAZEL, François; FAVRE, Pierre; [eds.]. "Aspects de la sociologie politique", *Revue
française de Sociologie* 24(3), jul-sep 83 : 365-594. [with contributions by François CHAZEL,
Michel DOBRY, Pierre BIRNBAUM, Daniel GAXIE, Pierre FAVRE]
4779   DOBRATZ, Betty A.; KOURVETARIS, George A. "An analysis and assessment of
political sociology", *Micropolitics* 3(1), 83 : 89-133. [USA]
4780   FÉLIX TEZANOS, José. *Sociología del socialismo español* (Sociology of the Spanish sociology).
Madrid, Tecnos, 83, 181 p.
4781   FILIPPOV, A. F. "Teorija politiki i 'političeskaja teorija' v sociologii N. Lumana"
(The theory of politics and the 'political theory' in the N. Luhman's sociology), *in: Voprosy
istorii i kritiki buržuaznoj sociologii.* Moskva, 1983 : 43-59.
4782   FREUND, Julien. "Sociologie générale et politique", *Année sociologique* 33, 83 : 273-299.
[Compte rendu bibliographique]
4783   JOSEPH, Lawrence B. "Neoconservatism in contemporary political science: democratic
theory and the party system", *Journal of Politics* 44(4), nov 82 : 955-982. [USA]
4784   KIGGUNDU, Moses N.; [et al.]. "Administrative theory and practice in developing
countries: a synthesis", *Administrative Science Quarterly* 28(1), mar 83 : 66-84.
4785   MAYER, Lawrence C. "Practising what we preach: comparative politics in the 1980's",
Comparative Political Studies 16(2), jul 83 : 173-194.
4786   SCHEMEIL, Yves. "D'une sociologie naturaliste à une sociologie politique: Robert Park",
Revue française de Sociologie 24(4), oct-dec 83 : 631-651.
4787   WASSENBERG, Pinky S.; [et al.]. "Gender differences in political conceptualization:
1956-1980", *American Politics Quarterly* 11(2), apr 83 : 181-203. [USA]

19200   POLITICAL DOCTRINES. POLITICAL THOUGHT
DOCTRINES POLITIQUES. PENSÉE POLITIQUE

19210   Political philosophy
Philosophie politique

4788   BUSINO, Giovanni. "La théorie politique et sociale de Norberto Bobbio", *Revue européenne
des Sciences sociales* 21(65), 83 : 185-198.
4789   ENEGREN, André. "Pouvoir et liberté. Une approche de la théorie politique de Hannah
Arendt", *Études* 358(4), apr 83 : 487-500.
4790   ENTMAN, Robert M. "The impact of ideology on legislative behavior and public policy
in the States", *Journal of Politics* 45(1), feb 83 : 163-182. [USA]
4791   KOMOROWSKI, Conrad. "Poland: the ideology of counter-revolution", *Political Affairs*
62(1), jan 83 : 16-21.
4792   LICHTER, Robert; ROTHMAN, Stanley. "The radical personality: social psychological
correlates of new left ideology", *Political Behavior* 4(3), 82 : 207-235. [USA]
4793   MERCADÉ, Francesc. *Cataluña, intelectuales políticos y cuestión nacional: análisis sociológico de las
ideologías políticas en la Cataluña democrática* (Catalonia, political intellectuals and national
question: a sociological analysis of political ideologies in democratic Catalonia). Barcelona,
Península, 82, 219 p.
4794   SUSUKI, Shuichi. "'Weber to Nietzsche' mondai no hihanteki kosatsu: M. Weber seijiron
hihan no sai-kento" (Max Weber and Nietzche: an analysis of Max Weber's political
theory), *Keiogijuku daigaku tetsugaku* 77, 83 : 83-112.

19220 Political power
Pouvoir politique

4795 COTTERET, Jean-Marie. "La légitimité du pouvoir et les nouveaux médias", *Revue des Sciences morales et politiques* 138(2), 83 : 209-222.

19230 Communism. Nationalism
Communisme. Nationalisme

4796 "Nacionalismos y las estructuras sociales en España" (Nationalisms and social structures in Spain), *Revista internacional de Sociología (Madrid)* 40(44), oct-dec 82 : 493-636.

4797 "Socialismo oggi" (Socialism today), *Schema* 5(9-10), jun 82 : 3-135. [with contributions by Roberto GUIDUCCI, Franco CAZZOLA, Bruno GROPPO, Emilio FRANZINA]

4798 "Special issue on French socialism", *Telos* (55), spr 83 : 3-239. [with contributions by Jean L. COHEN, Alain LIPIETZ, Jacques JULLIARD, Hugues PORTELLI, Bruno BONGIOUANNI, Richard P. SHRYOCK]

4799 "Werte des Sozialismus" (Values of socialism), *Einheit* 38(6), 83 : 524-550. [résumé en anglais, russe, français et espagnol, with contributions by Franck RUPPRECHT, Uwe-Jens HEUER, Karl A. MOLLNAU]

4800 ALMOND, Gabriel A. "Communism and political culture theory", *Comparative Politics* 15(2), jan 83 : 127-138.

4801 BOGGS, Carl. "The new populism and the limits of structural reforms", *Theory and Society* 12(3), mai 83 : 343-363. [followed by a response by Mark E. KANN: 365-373]

4802 BRUS, Wlodzimierz; KOWALAK, Tadeusz. "Socialism and development", *Cambridge Journal of Economics* 7(3-4), sep-dec 83 : 243-255.

4803 BUTENKO, A. P. "Protivorečija razvitija socializma kak obščestvennogo stroja" (Contradictions of the socialism development as a social system), *Voprosy Filosofii* 35(10), 82 : 16-29.

4804 CHIOZZI, Paolo. "Marcel Mauss: eine anthropologische Interpretation des Sozialismus" (Marcel Mauss: an anthropological interpretation of socialism), *Kölner Zeitschrift für Soziologie und Sozialpsychologie* 35(4), dec 83 : 655-679.

4805 CHOZA, Jacinto. "Cambio sociocultural y acción política en el problema de los regionalismos" (Sociocultural change and political action in the problem of regionalisms), *Revista de estudios políticos* (33), jun 83 : 147-167.

4806 CLEMENT, Wallace. "Regionalism as uneven development, class and region in Canada", *Zeitschrift der Gesellschaft für Kanada-Studien* (1), 82 : 63-74.

4807 DAHRENDORF, Ralf. *Die Chancen der Krise: über die Zukunft des Liberalismus* (The opportunities of crisis: on the future of liberalism). Stuttgart, Deutsche Verlags-Anstalt, 83, 240 p.

4808 FERGUSON, Kathy E. "Toward a new anarchism", *Contemporary Crises* 7(1), jan 83 : 39-57.

4809 FREITAG, Michel. "Discours idéologiques et langage totalitaire. Quelques considérations actuelles sur le fascisme et son idéologie", *Revue européenne des Sciences sociales* 21(65), 83 : 199-237.

4810 GERBER, Larry G. *The limits of liberalism, Josephus Daniels, Henry Stimson, Bernard Baruch, Donald Richberg, Felix Frankfurter and the development of the modern American political economy*. New York, NY, New York University Press, 83, viii-425 p.

4811 HIMMELSTRAND, Ulf. "Structural universals and historical specificities in defining socialism: some methodological and praxiological remarks", *Revue internationale de Sociologie* 17(1), apr 81 : 65-92.

4812 LACLAU, Ernesto. "Vers une théorie du populisme", *Civilisations* 31(1-4), 81 : 53-119.

4813 MACLEAN, Douglas; MILLS, Claudia; [eds.]. *Liberalism reconsidered*. Totowa, NJ, Littlefield, Adams; Rowman and Allanheld, 83, xvi-143 p.

4814 MARMORA, Léopoldo. "Populistes et socialistes: divergence et convergence. Notes sur la nation et la démocratie en Argentine", *Civilisations* 31(1-4), 81 : 185-243.

4815 MARTINS, Antonio J. "Bibliographie d'introduction au populisme latino-américain", *Civilisations* 31(1-4), 81 : 315-322.

4816 MEIDINGER, Claude. *La nouvelle économie libérale*. Paris, Presses de la Fondation Nationale des Sciences Politiques, 83, 280 p.

4817 NAHM, Andrew C. "Le nationalisme coréen: ses origines et son développement", *Revue de Corée* 15(1), spr 83 : 3-33.

4818 O'MEAGHER, Bruce; [ed.]. *The socialist objective: labor and socialism*. Sydney, N.S.W., Hale and Iremonger, 83, x-198 p. [Australia]

4819 REINKNECHT, Gottfried. *Nationalismus und kulturelle Identität in Asien und Südpazifik: (Auswahlbibliographie)* (Nationalism and cultural identity in Asia and the South Pacific: (a select bibliography)). Hamburg, Institut für Asienkunde, Dokumentations-Leitstelle Asien, 83, vii-218 p.

4820   SALTZMAN CHAFETZ, Janet; FUCHS EBAUGH, Helen Rose. "Growing conservatism in the United States? An examination of trends in political opinion between 1972 and 1980", *Sociological Perspectives* 26(3), jul 83 : 275-298.
4821   SEKELJ, Laslo. "Kommunizam i država u djelu Karla Marksa" (Communism and State in the works of Karl Marx), *Revija za Sociologiju* 11(1-2), 81 : 13-23.
4822   SMITH, Anthony D. "Nationalism and classical social theory", *British Journal of Sociology* 24(1), mar 83 : 19-38.
4823   STEIN, Steve. "Populism and the politics of social control in Latin America", *Civilisations* 31(1-4), 81 : 163-183.
4824   TRINDADE, Hélgio. "A questão do fascismo na América latina" (The question of fascism in Latin America), *Dados* 26(1), 83 : 53-76.
4825   TRINDADE, Hélgio. "La question du fascisme en Amérique latine", *Revue française de Science politique* 33(2), apr 83 : 281-312. [résumé en anglais]
4826   VEGA, Hector. "L'économie du populisme: le Chili des années 1960", *Civilisations* 31(1-4), 81 : 247-311.
4827   VILKOV, Ju. S. "Nekotorye aspekty ėvoljucii sovremennogo buržuaznogo nacionalizma" (Some aspects of the contemporary bourgeois nationalism evolution), *Naučnye Doklady vysšej Školy. Naučnyj Kommunizma* (6), 82 : 97-104.
4828   VOSTRIKOV, Ju. B. "Metodologičeskie problemy issledovanija socializma kak celostnoj sistemy" (Methodological problems of research on socialism as an integral system), *in: Problemy social'no-političeskogo razvitija socialističeskogo obščestva v sovremennyh uslovijah.* Moskva, 1982 : 172-196.
4829   WALICKI, Andrzej. *Philosophy and romantic nationalism: the case of Poland.* Oxford, Clarendon Press; New York, NY, Oxford, 82, 415 p.
4830   YAGI, Tadashi. "Anakisuto shakaigaku josetsu" (Introductory thinking of anarchist sociology), *Shakaigaku kenkyu* 45, 83 : 101-122.

19240   **Democracy. Dictatorship**
          Démocratie. Dictature

4831   "Democracia y Estado" (Democracy and State), *Revista mexicana de Sociología* 44(4), oct-dec 82 : 1095-1278. [Latin America]
4832   BOLLEN, Kenneth. "World system position, dependency, and democracy: the cross-national evidence", *American Sociological Review* 48(4), aug 83 : 468-479.
4833   BRACHER, Karl Dietrich. "Demokratie und Ideologie im Zeitalter der Machtergreifungen" (Democracy and ideology in the age of power seizures), *Vierteljahreshefte für Zeitgeschichte* 31(1), 83 : 1-24.
4834   BRAZZODURO, Marco. "Note su l'ideologia democratica" (Notes on the democratic ideology), *Revue internationale de Sociologie* 18(1-2-3), apr-aug-sep 82 : 5-11.
4835   HASHIZUME, Daisaburo. "Kindai seijigaku no konpon mondai" (The radical problem in modern politics), *Sociologos* 7, 83 : 120-128.
4836   LAMBERTI, Jean-Claude. *Tocqueville et les deux démocraties.* Paris, Presses Universitaires de France, 83, vii-325 p.
4837   MUCHA, Janusz. "Radykalizm w socjologii XX wieku" (Radicalism in sociology of 20th century), *Studia Socjologiczne* 88(1), 83 : 5-32.
4838   OBRADOVIĆ, Daniela. "Teorija o totalitarizmu u posleratnoj političkoj misli" (Theory of totalitarianism in postwar political considerations), *Sociologija* 25(1), 83 : 57-76.
4839   RODRÍGUEZ MANSILLA, Dario. *Formación de oligarquías en procesos de autogestión, la experiencia chilena entre 1967 y 1970* (Formation of oligarchies in self-management processes, the Chilean experience between 1967 and 1970). Santiago, Instituto de Sociología, Pontificia Universidad Católica de Chile, 82, 231 p.
4840   SCHAPOSNIK, Eduardo C. "Autoritarismo o fascismo" (Authoritarianism or fascism), *Desarrollo indoamericano* 17(76), apr 83 : 27-36. [Latin America]
4841   TIXIER, Pierre-Eric. "Démocratie directe et organisation. Pour une théorie du fonctionnement collectif", *Année sociologique* 33, 83 : 21-36.

19300   **CONSTITUTION. STATE**
          CONSTITUTION. ÉTAT

19310   **Political systems**
          Systèmes politiques

4842   "Apertura (La) en Brasil" (Opening in Brazil), *Revista mexicana de Sociología* 44(3), jul-sep 82 : 929-1071. [with contributions by Glaucio A. D. SOARES, David V. FLEISCHER, Bolivar LAMOUNIER]

4843 "État et société en Afrique noire", *Revue française d'Histoire d'Outre-mer* 68(250-253), 81 : 3-477. [with contributions by Yves PERSON, Kwame ARHIN, Boubacar BARRY, résumés en français et en anglais]

4844 "Pouvoirs (Les) africains", *Pouvoirs* 25, 83 : 1-148.

4845 "Systèmes étatiques africains", *Cahiers d'Études africaines* 22(3-4), 82 : 229-554.

4846 BADIE, Louis Bertrand; BIRNBAUM, Pierre. *Sociologie de l'État*. Paris, B. Grasset, 82, nouv., 250 p.

4847 BAYART, Jean-François. "La revanche des sociétés africaines", *Politique africaine* (11), sep 83 : 95-127.

4848 BIHARI, Mihály. "A politikai rendszer és környezete: funkciók és struktúrák rendszere" (The political system and its environment: a system of functions and structures), *Szociológia* 11(2), 82 : 215-231.

4849 CERASE, Francesco Paolo; MIGNELLA CALVOSA, Fiammetta. "Il ruolo dello Stato nell'attuale fase di sviluppo della società italiana. Note per un dibattito" (The role of the State in the present stage of development of the Italian Society. Notes for a discussion), *Revue internationale de Sociologie* 18(1-2-3), apr-aug-sep 82 : 193-202.

4850 DEBUYST, Frédéric. "État, démocratie et développement en Amérique latine", *Cultures et Développement* 14(4), 82 : 563-588.

4851 DIX, Robert H. "The breakdown of authoritarian regimes", *Western Political Quarterly* 35(4), dec 82 : 554-573.

4852 ÈLJAKOV, A. D.; KONDAKOV, V. V. "Političeskaja informacija i upravlenie socialističeskim obščestvom" (Political information and management of the socialist society), *Političeskaja Organizacija Obščestva i Upravlenie pri Socializme* (3), 82 : 101-113.

4853 GORIELY, Georges. "Un paradoxe historique: la social-démocratie allemande inspiratrice du bolchévisme", *Cahiers internationaux de Sociologie* 75, 83 : 197-214.

4854 HÖFFE, Otfried. "État minimal ou État social: réflexion philosophique", *Travail et Société* 8(2), jun 83 : 193-207.

4855 HUNEEUS, Carlos; NOHLEN, Dieter. "Sistemas políticos en América latina" (Political systems in Latin America), *Cuadernos hispanoamericanos* (390), dec 82 : 499-516.

4856 IGNATOV, Assen. "Quelques considérations sur les mécanismes cachés du système soviétique", *Documentation sur l'Europe centrale* 20(4), 82 : 206-217.

4857 MACHIMURA, Takashi. "Toshi shakairon no kokkaronteki isō: 'Atarashii toshi-shakaigaku' o megutte" (The theory of the state and urban sociology), *Shiso* 711, 83 : 78-96.

4858 MISZTAL, Barbara A.; MISZTAL, Bronislaw. "The issue of stability of the socio-political system in Poland. Revolutionary social processes and their totalitarian epilogue", *Revue des Pays de l'Est* 23(2), 82 : 1-26.

4859 OVSJANNIKOV, V. G.; SILANT'EV, S. G. "Sociologičeskie issledovanija političeskih otnošenij razvitogo socialističeskogo obščestvo: voprosy metodologii" (Sociological research on political relations of the developed socialist society: methodological questions), *Političeskaja Organizacija Obščestva i Upravlenie pri Socializme* (3), 82 : 33-44.

4860 PALMER, Ian. "State mechanisms and conditions of intervention: an examination of some recent official responses to the Aboriginal Land Rights demand", *Australian and New Zealand Journal of Sociology* 19(1), mar 83 : 3-32.

4861 PAPANOV, V. V. "Metodologičeskie aspekty issledovanija političeskih otnošenij razvitogo socializma" (Methodological aspects of research on the political relations of developed socialism), *Političeskaja Organizacija Obščestva i Upravlenie pri Socializme* (3), 82 : 27-33.

4862 PATJULIN, V. A. "Gosudarstvo i obščestvo: nekotorye aspekty vzaimootnošenij v kontekste istoričeskogo razvitija" (State and society: some aspects of their interrelations in the historical development context), *in: Socialističeskoe gosudarstvo i obščestvennyj progress*. Moskva, 1982 : 32-116.

4863 RYCHARD, Andrzej. "Social needs and the management system: the case of Poland", *Polish Sociological Bulletin* 54(2), 81 : 15-26.

4864 SHILS, Edward B.; ZUCKER, William. "Regulation: American versus European style", *International Social Science Review* 58(3), 83 : 168-178.

4865 SOLOV'EV, O. M.; SMIRNOV, B. V. "Struktura političeskoj sistemy obščestva razvitogo socializma" (Structure of the political system of the developed socialist society), *Političeskaja Organizacija Obščestva i Upravlenie pri Socializme* (3), 82 : 3-16.

4866 STRZELEWICZ, Willy. "Autorität und Freiheit in Staat, Gesellschaft und Erziehung" (Authority and freedom in State, society and education), *Hamburger Jahrbuch für Wirtschafts- und Gesellschaftspolitik* 27, 82 : 77-93.

4867 TOT, È. Ju. "Obščie i specifičeskie certy političeskoj organizacii socializma" (General and specific aspects of the socialism political organization), *Voprosy Filosofii* 35(9), 82 : 50-56.

4868   ZAGAJNOV, L. I. "XXVI s'ezd KPSS ob usilenii tvorčeski sozidatel'noj roli socialističeskogo
        gosudarstva" (The XXVIth Congress of the CPSU and the reinforcement of the socialist
        state creative role), *in: Socialističeskoe gosudarstvo i obščestvennyj progress.* Moskva, 1982 : 5-21.

        19320   Human rights
        Droits de l'homme

4869   "Censura y democracia" (Censorship and democracy), *Communicación* (40), jan 83 : 5-73.
        [Venezuela] [with contributions by José Ignacio REY, Berta BRITO, Marcelino
        BISBAL, Gilberto ALCALA, Gilberto NARANJO OSTTY, Gloria PERDOMO,
        Jesús M. AGUIRRE, Clarita MEDINA]
4870   "Droits (Les) de l'homme", *Cadmos* 6(21), spr 83 : 3-57. [with contributions by Friedrich
        Georg FRIEDMANN, Bernard DUPUIS, Robert SANTUCCI, Lucien BIANCO]
4871   "Mexican-Israeli conference on human rights", *Israel Yearbook on Human Rights* 12, 82 : 9-156.
        [with contributions by Jorge CARPIZO, Alberto SZEKELY, Diego VALADES, César
        SEPULVEDA, Ricardo MENDEZ SILVA]
4872   "Research and teaching of human rights", *Bulletin of Peace Proposals* 14(1), 83 : 1-114. [with
        contributions by José W. DIOKNO, Hiroko YAMANE, Musa BALLAM CONTEM,
        Riad DAOUDI, Hector FAUNDEZ-LESDEMA]
4873   BLAHOZ, Josef. "Les droits économiques, sociaux et culturels dans les conceptions des
        droits de l'homme du monde contemporain", *Annuaire de l'URSS et des Pays socialistes
        européens*, 82 : 175-188.
4874   BOVONE, Laura. "Libertà e utopia in Marcuse e Dahrendorf" (Freedom and utopia in
        Marcuse and Dahrendorf), *Studi di Sociologia* 20(3-4), jul-dec 82 : 273-296.
4875   DRAUS, Franciszk. "La dialectique de la liberté dans la pensée de Raymond Aron",
        Revue européenne des Sciences sociales 21(65), 83 : 143-184.
4876   DUFFY, P. J. "Article 3 of the European Convention on human rights", *International and
        Comparative Law Quarterly* 32(2), apr 83 : 316-346.
4877   FARACE, Alessandro. "Il 34e anniversario della dichiarazione universale die diritti dell'
        uomo" (34th anniversary of the Universal Declaration of Human Rights), *Affari sociali
        internazionali* 11(1), 83 : 5-16.
4878   GELSI BIDART, Adolfo. "Crisis y afirmación de derechos humanos" (Crisis and confirmation
        of human rights), *Revista de la Facultad de derecho de México* 31(118), apr 81 : 141-160.
4879   GRAY, J. *Mill on liberty: a defence.* London, Routledge and Kegan Paul, 83, xiii-143 p.
4880   GUANIERI, Giuseppe. "Les moyens non-judiciaires de protection et de promotion des
        droits de l'homme. L'action du Conseil de l'Europe", *Affari sociali internazionali* 11(2),
        83 : 53-64.
4881   O'MALLEY, Pat. "The invisible censor: civil law and the State delegation of press control",
        Media, Culture and Society 4(4), oct 82 : 323-337.
4882   OLLERO, Andrés. "Cómo tomarse los derechos humanos con filosofía" (How to consider
        human rights with philosophy), *Revista de estudios políticos* (33), jun 83 : 101-122.
4883   PEREZ, María. "Censura, autocensura y juego circular de información" (Censorship,
        self-censorship and circular game of information), *Revista de Ciencias Sociales de la Universidad
        de Costa Rica* 26(2), 83 : 43-54.
4884   PRESTON, Larry M. "Individual and political freedom", *Polity* 15(1), aut 82 : 72-89.
4885   RIVERO, Jean. "Vers de nouveaux droits de l'homme", *Revue des Sciences morales et politiques*
        137(4), 82 : 673-686.
4886   UNITED NATIONS. *Population and human rights: proceedings of the Symposium on Human Rights,
        Vienna, 29 June-3 July 1981.* New York, NY, UN, 83, 208 p.

        19330   Political representation
        Représentation politique

4887   "Electoral reform in China", *Chinese Law and Government* 15(4), wint 83 : 3-225. [with
        contributions by Weiyun XIAO, Jialin WU, Cheng LU, Gu ZHU]
4888   BRASIL DE LIMA, Olavo Jr.; ABRANCHES, Sérgio Henrique. "Representação eleitoral:
        conceitos e experiências" (Electoral representation: concepts and experiences), *Dados*
        26(2), 83 : 125-139.
4889   GIUSTI TAVARES, José Antonio. "Representação majoritária e representação proporcional:
        a controvérsia teórica e o impacto das fórmulas eleitorais sobre o processo político"
        (Majority and proportional representation: the theoretical controversy and the impact
        of electoral formulas on the political process), *Dados* 26(2), 83 : 155-179. [Brazil]

4890   MARTINS, Carlos Estevam. "A reforma do sistema eleitoral" (The reform of the electoral system), *Dados* 26(2), 83 : 141-153.

4891   PORRO, Nicola. "La rappresentanza fra subalternità e potere. Note in margine a convegno su poteri e controlli nell'Italia che cambia" (Political representation between inferiority and power. Notes about a meeting on power and control in changing Italy), *Critica sociologica* 65, 83 : 60-71.

19340   Government
Gouvernement

4892   BAYLEY, David H. "The police and political order in India", *Asian Survey* 23(4), apr 83 : 484-496.

4893   BUCK, Andrew J.; [et al.]. "Organization of police departments in the suburbs: new realities, new solution", *Annales internationales de criminologie* 20(1-2), 83 : 81-102. [USA]

4894   CHAPPELL, Henry W. Jr.; KEECH, William R. "Welfare consequences of the six-year presidential term evaluated in the context of a model of the US economy", *American Political Science Review* 77(1), mar 83 : 75-91.

4895   FRY, Louis W.; BERKES, Leslie J. "The paramilitary police model: an organizational misfit", *Human Organization* 42(3), 83 : 225-234. [USA]

4896   HOLLAND BAKER, Mary; [et al.]. "The impact of a crime wave: perceptions, fear and confidence in the policy", *Law and Society Review* 17(2), 83 : 319-335.

4897   MAHAJAN, Amarjit. *Indian policewomen: a sociological study of a new role.* New Delhi, Deep and Deep, 82, 198 p.

4898   MILLER, Larry S.; BRASWELL, Michael C. *Human relations and police work.* Prospect Heights, IL, Waveland Press, 83, xiv-178 p. [USA]

4899   NACHMIAS, David; FELBINGER, Claire. "Utilization in the policy cycle: directions for research", *Policy Studies Review* 2(2), nov 82 : 300-308.

4900   ROBERTSON, John D. "Inflation, unemployment, and government collapse: a Poisson application", *Comparative Political Studies* 15(4), jan 83 : 425-444.

4901   SMITH, Allen G.; LOUIS, Karen Seashore; [eds.]. "Multimethod policy research: issues and applications", *American Behavioral Scientist* 26(1), sep-oct 82 : 3-144.

19350   Parliament
Parlement

19360   Judiciary power
Pouvoir judiciaire

4902   "Judicial behavior: theory and methodology", *Political Behavior* 5(1), 83 : 7-153. [USA] [with contributions by C. Neal TATE, Gregory A. CALDEIRA, James L. CROYLE]

4903   CASTAN, Nicole. "La justice en question en France à la fin de l'Ancien Régime" *Déviance et Société* 7(1), mar 83 : 23-34.

4904   MAYNARD, Douglas W. "Social order and plea bargaining in the courtroom", *Sociological Quarterly* 24(2), spr 83 : 233-251. [USA]

4905   PALMER, Jerry; PEARCE, Frank. "Legal discourse and state power: Foucault and the judicial relation", *International Journal of the Sociology of Law* 11(4), nov 83 : 361-383.

19400   PUBLIC ADMINISTRATION
ADMINISTRATION PUBLIQUE

19410   Civil service. Technocracy
Fonction publique. Technocratie

4906   "Administration et société. Colloque IFSA, 27-28 janvier 1983", *Revue française d'Administration publique* (26), jun 83 : 7-245. [with contributions by Jacques MENIER, Céline WIENER, Pierre MAUROY, Jean-Marie DELARUE, Michel LA CLAINCHE]

4907   "Canadian public administration", *Canadian Public Administration* 25(4), wint 82 : 444-712. [with contributions by Kenneth KERNAGHAN, H. L. LAFRAMBOISE, V. Seymour WILSON, Audrey DOERR]

4908   "Management (Le) public", *Revue française d'Administration publique* (24), dec 82 : 5-102. [with contributions by Jean-Pierre NIOCHE, Charles R. WISE, Lois RECASCINO-WISE, Romain LAUFER, Jacques CHEVALLIER, Danièle LOSCHAK, Guy DESAUNAY]

4909   "Riforme (La) della publica amministrazione" (The reform of public administration), *Rivista trimestrale di Diritto pubblico* (3), 82 : 715-975. [Italy]
4910   BALDUCCI, Massimo. "Fonction publique en transtion: le cas italien", *Revue internationale des Sciences administratives* 48(3-4), 82 : 322-330.
4911   BOURGAULT, Jacques. "Les hauts fonctionnaires québécois: paramètres synergiques de puissance et de servitude", *Canadian Journal of Political Science* 16(2), jun 83 : 227-256. [résumé en anglais]
4912   BULLING, Manfred. "La structure de l'administration allemande", *Revue internationale des Sciences administratives* 49(2), 83 : 166-171.
4913   CAPPELLI, Peter. "Comparability and the British Civil Service", *British Journal of Industrial Relations* 31(1), mar 83 : 33-45.
4914   CATHERINE, Robert; THUILLIER, Guy. *L'être administratif et l'imaginaire.* Paris, Economica, 82, 123 p.
4915   CHACKERIAN, Richard; SHADUKHI, Suliman M. "Public bureaucracy in Saudi Arabia: an empirical assessment of work group behavior", *Revue internationale des Sciences administratives* 49(3), 83 : 319-322. [résumé en français]
4916   CHEVALLIER, Jacques; LOSCHAK, Danièle. "Rationalité juridique et rationalité managériale dans l'administration française", *Revue française d'Administration publique* (24), dec 82 : 53-94. [résumés en anglais et en espagnol]
4917   CHODAK, Szymon. "Etatization: its concept and varieties", *Research in Social Movements, Conflicts and Change* (5), 83 : 259-294.
4918   DAMGAARD, Erik. "The public sector in a democratic order. Problems and non-solutions in the Danish case", *Scandinavian Political Studies* 5(4), 82 : 337-358.
4919   DUPUY, François; THOENIG, Jean-Claude. *Sociologie de l'administration française.* Paris, A. Colin, 83, 206 p.
4920   EVELAND, J. D. "Some themes in the interaction of technology and administration", *Policy Studies Journal* 11(3), mar 83 : 409-418.
4921   FEICK, Jürgen; MAYNTZ, Renate. "Bürger im bürokratischen Staat: repräsentative Beurteilungen und Handlungseinschätzungen" (Citizens in a bureaucratic state: representative judgments and behaviour estimates), *Verwaltung* 15(4), 82 : 409-434.
4922   FELCMAN, Isidoro L. "Pautas para la definición de estrategias de investigación y diagnóstico institucional en la Administración Pública Argentina" (Rules to define strategies of investigation and institutional diagnostic of the Argentine public administration), *Revista Argentina de Administración Pública* 13/14, oct 82-mar 83 : 17-52.
4923   GARCÍA-ZAMOR, J. C.; MAYO-SMITH, I. "Administrative reform in Haïti: problems, progress and prospects", *Public Administration and Development* 3(1), mar 83 : 39-48.
4924   GILBERT, Charles E.; [ed.]. "Implementing governmental change", *Annals of the American Academy of Political and Social Science* 466, mar 83 : 1-205. [with contributions by James W. FESLER, Peter A. HALL, Eugene B. MCGREGOR, Alan D. DEAN, Eleanor CHELIMSKY]
4925   HEPER, N.; KALAYCIOGLU, E. "Organizational socialization as reality-testing: the case of the Turkish higher civil servants", *International Journal of Political Education* 6(2), aug 83 : 175-198.
4926   JOBERT, Bruno; MÜLLER, Pierre. "Participation, cogestion et changement social dans l'administration publique", *Revue française d'Administration publique* (27), sep 83 : 555-561. [France]
4927   KHAN, Akhtar Ali. "Political sterilization of public employees in India: a need for reform", *Political Science Review* 21(4), dec 81 : 21-39.
4928   KOEHN, P. "The role of public administrators in public policy making: practice and prospects in Nigeria", *Public Administration and Development* 3(1), mar 83 : 1-26.
4929   OLOWU, Dele. "The nature of bureaucratic corruption in Nigeria", *Revue internationale des Sciences administratives* 49(3), 83 : 291-296. [résumé en français]
4930   OULD DADDAH, Turkia. "Valeurs socio-culturelles et administration publique", *Afrique contemporaine* (125), mar 83 : 3-34. [Africa]
4931   PENAUD, Jeanne. "La haute fonction publique en France", *Rivista trimestrale di Diritto pubblico* (2), 83 : 660-676.
4932   RIDLEY, F. F. "Career service: a comparative perspective on civil service promotion", *Public Administration* 61(2), sum 83 : 179-196.
4933   STEINIGER, Wolfgang. "Die dänische Verwaltungsorganisation. Ein Beitrag zum Kommunalrechts Dänemarks" (The Danish administrative organization. A contribution to Denmark's communal law), *Verwaltung* 16(1), 83 : 81-102.
4934   SZENTPÉTERI, István. "Az igazgatás határai, társadalmi ellenőrzésének problémái" (The limits of administration, the problems of its social control), *Jogtudományi Közlöny* 38(12), 83 : 744-754.

4935 TANAKA, Toyoji. "Gyosei kanrisei ni okeru soshiki henkaku no katei bunseki" (A process analysis of organizational reform in public administration), *Shakaigaku hyoron* 34(1), 83 : 2-17. [Japan]
4936 TARKUNDE, V. M. "Falling standards in public life", *Radical Humanist* 46(6), sep 82 : 19-27. [India]
4937 WERNER, Simcha B. "New directions in the study of administrative corruption", *Public Administration Review* 43(2), apr 83 : 146-154.
4938 WITTKÄMPER, Gerhard W. "Möglichkeiten und Grenzen neuer Technologien in der öffentlichen Verwaltung" (Possibilities and limitations of new technologies in public administration), *Verwaltung* 16(2), 83 : 161-177.
4939 ZAFARULLAH, Habib Mohammad; KHAN, Mohammad Mahabbat. "Staffing the higher civil services in Bangladesh: an analysis of recruitment and selection process", *Public Administration and Development* 3(2), apr 83 : 121-133.

19420 Central government. Local government
Administration centrale. Administration locale

4940 "Fusie (De) van gemeenten in Belgie, een evaluatie na vÿf jaar" (The merger of communes in Belgium: an evaluation after five years), *Res publica* 24(3-4), 82 : 407-741. [résumé en anglais; with contributions by J. MICHEL, R. MAES, W. DEWACHTER]
4941 AMMONS, David N.; KING, Joseph C. "Productivity improvement in local government: its place among competing priorities", *Public Administration Review* 43(2), apr 83 : 113-120. [USA]
4942 CASTELLS, Manuel. "Local government, urban crisis and political change", *Political Power and Social Theory* 2, 81 : 1-19.
4943 DE MELLO, Diogo Lordello. "Modernización de los gobiernos locales en América latina" (Modernization of local governments in Latin America), *Revista interamericana de Planificación* 17(66), jun 83 : 185-202.
4944 DOWNS, Charles; KUSNETZOFF, Fernando. "The changing role of local government in the Nicaraguan revolution", *International Journal of Urban and Regional Research* 6(4), dec 82 : 533-548. [résumés en français, espagnol et allemand]
4945 GOULD, Harold A. "Who got a piece of the action? A century of urban politics in Faizabad municipality", *Contributions to Indian Sociology* 16(1), jan-jun 82 : 97-114. [India]
4946 KNEMEYER, Franz-Ludwig. "L'autonomie administrative des communes en Allemagne fédérale", *Revue internationale des Sciences administratives* 49(2), 83 : 178-186.
4947 WIATR, Jerzy J. "Samorząd społeczny w systemie politycznym Polski Ludowej" (Communal self-government in the political system of People's Poland), *Wieś Współczesna* 311(1), 83 : 3-7.
4948 WIATR, Jerzy J.; [ed.]. *Władza lokalna u progu kryzysu. 'Studium dwu województw'* (Local government on the verge of crisis. 'Study on two districts'). Warszawa, Uniwersytet Warszawski Instytut Socjologii, 83, 474 p.

19500 POLITICAL PARTIES. PRESSURE GROUPS
PARTIS POLITIQUES. GROUPES DE PRESSION

19510 Party systems. Political parties
Systèmes de parti. Partis politiques

4949 "Party activists in comparative perspective", *International Political Science Review* 4(1), 83 : 11-143. [with contributions by Alan ABRAMOVITZ, John F. BIBBY, Abraham BRICHTA, Roland CAYROL, Karlheinz REIF]
4950 "Political parties and the Madisonian model", *Political Science Reviewer* 12, aut 82 : 1-97. [with contributions by James PIERESON, Kenneth KOLSON, Paul K. POLLOCK]
4951 BELLIGNI, Silvano. "Sul sistema partitico dell'Italia contemporanea. Elementi per una rassegra della letterature sociopoliticologica" (On the party system of contemporary Italy. Elements for a review of socio-political literature), *Stato e Mercato* (8), aug 83 : 317-341. [résumé en anglais]
4952 BRASIL DE LIMA, Olavo Jr. "Realinhamento político e desestabilização do sistema partidário: Brasil, 1945-1962" (Political realignment and destabilization of the party system: Brazil, 1945-1962), *Dados* 25(3), 82 : 365-377.
4953 CHAIGNEAU, Pascal. "Le système de partis à Madagascar", *Penant* 93(781-782), dec 83 : 306-345.

4954   DI PALMA, Giuseppe. "Governo dei partiti e riproducibilità democratica: il dilemma delle nuove democrazie" (Party government and democratic reproductibility: new democracies' dilemma), *Revista italiana di scienza politica* 13(1), apr 83 : 3-36.

4955   DI TELLA, Torcuato S. " 'Partidos del Pueblo' en América Latina. Revisión teórica y reseña de tendencias históricas" ('Peoples Parties' in Latin America. A theoretical review and a survey of historical trends), *Desarrollo Económico* 22(88), jan-mar 83 : 451-483.

4956   GILMOUR, C. Edwin. "The future of the American party system", *India Quarterly* 38(1), mar 82 : 20-50.

4957   IYASU, Tadashi. *Seito habatsu no shakaigaku* (The Habatsu: a sociological study). Kyoto, Sekai Shisosha, 83, 334 p. [Japan]

4958   KEARNEY, Robert N. "The political party system in Sri Lanka", *Political Science Quarterly* 98(1), spr 83 : 17-33.

4959   MAKI, Dennis R. "Political parties and trade union growth in Canada", *Relations industrielles* 37(4), 82 : 876-886.

4960   MOODY, Peter R. Jr. "The erosion of the function of political parties in the post-liberal State", *Review of Politics* 45(2), apr 83 : 254-279.

4961   MÜLLER-ROMMEL, Ferdinand. "Parteien neuen Typs in Westeuropa: Eine vergleichende Analyse" (New type parties in Western Europe: a comparative analysis), *Zeitschrift für Parlamentsfragen* 13(3), sep 82 : 369-390.

4962   N'DONGOBIANG, M. "Le parti démocratique gabonais et l'État", *Penant* 93(780), jul 83 : 131-152.

4963   PASO, Leonardo. *Historia de los partidos políticos en la Argentina: 1900-1930* (History of Argentine political parties: 1900-1930). Buenos Aires, Directa, 83, 574 p.

4964   PASQUINO, Gianfranco. "Partiti, società civile, istituzioni e il caso italiano" (Parties, civil society, institutions and the Italian case), *Stato e Mercato* (8), aug 83 : 169-207. [résumé en anglais]

4965   RAMIREZ, Manuel. "El sistema de partidos en España tras las elecciones de 1982" (Party system in Spain after the 1982 elections), *Revista de estudios políticos* (30), dec 82 : 7-20. [see also ibid. pp. 81-109 by Rafael del AQUILA TEJERINA]

4966   ROWLAND, C. K. "The disintegration of American political parties: the evidence from 1980 nomination campaigns", *Tocqueville Review* 3(1), wint 81 : 183-194.

4967   SASAKI, Kōken. "Furukute atarashii 'Jishu kanriron' " ('Autogestion' of the French New Socialist Party), *Soka daigaku Soshiorojika* 7(2), 83 : 1-21.

4968   SELLE, Per; SVÅSAND, Lars. "The local party organization and its members: between randomness and rationality", *Scandinavian Political Studies* 6(3), sep 83 : 211-229.

4969   SIVINI, Giordano. "Solidarità e organizzazione nella sociologia del partito politico di Roberto Michels" (Solidarity and organization in the sociology of political parties by Roberto Michels), *Revue internationale de Sociologie* 18(1-2-3), apr-aug-sep 82 : 30-39.

4970   SOLBES, Jean; GRAY, Lawrence. "Les partis politiques aux États-Unis", *Recherches internationales* (8), trim. 2, 83 : 25-31.

4971   WARE, Alan. "Party decline and party reform", *Teaching Politics* 12(1), jan 83 : 82-96.

**19520   Pressure groups. Protest movements
            Groupes de pression. Mouvements contestataires**

4972   "German (The) Peace Movement", *Telos* (56), sum 83 : 119-192. [with contributions by Ingrid MEUSCHAL, Walter SUSS, Michael LUCAS, Axel HONNET, Otto HALLSCHEUET, Boris FRANKEL, Jeffrey HERF]

4973   "Interest intermediation: toward new corporatism(s)", *International Political Science Review* 4(2), 83 : 151-260. [résumés en français; with contributions by Gehrard LEMBRUCH, Bernd MARIN, Andrew COX, Jack HAYWARD]

4974   "Special issue on social movements", *Telos* (52), sum 82 : 3-77. [with contributions by Klaus EDER, Jean COHEN, Norberto BOBBIO, Du-Yul SONG, Bruno BONGIOVANNI]

4975   BRAND, Karl-Werner. *Neue soziale Bewegungen: Entstehung, Funktion und Perspektive neuer Protestpotentiale; eine Zwischenbilanz* (New social movements: origin, function and perspectives of new protest powers; a provisional appraisal). Opladen, Westdeutscher Verlag, 82, 206 p. [Germany FR]

4976   BROSZAT, Martin. "Zur Struktur der NS-Massenbewegung" (On the structure of national-socialism mass movement), *Vierteljahreshefte für Zeitgeschichte* 31(3), 83 : 52-76.

4977   BROWNE, William P. "Mobilizing and activating group demands: the American Agriculture Movement", *Social Science Quarterly* 64(1), mar 83 : 19-34.

4978   CASANOVA, José V. "The Opus Dei ethic, the technocrats and the modernization of Spain", *Social Science Information* 22(1), 83 : 27-50.

4979 COHEN, Jean L. "Rethinking social movements", *Berkeley Journal of Sociology* 28, 83 : 97-113.
4980 DENITCH, Bogdan. "Social movements in the Reagan era", *Telos* (53), aut 82 : 57-66.
4981 DIX, Robert H. "The varieties of revolution", *Comparative Politics* 15(3), apr 83 : 281-294.
4982 DUBET, F.; [et al.]. "A social movement: Solidarity", *Telos* (53), aut 82 : 128-136.
4983 DUBET, François. "Sociologie des mouvements sociaux", *Année sociologique* 33, 83 : 433-507. [Compte rendu bibliographique]
4984 FREEMAN, Jo; [ed.]. *Social movements of the sixties and seventies.* New York, NY, Longman, 83, xvii-382 p. [USA]
4985 GOLUBOVIĆ, Zagorka. "Istorijske ponke socijalnog pokreta u Poljskoj, 1980-1981" (Historical lessons of social movement in Poland, 1980-1981), *Revija za Sociologiju* 11(1-2), 81 : 43-55. [résumé en anglais]
4986 GURR, Ted Robert. "Outcomes of public protest among Australia's aborigines", *American Behavioral Scientist* 26(3), jan-feb 83 : 353-373.
4987 HORTON SMITH, David; PILLEMER, Karl. "Self-help groups as social movement organizations: social structure and social change", *Research in Social Movements, Conflicts and Change* (5), 83 : 203-233.
4988 JENKINS, J. Craig. "Resource mobilization theory and the study of social movements", *Annual Review of Sociology* (9), 83 : 527-553.
4989 KAWAMURA, Nozomu. "Citizen's movement against environmental destruction in Japan", *Tokyo toritsu daigaku sogo toshi kenkyu* 18, 83 : 99-109.
4990 LAW, Kim S.; WALSH, Edward J. "The interaction of grievances and structures in social movement analysis: the case of JUST", *Sociological Quarterly* 24(1), wint 83 : 123-136. [Johnstowners United to Stop another Tragedy]
4991 LAWSON, Ronald. "Origins and evolution of a social movement strategy: the rent strike in New York City, 1904-1980", *Urban Affairs Quarterly* 18(3), mar 83 : 371-395.
4992 LOCHMANN, Renate. "Die Friedensbewegung, die Ökologiebewegung und die Frauen-bewegung" (The peace, ecological and feminist movements), *Vorgänge* 21(5-6), 82 : 95-107. [Germany FR]
4993 LODGE, Tom. "The Paarl insurrection: a South African uprising", *African Studies Review* 25(4), dec 82 : 95-116.
4994 MARTINS, Antonio J. "L'espace populiste. Notes sur les mouvements populaires latino-américains", *Civilisations* 31(1-4), 81 : 23-51.
4995 MCADAM, Doug. "Tactical innovation and the pace of insurgency", *American Sociological Review* 48(6), dec 83 : 735-754. [USA]
4996 NARIO, Hugo; [ed.]. *Movimientos sociales. Los crímenes del Tandil, 1872* (Social movements. The crimes of Tandil, 1872). Buenos Aires, Centro Editor de América Latina, 83, 91 p.
4997 O'KEEFE, Michael; SCHUMAKER, Paul D. "Protest effectiveness in Southeast Asia", *American Behavioral Scientist* 26(3), jan-feb 83 : 375-394.
4998 OLIVER, Pamela. "The mobilization of paid and volunteer activists in the neighborhood movement", *Research in Social Movements, Conflicts and Change* (5), 83 : 133-170.
4999 SANT CASSIA, Paul. "Patterns of covert politics in post-Independence Cyprus", *Archives européennes de Sociologie* 24(1), 83 : 115-135.
5000 SCHÄFER, Wolf; [ed.]. *Neue soziale Bewegungen* (New social movements). Frankfurt-am-Main, Fischer Taschenbuch Verlag, 83, 128 p.
5001 SCHERER-WARREN, Ilse. *Movimientos sociais: um ensaio de interpretação sociológica* (Social movements: an essay of sociological interpretation). Florianópolis, SC, Curso de Pós-Graduação em Ciências Sociais, Universidad Federal de Santa Catarina, 83, 89 p.
5002 SCHLOZMAN, Kay Lehman; TIERNEY, John T. "More of the same: Washington pressure group activity in a decade of change", *Journal of Politics* 45(2), mai 83 : 351-377.
5003 SETHI, S. Prakash. "Corporate political activism", *California Management Review* 24(3), 82 : 32-42. [USA]
5004 SIISIÄINEN, Martti. "Uusien yhteiskunnallisten liikkeiden demokratia- ja organisaatio-ongelman teoreettisista juurista politiikan sosiologiassa" (On the theoretical origins of the problems of democracy and organization raised by new social movements), *Politiikka* 25(2), 83 : 103-117.
5005 SURANA, Pushpendra. *Social movements and social structure: a study in the princely states of Mewar.* New Delhi, Manohar, 83, 194 p.
5006 TOURAINE, Alain; [ed.]. *Mouvements sociaux d'aujourd'hui: acteurs et analystes.* Paris, Éditions ouvrières, Éditions Économie et Humanisme, 82, 263 p. [Colloque de Cerisy-La-Salle, 1979]
5007 TUÑON DE LARA, M. "Crisis económicas y movimientos sociales: el caso español, 1898-1934" (Economic crises and social movements: the Spanish case, 1898-1934), *Sistema* (52), jan 83 : 3-21.

5008   USEEM, Bert; ZALD, Mayer N. "From pressure group to social movement: organization dilemmas of the effort to promote nuclear power", *Social Problems* 30(2), dec 82 : 144-156.
5009   WALKER, Jack L. "The origins and maintenance of interest groups in America", *American Political Science Review* 77(2), jun 83 : 390-406.
5010   WALSH, Edward J.; WARLAND, Rex H. "Social movement involvement in the wake of a nuclear accident: activists and free riders in the TMI area", *American Sociological Review* 48(6), dec 83 : 764-780. [USA: Three Mile Island]
5011   WEBB, Keith; [et al.]. "Etiology and outcomes of protest: new European perspectives", *American Behavioral Scientist* 26(3), jan-feb 83 : 311-331.
5012   WILSON, Frank L. "Les groupes d'intérêt sous la Cinquième République. Test de trois modèles théoriques de l'interaction entre groupes et gouvernement", *Revue française de Science politique* 33(2), apr 83 : 220-254. [résumé en anglais]

19530   Political majority. Political opposition
Majorité politique. Opposition politique

5013   "Russian dissidents and their attitudes toward the non-Russian nations", *Nationalities Papers* 11(2), aug 83 : 190-254. [with contributions by Yaroslav YILINSKY, David KOWALEWSKI, Yakov SUSLENSKY, Sviatoslaw KARAVANSKY]
5014   GRILLI, Pietro. "L'opposizione politica nei sistemi non competitivi: una premessa analitica" (Political opposition in non-competitive systems: an analytical premise), *Revista italiana di scienza politica* 13(1), apr 83 : 65-102.
5015   KOWALEWSKI, David. "Establishment vigilantism and political dissent: a Soviet case study", *Armed Forces and Society* 9(1), aut 81 : 83-97.
5016   KRANE, Dale. "Opposition strategy and survival in praetorian Brazil, 1964-79", *Journal of Politics* 45(1), feb 83 : 28-63.
5017   LÉVY, Shlomit. "A cross-cultural analysis of the structure and levels of attitudes towards acts of political protest", *Social Indicators Research* 12(3), apr 83 : 281-309.
5018   LIJPHART, Arend. "The relative salience of the socioeconomic and religious issue dimensions: coalition formations in ten western democracies, 1919-1979", *European Journal of Political Research* 10(3), sep 82 : 201-211.
5019   MCCAUGHRIN, Craig. "Statics and dynamics of dissent", *Comparative Political Studies* 15(4), jan 83 : 405-423.
5020   SEIDENBERG, Dana April. *Uhuru and the Kenya Indians: the role of a minority community in Kenya politics, 1939-1963.* New Delhi, Vikas, 83, 198 p.
5021   SHIN, Myungsoon. "Political protest and government decision making: Korea, 1945-1972", *American Behavioral Scientist* 26(3), jan-feb 83 : 395-416.

19600   POLITICAL BEHAVIOUR. ELECTIONS. POLITICS
COMPORTEMENT POLITIQUE. ÉLECTIONS. POLITIQUE

19610   Political leaders. Political society
Leaders politiques. Société politique

5022   CARLSON, James M.; HYDE, Mark S. "The candidate oriented party activist", *Social Science Journal (Fort Collins)* 19(4), oct 82 : 79-92. [USA]
5023   MALIK, Yogendra K. "Role perceptions and role evaluation of Indian urban political elite: a Punjab case study", *Asian Survey* 23(9), sep 83 : 1062-1080.
5024   WELLS, William G. Jr. "Politicians and social scientists: an uneasy relationship", *American Behavioral Scientist* 26(2), nov-dec 82 : 235-249.

19620   Political attitudes. Political participation
Attitudes politiques. Participation politique

5025   "Nuevas formas de hacer política" (New forms of political action), *Nueva sociedad* (64), feb 83 : 23-96. [Latin America] [with contributions by Hartmut KARMER, Henry PEASE GARCIA, Rafael KRIES, Francisco MIERES]
5026   BLAKE, Donald E. "The consistency of inconsistency: party identification in federal and provincial politics", *Canadian Journal of Political Science* 15(4), dec 82 : 691-710. [résumé en français]
5027   BROMKE, Adam. "The revival of political idealism in Poland", *Canadian Slavonic Papers* 24(4), dec 82 : 335-357.

5028   BUNKER, Stephen G.; COHEN, Laurence E. "Collaboration and competition in two colonization projects: toward a general theory of official corruption", *Human Organization* 42(2), sum 83 : 106-114.

5029   CASSEL, Carol A. "Predicting party identification, 1956-80: who are the Republicans and who are the Democrats?", *Political Behavior* 4(3), 82 : 265-282. [USA]

5030   COOK, Timothy E. "Another perspective on political authority in children's literature: the fallible leader in L. Frank Baum and Dr. Seuss", *Western Political Quarterly* 36(2), jun 83 : 326-336.

5031   FENNELL, Phil; THOMAS, Philip A. "Corruption in England and Wales: an historical analysis", *International Journal of the Sociology of Law* 11(2), mai 83 : 167-189.

5032   GOMBÁR, Csaba. "Democratic politicising-political culture", *International Journal of Political Education* 5(4), dec 82 : 301-317.

5033   GRANSOW, Volker; OFFE, Claus. "Political culture and the politics of the social democratic government", *Telos* (53), aut 82 : 67-80. [Germany FR]

5034   GUTERBOCK, Thomas M.; LONDON, Bruce. "Race, political orientation and participation: an empirical test of four competing theories", *American Sociological Review* 48(4), aug 83 : 439-453.

5035   HIMMELWEIT, Hilde T. "Political socialization", *International Social Science Journal* 35(2), 83 : 237-256.

5036   HOOPER, Michael. "The motivational bases of political behavior: a new concept and measurement procedure", *Public Opinion Quarterly* 47(4), 83 : 497-515. [USA]

5037   JAIN, R. B. "Fighting political corruption: the Indian experience", *Indian Political Science Review* 17(2), jul 83 : 215-228.

5038   KERI, László. "Notes to the research on political socialization in Hungary", *International Journal of Political Education* 5(4), dec 82 : 291-299.

5039   LARAÑA RODRIGUEZ-CABELLO, Enrique. "Comunicación y política en la sociedad industrial avanzada. Los medios de comunicación colectiva y las campañas electorales" (Communication and politics in the advanced industrial society. Mass media and electoral campaigns), *Revista de estudios políticos* (29), oct 82 : 51-79.

5040   LOSADA, Rodrigo. *Identificación y participación política en Colombia* (Political identification and participation in Colombia). Bogotá, Fundación para la Educación Superior y el Desarrollo, 82, 234 p.

5041   LUPFER, Michael B.; ROSENBERG, J. P. "Differences in adults' political orientations as a function of age", *Journal of Social Psychology* 119(1), feb 83 : 125-133. [USA]

5042   MALIK, Yogendra K. "Sub-cultural variations and political socialization: the case of North Indian youth", *Journal of Asian and African Studies* 16(3-4), oct 81 : 223-237.

5043   MCDONALD, Michael A.; HOWELL, Susan E. "Reconsidering the reconceptualizations of party identification", *Political Methodology* 8(4), 82 : 73-91. [USA]

5044   MÜLLER, Edward N.; JUKAM, Thomas O. "Discontent and aggressive political participation", *British Journal of Political Science* 13(2), apr 83 : 159-179.

5045   PIERCE, John; HAGNER, Paul. "Levels of conceptualization and political belief consistency", *Micropolitics* 2(4), 83 : 311-348. [USA]

5046   POLLOCK, Philip H. III. "Are there two liberalisms? The partisan and demographic influences on two dimensions of political belief", *Sociological Focus* 16(4), oct 83 : 227-237.

5047   REICHEL, Peter. "Politische Kultur und Demokratie. Ein deutsches Strukturproblem" (Political culture and democracy. A German structural problem), *Vorgänge* 21(5-6), 82 : 41-55. [Germany FR]

5048   ROSE, Lawrence E.; WALGAHL, Ragnar. "The distribution of political participation in Norway: alternative perspectives on a problem of democratic theory", *Scandinavian Political Studies* 5(4), 82 : 285-314.

5049   SIGELMAN, Lee; FELDMAN, Stanley. "Efficacy, mistrust and political mobilization", *Comparative Political Studies* 16(1), apr 83 : 118-143.

5050   STERCK, Stefaan. "Kind en politiek" (Children and politics), *Res publica* 25(1), 83 : 3-19. [Belgium]

5051   WASMUND, Klaus. "The political socialization of terrorist groups in West Germany", *Journal of Political and Military Sociology* 11(2), spr 83 : 223-240.

5052   WAYMAN, Frank Whelon; STOCKTON, Ronald R. "The structure and stability of political attitudes: findings from the 1974-1976 Dearborn Panel Study", *Public Opinion Quarterly* 47(3), 83 : 329-346. [USA]

5053   WHITE, Stephen. "Political communications in the USSR: letters to party, State and press", *Political Studies* 31(1), mar 83 : 43-60.

5054   WINKLER, John D. "Determinants of political participation in a Canadian and a United States city", *Political Psychology* 3(3-4), wint 82 : 140-161.

5055 WORMALD, Eileen. "A political women: the myth of early socialisation", _International Journal of Political Education_ 6(1), apr 83 : 43-64.

5056 YOGEV, Abraham; SHAPIRA, Rina; TIBON, Shira. "Political socialization in an African national youth movement", _International Journal of Political Education_ 5(3), sep 82 : 211-223.

19630 Elections
Élections

5057 "Elections in the Pacific", _Political Science_ 35(1), jul 83 : 1-144. [with contributions by James JUPP, Alan CLARK, William TAGUPA, Barrie MacDONALD, Leulu Felise VA'A, Donald R. SHUSTER]

5058 BOTTIROLI CIVARDI, Marisa. "Un' analisi ecologica del voto politico. Il caso della Lombardia" (Ecological analysis of political voting. The case of Lombardy), _Politico_ 48(1), 83 : 55-90. [résumé en anglais]

5059 DELLI CARDINI, Michael X. "Political distillation: the changing impact of partisanship on electoral behavior", _American Politics Quarterly_ 11(2), apr 83 : 163-180. [USA]

5060 GERSCHMAN, Silvia. "O voto na favela" (Voting in favela), _Revista brasileira de Estudos políticos_ (56), jan 83 : 155-177. [Brazil]

5061 GIOVANNINI, Paolo. "Astensionismo elettorale e questione giovanile" (Electoral abstentionism and youth problem), _Revista italiana di scienza politica_ 12(3), dec 82 : 457-477. [Italy]

5062 HERIN, Robert. "Géographie des comportements électoraux dans les provinces d'Albacete, Alicante et Murcia (Sud-Est de l'Espagne)", _Revue géographique des Pyrénées et du Sud-Ouest_ 53(4), wint 82 : 356-380. [résumés en anglais et en espagnol]

5063 HOWELL, Susan E. "Campaign activities and State election outcomes", _Political Behavior_ 4(4), 82 : 401-417. [USA]

5064 KELLEY, Jonathan; MCALLISTER, Ian. "The electoral consequence of gender in Australia", _British Journal of Political Science_ 13(3), jul 83 : 365-377.

5065 KRAMER, Gerald H. "The ecological fallacy revisited: aggregate — versus individual — level findings on economics and elections, and sociotropic voting", _American Political Science Review_ 77(1), mar 83 : 92-111.

5066 LEWIS-BECK, Michael S. "Economics and the French voter: a micro analysis", _Public Opinion Quarterly_ 47(3), aut 83 : 347-360.

5067 MARTÍN VASALLO, José Ramón. _Las elecciones a Cortes en la ciudad de Salamanca, 1931-1936: un estudio de sociología electoral_ (Cortes elections in Salamanca, 1931-1936: a study of electoral sociology). Salamanca, Servicio de Publicaciones del Ayuntamiento de Salamanca, 82, 165 p. [Spain]

5068 MCARTHUR, Margaret. "The triennial poll on liquor; factors on voting behavior", _Political Science_ 34(2), dec 82 : 204-213. [New Zealand]

5069 MCIVER, John P. "Unemployment and partisanship. A second opinion", _American Politics Quarterly_ 10(4), oct 82 : 439-451.

5070 MONK-TURNER, Elizabeth. "Sex and voting behaviour in the United States of America", _Journal of Social, Political and Economic Studies_ 7(4), wint 82 : 369-376.

5071 RASMUSSEN, Jorgen. "The electoral costs of being a woman in the 1979 British general election", _Comparative Politics_ 15(4), jul 83 : 461-475.

5072 ROETTGER, Walter B.; WINEBRENNER, Hugh. "The voting behavior of American political scientists: the 1980 presidential election", _Western Political Quarterly_ 36(1), mar 83 : 134-148.

5073 SALISBURY, Bart R. "Evaluative voting behavior: an experimental examination", _Western Political Quarterly_ 36(1), mar 83 : 88-97.

5074 SCHNAPPER, Dominique; STRUDEL, Sylvie. "Le 'vote juif' en France", _Revue française de Science politique_ 33(6), dec 83 : 933-961. [résumé en anglais]

5075 THOMPSON, William R.; ZUK, Gary. "American elections and the international electoral-economic cycle a test of the Tufte hypothesis", _American Journal of Political Science_ 27(3), aug 83 : 464-484.

5076 TUCKEL, Peter S.; TEJERA, Felipe. "Changing patterns in American voting behavior, 1914-1980", _Public Opinion Quarterly_ 47(2), sum 83 : 230-246.

5077 WEATHERFORD, M. Stephen. "Economic voting and the 'symbolic politics' argument: a reinterpretation and synthesis", _American Political Science Review_ 77(1), mar 83 : 158-174.

5078 WOLFLE, Lee M. "Socialist voting among coal miners, 1900-1940", _Sociological Focus_ 16(1), jan 83 : 37-47. [USA]

5079 ZIMMER, Troy A. "Community and communality in voting participation", _Sociological Perspectives_ 26(2), apr 83 : 185-199. [USA]

**19640   Politics
           Politique**

5080   "Research on American politics", *Social Science Quarterly* 63(3), sep 82 : 517-588.
5081   BLUM, Linda M. "Politics and policy-making: the comparable worth debate", *Berkeley Journal of Sociology* 28, 83 : 39-67.
5082   FRANKEL, Philip H. "Consensus, consociation and cooption in South African politics", *Cahiers d'Études africaines* 20(4), 80 : 473-494.
5083   JASIŃSKA-KANIA, Aleksandra. "Rationalization and legitimation crisis: the relevance of Marxian and Weberian works for an explanation of the political order's legitimacy crisis in Poland", *Sociology (London)* 17(2), mai 83 : 157-164.
5084   MIRONESCO, Christine. *Le logique du conflit: théories et mythes de la sociologie politique contemporaine.* Lausanne, P. M. Favre, 82, 185 p.
5085   O'KANE, Rosemany H. T. "Towards a nomination of the general causes of coups d'État", *European Journal of Political Research* 11(1), mar 83 : 27-44.
5086   VASILIK, M. A. "Političeskaja žizn' razvitogo socialističeskogo obščestva kak kategorija naučnogo kommunizma" (The political life of the developed socialist society as a category of scientific communism), *Političeskaja Organizacija Obščestva i Upravlenie pri Socializme* (3), 82 : 16-27.

**19700   ARMY. MILITARY SOCIOLOGY
           ARMÉE. SOCIOLOGIE MILITAIRE**

5087   ENDERS, Samuel; ALEXIEV, Alex. "The ethnic factor in the Soviet armed forces", *Conflict* 4(2-3-4), 83 : 93-180.
5088   ESSER, Martin. *Das Traditionsverständnis des Offizierkorps: eine empirische Untersuchung zur gesellschaftlichen Integration der Streitkräfte* (Tradition understanding of the officer corps: an empirical research on the social integration of the military). Heidelberg, R. von Decker, 82, xx-354 p.
5089   FRUHLING, Hugo; PORTALES, Carlos; VARAS, Augusto. *Estado y fuerzas armadas* (The State and the armed forces). Santiago de Chile, FLACSO, 83, 204 p.
5090   KEMENY, Jim. "Professional ideologies and organizational structure: tanks and the military", *Archives européennes de Sociologie* 24(2), 83 : 223-240.
5091   NAGY, Emil. *Életmód, katonai életmód* (Way of life, military way of life). Budapest, Zrinyi Katonai Kiadó, 82, 206 p.
5092   SEGAL, David R.; SEGAL, Mady Wechsler. "Change in military organization", *Annual Review of Sociology* (9), 83 : 151-170. [USA]
5093   SEREBRJANNIKOV, V. V. "K voprosu o roli armii v žizni obščestva: kritika sovremennyh buržuaznyh koncepcij" (Question of the Army's role in societal life: critics of contemporary bourgeois conceptions), *Voprosy Filosofii* 35(12), 83 : 97-105.
5094   SMITH, A. Wade. "Public consciousness of blacks in the military", *Journal of Political and Military Sociology* 11(2), spr 83 : 281-300. [USA]
5095   THIEBLEMONT, André. "Les militaires sous le regard ethnologique", *Défense nationale* 39, jun 83 : 73-87. [France]
5096   WECHSLER SEGAL, Mady; SEGAL, David R. "Social change and the participation of women in the American military", *Research in Social Movements, Conflicts and Change* (5), 83 : 235-258.
5097   WEEDE, Erich. "Military participation ratios, human capital formation and economic growth: a cross-national analysis", *Journal of Political and Military Sociology* 11(1), spr 83 : 11-19.
5098   WOLPIN, Miles D. "Sociopolitical radicalism and military professionalism in the Third-World", *Comparative Politics* 15(2), jan 83 : 203-221.

**19800   INTERNATIONAL RELATIONS
           RELATIONS INTERNATIONALES**

**19810   International law. International organizations
           Droit international. Organisations internationales**

5099   GRAIZBORD, Boris. "Integración, diferencias regionales e interdependencia en la frontera de Mexico con Estados Unidos" (Integration, regional differences and interdependence in the frontier of Mexico with the United States), *Demografía y Economía* 17(1), jan-mar 83 : 1-20.

5100   JAYARAMU, P. S. "Super powers and the changing international system: a third world
         perspective", *India Quarterly* 38(2), jun 82 : 147-160.
5101   KNIEPER, Rolf; SMITH, Daniel. "The conditioning of national policy-making by inter-
         national law: the stand-by arrangements of the International Monetary Fund", *Inter-
         national Journal of the Sociology of Law* 11(1), feb 83 : 41-64.

19820   Foreign policy. Sovereignty
         Politique étrangère. Souveraineté

5102   BOISOT, Marcel. "Esquisse d'une psychologie du pacifisme", *Défense nationale* 39, nov
         83 : 63-74.
5103   COLARD, Daniel. "Les mouvements pacifistes européens", *Documents* 38(2), apr 83 : 3-16.
5104   FORGET, Philippe. "Pacifisme et idéologies", *Défense nationale* 39, jul 83 : 23-42.
5105   JAFFRE, Jérôme. "La politique étrangère et l'opinion française", *Tocqueville Review* 3(1),
         wint 81 : 174-182.
5106   RODRIGUEZ GARCIA, A. "Movimientos pacifistas del Estado español" (Pacifist
         movements in Spain), *Documentación Social* (52), jul-sep 83 : 213-218.

19830   International cooperation. War
         Coopération internationale. Guerre

5107   ARASZKIEWICZ, Halina. "Die Entwicklungshilfe der europäischen RGW-Länder im
         Ausbildungsbereich" (Comecon countries' development aid in the education field),
         Internationales Afrika Forum 19(3), trim. 3, 83 : 277-288.
5108   BRAILLARD, Philippe. "Quelques perspectives de développement de l'étude empirique
         des conflits internationaux", *Études internationales* 14(2), jun 83 : 219-236.
5109   BURLACKIJ, F. M. "Filosofija mira" (The peace philosophy), *Voprosy Filosofii* 35(12),
         83 : 57-66.
5110   CALSAMIGLIA, A. "Sobre la justificación de la guerra" (On the justification of war),
         Sistema (56), sep 83 : 25-61.
5111   COSTE, René. "L'Église catholique face aux problèmes de la guerre et de la paix au cours
         des siècles", *Défense nationale* 39, jun 83 : 55-72.
5112   FISKE, Susan T.; FISCHHOFF, Baruch; MILBURN, Michael A.; [eds.]. "Images of
         nuclear war", *Journal of Social Issues* 39(1), 83 : 1-180.
5113   KAUFMAN, Joyce P. "The social consequences of war: the social development of four
         nations", *Armed Forces and Society* 9(2), wint 83 : 245-264.
5114   KLENNER, Hermann. "Frieden und Menschenrechte" (Peace and human rights), *Deutsche
         Zeitschrift für Philosophie* 30(12), 82 : 1468-1480.
5115   LENG, Russell J.; GOCHMAN, Charles S. "Dangerous disputes: a study of conflict
         behavior and war", *American Journal of Political Science* 26(4), nov 82 : 664-687.
5116   MEDINA, Manuel. "La aplicación del concepto de estructura a la sociedad internacional"
         (The application of the concept of structure to the international society), *Revista de estudios
         internacionales* 3(4), dec 82 : 985-1003.
5117   NAHUŠEV, V. Š. "Nekotorye teoretičeskie i metodologičeskie aspekty internationalizacii
         žizni narodov" (Some theoretical and methodological aspects of the people's life inter-
         nationalization), *Vestnik Moskovskogo Universiteta. Serija Teorija naučnogo Kommunizma* (6),
         82 : 35-43.
5118   SCARDUELLI, Pietro. "La guerra nelle società primitive: una prospettiva evoluzionistica"
         (The war in primitive societies: an evolutionistic view), *Rassegna italiana di Sociologia* 24(3),
         jul-sep 83 : 361-402. [résumé en anglais]
5119   SREDIN, G. V. "Problemy vojny i mira v sovremennuju èpohu" (War and peace
         problems in the contemporary era), *Voprosy Filosofii* 35(10), 82 : 3-15.
5120   TJUŠKEVIČ, S. A. "Vojna-ugroza social'nomu progressu" (War is a threat for social
         progress), *Voprosy Filosofii* 35(12), 83 : 75-81.
5121   VOLKOGONOV, D. A. "Ugroza miru — mifičeskaja i real'naja" (Threats to peace:
         the mythical and the real ones), *Voprosy Filosofii* 35(12), 83 : 82-88.

19840   Disarmament. Weapons
         Désarmement. Armes

5122   FONTANEL, Jacques. "La question du désarmement", *Économie et Humanisme* 271, jun
         83 : 39-45. [see also ibid. 271, aug 83: 48-57 and 273, oct 83: 65-73]

5123   MCCUBBINS, Matthew D. "The policy components of arms competition", *American Journal of Political Science* 27(3), aug 83 : 385-406.

5124   MCLAUCHLAN, Greg. "E. P. Thompson on the nuclear arms race", *Berkeley Journal of Sociology* 28, 83 : 131-140.

20100   SOCIAL PROBLEMS
          PROBLÈMES SOCIAUX

20110   Applied sociology
          Sociologie appliquée

5125   "Recherche (La) en action sociale", *Informations sociales* (6), 83 : 2-94. [France] [with contributions by Bernard GUIBERT, Michel CHAUVRIERE; Jean-François LAE, Roger JAUDON, Liane MOZERE]

5127   *Social information of India: trends and structure.* Delhi, Hindustan Publishing Corporation, 83, xxiv-299 p.

5128   BERMAN, Jeffrey S.; READ, Stephen J.; KENNY, David A. "Processing inconsistent social information", *Journal of Personality and Social Psychology* 45(6), dec 83 : 1211-1224.

5129   BULMER, Martin. "Applied social research? The use and non-use of empirical social inquiry by British and American governmental commissions", *Policy Studies* 6, 82 : 55-82.

5130   BULMER, Martin. *The uses of social research. Social investigation in public policy making.* London, G. Allen and Unwin, 82, xv-184 p.

5131   BULMER, Martin; WARWICK, Donald P.; [eds.]. *Social research in developing countries: surveys and censuses in the Third World.* Chichester-New York, NY, John Wiley, 83, xviii-383 p.

5132   DAUDISTEL, Howard C.; [ed.]. "Applied sociology", *Teaching Sociology* 11(1), oct 83 : 3-112.

5133   HAWKINS, Darnell F.; [ed.]. "Social research and the courts", *Sociological Methods and Research* 11(4), mai 83 : 379-533. [USA]

5134   HELLEVIK, Ottar. *Sosiologisk metode for brukere av samfunnsforskning* (Sociological methods for the users of social research). Oslo, Universitetsforlaget, 82, 103 p. [Norway]

5135   INDIAN COUNCIL OF SOCIAL SCIENCE RESEARCH AND CENTRAL STATISTICAL ORGANISATION. *Social information of India: trends and structure.* Delhi, Hindustan Publishing Co., 83, xxiv-302 p.

5136   KUTYREV, B. P. " 'Social'naja fotografija' ili social'noe upravlenie?" ('Social photography' or social planning?), *Sociologičeskie Issledovanija (Moskva)* (1), 83 : 125-129.

5137   MATEJKO, Alexander J. "Utilization of social research. The Alberta case", *Sociologia internationalis* 21(1-2), 83 : 117-144. [Canada]

5138   MONTANDON, Clópâtre. "Problèmes ethiques de la recherche en sciences sociales: le cas d'une étude en milieu carcéral", *Schweizerische Zeitschrift für Soziologie / Revue suisse de Sociologie* 9(2), 83 : 215-233.

5139   SIEBER, Joan E.; [ed.]. "Values and applied social research", *American Behavioral Scientist* 26(2), nov-dec 82 : 149-280.

5140   WITZEL, Andreas. *Verfahren der qualitativen Sozialforschung: Überblick und Alternativen* (Processes of qualitative social research: overview and alternatives). Frankfurt-am-Main-New York, NY, Campus Verlag, 82, 136 p.

20120   Social pathology
          Pathologie sociale

5141   BASSIS, Michael S.; GELLES, Richard J.; LEVINE, Ann. *Social problems.* New York, NY, Harcourt Brace Jovanovich, 82, xix-586 p. [Edited by Robert K. MERTON]

5142   BROWN, Muriel; [ed.]. *The structure of disadvantage.* London-Exeter, NH, Heinemann Educational Books, 83, 210 p.

5143   CASTEL, Robert. "De la générosité au risque", *Actes de la Recherche en Sciences sociales* 47-48, jun 83 : 119-127. [Arriérés-mentaux, alcooliques, etc. en France]

5144   DEFLEUR, Melvin L.; [ed.]. *Social problems in American society.* Boston, MA, Houghton Mifflin Co., 83, xx-616-40 p.

5145   GDOWSKA-WILIŃSKA, Maria. *System zapobiegania wykolejaniu się społecznemu dzieci i młodzieży w środowisku wielkomiejskim* (The system of prevention of social demoralization of children and young people in urban environment). Warszawa, Wydawnictwa Uniwersytetu Warszawskiego, 83, 194 p. [Poland]

5146   HATANAKA, Munekazu. "Jūmin undō no tenkai ni okeru kansetsu shutai no yakuwari: Nagoya ni okeru Shinkansen kogai hantai undo o jirei nishite" (The role of the indirect components in civil unrest), *Okinawa kirisutokyo tanki-daigaku kiyo* 11, 83 : 47-60.

5147   JACOBS, Jerry. *Social problems through social theory: a selective view.* Houston, TX, Cap and Gown Press, 83, xii-155 p.
5148   KIRIČENKO, V. N.; [et al.]. *Social'nye problemy v perspectivnom planirovanii* (Social problems in perspective planning). Moskva, Ėkonomika, 82, 303 p.
5149   PALANCA, Vaifai. "La geografia del disagio sociale: Italia 1971-1981" (Geography of social unrest: Italy 1971-1981), *Politica ed Economia* 14(9), sep 83 : 40-48.
5150   STALLBERG, Friedrich Wilhelm; [ed.]. *Soziale Probleme: grundlegende Beiträge zu ihrer Theorie und Analyse* (Social problems: basic essays on their theory and analysis). Neuwied, Luchterhand, 83, ix-209 p.

20130   Disasters
         Catastrophes

5151   INTERNATIONAL CENTER OF GERONTOLOGY / WORLD HEALTH ORGANIZATION. WORKING GROUP. *Medical and social aspects of accidents among the elderly.* Paris, ICG, 83, 82 p.
5152   ODA, Toshikatsu; YAMAMURA, Etsuo. "Chiiki saigai to iryo keikaku ni kansuru ichikosatsu" (A study on community disaster and community medical service planning), *Toshi keikaku bessatsu* 18, 83 : 181-186.
5153   URANO, Masaki; WADA, Yushi. *Keikai sengem hatsureiji-to no panikku yosoku oyobi taisaku ni kansuru chosa* (The earthquake prediction and preparedness program concerning the social disorder in response to the short term warning announcement). Yokohama, Yokohamashi Somukyoku, Yokohamashi shobokyoku, Mirai Kogaku Kenkyujo, 83, 67 p.

20140   Poverty
         Pauvreté

5154   AIMEZ, Pierre. "Violences alimentaires et psychométamorphoses du corps féminin", *Social Science Information* 22(6), 83 : 927-940.
5155   ARGUELLO, Omar. "Pobreza y fecundidad en Costa Rica" (Poverty and fertility in Costa Rica), *Notas de Población* 11(32), aug 83 : 9-54.
5156   BOKOR, Ágnes. "Depriváció — társadalompolitika — szociálpolitika" (Deprivation — societal policy — social policy), *Társadalomtudományi Közlemények* 13(1), 83 : 126-143.
5157   CHAKRAVARTY, Satya Ranjan. "Ethically flexible measures of poverty", *Canadian Journal of Economics / Revue canadienne d'Économique* 16(1), feb 83 : 74-85.
5158   ESCUDERO, José Carlos. "Daños sociales por malnutrición" (Social damages raised from malnutrition), *Cuadernos médico-sociales* 25, sep 83 : 5-16.
5159   GOODWIN, Leonard. *Causes and cures of welfare: new evidence on the social psychology of the poor.* Lexington, MA-Toronto, ON, Heath, Lexington Books, 83, xviii-199 p.
5160   GOVAERTS, France. "Pauvres et pauvreté: discours, désignation langagière et marginalisation", *Revue de l'Institut de Sociologie* (3-4), 83 : 439-453.
5161   HUSAIN, M. G. *Psycho-ecological dimensions of poverty.* New Delhi, Manohar, 83, x-115 p. [India]
5162   KÜHRT, Peter. *Das Armutssyndrom: die Entstehung und Verfestigung von Sozialhilfebedürftigkeit in der Bundesrepublik* (The syndrome of poverty: origin and strengthening of social aid need in the Federal Republic). Weinheim, Beltz, 82, 100-xxxiv p.
5163   MARTINI, Gianfranco. "Quanti poveri sono fra noi? L'indagine della Comunità europea" (How many poor among us? European Community survey), *Affari sociali internazionali* 10(4), 82 : 5-18.
5164   MIĆUNOVIĆ, Dragoljub. "Lokova politička teorija svojine" (Locke's political theory of poverty), *Sociologija* 25(1), 83 : 39-55.
5165   MORRIS, David; MCALPIN, Michelle B. *Measuring the condition of India's poor: the physical quality of life index.* New Delhi, Promilla, 82, ix-100 p.
5166   OGIEN, Ruwen. *Théories ordinaires de la pauvreté.* Paris, Presses Universitaires de France, 83, 176 p.
5167   PARKINSON, J. R.; [ed.]. *Poverty and aid.* New York, NY, St. Martin's Press, 83, 264 p.
5168   PRAKASH, Brahm; DOSHY, Asha. "Urban poor: analysis and action", *Indian Journal of Social Work* 43(4), jan 83 : 455-465.
5169   PRIETO ESCUDERO, Germán; PRIETO YERRO, Claudina. "El fenómeno sociológico de pobreza en la moderna economía" (The sociological phenomenon of poverty in modern economy), *Revista de Economía política* 93, jan-apr 83 : 173-195.
5170   ROMÃO, Mauricio E. C. "Considerações sobre o conceito de pobreza" (Considerations on the concept of poverty), *Revista brasileira de Economia* 36(4), oct-dec 82 : 355-370. [Brazil]

5171   SARPELLON, Giovanni. *Rapporto sulla povertà in Italia: la sintesi della grande indagine CEE* (Report on poverty in Italy: synthesis of the large EEC survey). Milano, F. Angeli, 83, 304 p.

5172   SARVESWARA RAO, B.; DESHPANDE, V. N.; [eds.]. *Poverty, an interdisciplinary approach.* Bombay, Madras Institute of Development Studies, 82, 296 p. [India]

5173   SESHADRI, K. *Rural unrest in India.* New Delhi, Intellectual Publishing House, 83, xiii-192 p.

20150   Alcoholism. Drugs of abuse
Alcoolisme. Drogue

5174   "Psychology in the public forum: alcoholism", *American Psychologist* 38(10), oct 83 : 1035-1121. [with contributions by Rudolf H. MOOS, John W. FINNEY, Spark MATSUNAGA, William MAYER]

5175   ADLER, Israel; KANDEL, Denise B. "Risk periods for drug involvement in adolescence in France and in Israel: application of survival analysis to cross-sectional data", *Social Forces* 62(2), dec 83 : 375-397.

5176   ADLER, Patricia A.; ADLER, Peter. "Relationship between dealers: the social organization of illicit drug transactions", *Sociology and Social Research* 67(3), apr 83 : 260-278. [USA]

5177   ARMSTRONG, Hal. *Nous sommes tous des toxicos.* Paris, Éditions Clancier-Guénaud, 82, 247 p.

5178   BOYD, Neil. "The dilemma of Canadian narcotics legislation: the social control of altered States of consciousness", *Contemporary Crises* 7(3), jul 83 : 257-269.

5179   BRICEÑO PUENTE, Carlos. *Las drogas en el Perú* (Drugs of abuse in Peru). Lima, Pueblo Libre, Tip. SESATOR, 83, 236 p.

5180   BRUNETTA, Giuseppe. "Il fenomeno droga nel 1981" (Drug phenomenon in 1981), *Aggiornamenti sociali* 34(3), mar 83 : 219-229. [Italy]

5181   CASSWELL, Sally; SMYTHE, Margaret. "Alcohol consumption by women", *Australian and New Zealand Journal of Sociology* 19(1), mar 83 : 146-152. [New Zealand]

5182   COX, W. Miles; [ed.]. *Identifying and measuring alcoholic personality characteristics.* San Francisco, CA, Jossey-Bass, 83, 107 p.

5183   CRAIG, Richard B. "Domestic implications of illicit Colombian drug production and trafficking", *Journal of Inter-American Studies and World Affairs* 25(3), aug 83 : 325-350.

5184   DAMIANI, Paul; [et al.]. "Étude des distributions de consommation de tabac et d'alcool", *Journal de la Société de statistique de Paris* 124(2), trim. 2, 83 : 119-128. [France]

5185   DREHER, Melanie C. "Marihuana and work: cannabis smoking on a Jamaican sugar estate", *Human organization* 42(1), 83 : 1-8.

5186   FALK, Pasi; SULKUNEN, Pekka. "Drinking on the screen: an analysis of a mythical male fantasy in Finnish films", *Social Science Information* 22(3), 83 : 387-410.

5187   FOURNIER, Dominique. "Façons de boire, façons de voir...", *Social Science Information* 22(3), 83 : 411-434. [Mexique]

5188   GARCÍA MAS, M. P. "Metodología e investigación en el área de la salud mental. La perspectiva de un sociólogo en el área de las toxicomanías" (Methodology and research in the field of mental health. Sociologists approach to drug addiction), *Sociología* (1), 83 : 9-14.

5189   GLANTZ, Meyer D.; PETERSEN, David M.; WHITTINGON, Frank J.; [eds.]. *Drugs and the elderly adult.* Rockville, MD, US DHHS, National Institute on Drug Abuse; Washington, DC, United States Government Printing Office, METROTEC, 83, xiii-305 p.

5190   HIMMELSTEIN, Jerome L. "From killer weed to drop-out drug: the changing ideology of marihuana", *Contemporary Crises* 7(1), jan 83 : 13-38.

5191   HULL, Jay G.; YOUNG, Richard David. "Self-consciousness, self-esteem, and success-failure as determinants of alcohol consumption in male social drinkers", *Journal of Personality and Social Psychology* 44(6), jun 83 : 1097-1109.

5192   KOSKI, Patricia R.; ECKBERG, Douglas Lee. "Bureaucratic legitimation: marijuana and the drug enforcement administration", *Sociological Focus* 16(4), oct 83 : 255-273. [USA]

5193   KUKAWKA, Kazimierz. "Niektóre prawno-społeczne problemy przeciwdziałania alkoholizmowi" (Some legal and social problems of counteracting alcoholism), *Praca i Zabezpieczenie społeczne* 25(3), 83 : 1-10. [Poland]

5194   LASAGNA, Louis C.; LINDZEY, Gardner. "Marijuana policy and drug mythology", *Society* 20(2), feb 83 : 67-78.

5195   LÉVY, Marguerite F.; [et al.]. "Alcoholic women in industry", *International Journal of Group Tensions* 10(1-4), 80 : 120-129. [USA]

5196   MÄKELÄ, Klaus. "The uses of alcohol and their cultural regulation", *Acta Sociologica* 26(1), 83 : 21-31.

5197   MALVIN, Janet H.; MOSKOWITZ, Joel M. "Anonymous versus identifiable self-reports of adolescent drug attitudes, intentions and use", *Public Opinion Quarterly* 47(4), 83 : 557-566. [USA]

5198   MARSH, Alan; MATHESON, Jil. *Smoking attitudes and behaviour: an enquiry carried out on behalf of the Department of Health and Social Security.* London, HMSO, 83, xiv-185 p.

5199   MARSH, Jeanne C.; SHEVELL, Steven K. "Males' and females' perceived reasons for their use of heroin", *Social Service Review* 57(1), mar 83 : 78-93.

5200   ONNIS, Luigi. "La tossicomania: problema individuale o condizionamento sociale?" (Drug addiction: individual problem or social condition?), *Revue internationale de Sociologie* 18(1-2-3), apr-aug-sep 82 : 164-180.

5201   PERRIER, François. *L'alcool au singulier: l'eau-de-feu et la libido.* Paris, InterEditions, 82, 187 p.

5202   RICCARDO, Guerrieri. "Strategie d'intervento e di collocamento all'interno della organizzazione terapeutica per i tossicomani in Francia" (Intervention and location strategies within the therapeutic organization for drug addictors in France), *Critica sociologica* 65, 83 : 119-130.

5203   SCHREIER, James W. "A survey of drug abuse in organizations", *Personnel Journal* 62(6), jun 83 : 478-484.

5204   VAUGHN, Susan M. "The normative structures of college students and patterns of drinking behavior", *Sociological Focus* 16(3), aug 83 : 181-193. [USA]

5205   WHITE, Michael D.; LUKSETICH, William A. "Heroin: price elasticity and enforcement strategies", *Economic Inquiry* 21(4), dec 83 : 557-564. [USA]

20160   Crime. Delinquency
Délit. Délinquance

5206   "Comportements délictueux", *Bulletin de Psychologie* 36(5-10), apr 83 : 209-488. [France] [with contributions by J. BERGERET, P. G. COSLIN, L. BRUNET, C. FAUGERON, N. MAILLOUX, I. MUNNICH]

5207   "Crime (On) and victims", *Social Forces* 61(4), jun 83 : 1010-1043. [with contributions by Darrell J. STEFFENSMEIER, Mark WARR, Mark STAFFORD]

5208   "Crime in America", *Public Interest* (70), wint 83 : 22-65. [USA] [with contributions by James Q. WILSON, Mark H. MOORE, George L. KELLING]

5209   "Crime prevention", *Social Policy* 13(1), sum 82 : 47-53. [USA] [with contributions by Frank RIESSMAN, Joan McDERMOTT, Carol SHAPIRO, Lorraine GUTIERREZ, Mark D. LEVINE]

5210   "Criminalité internationale et coopération des États", *Revue juridique et politique. Indépendance et Coopération* 37(1-2), mar 83 : 11-565. [with contributions by Pasteur NZINAHORA, Cyrille NJEJIMANA, Ali AFKADA]

5211   "Critical issues in crime control policy", *American Behavioral Scientist* 27(1), 83 : 3-128. [with contributions by Edith Elizabeth FLYNN, Albert J. REISS Jr., William F. GABRIELLE Jr., Sarnoff A. MEDNICK, Marvin E. WOLFGANG, Alfred BLUMSTEIN, Herbert EDELHERTZ]

5212   "Dutch (The) Welfare State: social and legal control, crime and delinquency", *Contempory Crises* 7(2), apr 83 : 91-232. [with contributions by Martin MOERINGS, Han JANSE DE JONGE, Be BUITIWG, Nico JORG, C. KELK, Frans KOENRAADT]

5213   "Peur (La) du crime", *Annales internationales de criminoligie* 20(1-2), 83 : 115-157. [with contributions by J. P. GILBERT, V. AMANDA, H. SOUCHON]

5214   "Philosophie (La) de la justice pénale et la politique criminelle contemporaine", *Revue internationale de droit pénale* 53, trim. 4, 82 : 555-971.

5215   "Ville (La) et la criminalité. Quatre regards. Contribution française au Xe Congrès international de défense sociale (Thessalonique, 28 september-2 octobre 1981)", *Archives de politique criminelle* (6), 83 : 71-146. [with contributions by Mireille DELMAS-MARTY, Arlette FARGE, Vincent LAMANDA, Jean-Pierre DELMAS-SAINT-HILAIRE]

5216   ANTTILA, Inkeri. "Les nouvelles perspectives de la justice pénale spécialement dans les pays scandinaves", *Archives de politique criminelle* (6), 83 : 217-227.

5217   ARLACCHI, Pino. *Mafia, peasants and great estates.* Cambridge, Cambridge University Press, 83, 212 p.

5218   ARNOLD, William Robert; BRUNGARDT, Terrance M. *Juvenile misconduct and delinquency.* Boston, MA, Houghton Mifflin, 83, xiii-482 p.

5219   ARRAS, John D. "The right to die: on the slippery slope", *Social Theory and Practice* 8(3), aut 82 : 285-328.

5220   ARVISENET, Philippe d'. "Crimes, récidive et politique pénale", *Analyses de la SEDEIS* (36), nov 83 : 36-40. [France]

5221   BARAK-GLANTZ, Israel L. "Patterns of prisoner mis-conduct: toward a behavioral test of prisonization", *Sociological Focus* 16(2), apr 83 : 129-146. [USA]

5222   BERTELLI, Bruno. "Sistema penitenziario e inserimento sociale del condannato" (Penitentiary system and social insertion of the condemned person), *Ricerca sociale* 10(31), oct 83 : 37-61. [Italy]

5223   BLACK, Donald. "Crime as social control", *American Sociological Review* 48(1), feb 83 : 34-45.

5224   BLUM, Bill. "Crime and justice", *Socialist Review* 13(71), oct 83 : 131-141.

5225   BLUM-WEST, Steve; CARTER, Timothy J. "Bringing white-collar crime back in: an examination of crimes and torts", *Social Problems* 30(5), jun 83 : 545-554.

5226   BOLLEN, Kenneth A. "Temporal variations in mortality: a comparison of US suicides and motor vehicle fatalities, 1972-1976", *Demography* 20(1), feb 83 : 45-59.

5227   BOULOG, Bernard. "Le récidivisme", *Revue de Science criminelle et de Droit pénal comparé* (2), jun 83 : 199-207.

5228   BOWERS, Stephen R. "Law and lawlessness in a socialist society: the potential impact of crime in East Germany", *World Affairs* 145(2), aut 82 : 152-176.

5229   BRADY, J. P. "Crime, justice and community in socialist Cuba", *Annales internationales de criminologie* 20(1-2), 83 : 5-31.

5230   BULLINGTON, Bruce; KATKIN, Daniel; [et al.]. "Rhetoric and reality in the reform of juvenile justice policy", *Policy Studies Review* 2(2), nov 82 : 230-238.

5231   BURNS, George E.; LAKE, Donald E. "A sociological perspective on implementing child abuse legislation in education", *Interchange* 14(2), 83 : 33-53. [USA]

5232   BYRNE, John; YANICH, Donald. "Incarceration vs. community-based corrections: more than just politics", *Policy Studies Review* 2(2), nov 82 : 216-223.

5233   CAMUS, Jürgen; ELTING, Agnes. *Grundlagen und Möglichkeiten integrationstheoretischer Konzeptionen in der kriminologischen Forschung* (Bases and possibilities of the integration theoretical concepts in criminal research). Bochum, Brockmeyer, 82, iv-361 p.

5234   CARTER, Timothy J.; [et al.]; [eds.]. *Rural crime: integrating research and prevention.* Totowa, NJ, Allanheld, Osmun, 82, xvi-265 p.

5235   CATANI, M. "Questions posées par l'action d'un service de prévention spécialisé à l'égard d'une population maghrébine", *Annales de Vaucresson* 20, 83 : 51-88. [France]

5236   COLVIN, Mark; PAULY, John. "A critique of criminology: toward an integrated structural-Marxist theory of delinquency production", *American Journal of Sociology* 89(3), nov 83 : 513-551.

5237   CRONJÉ, Geoffrey. *The delinquent as a personality: the concept of bio-psychosociocriminological causality.* Pretoria, University of South Africa, 82, 717 p. [2 vols.]

5238   CUSSON, Maurice. *Le contrôle social du crime.* Paris, Presses Universitaires de France, 83, 342 p.

5239   DAVIDOVITCH, André; ROBERT, Philippe. "Sociologie criminelle", *Année sociologique* 32, 82 : 379-438. [Compte rendu bibliographique]

5240   DAVIES, Christie. "Crime, bureaucracy, and equality", *Policy Review* (23), wint 83 : 89-105.

5241   DAVIS, Robert. "Black suicide and social support systems: an overview and some implications for mental health practitioners", *Phylon* 43(4), dec 82 : 307-314.

5242   DELUMEAU, Jean. *Le péché et la peur: la culpabilisation en Occident, XIIIᵉ-XVIIIᵉ siècles.* Paris, Fayard, 83, 741 p.

5243   DI FORTI, Filippo. *Per una psicoanalisi della mafia: radici, fantasmi, territorio e politica* (For a psychoanalysis of the Mafia: roots, phantasms, territory and politcs). Verona, G. Bertani, 82, 206 p.

5244   DOBASCH, Russell P. "Labour and discipline in Scottish and English prisons: moral correction, punishment and useful toil", *Sociology (London)* 17(1), feb 83 : 1-27.

5245   DRIESSEN, Henk. "The 'noble bandit' and the bandits of the nobles: brigandage and local community in nineteenth-centry Andalusia", *Archives européennes de Sociologie* 24(1), 83 : 96-114.

5246   EKLAND-OLSON, Sheldon; BARRICK, Dennis M.; COHEN, Lawrence E. "Prison overcrowding and disciplinary problems: an analysis of the Texas prison system", *Journal of Applied Behavioral Science* 19(2), 83 : 163-176. [USA]

5247   FÉDÉRATION NATIONALE DES SERVICES SPÉCIALISÉS DE PROTECTION DE L'ENFANCE ET DE L'ADOLESCENCE. *L'enfant victime; les enfants maltraités par leurs parents: leur approche par le médecin, le magistrat, l'avocat, le travailleur social et le criminologue. Congrès organisé à Strasbourg, avril 1979.* Paris, Erès, 82, 137 p.

5248   FENNELL, John T. "Bands of violence: the crisis of America's prisons and jails", *Journal of Social, Political and Economic Studies* 8(1), spr 83 : 81-91.

5249   FIZE, Michel. "Les entrants en prison: un produit de la réaction sociale", *Déviance et Société* 7(2), jun 83 : 97-114. [France]

5250   FLEMING, Thomas; VISANO, L. A.; [eds.]. *Deviant designations: crime, law, and deviance in Canada.* Toronto, ON, Butterworths, 83, viii-493 p.

5251   FRAZIER, Charles E.; BROCK, E. Wilbur; HENRETTA, John C. "The role of probation officers in determining gender differences in sentencing severity", *Sociological Quarterly* 24(2), spr 83 : 305-318.

5252   FURNHAM, A.; HENDERSON, M. "Lay theories of delinquency", *European Journal of Social Psychology* 13(2), apr-jun 83 : 107-120. [résumé en français et en allemand]

5253   GARLAND, David; YOUNG, Peter; [eds.]. *The power to punish: contemporary penalty and social analysis.* London, Heinemann Educational Books; Atlantic Highlands, NJ, Humanities Press, 83, x-238 p.

5254   GHALI, Moheb; [et al.]. "Economic factors and the composition of juvenile property crimes", *Applied Economics* 15(2), apr 83 : 267-281.

5255   GLUCKLICH, Ariel. "Karma and social justice in the criminal code of Manu", *Contributions to Indian Sociology* 16(1), jan-jun 82 : 58-78. [India]

5256   GREENBERG, Jack. "Capital punishment as a system", *Yale Law Journal* 91(5), apr 82 : 908-936.

5257   GRISÉ, Yolande. *Le suicide dans la Rome antique.* Montréal, PQ, Bellarmin; Paris, Les Belles Lettres, 82, 325 p.

5258   HASTINGS, R.; [et al.]. "L'indemnisation des victimes d'actes criminels", *Déviance et Société* 7(4), dec 83 : 349-385.

5259   HENDIN, Herbert. *Suicide in America.* New York, NY, Norton, 82, 252 p.

5260   HINCHMAN, Lewis P. "Hegel's theory of crime and punishment", *Review of Politics* 44(4), oct 82 : 523-545.

5261   HIRSCHI, Travis; GOTTFREDSON, Michael. "Age and the explanation of crime", *American Journal of Sociology* 89(3), nov 83 : 552-584.

5262   HOLLINGER, Richard C.; CLARK, John P. "Deterrence in the workplace: perceived certainty, perceived severity, and employee theft", *Social Forces* 62(2), dec 83 : 398-418.

5263   HOSHINO, Kanehiro. "Boryoku soshiki no yobigun toshiteno shonentachi" (Fringe members of organized criminal gang), *Hanzai to hiko* 58, 83 : 89-116.

5264   JACOB, Herbert; [et al.]. *Governmental responses to crime: crime and governmental responses in American cities.* Washington, DC, United States Department of Justice, National Institute of Justice, 82, xvii-135 p.

5265   JANOFF-BULMAN, Ronnie; FRIEZE, Irene Hanson; [eds.]. "Reactions to victimization", *Journal of Social Issues* 39(2), 83 : 1-221.

5266   JESCHECK, Hans-Heinrich. "La peine privative de liberté dans la politique criminelle commune. Exposé comparatif de la situation en République fédérale d'Allemagne et en France", *Revue de Science criminelle et de Droit pénal comparé* (4), dec 82 : 719-732.

5267   JURAS, Roman. "Podkultura przestępcza — podkultura więzienna — drugie życie: związki i antynomie" (Criminal sub-culture — prison sub-culture — second life: connections and contradictions), *Zeszyty Naukowe Wydziału Humanistycznego Uniwersytetu Gdańskiego* 7, 83 : 31-40. [Spec. No Filozofia i Socjologia]

5268   KARAKASHEV, Veselin. *Problemi na opredeliane efektivnostta na nakazanieto lishavane ot svoboda* (Problems related to the efficiency of the punishment deprivation of liberty). Sofiĭa, Izd-vo na Bŭlgarskata Akademiia na Naukite, 82, 189 p. [Bulgaria]

5269   KIKUCHI, Kazunori; HORIUCHI, Mamoru; [eds.]. *Boryoku hiko* (Violent delinquency). Tokyo, Gakuji Shuppan, 83, 51 p. [Japan]

5270   KRAFCHIK, Max. "Unemployment and vagrancy in the 1980s: deterrence, rehabilitation and the depression", *Journal of Social Policy* 12(2), apr 83 : 195-213. [UK]

5271   LAYSON, Stephen. "Homicide and deterrence: another view of the Canadian time-series evidence", *Canadian Journal of Economics / Revue canadienne d'Économique* 16(1), feb 83 : 52-73.

5272   LITTLE, Craig B.; SHEFFIELD, Christopher P. "Frontiers and criminal justice: English private prosecution societies and American vigilantism in the eighteenth and nineteenth centuries", *American Sociological Review* 48(6), dec 83 : 796-808.

5273   LIU, Yih-Wu; BEE, Richard H. "Modeling criminal activity in an area in economic decline: local economic conditions are a major factor in local property crimes", *American Journal of Economics and Sociology* 42(4), oct 83 : 385-392. [USA]

5274   LUKSETICH, William A.; WHITE, Michael D. *Crime and public policy: an economic approach.* Boston, MA-Toronto, ON, Little, Brown, 82, x-305 p.

5275   LYNCH, Margaret A.; ROBERTS, Jacqueline. *Consequences of child abuse.* London-New York, NY, Academic Press, 82, xiii-226 p. [UK]

5277   MAHESHWARI, C. L. *The recidivists: a sociological analysis.* Agra, Arvind Vivek Prakashan, 83, ix-289 p. [India]

5278   MARTIN, Judith A. *Gender-related behaviors of children in abusive situations.* Saratoga, CA,
          R & E Publishers, 83, vii-135 p. [USA]
5279   MASUDA, Shūji. "Jidō gyakutai ni okeru seiteki bōkō no kenkyū" (Study of sexual
          exploitation in child abuse), *Shihoku gakuin daigaku ronshu* 52, 83 : 75-92.
5280   MATSUYAMA, Hiromitsu. "Nihon ni okeru jisatsu no shakaigaku-teki kenkyu: jisatsu
          cohort" (Sociological studies of suicide in Japan: suicide cohort), *Nihon daigaku
          Soshiorojikusu* 6, 83 : 29-42.
5281   MAXIM, Paul; PLECAS, Darryl. "Prisons and their perceived impact on the local
          community: a case study", *Social Indicators Research* 13(1), jul 83 : 39-58.
5282   MCBARNET, Doreen. "Victim in the witness box. Confronting victimology's stereotype",
          Contemporary Crises 7(3), jul 83 : 293-303.
5283   MCDOWALL, David; LOFTIN, Colin. "Collective security and the demand for legal
          handguns", *American Journal of Sociology* 88(6), mai 83 : 1146-1161. [Detroit, USA]
5284   MESSMER, Peter. *Arbeit und Abweichung: theoretische Überlegungen und empirische Untersuchungen
          zur sozio-ökonomischen Situation straffälliger und verwahrloster Jugendlicher* (Work and deviance:
          theoretical considerations and empirical researches on socio-economic situation of offender
          and vagrant youth). München, Deutscher Jugendinstitut, 82, 268 p. [Germany FR]
5285   MESSNER, Steven F. "Regional and racial effects on the urban homicide rate: the
          subculture of violence revisited", *American Journal of Sociology* 88(5), mar 83 : 997-1007.
          [USA]
5286   MILČINSKI, Lev; [ed.]. *Samomor in Slovenci* (Suicide in Slovenia). Ljubljana, Inštitut za
          Medicinske vede, Univerzitetna Psihiatrična Klinika v Ljubljani, 83, vi-333 p.
5287   MOENS, G. "Zelfmoord in België. Verloop van het geografisch zelfmoordpatroon
          (1968-1972 tot 1973-1977)" (Suicide in Belgium: evolution of the geographic scheme
          of mortality by suicide from 1968 to 1972 and from 1973 to 1977), *Bevolking en Gezin*
          (3), 82 : 269-282.
5288   MUSHENO, Michael C. "Criminal diversion and social control: a process evaluation",
          Social Science Quarterly 63(2), jun 82 : 280-292.
5289   NAGEL, Jack. "The relationship between crime and incarceration among the American
          States", *Policy Studies Review* 2(2), nov 82 : 193-200.
5290   NAGEL, Stuart. "Rationalism versus incrementalism in criminal sentencing", *Policy Studies
          Review* 2(2), nov 82 : 224-229.
5291   NAGLA, B. K. "The criminality of women in India", *Indian Journal of Social Work* 43(3),
          oct 82 : 273-282.
5292   NEEDLE, Jerome; STAPLETON, William Vaughan. *Policy handling of youth gangs.*
          Washington, DC, US Department of Justice, Office of and Institute for Juvenile Justice
          and Delinquency Prevention, 83, xiv-81 p.
5293   PACHECO, Angel. "Consideraciones sobre la criminalidad y la violencia: un examen crítico
          del concepto de socialización" (Considerations on criminality and violence: a critical
          examination of the concept of socialization), *Revista de Ciencias sociales* 22(3-4), dec 80 : 215-244.
5294   PALUMBO, Dennis J. "Community corrections: is it just another way of tinkering with
          the criminal justice system?", *Policy Studies Review* 2(2), nov 82 : 201-215.
5295   PATERNOSTER, Raymond; [et al.]. "Perceived risk and social control: do sanctions really
          deter?", *Law and Society Review* 17(3), 83 : 457-479. [USA]
5296   PETTIWAY, Leon E. "Mobility of robbery and burglary offenders: ghetto and nonghetto
          spaces", *Urban Affairs Quarterly* 18(2), dec 82 : 255-270.
5297   POITOU, Danièle. "Délinquance juvénile et urbanisation au Niger et au Nigeria", *Cahiers
          d'Études africaines* 21(1-3), 81 : 111-127.
5298   POOLE, Eric D.; REGOLI, Robert H. "Professionalism, role conflict, work alienation
          and anomia: a look at prison management", *Social Science Journal (Fort Collins)* 20(1),
          jan 83 : 63-70.
5299   RAJAN, V. N. *Whither criminal justice policy?.* New Delhi, Sagar, 83, 280 p.
5300   RANKIN, Joseph H. "The family context of delinquency", *Social Problems* 30(4), apr
          83 : 466-479. [USA]
5301   RAO, S. Venugopal. *Crime in our society: a political perspective.* New Delhi, Vikas, 83, 153 p.
          [India]
5302   RAY, Jacqueline W.; [et al.]. "Diversion: an alternative for youthful offenders", *International
          Journal of Group Tensions* 10(1-4), 80 : 139-146. [USA]
5303   RESNIK, Judith. "Women's prisons and men's prisons: should prisoners be classified
          by sex?", *Policy Studies Review* 2(2), nov 82 : 246-252.
5304   REUTER, Peter. *Disorganized crime: the economics of the visible hand.* Cambridge, MA-London,
          Massachusetts Institute of Technology Press, 83, xiv-233 p.

5305 ROTTENSCHLAGER, Karl. *Das Ende der Strafanstalt: Menschenrechte auch für Kriminelle?* (The end of the penal institution: human rights even for criminals?). Wien, Herold, 82, 285 p. [Austria]

5306 SAINZ SANCHEZ, E. "El accidente infantil como una de las fuentes para el estudio de los malos tratos" (Child accident as a basis for the study of child abuse), *Sociología* (1), 83 : 15-18.

5307 SALO, Mikko A. "Child abuse and low fertility. Theoretical perspectives", *Yearbook of Population Research in Finland* 21, 1983 : 118-129.

5308 SCHNEIDER, Leda. *Marginalidade e delinqüência juvenil* (Marginality and juvenile delinquency). São Paulo, Cortez Editora, 82, 156 p.

5309 SCHUMANN, Karl F. "Comparative research on legal sanctions: problems and proposals", *International Journal of the Sociology of Law* 11(3), aug 83 : 267-276.

5310 SCHWARZ, Norbert; BRAND, Julianne F. "Effects of salience of rape on sex role attitudes, trust and self-esteem in non-raped women", *European Journal of Social Psychology* 13(1), jan-mar 83 : 71-76.

5311 SESNOWITZ, Michael L.; HEXTER, J. Lawrence. "Economic determinants of theft: some empirical results", *Public Finance Quarterly* 10(4), oct 82 : 489-498. [USA]

5312 SHAMIR, Boas. "A cross-cultural comparison of prison guards' beliefs regarding the rehabilitation potential of the prisoners, the rehabilitative potential of the prison and their own supportive role", *International Journal of Comparative Sociology (Leiden)* 23(3-4), sep-dec 82 : 216-224.

5313 SHELEY, Joseph F. "Critical elements of criminal behavior explanation", *Sociological Quarterly* 24(4), 83 : 509-525.

5314 SHOTLAND, R. Lance; GOODSTEIN, Lynne. "Just because she doesn't want to doesn't mean it's rape: an experimentally based causal model of the perception of rape in a dating situation", *Social Psychology Quarterly* 46(3), sep 83 : 220-232.

5315 SINGH, M. P. *Crime and delinquency: problem of youth in contemporary society.* Delhi, UDH Publishers, 83, xxxi-87 p. [India]

5316 SMAUS, Gerlinda. "Mass médias et criminalité: état de la recherche en Allemagne et en Autriche", *Déviance et Société* 7(3), sep 83 : 248-268.

5317 SPICKENHEUER, J. L. P. *Bevolking en criminaliteit op de Nederlandse Antillen* (Population and criminality in the Netherlands Antilles). 's-Gravenhage, Ministerie van Justitie, Staatsuitgeverij, 82, 68 p.

5318 SRIVASTAVA, R. N. "Modern trends in criminology and steps toward correctional administration", *Indian Journal of Social Research* 23(2), aug 82 : 177-185.

5319 TÄHTINEN, Unto. *Non-violent theories of punishment: Indian and Western.* Helsinki, Akateeminen Kirjakauppa, 82, 148 p.

5320 TAKAHARA, Masaoki. " 'Gendaigata' shōnen hikō to itsudatsu kōdōron" (The contemporary type of juvenile delinquency and deviant behavior theories), *Hanzai shakaigaku kenkyu* 8, 83 : 187-201.

5321 THERRIAULT, Guy. "Le concept d'isotopie: un instrument sémantique pour l'analyse du discours criminologique", *Déviance et Société* 7(2), jun 83 : 115-152.

5322 THOMAS, Charles W.; HEPBURN, John R. *Crime, criminal law, and criminology.* Dubuque, IA, W. C. Brown, 83, xvi-603 p.

5323 THORNTON, Bill; RYCKMAN, Richard M. "The influence of a rape victim's physical attractiveness on observers' attributions of responsibility", *Human Relations* 36(6), jun 83 : 549-561.

5324 TITTLE, Charles R. "Social class and criminal behavior: a critique of the theoretical foundation", *Social Forces* 62(2), dec 83 : 334-358. [USA]

5325 TOURNIER, Pierre. "Le retour en prison. Analyse rétrospective de la cohorte des condamnés à une peine de trois ans et plus, libérés en 1973", *Déviance et Société* 7(3), sep 83 : 237-248. [France]

5326 UNNEVER, James D. "Direct and organizational discrimination in the sentencing of drug offenders", *Social Problems* 30(2), dec 82 : 212-225.

5327 VAN DEN BERG, Ger P. "The Soviet Union and death penalty", *Soviet Studies* 35(2), apr 83 : 154-174.

5328 VOLKOV, B. S. *Motivy prestuplenij: ugolovno-pravovoe i social'no-psychologičeskoe issledovanie* (The criminal motives: a penal-legal and socio-psychological research). Kazan', Izdatel'stvo Kazanskogo Universiteta, 82, 152 p.

5329 WARR, Mark; MEIER, Robert E.; ERICKSON, Maynard L. "Norms, theories of punishment, and publicly preferred penalties for crimes", *Sociological Quarterly* 24(1), wint 83 : 75-91. [USA]

5330   WARREN, Charles W.; SMITH, Jack C.; TYLER, Carl W. "Seasonal variation in suicide
          and homicide: a question of consistency", *Journal of Biosocial Science* 15(3), jul 83 : 349-356.
          [USA]
5331   WASSERMAN, Ira M. "Political business cycles, presidential elections, and suicide and
          mortality patterns", *American Sociological Review* 48(5), oct 83 : 711-720. [USA]
5332   WEIMER, David L.; REIXASCH, Karen. "A note on America's 'cloacal' jails", *Policy
          Studies Review* 2(2), nov 82 : 239-245.
5333   WILLIS, K. G. "Spatial variations in crime in England and Wales: testing an economic
          model", *Regional Studies* 17(4), aug 83 : 261-272. [résumés en français et allemand]
5334   WILSON, James Q. "Thinking about crime", *Atlantic* 252(3), sep 83 : 72-88. [USA]
5335   WOLF, Heinz E. "Forensische Psychologie in der DDR" (Bar psychology in GDR),
          Deutschland Archiv 16(9), sep 83 : 941-954.
5336   WRIGHT, Martin. *Making good: prisons, punishment, and beyond.* London, Burnett Books,
          82, 316 p.
5337   YAJIMA, Masami. "Hiko shonenzo no jisshoteki kenkyu: Seibetsu, seisekibetsu, gakusei
          seikatsubetsu sai o chushin ni" (A practical study on images of juvenile delinquents),
          Nagano daigaku kiyo 5(2), 83 : 71-87.
5338   YAJIMA, Masami. "Saikin no shonen hiko ni tsuiteno jakkan no comment" (A comment
          on recent juvenile delinquency), *Taisho daigaku counseling kenkyujo kiyo* 6, 83 : 21-28. [Japan]

20200   **SOCIAL POLICY**
          POLITIQUE SOCIALE

20210   **Social action. Social planning**
          Action sociale. Planification sociale

5339   "Area policy and area strategies: the origins and lessons of the British experience",
          International Journal of Sociology and Social Policy 2(2), 82 : 1-42.
5340   "Políticas sociales y planificación social" (Social policies and social planning), *Revista
          interamericana de planificación* 17(68), dec 83 : 5-215. [with contributions by Rolando
          FRANCO, Pedro DEMO, Richard BATLEY, Ray BROMLEY, Alberto VASCO]
5341   "Social welfare policy", *Policy Studies* 6, 82 : 535-588. [with contributions by Moncrieff
          COCHRAN, Jill KHADDURI, Raymond J. STRUYK, Charles S. RODGERS,
          Steven P. ERIE]
5342   ADAMY, Wilhelm. "Sozialabbau und Umverteilung in der Wirtschaftskrise. Zum Vergleich
          der Wirtschafts- und Sozialpolitik in Bonn und Weimar" (Social restrictions and income
          distribution in economic crisis. A comparison of economic and social policy in Bonn
          and Weimar), *WSI Mitteilungen* 36(10), oct 83 : 603-616.
5343   ANIOŁ, Włodzimierz. "Z zagadnień teorii polityki społecznej" (On the problems of the
          theory of social policy), *Polityka społeczna* 10(3), 83 : 5-8.
5344   ARELLANO, José P. "Las políticas sociales en Chile: breve revisión histórica" (Social
          policies in Chile: a brief historical overview), *Revista interamericana de planificación* 17(68),
          dec 83 : 132-150.
5345   BÉNÉTON, Philippe. *Le fléau du bien: essai sur les politiques sociales occidentales, 1960-1980.*
          Paris, Éditions R. Laffont, 83, 319 p.
5346   BERGSON, Abram. "Pareto on social welfare", *Journal of Economic Literature* 21(1),
          mar 83 : 40-46.
5347   BOLČIĆ, Silvano. *Razvoj i kriza jugoslovenskog društva u sociološkoj perspektivi* (Development
          and crisis of the Yugoslavian community in a sociological perspective). Beograd,
          Radionica SIC, 83, 227 p.
5348   CARDOSO, F. H. "Social policies in Latin America in the eighties: new options?",
          Alternatives 8(4), spr 83 : 553-571.
5349   CARDOSO, Fernando Henrique. "Las políticas sociales en la década de los años ochenta:
          nuevas opciones?" (Social policies in the 1980's: new options?), *Trimestre económico* 50(1),
          jan-mar 83 : 169-188. [Latin America]
5350   CARPENTER, Luther P. "France in 1968: a breakdown of the welfare state", *Tocqueville
          Review* 5(1), sum 83 : 74-96.
5351   COLOZZI, Ivo. "Degrado del sistema e opzioni soggettive. Una applicazione della teoria
          di Hirschman alla crisi del 'Welfare State' " (Crisis in the system and subjective options:
          an application of Hirschman's theory to the crisis of the Welfare State), *Studi di Sociologia*
          21(1), mar 83 : 14-28.
5352   COOK, Karen S.; HEGTVEDT, Karen A. "Distributive justice, equity, and equality",
          Annual Review of Sociology (9), 83 : 217-241.

5353   CRANACH, Mario von; HARRÉ, Rom. *The analysis of action: recent theoretical and empirical advances.* Cambridge-New York, NY, Cambridge University Press; Paris, Éditions de la Maison des Sciences de l'Homme, 82, xv-404 p.

5354   DEACON, Alan; BRADSHAW, Jonathan. *Reserved for the poor: the means test in British social policy.* Oxford, B. Blackwell and M. Robertson, 83, vi-228 p.

5355   DELORS, Jacques. "La dynamique du droit social et de la négociation collective comme donnée majeure de la politique économique", *Droit social* (1), jan 83 : 85-88. [France]

5356   DEMARIA, William. "Dialectics and domination: reflections on social action", *Australian and New Zealand Journal of Sociology* 19(1), mar 83 : 50-78.

5357   DESTREE, A. "Réformisme 'laïcisant' en Iran, Turquie et Afghanistan, 1920-1930", *Civilisations* 33(1), 83 : 167-186.

5358   DIXON, John; JAYASURIYA, D. L.; [eds.]. *Social policy in the 1980s.* Belconnen, ACT, Canberra College of Advanced Education, Australasian Social Policy and Administration Association, 83, v-302 p. [Australia]

5359   DONATI, Pierpaolo. "L'aide sociale et les services sociaux en Italie depuis 1950", *Futuribles* 63, feb 83 : 47-60.

5360   EDGELL, Stephen; DUKE, Vic. "Gender and social policy: the impact of the public expenditure cuts and reactions to them", *Journal of Social Policy* 12(3), jul 83 : 357-378.

5361   EYZENGA, Gerard. *Welzijn op de wip: een kritische beschouwing van actuele welzijnsvraagstukken* (Welfare on the balance: a critical examination of present welfare problem). Groningen, Wolters-Noordhoff, 82, 181 p. [Netherlands]

5362   FERGE, Zsuzsa. "Új és régi szociálpolitikai dilemmák" (Recent and old dilemmas of social policy), *Társadalmi Szemle* 38(8-9), 83 : 29-42.

5363   FETSCHER, Iring. *Vom Wohlfahrtsstaat zur neuen Lebensqualität: die Herausforderungen des demokratischen Sozialismus* (From the welfare state to the new quality of life: the challenges of the democratic socialism). Köln, Bund-Verlag, 82, 217 p.

5364   GANE, Mike. "Anthony Giddens and the crisis of social theory", *Economy and Society* 12(3), 83 : 368-398. [a review article]

5365   GIROD, Roger; LAUBIER, Patrick de; [comps.]. *La politique sociale dans les pays occidentaux: diagnostics, 1945-1980.* Lausanne, Réalités Sociales, 82, iii-128 p.

5366   GLAZER, Nathan. "The Reagan administration and social policy: is a counterrevolution under way?", *Tocqueville Review* 4(1), sum 82 : 118-126.

5367   GLENNERSTER, Howard; [ed.]. *The future of the welfare State: remaking social policy.* London-Exeter, NH, Heinemann, 83, 234 p. [UK]

5368   GRAYCAR, Adam; [ed.]. *Retreat from the welfare State: Australian social policy in the 1980'.* Sydney-Boston, MA, Allen and Unwin, 83, viii-206 p.

5369   GROMANN, Annette; DA COSTA REIS, Heraldo. "Execução de projetos sociais" (Implementation of social projects), *Revista de Administração municipal* 30(167), jun 83 : 28-43. [Brazil]

5370   GRØNBJERG, Kirsten A. "The Welfare State: prospects for the 1980s", *American Behavioral Scientist* 26(6), jul-aug 83 : 683-816. [USA]

5371   HAJJAR, Sami G. "Qadhafi's social theory as the basis of the third universal theory", *Journal of Asian and African Studies* 17(3-4), oct 82 : 177-188.

5372   HEKMAN, Susan. "Some notes on the universal and conventional in social theory: Wittgenstein and Habermas", *Social Science Journal (Fort Collins)* 20(2), apr 83 : 1-15.

5373   HENTSCHEL, Volker. *Geschichte der deutschen Sozialpolitik, 1880-1980* (History of German social policy, 1880-1980). Frankfurt-am-Main, Suhrkamp, 83, 317 p.

5374   HOPPE, Hans-Hermann. "Vom Konzept der Wohlfahrtsmessung der Theorie der Gerechtigkeit. Zur Begründung einer analytischen Theorie der sozialen Wohlfahrt" (The concept of measurement of social welfare in the theory of justice. The foundations of an analytical theory of social welfare), *Zeitschrift für Politik* 29(4), nov 82 : 403-428.

5375   INGLIS, Fred. *Radical earnestness: English social theory, 1880-1980.* Oxford, M. Robertson, 82, ix-253 p.

5376   IYER, V. R. Krishna. *Indian social justice in crisis.* Madras, Affiliated East-West Press, 83, 145 p.

5377   IZDEBSKI, Mieczysław. "Organizacja systemu pomocy społecznej" (Organizational schemes of social welfare), *Praca i Zabezpieczenie społeczne* 25(5-6), 83 : 20-26. [Poland] [continued in ibid. 25 (7), 1983 : 22-30]

5378   JACOME, Nicanor. "Evolución de la política social ecuatoriana, 1963-1979" (Evolution of social policy in Ecuador, 1963-1979), *Revista interamericana de Planificación* 17(68), dec 83 : 183-193.

5379   JASSO, Guillermina. "Fairness of individual rewards and fairness of the reward distribution: specifying the inconsistency between the micro and macro principles of justice", *Social Psychology Quarterly* 46(3), sep 83 : 185-199.
5380   JAYASURIYA, D. C. *Law and social problems in modern Sri Lanka.* New Delhi, Sterling Publishers, 82, vi-144 p.
5381   KANFER, Frederick H. "Soziale Kommunalpolitik und Implementation kommunalen Wandels: ein psychosoziales Modell" (Communal social policy and the improvement of changes in the commons: a psycho-social model), *Sociologia internationalis* 20(1-2), 82 : 55-86. [résumé en anglais]
5382   KARKAS, Katalin. "A társadalompolitika és intézményei Norvégiaban" (Social policy and institutions in Norway), *Közgazdasági Szemle* 30(6), 83 : 729-739.
5383   KARS-MARSHALL, Cri. *Sociaal beleidsonderzoek in ontwikkelingslanden: een vergeljkend kader* (Social policy research in developing countries: a comparison framework). 's-Gravenhage, VUGA, 83, 270 p.
5384   KLEES, Bernd. "Ordnungspolitik als Sozialpolitik" (Order policy as social policy), *Frankfurter Hefte* 37(12), dec 82 : 28-38. [Germany FR]
5385   KORPI, Walter. "Strategie di politica sociale. Il caso svedese" (Strategies of social policy. The Swedish case), *Stato e Mercato* (6), dec 82 : 401-427. [résumé en anglais]
5386   KOTYREV, B. P. "Social'noe razvitie i planirovanie" (Social development and planning), *Izvestija Sibirskogo Otdelenija Akademii Nauk SSSR. Serija Obščestvennyh Nauk* 20(1), 83 : 27-33. [USSR]
5387   KRAVČENKO, A. I.; FROLOV, S. F. "Social'noe planirovanie v socialističeskih stranah" (Social planning in the socialist countries), *Sociologičeskie Issledovanija (Moskva)* (1), 83 : 187-188.
5388   KRUTOVA, O. N. *Čelovek i istorija: problemy čeloveka v social'noj filosofii marksizma* (Man and history: the human problems in Marxism social philosophy). Moskva, Politizdat, 82, 208 p.
5389   LANDIER, Hubert. "Un bilan social de septennat présidentiel", *Tocqueville Review* 3(2), aut 81 : 394-410. [France]
5390   LAUBIER, Patrick de. *Idées sociales: essai sur l'origine des courants sociaux contemporains.* Fribourg, Éditions universitaires, 82, 161 p.
5391   LLOYD, Christopher; [ed.]. *Social theory and political practice.* Oxford, Oxfordshire, Clarendon Press; New York, NY, Oxford University Press, 83, ix-182 p.
5392   MACPHERSON, Stewart. *Social policy in the Third World: the social dilemmas of underdevelopment.* Totowa, NJ, Littlefield, Adams; Allanheld, Osmun, 82, 220 p.
5393   MAIER, Ferdinand. *Zur Herrschaftslogik des sozialen Handelns: eine kritische Rekonstruktion von Max Webers Gesellschaftstheorie* (On the power logic of social action: a critical reconstruction of Max Weber's theory of society). Königstein/Ts., Forum Academicum, 82, 229 p.
5394   MALYAROV, O. V. *The role of the state in the socio-economic structure of India.* New Delhi, Vikas, 83, 463 p.
5395   MCCASHIN, Anthony. "Social policy: 1957-82", *Administration (Dublin)* 30(2-3), 82 : 203-223. [Ireland]
5396   MCNALL, Scott G. "Variations on a theme: social theory", *Sociological Quarterly* 24(4), 83 : 471-487.
5397   MILLS, Don. "Alternatives of social policies for Latin America and the Caribbean in the eighties", *Planning Bulletin* 9, 82 : 17-22.
5398   MOLITOR, Bruno. "Der Mythos des Sozialen" (Myth of the social), *Zeitschrift für Wirtschaftspolitik* 32(2), 83 : 131-149.
5399   MORALES, Eduardo. *Políticas sociales y sistema político. Antecedentes, situación actual y perspectivas* (Social policies and political system. Past, present and perspectives). Santiago de Chile, FLACSO, 83, 34 p. [Chile]
5400   MUSHKAT, Miron. "Some critical observations on prevailing approaches to social programme evaluation", *Sociologia internationalis* 21(1-2), 83 : 105-116.
5401   O'HIGGINS, Michael. "Rolling back the welfare state: the rhetoric and reality of public expenditure and social policy under the Conservative government", *Yearbook of Social Policy in Britain*, 82 : 153-178.
5402   PAIGE, Jeffery M. "Social theory and peasant revolution in Vietnam and Guatemala", *Theory and Society* 12(6), nov 83 : 699-737.
5403   PEMBERTON, Alec. "Marxism and social policy: a critique of the 'contradictions of welfare'", *Journal of Social Policy* 12(3), jul 83 : 289-307.
5404   PILCH, Jolanta. "Oświata i kultura w polityce społecznej wobec ludności wiejskiej" (Education and culture in social policy towards the rural population), *Biuletyn Instytutu Gospodarstwa Społecznego* 26(1), 83 : 112-123. [Poland]

5405   PITSCHAS, Rainer. "Armut des Sozialstaats und kommunale Sozialpolitik. Über Prioritäten der Ressourcennutzung im Jugendhilfe- und Sozialwesen" (Poverty of the social State and communal social policy. On priorities of resources utilization in youth care and social services), *Verwaltung* 15(4), 82 : 473-501.

5406   RACINE, Luc. "Paradis, âge d'or, royaume millénaire et cité utopique. Note sur la différenciation des formes de l'état idéal de perfection sociale", *Diogène* 122, apr-jun 83 : 130-147.

5407   RAMAKRISHNA, V. *Social reform in Andhra, 1848-1919.* New Delhi, Vikas, 83, 241 p.

5408   REISCHAUER, Robert Danton; MEYER, Jack A. *The impact of social welfare policies in the United States.* New York, NY, Conference Board Report No. 823, 82, v-26 p. [Edited by Edgar R. FIEDLER]

5409   RYDENFELT, S. *The rise and decline of the Swedish welfare State.* Lund, Lunds Universitet, Nationalekonomiska Institutionen, Meddelande 75, 83, 55 p.

5410   SAAVEDRA, María Josefa. *Política del bienestar social* (Social welfare policy). La Paz, Librería Editorial 'Juventud', 82, 89 p.

5411   SCHRAM, Sanford F.; TURBETT, J. Patrick. "Civil disorder and the welfare explosion: a two-step process", *American Sociological Review* 48(3), jun 83 : 408-414.

5412   SCHWEIDER, Saundra K. "The sequential development of social programs in eighteen welfare states", *Comparative Social Research* 5, 82 : 195-219.

5413   SEGRE, Sandro. "Natura ed agire sociale nelle concezioni di Marx e Weber" (Nature and social action in Marx' and Weber's thought), *Critica sociologica* 67, 83 : 69-84.

5414   SEIDMAN, Steven. "The enlightenment of the origins of modern social theory", *Journal of the History of Sociology* 5(1), 83 : 66-90.

5415   SHALEV, Michael. "Politica di classe e welfare state" (Class policy and welfare state), *Stato e Mercato* (6), dec 82 : 465-493. [Western Europe] [résumé en anglais]

5416   SHARMA, Ram Nath. *Indian social problems.* Horsham, W. Sussex, J. K. Publishers, 82, vi-458 p.

5417   SINHA, Balbir Sahai. *Law and social change in India.* New Delhi, Deep and Deep, 83, 431 p.

5418   ŠOL'COVA, M. "Social'naja politika ČSSR — put' k real'nomu blagosostojaniju naroda" (The Czechoslovakia social policy: the way to a real welfare people), *in: Social'naja spravedlivost' i puti eě realizacii v social'noj politike. I.* Moskva, 1982 : 104-110.

5419   TAKEGAWA, Shogo. "Taisengo igirisu ni okeru shakai seisaku to fubyodo" (Social policy and inequality in post-war Britain), *Kikan shakai hosho kenkyu* 18(4), 83 : 463-477.

5420   TAREMENKO, G. "Voprosy social'noj politiki v evropejskih stranah SĚV" (Social policy problems in the CMEA European member countries), *Planovoe Hozjajstvo* 59(6), 83 : 108-113.

5421   TASHIRO, Fujio. *Shakai fukushi to kirisutokyo* (Social welfare and Christianity). Tokyo, Aikawa Shobo, 83, 134 p.

5422   TAYLOR-GOOBY, Peter. "Legitimation deficit, public opinion and the Welfare State", *Sociology (London)* 17(2), mai 83 : 165-184.

5423   TAYLOR-GOOBY, Peter. "Two cheers for the Welfare State: public opinion and private welfare", *Journal of Public Policy* 2(4), oct 82 : 319-346. [UK]

5424   TERNY, Guy; [ed.]. "Efficacité (L') des politiques sociales", *Revue d'Économie politique* 93(3), mai-jun 83 : 311-395. [Congrès de l'Association française de science économique; résumé en anglais]

5425   TOŠČENKO, Ž. "Social'noe proektirovanie: metodologičeskie osnovy" (Social planning: methodological bases), *Obščestvennye Nauki* (1), 83 : 54-65.

5426   TRATTNER, Walter I.; [ed.]. *Social welfare or social control? Some historical reflections on 'Regulating the poor'.* Knoxville, TN, University of Tennessee Press, 83, 161 p.

5427   TREGUBOV, A. I.; [ed.]. *Social'no planirovanie v stranah SĚV i učastie v nem profsojuzov* (Social planning in the CMEA countries and the trade unions participation in it). Moskva, Vysšaja Škola Profsojuznogo Dviženija VCSPS imeni N. M. Švernika, 82, 117 p.

5428   TRYFAN, Barbara. "Działalność socjalna na rzecz rodziny wiejskiej w RFN" (Welfare work for a rural family in the Federal Republic of Germany), *Wieś Współczesna* 316(6), 83 : 138-144.

5429   TUBENCHLAK, James. *Crise social e delinqüência* (Social crisis and delinquency). Rio de Janeiro, Livraria Freitas Bastos, 81, 95 p. [Brazil]

5430   UNIVERSITÉ DES SCIENCES SOCIALES DE GRENOBLE. CENTRE D'ÉTUDE ET DE FORMATION SUR LA PLANIFICATION ET L'ÉCONOMIE SOCIALES. *Décentralisation et politiques sociales: actes.* Paris, CEPES, Association Internationale Futuribles, 83, 379 p.

5431   VAN DE VALL-CHERJL BOYAS, Mark. "A paradigm of social policy research (SPR) in advanced social systems: empirical analysis", *Revue internationale de Sociologie* 17(1), apr 81 : 93-111.

5432   VAN SNIPPENBURG, L. B.; LETTERIE, J. W. "Welsijnsbeleid: landenvergelijkend
        empirisch onderzoek nader bekeken" (Welfare policy: a review of cross-national research),
        Sociologische Gids 30(2), mar-apr 83 : 94-113.
5433   VAN VUGHT, Frans A. *Experimentele beleidsplanning* (Experimental policy planning).
        's-Gravenhage, VUGA, 82, 381 p.
5434   VESSILLIER, Elisabeth. "La production sociale dans les pays de l'Est. Faits et
        controverses", *Analyses de la SEDEIS* (36), nov 83 : 27-31.
5435   VIEIRA, Evaldo Amaro. *Estado e miséria social no Brasil, de Getúlio a Geisel, 1951 a 1978* (State
        and social poverty in Brazil, from Getulio to Geisel, 1951 to 1978). São Paulo, Cortez
        Editora, 83, 240 p.
5436   VOLKOV, Ju. E. "Social'naja politika sovetskogo gosudarstva i stanovlenie besklassovoj
        struktury obščestva" (Social policy of the Soviet State and future of a classless society),
        Sovetskoe Gosudarstvo i Pravo 56(2), feb 83 : 3-12.
5437   WATSON, David. "Making reality intelligible: the relation between philosophical analysis
        and the study of social policies", *Journal of Social Policy* 12(4), oct 83 : 491-512.
5438   WHITELEY, Paul; WINYARD, Steve. "Influencing social policy: the effectiveness of
        the poverty lobby in Britain", *Journal of Social Policy* 12(1), jan 83 : 1-26.
5439   WOLFSON, Dirk J. "On the social selectivity of public spending programmes", *Netherlands
        Journal of Sociology* 19(2), oct 83 : 181-197. [Netherlands]
5440   YAMAZAKI, Keiichi. "Shakaiteki koiron to ethnomethodology: Shakaiteki koi ni okeru
        kisoku to relevance" (Social action theory and ethnomethodology: rule and relevance
        in social action), *Sociologos* 7, 83 : 88-106.
5441   ZALHER, Hans F. "Introduction au droit social allemand", *Revue française des Affaires sociales*
        37(1), mar 83 : 7-62.
5442   ZIELONKA, Jan. "Social philosophy and the Polish experiment", *Sociologische Gids* 30(2),
        mar-apr 83 : 82-93.
5443   ZVORYKIN, A. A.; GUR'JANOV, S. T. *Prikladnye aspekty social'nogo upravlenija* (Applied
        aspects of social management). Moskva, Izdatel'stvo Moskovskogo Universiteta, 83, 330 p.

        **20220   Social security
                   Sécurité sociale**

5444   "Conceptions de la Sécurité sociale au Canada", *Revue internationale de Sécurité sociale* 36(2),
        83 : 258-284.
5445   "États protecteurs en crise", *Futuribles* 66, mai 83 : 3-89. [with contributions by Hughes
        de JOUVENEL, Yves GUILLOTIN, Gérard MARTIN, Naohiro YASHIRO]
5446   ALBER, Jens. "Einige Grundlagen und Begleiterscheinungen der Entwicklung der Sozial-
        ausgaben in Westeuropa, 1949-1977" (Some causes and concomitant manifestations
        of social security expenditure development in Western Europe, 1949-1977), *Zeitschrift
        für Soziologie* 12(2), apr 83 : 93-118.
5447   BARTELS, Hans-Joachim. "Das Sozialversicherungs- und Versorgungsrecht in der DDR"
        (Social insurance and protection law in the GDR), *Jahrbuch für Ostrecht* 23(1-2), 82 : 9-81.
5448   BILINSKY, Andreas. "Das Sozialversicherungs- und Versorgungsrecht in der Sowjetunion" (So-
        cial insurance and protection law in the Soviet Union), *Jahrbuch für Ostrecht* 23(1-2), 82 : 83-152.
5449   BOISARD, Pierre. "La politique familiale en France, 1960-1980. Bilan et perspectives",
        Travail et Société 8(4), oct-dec 83 : 445-456.
5450   BRAMANTI, Donatella. "Anziani e politica sociale" (Aged and social policy), *Vita e pensiero*
        66(3), mar 83 : 44-52. [Italy]
5451   BRUCHE, Gert. *Die französische Arbeitslosenversicherung: Grundzüge und Strukturmerkmale nach
        der Reform von 1979/80* (The French unemployment insurance: essential features and
        structural characteristics after the 1979/80 reform). Berlin, Wissenschaftszentrum Berlin,
        82, 34 p.
5452   BÜRGISSER-PETERS, Petra. *Verteilungswirkungen der staatlichen Altervorsorge in der Schweiz*
        (Distribution effects of the state old age insurance in Switzerland). Zürich, Schulthess
        Polygraphischer Verlag, 82, vi-329 p.
5453   BUTLER, Peter M.; SMITH, Ron. "The worker, the workplace, and the need for
        unemployment insurance", *Canadian Review of Sociology and Anthropology* 20(4), nov
        83 : 393-412. [Canada]
5454   CATRICE-LOREY, Antoinette. "La Sécurité sociale et l'État en France: quelle autonomie
        de gestion pour l'institution?", *Revue internationale de Sécurité sociale* 36(2), 83 : 213-228.
5455   COENEN-HUTHER, Josette. "Médicalisation et définition de la situation: le cas
        d'institutions de placement à long terme pour personnes âgés", *Schweizerische Zeitschrift
        für Soziologie / Revue suisse de Sociologie* 9(2), 83 : 313-336.

5456   DAVIS, Lynne. "Now you see it, now you don't: the restructuring of Commonwealth government child care policy, 1972-1982", *Australian and New Zealand Journal of Sociology* 19(1), mar 83 : 79-95.

5457   DELEECK, H. "Les cotisations à la sécurité sociale et leurs conséquences sur la distribution des charges sociales et sur l'emploi", *Revue belge de Sécurité sociale* 25(2), feb 83 : 302-319.

5458   DELEECK, Herman. "Voorstellen voor de toekomstige struktuur van de sociale zekeheid" (Proposals for the future structure of social security), *Economisch en Sociaal Tijdschrift* 37(6), dec 83 : 661-675. [Belgium]

5459   DINGWALL, Robert; EEKELAAR, John; MURRAY, Topsy. *The protection of children: state intervention and family life.* Oxford, B. Blackwell, 83, x-286 p. [UK]

5460   DUMONT, Jean-Pierre. "La Sécurité sociale dans le monde", *Revue française des Affaires sociales* 37(3), sep 83 : 49-67.

5461   FLORESCU, Jean. "Das Sozialversicherungsrecht der Sozialistischen Republik Rumänien" (Social insurance law of the Romanian Socialist Republic), *Jahrbuch für Ostrecht* 23(1-2), 82 : 245-285.

5462   FREEMAN, Gary; ADAMS, Paul. "The politics of social security: expansion, retrenchment, and rationalization", *Sage Yearbooks in Politics and Public Policy* (10), 82 : 242-261. [USA]

5463   FURNHAM, Adrian. "Attitudes toward the unemployed receiving social security benefits", *Human Relations* 36(2), feb 83 : 135-149.

5464   GOROSQUIETA, J. "Política para la mejora de la Seguridad Social" (Policy to improve social security), *Revista de Fomento social* 37(151), jul-sep 83 : 261-271.

5465   GROSS, Johanna. "Sozialleistungssystem der BRD unter Anpassungszwang" (Social allowances system in the GFR under adaptation constraint), *IPW Forschungshefte* 18(3), 83 : 4-128. [résumés en russe, anglais, espagnol et français]

5466   HABER, William. "Social security in the United States: an ongoing debate", *International Journal of Social Economics* 10(6-7), 83 : 21-28.

5467   JESSEL-HOLST, Christa. "Das Sozialversicherungs- und Versorgungsrecht Bulgariens" (Social insurance and protection law in Bulgaria), *Jahrbuch für Ostrecht* 23(1-2), 82 : 201-243.

5468   KOMAROVA, D. "Sovetskaja sistema social'nogo obespecenija" (The Soviet system of social security), *Kommunist (Moskva)* 58(18), dec 82 : 60-67.

5469   KURZYNOWSKI, Adam. "Sytuacja rodzinna ludzi starszych a ich uczestnictwo w ośrodkach dziennego pobytu" (Family situation of elderly people and their participation in daytime centres), *Studia demograficzne* 21(1), 83 : 35-68. [Poland]

5470   KURZYNOWSKI, Adam. "Urlopy i zasiłki wychowawcze dla młodych matek" (Leaves and rearing allowances to young mothers), *Biuletyn Instytutu Gospodarstwa Społecznego* 25(4), 82 : 47-67. [Poland]

5471   KURZYNOWSKI, Adam. "Wybrane elementy polityki rodzinnej w Polsce" (Selected elements of family policy in Poland), *Biuletyn Instytutu Gospodarstwa Społecznego* 26(1), 83 : 35-71.

5472   LANTSEV, Mikhail S.; SHCHENNIKOV, Lyndmila. "Sécurité sociale et services en faveur des personnes âgées en URSS", *Revue internationale de Sécurité sociale* 35(4), 82 : 598-613.

5473   LISOWSKI, Adam E. "Instytucjonalne formy zaspokajania potrzeb ludzi starych w środowisku zamieszkania" (Institutional forms of meeting the needs of old people in their residential environment), *Biuletyn Instytutu Gospodarstwa Społecznego* 25(3), 82 : 131-145. [Poland]

5474   LOVELACE OPPONG, J. "Care of the aging in Ghana", *Planning and Administration* 10(2), aut 83 : 36-41.

5475   LYGRISSE, Jean. *Histoire de la sécurite sociale en Algérie: 1830-1962.* Paris, Association pour l'Étude de l'Histoire de la Sécurite Sociale, 83, 229 p.

5476   MILLS, Catherine. "Le système social à l'épreuve de la crise", *Revue française des Affaires sociales* 37(3), sep 83 : 103-132. [France]

5477   MOSLEY, Hugh. "Social security in the United States and the Federal Republic of Germany: a comparison of public and private systems", *Policy Studies Journal* 11(3), mar 83 : 492-503.

5478   OLSEN, Lenore. "Services for minority children in out-of-home care", *Social Service Review* 56(4), dec 82 : 572-585.

5479   ORDEIG FOS, José María. *El sistema español de Seguridad Social* (The Spanish social security system). Madrid, Editoriales de Derecho Reunidas, 82, xvi-522 p.

5480   ORTEGA, Victorino. "Reforma de la seguridad social y crisis económica" (Reform of social security and economic crisis), *Revista de Fomento social* 37(151), jul-sep 83 : 249-259. [Spain] [see also ibid., Javier GOROSQUIETA, 261-271]

5481   PALARD, Jacques. "La politique de la vieillesse et les relations centre-périphérie en France", *Sociologia internationalis* 20(1-2), 82 : 117-134. [résumé en anglais]

5482   PUHEK, Ivan. "Socijalisticki oblici društvene zaštite" (Socialist forms of social protection), *Politička Misao* 19(2), 82 : 61-75. [Yugoslavia]

5483   REMAN, Pierre. "La sécurité sociale aux portes de la dualisation", *Revue nouvelle* 39(4), apr 83 : 386-402.
5484   ROSSI, Giobznnz. *La famiglia assistita* (Aided family). Milano, F. Angeli, 83, 107 p. [Italy]
5485   RUPP, Laszlo. "Das Sozialversicherungs- und Versorgungsrecht Ungarns" (Social insurance and protection law in Hungary), *Jahrbuch für Ostrecht* 23(1-2), 82 : 287-329.
5486   SCHMIED, Erich. "Die soziale Sicherung in der Tschechoslowakei" (Social insurance in Czechoslovakia), *Jahrbuch für Ostrecht* 23(1-2), 82 : 153-200.
5487   SOLOV'EVA, L. I. *Problemy social'nogo obespečenija v stranah EĖS* (Problems of social security in the EEC countries). Moskva, Nauka, 83, 255 p.
5488   SPINNARKE, Jürgen. *Soziale Sicherheit in der Bundesrepublik Deutschland* (Social security in the Federal Republic of Germany). Heidelberg, C. F. Müller, 82, 119 p.
5489   SWIDLER, Steve. "An empirical test of the effect of social security on fertility in the United States", *American Economist* 27(2), 83 : 50-57.
5490   TREAS, Judith. "Trickle down or transfers? Postwar determinants of family income inequality", *American Sociological Review* 48(4), aug 83 : 546-559.
5491   WALKER, Alan; [ed.]. *Community care: the family, the state, and social policy*. Oxford, B. Blackwell and M. Robertson, 82, xiii-221 p.
5492   WOLLAST, E. "Les stratégies de décision en matière de besoins de services de santé pour les personnes âgées en Belgique", *Gérontologie et Société* 25, jun 83 : 80-86.
5493   YAMASHITA, Kesao; [ed.]. *Rojin fukushi: sono genjitsu to seisaku kadai* (Welfare for the aged: its realities and government policies). Tokyo, Kawashima Shoten, 83, 265 p. [Japan]

20300   **SOCIAL WORK**
         TRAVAIL SOCIAL

5494   "Special issue on the privatization of social work: the new non-federalism", *Urban and Social Change Review* 16(1), wint 83 : 3-32. [cont. in ibid. 16 (2), sum 83: 2-26, with contributions by Barbara B. FEINSTEIN, Frank OKRASINSKI, Paul M. ROMAN, Mimi ABRAMOVITZ, Irwin EPSTEIN, Margaret GIBELMAN, Harold W. DEMONE]
5495   BAILEY, Roy Victor; LEE, Phil; [eds.]. *Theory and practice in social work*. Oxford, Basil Blackwell, 82, viii-238 p.
5496   BIERHOFF, Burkhard. *Das Theorie-Praxis-Verhältnis: Überlegungen zum Handlungswert theoretischer Ansätze für soziale Praxis, am Beispiel der ausserschulischen Jugendarbeit* (The theory-practice relationship: considerations on the handling value of the theoretical approaches in social practice, by the example of the extra-scholar youthwork). Schwerte, H. Freistühler, 82, 577 p.
5497   BOWKER, Joan P.; [ed.]. *Education for primary prevention in social work*. New York, NY, Council on Social Work Education, 83, 92 p.
5498   GIACOMINI, Maria Rita; HAYASHI, Maria; PINHEIRO, Susie de Albuquerque. *Trabalho social em favela* (Social work in favela). São Paulo, Cortez Editora, 82, 89-2 p. [Brazil]
5499   KARLSSON, Kurt. *Socialt arbete en bok om ideologi, metoder och organizationsformer* (Social work: a book on ideology, methods and forms of organization). Malmö, LiberHermod, 82, 155 p.
5500   RAAB, Erich. *Schulsozialarbeit in der Bundesrepublik* (School social work in the Federal Republic). München, Deutsches Jugendinstitut, 82, 70 p.
5501   REES, Stuart; WALLACE, Alison. *Verdicts on social work*. London, E. Arnold, 82, vii-192 p.
5502   SWEDNER, Harald. *Socialt Arbete* (Social work). Lund, Liber Förlag, 83, 224 p. [Sweden]
5503   THORMAN, George. *Helping troubled families: a social work perspective*. New York, NY, Aldine Publishing Co., 82, xii-191 p.

20400   **SOCIAL SERVICES**
         SERVICES SOCIAUX

20410   **Medical sociology. Medicine**
         Sociologie médicale. Médecine

5504   "Aspects de la médecine en Afrique", *Présence africaine* (124), trim. 4, 82 : 5-137. [with contributions by Marc SANKALE, Conla A. A. QUENUM, Issa Boubou HAMA, Yvette PARES]
5505   ALONSO HINOJAL, I. "La sociología, la sanidad y la salud: análisis de su espacio específico" (Sociology, sanitary conditions, health: analysis of the specific field), *Sociología* (1), 83 : 6-8.

5506 BANNERMAN, Robert H.; BURTON, John; CHEN, Wen-Chieh. *Traditional medicine and health care coverage.* Geneva, World Health Organization, 83, 342 p.

5507 BOULOUGOURIS, John C.; [ed.]. *Learning theory approaches to psychiatry.* Chichester-New York, NY, Wiley, 82, xxi-262 p.

5508 GLASSNER, Barry; MORENO, Jonathan D. "Clinical sociology and social research", *Sociology and Social Research* 66(2), jan 82 : 115-126.

5509 GUYOT, Jean-Claude. *Quelle médecine pour quelle société?.* Toulouse, Privat, 82, 366 p.

5510 MAÎTRE, Jacques; LÉVY, Emile. "Sociologie et économie de la santé", *Année sociologique* 32, 82 : 515-516. [Compte rendu bibliographique]

5511 NERI, Aldo. *Salud y política social* (Health and social policy). Buenos Aires, Hachette, 82, 261 p. [Argentina]

5512 RIDDER, Paul. "Tod und Technik: Sozialer Wandel in der Medizin" (Death and technique: social change in medicine), *Soziale Welt* 34(1), 83 : 110-119. [résumé en anglais]

5513 STROTZKA, Hans. "Sozialpsychiatrie. Entwicklung, Stand und Chancen — mit besonderer Berücksichtigung Österreichs" (Social psychiatry: evolution, State and trends especially in Austria), *Journal für Sozialforschung* 23(2), 83 : 169-184.

5514 VOGT, Irmgard. "Frauen als Objekte der Medizin: das Frauensyndrom" (Women as objects of medicine: the female syndrome), *Leviathan* 11(2), 83 : 161-199.

5515 WAKASA, Mamoru; OYAMA, Osamu; SHIMANOUCHI, Norio; [eds.]. *Hoken shakaigaku: riron to genjitsu* (Medical sociology: theory and practice). Tokyo, Kakiuchi Shuppan, 83, 283 p.

5516 WRIGHT, Peter; TREACHER, Andrew; [eds.]. *The problem of medical knowledge: examining the social construction of medicine.* Edinburgh, Edinburgh University Press, 82, 232 p.

5517 YOYO, Michel. "Médecine et société à La Martinique", *Bulletin d'Information du CENADDOM* 13(69), trim. 1 83 : 40-47.

5518 YUSTE GRIJALBA, Francisco Javier. *Ensayos sobre medicina preventiva y social* (Essays on preventive and social medicine). Madrid, Akal, 82, 148 p.

**20420 Public health
Santé publique**

5519 "Community development and primary health care", *Community Development Journal* 18(2), apr 83 : 97-197. [with contributions by Alessandro ROSSI-ESPAGNET, Helen ROSEN-THAL, Audrey AARONS]

5520 "Health and population planning", *Pakistan Year Book* (10), 83 : 303-316. [Pakistan]

5521 "Health care policy", *Policy Studies* 6, 82 : 347-444. [with contributions by Lawrence D. BROWN, David MECHANIC; Carroll L. ESTES, Philips R. LEE, Peter McMENANIN, Uwe E. REINHARDT]

5522 "Infanzia e salute: prospettive sociologiche e di politica socio-sanitaria" (Childhood and health: sociological and socio-health policy), *Ricerca sociale* 10(29), 82 : 7-169. [Italy] [with contributions by Pierpaolo DONATI, Sergio NORDIO, Claudio STROPPA, Juo COLOZZI]

5523 ABEL-SMITH, Brian. "L'efficacité économique dans la prestation des soins de santé", *Revue internationale de Sécurité sociale* 36(2), 83 : 181-198.

5524 BEGUN, James W.; LIPPINCOTT, Ronald C. "A case study in the politics of free-market health care", *Journal of Health, Politics Policy and Law* 7(3), aut 82 : 667-685.

5525 BERKI, S. E.; [ed.]. "Health care policy in America", *Annals of the American Academy of Political and Social Science* 468, jul 83 : 9-263.

5526 BOSE, Ashish; DESAI, P. B. *Studies in social dynamics of primary health care.* Delhi, Hindustan, 83, xvi-228 p.

5527 BOSSERT, Thomas John. "Can we return to the regime for comparative policy analysis? Or, the State and health policy in Central America", *Comparative Politics* 15(4), jul 83 : 419-441.

5528 CARLIER, Alain. "La liberté de prescription des médicaments en milieu hospitalier", *Revue française des Affaires sociales* 37(1), mar 83 : 81-90.

5529 CHAMPAGNE, François; [et al.]. "Le système de soins au Québec: une organisation visant l'équité et le respect des libertés individuelles", *Revue française de Finances publiques* (2), 83 : 57-79.

5530 CHESTER, T. E.; ICHIEN, Mitsuya. "Health care in Japan", *Three Banks Review* (137), mar 83 : 17-26.

5531 DELASSUS, J. M.; VERRIERE, E. "La santé mentale à La Réunion", *Bulletin d'Information du CENADDOM* 13(69), trim. 1 83 : 20-30.

5532 DELIEGE, Denise. "Participation de la population au système de santé", *Cahiers de Sociologie et de Démographie médicales* 22(4), dec 82 : 327-348. [Belgium]

5533   DÍAZ-BRIQUETS, Sergio. *The health revolution in Cuba*. Austin, TX, University of Texas Press, 83, xvii-227 p.
5534   DOWNING, Theodore E.; NEW, Peter K. "The politics of health care in Nicaragua before and after the Revolution of 1979", *Human Organization* 42(3), aut 83 : 264-272.
5535   DURAN, Ma. A. "Desigualdad social y salud" (Social inequality and health), *Sociología* (1), 83 : 19-23.
5536   ELLENCWEIG, Aui Yacar. "The new Israeli health care reform: an analysis of a national need", *Journal of Health, Politics Policy and Law* 8(2), sum 83 : 366-386.
5537   EVANS, Robert G. "Health care in Canada: patterns of funding and regulation", *Journal of Health, Politics Policy and Law* 8(1), spr 83 : 1-43.
5538   GONZÁLEZ RODRIGUEZ, B. "Aspectos metodológicos de la investigación en el área de la salud mental" (Methodological aspects of research in the field of mental health), *Sociología* (1), 83 : 88-90.
5539   GOSTIN, Larry. "Contemporary social historical perspectives on mental health reform", *Journal of Law and Society* 10(1), sum 83 : 47-70. [UK]
5540   GROTE-JANZ, Claudia von; WEINGARTEN, Elmar. "Technikgebundene Handelsabläufe auf der Intensivstation: zum Zusammenhang von medizinischer Technologie und therapeutischer Beziehung" (Performance in intensive care: medical technology and the therapeutic relationship), *Zeitschrift für Soziologie* 12(4), oct 83 : 328-340.
5541   HAAVIO-MANNILA, Elina. "Caregiving in the Welfare State", *Acta Sociologica* 26(1), 83 : 61-82.
5542   HESSLER, Richard M.; TWADDLE, Andrew C. "Sweden's crisis in medical care: political and legal change", *Journal of Health, Politics Policy and Law* 7(2), sum 82 : 440-459.
5543   JONES, William R. "La clinique dans trois types de société au Moyen Âge", *Diogène* 122, apr-jun 83 : 95-110. [Byzantin, latin, islamique]
5544   KADUSHIN, Charles. "Mental health and the interpersonal environment: a reexamination of some effects of social structure on mental health", *American Sociological Review* 48(2), apr 83 : 188-198.
5545   KENNEDY, Catherine A.; KING, James A.; MURACO, William A. "The relative strength of health as a predictor of life satisfaction", *International Social Science Review* 58(2), 83 : 97-102.
5546   KURTZ, Richard A. "Perceptions of medical clinics in Kuwait", *Journal of Asian and African Studies* 17(3-4), oct 82 : 208-217.
5547   LEROY, Xavier. "L'accès aux soins médicaux. Analyse régionale de l'offre et de la consommation. Elaboration d'une politique visant à leur adéquation", *Revue belge de Sécurité sociale* 24(11-12), dec 82 : 881-1030. [continued in 25 (1), jan 83 : 3-18]
5548   MARSELLA, A. J.; WHITE, G. M.; [eds.]. *Cultural conceptions of mental health and therapy*. Dordrecht, D. Reidel Publishing Co., 82, 416 p.
5549   MCLURE, Walter. "Implementing a competitive medical care system through public policy", *Journal of Health, Politics Policy and Law* 7(1), spr 82 : 2-44.
5550   MENZEL, Paul T. *Medical costs, moral choices: a philosophy of health care economics in America*. New Haven, CT-London, Yale University Press, 83, xi-260 p.
5551   OSGOOD FIELD, John; ROPES, George. "The influence of the health system on the recorded incidence of infant mortality and birth rates in rural Egypt", *Égypte contemporaine* 73(387), apr 82 : 25-59.
5552   PICHERAL, Henri. "Géographie médicale, géographie des malades, géographie de la santé", *Espace géographique* 11(3), sep 82 : 161-174.
5553   REINHARDT, Uwe E. "Health insurance and health policy in the Federal Republic of Germany", *Policy Studies* 6, 82 : 431-444.
5554   ROGLER, Lloyd Henry; [et al.]. *A conceptual framework for mental health research on Hispanic populations*. Bronx, NY, Hispanic Research Center, Fordham University, 83, vii-101 p.
5555   SINDELAR, Jody L. "Behaviorally caused loss of health and the use of medical care", *Economic Inquiry* 20(3), jul 82 : 458-471. [USA]
5556   TORELLI, Maurice. "Médecine et culture", *Revue juridique et politique. Indépendance et Coopération* 37(3), jun 83 : 603-616.
5557   VÅGERÖ, Denny. "The evolution of health care systems in England, France and Germany in the light of 1848 European revolutions", *Acta Sociologica* 26(1), 83 : 83-88.
5558   WILLIAMS, Rory. "Concepts of health: an analysis of lay logic", *Sociology (London)* 17(2), mai 83 : 185-205.

20430   Hospitals
Hôpitaux

5559   "Linking health care and social services — international perspectives", *Social Service Delivery Systems: an International Annual* 5, 82 : 1-304. [with contributions by William J. TENHOOR, Erik HOLST, Hirobumi ITO, Karin TENGWALD, George WALLS, George TSALIKIS, Jacques FOURNIER, Nicole QUESTIAUX]

5560   "Sommes-nous malades de la santé?", *Projet* (179-180), dec 83 : 929-1097. [with contributions by P. GALLOIS, P. CORNILLOT, A. FAVEL, M. GAGNEBIN, A. d'HOUTAUD]

5561   BERGSTRAND, Curtis R. "Big profit in private hospitals", *Social Policy* 13(2), aut 82 : 49-54.

5562   CABANIS, Jean-Noël; LAVIGNE, Claude. "La décentralisation et les espoirs des hôpitaux publics", *Revue française des Affaires sociales* 37(1), mar 83 : 119-134.

5563   CHAPERON, Jacques; [et al.]. "La santé de première ligne: les pratiques de groupe en France", *Revue française des Affaires sociales* 37(1), mar 83 : 63-79.

5564   DE VRIES, J. L.; [et al.]. "Analysis of cost and coverage of government financed primary health care services in Tanzania", *Socio-Economic Planning Sciences* 17(1), 83 : 39-47.

5565   DEMICHEL, André. "La réforme hospitalière: éléments pour une problématique", *Revue française de Finances publiques* (2), 83 : 107-115.

5566   HARRISON, Deborah H.; KIMBERLY, John R. "Private and public initiatives in health maintenance organizations", *Journal of Health, Politics Policy and Law* 7(1), spr 82 : 80-95.

5567   KIESLER, Charles A. "Public and professional myths about mental hospitalization: an empirical reassessment of policy-related beliefs", *American Psychologist* 37(12), dec 82 : 1323-1339. [USA]

5568   NAJMAN, J. M.; [et al.]. "Politics, policy and performance: the primary prevention of disease in two community health centres in Queensland", *Australian and New Zealand Journal of Sociology* 19(3), nov 83 : 385-490. [Australia]

5569   WORLD HEALTH ORGANIZATION STUDY GROUP. *Research for the reorientation of national health systems.* Geneva, WHO, 83, 71 p.

20440   Social workers
Travailleurs sociaux

5570   BEBBINGTON, A. C.; DAVIES, Bleddyn. "Equity and efficiency in the allocation of the personal social services", *Journal of Social Policy* 12(3), jul 83 : 309-329.

5571   EAGLSTEIN, A. Solomon; PARDES, Yosef. "A formula for determining social worker position based upon the Pardes method", *Social Indicators Research* 13(1), jul 83 : 59-68. [in regional councils]

5572   GÖSCHEL, Albrecht; [et al.]. "Infrastructural inequality and segregation: theory, methods and results of an empirical research project carried out in 12 large towns in West Germany", *International Journal of Urban and Regional Research* 6(4), dec 82 : 503-531. [résumés en français, espagnol et allemand]

5573   KAKABADSE, Andrew. "Bureaucracy and the social services: a comparative study of English social service departments", *International Journal of Social Economics* 10(5), 83 : 3-13.

5574   KATZ ROTHMAN, Barbara. "Midwives in transition: the structure of a clinical revolution", *Social Problems* 30(3), feb 83 : 250-283.

5575   LA HAYE, Jacques. "Pour un modèle de prévision de la main-d'oeuvre médicale au Québec", *Cahiers québécois de Démographie* 11(2), aug 82 : 195-226.

5576   LIMA, Arlette Alves. *Serviço social no Brasil: ideologia de uma década* (Social service in Brazil: ideology of a decade). São Paulo-SP, Cortez Editora, 82, 111 p.

5577   MAKISATO, Tsuneji. "Shisetsu shakaika no totatsuten to kadai: Iwayuru shogu no shakaika o chushinni" (A landmark and issue in socialization of welfare institution: with special reference to the socialization of institutional care), *Osaka furitsu daigaku shakai mondai kenkyu* 33(1), 83 : 119-151.

5578   MATHEWS, Gary. "Social workers and political influence", *Social Service Review* 56(4), dec 82 : 616-628.

5579   MATSUHARA, Ichiro. "Jumin no Rinhokan riyoken, service jukyuken no kento" (The right to social services in community center), *Kansai daigaku shakaigakubu kiyo* 15(1), 83 : 217-231. [Japan]

5580   MATSUHARA, Ichiro; HASHIMOTO, Yoshiro; AKASHI, Takayuki; [eds.]. *Shakai fukushi kenshu no hyoka: fukushi jimusho, hoikujo, shakai fukushi kyogikai shokuin ni taisuru chosa* (Evaluation systems of training programs for social service workers). Osaka, Fukushi Shakaigaku Kenkyukai, 83, 67 p. [Japan]

5581   MAYER-RENAUD, Micheline; LE DOYEN, Alberte. *L'intervention sociale: actes du colloque de l'Association canadienne des sociologues et anthropologues de langue française.* Montréal, Éditions Coopératives A. Saint-Martin, 82, vii-384 p.

5582   PATHAK, Shankar. *Social welfare manpower: a regional study.* Delhi, Suruchi, 83, 105 p. [India]

5583   PAULA FALEIROS, Vicente de. "Les centres sociaux urbains au Brésil", *Revue internationale d'action communautaire* 8(48), aut 82 : 191-195. [résumés en anglais et en espagnol]

5584   PAWLUCH, Dorothy. "Transition in pediatrics: a segmental analysis", *Social Problems* 30(4), apr 83 : 449-465. [USA]

5585   RAI, Gauri S. "Reducing bureaucratic inflexibility", *Social Service Review* 57(1), mar 83 : 44-58.

5586   TURGEON, Jean. "Les médecins diplômés du Québec inscrits à la régie de l'Assurance-maladie du Québec (RAMQ) au 30 mars 1980", *Cahiers québécois de Démographie* 11(2), aug 82 : 227-252.

5587   TWAIN, David. *Creating change in social settings: planned program development.* New York, NY, Praeger, 83, vii-211 p.

AUTHOR INDEX
INDEX DES AUTEURS

Aaron, Daniel, 1799
Aballea, François, 3184
Abbott, Andrew, 1210
Abbott, John C., 2127
Abbruzzese, Salvatore, 4107
Abdulgani, H. Roeslen, 1681
Abel-Smith, Brian, 5523
Abeles, Marc, 3761
Abgarjan, Ě. A., 129
Abgarjan, R. Ě., 129
Abmeier, Klaus, 1753
Abowd, John M., 4011
Abraham, Gary, 1463
Abraham, Georges, 498
Abrahamse, Allan F., 3588
Abrams, Philip, 1
Abranches, Sérgio Henrique, 4888
Abrosoli, Luigi, 1857
Abul'hanova-Slavskaja, K. A., 556
Accardo, Alain, 2
Acedo, Clemy Machado de, 345
Adair, Philippe, 3623
Adam, Franko, 147
Adam, Heribert, 3390
Adamchak, Donald J., 2817, 3564
Adams, Paul, 5462
Adams, Robert McCormick, 3
Adamy, Wilhelm, 5342
Addi, Lahouari, 4108
Adewumi, J. B., 3646
Adhikari, Shyam Prasad, 3647
Adler, Israel, 5175
Adler, Laure, 3016
Adler, Patricia A., 5176
Adler, Peter, 5176
Aebischer, Verena, 1546
Agafonov, N. T., 3762
Agar Corbinos, Lorenzo, 3488
Aggarwal, J. C., 1924
Aggarwal, Y. P., 716
Agger, Ben, 232
Aghajanian, Akbar, 3323
Aglietta, Michel, 4003
Agnew, Robert S., 568
Agnihotri, U. S., 2245
Ágó, Erzsébet, 1080
Agudelo Mejía, Santiago, 4467
Aguirre, Benigno E., 901
Agulhon, Catherine, 4468
Agulhon, Maurice, 3802
Ahmed, Akbar S., 1337, 3565
Ahn, Byong Man, 3566
Ahponen, Pirkkoliisa, 947
Ahrne, Göran, 2256
Aikara, J., 1925
Aimez, Pierre, 5154
Ajsen, Icek, 644

Akaoka, Isao, 4374
Akashi, Takayuki, 5580
Akers, Ronald L., 1081
Akhavi, Shahrough, 1338
Akiba, Setsuo, 233, 3763
Aktouf, Omar, 733
Al-Omaim, Musa'ad, 2840
Al-Shami, Ibrahim, 2020
Alba, Richard D., 3324
Albanese, Robert, 758
Alber, Jens, 5446
Alberdi, Ines, 2923
Albornoz Peralta, Osvaldo, 4602
Albrecht, Richard, 1682
Albrecht, Sandra, 4714
Alcalay, Rina, 692
Alcandre, Jean-Jacques, 2021
Alcobensas Tirado, Maria Pilar, 2973
Aldgate, Anthony, 1747
Aldrich, Robert, 2996
Alegría, Juana Armanda, 3217
Alek-Kowalski, Tadeusz, 1507
Alekseev, S. S., 1251
Aleš, Milan, 2727
Alessi, Louis de, 3974
Alexander, Jeffrey C., 444
Alexiev, Alex, 5087
Alexis, Marion, 4603
Alibar, France, 3218
Allcock, John B., 4757
Allen, Luther A., 3764
Allen, Michael, 346, 3219
Allen, Sheila, 2555
Allers, Robert D., 3017
Allie, Robert, 1926
Almarcha Barbado, María Amparo, 2022, 2023
Almeder, Robert, 1240
Almeida, Maria Suely Kofes de, 3086
Almond, Gabriel A., 4800
Alonso Baquer, Miguel, 1464
Alonso Hinojal, I., 1858, 5505
Alperovich, Gershon, 2728
Alpers, Svetlana, 1824
Alston, Jon P., 2439
Alt, James, 743
Altbach, Philip G., 1859, 2024
Althabe, 671
Althaus, Paul G., 3567
Altieri Leonardo, 800
Altman, Irwin, 3610
Altmann, Norbert, 4604
Aludaat, K., 2025
Alvarez Reguillo, Lino, 3765
Alvarez, Gabriel C., 2513
Alvarez, María de la Luz, 3087
Alvarez, Vladimir, 2661
Alvira, Francisco, 347

Burton, John, 5506
Busch, Adelheid, 1873
Bushkovitch, Paul, 2237
Busino, Giovanni, 4788
Buss, Andreas, 1353
Buss, Terry F., 4228
Büssing, André, 4380
Bustamante, Jorge A., 3498
Butenko, A. P., 4803
Butler, Kenneth G., 1255
Butler, Peter M., 5453
Butler, Richard J., 3396
Buttel, Frederick H., 2304
Byrne, John, 5232
Byrnes, Heidi, 1548

Cabanes, Robert, 747
Cabanis, Jean-Noël, 5562
Cabrerizo Plaza, Florencio, 4135
Cadwallader, Mervyn L., 1996
Cagiano de Azevedo, Raimondo, 2926
Cagigal, J. M., 4760
Cahn, Meyer Michael, 42
Caire, Guy, 4683
Cairncross, Alec, 4259
Cakunov, V. V., 2498
Caldarola, Carlo, 1300
Čaldarović, Ognjen, 3787
Calderon, R., 3456
Caldwell, J. C., 2822
Caldwell, Pat, 2822
Calhoun, Craig, 1190, 4615
Callan, Victor, 2638, 2927, 2928
Callon, Michel, 199
Calot, Gérard, 2920
Calsamiglia, A., 5110
Calvert, Peter, 2265
Camacho, Daniel, 867
Camarero González, Arturo, 2033
Camboredon, Jean-Claude, 3660
Cambre Mariño, Jesus, 1874
Camburn, Donald, 2617
Camerini, Massimo, 1093
Campagnac, Elisabeth, 927
Campani, Giovanna, 4280
Campbell, Jennifer, 1073
Campbell, Paul R., 2528
Campbell, Richard T., 2352
Camus, Jürgen, 5233
Camusi, Maria Pia, 4476
Cancian, Francesca M., 2034
Canning, Claire, 3897
Cannon, Robert A., 2142
Cao Garcia, Ramon, 1932
Capel Martínez, Rosa María, 4281
Caplow, Theodore, 425, 3099, 3768
Capo, Hounkpatin C., 1621
Capobianco, Michael, 707
Cappadocia, Ezio, 1094
Cappelli, Peter, 4913
Caputo, Cataldo, 2517
Carabaña, J., 1227, 2035, 3024
Carapico, Sheila, 3736

Carbonnier, Jean, 1256, 1257
Cardoso, Ciro Flamarion Santana, 2238
Cardoso, F. H., 20, 4040, 5348, 5349
Carinci, Franco, 4684
Carlier, Alain, 5528
Carlson, Elwood, 2877
Carlson, James M., 5022
Carlson, John E., 4112
Carman, Roderick S., 1095
Carnevale, Peter J. D., 821
Caro, Jean-Yves, 117
Caron, Jean, 1549
Carpenter, Luther P., 5350
Carpenter, Peter, 2036
Carpentier, Jean-Baptiste, 1577
Carr, Shirley G. E., 2562
Carracedo, Orlando, 4113
Carrannante, Leonarda Roveri, 3039
Carrier, James G., 575
Carroll, Glenn R., 2829
Carter, Michael J., 4192
Carter, Timothy J., 5225, 5234
Cartier, Michel, 2734
Cartwright, D., 855
Cartwright, Rosalind L., 3232
Casali, Elide, 1805
Casals, Ignasi, 2697
Casanova, José V., 4978
Casco Montova, Rosario, 3661
Casella, Mario, 4041
Caselli, Graziella, 2823
Cashmore, Ernest, 3333
Caspi, Dan, 868, 3440
Cassá, Roberto, 3981
Cassel, Carol A., 5029
Casswell, Sally, 5181
Castan, Nicole, 4903
Castel, Robert, 5143
Castells, Manuel, 3788, 4942
Castillo Alonso, Juan José, 4169
Castro, Luis J., 3457
Catani, M., 529, 5235
Catanzaro, Raimondo, 2175
Catherine, Robert, 4914
Catrice-Lorey, Antoinette, 5454
Cavallaro, Renato, 360
Cavanagh, Darol M., 2038
Cazemajou, Jean, 3334
Cealis, Roza, 3499
Cebula, Richard J., 4589
Ceccarelli, Fabio, 928
Cecez, Momir, 4711
Cendales G., Lola, 2108
Cerase, Francesco Paolo, 4849
Cerroni, Umberto, 445
Certeau, Michel de, 1578
Čertihina, È. S., 4299
Česáková, Dana, 4477
Cesare, Bianca Maria, 3233
Cestaro, Antonio, 2266
Chabbi, Morched, 3789
Chabrol, Claude, 435
Chackerian, Richard, 4915

Spivey, W. Austin, 2315
Spöhring, Walger, 4697
Spoormans, H., 2332
Spores, John M., 1237
Squires, Gregory D., 122
Srb, Vladimír, 2783
Sredin, G. V., 5119
Srikantan, K. S., 2982
Srirantia, Santhebachahalli G., 2756
Srivastava, R. N., 5318
Srivastava, R. S., 2718
Srivastava, Suresh C., 4579
Srubar, Ilja, 2486
Staatz, John M., 3999
Stack, Steven, 1468, 4006
Stager, Susan F., 549
Stagl, Justin, 909
Stahura, John M., 3936
Stallberg, Friedrich Wilhelm, 5150
Štambuk, Maja, 3600, 3727
Stame, Nicoletta, 2200
Stamm, Anne, 2178
Stan, Charlotte M., 697
Stankiewicz, Janina, 4099
Stapleton, William Vaughan, 5292
Stąporek, Bolesław, 2049
Stappers, J. G., 1758
Starbuck, William H., 756
Staroverov, V. I., 3728
Starrs, Chris, 2292
Starski, Stanislaw, 2333
Startup, Richard, 451
Startz, Richard, 4203
Stasiak, Andrzej, 3729, 3937
Statera, Gianni, 144
Stauder, Paulo, 308
Steady, Filomina Chioma, 4338
Stebbins, Robert A., 1152
Steele-Perkins, Chris, 3774
Steenbergen, Bart van, 2433
Stefanile, Claudio, 3185
Stehlík, Jiří, 2784
Stehr, Nico, 1528
Stein Greenblat, Cathy, 3013
Stein, Nancy Wendlandt, 102
Stein, Steve, 4823
Steinberg, Laurence D., 4493
Steiner, Gibert Y., 2983
Steiniger, Wolfgang, 4933
Stenning, Philip C., 1066
Stepanov, I. G., 1164
Stephenson, Stanley P. Jr., 4339
Sterck, Stefaan, 5050
Stern, J., 2858, 4244
Stešenko, V. S., 2984
Steszenko, Walentyna S., 2785
Steven, Rob, 2334
Stevenson, Wayne, 4245
Stewart, A., 2214
Stewart, Abigail J., 3441
Stewart, John, 1536
Stewart, Joseph Jr., 2229
Stewart, Mark B., 3442

Stewman, Shelby, 4523
Stežko, Z. V., 2201
Stidham, Ronald, 2616
Stiens, Gerhard, 2828
Stier, Frances, 3472
Stimson, Robert John, 3938
Stinchcombe, Arthur L., 342, 3973
Stockton, Ronald R., 5052
Stoetzel, Jean, 1070
Stoïchev, Todor Stoïchev, 309
Stokes, C. Shannon, 3186
Stoljarova, L. I., 3998
Stolte, John F., 550
Stolte-Heiskanen, Veronica, 840
Stone, Carl, 4425
Storižko, A. I., 1243
Stoto, Michael A., 401
Strassoldo, Raimondo, 4100
Stratton, Jon, 1839
Strautyn', A., 3187
Stray, S. J., 887
Streiff-Fenart, Jocelyne, 4340
Streitwieser, Mary L., 3939
Strel'cov, N. N., 310
Strém, Kálmán, 1840
Stresius, Lothar, 311
Strinati, Dominic, 4580
Strommen, Ellen A., 509
Strong, John R., 1606
Strothmann, Dietrich, 1436
Strotzka, Hans, 5513
Strudel, Sylvie, 5074
Struyk, Raymond J., 3964
Strzelecki, Zbigniew, 2546
Strzclewicz, Willy, 4866
Stuart, Robert C., 3940
Stuart-Fox, Martin, 312, 2429
Stukin, Kazimierz, 4136
Sturmthal, Adolf, 4246
Subramaniam, V., 1397
Šučenko, V. A., 313
Suchocka, Renata, 3730
Sudakov, V. I., 314
Sudman, Seymour, 430
Sufin, Zbigniew, 2230
Sugaya, Yoshiko, 3188
Sugimoto, Atsuo, 1165
Sugioka, Naoto, 829, 3731
Sugrue, Noreen M., 2431
Suh, Sang-Mok, 4008
Sujatozel'kaja, A. V., 2487
Sułek, Antoni, 1071
Sulkunen, Pekka, 5186
Sullivan, Charles A., 4270
Sumichrast, Michael, 3931
Sumioka, Hidetake, 2488
Sumitani, Akio, 825
Summerfield, Angela B., 605
Summers, C. W., 4596
Šumratov, B. I., 4211
Sundbo, Jon, 4452
Supek, Rudi, 402, 1166
Supraptilah, Bondan, 2918

SUBJECT INDEX

Abandoned children, 2658
  USA, 2647
Ability grouping, 723
  USA, 2132
Abortion, 2923, 2924, 2976, 2991
  Africa, 2934
  Australia, 2927, 2928, 2990
  Belgium, 2988
  Hawaii, 2932
  New Zealand, 2969
  Poland, 2967
  Spain, 2973, 2987
  USA, 2941, 2944, 2948, 2983
Absenteeism, 4447, 4450
  Canada, 4443
  Denmark, 4452
  Spain, 4445
Academic achievement, *use* Academic success
Academic aptitude, 575
Academic freedom
  USA, 1950
Academic profession, 787
  Chile, 2167
  USA, 2166
Academic success, 1946, 2128, 2131, 2133
  Canada, 2135
  Hungary, 2134
  New Zealand, 2130
  United Kingdom, 2130
Access to education, 1966
Accidents, 5151
Acculturation
  USA, 1037
Achievement, 362, 582, 4098
  USA, 616
Achievement motivation, 1913
Action, 571, 600, 606, 608, 611, 756, 2199
  India, 393
Action research, 147
Action theory, 69, 242, 264, 268, 290, 304, 308, 310
Administration, *use* Public administration
Administrative control, 769, 773, 796, 809, 4554
Administrative corruption
  India, 4936
  Nigeria, 4929
  USA, 4937
Administrative organization
  USA, 4920
Administrative reforms
  Haiti, 4923
  Italy, 4909
  Japan, 4935
Administrative sciences
  developing countries, 4784
  USA, 4777

Adolescents, 530, 549, 638, 1048, 1081, 2356, 2677, 2808, 2887, 2920, 3430
  Belgium, 2670
  France, 1641, 2975, 5175
  Israel, 5175
  Spain, 1074
  USA, 5197
Adopted children
  Denmark, 2657
  Japan, 2659
Adorno, Theodor W., 237, 298, 311
Adult education, 2098, 2105, 2111
  Germany FR, 2090, 2095
  India, 2114
  Italy, 2113
  Latin America, 2108, 2116
  United Kingdom, 2099
  USA, 2086, 2100, 2104, 2113
Adulthood, 2686
Adults, 1041
Advertising, 1592, 1663, 1664, 1666, 1667
  Norway, 1710
  USA, 1665
Affiliation, 660
Afghanistan
  secularization, 5357
  social reforms, 5357
Africa
  abortion, 2934
  art, 1782
  biographies, 207
  brain drain, 4459
  Churches, 1432
  cinema, 1763
  culture, 977
  demography, 2530
  dropout, 2013
  economic and social development, 1763
  emigration, 3537
  ethnicity, 3381
  family, 3280
  forced migration, 2241
  history, 977
  intellectuals, 2383
  language policy, 1619
  marginality, 1128
  medicine, 5504
  modernization, 3923
  national identity, 1619
  national language, 1619
  novels, 1807
  occupations, 4458, 4459
  political socialization, 5056
  political systems, 4844, 4845, 4847
  proletariat, 1128
  public administration, 4930
  refugees, 3479

agricultural enterprises, 2579
capitalism, 1279
child care, 5456
children, 2638
class consciousness, 2267, 2285
collective bargaining, 4089
crime, 3160
cultural pluralism, 965, 2144
curriculum, 2038, 2144
educational needs, 1974
educational planning, 1976
educational policy, 1977
electoral sociology, 5064
elite, 2392
ethnic groups, 3336, 3380
family, 3113
family planning, 2958
family relations, 3160
feminism, 3243
health services, 5568
higher education, 2036, 2038
historical demography, 2529
immigrant assimilation, 3523
immigrants, 3482, 3497, 3548
income inequality, 2580
indigenous population, 1638, 1997, 3231,
    3328, 3360, 4860, 4986
labour law, 4595
land property, 4860
language, 1638
law, 1279
lawyers, 4556
middle class, 2285
migration, 3471
militancy, 2169
new technologies, 4089
nicknames, 2529
occupational choice, 4521
occupational prestige, 4482
political participation, 2169
population, 1976, 2533, 2539
press, 3548
protest movements, 4986
refugees, 3503
school attendance, 2012
sex differentiation, 2580
sex discrimination, 2618
sex roles, 2593
social conditions, 93
social inequality, 2234
social policy, 5358, 5368
socialism, 4818
sociology, 93
sport, 4759
State intervention, 4860
strikes, 4699
teachers, 2142, 2164, 2169
towns, 3938
trade unions, 4618
unemployment, 4251
urban life, 3938
urbanization, 3881
violence, 3160

voting behaviour, 3237
wage discrimination, 2580
welfare State, 5368
women, 2579
women's participation, 3235, 3237, 3308,
    3313
women's status, 3231, 4759
workers' participation, 4728
youth, 2662
Austria
    aged, 2700
    antisemitism, 3418
    criminal justice, 5305
    criminology, 5316
    educational policy, 1923
    ethnic groups, 3343
    national minorities, 3344, 3348
    primary education, 2159
    social psychiatry, 5513
    trade unions, 4605
Authoritarianism, 869, 870, 873, 874, 876, 4543
    Brazil, 2394
    Latin America, 867
Authority, 805
Automation, 2309, 4440
    France, 4062
    Japan, 4071
Automobile industry
    USA, 4564
Automobiles, 4126
    United Kingdom, 4115
    USA, 4128

Balance theory, 863
Bangladesh
    child mortality, 2825
    civil service, 4939
    culture, 938
    female labour, 2594
    fertility, 2891, 2901
    infant mortality, 2825
    Islam, 1344
    marriage, 3025
    mortality, 2841
    peasants, 2901, 3738
    population, 2536
    rural areas, 2594
    rural society, 3739
    sex differentiation, 2841
    villages, 3649
    women, 2594
Bank management
    Italy, 4152
Banks
    France, 4691
    Italy, 4152
Barbados
    urban development, 3905
Bargaining, 670, 673, 680, 682, 685, 688,
    1157, 4904
Barristers, *use* Lawyers
Barthes, Roland, 281
Baruch, Bernard, 4810

Basic education, 2107
  Latin America, 2108
Baudrillard, 815
Beauvoir, Simone de, 3315
Behaviour, 847, 848, 849, 850, 3610
Behavioural sciences, 3, 42, 744
  USA, 4064
Behaviourism, 261
Belgium
  abortion, 2988
  adolescents, 2670
  aged, 3468
  care of the aged, 5492
  Catholicism, 1359
  child mortality, 2844
  children, 5050
  communication, 1609
  day care centres, 1998
  employment, 4157
  evolutionism, 248
  family, 3145
  family relations, 4253
  foreigners, 3338
  frontier workers, 4292
  health, 5532
  housing policy, 3823
  humanization of work, 4383
  immigrant assimilation, 3507
  local government, 4940
  marital status, 3081
  medical care, 5547
  migration, 3468, 3477
  penal law, 1289
  political socialization, 5050
  population censuses, 2788
  population growth, 3477
  population policy, 2943
  regional planning, 4157
  research centres, 11
  school age population, 1998
  secondary education, 2007
  social security, 5457, 5458, 5483
  sociology, 11
  suicide, 5287
  theatre, 1846
  unemployed, 4253
  working time arrangement, 4369, 4388, 4436
  youth unemployment, 4229
Belief, 609, 880, 881, 889
Benin
  literacy, 2097
  revolutionary movements, 2097
Benjamin, Walter, 1784
Bibliographies, 10, 186, 188, 215, 515, 1256,
    1257, 1320, 1393, 1458, 1526, 1531,
    1905, 2178, 2271, 2612, 2849, 3454,
    4173, 4610, 4782, 4815, 4983, 5239,
    5510
  Germany FR, 1096
  USA, 3362
Big enterprises
  USA, 2310
Bilingual education

Latin America, 2087
  Spain, 2110
Bilingualism, 1614
  Canada, 1637, 1642, 1645, 1646
  France, 1616
  USA, 1654
Biographies, 205, 208, 209, 212, 529, 917, 1122
  Africa, 207
Biological family, *use* Nuclear family
Biology, 928, 2189
Birth, 2905
  developing countries, 2912
  USA, 3282
Birth control
  Puerto Rico, 2972
Birth intervals, 2910
Birth order, 2885
Birth spacing
  Kenya, 2962
  USA, 2959
Black Africa
  political systems, 2211
  social pluralism, 2211
Blacks
  Brazil, 1136
  South Africa, 3862, 4630, 4662
  United Kingdom, 3333
  USA, 542, 899, 1847, 2360, 2564, 3213,
    3316, 3362, 3441, 3936, 5034, 5094,
    5241
Bobbio, Norberto, 4788
Bolivia
  peasant organizations, 3689
  social policy, 5410
Botswana
  collective farming, 4120
Boudon, Raymond, 2174, 2181
Bourdieu, Pierre, 2, 16
Bourgeois society, 918, 1239, 1242, 1941, 4827
  France, 3993
Bourgeoisie, 1040, 2332
  Latin America, 2255
Bowles, Samuel, 1877
Brain drain
  Africa, 4459
  Andean countries, 3536
Brazil
  authoritarianism, 2394
  Blacks, 1136
  broadcasting, 1683
  Catholic Church, 1422, 1425
  child labour, 4274
  child neglect, 3108
  cinema, 1707
  cultural property, 935
  culture, 958
  delinquency, 5429
  democratization, 1699, 1903
  economic and social development, 2882
  education, 1903, 1908
  educational policy, 1959
  electoral systems, 4890
  elite, 2394

entrepreneurs, 4040
ethnic minorities, 1308, 1309, 3359
family, 2472, 3086
fertility, 2882
higher education, 2043, 2066
housing, 3798
housing policy, 3916
juvenile delinquency, 3108, 5308
kinship, 3359
labour movements, 4680
leisure, 4743
literacy, 2102
marginality, 5308
mass communication, 1425
middle class, 3359
miscegenation, 914
national identity, 914
party systems, 4952
political corruption, 5028
political opposition, 5016
political representation, 4888, 4889
political systems, 4842
politics, 995
population movement, 2739
poverty, 2472, 5170
press, 1699
race, 3378
race relations, 1136
religion, 1308, 1309, 3359
religious syncretism, 1308
school attendance, 4274
slums, 3798, 5060, 5498
social change, 2472
social conditions, 5429, 5435
social policy, 5369
social protest, 1136
social services, 5576, 5583
social work, 5498
society, 995
State, 2394
towns, 3857
universities, 2069, 2075
urban planning, 3865
urbanization, 3782
value systems, 958
voting behaviour, 5060
women's education, 3294
Breast-feeding
Pakistan, 2651
Yemen, 2940
Brigandage
Spain, 5245
Broadcasting, 1670
Brazil, 1683
German DR, 1691
Germany FR, 1415, 1691
Brotherhoods
Western Africa, 1417
Buddhism, 1353, 1401, 1403
Burma, 1394, 1396
India, 1397
Korea R, 1335
Laos, 312

USSR, 1352
Bulgaria
industrial sociology, 4176
production collectivities, 4176
punishment, 5268
religious practice, 1491
social classes, 2299
social security, 5467
social stratification, 2299
sociolinguistics, 1567
sociology, 51
Bureaucracy, 779
China, 762
developing countries, 781
Japan, 776
United Kingdom, 778, 5573
USA, 766, 5585
Bureaucratic control, 754, 767
Bureaucratic organization, *use* Bureaucracy
Bureaucratization, 787, 794
Burial, *use* Funeral rites
Burma
Buddhism, 1394, 1396
Burundi
rural development, 3664
Business cycles
USA, 5331
Business economics
USA, 4051
Business management, 1240, 3975, 4053,
4055, 4057, 4060
USA, 2034, 4039, 4044, 4049, 4059
Business organization, 4061
United Kingdom, 4058
Business planning, *use* Corporate planning

Cameroon
religious movements, 1481
women's participation, 3284
women's status, 3284
Canada
absenteeism, 4443
academic success, 2135
aged, 2698, 4014
bilingualism, 1637, 1642, 1645, 1646
capital, 812
capital punishment, 5271
Catholicism, 1367, 2010
childhood, 2652
Christianity, 1348
cinema, 2162
civil servants, 4911
class behaviour, 3403
class identification, 2324
continuing education, 2106
cooperatives, 3982
cultural pluralism, 954, 3363
delinquency, 5250
deviance, 5250
disability, 2796
divorce, 3042
dropout, 1994
drug addiction, 5178

foreign workers, 4318, 4323
foreigners, 3340
health policy, 5553
higher education, 2077
housing policy, 3813, 3832
immigrants, 3509, 3551
immigration, 3480
immigration policy, 3493, 3560
individualism, 547
industrial sociology, 4179
information policy, 181
information sciences, 181
information technology, 181
juvenile delinquency, 5284
labour market, 686, 2077
labour relations, 4604, 4629
labour supply, 4197, 4435
local government, 2443, 4946, 5381
mass education, 1734
mass media, 1721, 1734
media, 1675
migrant workers, 4332
migration research, 3560
military personnel, 5088
minority groups, 710
mortality, 2828
parent-child relations, 3119
part-time employment, 4237
peasants, 3716
penal sanctions, 5266
personnel management, 4604, 4629
political culture, 5033, 5047
political socialization, 5051
population movement, 2751
poverty, 5162
press, 1677, 1729
primary education, 2159
prostitution, 2999
public administration, 4912
religious movements, 1485
rural areas, 3093, 5428
rural development, 3958
secularization, 1496
social action, 5428
social change, 2443
social consciousness, 4323
social history, 2421
social integration, 3340, 5088
social legislation, 5441
social movements, 4972, 4975, 4992
social policy, 1895, 2443, 5342, 5381, 5384
social protest, 4975
social security, 4303, 5465, 5477, 5488
social services, 5572
social structure, 2183
social work, 5500
socialization, 1096
sociological research, 4179
sociological theory, 285
sociology, 50, 64, 68
songs, 1831
strikes, 4696, 4697
students, 2018

teachers, 2165
television, 1682
terrorism, 1117, 5051
towns, 3831
trade unions, 4603, 4605
unemployment, 4243, 4255
universities, 2021
urban areas, 3891
urban development, 3958
urban planning, 3752
urban renewal, 3785
urbanism, 3863
value orientation, 547
value systems, 1055, 1496
vocational education, 4514
vocational training, 4498
women, 2553, 3340
women workers, 4303
work organization, 4732
work place, 4197
workers' participation, 4732, 4734
working conditions, 4390
working time, 4370, 4376
working time arrangement, 4372, 4435, 4439
works councils, 4604, 4629
youth, 1096
youth employment, 5284
youth unrest, 2678
Ghana
    care of the aged, 5474
    Christianity, 1378
    class conflicts, 2300
    ethnicity, 3364
    housing, 3777
    literacy, 2089
    press, 1773
    residential mobility, 3860
    social development, 2471
    trade unionism, 4612
    witchcraft, 1326
Giddens, Anthony, 5364
Gifted children, 2637
    USA, 2643, 2650
Gintis, Herbert, 1877
Girls, 1095
Goffman, Irving, 548
Goldmann, Lucien, 269
Gouldner, Alvin W., 230
Government, 4900
Government spending, *use* Public expenditures
Graduates, 2058
    Canada, 4494
    India, 2250
    Indonesia, 2062
    Poland, 2083
Gramsci, Antonio, 245, 1254
Graph theory, 477, 478, 479, 480, 481, 482
Greece
    class formation, 2323
    internal migration, 3580
    politics, 2323
    press, 1736
    villages, 1112

rural development, 3697, 4109
rural society, 3648
schooling, 1938
skilled workers, 4481
social change, 2462, 2489, 2491, 2492
social conditions, 2720
social history, 2426
social inequality, 2134
social security, 5485
social stratification, 2210
social structure, 2675
socialist society, 3991
sociology, 59, 60
teachers, 2148
technocracy, 2397
technological change, 4046
theology, 1306
villages, 3648, 3654, 3723, 3988
vocational training, 4481
women's employment, 4308
youth, 2675
Hunting
    France, 3650, 3658, 3659, 3660, 3690,
       3717, 3737, 4105, 4762

Identification, 664
Identity, 524, 525, 528, 532, 536, 541, 545,
    548, 610, 664, 838, 855, 1170, 1383,
    2146, 4132, 4275, 4301, 4321, 4340
    Guatemala, 3347
    New Zealand, 1315
Ideology, 30, 331, 403, 890, 891, 892, 894,
    896, 898, 1145, 2386, 3192, 4833, 5090
    Tanzania, 897
    USA, 899
Illegal immigration, 3518
    France, 3499, 3533, 3534
    USA, 3492, 3517
Illegitimacy, 2877
    Sweden, 2951
Illiteracy
    Yugoslavia, 2101
Illness, *use* Diseases
Image, 855, 1470, 3911, 4042
Imagination, 70, 595
Immigrant assimilation, 3483, 3530
    Australia, 3523
    Belgium, 3507
    France, 3496
    Sudan, 3506
    USA, 3225
Immigrants, 3516, 3520
    Australia, 3482, 3497, 3548
    Canada, 3352, 3403
    Chile, 3488
    France, 3491, 3495, 3528, 3555
    Germany FR, 3509, 3551
    Israel, 669
    Morocco, 3558
    Netherlands, 3545
    North Africa, 4340
    Sweden, 3519
    United Kingdom, 3501

    USA, 3350, 3490, 3494, 3524, 3543, 3553,
       3554, 3562
    Yugoslavia, 3513
Immigration, 3546
    Argentina, 1341, 3559
    France, 3527
    Germany FR, 3480
    Italy, 3485
    Saudi Arabia, 3532
    Uruguay, 3547
    USA, 3498, 3508, 3514, 3535, 3539, 3544
Immigration law
    USA, 3515
Immigration policy
    Canada, 3556
    France, 3504
    Germany FR, 3493, 3560
    USA, 3484, 3500, 3561
Impoverishment
    Tunisia, 3685
Incest taboo, 3006
Income distribution, 4037
    Canada, 4239
    Switzerland, 5452
    United Kingdom, 1930
    Uruguay, 4033
    USA, 4026
Income inequality, 2774, 4017, 4027
    Australia, 2580
    USA, 2358, 4034, 5490
India
    action, 393
    administrative corruption, 4936
    adult education, 2114
    aged, 2718
    ageing, 2699
    agricultural policy, 4124
    area studies, 92, 419
    attitudes, 853
    Buddhism, 1397
    castes, 1498, 2221, 2239, 2242, 2243,
       2245, 2247, 2248, 2249, 2250, 2274
    Catholic Church, 2243
    Christians, 1402
    civil servants, 4927
    class differentiation, 853, 2348
    class formation, 2223, 2330
    clergy, 1440
    colonialism, 3683
    community power, 3725
    cooperative sector, 3997
    crime, 5301
    criminal justice, 5255
    cultural change, 4124
    cultural environment, 2781
    cultural level, 1964
    cultural policy, 1008
    delinquents, 5276
    demographic research, 2964
    demographic transition, 2735
    disabled persons, 2810
    divorce, 3041
    dowry, 3054, 3077

social change, 4891
social classes, 2266
social conflicts, 675
social history, 5257
social integration, 2809
social structure, 2175, 2190
social success, 2403
social unrest, 5149
sociologists, 115
sociology, 53, 113, 302
sociology of family, 3107
sociology of law, 1288
State intervention, 4849
strikes, 4697
suicide, 5257
teaching of sociology, 1875
terrorism, 1090, 1094
urban areas, 675
value, 1044
voting behaviour, 5058
welfare State, 4559
women workers, 4277
women's status, 3233, 3241, 3286, 3297, 3307
working conditions, 4277
youth, 1469, 5061
Ivory Coast
rural-urban migration, 3583
villages, 3672

Jamaica
attitude to work, 4425
drug addiction, 5185
Japan
administrative reforms, 4935
adopted children, 2659
aged, 2724, 3140
attitude to work, 969, 4374, 4408
automation, 4071
bureaucracy, 776
care of the aged, 5493
Christianity, 1386
class consciousness, 2338
class struggle, 2293
community development, 3635, 3636, 3637, 3639
conflicts, 684
consumer behaviour, 2076
cultural change, 1018
cultural values, 1016
customs, 1448
delinquency, 5269
disaster relief, 5152
divorce, 3018, 3047
educational opportunities, 3254
emigrants, 3353, 3359
employees, 4549
environmental protection, 4989
ethnic minorities, 3385
ethos, 1246
family, 2298, 3179, 3189, 3204, 3205
family history, 2628, 3177
family life, 2076, 3157
family planning, 2933

family relations, 2060
family structure, 2843
farmers, 3731
female labour, 4349
feminism, 3301
fertility, 2871, 3155
festivals, 1187, 1199, 1205
fishing villages, 3733
folk culture, 1186
funeral rites, 1445, 1448
generation conflicts, 2628, 2632
health insurance, 5530
higher education, 2056
hotel industry, 4428
households, 2583
housing, 3153
industrialization, 4119
inheritance, 2628
joint family, 3153
journalism, 1703
juvenile delinquency, 5338
labour relations, 4374, 4581, 4584
leadership, 829
leisure, 4748
libraries, 191
life styles, 4748
local communities, 3632
local government, 3632
mass media, 1718
medical care, 5530
mortality decline, 2843
music, 1835
neighbourhood, 3763, 3854
noise control, 1114
occupational life, 4496
occupational safety, 4496
painting, 1826
parent-child relations, 3140
patriarchy, 3155
patrilineal descent, 3130
peasantry, 3177
peasants, 3706
personnel management, 4368
political parties, 4957
population composition, 2786
population distribution, 2762
population movement, 2736
population policy, 2736
preschool education, 2003
press, 1760, 1761, 1762
primary schools, 2151
professors, 2415
religion, 1305
religious affiliation, 1482
rites, 1187
rural communities, 3885
rural society, 3706
rural-urban migration, 3607
school adaptation, 2015
scientific and technical progress, 4074
scientific community, 150
social behaviour, 1016, 1106
social change, 2439

social classes, 2334
social groups, 3874
social indicators, 469
social mobility, 2415
social movements, 4989
social participation, 3731
social policy, 3961
social promotion, 4119
social protest, 1114
social services, 5579
social stratification, 2298
social unrest, 5146
social welfare, 469
social workers, 5580
society, 996
student behaviour, 2076
students, 2060, 2071
suicide, 5280
teachers, 2151
technology assessment, 4078
theatre, 1852
towns, 3875, 3892, 3960
trade unions, 4632
training, 5580
universities, 2048
university campus, 684
urban communities, 1187, 3874, 3885,
  3888, 3961
urban life, 1199
urbanization, 3885, 3886
value judgment, 329
villages, 3711
way of life, 969
women, 2615
women workers, 4320
women's education, 3254
women's status, 2724, 3223, 3302, 4320
workers, 2338
working class, 2298
working conditions, 4413, 4428
youth, 2685, 3731
Jews, 3146
  Argentina, 1341, 1374
  France, 1354, 1391
  India, 1385, 1402
  Poland, 1362
  United Kingdom, 2831
  USA, 1346, 1355, 2663, 3553
  USSR, 1373, 3541
  voting behaviour, 5074
Job creation, *use* Employment creation
Job enrichment
  France, 4409
Job evaluation, 4256
Job opportunities, *use* Employment opportunities
Job requirements, 4486
Job satisfaction, 3464, 3520, 4380, 4393,
  4395, 4397, 4407, 4410, 4431, 4446,
  4453
  Canada, 4429
  Israel, 4534
  Spain, 4426
  USA, 4389

Job search
  United Kingdom, 3877
  USA, 4224
Job security, *use* Employment security
Joint consultation, 4704
Joint family, 4015
  Japan, 3153
  Senegal, 3161
Joint management, *use* Workers' participation
Jordan
  students, 2025
Journalism, 1685, 1754, 1772
  Israel, 1749
  Japan, 1703
Journalists
  France, 1748
Journey to work, *use* Commuting
Judaism, 494, 1364, 1376
  Israel, 1366
Judicial behaviour, 4905
  USA, 4902
Judiciary power
  France, 4903
Jury, 639, 704
Justice, 1255, 1260, 1262, 1278, 1280, 1285
Juvenile delinquency, 5218, 5320, 5337
  Brazil, 3108, 5308
  Germany FR, 5284
  India, 5315
  Japan, 5338
  Niger, 5297
  Nigeria, 5297
  Poland, 5145
  USA, 5230, 5254, 5292, 5302

Kampuchea
  refugees, 3557
Kant, Emmanuel, 522
Kenya
  alienation, 4377
  attitude to work, 4377
  birth spacing, 2962
  child mortality, 2848
  engineers, 4458
  fertility, 2962
  fertility decline, 2884
  housing, 3849
  internal migration, 3604
  political minority, 5020
  population growth, 2729
  rural population, 3111
  social science research, 139
  teacher training, 2163
  theatre, 1850
  working conditions, 4377
Kibbutz
  Israel, 1048, 1366, 4130
Kinship, 3128, 3180
  Brazil, 3359
  India, 3112, 3138
  Italy, 3089
  Southeastern Asia, 3194
  United Kingdom, 3606

Marx, Karl, 61, 90, 223, 225-26, 231, 244,
    263, 273, 287, 931, 1101, 1105, 1139,
    1162, 1304, 1323, 2217, 2450-51, 2486,
    2490, 3246, 4000, 4177, 4351, 4438,
    4821, 5413
Marxism, 35, 222-29, 231-33, 235-36, 251,
    257, 262, 265, 270, 282, 286, 294, 296,
    305, 309, 315, 317-18, 325, 445, 916,
    976, 1148, 1164, 1283, 2425, 2470,
    2494, 3804, 3842, 3994, 4101, 4200,
    5083, 5388, 5403
    China, 21, 45
    Laos, 312
    Poland, 279
Mass communication, 1065, 1601, 1607, 1669,
    1689, 1715, 1717, 1728, 1731, 1753
    Brazil, 1425
    France, 1743
    Hungary, 1759
    Indonesia, 1681
    Mexico, 1720
Mass culture, 916, 990, 1688, 1787
    Spain, 4745
    United Kingdom, 1006
Mass education
    Germany FR, 1734
    India, 1925
    Vietnam, 1991
Mass media, 1180, 1556, 1557, 1643, 1672,
    1674, 1688, 1725, 1735, 1744, 1746,
    1754, 1756, 1758, 1764, 4795, 5039,
    5316
    France, 1679
    Germany FR, 1721, 1734
    Japan, 1718
    Mexico, 1701
    Pakistan, 1673, 1733
    Spain, 1726
    Tunisia, 1712, 1714
    USA, 102, 1708, 1739, 1740, 1767, 1768
    USSR, 1730
    Yugoslavia, 1742
Mate selection, 3033, 4340
    Germany, 3022
    Mexico, 3056
    USA, 3634
Materialism, 237, 319
Mathematical analysis, 450, 472
Mathematical methods, 447
Mathematics, 129, 446, 451, 1825
Mauritania
    slavery, 2244
Mauritius
    labour law, 4597
Mauss, Marcel, 4804
Mazdeism, *use* Zoroastrianism
Mead, George H., 293, 2431
Meaning, 1626
    India, 393
Measurement, 420, 4354, 5157
Media, 1671, 1704, 1727
    Germany FR, 1675
    Norway, 1710

Switzerland, 1755
Mediation, 4705
Medical care, 5519, 5523, 5526, 5540, 5541, 5543
    Belgium, 5547
    Canada, 5529, 5537
    France, 5528, 5557
    Germany, 5557
    Israel, 5536
    Italy, 5522
    Japan, 5530
    Kuwait, 5546
    Nicaragua, 5534
    Sweden, 5542
    United Kingdom, 5557
    USA, 5524, 5525, 5549, 5550, 5555
Medical costs, *use* Health expenditures
Medical economics, *use* Health economics
Medical personnel
    Canada, 5575
Medical sociology, 5505, 5510, 5515
Medicinal drugs, *use* Drugs
Medicine, 1092, 2807, 5506, 5509, 5512,
    5514, 5516
    Africa, 5504
    Italy, 1327
    Martinique, 5517
Medina Echavarría, José, 20
Mediterranean countries
    television, 1750
    women's status, 3210
Meetings, 158
Mental diseases, 639, 2589, 2803, 2806
    Tunisia, 2814
Mental health, 1265, 5188, 5538, 5544, 5548
    Reunion Island, 5531
    United Kingdom, 5539
    USA, 5554
Mental hospitals
    USA, 5567
Mental retardation, 2812
Mentally disabled, 2799, 2804
    USA, 2813
Merton, R. K., 272
Messages, 1602
Methodology, 400
Mexico
    child mortality, 2847
    class struggle, 2270
    contraception, 2985
    drinkers, 5187
    economic recession, 4003
    emigrants, 3225, 3492
    emigration, 3498
    family planning, 1720
    indigenous population, 3321, 3345
    infant mortality, 2847
    labour disputes, 4681
    labour movements, 4601
    labour relations, 3663
    labour supply, 4191
    land tenure, 3663
    mass communication, 1720
    mass media, 1701

Latin America, 3735
Spain, 3719
Peasants, 5217
Asia, 3644
Bangladesh, 2901, 3738
Germany FR, 3716
India, 3651
Japan, 3706
Sri Lanka, 2979
Sudan, 3698
Pediatricians
USA, 5584
Peer groups, 701, 702
Penal law, 1227, 1282, 1287, 5214
Belgium, 1289
China, 1272
France, 1247, 1263, 1411, 5325
Italy, 1277
Switzerland, 1268
Penal sanctions, 3467, 5309
France, 5266
Germany FR, 5266
Scandinavia, 5216
USA, 5251, 5289, 5290, 5329
Penitentiary system, 579
Italy, 5222
USA, 5230, 5232, 5246, 5294, 5298, 5303,
5332
Pension schemes
France, 2704
Pensions, *use* Retirement pensions
Perception, 1658
Perception of others, 638
Performance, 597
Performers, 1785
Periodicals, 213, 214
Personality, 556, 557, 558, 559, 560, 561,
563, 850, 932, 1000, 4084
Personality assessment, *use* Personality
measurement
Personality development, 562, 564, 565, 839,
948, 1212, 1235, 1853
Personality measurement, 443
Personnel management, 2258, 4352, 4356,
4360, 4361, 4364, 4365, 4367
France, 4359
Germany FR, 4604, 4629
Indonesia, 4357
Japan, 4368
Netherlands, 4432
United Kingdom, 4368
Personnel supervision, *use* Personnel management
Persuasion, 881, 1591, 1592
Peru
child mortality, 2868
class domination, 2259
community development, 2868
divorce, 3037
drug addiction, 5179
fertility, 2880
housing, 3894
infant mortality, 2868
internal migration, 3592

land reforms, 2740
regional disparities, 3592
rural women, 2740
women's employment, 4291
Petroleum industry
Mexico, 2270
Phenomenology, 241, 292, 301
Philippines
family planning, 2986
housing, 3843
informal sector, 3581
labour migration, 3581
rural development, 3688
rural-urban migration, 3603
sexual behaviour, 3007
social classes, 3950
urban population, 2725
urbanization, 3603, 3950
Phillips curve, 4700
Philosophers
France, 119, 126
Philosophy, 17, 63, 245, 256, 257, 275
France, 119, 126
USSR, 280, 313
Physicians, 2863, 4527
Canada, 5586
France, 4457
Piaget, Jean, 1213, 1588
Pilgrimages
India, 1964
Planned economy, 4216
Planned parenthood, *use* Family planning
Planning
Latin America, 757
Playing activities, 918, 4766
Plural society, *use* Social pluralism
Pluralism, 1764
Poetry
India, 1803
USA, 1801
Poland
abortion, 2967
aged, 2719, 3602, 4753
agricultural enterprises, 4122
agricultural workers, 4136, 4535
alcoholism, 5193
aspirations, 2683, 4326
attitude to work, 4385, 4392, 4416, 4535
attitudes, 1124, 4326
care of the aged, 5469, 5473
career development, 2083
Catholic Church, 1427
Catholicism, 1230, 1398
Christianity, 1379
Church and State, 1489
class conflicts, 2337
class structure, 2291
class struggle, 2333
clubs, 4753
collective farming, 4122
commuting, 3608
contraception, 2967
crime prevention, 5145

Religious integrism, 1473
Religious life
    Central America, 1458
Religious movements, 1480
    Cameroon, 1481
    Germany FR, 1485
    India, 1498
    Malaysia, 1488
    Mexico, 1483
    Netherlands, 1495, 1501
    Polynesia, 1499
    Scotland, 1479
    Spain, 1484
    United Kingdom, 1475, 1476
    USA, 1474, 1493
Religious participation
    Chile, 1502
    USA, 1486
Religious practice
    Bulgaria, 1491
    France, 1492
    New Zealand, 1487
    Poland, 1451
    USA, 1500
Religious revival
    USA, 1474
Religious symbolism, 1363
Religious syncretism
    Brazil, 1308
    Malaysia, 1488
Remarriage
    United Kingdom, 3040
Research, 4901
Research and development
    China, 148
Research centres
    Belgium, 11
Research foundations, 155
Research institutions, *use* Research centres
Research methods, 144, 362, 383, 399, 2085, 4747
Research techniques, 389
Research workers, 125
Residence, 3860
    Poland, 3951
    Senegal, 3161
Resident satisfaction, 3897
    Canada, 4014
    Nigeria, 3806
    USA, 3836, 3861
Residential areas
    Hungary, 3948
    USA, 3871
Residential mobility, 3855, 3953
    Colombia, 3808
    Ghana, 3860
    Togo, 3860
    USA, 3791, 3927, 3936, 3955
Residential segregation, 3906
    Netherlands, 3426
    USA, 3753, 3837, 3873, 3930, 3939, 3959
Resource allocation, 3063
Responsibility, 854, 1216, 1218, 1226, 1243, 5323
Retired persons, 2709, 2713

France, 2704, 2715
India, 2692, 2693
Netherlands, 3569
USA, 2691
Retirement, 4444, 4449
    France, 3163
Retirement pensions, 4322
Return migration, 3481, 3540, 3550
    Algeria, 3522, 3529
    Ireland, 3511
    Newfoundland, 3511
    Portugal, 3542
Reunion Island
    mental health, 5531
Revolt, 2109
Revolution, 2451, 2468, 2470, 2496, 3665
    Angola, 2465
    China, 2380, 2463
    developing countries, 2458
    France, 2419, 2459, 2479
    Germany, 2423
    Mozambique, 2465
Revolutionary movements, 3246, 4981
    Benin, 2097
    Germany, 2097
Rewards, 2131, 5379
Ricardo, D., 2517
Richberg, Donald, 4810
Rickert, H., 1169
Riesman, David, 98
Right to work, 4238
    USA, 4589
Risk, 835, 4098
Rites, 934, 1443, 1446, 1449
    France, 3659
    India, 2243
    Japan, 1187
    Poland, 1451
    Tunisia, 1450
    USSR, 1444
Ritual, *use* Rites
Robotics, 4066, 4070
    USA, 4068, 4090
Role, 343, 839, 841, 845, 884, 1121
Role attribution, *use* Role prescription
Role conflicts, 843
    Finland, 840
Role perception, 833
Role playing, 836
Role prescription, 838
Role taking, 835
Role theory, 834, 837, 842, 844
Romania
    agrarian reforms, 3667
    customs, 1200
    fairy tales, 1814
    fertility, 2888
    folk culture, 1200
    manpower utilization, 4262
    occupational mobility, 4489
    rural development, 3714
    rural life, 3667
    self-management, 772

class conflicts, 2343
fertility, 3068
marriage, 3068
penal sanctions, 5216
social mobility, 2412
social structure, 2412
Schizophrenia, 1536
Schleiermacher, Friedrich, 1314
School achievement, *use* Academic success
School adaptation
  Japan, 2015
  USA, 2797
School administration, 2016
  India, 2014
  Italy, 2011
  USA, 2017
School age population
  Belgium, 1998
School attendance
  Australia, 2012
  Brazil, 4274
School desegregation
  USA, 1922, 1933, 1952, 1961, 1975
School environment
  USA, 2564
School failure
  Latin America, 2129
School leaving
  United Kingdom, 1930
School management, *use* School administration
School population
  USA, 937
Schooling
  France, 1927
  Hungary, 1938
  United Kingdom, 1930
  USA, 1877
Schools, 2004
  New Zealand, 2005
  USA, 2132
Science, 331, 446, 1234, 1504, 1508, 1509,
    1510, 1511, 1512, 1520, 1537, 1538,
    1539
  German DR, 1506
  Latin America, 1521
  socialist countries, 1529
  USSR, 1218
  Yugoslavia, 1535
Science policy, 152, 157
  Arab countries, 151, 156
  Netherlands, 153, 153
Sciences of man, *use* Social sciences
Scientific and technical progress, 1446, 1526,
    2435, 4073, 4084, 4092
  Japan, 4074
  USSR, 4085
Scientific communication, 219
Scientific community, 158, 160, 219
  Japan, 150
  Netherlands, 159
Scientific cooperation, 154
  Latin America — Spain, 149
  Spain — Latin America, 149

Scientific discoveries, 1576
Scientific progress, 4069
  USSR, 4095
Scientific publications, 218, 219, 220
Scientific research, 1510, 4098
Scientific thought, 253, 1515
Scientists, 120, 124, 125, 160, 1243, 4098
  Finland, 840
  United Kingdom, 123
Scientology, 1534
Scotland
  Protestantism, 1479
  religious movements, 1479
Sea, 54
Sea transport, 792
Seafarers
  Poland, 4545, 4546
Secondary education
  Belgium, 2007
  Canada, 1994, 2001
  France, 2008
  Spain, 1993, 2009
  USA, 1996
  Zaire, 2000
Secondary groups, *use* Complex organizations
Secondary schools
  USA, 599, 1992
Secondary sector, *use* Industrial sector
Secret societies
  Cuba, 1435
Sects, 1342, 1418, 1420, 1426, 1438
  France, 1411
  Guadeloupe, 1419
  USA, 1408, 1423, 1437
Secularization
  Afghanistan, 5357
  Germany FR, 1496
  Iran, 5357
  Turkey, 5357
Self-assessment, *use* Self-evaluation
Self-attention, 533
Self-concept, 532, 534, 552, 555, 645, 2315, 3232
Self-esteem, 530, 535, 540, 542, 544, 546,
    549, 554, 2621, 4254, 5191
Self-evaluation, 526, 550, 551, 1073, 1278,
    3012, 3023
Self-help, 4987
Self-management, 775, 4967
  Romania, 772
  Yugoslavia, 777, 1742
Self-perception, 537, 553, 648, 4545
Semantics, 1558, 1649, 5321
Semiology, 1554, 1622, 1894
Semiotics, 1557, 1563
  USA, 1561
Senegal
  craftsmen, 3671
  joint family, 3161
  migration, 3671
  polygamy, 3060
  residence, 3161
  rural communities, 3671
  trade unions, 4642

Strikes, 4006, 4685, 4689, 4698
    Australia, 4699
    France, 4693, 4697
    Germany FR, 4696, 4697
    Italy, 4697
    United Kingdom, 4694, 4695, 4697
    USA, 871, 4404, 4686, 4690, 4716
Structural analysis, 348, 370, 375, 405, 412,
    703, 898
Structuralism, 249, 259, 269, 281, 288, 315, 320
Student behaviour
    Japan, 2076
    USA, 2028, 2047
Student housing, 3825
Student movements
    France, 2057
    Spain, 2033
    Uruguay, 2051
Students, 1234, 2084
    China, 2029
    France, 2029, 2063, 2357
    Germany FR, 2018
    Japan, 2060, 2071
    Jordan, 2025
    New Zealand, 2130
    Poland, 2049, 2055, 2070, 2085, 3730
    United Kingdom, 2080, 2130
    USA, 2071, 2080, 3427, 5204
Subculture, 5267
    USA, 983, 5285
Subjectivity, 336
Suburban areas
    France, 3900
    USA, 3871, 3936
Sudan
    agricultural workers, 4538
    demographic transition, 2771
    emigration, 3532
    everyday life, 2578
    housewives, 2578
    immigrant assimilation, 3506
    middle class, 2578
    peasants, 3698
    religion, 1322
Sugar cane
    Caribbean, 2240
Suicide, 1088
    Belgium, 5287
    Italy, 5257
    Japan, 5280
    USA, 5226, 5241, 5259, 5330, 5331
    Yugoslavia, 5286
Superannuation, *use* Retirement
Surnames, *use* Nicknames
Survey analysis, 361
Surveys, 380, 423, 426, 428, 430, 431, 4026
    Africa, 427, 432
Sweden
    class structure, 2613
    collective bargaining, 4628
    family, 3098
    female labour, 2413
    fertility, 2890, 2899, 3155

    higher education, 2068
    housing policy, 3794
    illegitimacy, 2951
    immigrants, 3519
    intellectuals, 2372
    labour law, 4596
    labour market, 686
    labour relations, 4562
    medical care, 5542
    occupational mobility, 4511
    patriarchy, 3106, 3155
    political opinion, 1770
    press, 1770
    sex equality, 2622
    social classes, 2256
    social mobility, 2406, 2413
    social policy, 5385
    social work, 5499, 5502
    trade unions, 4628
    unemployment, 4255
    urban communities, 3904
    welfare State, 5409
    women, 2613
    women workers, 3106
    women's employment, 4290
    women's status, 3106
    workers' participation, 4731
    working class, 3106
Switzerland
    care of the aged, 5452, 5455
    Churches, 1434
    cultural identification, 3329
    foreign workers, 4283
    foreigners, 3319, 3329
    income distribution, 5452
    marriage, 3045
    media, 1755
    migrant workers, 4332
    penal law, 1268
    politics, 1434
    primary education, 2159
    quality of life, 4036
    religion, 1434
    social inequality, 3045
    sociological research, 134
    value systems, 1056, 1434
Syllabus, *use* Curriculum
Symbolic interaction, 1581
Symbolism, 413, 1595, 3890
Symbols, 1593, 1594, 1687, 2836
Syndicalism, *use* Trade unionism
Systems analysis, 363, 395, 409, 898, 950,
    1060, 2213, 2440, 4211
Systems of education, *use* Educational systems
Szabó, Ervin, 1527
Szczurkiewicz, Tadeusz, 507

Taiwan
    fertility, 3572
    industrialization, 4140
    intellectuals, 2370
    internal migration, 3572
    urbanization, 3928

student movements, 2051
USA
  abandoned children, 2647
  ability grouping, 2132
  abortion, 2941, 2944, 2948, 2983
  academic freedom, 1950
  academic profession, 2166
  acculturation, 1037
  achievement, 616
  administrative corruption, 4937
  administrative organization, 4920
  administrative sciences, 4777
  adolescents, 5197
  adult education, 2086, 2100, 2104, 2113
  advertising, 1665
  age, 4469
  aged, 584, 617, 2360, 3807, 3965, 5189
  ageing, 2687
  agricultural education, 2123
  agricultural mechanization, 4343
  agricultural workers, 3459, 4343, 4540
  alcoholism, 1159, 5174, 5195
  alienation, 1159
  antisemitism, 3428
  architecture, 3814
  armed forces, 5092
  art, 1796, 1992
  artists, 1780
  associations, 749
  attitude to work, 4398, 4408, 4417
  attitudes, 2310
  automobile industry, 4564
  automobiles, 4128
  behavioural sciences, 4064
  bibliographies, 3362
  big enterprises, 2310
  bilingualism, 1654
  birth, 3282
  birth spacing, 2959
  Blacks, 542, 899, 1847, 2360, 2564, 3213,
    3316, 3362, 3441, 3936, 5034, 5094,
    5241
  bureaucracy, 766, 5585
  business cycles, 5331
  business economics, 4051
  business management, 2034, 4039, 4044,
    4049, 4059
  capital accumulation, 3899
  capital punishment, 3398, 5256
  care of the aged, 3964
  career development, 3463, 4336
  career planning, 4485
  Catholics, 3634
  causes of death, 5226
  child abuse, 5231, 5278
  child care, 5478
  child neglect, 3166
  children, 2656, 3035
  choice, 1028
  cinema, 3168
  citizens, 3624
  civil servants, 871
  civil service, 4337

class formation, 2329
class identification, 2304
class structure, 2314, 2349
clinical psychology, 516
collective agreements, 4716
collective bargaining, 4628, 4707
collective behaviour, 5283
community, 893
community development, 3630, 3631
community membership, 3634
community participation, 5079
commuting, 3588
conservatism, 4820
consumer behaviour, 4144
contraception, 2937
cost of living, 4589
courts, 4904, 5133
crime, 617, 766, 1108, 4896, 5207, 5234, 5304
crime prevention, 5209, 5211, 5264, 5283
criminal justice, 5224, 5225, 5264, 5272, 5322
criminal sentencing, 5295, 5326
cultural change, 1014
cultural patterns, 973
cultural pluralism, 937
cultural values, 1028
culture, 956
death rate, 2829
delinquency, 2558, 5208, 5240, 5264,
  5289, 5300, 5324, 5334
deontology, 1210
deregulation, 4864
desegregation, 1135
deviance, 1108
disabled children, 2797
disabled persons, 2793, 2800
dismissals, 4455
divorce, 2893, 3017, 3035, 3041
drinkers, 5204
drug addiction, 2047, 5192, 5194, 5197,
  5199, 5203, 5326
drug dealers, 5176
drugs, 5189
dual economy, 3976
economic hardship, 3052
economic performance, 1989, 4568
economic recession, 3069, 4242
education, 1911, 1914
educational development, 1989
educational innovations, 2136
educational policy, 1990, 2229, 2672
educational reforms, 1981
electoral campaigning, 5063
electoral sociology, 5059
elite, 2365
employees, 4646, 5225
employment, 4578
employment discrimination, 4257, 4258,
  4267, 4270
employment policy, 4226
entrepreneurs, 4050
environment, 3609
equal opportunity, 2229
ethnic groups, 1708, 2833, 3350, 3380

Works councils
  Germany FR, 4604, 4629
  USSR, 4669
Works of art, 1781, 1784
World population, 2538
Writers
  Latin America, 1816

Yemen
  breast-feeding, 2940
  contraception, 2940
  fertility, 2940
  modernity, 1209
  rural communities, 3736
  traditionalism, 1209
Young workers, 1052, 4302, 4328, 4342
  Poland, 2055, 4326
Youth, 525, 546, 960, 1711, 1840, 2665,
    2681, 2684, 4620, 5496
  Australia, 2662
  Chile, 1502
  China, 2679
  developing countries, 2668
  France, 1131
  Germany, 2667
  Germany FR, 1096
  Hungary, 2675
  India, 2679, 2680, 4087
  Italy, 1469, 5061
  Japan, 2685, 3731
  Netherlands, 3048, 3354
  Poland, 2676, 3149
  Sri Lanka, 4533
  Tunisia, 2664
  United Kingdom, 2671
  USA, 1465
  USSR, 2649, 2666, 2669
  Yugoslavia, 3053
Youth employment
  Germany FR, 5284
Youth organizations, 2084, 2674
  Africa, 5056
  USA, 2663
Youth policy
  France, 2660
  Latin America, 2661
  USA, 2672
Youth unemployment
  Belgium, 4229
  Canada, 4239, 4250
  Denmark, 4248
  France, 4222, 4247
  United Kingdom, 4254
  USA, 4235, 4245, 4339
Youth unrest
  Germany FR, 2678
  Western Europe, 2682
Yugoslavia
  agricultural production, 4131
  antisemitism, 3439
  attitudes, 3053
  economic conditions, 5347

  educational systems, 1943
  emigration, 3487
  ethnic groups, 3370
  family, 3021
  family farms, 4118, 4137
  family relations, 3066, 3152
  higher education, 2046, 2067
  illiteracy, 2101
  immigrants, 3513
  information sources, 174
  inheritance, 4118
  interethnic relations, 3414
  internal migration, 3591
  marriage, 3021, 3053, 3066
  mass media, 1742
  population composition, 2769
  press, 1723
  production factors, 4131
  professors, 2046
  rural areas, 2101
  rural development, 3727
  rural-urban migration, 3593, 3600
  science, 1535
  self-management, 777, 1742
  social change, 1166, 4757
  social conditions, 5347
  social development, 2186
  social integration, 1154, 1160, 1166
  social sciences, 14
  social security, 5482
  social stratification, 2215
  social structure, 2186, 2198
  sociologists, 121
  sociology, 174
  suicide, 5286
  teaching of sociology, 121
  technological change, 777
  tourism, 4757
  workers' self-management, 4709, 4711,
    4725, 4729
  youth, 3053

Zaire
  colonial history, 1888
  educational reforms, 2000
  family planning, 2953
  history of education, 1888
  secondary education, 2000
  urbanization, 3784
Zambia
  housing, 3829
  housing policy, 3853
  marriage, 3020
  migration, 3460
  ruling class, 2381
  rural development, 3460
  women's employment, 4314
Zimbabwe
  ageing, 2703
  women's status, 3312
Znaniecki, Florian, 367
Zoroastrianism, 1384

INDEX DES MATIÈRES

histoire, 977
identité nationale, 1619
intellectuels, 2383
langue nationale, 1619
marginalité, 1128
médecine, 5504
migration forcée, 2241
milieu urbain, 427
modernisation, 3923
organisations de jeunesse, 5056
politique linguistique, 1619
population urbaine, 1128, 2748
professions, 4458, 4459
prolétariat, 1128
réfugiés, 3479
romans, 1807
socialisation politique, 5056
sous-développement, 3923
statut de la femme, 3060, 3280
systèmes de valeur, 4930
systèmes politiques, 4844, 4845, 4847
technologie, 4076
travailleurs, 2748
vie urbaine, 3800, 3819
villes, 3800, 3809, 3819
Afrique au Sud du Sahara
classe ouvrière, 2271
développement rural, 3653
éducation, 1904
État, 4843
Islam, 1356
langues, 1621, 1648
société, 4843
statut de la femme, 3253
Afrique Centrale
administration publique, 1459
sacré, 1459
Afrique du Nord
chamanisme, 1332
immigrants, 4340
Islam, 1393
statut de la femme, 3285
Afrique du Sud
alphabétisation, 2094, 2096
apartheid, 3399, 3401, 3413, 3417, 3429, 3434, 3449
capitalisme, 3393, 3395
discrimination raciale, 3433
Église catholique, 3429
Église et État, 1503
Églises protestantes, 1414
Hindouisme, 1369
logement, 3862
mouvements contestataires, 4993
Noirs, 3862, 4630, 4662
politique, 5082
population, 2528
psychologie sociale, 497
racisme, 3400
relations du travail, 4662
relations raciales, 3393, 3395, 5082
ségrégation raciale, 3419
syndicalisme, 4662

syndicats, 4630
villes, 3921
violence, 1173
Afrique méridionale
statut de la femme, 3216
Afrique noire
pluralisme social, 2211
systèmes politiques, 2211
Afrique occidentale
bibliothèques, 195
communautés religieuses, 1430
confréries, 1417
Islam, 1343, 1417, 1430
maladies, 2811
politique culturelle, 1022
rôles sexuels, 2601
ségrégation raciale, 3406
Afrique orientale
Christianisation, 1477
dot, 3076
enseignement supérieur, 2054
Afrique tropicale
maladies, 2791
âge, 845, 2627, 2634, 2829, 3450, 4395, 5041, 5261
États-Unis, 4469
âge adulte, 2686
âge au mariage
Chine, 3083
Espagne, 3456
Agression, 667, 669, 1179
Agressivité, 668, 2790
Agriculteurs, 2350
Argentine, 3718
États-Unis, 2304, 3721
Japon, 3731
Pays en développement, 3713
Pologne, 4136
Royaume-Uni, 3732
Agriculture, 4132
France, 4402
Agriculture à temps partiel
Pays de la CEE, 4106
Agriexploitation
Tanzanie, 4127
Agriexploitation collective
Botswana, 4120
Pologne, 4122
Aide à l'enfance
Australie, 5456
États-Unis, 5478
Royaume-Uni, 5459
Aide au développement, 2111
Europe orientale, 5107
Aide aux gens âgés
Belgique, 5492
États-Unis, 3964
France, 5481
Ghana, 5474
Italie, 5450
Japon, 5493
Pologne, 5469, 5473
Suisse, 5452, 5455

coopération scientifique, 149
Espérance de vie
    Canada, 2866
    Pologne, 2837, 2838, 2839, 2846
Estime de soi, 530, 535, 540, 542, 544, 546,
    549, 554, 2621, 4254, 5191
Établissements humains, 3621, 3622
    Amérique latine, 3620
    URSS, 3626
État, 222, 981, 4821, 4846, 4857, 4862, 5089
    Afrique au Sud du Sahara, 4843
    Amérique latine, 4831, 4850
    Brésil, 2394
    Canada, 812
État providence, 722, 4854, 5351, 5363, 5405,
    5541
    Australie, 5368
    États-Unis, 5370, 5411
    Europe occidentale, 5415
    France, 5350
    Italie, 4559
    Royaume-Uni, 5367, 5401, 5422, 5423
    Suède, 5409
États-Unis
    abandon d'enfant, 3166
    accidents du travail, 4404
    accidents nucléaires, 5010
    accomplissement, 616
    acculturation, 1037
    accumulation de capital, 3899
    activité militante, 871
    adaptation scolaire, 2797
    administration locale, 4346, 4941
    administration publique, 4924
    administration scolaire, 2017
    adolescents, 5197
    âge, 4469
    agriculteurs, 2304, 3721
    aide à l'enfance, 5478
    aide aux gens âgés, 3964
    alcoolisme, 1159, 5174, 5195
    aliénation, 1159
    allocations familiales, 5490
    alphabétisation fonctionnelle, 2103
    aménagement urbain, 3748, 3887
    amitié, 655
    antisémitisme, 3428
    appartenance à la collectivité, 3634
    architecture, 3814
    art, 1796, 1992
    artistes, 1780
    assimilation des immigrants, 3225
    associations, 749
    attitude envers le travail, 4398, 4408, 4417
    attitudes, 2310
    attitudes politiques, 5022, 5041, 5052
    attitudes raciales, 3415, 3427
    autogestion ouvrière, 4736
    automobiles, 4128
    avortement, 2941, 2944, 2948, 2983
    bandes, 5292
    besoins de logement, 3818, 3964, 3965
    bibliographies, 3362

bibliothécaires, 198
bibliothèques, 2086
bien-être social, 4214
bilinguisme, 1654
budgets familiaux, 5490
bureaucratie, 766, 5585
buveurs, 5204
cadres, 4442
cadres moyens, 4552
cadres supérieurs, 4134
cafés, 4761
campagne électorale, 5063
campus universitaire, 3011
Catholiques, 3634
causes de décès, 5226
changement culturel, 1014
changement social, 2034, 2448, 2456,
    2552, 2557, 4421
châtiment, 5329
chefs d'entreprise, 4050
choix, 1028
choix d'une profession, 4484, 4485
choix du conjoint, 3634
chômage, 4217, 4226, 4228, 4230, 4233,
    4241, 4242
chômage des jeunes, 4235, 4245, 4339
cinéma, 3168
citoyens, 3624
classe moyenne, 3878
classe ouvrière, 2281, 2317
classes sociales, 2256, 2310, 2311, 3282, 5324
collectivité, 893
compagnies d'assurance, 1051
comportement collectif, 5283
comportement de l'étudiant, 2028, 2047
comportement du consommateur, 4144
comportement électoral, 3341, 5070, 5072,
    5073, 5076, 5078
comportement judiciaire, 4902
comportement politique, 4228, 5036, 5045
comportement religieux, 1465
comportement sexuel, 2994, 3004
condamnation pénale, 5295, 5326
conditions de travail, 4568
conditions de vie, 3114
conditions sociales, 8
conflits raciaux, 3392, 3407, 3412
conservatisme, 4820
contraception, 2937
conventions collectives, 4716
corruption administrative, 4937
coût de la vie, 4589
crise politique, 5331
culture, 956
cycle de vie, 3791, 3836
cycles économiques, 5331
délinquance, 2558, 5208, 5240, 5264,
    5289, 5300, 5324, 5334
délinquance juvénile, 5230, 5254, 5292, 5302
délits, 617, 766, 1108, 4896, 5207, 5234,
    5304
déontologie, 1210
déréglementation, 4864

1161, 1181, 2195, 2654, 3085, 4302, 5293
Allemagne RF, 1096
Pologne, 2141
Socialisation politique, 814, 3202, 5030, 5035, 5055
Afrique, 5056
Allemagne RF, 5051
Belgique, 5050
États-Unis, 2577, 3296
Hongrie, 5038
Inde, 5042
Socialisme, 916, 972, 997, 1235, 1527, 2468, 4037, 4797, 4799, 4802-04, 4811, 4828, 4867, 5363
Argentine, 4814
Australie, 4818
Espagne, 4780
France, 4798
Royaume-Uni, 963
Tanzanie, 2312
Société, 920, 936, 988, 1318, 2409, 2597, 4100
Afrique au Sud du Sahara, 4843
Brésil, 995
Inde, 984
Irlande, 955, 979
Japon, 996
Pologne, 961
République dominicaine, 966
Royaume-Uni, 939, 962
Société bourgeoise, 918, 1239, 1242, 1941, 4827
France, 3993
Société capitaliste
relations interethniques, 3402
relations raciales, 3402
Société civile
Europe orientale, 970
Société de consommation, 916
Société dualiste, 2217
Société industrielle, 1057, 2501
Société internationale, 5116, 5117
Société paysanne, 3668
Société post-industrielle, 2497
Société rurale, 3680, 3695, 3740
Bangladesh, 3739
Espagne, 3700
Hongrie, 3648
Inde, 3739
Italie, 2701
Japon, 3706
Pologne, 3715
Thaïlande, 3694
Société socialiste, 885, 896, 948, 976, 985, 1000, 1013, 1062, 1226, 1261, 1539, 1897, 2173, 2185, 2350, 2449, 2542, 3187, 3983, 3990, 3994, 3998, 4077, 4150, 4852, 4859, 4861, 4865, 4868, 5086
Allemagne RD, 2588
Hongrie, 3991
URSS, 3989
Société traditionnelle, 875
Asie du Sud-Est, 2505

Société urbaine, 4544
Danemark, 4305
États-Unis, 3756, 3878
Inde, 3783
Mexique, 3775
Sociétés développés
changement social, 4082
Sociétés savantes
France, 170
Sociétés secrètes
Cuba, 1435
Sociographie
Pays-Bas, 416
Sociolinguistique, 1545, 1551, 1553, 1562, 1564, 1565, 1589, 1641
Bulgarie, 1567
Israël, 1550
Malaisie, 1547
Sociologie, 1, 2, 12, 16, 23, 31, 39-41, 46, 48, 52, 54-56, 61, 63, 65, 69, 74-75, 78-79, 83-84, 108-12, 149, 215, 221, 444, 449, 507, 513, 552, 2422
Allemagne RF, 50, 64, 68
Amérique latine, 20, 87
Australie, 93
Belgique, 11
Bulgarie, 51
Canada, 43, 47, 81
Chine, 21, 45, 105
Corée R, 111
États-Unis, 8, 26, 27, 66, 68, 98, 353, 392, 1171, 3274
France, 85
Hongrie, 59, 60
Inde, 92
Italie, 53, 113, 302
Pays-Bas, 18
Pologne, 25, 106
Roumanie, 24
Royaume-Uni, 88
Tchécoslovaquie, 13
URSS, 35, 91
Yougoslavie, 174
Sociologie appliquée, 19, 5132, 5139
Sociologie criminelle, 5237, 5239
Sociologie de l'art, 1789, 1793
Sociologie de l'éducation, 892, 1861-62, 1869, 1882, 1887, 1898, 1901-02, 1907, 1912, 1915
Espagne, 1858, 1900
Italie, 1875, 1883
République dominicaine, 1879
Royaume-Uni, 1864
Sociologie de la connaissance, 117, 1505, 1507, 1512, 1514, 1517, 1522-26, 1528, 1531, 1533, 1536, 1540-41, 1543
Allemagne, 1516
États-Unis, 1513
Sociologie de la culture, 908, 909, 911
Sociologie de la famille, 3105, 3129, 3154
États-Unis, 3095, 3199
Inde, 3120
Italie, 3107